# PASOLINI REQUIEM

PANTHEON BOOKS ▬ NEW YORK

BARTH DAVID SCHWARTZ

# PASOLINI
# REQUIEM

*Acknowledgments to reprint previously published material
can be found on page 753.*

Library of Congress Cataloging in Publication Data

Schwartz, Barth David.
Pasolini requiem / Barth David Schwartz.
p.    cm.
Includes bibliographical references and index.
1. Pasolini, Pier Paolo, 1922–1975.    2. Motion picture producers and
directors—Italy—Biography.    3. Authors, Italian—20th century—
Biography.    I. Title.
PN1998.3.P367S39      1992
858'.91409—dc20
[B]    90-53403
ISBN 0-394-57744-2

Book design by Fearn Cutler
Manufactured in the United States of America
First Edition

*To my Parents*

# CONTENTS

# ACKNOWLEDGMENTS

This book was written over many years and in many places, beginning in San Francisco in the winter of 1975 and coming to term in Amsterdam more than fifteen years later. The research has taken me from Los Angeles to New York; it has traveled with me to teaching posts in the American Midwest, Tunisia, and Malaysia.

In Italy, I have learned from Pasolini the length and breadth of the Peninsula, from Gorizia—as Austrian as it is Italian—to Agrigento, where the radio signal from Tunis comes in clear. And Pasolini gave me Rome, a city I have come to love (and to hate) as much as any who know her well.

The following is a partial list of only those persons who aided me most, and to whom I express my deepest gratitude for their patience and goodwill:

In Stockholm:

Claës Bäckstrom, René Coeckelbergh, Ulla-Britt Edberg, Goran Grieder, Bengt Holmquist, Tom Johannesson, Carl-Johan Malmberg, Ignas Schneynius, Nils Petter Sundgren, Kristina and Mats Valinger, Anna-Lena Wibom.

In Amsterdam:

Marie-Rose and Maarten Asscher, Toenke Berkelbach, Hubert de Boer, Sylvia and Carel de Vries, Eveline and Jan Koolhaas, Koosje and Teun Koolhaas.

In the United States:

Patricia and James Atwater, Don Baker, Roberto Barazzuol, Darryl Beach, David Butler, Jeff Cothran, Agnese Galleani, Carol and James Geist, Alberto Grimaldi, Michael Hoban, Richard Keresey, Cecilia Galiena Knox, Felicity Mason, Bruce McKee, Buddy Mear, John Jay Orcutt, Barbara and Charles Pierce, Robert White Rich, David Schorr, James P. W. Thompson, Francesca Valente.

In Britian: Raymond Leppard, Una Marchetti, Terence Stamp.

In Italy: Mirella Acconciamessa; Alberto Arbasino; Beatrice Banfi; Giorgio Bassani; Attilio and Bernardo Bertolucci; Laura Betti; Alfredo Bini; Mauro Bolognini; Gianni Borgna; Anna and Aldo Bravi; Prof. Gian Piero Brunetta; Avv. Bruno Brusin; Avv. Guido Calvi; Graziella Chiarcossi; Sergio and Franco Citti; Mario Coffaro; Furio

Colombo; Claudio, Piero, and Fulvia Colussi; the late Gino Colussi; Franco Cordelli; Marinella, Elena, Floriano, and Ilaria Dall'Armi; Ninetto Davoli; Elsa De Giorgi; Luciano De Giusti; Tonino Delli Colli; Danilo Donati; Bruna Durante; the late Dr. Fausto Durante; Alessandra and Francesco Durante; Dante Ferretti; Giovanni Forti; Franco Fortini; Avv. Alessandro Galiena; Cesare Garboli; Avv. Michele Gentilone; Franco and Massimo Giacometti; Dr. Luigi Giorgi; Claudio Giunnelli; Enzo Golino; Davide Grieco; Avv. Guido Guasco; Carla, Marcello, Marco, Paolo, Fabio, and Virginia Iannarelli; Nicoletta Lazzari; Avv. Rocco Mangia; Dacia Maraini; Avv. Nino Marazzita; Fabio Mauri; Leonardo Mondadori; Noris Morano; the late Alberto Moravia; the Hon. Giorgio Napolitano; the late Enrichetta Colussi Naldini; Nico Naldini; Avv. Teresa de Simone Niquesa; Carlo Orsi; Silvana Mauri Ottieri; Piero Ottone; Lucia Pallavicini; Marcello Panza; Marsilio, Natalia, and Novello Papafava; Dino Pedriali; Riccardo Peloso; Rosanna Rossanda; Roberto Roversi; Avv. Giuseppe Santarsiero; Aggeo Savioli; Prof. Gianni Scalia; the late Leonardo Sciascia; Enzo Siciliano; Mario Soldati; Rodolfo Sonigo; Lorenzo Tornabuoni; the Hon. Aldo Tortorella; Davide Tortorella; Franco Tosi; the Hon. Antonello Trombadori; the late Fr. Davide Mario Turoldo; Marta and Gaspare Vesco; the Hon. Paolo Volponi; Wilton Wynn; Giovanni Zanalda; Marisa, Andrea, Gian Maria, and Fabio Zanzotto.

The unstinting assistance of certain persons has been crucial to the making of this book and merits special thanks. They are Fiorentino Amodio, Prof. Jean Carol Dillon, Dr. Martin Peretz, Giuseppe, Maria, and Alessandra Zigaina. In addition I wish to express my gratitude to Erroll McDonald. Yoji Yamaguchi, and Grace McVeigh of Pantheon Books, and to Andrew Wylie, Deborah Karl, Bridget Love, and Susan Schorr of Wylie, Aitken and Stone (New York), and Sally Riley of Aitken and Stone (London).

And last, but first, to Jerry W. Hibbitts.

# PART I

# 1

> *Yes, certainly it is worthwhile knowing poets, but it is not really so*
> *indispensable, otherwise how could one ever know those already*
> *dead?*
>
> *—Pier Paolo Pasolini*

# THE WHITE
# BOATS OF WAXHOLM

He could not have chosen a better time for the journey north. Only
a few weeks before, he had wrapped up *Salò, or the 120 Days of
Sodom;* only its dubbing into French, the language of its coproducers,
needed his supervision before a winter release. It would open commercially in Milan, timed to coincide with a premiere at the new
Paris Film Festival.

He had assembled his recent articles from the daily *Corriere della
sera* and its sister publication *Il mondo:* his polemics on politics and

sex, against television and compulsory schools—scandalous essays that had made him famous throughout Europe and even more than ever, if that were possible, the talk of Italians. His pulpit had been no less than the front page of the semiofficial journal of Italy's ruling class, a national readership like no other granted an intellectual in living memory. His position was unique: He had power without office, influence without privilege, notoriety in his own country and respect abroad. Livio Garzanti in Milan, his publisher of twenty years, would soon issue the articles as a book, and then the next, inevitable round of outrage and response, of proclamations and rebuttals would begin.

Pier Paolo Pasolini flew to Stockholm on Monday, October 27, 1975. In fewer than three hours, he went for a four-day visit to a place where people still stood in line without jostling and generally treated one another with more delicacy than do Romans. He was welcomed by an attentive public, one perhaps even too respectful. He was their guest of honor, even if they knew only the films and not the poetry, the novels, the criticism and understood only vaguely what an extraordinary place he held on the Italian scene. By now, his was a stance of radical isolation, but in a society that did not share the Nordic myth of the heroic outsider. Swedes might believe one could come alone to insight, returning with it from the cold to the tribal campfire; Italians left alone are condemned to death.

His hostess was Lucia Pallavicini, chief of the Italian Cultural Institute in Sweden and a veteran diplomat at international exchange. A blond, fine-boned woman who spoke with the elegant French "r" of the Italian upper class, she was well connected in Stockholm's tight artistic circles. Swedish journalists and her colleagues from other foreign cultural foundations could count on late-night suppers in her Institute apartment, ones with pasta properly cooked and even bottles of wine left open on the table, something special in Sweden, where it is doled out by the expensive glass. Cultural page copy could be found here, and interesting and important visitors long after Stockholm, sober even drunk, had rolled up its sidewalks.

Pallavicini believed this, her latest visitor, to be the sole Italian candidate for the Nobel Prize in Literature after Eugenio Montale, who had won just that year. But Pasolini was altogether another type, nothing like Montale who was an ever-so-bourgeois Milanese poet— cosmopolitan, double-breasted, ironical, and absolutely *comme il faut*. They were bitter personal enemies, though respectful in public about their work. Pallavicini's intention was, in a dignified manner, to expose and promote Pasolini in the right circles: to key literati in the orbit of the Swedish Academy, to those critics whose opinions count in that most intimate of worldly yet provincial capitals. The Nobel Prize may be of the entire world, but is also only a decision by a few men meeting in a room in one city.

A public program was needed, several days of events. The Svenska Filminstitutet (flush with cash thanks to Sweden's seventies' boom, and housed in an efficient new building) had collected his films from the first, starting with *Accattone* in 1961. They had already planned a retrospective of his film work to stretch over two months: ten prints from their own archives, spanning his output up to the last released film, *The Thousand and One Nights*. It was arranged that the director would attend a screening of October 29 and answer questions afterward about a still mysterious latest film, *Salò*. The international gossip was that it was deeply shocking, a movie to walk out of.

A coincidence made the schedule right: Pasolini's *Le ceneri di Gramsci* (The ashes of Gramsci), a book by now part of what Italians call "the canon" of their poetry, had never been translated into Swedish. Somehow, the big Stockholm publishers had dropped the cross-culture ball: "as so often the case, asleep," at least in the opinion of René Coeckelbergh, a Swede of Flemish origin whose new, tiny firm saw its chance to include Pasolini in a line of eight foreign poets, brought for the first time into Swedish. He had bought the translation rights for a pittance and ordered a print run of two thousand copies, reasonable in a country of eight million people no more given to buying poetry than any other.

Plans were settled: the book's publication date was set to coincide with the days of the visit; the publisher would line up an important Swedish actor to read from the poems on Tuesday, October 28, at eight o'clock at the Institute's headquarters. Pallavicini handled the mailing of announcements and sold tickets; Coeckelbergh's role was to take the poet-director-journalist-critic to lunch; Pallavicini would deliver the appropriate literary critics. The Italian Foreign Ministry would pay for the air ticket to and from Rome and their guest would stay, as was normal, in the Italian Institute's visitors' apartment.

She met her honored visitor at Arlanda airport, but he did not come alone, as invited. He brought along the one after his mother whom he had loved most in the world, actor Giovanni ("Ninetto") Davoli. The truth was, theirs was a relationship now fueled by its past; Pasolini settled for the company of this family man who would later deny his claim to fame: that Pier Paolo Pasolini had loved him. Only foreigners could be convinced by the denial. Italians understood perfectly well that loving Ninetto had brought Pasolini joy but also a frustration unto death; understood that the lovers had long ago become father and son, and that while Ninetto had reciprocated with a fiercely beautiful devotion (the sort Swedes call "characteristically Mediterranean"), it was not sexual rapture. Ninetto loved him as he could but he could not save him.

For the first night in Stockholm, Pallavicini had arranged an interview for Ulla-Britt Edberg, a cultural affairs reporter and theater critic at the conservative daily, the *Svenska Dagbladet*. Like almost everyone else, she conducted her interview in French. She sat on a sofa in Pallavicini's *salone* (sipping a glass of wine; he took only fruit juice) and confronted a man whose face she recalled more than a dozen years later, even after hundreds of other interviews.

> I can usually open people. But he was like a rock, not coming to you at all, no gestures. And those eyes—they were like, well, black marbles, but soft behind the tinted lenses. He never seemed bored. He made it clear that he was not unwilling to answer questions. He was just deeply inside himself, I'd say almost autistic even, and yet when I hit on a subject that interested him, he became very articulate, speaking clearly and in detail. I never met anyone like him . . . so self-contained.

She noticed his thin lips and how even at fifty-three he had no "middle-aged softness" about him ("as even Ingmar Bergman now had"); "he was muscular, tight and hard, his body like a circus tightrope walker."[1]

The results of their brief talk appeared in print the next morning, with a photo of him standing closed-faced in front of the Royal Dramatic Theater near his hotel, wearing a coat with a shearling collar and the striped sport shirt in which he was to die. Under the headline "Enormous and Turmoiled Rings Emanate from Pasolini," she wrote, "When he writes [essays] about politics, as recently in Italian newspapers, they just boil. He makes you worried."

He told her, as he had journalists for years, that he wanted to live in Morocco, not Italy, where "we live in a tragic situation." He said crime was everywhere, worse than ever before, something "pitiless and without rules." The ruling Christian Democrats, he said, ought to be "put on trial" and explained that while other countries (presumably including Sweden) had some "antidote" to the "violence" of industrialization and American-style consumerism, Italy was "defenseless," a victim of "what he does not hesitate to call cultural genocide."

Since he was famous as the poet of the poor, the champion of the *borgate*, the Roman slums, she asked his feelings about them. About "the people . . . *il popolo*," as opposed to the bourgeoisie. "They are like children," he said, "they have a sense of the comic but not of humor." "As for myself, I've become more humoristic," he said without smiling, "which means I have become more bourgeois."

The interview done, Edberg stayed to dinner at Pallavicini's renowned table. Other guests included Anna-Lena Wibom, director of the Filminstitutet, Ninetto, literary critic Bengt Holmquist (writing in the morning newspaper *Dagens Nyheter*), and Pallavicini's translator for public events, Tom Johannesson. A banker by profession but Italian-Swedish translator by passion, he was a formal and punctilious man, even prim, who prided himself on being invisible but at hand when needed. Edberg noted that after dinner, "Pasolini just disappeared . . . I assumed he went into his apartment at the Institute. He was just gone."

The Italian Institute's official guest quarters was within the complex, close enough to the director's apartment for easy entertaining, fully furnished, but with its own entrance. After one night there with Ninetto, the next morning—on Tuesday—Pasolini asked to be provided with a hotel room. Pallavicini was not surprised—he was known for his noctural adventures, had written of them explicitly in his poetry. She thought he just wanted more independence, or Ninetto did, and she was happy to provide it.

As in the past, he called the Hotell Diplomat—written with two *l*'s in Swedish. "Diplomat" somehow fit because of the many embassies located nearby and because some countries even rented suites to house their official delegations; the Yugoslav ambassador was assassinated in his top-floor office, above the hotel, by a Croatian separatist a year before Pasolini's stay.

He signed the register on October 28, describing his profession as *écrivain* in French, not *cinéaste*; born in Bologna, March 5, 1922; current address via Eufrate, 9, Rome. Ninetto signed as *attore*, born in Rome, October 11, 1948, current address via Titto Labigno, 173, also Rome. They shared room 301, 238 Swedish crowns per night.

The evening of October 28 at the Italienska Kulturinstitutet was for Pasolini-as-writer. Pallavicini piled his books on a table near a microphone. Before a crowd of more than five hundred, an actor read from the new Swedish translation of *Le ceneri di Gramsci* and Pasolini answered questions from the floor. Pallavicini recalled:

> He was incredibly sweet, you really noticed that. If a question were banal, even stupid, he tried to understand what the speaker was driving at. When they were courteous, he was courteous; when someone was a bit provocatory,

he was also courteous. I've participated in hundreds of such meetings in my life, and he was one of the very best ever—his incredible *mitezza* [gentleness, also the word for meekness] struck you in his manner, so patient, so in contrast to the violence in his films, like the one that he was then working on, going to Paris from Stockholm to dub. It went very well, his visit, a real success.

He did not mention *Vas* (also with the working title *Petrolio*), the novel-in-progress he had been writing for several years, one he told a few friends would have "everything" in it and take five more years to complete. No one save Alberto Moravia had read it, but word was he had reached six hundred pages already and gone into detail about his intimate life, the life about which every Italian had an opinion. But he told *Ceneri*'s translator (who later wrote about it in the *Göteborgsposten*) that he was working ". . . on a novel about consumer society, which in the end sells people and consumes itself . . . it is one, or more, very political novels." When asked: "Will it be an Italian tragedy?" Pasolini answered "softly": "It will probably be for my heirs to take care of that." And the Swedish translator wrote: "That is one of the few times I see him smile."[2]

The next night was for Pasolini-the-filmmaker. Wibom's Filminstitutet had borrowed a print of his 1966 *Uccellacci e uccellini* (Hawks and sparrows; rendered *Big Birds and Little Birds* in Swedish: *Snalla faglar och stygga*) from the film archives in Helsinki. It would be shown at seven and a screening of *Oedipus Rex* (in Swedish, *Kung Oidipus*), made a year later, would follow, at nine. One film of ideology and one of mythology. Then question-and-answer.

The previous afternoon, October 28, Pasolini arrived with Ninetto at the Institutet, punctual as always. They lunched with Wibom and Bengt Holmquist, then writing frequently on Italian literature. "I think we struck it off immediately," Holmquist remembered, "because we shared a sense of the absurd. He seemed nervous to me, I had the feeling this was someone to whom something terrible could happen at any time." They exchanged addresses, and Pasolini asked Holmquist to call the next time he came to Rome.

Instead, Holmquist wrote an obituary in the morning *Dagens Nyheter* of November 3:

His was a talent of seldom-seen breadth . . . to get the equivalent, you would have to have Sartre, Böll, Bergman in the same person. To see him in action was an event in itself, how nicely he turned all kinds of questions into something meaningful, how simply and clearly he would clarify the most complicated phenomena. That there was concern under the surface was easy to see, but it didn't seem to be about his personal life or conflicts. His concern for what was happening in Italy was so much stronger. Not that he had given up hope, but for a long time he had seen the evil signs growing.

Before an early dinner in the Institute's restaurant, the no-nonsense Wibom gave her guests what she calls "a detailed and lengthy tour."

> We show off a bit for important directors who come here, making a small spectacle of our computerized microfiche system, the up-to-date documentation center . . . We push a few buttons and all the data on them comes up, a sort of show-and-tell. He talked about the future of the prints of his films. He was worried about how they were being preserved, or rather not, in Italy.

He talked to her about the disappearance of traditional cultures, how everything was getting to be the same everywhere, homogenized and evened out. Not one to shrink from animated differences of opinion, she explained how it seemed to her that one could go "a few feet off any main street in Italy and find special things, dialects" and how remarkable it was that after three centuries of mass tourism the Italians had kept their distinct identity, and had changed so little. "He had his own opinions, of course, and I never imagined I would do anything to change them, not that I meant to."

The film showings on October 29 went smoothly, the audience plugged into earphones providing near-simultaneous translation. Artist Claës Backström thought how "innocent" the questions were, how mild-mannered were the Swedish intellectuals of post-1968 gathered there, "ignorant of the world, reading about revolution as though something faraway, abstract, just an idea." The films finished, Pasolini went to the front of the room and invited questions. They stayed mostly on the level of technique. Pasolini answered fully, in rounded responses that were, if not rehearsed, then at least perhaps expressions of thoughts he had had before. Occasionally, he turned to Johannesson and said, "You know what I would say, go ahead and answer."

He did not tell his listeners that his Italy was neither the one of Mussolini's rhetorical "saints, poets, and navigators," nor that of a Nordic nightmare of thieves, layabouts, and gigolos. Rather, it was a country like theirs, but one whose people was its own worst enemy. They certainly worshiped different myths, had different ideas of sin, love, and death. His audience were people who expected not only a job and a good apartment (with the help of a State they trusted), but a house in the country, a Volvo, sex education, abortion and divorce

on demand, no censorship; to pay their taxes and receive in exchange excellent medical care, schools, and police protection (what
little was needed; Olof Palme had not yet been shot on the street).
For most of them, Italy was a place to visit on a charter flight, known
for lots of art, one big museum with a *cappuccino* afterward. If metaphor were wanted, their country was a garden, his an antheap;
Swedes were almost incapable of being together, Italians almost unable to be alone.

He could hardly explain, then and there, that the subproletariat
of the Roman *borgata* shared with the poor at the edges of Europe
(and all Asia, all Africa) a vitality rooted in not obeying rules; that
their living by instinct and impulse—what he so loved—was now
being effectively tamed, once and for all, by what he called the
"moralism" of "neo-capitalism's false tolerance." And that this was
the same set of life-denying strictures which condemned him to "mar-
ginality" (regardless of "success") because of what he believed to be
his innate differentness.

He gave another interview, remarking that "the intellectual's role,
is not to have any role—to be the living contradiction to every role."
Once, the artist's job was to fight for sexual freedom and freedom of
speech, but

> today the bourgeois power exercises a false tolerance which allows sexual
> freedom and a certain freedom of speech. The artist's duty is to reveal the
> false tolerance which makes people unhappy and places upon them even
> heavier duties instead of giving freedom. I myself have too much freedom
> in my work. That is a false freedom.[3]

He may have thought Sweden had traipsed after what he called
"the siren of neo-capitalism," living in a consequent "horrible existential vacuum." And yet, to the extent such a phenomenon existed
in 1975, it was a nonconformist country, a place of beneficent socialism whose prime minister had publicly chided the American president about Vietnam.

Everyone seemed satisfied with the question-and-answer session.
At one point, in the course of answering an inquiry about public
reaction to his newspaper articles against abortion and for a ban on
compulsory secondary education and television, he said matter-of-
factly, almost in passing, that he expected to be killed, murdered.
This elicited no follow-up, no comments.

There had been talk of a gathering at Pallavicini's home after the
screenings, but such plans were suddenly called off. It seemed that

he and Ninetto had argued and agreed to go their separate ways. Pasolini asked Wibom to show him some nightlife, some of the then-famous wild Swedish sex clubs. She was happy enough to do so but pleased to have along two Frenchmen from that country's cultural institute ("they always invite each other, these institutes"), one of whom would drive. Ninetto went elsewhere.

This tour of Stockholm-by-night seems to have been the only advice, the only guidance Pasolini sought. Every time Johannesson picked him up at his hotel, he never mentioned where he had been in his free time; the discreet interpreter never inquired. He did not seem to want to know about shopping, museums, and the like. While he asked about Swedish politics, he was happy to leave matters at the level of light conversation. If he had wanted to learn about cruising in Humlegarden, the gay bar called the Piper Club, the porno flicks, and Arab hustlers around the intersection of Klara Norra Kyrkogata and Gamla Brogatan, he could have found out easily enough, and without comment. This was not Rome but Stockholm with two dozen known, open homosexual meeting places. Had he wanted to know the scene at the Central Station's public facilities (nervous men peering through the crack where pissoir partitions do not reach the walls, space enough to pass a hand) he could have. If he had a guidebook to sex, it did not appear. "We assumed he was a skilled hunter," said Coeckelbergh, "and left it at that."

Wibom chose a place called the Lido. Its showing of porno films made it a registered cinema to which she had a pass, as she had to all Stockholm's screens. "We looked around, had something to drink, and soon he suggested we leave," she says. The shows were not nonstop and something about sitting in the dark waiting for the strip act to begin made them uncomfortable. Next was the Chat Noir, "a much more elegant place" according to Wibom, "with topless waitresses." The hefty entrance charge was paid, some food ordered, and a man and a woman appeared. To the steady patter of risqué jokes, they undressed. They then copulated on stage. At some point, about midnight, Wibom excused herself. "I had a husband and children," she said later, "and he was all right, in good hands, nothing more for me to be concerned about."

The next morning, Pasolini appeared at the Filminstitutet. He remarked to Wibom that the show had been "appalling, worse than *Salò*." But she had not seen the still unreleased film, and may not have remembered his attack on heterosexual coupling, did not know that he had written that marriage was "a funeral rite." When reporters called her from Italy four days later, she told them only about how his films had been well received, many satisfactory interviews made. She said nothing about the visit to the Chat Noir.

On Thursday, October 30, he met reporters at the Institute and answered questions about the Nobel. Since Montale was "already considered a great poet in Italy and will be in all of literature," he said it would have been better to give the Prize to Sandro Penna, "always destined to be a poet at the margins, not known, even despised, whereas in fact he is a very great poet, as much as Montale."[4] Shortly before his death, Penna told a reporter (who probably had to pay dearly for the interview, which Penna considered work to be compensated), "I am not a homosexual. I am a pederast." Importing André Gide without proper citation, he declared, "Homosexuality is a privilege." The highly eccentric Penna's invisibility, even in Italy, was not for lack of Pasolini's efforts on his behalf. In March 1970, he made sure Garzanti published Penna's collected work, and wrote in the preface that his friend was "perhaps the greatest and most joyful living Italian poet."[5]

That day, Coeckelbergh took Pasolini and Ninetto to lunch, to an island-park called Djurgården, a public space dotted with luxury villas. At the Lidingöbro Värdshus, literally, "Inn at the bridge to Liding Island," they found a glassed-in terrace for cold weather (they sat outside) and excellent seafood. Coeckelbergh recalls Pasolini talked about consumer culture, the " 'Americanization' of Europe," of Italy and Sweden; he seemed to his publisher "more introverted than when I had known him in the sixties." When he criticized, he seemed to his host "like a lion, on the attack by way of defense." Ninetto followed every girl (their long legs made him call them "*cavalle*," horses) with his eyes, making a show of it. "The atmosphere at the table was tense," Coeckelbergh says, "and Pasolini finally told Ninetto he was vulgar (*sei volgare*), and to shut up."

That afternoon, Pasolini addressed about sixty students in a top-floor, windowless room at the Filminstitutet, a combined gathering of the film practice and theory-history departments of the University of Stockholm. The event was organized by a film teacher named Carl-Johan Malmberg.

Pasolini talked about *Salò*, but only metaphorically, saying sex was "a symbol of power." If the students—used to State-issued contraceptives available on demand from their high school years—did not quite understand (Malmberg later admitted he did not), no one asked for clarification. Through a student interpreter, he told them

"Young people have become ugly"; the well-mannered Swedes did not flinch. Someone asked how he had "managed" to get the infant to smile at the father in the opening scene of *Oedipus*, just as the script required. "These are among the gifts from reality that you get as a filmmaker," he answered, and Malmberg remembered the phrase for a decade.

Malmberg asked the question others had already posed: Why had he "given up" his ideological films, the "committed" movies that he was known for, to make apparently escapist, even reactionary fables out of Chaucer and Boccaccio and the *Arabian Nights*. And Pasolini answered, as he had in countless interviews, that these were his "most ideological films of all," because they showed life "before the body had become merchandise," before the cash nexus had invaded social life and all had become obvious, necessary, and preordained. They were a rebuke, he explained, and added, "but I don't believe in them anymore."

The encounter over, Malmberg made a point of meeting Pasolini at the classroom door.

> I thanked him, in French, for providing the students the most stimulating encounter we had ever had. He looked hard at me, saying nothing. Then he smiled and thanked me and gestured that I ought to go ahead. I think he said "youth first" and I had the odd sensation that I had proceeded ahead, leaving him behind, really leaving him. Of course, I wish now I had spoken with him more. One does not imagine someone passing out of a classroom door to his death.

Years later, Malmberg still recalled Pasolini's "extreme presence in a room," that he was "a person who makes you wonder . . . who let the world project, in all its particles, on himself . . . [one] whose need for personal synthesis must give way to their hunger for variety, [one of those who] say yes to the non-uniting contradiction and to the changeable, [with] a need to be where the world was creating itself anew, something that led him to create the world anew more than other people. The Now was all that counted . . . he said no to the ready-made lethargy of memory."[6]

During one of these evenings—Tuesday or Wednesday—Wibom saw Ninetto dining alone at the KB restaurant, which she calls "an intellectuals' hangout."

On Thursday evening, Pasolini was guest of the Swedish Film Critics' Association, the Svenska Filmkritikerforbundet. Hans Schiller, film critic for the *Svenska Dagbladet*, sent out a notice: "We have succeeded in securing the presence of Pier Paolo Pasolini for an encounter at the Film Club's room in the Filminstitutet, at 8 P.M. on October 30. Actor Ninetto Davoli will also be present."

Afterward, a farewell dinner convened at the famous Gyldene Freden (the Golden Peace) restaurant, a luxurious establishment owned by the Swedish Academy, housed in a seventeenth-century building in the Österlånggatan in the old city, called Gamla Stan. Tourists are directed to the cellars, but do not complain because of the vaulting, thick pillars, and antique feeling of the place. Important people and locals with money to spend are directed to the ground floor: their table was here—Pasolini, Schiller, Pallavicini, Johannesson, Nils Petter Sundgren—then writing for the tabloid *Expressen* and Sweden's leading TV film critic—and perhaps others, but no one remembers.

The "Immortals," eighteen members of the Swedish Academy, hold their Thursday dinner meetings in a private room up one flight. Soon after Pasolini and his company were seated, a group of Academicians filed in—Henry Olsson, Karl-Ivar Stahle, Karl Ragnar Gierow in his signature black glasses. Johannesson spotted Anders Österling, the Academy's ninety-one-year-old "Permanent Secretary." Since 1941, it had been he who announced the Nobel Prize–winner for Literature to the world's press. Someone pointed him out to Pasolini, who said of Österling, "I've read some of his poetry."

So, on his own initiative, Johannesson cornered the old man— Swedish translator of Montale, Quasimodo, Ungaretti, Saint Francis, Petrarch, Tasso—in the cloakroom: Would Österling like to meet Pasolini, just to say hello? No, he had a cold, did not feel well, wanted to go home. "Give him my best regards, but let's make it another time," he answered, and disappeared into the Stockholm late-October night, arrived early as it does that time of year.

Less than a week later, Sundgren published "A Last Meeting with Pasolini" in *Expressen:*

> We talked lightly about the decline of humanistic culture and he said there was no longer any dialogue between Marxists and Catholics in Italy because there are no Catholics or Marxists in the old sense, that the power of the Catholic Church had been destroyed with that of the Italian peasant society, destroyed by a consumer culture imposed from above.[7]

Sundgren recalled Pasolini remarked that "the villages are emptied of people, as are the churches" and added "soon there will be only hens and old people in the countryside." He told his attentive hosts that even the Communist Party had adapted to the consumer society, leaving only the belief in "holy consumption." "In my last three films, *Decameron, Canterbury Tales,* and *The Thousand and One Nights,* I wanted to show how eroticism was a warm, life-giving power for people, before it changed into a commerce of our time. My films are antipornographic." And after *Salò* ("set in 1945 because the end of the war marks the beginning of our own time, when eroticism is perverted into commerce"), he said he intended to "make a couple more films and then I'm going to write novels and articles."

About midnight, Johannesson drove Pasolini back to the Diplomat and they chatted for a few minutes in its first-floor lobby, a functional space outfitted with two sofas and a table, just enough for a hotel with a tearoom that closes at seven and is proud of it. Johannesson asked Pasolini to inscribe his prized first edition of *Le ceneri di Gramsci,* one he had bought in 1962 in Palma di Montechiaro, a Sicilian town laid out like a chessboard by the grandfather of Giuseppe di Lampedusa, who set part of *The Leopard* there, calling it Donnafugata. Carlo Levi, attending a conference with Johannesson, had told him, "Buy this book, you don't know this poet yet in Sweden, but you will."

Pasolini asked that he leave him the book overnight; he would give it to Pallavicini the next morning when she came to take him to the SAS morning flight to Le Bourget. As they parted, Johannesson said, "Let's go out for dinner in Rome, to an inexpensive but good place." Pasolini answered, "I've got money, let's just go to a good place."

The bow-fronted window of room 301 offers a view of Stockholm a travel brochure could tout. To the left lies the "Ship Island," *Skeppsholmen,* its museums of modern and Asian art invisible at night. Looking out, Pasolini could have seen the Sailors' Church (the Skeppsholmen Kyrkan), its low, flat dome atop an elegant ochre façade brilliant gold by day, softly floodlit at night. Behind it rises the dignified Swedish Baroque spire of St. Catherine's. In the dark, when the ability to perceive depth vanishes, the spire, the church and Skeppsholmen all appear to occupy the same plane. Next to them, although really in front, the yellow neon sign that announces the waterfront headquarters of the WAXHOLMSBOLAGET—the "Waxholm Company"—which operates white ferry boats to and from a resort of that name in the Archipelago.

Strindberg wrote about these white boats in *The Red Room* almost precisely a century before: it was "the first Swedish social novel," students are told, one of those classics his countrymen know about more than read. How much Pasolini had in common with that Swedish rebel without hobbies: their polyvalent genius, moving freely among media, their love of drawing and painting (both painted occasionally but intensively, for a few days at a time; both used color for structure). Even their fascination with alchemy. Did Pasolini know Strindberg wrote a history of his country as seen through the eyes of its lower classes (*The Swedish People*) and that he found Italy's cities and coasts already polluted, save for Venice, a hundred years ago? How it would have interested him to know Strindberg dismissed industrialization as "a useless luxury" and spent a decade writing *Inferno*, about what he called "the religious crisis that was assailing men's consciences all over Europe, after the decline of positivism." And that, like Pasolini, he had been accused of blasphemy for which he narrowly escaped prison? Did Pasolini know that Strindberg called the world "a shit-hole"?

Opposite the title page in Tom Johannesson's edition, Pasolini wrote:

> To Tom
> My translator *in ore*[8] exquisite and therefore not less vulnerable, in homage to his (mimetic) eloquence.
>
> Pier Paolo Pasolini

Then he added:

> Stockholm, Hotell Diplomat—during a night strangely warm of eighteen years after, my shoulders to the sea, to my right the Institute and the Institutet, and on my left the Old "Stan," cold—on my cornea the Academicians in the restaurant and in my ears the sound of a language that one asks oneself about, knowing one cannot have the answers . . . and in my heart the thread of a life (mine) which no longer interests.
>
> 30 October 1975.

Pasolini could not have slept as late as he usually did that night. SAS flight 561 departed for Le Bourget on Friday the 31st punctually at 8:55 A.M.; DC–9s at Arlanda were rarely backed up, as at Milan or Rome. When Pallavicini gathered Pasolini and Ninetto at the hotel, they seemed on excellent terms. The actor flew directly to Rome; Pasolini was to spend only a half-day in Paris, working on the dubbing of *Salò*. He was to be back in Rome the same evening, so he and Ninetto agreed to meet for dinner. On Saturday, November 1, they would get together in the San Lorenzo district: Pasolini with Ninetto, his wife, and their two sons.

# 2

*Do not despise the sensibility of any man. The sensibility of each man is his genius.*

*—Charles Baudelaire*

*It seemed as if the gods, in reward for his devotion to them, had given him a death which, for its swiftness and its opportunity, he might well have desired.*

*—Walter Pater on the murder of Winckelmann*

# AL POMMIDORO

Tourists never visit San Lorenzo. By 1975, even Romans who did not live there avoided the neighborhood after dark. Those over fifty or sixty recall with sadness when the quarter was different: *popolare*, a district of working poor, of stonecutters who furnished funeral statues and stone flower urns to the nearby cemetery of Campo Verano and of their wives (one per lifetime) who took care of the children, and of children who were not delinquents. They recall how the *quartiere* had its own personality and pride, its dialect distinct from

Rome's many other voices, one heard in shops and cafés whose owners were not, as later, bullied into paying protection money by teenage gangs. Then socialism thrived in San Lorenzo, and old-school
anarchists could still be found. Before Benito Mussolini took over
and muzzled all opposition, San Lorenzinos opposed to the new-
fangled Fascist movement had catcalled at the future Duce's men.
By the 1970s, San Lorenzo still housed a few granite-and-marble
works: the firms of Adriano Frioli and Dante Guagnelli kept up the
tradition. But they were outnumbered by the unemployed and by
extremist, extra-parliamentary political activists, predecessors to the
Red Brigades. San Lorenzo had become infamous for *la malavita*,
synonymous with drug dealers and their customers, thieves and their
fences, prostitutes and their protectors. Well-off Romans, *gente per
bene*, considered it a neighborhood where one risked a handbag
snatched, car broken into, or worse.

Later, matters improved. With the 1980s, San Lorenzo attracted
"urban pioneers" from the middle class; it is, after all, adjacent to
the always expanding medical (and morgue) complex of the University, convenient to the train station, and not all that far from the
Spanish Steps. Today it is full of intellectual types, *dottori*—degree-
holders—who have flocked there, now that foreigners have taken over
Trastevere, and Africans and Arabs the district between the station
and Piazza Vittorio. Newcomers and their realtors praised it as "the
last truly Roman neighborhood." But that was yet to come.

Much of San Lorenzo's bittersweet memory for the better old days
is linked with regret at what happened one summer day in 1943. The
neighborhood has the sorry distinction of being the only part of Rome
bombed by the Americans, intent on destroying the rail-links that let
the Germans hold on after Anzio. Here came the shove that pushed
Mussolini out of power. San Lorenzo became a target 1,134 days after
the war began in Italy, its bad luck that the Nazis were moving
equipment and reinforcements for the Sicilian campaign through the
central train station and the Tiburtino substation at its edge, storing
supplies in vast marshaling yards—375 acres of depot—all hard by
where people lived. The Fascist regime had built some air raid shel-
ters, but no one thought they would ever be used. Many people did
not know where they were; besides, there wasn't time. At about eleven
on the already stifling Monday morning of July 19, weddings were
starting (people sensed the war was ending) and apartments were
occupied; the streets were thronged with people going about the business of living as best they could with wartime rationing and the black
market. No Roman expected to die because of an entire trainload of

ammunition parked almost adjacent to schoolyards and apartment blocks and exploding in the heart of town. Did not the slogan carved on the walls and over the doorposts of public buildings say it: *Il Duce ha sempre ragione* (The Duce is always right)?

As the Yanks piloted their B-42s in eighty-six-degree heat, Hitler was meeting Mussolini, to dismiss his plea that the German factories deliver two thousand more planes for the Italian air force: they were more pressingly needed on the Russian front.

The bombs fell not only on the rail lines but into the Campo Verano burial ground: on its brick walls, on the tombs, and on the stone filing-cabinet *columbaria* where some families put their beloved dead above ground. The outrage was not only that the living were killed but that the bombing disturbed the peace of the dead, a quiet that not even the trams screaming on the busy Viale Regina Margherita could trouble. Seven hundred to twelve hundred died, with as many wounded.

By two that afternoon when the smoke cleared, both the king and the pope came—separately—to inspect and to reassure. When Vittorio Emanuele descended from his car, the men and women of San Lorenzo jeered him in the streets. Some even threw back the banknotes his staff gave to the walking wounded. The scene made the seventy-six-year-old monarch tremble, and drove home the conviction it took him twenty years to reach: that Mussolini had to go, and within that week.

In mid-afternoon's most intense heat, the Holy Father arrived. Long-silent Pius XII had heard the explosions from inside the Vatican, and was driven across town in his black Mercedes with papal yellow-and-white flags flying. It was the first time he had left his separate state of the Holy See since June 1940. As he walked among the people, he wept. He climbed the steps of San Lorenzo-outside-the-Walls and recited the De Profundis. People later talked about how the blood of the raid's victims stained the hem of his white linen cassock. Five days later, on Saturday, July 24, the Grand Council of Fascism—the rubber stamp junta Mussolini created for window dressing—voted the Duce out of office.

Dina, the twenty-eight-year-old wife of Ettore Bravi, died in the San Lorenzo air raid. She fell in the rubble of her family restaurant's basement, two baby girls in her arms. Her family buried and mourned her as did the survivors of over 119 others who were crushed in the rubble of the direct hit of the square. During the next, horrible months, when the Germans took Italians off the streets and shot them as the Allies moved north, Ettore and his eight-year-old son Aldo did what they could to survive. What else did they have but the hole-in-the-wall café, a wine-shop really, for rebuilding? Friends joined in to help. Soon the wine from Monte Portio started arriving again, to be sold in quarter, half, and full liters to a clientele that needed the stuff more than ever. The place stuck to what it did best: serving drink. They poured decent *vini da tavola*, usually by the glass, brimming beakers of raw, brilliant reds, and tannic whites from the city's castle country, the outskirts' *castelli romani*.

In those first, toughest years, the Bravis' place remained the domain of the *carrettieri*, burly men who worked as stevedores at the port of Ostia, or as masons, or perhaps as teamsters when a truck with four decent tires could be found. To pass through the doorway, customers shoved aside cheap strands of multicolored plastic beads. Inside were not much more than the two front rooms of a converted apartment, enlarged and equipped with a professional, oversized refrigerated case and a barely-more-than-domestic-scale stove.

Customers came because Aldo's paternal grandmother Clementina bantered with them, giving as good as she got. She told stories in *romanesco*, listened to their troubles, doled out abundant portions of sure-fire salves of drink and sympathy. So wide she needed two chairs to sit down, she also could throw two drunks out of her place at the same time, unaided.

When Ettore died at only forty-eight, Aldo took over. He had married a girl from Sabina, named Anna, a woman both efficient and loving, expansive and reliable. They did not have sons, but their three daughters married, and that gave hope for the future of the business. In the days before the *malavita* ruined San Lorenzo, the Bravis' was an excellent location, facing directly onto the piazza. The sons-in-law worked; Anna oversaw the kitchen, Aldo brought in fresh game he shot, their daughters waited on tables. Aldo is an avid hunter, like his father, and when his day in the country goes well the refrigerated case (dubbed the *riserva di caccia*, game cooler) is stocked with pheasants and quail, hare and boar which pass over the charcoal en route to a plaid-clothed table, following the pasta course, a plate of artichokes on the side.

The now successful enterprise needed a catchy name. At least three versions can be heard in San Lorenzo about how it came to be called Al Pommidoro (At Tomato's). One looks to Clementina, even at a young age a large woman, round and flushed with wine. She looked like a rotund and ripened tomato—a *pomodoro*.

Another tale, one which old-timers in the district recite but the family deny, is that the place took its name from Ettore's red nose, distinctive in his otherwise pallid, handsome face. The more decorous explanation Aldo tells (and he should know) is that it arose from his father's skill at getting along with all sorts of people, always ready with the right word whether for a fancy doctor from the nearby clinics or for a thief recently freed from the prison of Regina Coeli and returned to the neighborhood.

"Calling the place after a tomato was right," says Aldo. "That's how my father was—like tomato—mixing well with everything."

Aldo was lucky to have married the tranquil Anna. She was happy to cook and to greet faculty people who now came for lunch from the University and the journalists from *L'unità*, the Communist Party daily, and from the left-leaning, but not Party-official *Paese sera*, both headquartered nearby. She left Aldo free to deal with other problems, like the decline of the neighborhood all around them.

Some of the new toughs in San Lorenzo took to extortion, often to support a drug habit. Money paid the right people could keep a merchant's windows unbroken, his awnings intact. They once called on Aldo and eyed his prized English setter, Brio. "Too bad if Brio were to take sick, Aldo," they said, "even die." But Bravi refused to be intimidated, would not take the hint and pass them an envelope, a *busta* of protection money, every month. He told the father of one of the gang's leaders that if anything happened to the dog, he would shoot whomever he thought responsible. Because Aldo was known in the neighborhood for his skill with a hunting rifle, that put an end to it.

But the incident worried him, and he never told Anna about it. Instead, he started closing earlier on weekends and holidays when the hoods were out and looking for trouble. He made of their presence justification to lower the heavy, corrugated iron gate over the door and windows and go for a little bird hunting and peace of mind.

The holiday weekend of November first and second, the Bravis planned a respite, the reward for a certain economic well-being achieved. This was the weekend of the dead, what the English and Americans call Halloween. Protestant countries ignore the dead on that day, losing them in the shuffle of kids and candy. But here the day of Ognissanti, of all the saints, was still observed separately from that of Ognimorti. On Ognissanti Sunday, this year the second of November, Italians buy more bouquets than anytime save at Easter and families crowd Campo Verano. The Bravis had their dead to commemorate, but the best way to celebrate the living was to gather together in the open air, not slave in the kitchen and wonder if some hooligans were out for mischief.

Roman evenings were cold now, and rain was predicted soon. By eight on Saturday, the evening had turned fast to night the way it does in big cities, making its arrival known because streetlights and house windows were lit, car headlights shone.

The wind picked up, but not enough to cause worry. The next day, Aldo and Anna, their daughters and sons-in-law would eat, laugh, and work in their productive garden at Moricone, bursting in spring with cherries enough to preserve and enough left over to sell, and have a good lunch followed with a sweet nap. They planned to keep the restaurant closed Monday as well as Sunday, observing the tradition of the *ponte*, the bridge connecting Sunday the second with Armistice Day on Tuesday the fourth.

When a couple at the back of the restaurant paid their bill and left, Anna stepped forward to lower the *saracinesca*, the zinc-coated shutter on rollers that sealed the entrance from the street and anything that could come from it. She brought it almost to the ground, but not completely: that way diners knew they should finish and leave. It also put on notice those arriving for dinner—nine is a normal dinner hour in Rome—that they should go elsewhere this night.

But before Anna could call the day done, a man came in for his life's last meal.


Aggeo Savioli and his wife, who writes under the name Mirella Acconciamessa, are in the business of being observant. They were both journalists on the staff of the official Italian Communist Party daily, *L'unità:* she in general assignments, he an editor of the influential *spettacoli* section, charged with seeing to the smooth output of a massive volume of book reviews, interviews, film, theater, and music criticism.

The Saviolis remember almost every detail of what happened at about nine o'clock that Saturday night, she well enough to chronicle it for her paper a few days later, when everyone wanted to know everything possible about what occurred. They had called for their bill, ready to depart for Trastevere where Aggeo had tickets to a play, "something underground," he was to review.

The Bravis and the Saviolis recall spotting the trousers and ankle-length boots at the same time; someone they knew was standing outside and wanted to come in. Anna remembers that she was standing in her apron and her three daughters were nearby. Anna's brother called out, certain he recognized the clothes of one of the restaurant's regular clients. He was sure he did not say, "Anna, there's someone outside" but rather, "Anna, it's Pasolini." She hurried to lift the shutter, and seeing it was indeed, urged him to enter.

"He insisted he would go somewhere else," she says, "said that he didn't want to bother us. Of course, I told him it was no trouble at all and he should come in and be comfortable." And so he did: He liked the Pommidoro because the Bravis were living links to the days of the war and the Resistance. He loved talking with Anna, who speaks uncontaminated Roman dialect. As they chatted, he invited them to visit him at his place near Viterbo, talked about coming to play in a benefit soccer match near their country place.

Journalist Acconciamessa now saw her chance for a scoop, an exclusive interview. Pasolini was written about in the newspapers every day: sometimes as a bit of news, occasionally an interview, or critical pieces by Italy's most famous writers attempting to answer his polemics. And there was the growing scandal over _Salò_. It had not been released, but the heat was up about it; how it was violent and pornographic, pushing to the limits the liberal tolerance he condemned as purely nominal, always false, no more than "a more refined form of condemnation."[1]

One knew little for certain, but those who claimed some insider information reported that what happened on the closed set at Cinecittà was the most upsetting film ever made by a serious artist, a product more appropriate to X-rated cinemas than to legitimate screens and the wider public. People said its homosexuality, sadomasochistic violence, and despair were autobiographical—or what they imagined to be autobiographical—and far too much so for comfort. The critics were braced for his upping the ante yet again.

Acconciamessa thought nothing could be better than to find herself here in this little restaurant with him on an off-day, a chance to ask her questions about his version of his "giving scandal." She would just go up to him and hail him the way Romans do, by his last name only. He knew her: They had talked at the time of _Canterbury Tales_ three years before. But at the last moment, she claims she thought better of it somehow, changed her mind. She says she looked at him and decided to give him a moment's peace from the controversy that always surrounded him, from the outrage that seemed to cling to him as tightly as the skin "stretched taut over his fifty-three-year-old face."

So she simply welcomed him and reminded him of the last time they had met. She wanted to be sure he remembered her—he was very good copy indeed—for the next time. Seeing Brio, she seized upon the dog as the right topic and started talking about dogs and their characters. She seemed to think he said he preferred cats, but it hardly mattered. They were both willing to talk of nothing, to take a rest from work.

Anna interrupted, calling from the kitchen to ask whether Pasolini expected someone, or would he be eating alone. Yes, he answered, he was expecting people any moment—Ninetto Davoli, his wife, their two sons—the first named Pier Paolo, the second Guido, like Pasolini's younger brother, a Partisan killed in the war.

Then he ducked under the lowered shutter, and stepped outside, amid the parked cars in the Piazza dei Sanniti, patient until Ninetto arrived.

Only then did the women talk. They stood near the door and spoke about him, looking at his back as they did so; he was just beyond their hearing, within their vision under a streetlamp and in the reflected neon of the cinema marquee where another porno movie was playing. Mirella, always working, noted it was *Two Hookers in Pigalle*. They joked about how Pasolini might, in fact, be waiting for some other young man so he could go off with him and "cuckold Ninetto." Theirs was a duet of approval, nurturing, sympathic, a comic duet out of the laughing Mozart, spoken without prejudice and in the same terms as if Pasolini had been a notorious luster after young females rather than males. Their gentle humor was insiders' insight, for both knew Ninetto had been the only one of the thousands of young men whom Pasolini really loved. In the gossip-ridden Roman world that believes it knows all, Anna and Mirella understood the relationship even without having read the anguished sonnets Pasolini had written more than four years before. Ninetto was in the army then, given a day off from the brig in Arezzo where he had been sent for some infraction, and Pasolini had gone to visit him there. He was so crazy about the boy, whom he had given a career as a comic actor, that even Maria Callas—Pier Paolo's friend, star of his *Medea* then in production—had become curious about her friend's passion and went along, thinking he must be someone extraordinary. Callas met Ninetto, but decided she was not overly impressed. But then none of Pasolini's *mondain* circle saw in Ninetto what Pier Paolo did. The *paparazzi* followed and the picture appeared in all the tabloids: Ninetto in uniform, flanked by Pasolini and Callas, two loving parents who, in fact, were parents neither one.

When Ninetto married, Pasolini told Alberto Moravia and the novelist's former wife, Elsa Morante, that he "wanted to die," that it hurt so badly he wished to cease to be. He made what scenes he could to stop the marriage, but Ninetto was a normal boy—he wanted a wife and family. But Pasolini continued to cast his protégé in his films, with leading roles in all three parts of the *Trilogy*, but not in *Salò*. Their next project called for him to star opposite the great Neopolitan comic Eduardo de Filippo in a film set in contemporary Naples, Paris, and New York. They had to discuss that tonight.

Pasolini stood near his silver Alfa Romeo 2000GT; he loved it because it was fast in a country with no speed limits, was elegantly shaped in a culture where such matters count. The car was clean, inside and out, because his young second cousin Graziella, a university student who lived with him and his mother, Susanna, had washed it that afternoon. Now it shone an unusual color, as though itself phosphorescent, something silver metallic that glowed yellow, reflecting the square's sulphur streetlamps.

Mirella stood alone, waiting for him as he waited for Ninetto to arrive. A few days later, she told her readers, "I thought that like that, his back to the light, Pasolini seemed younger, and the lines in his face almost vanished."

What happened next is not clear. Acconciamessa says a boy appeared, one she didn't get much of a look at, and that Pasolini gestured him over and they spoke. She was not sure, even thinking hard about it, whether he seemed to have arrived by appointment and with some sense of purpose or only happened by and Pasolini caught his eye. Or rather he caught Pasolini's. The director was always on the lookout for new youths to meet and had long ago stopped being shy about accosting them. His direct manner seemed admirably fearless to some, scandalous to others, foolhardy to almost all; to Acconciamessa—who had many homosexual friends in the arts—it was simply a matter of fact.

The two stood and spoke for only a moment and the women could not hear them. They could not tell whether Pasolini and the youth talked as though it was their first meeting or they already knew one another. But Pasolini knew so many boys in the *borgata;* Anna and Mirella understood that this was one encounter among countless others, perhaps not even the first of what might yet be several this night. The boy moved on.

What is sure is that Ninetto now arrived with his wife and sons. He drove a white BMW. The movies had made him more money than he ever imagined—he had taken to dressing out of pricey shops around the Spanish Steps. After embraces all around, the group entered for dinner. The restaurant's stock was low and Pasolini ate only a beefsteak and fried potatoes, no pasta. The others took some home-made sausages, a bit of fruit. It was about nine-thirty, perhaps a quarter to ten.

The new film's role would be difficult and Ninetto had succeeded as a comic actor by playing himself. Getting straight what his friend Pier Paolo—" 'Pa" in Roman slang—wanted was critical. Ninetto needed to know what his tone was to be as he roamed the streets of several cities in search of the truth, following "the comet of ideology." Pasolini kept changing the cities in his search to find just the right modern counterparts to the ancient world. The script's working title was *Ta kai ta*, ancient Greek for "This and That," but he also called it *Porno-teo-kolossal*. As usual, he was ready to start work even before his previous film was released.

At first, the script called for shooting in Stuttgart, but Istanbul popped up in conversation and as quickly disappeared. Pasolini talked of New York, about Naples. He showed Ninetto his crayon sketches of certain scenes. He often did this, drawing many quick sketches, primitive story boards. He always saw his films in his head, and drew them as so many stills, so that the making became a mechanical process of transferring his clear picture into action before cameras. As usual, they also talked soccer scores. Pasolini and Davoli agreed the actor would take home a rough script and read it over.

Ninetto's infant son, Pier Paolo, had tired. Anna recalls at 10:20 Pasolini looked at his watch and said, "Anna, please make up my bill. Otherwise I'll be late [*faccio tardi*]." That's all he said: she assumed it meant he had an appointment, was going to see someone he knew, where he was expected. He always paid by check, writing the bill upwards to twenty-five or thirty thousand lire and taking cash back. This time—Anna thinks it is the only time this happened—he wrote the exact amount due, eleven thousand, on his account at the Cassa di Risparmio di Roma (the Rome Savings Bank) on via Giancinto Carini in Monteverde Vecchio, the street where he had lived before moving to via Eufrate, in EUR. Anna believes he did not want to carry any cash with him where he was going, that he felt safer that way.

She has kept the check in a plastic folder and takes it out to show people who have a reason to ask, like the TV crew which later came to reconstruct that evening for a series about famous unsolved crimes.

Their last customers gone, the Bravis closed the Pommidoro immediately and left the next morning for Moricone, before the first reports of what happened. They heard the news from Anna's mother, who heard it on the radio. "When we came back to town and I opened up, I saw their glasses still on the table as they had left them," Anna says. "And when I saw the oil in the frying pan, the one I had used to cook his potatoes, I started to cry."

As they parted, Pier Paolo and Ninetto agreed to talk the next day, Sunday, November 2, the holiday dedicated to the dead. "I thought he was going home," Ninetto later told the reporters, "I said, 'Ciao 'Pa, we'll be in touch.' He also said 'Ciao,' as though it were nothing at all. He seemed only a bit melancholy." The Bravis saw Ninetto leave with his family, going one direction in his car, and Pasolini leave alone, going another way, in his.


The via Tiburtina would have been Pasolini's most direct route to the central train station. But no one knows for certain that he arrived that way. He could, after some turns, have taken the via Cavour straight there, passing behind Santa Maria Maggiore on the way.

The paved station square, utilitarian and without charm, is Rome's principal transport hub, just the sort of place to look at someone without being seen to do so, to do business without drawing attention to yourself, not a destination in itself. Nice people not taking a bus or train avoided the area entirely, leaving it for gypsies to hustle passersby and for Africans—some still in native dress but without proper papers—who set up illegal shop on its sidewalks to sell out of suitcases cheap watches and wooden carvings of elephants, belts, and sunglasses guaranteed to fall apart.

Here the hustlers, amateur and professional, gathered in bars clustered around the Moderno and Modernetta porno movie houses; the attraction that night at the first was *Porno West,* at the second *La mia carne brucia di desiderio* (My flesh burns with desire). Bars on both sides of the piazza were known for the trade; under the nervous eyes of tourists, the boys (careful of informers and undercover cops) swapped stories, smoked cigarettes, and looked, trying not to look obvious, for customers. Competition for the good ones, for johns who signaled their interest by ordering a light beer (*una chiara*), had been intensifying recently. During 1973–74, Roman police ran in more than 150 boys, newcomers to the trade, many come to the big city from the provinces with nothing to sell but themselves. They drove prices down and threatened established connections between long-time hustlers and their steady clients.[2]

On one side of the square, going toward the center of town, two curved buildings faced with gigantic colonnades flank a fountain, as though protecting it from the city or sheltering those within from view. The luxurious Grand Hotel sits in between the station square and the fountain. It turns its side against the seaminess of the Piazza dell'Esedra, renamed the Piazza della Repubblica. In best Roman ironic fashion, ambassadors and big-time businessmen discuss deals in the bar of this elegant hostelry only yards from where young Libyans, Tunisians, Moroccans, and Egyptians go to find a queen, a *checca*, who will pay for the right to grope a crotch in the nearby movie theaters' back rows.

Facing this spot, where the Fountain of the Naiads now stands, Emperor Maximilian started construction of vast brick baths in A.D. 298, a job finished seven or eight years later by Diocletian. Art collections and libraries, not just steamrooms and cloisters, were built into the complex surrounding small gardens of clipped box, ivy, and bay trees. More than a dozen centuries later, at the unification of Italy, a national collection of paintings and antique sculpture, the Museo Nazionale Romano, was installed here, an island of rarely disturbed peace amid the bus fumes and careening taxis. Romans still call it the Museo delle Terme (the Museum of the Baths). As everywhere in Italy, a pagan monument accommodated a Christian one.

The bits of garden separating the museum from the hustlers' bars are nothing Diocletian would recognize. With the cloisters gone, they are not more than a passageway with plants, a sort of no-man's-land. Some scrubby bushes no one tends offer a hint of privacy for boys and men who want to ask for a cigarette, make small talk, and perhaps go somewhere more private. The footpaths among the bushes take their tone from the piazza itself: lots of people in motion, some who want to panhandle, some seeking to invite, others seeking an invitation.

Pasolini had been here before. He might easily have made a pickup elsewhere, on any of the city's most-traveled streets and most-visited monuments. He could have joined the walkers cruising the hill called Monte Caprino next to Michelangelo's buildings atop the Capitoline hill, or worked the pissoirs along the Tiber or the edges of the Circo Massimo. Hundreds of boys, maybe thousands, had come into his nights and out again, uncounted sexual encounters that not always included a handshake, frequently no names or only false ones (he usually told his own), and few particulars about work or residence. Sometimes he paid; sometimes he didn't. Occasionally, the encounter was warmer, perhaps extending through eating together, a drink, a second meeting. But not necessarily. It was understood by both parties (assuming they were two and not a group) that the intersection might last minutes or start something to endure a lifetime. One took one's chances.

His 1955 novel *Ragazzi di vita* had put the phrase, literally "boys of life," into Italian usage just as it named the type he liked: poor, uneducated, forgotten, often petty criminal youths whose Rome had nothing to do with nightclubs, sidewalk cafés, shopping, or coins in the Fountain of Trevi. His were the gritty neighborhoods out past the end of the bus lines, places where the cute little urchin sold his ass, lived out of garbage pails, dealt in stolen goods, and picked pockets rather than stand around waiting for tips behind a bar. The margins of the city inhabited by the dispossessed were his symbolic territory, so much so that the press had come to call those quarters "pasolinian." And much of his art had been about the lives of those whose names do not make it into the newspapers, save when they are arrested.

Loving slum boys, both in the abstract and in fact, was his link to the vitality of life itself and to death. In 1969, he wrote "Lines from the Testament," a poem which appeared in his last collection of verse.

> Sex is a pretext. For however many the encounters
> —and even in winter, through streets abandoned to
> the wind,
> amid expanses of garbage against distant buildings,
> there are many—there's only moments in the
> solitude;
> the livelier and warmer the sweet body
> that anoints with seed and then departs,
> the colder and deathlier the beloved desert around
> you;
> like a miraculous wind, it fills you with joy,
> it, not the innocent smile or troubled arrogance
> of the one who then goes away; he carries with him a
> /youthfulness
> awesomely young: and in this he's inhuman
> because he leaves no traces, or, better, only one
> trace
> that's always the same in all seasons.
> A boy in his first loves
> is nothing less than the world's fecundity.
> It is the world that thus arrives with him,
> appearing, /disappearing,

like a changing form. All things remain the same—
and you'll search half the city without finding him
again;
the deed is done; its repetition is ritual. And
the solitude's still greater if a whole crowd
waits its turn: in fact the number of disappearances
grows
leaving is fleeing—and what follows weighs upon the
present
like a duty, a sacrifice performed to the death
wish.
Growing old, however, one begins to feel weary
especially at the moment when dinnertime is over
and for you nothing is changed; then you're near to
screaming / or weeping;
and that would be awesome if it wasn't precisely
merely / weariness
and perhaps a little hunger. Awesome, because that
would mean
your desire for solitude could no longer be
satisfied,
and what isn't considered solitude is the true
solitude,
the one you can't accept, what can you expect?
There's no lunch or dinner or satisfaction in the
world
equal to an endless walk through the streets of the
poor,
where you must be wretched and strong, brothers to
the dogs.[3]

The boys were the excuse, and also the concrete, touchable proofs of an idea that is no good without a body. He believed that in the encounters, no one was hurt; and if anyone, it was he. He found tenderness and humanity in what the mass of people think the icy dealings of automata. Unless one chooses not to believe him, Pasolini found this life an idyll, almost to the end, when everything changed; the boys' was God-given beauty, a confirmation he required that he was alive, that the world was there and he was in it, that he could take it in his hands, and be taken in its hands, be loved and love it.

When he came to Rome, just as the century reached midpoint, just as the nightmare 1940s passed into the stupidly optimistic 1950s, he found a world altogether different from how it was this night. Into this more innocent Rome, one he found both "ferocious" and "teeming," a more innocent Pasolini had thrown himself with the ardor of a young man in love with life itself. Right on the front page of the *Corriere della sera,* he had written about how it had changed, how the Italians had mutated "anthropologically," and become a nation of what he believed protocriminals, ruined by consumerism, television, and compulsory secondary education. Some people thought he was one of those doing the ruining, that the contradiction between accusing boys of being criminal and paying them for sex was going too far, stretching artistic complexity to the point of plain hypocrisy.

Behind the wheel of his Alfa 2000GT, he looked quite able to take care of himself: he dyed his hair, dressed as the boys did, and could talk that way too. He understood their schemes to cadge a gold lighter or "a loan." But he was here because this was what he always did, and because he needed to be here. He confessed in print, for anyone to read:

> Thousands of them. It's impossible to love only one
> of them.
> Each has his own new or ancient
> beauty, which all share: dark,
> blond, slender, brawny, it is
> the world I love in him . . .
> . . . at times
> I think nothing else has the wonderful
> purity of this feeling. Better death
>
> than to renounce it! I must defend this
> desperate awesome tenderness,
> which, like the world, was mine at birth.
>
> Perhaps no one's ever lived at such peaks
> of desire—funereal anxiety which
> fills me as the sea its breezes.
>
> Slopes, hills, grass a thousand years old,
> landslides of flowers or garbage, branches
> dry or glistening with dew, the air
>
> of the seasons, with their recent
> and ancient sunlit walls . . . all this
> hides me and my (you laugh!) young friends
>
> in whom no act is dishonest
> because their desire is without tragedy
> since their sex is whole and fresh.

I couldn't, otherwise. Only the wholesome
normal healthy son can kindle my
darkly dazzling thought; and in only one way

do I resemble him, in the infinite
reascertaining of the lilylike
secret of his impure groin.

And a thousand times this act has to be
repeated, because not to
means to feel death like a frenzied pain

unequaled in the living world. . . .
I don't conceal it, I who've never concealed
anything: the unrepressed love that invades me,

love for my mother, has no room
for hypocrisy or cowardice! Nor am I right
because I'm different; I don't know

your God; I'm an atheist: prisoner
only of my love, but in all else I'm free,
in every judgment, every passion.

I am a free man! Freedom's
honest food is tears; well, then I'll weep.
It's the price of my legitimating my desire,

yes, but love's worth all I have.
Sex, death, political passion, these
are the simple objects to which I give

my elegaic heart. . . . My life
possesses nothing else.[4]

In 1964, in other lines from the same poem, he assigned the roles
and described the players:

In reality, I'm the boy, they're
the adults. I, who by the excess of my presence

have never crossed the border between love
for life and life . . .
I gloomy with love, and all around me the chorus

of the happy, for whom reality's a friend.

# 3

*"Once I walked around Rome and Rome smiled at me, made me happy. Now it makes me afraid. Rome today smells of death."*

*He suffered both from persecution and from a sense of persecution, and the two did not always coincide.*
                              *—Muriel Spark on Cardinal Newman*

# IN SEARCH
# OF GENNARIELLO

Pasolini at the station did not play the naïf. On the contrary, he was experienced in the street sex game and knew what he wanted. The boys he preferred had to have a certain look: He had a type—not a preference, but a fixation—and never varied from it.

He described his obsession in one of his last essays, a long letter to an imaginary Neapolitan boy named Gennariello, age fifteen. He printed it in the weekly magazine *Il mondo*.

First of all, you are, and should be, very nice-looking. Not perhaps in the conventional sense. In build you can be small and indeed even a little skinny; your features can already show the marks which in later years will inevitably turn your face into a mask. But your eyes must be black and shining, your mouth a little wide; your face fairly regular; your hair must be short at the neck and behind the ears; whereas on your brow I have no difficulty in granting a kind quiff, warlike and perhaps a little exaggerated and ridiculous. I would not mind if you were a bit of a sportsman and therefore slim in the hips and solid in the legs. As for the sport, I would prefer you to like soccer so that now and again we can have a game together. And all this—all this about your body let us be clear, has not in your case any practical or interested aim; it is a pure esthetic thought, one moreover that puts me at my ease. Let us understand each other: if you were ugly, really ugly, it would be all the same provided you were as likeable and normally intelligent and affectionate as you are. In that case, it is enough if your eyes are laughing—just as if instead of being a Gennariello you were a Concettina.[1]

Two issues later, he warned the readers of the "Letter to Gennariello," in what he called his "little instructional treatise":

We shall have a lot to say about sex. It will be one of the most important of our topics and I shall certainly not lose the chance to tell you some truths in this connection even if they are simple ones which nevertheless will, as usual, greatly shock Italian readers, who are always ready to cut dead the reprobate and turn their backs on him. Well, in that sense I am like a Negro in a racist society which has felt the need to indulge in a spirit of tolerance. That is to say, I am tolerated.[2]

To appeal to him, the boys need not be intelligent in the usual sense, and certainly not intellectual. He preferred that they had not gone past high school, and made no secret of his visceral dislike for the brainy sort, whom he scorned as presumptuous, guilty, and plagued with what he called "petty bourgeois anxiety." Innocence of a kind would do better, or at least formal ignorance; better was plenty of *furbizia*—street smarts, everyday cunning. He spoke of it as another kind of wisdom, somehow uncorrupted, sweet even when rough because it was the aggression of society's powerless marginals. The boys' lack of conventional manners was only the absence of an undesirable sophistication. Even at the height of his fame as a film director, known far beyond literary circles, he sought out the company of such boys, never minding if they were bumpkins, awkward, or even outrageous in social situations. When Ninetto "made a fool of himself" and shocked grand ladies of the Roman salons, Pasolini only smiled and explained gently that he ought not to worry, that the apparently scandalized "could not help themselves."

Some of his friends accused him of willful blindness. He seemed absurd, was making a *brutta figura*, insisting that the punks were somehow wise in a way others did not see. He even listened to his boys' banalities with respect, seeming to prefer their observations to those of important writers like Giorgio Bassani, who stopped frequenting Pasolini because of it.

But toward the end, he changed his mind. He turned on them with the fury of a lover betrayed, condemning them as a "calamity," a generation both unhappy and criminal as no other had ever been.

His poetry throughout the fifties and his films up to 1968 were grounded in love of the *borgata*, the slum world no one else wanted to know about. The erotic link he had to the slums was also a utopian vision of the *popolo* and an ideological commitment to the Left. But after 1968 he began to see the young as "victims" of a consumer culture that turned the willing boys into monstrous hustlers. The metamorphosis of his angels into demons meant his inspiration had dried up around him, leaving him on a lake of salt. The boy he met in the piazza the night of November 1, 1975, was no more than an infant when Pasolini published the book of poems called *The Religion of My Time*. He had written then,

> my loves of pure sensuality
> repeated over and over in the sacred valleys of lust,
> sadistic, masochistic, the trousers
> with their warm sack
> where a man's destiny is marked
> —are acts I perform, alone
> in the midst of a wondrously convulsive sea.
>
> Bit by bit, the thousands of sacred gestures,
> the hand on the warm swelling,
> the kisses, each time to a different mouth,
> always more virgin,
> always nearer the enchantment of the species,
> the norm that makes tender fathers of sons. . . . [3]

By the time they met, though, there were no more "tender fathers."

> These last years I have studied these sons for a long time. In the end my judgment, however unjust and pitiless it may seem, even to myself, is one of condemnation. I have tried to understand, to pretend not to understand, to rely on exceptions, to hope for some change, to consider the reality young

people represent historically—that is beyond subjective judgments of good or evil. But it has been useless. My *feeling* is condemnatory. . . . In the end—that is today, at the beginning of 1975—my feeling, I repeat is one of condemnation . . . more than a condemnation, my feeling, in fact, is a "ceasing to love. . . ."[4]

In 1975, at the age of fifty-three, Pasolini himself was beyond change. Even if the boys had turned mean,[5] he could only repeat the same gestures toward them. The particular beauty the boys should have, his behavior with them, including some roughness, the obligatory rituals of nightly cruising whatever the weather or his fatigue—these were frozen now in ritual.

He once wrote that he would have driven "a thousand miles" for such an encounter as tonight's at the station. Those who traveled with him to make movies believed it. After Pasolini was dead, his first producer Alfredo Bini wrote about dragging him out of Bedouin tents, beaten bloody for his importunities.[6] Others hint, always vaguely but persistently, that every city he visited in Africa, Asia, South and North America became a place for cruising, no matter the danger. They point to his writings about India and Africa, peopled with boys he met at all hours and anywhere. It was understood by his film troupes that when work was done, Pasolini would disappear to take enormous risks; like clockwork he vanished from location after dinner, or after ten when he was in Rome.

He went around dressed like his boys, tight jeans and jean jacket cinched at the waist, polyester shirts far cheaper than he could afford, often with loud patterns. In the sixties and seventies, he took to wearing ankle-high boots and wide leather belts with oversize buckles. His silver Alfa became known not only to the movie people who saw it parked at Cinecittà, or to the journalists who knew that its arrival meant news, or to his friends among the literati who would never dare to drive such a flashy symbol of money; it was also known to boys who had seen him move in and out of the slums, boys who recognized it because those who work the streets make it their business to remember cars.

Antonio Nori's bar stands only yards from the train station, at the end of via Daniele Manin, where the street dissolves into the Piazza dei Cinquecento. His father and his grandfather had owned it before him. It always offered food—*tramezzini* stuffed and cut on the diagonal, or sandwiches grilled to burn black stripes onto the breadrolls, leaving the spinach-and-mozzarella filling cold inside—and the dazzling variety of drinks served by any good Roman bar—dozens of *digestivi* and *aperitivi,* beer on tap served in dimpled mugs, house wine by the glass, fresh-squeezed orange, grapefruit, and lemon juice with fizzy water in summer. The centerpiece, of course, was a huge machine for making the coffee that glues Roman social life together. In 1975 the bar was open twenty-four hours a day. At night, its sidewalk tables each bore an electric lamp which let down pools of light on the orange and red tablecloths and onto the green plastic chairs made of cord wrapped around a tubular frame. "It was really beautiful," Nori says proudly, "always the same: none of that ever changes."[7] But people stole the lamps, so Nori replaced them with white-and-green plastic ashtrays to advertise his private-brand coffee.

The last months of 1975 were the peak of the bad times, when the traffic of the *malavita* kept good customers away. By Nori's own admission, his bar was a place where drug deals were made until the police clamped down hard throughout the station district. And then there were the hustlers. Nori does not think most of the boys were professionals, just kids "willing to do it sometimes for men willing to pay." He is a man who makes it his business to mind his own business; so long as no one bothers other customers, what they do is their affair alone. "All sorts of people come here and some for that," he says of the skin trade around his premises. "I saw Pasolini here all the time: he was a regular," and not at this bar alone, but also at the "Dey" down the street and the "Indipendenza" across the gigantic square.

When Pasolini arrived at Nori's this particular night, all the witnesses agree that he pulled to the curb and lowered the window on the passenger side. The boys on the sidewalk, even those inside the bar, could have seen his face; turning his head from the driver's side, he would have been on a sight-line with their crotches. To talk with him, they had to kneel or bend over at car-side so as not to speak over the silver Alfa's roof. Some evidence suggests that Pasolini was cautious. He kept the door locked on the passenger side and talked through that window without rolling it all the way down. He had reason to be careful.

Several days later, when everyone had a story to tell, some drag queens told reporters that they had been the first to recognize Pasolini, had rushed up to his car, asking him to "take us for a ride," just a spin, *due passi.* He refused and moved the car forward along the curb toward a group of teenage boys standing in the doorway of the bar. Stefano Deidda, Adolfo De Stefanis, Claudio Seminara, and Giuseppe Pelosi, called "Pino."

Claudio and Pino did everything together. They'd pooled their cash to buy an old white Fiat 850, although only one of them had a driver's license. They went to a dance hall together with that intense male bonding of Mediterranean adolescents, and to the porno flicks together. That's where they later said they'd been earlier in the day—they told the inquiring magistrate—after dancing at a neighborhood place with some girls they knew. In the late afternoon, they'd come to the station square to catch the film at the Moderno. But they claimed they changed their minds. Instead, they came to this bar, where the faggots hung out.[8]

They themselves weren't queer, of course—they hated queers as did everyone else—but they were perhaps not unwilling to make some money off them if the occasion presented itself. Everyone knew the difference between going with a queer and being one. Those guys, kind of women really, either went to their knees or bent over. So long as the roles were always kept very clear—who did what to whom—then it was harmless enough. A *maschio* was no less virile for letting a fag service him. Lots of perfectly normal guys had tried it, even more than once. No one was shocked at the arrangement. It would be perfectly reasonable for them to use the money earned this way to buy gifts for their girl friends, take them on dates. Their *figura* was not at issue, but only so long as the players stayed within their assigned roles.

Pasolini spoke first to Claudio, smooth-skinned and pretty, his hair in blond waves like a del Sarto angel, his forehead high and clear. But his manner was too refined to be sexy and he was slim like a girl: Pasolini liked them more masculine of affect.

Then he spotted Pino. Behind the wheel of his car, he must have been struck by the boy's resemblance to Ninetto and to the Gennariello of his imagination: the black eyes, the mound of ringlets high in front, the small waist and strong legs, the straight, wide mouth. His pants (tight, without pockets) displayed the goods, a cheap shirt and jacket did justice to his chest and shoulders, and boots with heels made him taller. To justify the nickname they themselves made up, "Pino *la rana*" (Pino the frog), news reporters later claimed that his eyes bulged, but they did not. Pino Pelosi was a good-looking kid from the lower class, seventeen years old, with a record of juvenile delinquency that had "put him in" three times, rough but not scabrous—exactly the type Pasolini preferred.

Pino remembers, "Pasolini asked for directions, I think, but I

understood immediately what he wanted."[9] He says Pasolini offered
him a ride and something to eat. The boy, who was car-crazy, might
also have sensed the chance to drive the Alfa. But everyone who was
there at the time understood what everyone else wanted: For money,
the kid was willing to go for a spin and allow himself to be felt up.
He'd allow a blow-job for, say, twenty thousand lire, but that was
all. "There's a limit," he said more than a decade later, "I would go
that far but then there's a wall, no further.[10] He says that at seventeen
he was "confused" and "immature," even afraid. "But you suppress
the fear," he says. It was such an easy way to get cash, other guys
did it, and it certainly did not make him a fag.

True or not, this is the version he gave to the Tribunal. Pelosi
never denied that he accepted the offer from a stranger and that he
was willing to have his pants opened as well. The rest of his story,
repeated for ten years and more, follows from there: a tale of a *bravo
ragazzo*, fallen temporarily on bad times, defending himself against
the attack of a psychopath, a well-known homosexual and corruptor
of minors, a rich man bribing the slum kid for his body. That didn't
make him a killer, he argued, or part of a plot.

Some of the press explained it differently: that Pino recognized
Pasolini at once because they had met before or because he had seen
his picture in the papers or on TV. They say he came directly over
and offered himself, having his own idea of how the night would end.


Within minutes of their leaving the square in Pasolini's car, he and
Pino were back. In the excitement of the pickup, Pino claims, he
had forgotten the car he and Claudio owned, what ought to be done
with it if he were late. Making arrangements for the Fiat was sensible.
One never goes out at night with a fag without a plan, and it was still
early on a Saturday night on a holiday weekend, and one had to be
ready for all sorts of adventures. The boys spoke for a while on the
sidewalk and Claudio took the keys, agreeing to drop the heap near
Pino's grandmother's place in the *borgata* and to leave the keys under
the seat, if he were not back soon. When the police interrogated
Claudio later, he said Pino's only explanation was "This one will take
me home afterward."[11]

Pino has always stuck to the story that he told Claudio only that
he was "going for a ride" and would be "right back." He made their
powwow out to be so many giggling girls at an American high school
prom, compelled to report every move to one another. In his version
of events, he presented himself to the court as solicitous of his

friends' convenience and feelings, the stuff of responsible adult behavior.

But the police, the press, and the courts worried over this sidewalk conference. Surely this was the chance for making a plot. In these moments the boys could have agreed to meet in a certain isolated spot where they could beat up the *frocio* and take his wallet, maybe steal the car, and let him walk back to the ritzy neighborhood where he probably lived.

When the magistrate questioned Seminara, Deidda, and De Stefanis, the boys added a detail which was confirmed by a self-described hustler who came forward at Pelosi's trial the next April. Someone Pino did not know, and did not see, called out to him as he was about to get into Pasolini's car for the second time, "Pino, don't go with that one. That's Pasolini, and he'll try to fuck you in the ass"—friendly advice from one street whore to another. Pino's lawyer did not pursue the matter, suggesting as it does that he was not, as he claimed, the good boy in a bad place, and that he knew about Pasolini from the start. Pino dismissed the story and steadfastly held that he knew the man only as Pier Paolo—not " 'Pa" in dialect as Ninetto called him, no last name, no reputation, nothing more.

Whatever he knew, he was soon in the car again, as Pasolini swung away from the curb and headed for the outskirts of the city. Hunter and prey—whichever was which—had connected.


The Alfa's seats put Pino and Pier Paolo close together, separated only by the wood-topped gearshift not perpendicular to the floor but angled steeply forward, almost up to the dash. They would have felt the cobblestones under the tires, their impact increased by the speed the car reached without strain.

Within two minutes, they could have moved fast around the Esedra fountain and into the via Nazionale, aiming for the Piazza Venezia where the top of the Altare della Patria monument (dubbed the "Wedding Cake" by English soldiers garrisoned in Rome during World War II) was visible at the bottom of the hill. The Nazionale had been blasted through the maze of layered Rome in the first enthusiasm of the united kingdom for making the city a capital equal to Paris.

The car's silver skin reflected in the shopwindows packed with goods that spill onto the sidewalk every morning to be tucked away every night—"best prices in Rome," signs claim in English, German, and Japanese. In Pasolini's novel *Una vita violenta*, Tommaso Puzzilli had walked down this street, a boy just like Pino, except that he came from Pietralata *borgata* instead of Pino's Guidonia. He had looked in the shopwindows and wanted what they had to sell, the life they offered. The windows were dark now, of course. Pelosi claims that at some point along this route, Pasolini put his hand on his thigh, touched his crotch. Pino admits he did not resist.

A little farther on the left rise the markets of Trajan, their brick vaults amazingly intact. A sharp turn and they roared past Trajan's Column, once the focal point of a splendid complex now gone. The Roman Forum was on their right, the ancient heart of the city.

They had to make almost a full circle, clockwise around the Colosseum. The area under the arches of the arena was well known for pickups; it would have been difficult for them not to notice the boys hanging around, leaning on the railings. Three weeks later, *Oggi* magazine sent a reporter to talk to the hustlers. One explained how business had fallen off after Pasolini was killed: Everyone was afraid, he said, was staying home. Another said he knew Pasolini well, considered him "a friend," but without sex. Eighteen-year-old "Marco" said he was not able to return to the streets for five nights after the killing, that he saw Pasolini drive by that Saturday night "at about nine o'clock," but that is impossible. "Marco" said he had never had much luck with Pasolini, who seemed to prefer what the young hustler called "more masculine types" than he.

Pasolini knew the ancient poets; he had taught them and their languages in a high school after the war. He had made films of Sophocles' *Oedipus* and Euripides' *Medea*, and had directed a production of Aeschylus' *Oresteia* transposed to black Africa. At the age of seventeen, Pino's age, Pasolini was by his own account "reading a book and a half a day," discovering the new French cinema, Freud, modern poetry and painting. He was captain of the soccer squad of the Bologna University literature department, talked of directing a student production of Calderón's *La vida es sueño*, sketched the outline of a study on contemporary Italian painting, and consumed poetry by the yard—Cecchi, Montale, and Ungaretti. He filled notebooks with "lists of the contemporary authors 'to be read,' " and passed long hours "on the smooth, enemy benches of the library" absorbing the latest in criticism and poetry, the magazines that addressed what culture was and ought to be in the deepest years of Mussolini.

Pelosi barely managed in school. At seventeen, he had a criminal record for petty theft and was a veteran of youth detention centers, his schooling under tutelage of the police and the courts already begun. He would never have a career, only jobs and then not for long, never rise out of the underclass. All the Republic's talk about building democracy and equality, all the debates over opportunity did not change life for boys like him. Economic boom or not, he was living out a hobbled birthright, inherited from his father and his father before him. Without skills, he had left school at an age not greater than prewar poor boys had. His worldly ambition consisted of getting enough to get by, on one side of the law or the other.

He later said that Pasolini asked him about himself. He could talk about his last job working for his uncle, a baker in Garbatella. Pino delivered breadrolls pressed into a shape to resemble roses and so called *rosette*. Romans love them for their crust and their hollow insides. It was hard work and dirty, lifting giant sacks of flour, baking in the middle of the night to delivery so housewives could buy before noon. Pino hated lugging the heavy crates, and had argued with his uncle. He always hated to be crossed or told what to do, and they had parted ways.

If he had been accommodating, he might have had a steady paycheck as his father had delivering packages, or his sister, who worked in a high-class butcher shop in via della Croce, while dreaming of becoming a stewardess. But he knew better. Exactly like the boys in Pasolini's novels, he understood he could do far better grabbing gold chains from necks and wrists, snatching an occasional handbag, picking a pocket and then graduating to apartment heists, burglarizing stores, and dealing a bit in stolen goods. He would probably not get caught, and if he did, he did. Then, back inside, he could move to the higher stages of the trades taught in prison, the fine points of getaway cars and unhooking alarms. The jails of Regina Coeli and Rebibbia are great centers of learning. Pino was about to register for a long course.

Pasolini liked sex in the open air, so he chose to bring Pelosi to Ostia on the coast south and west of Rome. His poetry speaks of outdoor sex frequently; many of his films include such scenes in fields. It was not odd, certainly not a homosexual monopoly. Roman couples, forced to live with their parents into adulthood, mate in borrowed cars, or the first of their own: They line the via della Camilluccia every night, out where Mussolini's mistress Claretta Petacci had lived. Romans have been known to copulate virtually in plain sight, inside their cars atop the Janiculum, near the equestrian statue of Anita Garibaldi. They park every which way, tucked into every grassy patch, under every spot where the city's umbrella pines lend a shadow. The via Appia, pride of ancient Rome's public works, turns into a nightly drive-in movie without the film, couples in every back and front seat for miles. On Sunday mornings, discarded rubbers litter the ground like so many empty ammo shells on a battlefield from which the dead and the wounded have disappeared.

Pasolini would have had no trouble asking Pelosi what he was willing to do. He never shrank from using the words he needed to tell what it was, exactly, that he wanted. Among film crews, he was famous for speaking softly but for being absolutely clear about his requirements, which had to be met the first time.

If Pino had really been Gennariello, Pasolini could have complimented him in Neopolitan. He could have said, *"Tiene nu bellu pesce"* (You've got a nice cock), agreed that he was to pay *vint' mila lire* (twenty thousand lire) if allowed to give him a blow-job—*"t' facc' nu bucchino"*—or use his hand to make him come, *"t' o' facc' in mane."* And if Pelosi demurred, muttering about how disgusting were the *ricchione*, the fags, Pasolini could gently doubt the boy was as innocent as he claimed. "Is this really your first time?"—*"Ma chesta è 'a primma vota pe' te'?"* But he would stop there, knowing better than to ask, "Would you like to take it in the ass?"—*"t' 'o fai mettere 'n culo?"* The answer then would be, *"Io facc' l'omm"*—"I'm the man."

But such conversation was impossible. Pelosi might have had the sangfroid to say what was acceptable sex and what not. It would have broken the atmosphere, eliminated the tease, the chase, the reluctance feigned, the conquest savored, the sweet reassurance that he, after all, had only "played the man." He has always insisted that he never would have agreed to bend over to "take it in the ass," and those who claim to understand such boys believe him. Pelosi told the court they never talked past agreeing "to do something." What happened at Ostia, he has always claimed, was an unwelcome surprise.

Both were playing a kind of Russian roulette. Maybe, by chance, both could emerge satisfied. If they were lucky, the appropriate muscles would contract, heartbeats rise, and release follow. Perhaps Pasolini was skilled enough to overcome such a tentative tough-guy's prudish *machismo*, his resistance to abandon. Pasolini, an experienced technician of sexual arousal, certainly knew when to insist and when to rest, when to go faster and when to pause, when to speak and when to be silent.

They would, at best, grapple with each other for a few moments, making the motions that lovers make. Pelosi was not the type to be kissed on the mouth. All Pasolini's calculations had to be right the first time, lest the ride back to the station be uncomfortable for them both. But since money was to change hands, it was Pasolini, the customer, who had to be satisfied. Perhaps, though, Pelosi did not see it this way, perhaps even that was beyond him. Jean Genet, asked about what happened that night, said, "All the Italians are gigolos, none professionals." Pelosi would not have imagined, not understood, that it was his job to please.

They were on the viale Ostiense now, modern asphalt poured wide over the ancient Ostia road. It makes part of a ring highway around the city, an almost perfect circle encompassing the historic center, the slums, and even some fields where a few shepherds, pathetic leftovers, watch sheep that watch bulldozers. As it turns toward the southwest, the road eventually reaches Fiumicino where Leonardo da Vinci Airport sits, although no one, not even foreigners, calls it that. The Tiber here is not the tawny blond it is far upstream, rich with the silt of inland mountains, but a poisoned, chemical yellow, long polluted at the stretch where it bends at the bottom of a trash-strewn slope. Pino had been promised a meal and Pasolini knew where to go, a trattoria that workers from the nearby wholesale markets used, a simple place overlooking the river, called Al Biondo Tevere.

If the stench from traffic fumes were not so overpowering, one might sit out front in the graveled garden. But that gray November, everyone went inside and left the clearing for parking cars. Besides, only from the inside can one look down the slope and over the tin-roofed shanties along the river bank, hovels set wherever some ground allows a city-dweller his unzoned patch of vegetables. At night, with everything dark and only electric lights, the place is appealing in a grimy, big-city way.

They knew Pasolini here as they knew him at the Pommidoro. Pino remembered how he was greeted as "*dottore*" when they walked in. Seated at a table with the requisite red-and-white check tablecloth topped with oiled paper, Pino ordered a glass of beer, spaghetti with oil and garlic, and a quarter of a roasted chicken. Pasolini only sipped a glass of beer as he listened to the boy talk, answering questions about his life.

A few weeks before, Pasolini had written his old friend Antonello Trombadori, art critic, editor, and Communist Party parliamentary deputy through four legislatures. The note was hand-carried by its subject who hoped to have a job from the politician—the usual thing, perhaps a guard somewhere, or keeper of a Party-owned garage, or an apprentice mason or carpenter.

Dear Antonello,

Here is Pasqualone Casau, the boy I spoke to you about. He is a *trasteverino*, a little rough [*un po' rozzo*], but he really is in need.[12]

He had intervened for boys he knew in this way for thirty years. Had matters gone differently, he might well have written such a note the next morning for the boy facing him now, one also really in need.

# 4

*Even when the facts are known, they have often not been suffi-
ciently submitted to criticism, elaboration, and synthesis; the true
and the false exist together, the important alongside the unimpor-
tant, in tendentious personal memoirs, newspaper columns, and the
self-justifying chronicles of official reports.*
                                        *—Denis Mack Smith, Italy*

# THE IDROSCALO, OSTIA

Out on the Ostiense, the city was either sleeping or celebrating
through the long holiday weekend. If a car had followed them, a
white Fiat 850 or any other car, Pasolini did not act as if he had
noticed it, changing his route. No trace of any kind was found of a
second vehicle: not tracks, not paint chips, no eyewitnesses, nothing.
But then it rained hard at the murder site before the investigators
went to work.

After the wholesale markets and over a bridge, the Ostiense yields

to the via del Mare, finally running out of pavement as it approaches
the Idroscalo, the old seaplane station near where the Tiber empties
into the sea, where Dante had souls embark for Hades. Now potholes
must have slowed the Alfa considerably. If not, its tight springs ex-
aggerating the ups and downs would have sent them bouncing off the
roof. On this track with no name, the headlights picked out the edges
of the holes and made moon craters of them, very white at the edges,
blackest black inside. The sea, winter gray, was about fifty yards
farther. They could have smelled it but not seen it in the dark.

They might have seen, after a bit, the edges of shacks—*case abusive* they are called, because "abusive" of the law—thrown up by
people who wanted a garden, someplace out of the city where the air
breathed of something other than auto exhaust. Pasolini had described the place precisely in his second novel, *Una vita violenta*[1]:

> Pietralata lay there, against the mounds of the Aniene and the grey sky: the
> old buildings to the right, and beyond, all the arc of the development's blocks
> and the rows of little houses, like a native village, with an odor of heated
> garbage so strong it was overwhelming. Every now and then there was a puff
> of cooler wind, a breeze from the sea, and then the stink of houses full of
> rags, rubble, and kids' pee mingled with the smell of the mud.

The *casette,* usually single rooms built of pressed board and corrugated iron, mostly were without electricity. The better-off squatters
brought generators with them or lit bulbs and ran televisions from
their car engines. It was not a proper neighborhood: no municipally-
made street signs, no paved sidewalks, no schools, no sewers, no
post office, not even a bar. It was nothing to see, except that to
Pasolini it was somehow better than the salons of Roman hostesses
or the villas of the rich.

Pelosi says Pasolini seemed to know where he was going. It was,
in fact, just where he had shot some footage the year before.
When he reached a clearing of hardened earth, an open field used at
times for soccer, he cut the engine. They sat a minute. No one knows
whether they spoke. Pelosi says Pasolini removed his glasses, undid
the boy's pants and bent over, awkward though it might have been,
sitting side by side. There was no resistance: "He took my cock in
his mouth for about a minute," Pelosi told the judges, "but he didn't
complete the blow-job."[2] Years later, he says that he did complete
it, and that all the autopsies—which found no trace of semen in
Pasolini's mouth—were simply wrong. "He could have spit it out,"
Pelosi says, unperturbed by the claims of scientific inquiry.[3] Much

later, analysis of a handkerchief found under the driver's seat showed traces of what the press delicately called "*liquido maschile*," although Pasolini's friends were able to keep this detail out of the papers at the time since it suggested Pasolini was the *corruttore*.

"*Me ho fatto una sburata*," Pelosi might have said in Roman street talk, "I've shot my wad." And that was that for *amore:* You concede the *frocio* the privilege of paying to service you, making sure your own mouth stayed closed tight, hands preferably locked behind your head or anchored lead-like at your side.

Pelosi first claimed he got out of the car because he wanted a cigarette. Later, he said it was because he wanted to pee—nothing incompatible in that—and still later, that Pasolini ordered him out.

From this point, his narrative unfolded in shorthand, is full of gaps. He says that while he was standing, facing into the dark, tucking his cock back into his pants, Pasolini approached him. What Pelosi told the police was all taken down, word for word, and passed with greater speed into the press than the police files:

> He made me lean over a metal fence and came down behind me, pushing against me, trying to pull my pants down. I, instead, told him to stop it, but he picked up a stick, the kind that are used in gardens, and he tried to stick it up my ass, or at least he pushed it against my ass without even having lowered my pants.[4]

"He made noises," Pelosi said, "stuff that made no sense, that I couldn't understand."[5]

> So I grabbed a piece of wood and turned around and said to him, "But have you gone nuts?" This Paolo didn't have his glasses on, he'd left them in his car, and to look at him in the face, it seemed to me the face of a crazy man, so much so that I was afraid. I ran off in the direction of the paved road, over the muddy part, and he followed me. Since I was wearing boots with heels on them, I got all loaded down and I fell. I felt Paolo on top of me, moving his shoulders and I could tell he wanted to start again so I turned around, and then this Paolo hit me on the head right there at the point where I have the scar. . . . After I took that hit, I grabbed the stick from him with both hands and managed to get him away from me. I ran off again and again he caught up with me. He started hitting me again with the stick, now I remember it was a green board, he hit me on the temples and various places on my body. I saw, lying on the ground, a board with writing on it . . . and I broke it over his head but even this didn't make him stop. He didn't seem to feel anything.[6]

The fight effectively ended with two massive kicks to the groin, made almost deadly by the strength of Pino's thighs and the points on his boots. "They saw I was much smaller than he, that he was so strong and in such good shape. But if you kick anyone, no matter how big he is, that hard and *there*, he's out."[7] Pasolini fell and Pelosi continued to hit him around the head and chest.

> I grabbed him by the hair and pulled his head down and gave him two kicks in the face. Paolo staggered but still found the force to punch me in the nose. With one of the two pieces of the board I hit him over and over until I heard him fall to the ground and gasp. I took off for his car then, carrying the two pieces of board with me but I threw them away as I did the green board, throwing all that near the fence and near the car. Then I got inside the car and fled in it. I was very shaken and it took me a while to start the car and turn on the lights. In my flight, I didn't know whether I passed over his body or not.[8]

But the Alfa did pass over Pasolini's body. Pelosi denies claims by some experts that the car passed over the body twice, once backward and then forward, before he drove away and headed back toward Rome. "All I wanted to do was to get away," he told the court. "I didn't think he was dead, but at that moment, since the main thing was to go and get my car, I didn't care that if I left Pasolini there, he might die of his wounds."[9]

The wounds made for gory viewing when they laid Pasolini out the next morning at the University hospital mortuary, on a stainless steel examining table outfitted with a steel cylinder for a pillow. When *L'espresso* carried the pictures three years later on the occasion of Pelosi's appeal, the issue sold out. Under the headline "Massacre of a Poet," it showed a half-dozen color shots: Pasolini seen from above, naked, lying on his stomach on the shining gurney, close-ups of his face both from the front and side, bruised badly around the right temple, the right ear almost cut through. As if this were not enough, the next page had a small insert of the three wooden boards the coroners had studied. The bulk of the page was given over to a color photo taken at the murder site, probably within the first hour after Pasolini was found. His face is blotched with blood. His right arm lies across his blue-green undershirt, resting gently as a child's in sleep, the left arm folded above it but torn open at the elbow, the skin just below the shoulder ripped away almost to the elbow.[10]

Some text was run from the autopsy report:

> When Pasolini was found, he was lying on his back, a bloody arm twisted, the other hidden beneath the body. The hair was matted with blood. The arms were blackened with bruises and reddened with blood, as were the hands. The fingers of the left hand were fractured and cut. The left jaw was fractured. The nose was flattened, and bent to the right. The ears were cut in half, and the left one twisted. Wounds on the shoulders, the thorax, the loins. A deep laceration at the nape of the neck. A bruise at the testicles, wide, deep. Ten ribs broken, and the sternum. The liver lacerated at two points. The heart burst.[11]

Many readers wrote angry letters to the editor when this appeared. One said he could not look at the photos without wincing: Dirt ground into the skin, seeming to mix with blood, was too close to the grave, the body's repossession by the earth too blunt. The editors declared they had done enough for their readers' sensibilities by holding the photos until the first shock of the murder had passed. Now that Pelosi's appeal was coming to a hearing, publication was their duty; anticipating attack, they wrote that the pictures "cast on the matter of Pier Paolo Pasolini's killing an atrocious but vivid light—one more vivid than any closing speech by a prosecutor or any sentence."

But what the photos showed had not killed him. The kicks and blows rendered him helpless, bleeding slowly on the ground, but not dead. Had the assault stopped at this point, the victim might have survived. A trio of coroners concluded death was caused by "rupture of the heart and hemorrhage, a traumatic rupture which initiated from the side of the right ventricle."[12] Pelosi never denied driving over Pasolini's body—traces of hair and blood were found on the car's underchassis—and it was this that crushed his thorax and killed him. Until then, his soul's container was seriously bruised but not yet broken asunder: His heart still pumped and his nerves still sent messages to the brain. The electrically charged meat of synapse and dendrite, the chemistry of sodium and potassium that connects body and soul, still made the muscles twist and the lungs suck air. Then a moment came—or is it not so fine as "a moment"?—when consciousness failed but life went on. While he lay dying, his digestion proceeded, his fingernails and hair still grew. Descartes said the body is a machine animated by a ghost. When the car passed over Pasolini, Descartes' ghost pulled back from the machine, leaving not all at once but slowly. Or so we like to think. Perhaps instead the ancient

Greeks were correct: The Moirai, who allot and spin the thread of life, simply snip it.

Scientists have found that considerable loss of blood induces chemical and psychological reactions favorable to hallucinatory experience. What are the hallucinations of a dying poet, the last mind-pictures of a film director? In the photographs of the body, Pasolini looks surprised, mouth open, no anguished contortion of features, apparently more stunned than pained. Why should he have been surprised? Once he had told Alberto Moravia, "You know, every time I go cruising I feel like I'm risking my life." After such a life, what could have surprised him at this final moment?

To many, Pasolini's death seemed another straightforward homosexual crime (*un tipico delitto omosessuale*). For years, as police calls came late at night from isolated places into the offices of *Il messaggero*, Sergio De Risi, veteran of the paper's *cronaca* section, told his colleagues, "It's either a *frocio* or a *putana*."[13] He was usually right. It was only to be expected; it happened all the time. But so much about this death in particular is conjecture and a public record of contradictory confession, self-interested testimony, and mounting public confusion. Little aside from the precision of the autopsy reports is sure.

When they found Pasolini and turned him over for the photographs, some reports say his belt buckle was open and zipper partially lowered. Pino's explanation is that, "in the violence of the struggle," a phrase he uses to dismiss many problem details, Pasolini's pants came open. Coroners, unafraid to say words even policemen resist, probed the boy's asshole for semen and Pasolini's too. They found none, so the answer came from the laboratory. They had not engaged in anal intercourse.

But even these reports are not certain. Another version in other official reports has it that, when they found the body, the pants were closed and the zipper up and that the police undid them so that Ninetto could check the laundry mark inside the waistband when he was called to identify the corpse. Or then again, maybe Pelosi, if he acted with accomplices, tampered with the pants, opened them to make Pasolini look sexually involved.

So much is lost. The few seconds between Pelosi's leaving the car and the first blow are gone. He claims he thought only of defending himself from Pasolini's attack; "fighting for my life," he says.[14] And some people who claim they knew Pasolini well are sure he taunted the boy, asserting his rights as a customer over the hustler. They contend Pasolini's only satisfaction was in being beaten, that he was prepared to do whatever was needed to arouse his boys to anger. They insist that Pasolini was lean, hard from his shoulders to the waist, with legs sinewy from playing soccer every weekend, running in play until he dropped. But Pelosi was also in good shape and had the hard, naturally strong body of an active and vain seventeen-year-old. He had no more experience as a street fighter than Pasolini did, but he did have a thirty-six-year advantage.

And yet, some others claim, Pelosi ought to have shown more damage, should have emerged from the struggle with more visible punishment. When the police picked him up within the hour, he showed barely a scratch. There was a small scrape at the nose, as though he had been hit, but no blood, no broken bone, no bruises. Where was the blow that incited such violent self-defense? Before he had a chance to kick Pasolini in the groin and drive blows to his head with a plank, how was he not bloodied too? Pelosi found it convenient to claim X rays that showed blows to his head have "disappeared" from the hospital. But without first-class police intelligence, with only Pelosi's insistence on self-defense, the rest is hearsay, the biased reconstructions of paid consultants, or sheer guesswork.

Many think the understanding between Pasolini and Pelosi unraveled in a moment, that Pasolini might have resented coming all this way only to be thwarted. The boy claimed he always meant only to take the ride and the meal, allow himself to be given a hand-job (*una sega*) or a blow-job (*un pompino*), and pocket the cash: *punto e basta*. He portrayed Pasolini as "monstrous" and violent, the aggressor, as "Dr. Jekyll and Mr. Hyde."[15] The same epithets were applied by Leonardo Sciascia, for whom Pasolini was at once "a great intellectual" and "a split personality" who "knew himself too well" to allow psychiatry near him, who "wanted to understand, but not to change."[16]

The hairline to violence was crossed as quickly and irreversibly as excitation can turn to ejaculation. "I have an infinite hunger for love / for the love of bodies without souls," Pasolini wrote,[17] and people read the line as prophecy. Pelosi claims that when he resisted "playing the woman," Pasolini said to him, "I'll kill you," and that the phrase did not seem the usual street bravado but a warning, not metaphoric but a threat to be taken literally. He might have understood that now he was only a body without a soul, and that Pasolini felt free to do anything to such a person, to one without a spirit.

Pasolini's friends vehemently denied this possibility, as well as the suggestion that he reacted with violence to the threat of a holdup.

Moravia told the press his friend was quite incapable of violence, but had been its victim, even recently when someone who called Pasolini "friend" had made off with his car at gunpoint one night at the Baths of Caracalla. Sergio Citti said:

> I knew him for twenty-five years . . . It is impossible that a man like Pier Paolo could do violence to a boy like this because he failed to satisfy certain of his wants. It's absurd, ridiculous. Pier Paolo was an intelligent man, and I, who knew him, know what would have been his reaction, a laugh, a laugh and that's all. He studied people. He had had two or three such misadventures before and all he did was fork over the money. In front of a holdup, that's how he reacted: he laughed it off. He was too intelligent to have a violent reaction.[18]

Pelosi admitted to a violent temper, and repeated for more than a decade that the eggshell enclosing his rage had cracked with Pasolini's first blow. He insisted that a seventeen-year-old from his background could not be expected to have understood what he was doing, or to calculate and control his actions at that moment.

The police found Pasolini awash in blood, his skull battered, one ear almost off, his fingernails flattened, and a line of broken bones across his fingers, as though he raised his hand to fend off the blow of a strong, elongated weapon. Pelosi claims in the course of the struggle he had found a straight plank, one with an address hand-painted on it. The makeshift sign was rotted and falling apart, but he grabbed it and brought it down on Pasolini's head and beat him about the body. Such a plank was found at the scene, smashed and blood-stained, marked with the words "via dell' Idroscalo, 93." But the next day, local people readily complied with news photographers' requests to pose with the split wood, obliviously layering it with their own fingerprints: What the press gained in graphic coverage the State lost as reliable evidence.

And yet, the fractures in Pasolini's left hand and the scale of the wounds suggest far more than what a rotten wooden plank could do in the hands of a single teenager, even a strong one, who was acting alone. It makes far better sense, many have claimed, to assume Pelosi had help. Others would have pinned Pasolini and held his arms, while he managed to free one hand to ward off an attack from a crowbar or iron pipe. Such blows would account better for the broken bones in Pasolini's fingers, shattered straight across. And these others would have taken the weapon with them, the job done.

Pelosi says that after the first attack, he started to run and heard Pasolini chasing him. He claims Pasolini overtook and tackled him, pushing him into the dirt. But Pelosi was not dirty when the police picked him up, and the authorities' reconstruction of the events suggested it was Pasolini who ran from his killer—or from his killers—losing blood until he fell unconscious.

After the chase, Pelosi says, they were about eighty yards from the car. "I kicked him once or twice in the balls," hard enough that his head bowed, exposing the skull for an unimpeded blow. The blow was hard, especially for a man who offered no resistance, either because he was restrained or because his head was already down and bleeding. The team of coroners documented hemorrhage-scale damage to the groin, smashed as hard as possible by someone striking without mercy. It was the kind of direct hit that suggests not a fight between equals but the purposeful beating of a helpless man, a torture victim in the hands of pitiless captors. To Faustino Durante, the forensic pathologist hired by Pasolini's mother, the damage to the cranium also seemed so extensive—sizable patches of hair and skin torn out—as to cry out that his arms had been pinned behind him, that he had been beaten by one or more persons while others held him immobile.

Durante also rejected Pelosi's claim that he drove over Pasolini's body unwittingly, killing him only in his panic to get away. On Wednesday, November 5, Durante went to the murder site himself, bringing oversized sheets of paper, pencils, rulers, and cameras to make his own sketches and measurements. He drew the shacks, noted where the body was lying, the location of the car, the distances and angle needed for the boy to get the vehicle around Pasolini and onto the exit road. His photos captured the print of tire treads passing over Pasolini's back. Pelosi seems to have tilted, shifting the wheels a little: The tracks were of the left front and rear wheels, and they moved up and across from the lower right of the body, from the waist toward the neck, toward the right shoulder. By Durante's measurements and his analysis of the Alfa's turning radius, Pelosi must have tried to go straight over the body in a deliberate line. The least effort—even an experienced driver's unthinking reflex—would have let him drive around it. Durante's conclusion was that Pelosi went out of his way to drive over Pier Paolo, killing him not incidentally but with determination.

Pasolini was wearing a *canottiera* when they found him, a blue-green strapped singlet of a kind that clings to the belly, once worn only by workmen but adopted by homosexuals all over the world. It was bunched up on his body from the waist, letting his flat stomach show, the right strap down over his shoulder. His overshirt was found not far away. It bore a large red stain, round and dried by morning, in the center of the back, and was (press reports claimed) neatly folded, arms in place, all its buttons closed, laid out near the body as though just delivered by some macabre laundry.

What could this mean? Did Pasolini, not yet felled by the kick to his crotch, remove his shirt and hold it over his wounds? Did this reflex action of trying to stanch the flow of blood down his face take his arms out of play, making him vulnerable to the kick? If not that, then who folded the shirt? Wouldn't Pasolini have ripped the shirt off, instead of folding it so neatly? Could he possibly have walked away from the fight, thinking it over, and taken time to double the fabric to make a better bandage? Or if Pino had panicked, as he claims, and bolted for the car, when would *he* have stopped to arrange the shirt, and why? If an accomplice, a fellow assassin, folded the shirt, why did he leave it there, perhaps with his fingerprints on it? Why not take it away?

Perhaps these are all false questions. Perhaps an overzealous police officer thought the shirt would somehow be better evidence if picked up and arranged as though on a shop shelf, better able to go neatly in a bag and back to the lab. Perhaps the shirt only seemed neat, and was really thrown down by Pasolini or ripped from his grasp, and the notion that someone had deliberately arranged it is a desperate fantasy like so much else. Perhaps the folded shirt was only a bit of gore invented by the press, an extra touch embroidered by reporters who could not resist melodrama, kept alive in the absence of a definitive denial by the police or the courts. No answers were, or can be, given.

Was Pino set up to take the rap? Was he supposed to become *lo specchietto per le allodole*—a decoy like hunters use, a way to draw off the heat?

The police waited to conduct their investigation for many hours after the body was found at dawn. Later, after the heavy rains, tire tracks, footprints, and other possible evidence were lost.


Within an hour after they found the body, the murder site was swarming with reporters and onlookers. The police did set up a barrier, just some cloth tape, but a bunch of kids ducked under it and started kicking a soccer ball, and too many people were allowed too close to the cadaver for any sort of decent evidence-gathering. The police did nothing to seal off the scene effectively. Within hours any prints that might have been made by a second vehicle disappeared in the footfalls of the kids playing around the body and the obliterating tracks of official cars.

By the next day, the clearing amid the shacks had become a place of morbid pilgrimage. Newspapers reported cars lined up nearby, disgorging families still on holiday and foreigners carrying maps. Technical discussions about whether Pasolini's headlights were on or not could be overheard. Someone built an oval of eighteen stones and at one end planted a cross of two sticks held together with a nail. When *Il messaggero's* Lucia Visca visited a week later, someone had painted "P. P. Pasolini" on the cross in a trembling hand. Someone else tore Pasolini's photo out of a newspaper, covered it in plastic, and laid it at the foot of the cross. A tin can stood nearby filled with flowers. In all, three vases were filled, and more flowers were laid on the ground. On Sunday night, after the corpse was gone, some people lit candles where the police had found it. Others reenacted the scene, measuring off the steps from the gate where Pasolini was supposed to have first fallen to the spot where they found the body. Some knocked on the doors of the shacks, interrogating the inhabitants. A man arrived in a taxi and bowed his head at the site, but when a reporter asked if he was a friend of Pasolini's he said, "No," and quickly left. People kept coming, even when it rained so hard that cars had to be pulled out of the mud.

November 17 brought more downpour, flooding the city, knocking out electricity for hours, and closing bridges. At the murder site, the wind reached seventy kilometers an hour and water submerged the so-called Tomb of Pasolini. Any physical evidence was now definitively erased.

When the Tribunal finally visited the site four months after the crime, on the morning of Tuesday, March 9, they had to stand around the rude monument—a testimony and a rebuke for the slow, sloppy police work which made a professional inquest impossible. The press claimed at least six serious errors had been made: (1) Pasolini's body was moved without allowing for prior inspection by a coroner; (2) the zone was not properly sealed off, so that people moved over it at will; (3) various objects—the sticks used as weapons, the overshirt, the car itself—were moved before forensic investigators arrived; (4) exact measurements of the distance of the corpse from the car and the location of physical evidence were not made; (5) the car stayed in a police garage in Ostia (and then one in via Gregorio VII) when it ought to have been in the hands of experts for examination; (6) the first questioning of inhabitants of the area did not begin until seventy-two hours after the crime, time for both fear and indifference to set in.

Three years later, a garden grew at the spot, unofficially dedicated to Pasolini.

The official report of the Squadra Mobile of Lido station best tells what happened after Pasolini stopped moving. Patrol-car partners Antonio Cuzzupè and Giuseppe Guglielmi signed and swore to the typed version, attesting to the arrest they made:

> PELOSI, Giuseppe, of Antonio and Paoletti Maria, born at Rome 28 June 1958, resident at Guidonia, district of Sette Ville, via Fusinate, 5; unmarried, holds a record, unemployed.

The term for "unemployed" is particularly tough: *nulla facente*— literally, "doing nothing."

> The year 1975, the 2nd day of November, in Ostia Lido, at the local office of the *carabinieri* at 2:30 in the afternoon. We, the undersigned, belonging to the force assigned to this station and serving then in the Nucleo Radiomobile, refer the following to whoever has the right to know it.[19]

At about one-thirty that morning they were proceeding down the Ostia breakwater at a section called the Lungomare Duilio in a squad car (they are fast, and so called *gazzelle*, "gazelles") with signal name Gazza 2. They were on routine surveillance, when "we saw pass us going in the other direction from our own an Alfa Romeo GT with the license Rome G69996, at a high speed, driven by a young man." When reporters asked, they estimated Pelosi was moving at over 100 miles an hour.

They radioed their station to set up a roadblock, doubled back, sped up, and pursued until they caught up with him at a restaurant called "Tibidabo." Pulling Gazza 2 next to the Alfa, they motioned for the driver to pull over and stop. Before they could reach him, though, the boy floored the car (*tutto gas*) and shot off "in precipitous flight" (*precipitosa fuga*), "bouncing off" (*pizzicando*) the curbstone.

> We, the undersigned, went after him and caught up about seven hundred to eight hundred meters later, forcing him with our car over against a wall. In the meantime, Officer Cuzzupè took out his gun. The young man got out of his car and, weeping and crying, tried to get away. He was immediately stopped and accompanied to this office, where he was identified as PELOSI Giuseppe, and spontaneously confessed to having stolen the car in Rome a short time earlier.[20]

Police records soon showed he was seventeen years and four months old, and known to the police and the courts for hustling (*teppismo*) and auto theft. He had been released from the Casal del Marmo, a youth correctional facility, only six weeks before. When finally forced over, Pelosi had braked hard; he complained almost at once that his head had been thrown forward against the steering wheel, cutting the skin slightly on the bridge of his nose.

The officers did not know that when Pino sped past, going the wrong way on a one-way street, he had already made one stop. He had seen a fountain, one of those municipally-maintained street pumps, in the via delle Caserme near the Piazza Scipione Africano. He had stopped to wash his face and rinse the blood from a trouser cuff, but the police did not notice any dampness there.

Pino kept them distracted by talking fast, and they had no reason to think this was more than auto theft. "I knew that they would find that the car was not mine," he said, "that I had a record, so I had to try and escape. I only stopped because they pointed a machine gun at me, through their passenger window.[21]

He needed to explain himself and seem to be just another *borgata* punk, caught in an everyday occurrence, nothing more. He pointed to the scratch on his nose and told them he hit it on the steering wheel. Later, he claimed this was a deliberate lie, that the scratch came from Pasolini's blow. He also claimed he had a deep cut on his neck. The officers took him to the emergency room of a communal clinic in the neighborhood, where a note was made of a "laceration and contusion at the hairline."[22] It was held to be nothing serious, treated on the spot, and that was that. There were no other bruises, wounds, bites, or scratches—none.

The police searched the Alfa immediately and found Pasolini's registration inside. Cuzzupè drove the car to the station: not bothering with fingerprinting the wheel or wearing gloves. He later said, "I didn't pay much attention to what was in the car then, being busy following the squad car that was ahead of me, carrying Pelosi."[23] When they arrived at the station, the police sent notice to Pasolini's cousin Graziella Chiarcossi, who shared a home with him and his mother on via Eufrate. They told her what they knew, only that her cousin's car had been found, driven by a boy who admitted stealing it.

At the Lido station, Pelosi insisted that the officers wait while he looked around the back seat of the squad car. He said he was missing his Marlboros and a lighter. But the search had to wait until after he was booked and transferred to the Casal del Marmo detention center. The head of the station, Vice Brigadier Luigi Vitale, recalled that it was only after they had brought him to the Casal that Pelosi began talking specifically about a ring. He made much show of the need to find it, indicated where he wore it, pointed to the light-colored skin on his finger where it had been. At about 4 A.M., Pino said, "Please, I'd like to have my cigarettes which I left in your car, and also my ring which fell off when you picked me up." They had him describe it, and looked for it inside the Alfa. They even agreed to go back to the stretch of road where they had stopped him and look there, using their headlights.

Vitale tried to be efficient or, at least, to protect himself. He went to the trouble of stating in his official report of November 5, "I can assure you that if the ring had been found, it would have been returned. I am speaking also of the lighter and the cigarettes which also were not recovered." He added, "He said he had stolen the car in Rome and came to Ostia to accompany a friend: I confirm that when it turned out that the car was the property of Pier Paolo Pasolini, he did not manifest any particular emotional reaction."[24]

Pino claims to this day that the police helped themselves to his lighter. But those who believe he did not act alone that night explain this commotion over lost trinkets differently: His accomplices took the cigarettes, lighter, and ring, their mysterious disappearance one more bit of circumstantial evidence of a conspiracy. Since Pelosi was eight months short of legal majority, he and his partners needed to ensure that the crime was solidly pinned on him, and quickly. The ring left at the murder site was the link, clumsy and obvious, but nonetheless a connection. Pelosi, the theory goes, was only putting the officers on the scent, as planned.

It is possible, of course, that he just wanted his ring back. The officers noticed how sincerely Pino cried, really hard, because no one could find his Marlboros or his lighter. That's all he asked for at first, before the ring. He insisted they check the inside of the car for him, look under the seat, in the glove compartment; the police accommodated him. No one thought about murder then. It was plainly a case of a two-bit delinquent who had graduated to car theft. It was obvious he was inexperienced, driving the wrong way on a one-way street, bawling like a baby over the lighter. Everyone knew how adolescent boys get agitated about watches and sunglasses, lighters and key-rings, little stuff that lent them a feeling of ownership, of adulthood. It all made sense.

Officers Cuzzupè and Guglielmi had picked Pelosi up a little before 1:30. They informed their superior, Vitale, about 2:00 and he also wrote up a report, repeating the facts contained in the documents of the arresting officers. By 3 A.M. the formalities needed to transfer Pino to the Casal del Marmo were complete. He was formally arrested and charged with auto theft at 4.

The owners of the *case abusive* near the Idroscalo had all slept soundly that night: A handful made sworn statements to that effect. No, they had not seen headlights nor heard a scuffle, no running and no cries. Some insisted they had not been near their shacks for months. One man was especially tight-lipped, concerned that his name stay out of the papers: He was spending the night with a woman not his wife. Romans long ago learned to hear, see, and say nothing when trouble breaks.

But early on Sunday morning, November 2, one of the residents, Maria Teresa Lollobrigida, housewife, forty-six, stepped forward as if on stage. Hers was a minor part but she played it with gusto. She was to tell her little story many times, with fresh enthusiasm for each reporter willing to listen, happy to pose again and again for each photographer willing to take her picture, pointing to the place where she first saw him.

Her husband, Alfredo Principessa (Italian women keep their maiden names for legal purposes), made a formal statement for the police, duly reported in the press.[25]

> About 6:30 this morning, my wife, Maria Teresa Lollobrigida, and I, along with our two children, Gianfranco, 27, and Mimma, 23, arrived in our car at the via dell' Idroscalo in Ostia, where I have a little house.

(The family went there every weekend to work the garden. "The ground is really hard," Alfredo added, "but in summer the air there is good.")

> As my wife got out of the car, she exclaimed, "They're always throwing their trash and garbage in the street," and went toward a mound of trash to move it. But when she got within a few steps, she realized it was a male cadaver.

Maria Teresa said "garbage" in Roman dialect, the dictionary Italian *"immondizie"* coming out *"monnezza."* She was made for TV news: Lollobrigida in her housedress, pointing an arm fleshy above the elbow, calling "garbage" the remains of an artist whose poetry and films themselves so often called up the garbage-strewn hillsides of the urban periphery. The press knew a character "just stepped from

the pages of Pasolini" when they saw one. The cover photo of *L'espresso* on November 9 showed Pasolini in three-quarter face, his hair
soccer-sweat damp, a drop hanging from his nose. He is grinning,
his eyes bright. Inside, a bold-face sidebar gave Maria Teresa her
moment, quoted in the glory of full Roman dialect:

> *Ma chi e quer fijo de mignotta che ha scaricato 'sta monnezza sotto casa mia?
> Me so' detto appena l' ho visto: pareva un sacco di stracci. E invece era n'
> omo. Morto.*

> And who'sa son-of-a-bitch threw this garbage in fronta my house? But no
> sooner I say it than I saw him: seemed to be a sacka rags. But instead,
> wuzza man. Dead.

By 7:50, police from the Ostia station were at the scene. The body
was in a clearing full of stones and ruts. A bloody shirt (the collar
tag said "Pasolini") was at the edge of a playing field marked off only
by a gate of two poles. Bloody sticks were also found nearby, and a
plank stained with a mixture of blood and brain matter. A reporter
noted that the police scientific officer found skin under Pasolini's
fingernails and leapt immediately to the conclusion that this proved
Pasolini attempted a defense.

About ten feet away, another so-called scientific officer found a
ring half-buried in the mud, "the kind of thing one buys at a country
fair, something imitation." Vice Brigadier Vitale reported everything
to do with the ring to his superiors, suggesting it "might not be
extraneous" to the case. Another squad car arrived from Lido station.
"We are looking for a ring with a red stone in it. Be careful not to
stamp down the dirt, the ring is important." An inspector took it out
of his pocket. "Here it is. We knew it had to belong to the assassin.
It had blood all over it and it could not belong to the victim. It is a
different size."[26]

At 10:40 A.M. the police took a statement from Ninetto Davoli:

> This morning, at about 7:30, I received a telephone call at my home from
> Pasolini's cousin who lives with him at via Eufrate 9, named Graziella. She
> told me that Pier Paolo had not come home that night and that at about 1:30
> she had been awakened by carabinieri who came to say that his car had
> been found.

> She was taken to the EUR station early the next morning and from there
> called me to see if I knew anything. She told me she was very worried
> because Pier Paolo's mother would be awakening soon. She wanted to be

there then to tell her Pier Paolo had not come home that night because he'd stayed the night at my place. I repeat that Graziella was planning to tell this to Pier Paolo's mother in order not to shock her.

I specify this because every time Pier Paolo was out late, he called me and called his family so that none of us would worry.

I dressed right away and went to his house, where Graziella had returned. I honked and she came down and we sat and talked about where Pier Paolo might be. I left Graziella then and on my own initiative drove over to the carabinieri station at EUR. The police there repeated to me what Graziella had said, but added that a corpse had been found at the Idroscalo at Ostia, and they asked me to go and have a look. There, as I have said, I immediately recognized the body shown to me to be that of Pier Paolo Pasolini.

As far as I know, Pier Paolo did not know anyone in that neighborhood, but he knew the area because, for several years, I went with him from time to time to play soccer in the field nearby.

Recently, I have paid no attention to whom Pier Paolo frequented. But I want to say that, because of his work, he knew a great many people.

Yes, I would add, now that I think of it, three or four months ago, we came here to play soccer, he and I and some film technicians from a production house.

I have nothing to add.[27]

At ten that morning, Pelosi was still trying to convince police interrogators that he had found Pasolini's Alfa in a parking lot on the via Tiburtina. At eleven, questions began to be asked with an eye to bringing charges against him for voluntary homicide. Pino confessed:

The deal was clear, I was supposed to play the man. But then he wanted to reverse the roles. I said no. He insulted me and we started hitting one another, and then I didn't see anymore. I didn't see that the plank had nails in it. He hit me too . . . he ran away. Then he fell. I took his car, I didn't understand anything, maybe I ran over him. He was crazy. I didn't understand.[28]

His rage had triggered: "Only I was supposed to play the man [*il maschio dovevo farlo solo io*]; not take turns."

# 5

*I'm only sorry that they fixed my image in a cliché which did not even help me to understand myself.*
— *Pier Paolo Pasolini*

*Everything summons us to death; nature, as if envious of the good she has done us, announces to us often and reminds us that she cannot leave us for long that bit of matter she lends us, which must not remain in the same hands and which must eternally be in circulation; she needs it for other forms, she asks it back for other works.*
— *Jacques Bossuet*, Sermon sur la mort

# LUNEDI, 3.xi.75

The long holiday weekend was normally a stretch of flat days for the press, nothing much to write about.

Those who followed the world outside the peninsula were worried about Spain after Franco, the dictator-who-might-not-have-been but for the tanks, planes, mustard gas, and fifty thousand troops Mussolini sent him in 1936. As the Generalissimo lay dying, Juan Carlos, the king-to-be, was off in the Sahara on what must have seemed a tragicomic venture several decades too late, to impose European imperial dreams on Morocco.

Closer to home, the Lazio soccer team, adored to madness by its Roman fans, played to a 1–1 draw against Bologna in front of forty thousand disappointed spectators. And the Roma squad was playing Como away, and that contest too fizzled out, 0–0.

Radio and television were ahead of the print media breaking the news. From mid-morning Sunday, the murder was reported evey hour across the nation, from Chiasso in the north, where Italian trains give way to Swiss conductors, to Ragusa in Sicily, on the same latitude as Tunis. Special bulletins broke into normal programming. One could not enter a bar for coffee or a *pasticceria* for a cake without encountering the news broadcast that was the center of discussion.

The newspapers began Monday morning with full front-page coverage, large-print headlines that shouted "*Assassinato* Pasolini." Editors started designing multi-page stories and assembled squads of reporters to blanket every aspect of the crime. Special pages were planned so that newspapers could bring in every possible bit of hard news, comment, and opinion not only on Pasolini's life and death but on his unique place in Italian culture.

The great majority of Italian newspapers are unashamedly partisan, proud of a political tradition that long has made them the point sheets for politicians and their industrialist or party owners. No reporter or editor takes too seriously Anglo-American talk about separating fact from opinion. Italy is an old country, cynical and innocent at once, skilled in the ways of survival. Its people understand that whoever tells the news has the power to make it. That is why the ruling Christian Democrats kept firm control over the State television, and why the Socialists and their allies maneuvered (with final success) to have their own second channel. As with everything else, Italian reality was carved into spheres of influence and peaceful coexistence. No one looked for agreement in the press on anything: "Objectivity" was the smokescreen of hypocrites, intent on a secret agenda.

Pasolini's death soon proved to be a political gold mine across the Italian spectrum. The far Right brayed that another pervert gone made the world a bit safer for right-thinking people, and, as expected, the far Left cried ink crocodile tears over him. Already on November 4, the Right-wing *Il secolo d'Italia* announced, "The murderer was alone." Not everyone resorted to hand-wringing and eulogy. Novelist Vasco Pratolini stated straightforwardly that he believed "the Fascists" had done it. In Milan someone spray-painted "Matteotti–Pasolini, Killed by the Fascists" on the sides of buildings; photos of the graffiti appeared nationwide within a day.

For many, the murder seemed proof that the neo-Fascists were fighting back, resisting the country's drift toward the Left, the slide to compromise with the Communist Party (PCI, Partito Comunista Italiano) then being engineered by Prime Minister Aldo Moro. Maybe, they reasoned, the murder of Pasolini, a man so visible, so much a symbol, was the opening volley of a silent war to crack down on the Left. It seemed possible. Hadn't the Interior Ministry's own thugs staged a fake coup in Milan, pushing a man from a police station window and blaming it on the anarchists? Most Italians believe anything possible in the land of the Renaissance and of Fascism, of Surrealism and the Counter-Reformation.

For details, people went to the printed press. When everything else in Italy seemed losing ground, the ritual of stopping at the corner kiosk for the papers had held on. Many people bought two: one published by their political party, and the other the *Corriere della sera*.

Indisputably Italy's leading daily in 1975, the *Corriere* was one year short of celebrating its centennial. Unlike many papers, the *Corriere* was always privately owned and not the subsidized mouthpiece of a political party. From the first, it thought of itself as speaking for and to all enlightened national opinion. The paper liked to think it made governments, not the other way around. People trusted the *Corriere*, even though they knew it to be the voice of Italy's Establishment, or perhaps because of that. And so, when Piero Ottone, its new editor, offered Pasolini carte blanche in 1974 to write long essays on topics of his choice under the rubric "Open Tribune," that alone was a laying on of hands, recognition of his stature as Italy's most controversial, and brilliant, moralist.

On Monday, November 3, the *Corriere*'s Rome and Milan editions were headlined "Pasolini Assassinated at Ostia." There was no need to include his first name: He was a public figure every Italian knew about. Over the declaration appeared an "eyebrow" subheadline: "The tortured body of the writer found in a clearing two hundred meters from the sea," and beneath the head, "The killer (17 years old) captured, confesses." The first page ran a picture of Pasolini wearing glasses, smiling slightly; next to it, a mug shot of Pelosi released by the police, and a photo of the corpse covered with a bloody sheet, two officers in the background, beyond them a crowd of rubberneckers.

The first three pages of the paper were devoted almost entirely to Pasolini: articles about the crime itself, the "Pasolinian" character of the murder site, the dead man's mother, his connections, and his work. Ulderico Munzi wrote the lead article, a breathless sketch of Pasolini's last hours from his dinner with Ninetto at the Pommidoro to his death. The details were such as could be pieced together at the time, and what was not (or could not) be known, Munzi augmented with speculation or liberal fantasy in the dramatic style of Italian journalism. Of the deadly fight in the clearing, for example, he wrote:

> Pasolini wanted to calm the boy. He called him by his nickname—*rana*, frog—which his friends use because of his eyes which bulge a little. "Frog" is something the boy would have shared with Pasolini a little beforehand.

No evidence exists that Pasolini tried to calm Pino, or even that Pino was ever called "Frog" by anyone, much less by Pasolini. Still, he is "Pino the Frog" consistently in Munzi's articles over the next weeks.

Munzi also sketched Pelosi's life: how he had worked as a baker's boy, how he went to school only until the age of twelve, how he lived with his father and mother in a modest house "on the side of a dusty hillside." Signora Pelosi talked about her son. As a boy, she said, "he was an angel, but as he got older he was ruined. We all had to work to survive; we saw him so little." His parents were given to wondering aloud why Pino was not more like his sister, two years older than he; she was a good girl, with nice friends.

Pino's mother slipped him a thousand lire every day "for cigarettes" and wondered what he did with himself all day and all night. "Nobody was able to pay attention to that boy," she said. "We sometimes saw him in the evening, at dinner when he didn't come home late. He never talked about himself, about what he was doing." She tried to develop his interests: made him visit a swimming pool, bought him a guitar. "The other day we saw a good movie, *Roma violenta*, a police story. I said to him: 'Go and see it and learn how to live, see what can happen.' And he said, 'What do you care?' "[1]

Italians are not embarrassed to have mothers. Pier Paolo's devotion to his went further: Susanna Pasolini was a participant in his work and the center of his life. His poem "Prayer to My Mother" reads in part, "You are my mother and your love's my slavery: / My childhood I lived a slave to this lofty / incurable sense of an immense obligation."[2]

Throughout the years, Susanna occasionally appeared in articles about her son, for example, photographed serving lunch to Pier Paolo and his friends. Invariably, she is the inwardly smiling *"mammetta,"* the little mother, hovering in the background, ready with welcoming words to her sons' friends, happy at his happiness, proud in his success, always wearing the locket photo of Guidalberto, the second-born son she had to bury. Pier Paolo made her a movie star of sorts. In his *Gospel According to Matthew*, he cast her as the aged Mary, running toward Golgotha and collapsing at the foot of the Cross. The still of her as *Mater dolorosa*, screaming and falling as she sees the Crucifixion, was widely reproduced. Monday's *Corriere* ran an article by Fabrizio De Santis headlined "The Grief [*dolore*] of the Mother When She Found Out." Its tone is melodramatic, the sufficient facts heightened by the editors' decision to print the whole article in italics. It began, "A dark shadow behind a window, an inhuman scream: These will remain for some of us the death of Pier Paolo Pasolini." De Santis' stakeout was the sidewalk in front of via Eufrate 9 in EUR where Pasolini had lived. It was, he noted, "the most modest house in the neighborhood, without expensive bits of brass and rare woods, no balconies festooned with rare flowers."

Pier Paolo's cousin Graziella kept the news from Susanna as long as she could, and at least she could make sure it did not come from strangers or the media. A friend was posted at the door to stand guard and turn away the curious. De Santis saw a car of young people drive up and ask if they could pay their condolences. Perhaps they were members of the Young Communist Federation of Rome. No matter: They were firmly discouraged.

Susanna, he wrote, "was used to being alone." He explained that, since Pier Paolo often spent the night out or returned as late as 2 A.M., his mother had taken to visiting with the hall porter. Even modest apartment blocks in better suburbs like EUR employ a *portiere* to receive and distribute mail. The reporter continued his vigil.

> Then, a little after one o'clock—a very high scream shattered the air, followed by another and yet another. They are howls with nothing human about them—howls of a wounded animal being torn apart. They fade and then they start again, higher yet. Pier Paolo's mother knows. . . .

> There came to mind the scene of the *Gospel* with Susanna-Madonna held up by pitying hands before Christ crucified.

Graziella could not bring herself to speak the news. It came instead from Pier Paolo's confidante, the actress Laura Betti.

De Santis observed that Susanna reacted like a "humble woman of the South." Women of Friuli, Susanna's home, do not scream, and compared to many Italians to the south of them, they hardly talk. Undemonstrative to the point of dourness, a characteristic usually attributed to Friuli's long occupation by stiff-necked Austria, *friulani* joke among themselves that they wear an emotional *scorza*, (a "bark") and live trapped inside. Susanna was not usually a woman to show her emotions and in this she was true to regional type.

Looking back at age eighty-six, Susanna's youngest sibling Gino recalled that she never discussed with him his nephew's homosexuality.[3] To do so would be, in part, a tacit acknowledgment of Gino's own such nature. Gino had left home and established himself in Rome as a connoisseur of antiques, an unmarried gentleman of discretion, who lived quietly and did not approve of Pier Paolo's flamboyant way of life. But the family reticence went further than this. Susanna never discussed the central issue of her family life even with her sister Enrichetta, whose only son, Nico, was also homosexual; nor is it certain that she confided in her other sister, Giannina, widely believed to be a lesbian. Decades, entire lives, generations passed in silence.

Susanna withdrew further into herself after Pier Paolo's death. She did not attend the public funeral staged a few days later by the Italian Communist Party, though she attended the burial in her home village of Casarsa. She retreated from the world, was placed in a rest home in Udine, and died in 1981. Now she lies beside Pier Paolo in the Casarsa cemetery: mother and son under matching tombstones. All four Pasolini rest here—Pier Paolo, Susanna, her husband Carlo Alberto, their son Guidalberto—in a burying ground cleared and walled in amid cornfields, at the end of a traditional row of poplars.

But unlike other old Casarsese families, they do not lie together: Carlo Alberto and Guidalberto are buried on one side of the cemetery's front gates; Susanna and Pier Paolo are adjacent, but on the other side. Architecture has honestly, permanently rendered in death the fissure that ran through the family in life.

On page 2 of the *Corriere*, Fabrizio Dragosei wrote from Florence about the Fifteenth Congress of the Radical Party. Pasolini was scheduled to address the gathering on Tuesday and his talk would have been newsworthy, as usual.

He planned to discuss the "DC Trial," his Bertrand Russell-like proposal to put the entire leadership of the Christian Democrats on trial, literally in the docket. Pasolini would have them all, from Andreotti to Fanfani, treated as common criminals, and with them the entire history of the Italian Republic from 1948 would be called to account. Right on the front pages of the *Corriere*, Pasolini accused them of the worst abuses, with creating in the Italy of 1975 something "degraded." Using the first person, as had Zola, he accused them of destruction of the environment, cynical dealing with the far Right and the CIA, personal corruption, the collapse of the schools and all civic and human values. He charged them with destroying Italy in a way worse than had Facism.[4]

But he planned to use the forum of the Radical Party Congress for more than denouncing the Right. He also had a few words for the Radicals themselves, who had come to find him a difficult and unpredictable fellow traveler. He was too independent even for this party of independents. Who else had the stature to tell those who favored divorce and abortion and gay rights that he was not with them? He was still for the Communists, the PCI, that slow-moving, often rigid party of the workers and peasants but never led by them, the party that had worked so hard, but not always so well, to shuck off Stalinism.

What had he prepared to tell the idealistic Radicals, at the height of the terror of the Red Brigades?

> **A.** The most lovable people are those who do not know they have rights.
> **B.** Those people who, while knowing that they have rights, do not claim them or actually renounce them, are also lovable.
> **C.** Those people who fight for the rights of others (above all for those who do not know they have them) are very sympathetic.
> **D.** In our society there are exploiters and exploited. Well, so much the worse for the exploiters.

As Dragosei reported, Party Secretary Spadaccia broke into the proceedings to take the microphone.

> Among us, Pier Paolo Pasolini was most out-in-the-open [*scoperto*], the most defenseless. His articles, his interventions mirrored a practice of "provocation" which is also the strategy of the Radicals. We argued with him about his position on abortion, but that happened with the frankness that characterizes a relationship among comrades.

Angelo Pezzana also addressed the gathering. He was the head of FUORI (literally "out," as in "out of the closet"), the Fronte Unitario Omosessuali Rivoluzionari Italiani, and now took the opportunity to use Pasolini's death to make a point about his own movement. Pasolini's death, he told the Radicals who had made common cause with his group, was no different than what was risked every day "by hundreds and hundreds of unknown homosexuals who pay with their lives for the violence in our society. Their names say nothing and the newspapers do not dedicate a line to them."

The Congress applauded; gay rights, after all, constituted an important plank in the Party's platform. But many in the gathering knew that Pasolini himself did not think sexuality the basis for either political philosophy or a political movement. For him, homosexuality was not the stuff for public policy but for private Calvary. He was not interested in voluntary organizations to promote individual liberation; he once said, "Civil rights have nothing to do with class struggle."[5] And the least attractive world he could imagine was one where homosexuals were like everyone else. In that, he was of another generation, out of another world: anguished and marginal, from the days when homosexuals were called *diversi* (literally, "different"), not *gay*. Co-opting him, whether in the name of normalization or cure, would have destroyed the alienation that was essential to his desperate creativity. The Radicals believed in psychiatry; Pasolini stood with tough, imprisoned Antonio Gramsci, who thought intellectuals should be their own psychologists.

Marco Pannella, the party's founder and firebrand *éminence grise*, spoke last. He described Pasolini as a kind of "lay saint" with "grace, love, rigor, intelligence, fantasy," who wanted to "save his assassins." He told Party members Pasolini's death was "Christian, revolutionary, Socratic. . . . Pier Paolo wanted to die in order to save."

A letter to the editor of the Right-wing *Il secolo d'Italia* later attacked Pannella as an "apostle of abortion" who would "find his saints in the mud of the Ostia beaches." As for the *Corriere della sera*'s reporting the Radical Party's reaction in such detail—that only became further proof that the paper had "descended several steps from the very high level of prestige and culture in which it had been held until recently."

To cover Pasolini's stunning diversity, the *Corriere* commissioned a group of articles for its third page, laid out under an indisputable headline: "The Tragic Death of Pier Paolo Pasolini, the Most Discussed Writer-Director of the Past Twenty Years." Each examined a different aspect of his vast, multifaceted talent. Literary critic Piero Citati, who had known him for many years, wrote a general appraisal.

> He seemed to have made a bet with himself: to put to the test in every
> medium his unlimited sensibility, provoke with all the weapons of intelli-
> gence and culture, baptize it always in new forms like a mannerist of the
> Cinquecento or one of the decadents from the start of this cen-
> tury . . . Everything seemed to work out well, almost as though he discov-
> ered inside himself such treasures that only decades could exhaust.[6]

The *Corriere* asked Carlo Bo to evaluate Pasolini the writer. There
was elegance in this choice: Bo, Rector of the University of Urbino,
was a staunch Catholic of well-known probity, and a respected literary critic of the old school. He had admired Pasolini's poetry early
on and had risen to his defense more than a decade ago, when the
government tried to ban his first novel, *Ragazzi di vita*, for obscenity.
When the chief judge asked him if he found the book immoral, he
had replied, "I find it profoundly religious." His endorsement was
like a parish priest's defense of the village harlot, and Pasolini's
acquittal was guaranteed.[7]

In the traditional rhetoric still flourishing in Italian universities,
Bo recapitulated what he called "one of the most impassioned, polemical, and often contradictory literary careers of our time." He
explained how Pasolini started writing in Friuli, influenced by the
great masters such as Pascoli and by the early Montale; he moved
through each of Pasolini's published volumes of verse, before coming
to his main point—that Pasolini, even when his citations were out of
contemporary events and "ran the risk of losing his voice in the noise
of his time," nonetheless remained a poet, a poet "even though" a
man of the news.

This possibility was not self-evident in Italy, where poets generally
write of things higher than the ordinary, and where they are rewarded
with indifference in life and a street named after them once they are
dead. Bo argued that Pasolini was an innovator in this regard:
". . . he knew how to drag himself out of everyday context and go
beyond the long poetic codification of the twentieth century." Pasolini
managed to find a voice roughly like Auden's, but coming not in
England after Hardy or in America after Whitman, but in Italy after
the otherworldliness of Fascist-imposed hermeticism. His two novels,
*Ragazzi di vita* and *Una vita violenta*, were credited with making "a
revolution of rhetoric and literary customs."

> His characters made of violence a way, if not of liberation, then at least of
> demanding citizenship. . . . This was not a coda to neo-realism, but of some-
> thing else that was even more important: Pasolini brought to his portrait of

little, squalid odysseys lost in the mud of the Roman periphery a capacity for love and pain.

Bo made a Christian defense of the heretical, blasphemous Pasolini. He read the confluence of Pasolini's art and life in a way ironically similar to that of the agnostic Radical Pannella.

> The writer did not just make literature, but inserted himself without reserve or calculation into the very river of human misery, transforming the recorder of classic *miserabilismo* into a confession of clearly religious nature, founded on the concept of sin.

The older man understood and forgave the younger Pasolini's frenzy: "as always happens to those who are driven by a natural force," it happened to Pasolini

> frequently to err and clamorously so, or to lose himself in a labyrinth of sophisms and contradictions. But this behavior came out of his good faith [*sua buona fide*] and the certainty which gave him a profound insight into reality. This explains the frantic rhythm of his work, the wealth of his talents. . . .

Pasolini the man of the cinema was the topic of the *Corriere*'s veteran film critic Giovanni Grazzini.[8] He called Pasolini "one of the masters of our cinema" and "a sovereign example of creative intelligence." No one else in the postwar era (save Fellini, "from whom he was a thousand miles distant") was, in fact, "the total author" in whom everything connected: "the experience of life, understanding of culture, political debate, and figurative gesture." What coherence there was in his work and in his vision straddled the categories by which Italian cinema was usually understood: he was at the same time "lyrical and problematical, Catholic and Marxist, crude realist and exquisite mannerist."

His earliest films, concerned with Italy's postwar slums, "already had many of the crucial themes of Pasolini's poetic cinema": the mixture of squalor and spiritualism, fantasy and misery. Up until *Uccellacci e uccellini* (Hawks and sparrows), his scathing fable of the Italian Left, Pasolini could have been classified as an ideological filmmaker and a polemicist. But his release of *Gospel According to Matthew*, dedicated to "the dear, sweet, and familiar memory of John XXIII," changed that perception. It was a rendition of the Scriptures so pious that Catholics embraced it enthusiastically and Marxists stood stunned by what seemed a betrayal by one of their own.

Pasolini's films seemed to run through periods: the "mythic period" of *Oedipus Rex*, *Theorem*, and *Medea*—ancient fables he made modern and contemporary parables which he filmed as though timeless—followed by what Grazzini called Pasolini's "third path," the *Trilogy of Life* begun in 1971—*Decameron*, *Canterbury Tales*, and *Thousand and One Nights*. They were films "inspired by the joy of living and narrating happily."

> His hope for revolution disillusioned, nauseated with semiological seminarians and struck by the degradation of social life, this "reactionary of the Left" who has lost faith in history loses himself in the classic medieval stories in order to sing simple feelings, the delight of the flesh, and the downgrading of rationality.

Pasolini rendered in them a utopian world of innocents living one day at a time, following the wisdom of their instincts in exotic settings—a voluptuous escapism that struck exactly the right chord with the moviegoing public in Europe and the United States. Again, Pasolini was understood and classified, but now as "nostalgic" and "reactionary." No sooner was the *Trilogy* completed, however, than he published a "Disavowal" of them as the preface to the edition of their screenplays.

He turned his camera to *Salò:* the horrifying world of absolute power gone mad, of the Marquis de Sade's thanatocracy set in an all-too-real historical time and place, in Mussolini's puppet Republic of Salò, propped up by the Nazis. Grazzini said that the later Pasolini was seized by a "spasm," that *Salò* was the beginning of a study of evil, feelings "animated by a pained rage." But his death left this new direction on the screen uncertain. "Come to scandalize," Grazzini wrote, "Pasolini left us more neurotic but richer."

Columnist Lietta Tornabuoni had yet a different assignment from the *Corriere*. While Bo, Catholic professor, wrote of Pasolini in an almost religious vein, and Grazzini reviewed his achievement in film as "provocative and sincere," Tornabuoni was to be hard-nosed and worldly about Pasolini the man. If the rest of the third page was in the business of canonizing the artist and intellectual, she brought him back, all too human, into the world of contemporary Rome.

Her charge was in her headline, "The Difficult Choice to Be 'Against.' " Pasolini, she wrote, for years represented for many the emblem of scandal, the personification of provocative transgression. Radio sketches and humorous weeklies cited him as the prototype of indecency. The right-wing newspapers attacked him with unrelenting vulgarity. The Fascists assaulted him, beating him up, tossing red paint at him; in court he was charged with armed robbery against a gas station attendant at San Felice Circeo.

Anti-conformist, difficult, extreme, Pasolini certainly would not appeal to the Romans' lazy cynicism: he was never really integrated even in the ambience of the literati and the intellectuals. Among writers, his true friends were truly few. Even in Roman intellectual circles, Pasolini was made to feel ill at ease because of his differentness ["*diversità*," meaning his homosexuality]. In salons or literary ceremonies, the "right" people never sought him out; he had, instead, friends among the people, anonymous and dangerous. . . . He had no taste for eating and drinking, didn't gossip, and never participated in distracted conversations about nothing in particular.

Other writers did not understand very well the "myth of youth" which obsessed him at the age of fifty-three—his boyish clothes (jackets, jeans, heeled boots), his elegant slimness, the vanity of his fast and extravagant cars. They did not understand his physical vitality—the soccer games played with boys at the edge of town, the challenges of *braccio di ferro* [a version of arm-wrestling] or *ditate* [roughly the game of "rock-paper-scissors"], the muscular strength he had developed or conserved. . . . Movie people accepted poorly his vast success as a director. Leftist intellectuals barely pardoned his visceral, "innocent," contradictory way of intervening in matters of politics—against the student demonstrators at the time of his famous poem in support of the police; against divorce; against abortion; against contemporary permissiveness; against growing criminality; against distorted progress and in praise of an ancient time "when there were fireflies"; against the governing class, called to the bar of a global "trial" without appeal; for the abolition of schools and of television.

She said the same intellectuals laughed behind his back when he faced down a lecture hall full of hostile students in 1969, and a piazza full of angry people in 1973 at one of his films' premieres. They called him "macho" with unconcealed sarcasm. When Pasolini proclaimed "Narcissism—the sole consoling force, sole salvation," they also laughed, although he knew perfectly well how it sounded and why he had come to think it a desperate truth.

She reported that the mandarins of Roman culture jeered when Pasolini cultivated Maria Callas, or was polite to Lady Bird Johnson, or attended benefit evenings at the Paris Opera, sitting between Mme. Pompidou and the Baroness Rothschild. "What kind of Communist was this?" they asked, forgetting that he was, first, intensely egalitarian. How could they, who were deeply status-conscious and often snobbish *arrivistes,* understand that he treated the powerful and famous in the same way as he did, say, Ninetto, and Ninetto in the same way as he did all the famous?

"In twenty-six years in Rome," she wrote, Pasolini was "the man most discussed, commented on, contested—and also, most insulted with the persecuting and racist mockery which is reserved for homosexuals." And she closed her farewell with some lines of his verse:

> And what will my "private" life count
> miserable skeletons, without life,
> neither private nor public, blackmailers,
> what difference do my words make, or will they make,
> I will be there, after death, in the spring,
> to win the wager.[9]

# 6

*Objective? See Italy objectively? Not be partisan? Maybe flying over the country in a Boeing, looking down. Otherwise, never.*
—*Giuseppe di Dio of* Il messaggero

# CAMPO DEI FIORI

Pasolini's murder closed the book on his long and tortuous relationship with the Italian Communist Party. For twenty years, payrolled operatives on its staff and ideologically correct critics within its sphere of influence had taken to the pages of its magazines and newspapers sometimes to praise and defend him, but more often to attack. He had been a perennial problem, difficult, *scomodo*, for decades. He announced he was with, and of, the Party because it was the only force set against reaction after the war, and he defended the PCI when it was attacked. But increasingly toward the end of his life, he turned around and accused the workers' vanguard of Fascist conformity.

One forum for his encounters was *Rinascita*, the PCI's monthly culture and current affairs magazine, founded and long run with an iron hand by Party leader Palmiro Togliatti himself. In its pages, reviews of Pasolini's novels and films appeared, sometimes following a hard ideological line, sometimes not. Because the PCI was in fact made up of different currents, each with its own influence and followers, the line wavered as editorial personnel changed. Pasolini's reception also varied with events and alliances in the broader political and cultural life of the country. In the fifties, he was useful as something with which to beat the Right over the issue of censorship. In 1968, he was less useful when he accused the Party of sitting on its hands. Sometimes he was a whipping boy, sometimes a hero, always a lightning rod.

Orthodox Marxist critics were frequently annoyed at the lack of correct ideology in the protagonists of Pasolini's novels and films. Long steeped in the tenets of socialist realism, some read novelistic plots for ideological lesson: Art was strictly to serve as moral exemplar. In this, as in so much else, the PCI mirrored doctrinaire Catholic criticism, which also practiced what Italians call prospectivism.

No sooner did the hard-liners lambaste him than others under the PCI's broad postwar umbrella came to his defense. Matters never remained simple between Pier Paolo and the Party: after cutting attacks on his novels in the latter half of the fifties, the PCI rose to his defense when he was charged with blasphemy for his film *La ricotta* in 1963. Even as the conservative press exaggerated his disagreements with the leadership and exulted in them, *Rinascita's* editor wrote asking that he contribute articles, and sent Togliatti's *cordiali saluti,* his best wishes.

The PCI daily newspaper, *L'unità*, was not merely a vehicle of editorial opinion but the official line of the most influential wing of postwar Italian culture. With its approval, doors opened at Party publishing houses and conferences. One either joined the roll of the blessed or, fallen from grace, a kind of Index. Service to the Left or Right ultimately mattered less than simply having an ideological home and the protection of allies. Pasolini broke a cardinal rule of Italian life: he refused to take sides, seeking shelter in alliances. He refused to exchange unquestioned loyalty for security.

But no such complication blurred *L'unità's* issue of November 3. The Party's top echelon took over the center of page one to state its official position on his life and his death. Unsigned (it emanated from the editorial staff with the blessing and guidance of the inner circle of the Central Committee), the declaration was nothing less than a final tally on Italy's twentieth-century "civil poet" of the Left.

> The atrocious end of Pier Paolo Pasolini deprives Italian culture of a high critical genius and the democratic movement of a true militant, animated by intense civic passion. We believe we speak truly when we say that the news of his death has struck the mind of each of us in the most shocking manner, setting off reflections on the very themes and problems to which he always dedicated his enormous labors as artist and student.[1]

The statement noted that his death mirrored the violence of his life "almost as though he sought this epilogue." Magnanimity came easier toward the silent dead than toward the pugnacious living.

The paper's political bosses knew its readers were familiar with Pasolini's public battles with the Party—how he had been expelled from its ranks in 1949 as "morally unfit," and how he had been nearly blocked by Togliatti personally from appearing in the Party's publication *Vie nuove* because "such a man is unfit for family readers." Readers might recall too how, the very year he was killed, he had likened the PCI leadership to a new version of Fascism. So, the leadership decided to clear the air about its history with Pasolini in the first issue of *L'unità* after his death, the one encounter with him when they could be sure of having the last word.

> He was, right until the end, our attentive interlocutor, committed, sharp, without concession. In our many discussions with him, we certainly were sometimes right and, other times, equally certainly wrong. It was easy "to be right" against Pasolini, calling him back to concrete historical reality from his paradoxes and exaggerations which sometimes seemed intent on avoiding history. But we certainly erred when, beyond his paradoxes and his exaggerations, we could not gather the truthful perspective which he tried to transmit, and which he suffered with his own existential being.[2]

With this collective *mea culpa*, *L'unità* also indicated a common bond between the masses in Western Europe's largest Communist party and Pasolini, the refined intellectual: That is, they shared an enemy. The Party closed its eulogy:

> The fascists always hated him, for he was the symbol of all they opposed, civilization, culture, the restlessness of inquiry. . . . At every decisive moment, he was present and on the right side.
>
> His death is a tragedy for this society.[3]

The same number also contained an appreciation of Pasolini by author Paolo Volponi. Pasolini had, in part, discovered Volponi and had published some of his early work in the pages of *Officina,* the magazine he edited with Francesco Leonetti, Franco Fortini, and Roberto Roversi in the late fifties. When Volponi's first novel, *Memoriale,* appeared in 1962, Pasolini called him "an elegiac Marxist." He had his chance for elegy now:

> Pasolini is a great poet, and a great master for our entire culture. He accepted living without rest, with the stubbornness always to be teaching. . . .
> The most beautiful image in Pasolini is of "humble Italy" [*l'umile Italia*], of an innocent . . . people, hungry for history. . . . His poetry is *popolare* because when his solo voice was raised, it always seemed to rise from a chorus alive in the background and ready to respond.[4]

In the quarter century from 1950 to 1975, the Party line on Pasolini had shifted from excommunication to lay canonization. The far Right complicated the ironies: on Tuesday, November 4, *Il secolo d'Italia* wrote that, at the end, Pasolini was moving in their direction, "becoming a reactionary writer," and that he had been "killed by the Marxists," that "mentally, the Communists had already eliminated him."

Many of the senior officers of the PCI were in Bari that week, participants in a conference that began on Sunday. *L'unità* reached them by phone to gather their reactions to the murder for printing in Monday's edition: They were eloquent but brief. Enrico Berlinguer, the sad-faced Sardinian head of the Party, sent Susanna Pasolini a telegram of condolence. In this, he was one with many of Italy's leading politicians—Prime Minister Aldo Moro, Vice Premier Ugo La Malfa—with the notable exception of President of the Republic Giovanni Leone, who kept silent.

In the meantime, Pasolini's friends painter Giuseppe Zigaina and actress Laura Betti were pushing the Party to make a more public demonstration of its commitment to Pasolini's memory. Zigaina had been Pasolini's friend for thirty years, one of that generation of intellectuals who came to adulthood with the collapse of Fascism and saw in Communism the best hope for Italy in the dark years of the late 1940s. The Party was for them the moral heir of the Resistance, and the shock of their lives came from the manifestations of Stalinism in the repression of Hungary and Czechoslovakia abroad and in the rigidity of Togliatti's Party discipline at home. Many found it difficult to stay loyal to the PCI; sometimes they did so because there was nothing better.

Zigaina was both a *compagno* to the Party and a man of cultural stature established enough to be able to speak on the telephone directly with Giorgio Napolitano, member of the PCI Directorate. He offered the Party a chance to show where it stood on "the question of Pasolini." "Do you want Pier Paolo, or should his friends and family bury him now in Casarsa?" He added in not completely mock threat, "Or do you want us to give him to the Radicals?" Zigaina proposed that Pasolini lie in state in the atrium of PCI headquarters. But Napolitano explained that such an honor had not even been paid to Togliatti; no one could lie in state there save, perhaps, another Gramsci.[5]

The PCI leadership had to worry about the comrades who did not think Pasolini "one of us." The hard-liners had never stopped suspecting that the emphasis both in his art and his life on individual experience and the sanctity of the ego was reactionary. What did this almost Catholic interest in the soul have to do with the inevitable triumph of the working class through revolutionary dialectic, an orderly process led by a Central Committee, and Executive Committee, all under the guidance of a discipline-setting Secretariat? Even, what business had a Marxist party with practicing Catholics in its ranks, staging what approached a requiem mass?

Such qualms, however, were not now to carry the day. Most comrades thought Pasolini unique enough and comrade enough for some form of official recognition. Napolitano told Zigaina that the Party did, indeed, want to show its sorrow publicly; but perhaps it would be best if the sponsorship did not come directly from the highest reaches of the PCI. Communist members of the Rome city council had just been humiliated when the Christian Democrats blocked their proposal for municipal commemoration of the dead poet. The Fascist newspaper had crowed in a headline, "The Campidoglio Will Not Celebrate the Lay Seer P. P. Pasolini," and continued, "Finally, the Communists decided not to press the point, one they were certain to lose, calling for beatification of their new lay saint" in the ancient hall at the heart of the city.

The entire operation had to be carefully stage-managed to avoid a public relations fiasco. Pasolini went down well enough with the young, but the Party was not made of students. Its base was in well-off workers and farmers, many of whom remembered the Resistance, family-types who had no sympathy with Pasolini's way of life. They may not have seen *Salò* but they had heard about it. They knew he was a practicing homosexual with a preference for teenagers, a difficult character who shocked people.

To many party loyalists, art had little to do with politics and politics even less to do with art. They saw themselves as working to construct a Marxist party, one beginning to become independent of Moscow, in a country until recently agricultural and among people who were unwilling to break with the Church. Someone like Pasolini seemed to the rank-and-file too full of theory and mitigating circumstances, hedged with reservations and ready with reasons not to conform to discipline. He was both too worldly for the ascetic and morally rigid wing of the Party and too closely identified with low-life for the radical chic, the decorative Communists who hover at the Party's cultural fringes, because it is warmer there than on the ignorant Right.

Zigaina's contacts in the PCI quickly found an acceptable compromise: the event would be sponsored by the Rome section of the Party's Youth Federation, the FGCI, headed by the young film enthusiast Gianni Borgna. This seemed fitting. Pasolini had written of the young generation of Communists as the best hope for the future of what Pasolini once called a "horribly dirty" country. It had been their round tables he had addressed, they, and not "the fathers," whom he had invited to his home in via Eufrate for discussion groups, they who had energy and hope.

Organizing for street politics is the bread-and-butter of all the Italian parties. Young operatives like Borgna were experienced at taking politics to the piazza: volunteers were not lacking to make the needed calls, negotiate with the city to close certain streets, alert the media (who, in this case, hardly needed alerting), erect a platform, and install a sound system. They wrote announcements, had them printed, then glued them on walls all over Rome.

> The Roman people express sorrow and dismay at the tragic and violent death of PIER PAOLO PASOLINI, among the most significant students of today's Italy, animated by an intense civic passion, who gave voice and human form to the lived experience and to the fight for liberty of the poorest and most oppressed of the city.

> The Communists of Rome remember in PIER PAOLO PASOLINI a comrade of so many cultural and political battles, a committed and authentic interpreter of the workers' democratic movement and of the great effort to construct a society with greater freedom, humanity, order, and justice.

> The funeral will take place on Wednesday, November 5, at five in the afternoon, starting from the House of Culture in the Largo Arenula.

(signed) Roman Federation of the PCI Federation of Italian Communist Youth (FGCI)

*Il secolo d'Italia* printed a quick response:

> The Roman people . . . not only do not share but regard with repugnance and disgust a life which, with perversion and crime, wove himself an apologia. . . . Now he will not annoy any more.

And on November 7, it ran a long article ridiculing as "grotesque" the "posthumous escalation of the *pasolinidi*," and lambasted the liberal press for working to make of him "a martyr saint." It is true that *Paese sera* remarked that "We know that especially toward the end Pasolini received threats from the Fascists," but the far Right inevitably rejected as absurd any notion that the crime was political rather than personal. *Il secolo* accused the very people who saw a conspiracy of conspiracy, and pointed a finger at the PCI.

Not everyone on the Left lined up to pay Pasolini homage. Luigi Pintor was part of a dissident group expelled from the PCI by the Central Committee in 1969 with much fanfare and recrimination all around. Their crime was "factionalism"; their own accusation that the PCI was too pro-Soviet in foreign policy and too reactionary on civil liberties. Pintor, Rossana Rossanda, and a few others started their own newspaper that summer—*Il manifesto*, with no advertising, no photos, but sixty thousand copies a day of six pages of solid politics, six columns across, under the heading "Proletarian Unity for Communism."

On Thursday, November 6, Pintor's article appeared:

> I do not believe Pasolini was a combination of Saint Francis, Ché Guevara, Savonarola, and Gramsci, as he is made to appear in the obituaries and posthumous panegyrics. It will seem mean of me to say it, but I believe something essential is missing . . . in the sensibility of someone who knows how to travel the streets of poor neighborhoods in a car of many cylinders, hateful symbol of violence, superiority and abuse.[6]

The neo-Fascist MSI (Movimento Sociale Italiano) had a good laugh at that: They quoted the article with glee and thanked him in their paper the next day.

Costanzo Costantini, writing in *Paese sera* on November 4, did not bother with circumlocution:

He was engaged in ideological violence against the very underclass of society he appeared to champion. It was Pasolini who, after all, was debasing these boys, paying them for prostitution and keeping them in a vicious life cycle. . . . With the death of Pasolini, part of our society feels itself freed of a burden, or at least of a restless and disturbing conscience, one which questioned itself as well as our individual and common destiny. It is said that, after all, "an abnormal" is dead; that he became the victim of a crime of a certain setting; that it was only to be expected. They never forgave him for being "an abnormal," but that in another sense: [he was] skilled more than other people, more intelligent than others, more lucid than others, aware and vigilant more than others. They never forgave him his success, found in any field he endeavored.[7]

The same week, Rossana Rossanda wrote on *Il manifesto*'s front page, "With a moving unanimity from Left to Right, the Italian press weeps for Pier Paolo Pasolini." But the truth was,

he did not please anyone, not us, not the Left because he battled against 1968, the feminists, abortion, and disobedience. And not the Right because his sallies came accompanied with discomforting reasoning, unusable for the Right, suspect. He especially did not please the intellectuals because he was the opposite of what they in general are, cautious distillers of words and positions, pacific exploiters of the separation between "literature" and "life" . . . this almost total unanimity is certainly the second heavy vehicle which passes over Pasolini's body.

She ridiculed her former Party comrades for their sudden *autocritica* and the Radical Party for "signing him on post mortem": "everyone now thinks to use him to their own profit."

I think that Pasolini—if one can imagine such a gesture from a man so gentle—would have spit on this fervor and these side-shows. I think that if he had emerged alive, he would have taken the side of the seventeen-year-old who beat him to death. Cursing him, but with him. . . . He will have a bourgeois funeral, and after a while the City of Rome will name a street after him. They will kill him better, his real enemies, than did that boy the other night.

The public was invited by the young Communists of Rome to pay homage to Pasolini at coffin-side on Wednesday, November 5. The place chosen for the lying-in-state is within sight of PCI headquarters in the via della Botteghe Oscure, but pointedly not in it. Instead, Pasolini's body was brought to the Party's Casa di Cultura, not more than a large apartment in a palazzo built in 1890 in an architectural style proud to be ponderous. The Party unit shares the building with a dozen other tenants, up a flight of narrow stairs made even less passable by the addition of an elevator in the center, one of those which carries four people with discomfort, forcing them to fall on one another to let the impractical double doors swing open and close. Pasolini had been there for debates. It was symbolically correct.

Its advantage is its location, a short walk from the Piazza Venezia and close to the Campo dei Fiori. To this most popular and tumultuous of Roman squares Pasolini's coffin was to be carried after the public had its chance to file past. It was here in the Campo that the people would say its farewell. Nearby was the Theater of Pompey, where Caesar was stabbed, and adjacent to the buildings which have since risen on its curved foundations, the Campo dei Fiori (Field of Flowers), once a meadow.

The Casa di Cultura rubs shoulders not only with monuments; it is also crammed in among sandwich shops, bars, and newsstands, and shaken with relentless traffic passing from the Piazza Venezia down the via Arenula, past the Ministry of "Mercy and Justice" and the Juvenile Court where Pino Pelosi was to be tried.

On Wednesday morning, a hearse brought Pier Paolo from the morgue in a plain, sealed oak coffin. He was to stay until late the next afternoon, plenty of time for the public to sign a book of condolence and shuffle past, slowly and in single file. That done, he would be brought to the Campo and laid on a platform, for speeches to be made over his body. Then a funeral operator would drive him north to Friuli for a second service and burial in the cemetery where his father and brother lay. The town of Casarsa had offered a temporary columbarium, an act of homage until his own gravesite next to the cemetery wall was prepared.

*La salma*—the mortal remains—was placed in the main room. A red flag covered one wall, potted plants to the sides. Flower arrangements had been arriving since the day before, more than a dozen wreaths, each big enough for a man to stand inside. A single bunch of white flowers—fragrant tuberoses, chrysanthemums, and carnations—with a ribbon that read "*La tua mamma*" lay atop his box, which was closed tight with three metal bands. Its lid bore a large bronze cross. Four men were posted at the corners, volunteers who took turns standing vigil.

Enrico Berlinguer, General Secretary of the PCI, arrived at 1:45. He stood graven-faced at the coffin's side while photographers took his picture. The "Internationale" was not sung, and Berlinguer did not make commemorative comments. In those days, he was busy extricating Italian Communism from Moscow, piecing together the program of "Eurocommunism" to be announced five years later. Everyone knew his wife attended Mass, but he did not make the sign of the cross.

Italians of every sort, the famous mixed with the unknown, climbed the stairs and filed past the coffin throughout the morning and into Wednesday afternoon. On Thursday, a line formed for an hour outside the Casa before its doors opened at 10:30. The mourners packed the halls inside and stood shoulder-to-shoulder on the sidewalk. They waited quietly, moved forward slowly, propelled by the better and the lesser emotions that come at the death of one who has stood out from the crowd.

The thousands of posters distributed throughout the city announcing the commemoration had struck home, but not to everyone in the same way. Many announcements were defaced before their glue had dried. Arturo Dalla Vedova, a forty-six-year-old Jesuit priest and former member of the faculty at the Papal Gregorian University, had followed the work crew. About seven in the morning of November 6, police found him near the PCI headquarters crossing out the *P*'s in Pasolini's name with a marking pen to write *porco* (pig). Across the top of every announcement he could find, he scrawled *capralo*—his version of *capraro* (goat-bugger)—*blasfemo, frocio,* or *perverto* (misspelling of *pervertito*).

When he was brought to trial, he told the magistrate that he had no personal hatred of Pasolini, but "I felt the need publicly, courageously, clamorously—but with dignity—to express my outrage at the radical-Communists' ignoble exaltation of a man who was so debatable a hero and saint." Sentenced to four months in prison and a fine of thirty thousand lire, he was later subjected to psychiatric examination and deemed not punishable at law because he was "not responsible for his actions."[8]

Late Thursday afternoon, Pasolini's closest friends began to assemble at the Casa to escort his body to the Campo dei Fiori. Bernardo Bertolucci arrived, red-eyed from crying and ready to do service as a pallbearer. The posted vigils now included Ettore Garofalo who had starred opposite Anna Magnani in Pasolini's *Mamma Roma*, Ninetto, Franco Citti, and Sergio Citti. In 1960, Pasolini had written that Sergio was his "only real friend: one of those friends you can count on when you're sick or in danger, when you croak." Sergio wrapped a red soccer jersey—Pier Paolo's number 11—around the coffin and knotted the sleeves to the handles on either side of the casket. It was not a silly gesture: Pasolini had written in all seriousness that "soccer is the last sacred ritual of our time," and "my sole consolation," taking the place of the Mass and substituting as a community rite for theater or cinema.

Others joined the rotating guard of honor: Antonello Trombadori, a leader of the Resistance, art critic, editor of the PCI's *Il contemporaneo*, and later a Communist deputy in Parliament; later, the directors Elio Petri, Francesco Rosi, Paolo Taviani and his brother Vittorio.

Those who filed past laid flowers, touched the coffin, sometimes murmured. They signed the book of condolence. The first was no one famous at all, someone with the name of the Italian everyman, Mario Rossi. One woman wrote, "I am here with my baby of two years old because she too will know who you are, who you were, and who you will be with time." Another, "We will never forget this terrible outrage against culture and life. We will continue with you in the struggle and in poetry." Someone signed "in the name of the free people of Portugal," someone else, "a schoolmate from the Liceo Galvani in Bologna."

At five o'clock, an hour later than had been planned, the last visitors signed. The doors were closed and locked so that the pallbearers could assemble the wreaths, hoist the coffin, and prepare the procession. Just then, a loud, insistent knocking demanded entrance. From inside, the guardians shouted through the door that it was too late to sign the book and that whoever was there should proceed directly to the Campo. The knocking rose to pounding and some inside became concerned, thinking it might be one of those squads of neo-Fascist punks, like the one that threw ink bottles at the screen during the premiere of *Accattone* fifteen years before and assaulted Pasolini in the cinema's lobby.

A reporter for *L'unità* went to have a look. Outside he found Oriana Fallaci, celebrity journalist of celebrities, with her lover, the Greek opposition leader Alessandro Panagoulis. Knowing that the next day's newspapers would list the important visitors at the lying-in-state, she insisted that she be let in and her name recorded in the book of condolences. She and Pasolini had known each other and they always followed each other's work, each respecting in the other a genius for polemic and self-promotion. During the weeks that followed the murder, Fallaci created a sensation with her series of articles in *L'Europeo* claiming that Pasolini had been assaulted and killed by a group, by Pelosi together with two hoodlums on motorcycles "pretty well known in the drug scene." She said she had discovered an eyewitness to the crime, one indicated to her by a paid informer, whose name she ultimately declined to reveal, citing her rights as a journalist under Italian law. Her claims were widely reprinted as fact. When the police investigated her story, however, as did newspapers and teams of independent researchers, no one was able to confirm what she had written. Nonetheless, her articles made best-selling issues for her employers' magazine.

Thursday afternoon was cool but not cold, with wisps of clouds very high in the sky. The reigning color was Communist red. The crowd in the streets outside the Casa di Cultura had been growing for four hours; it was estimated at over ten thousand. They crowded the nearby streets. They waited quietly for the coffin to appear in the doorway. Some thought that there might be some violence, but they misunderstood the restlessness of the crowd: It was frustration at fate and grief at tragedy, not simple anger. As the cortège prepared to move, photographers hustled for position, knowing pictures of Pasolini's funeral would sell well to the press throughout the world.

As the coffin came into view, high on the shoulders of Pier Paolo's friends, people started to applaud. The sound—something incongruous to northern ears—grew and grew. It astonished because so many thought Pasolini well known, much debated but little loved, and it stunned because it broke a deep silence, as though the ancient Church procedure of canonization by acclamation had been suddenly and strangely revived. Pasolini would have the Church's Mass in Casarsa tomorrow, but today in Rome he was being sent on his way with the salutation and farewell of the people.

The men carrying the casket moved slowly toward the Campo dei Fiori at the tail of a ramshackle procession: First, the red flags dressed in mourning, then the funeral wreaths each requiring two men to carry, and finally the coffin itself. Applause spread through the streets like a long wave. It echoed from the buildings and set a flock of starlings to flight. *L'unità* reported, "On such a Roman November afternoon, the day begins to end and the birds rise toward a sun justly called blood-red." Fists rose in the revolutionary salute, some people tossed flowers, others lifted bouquets in the air as if to show them to the dead man. Many seemed frantic to touch the coffin. Pallbearer Bernardo Bertolucci recalled later the feeling that he might lose his grasp and be swept off his feet at any moment.

The Campo was not simply one site among others for the ritual, but the one God-as-genius-stage-manager would have ordered. Every morning and all day Saturday, it houses Rome's liveliest fish, fruit, and vegetable market, its white canvas umbrellas keeping sun or rain off the goods for sale. Tourists make the mistake of believing those who work the Campo's food stalls are poor because picturesque.

But the Campo has not always been dedicated to the stuff of life. It has also been a place of execution. Here, two renegade priests died for their efforts to dispatch Pope Urban VIII with black magic. Here, in 1600, the Church burned the great Giordano Bruno alive, partly because he was a Copernican who had dared to write that one's understanding of the world may depend on where one is in it: The reason we do not sense the earth's rotation around the sun is because we share in it. Newly liberated from the temporal power of the popes, the people of Rome erected a statue of Bruno in 1889 at the exact spot in the center of the Campo where he died. He stands now facing toward the Vatican, brooding and in defiance, his head hooded under a bronze cowl.

Volunteers from the Communist Youth Federation had constructed a platform of used two-by-fours at the southeast end of the piazza in front of the little movie house called the Farnese, next to a small *rosticceria* thick with smells. This was to be Pasolini's bier, brightly lit in the falling darkness by photographers' halogen lamps. Three speakers were chosen to do him honor: Gianni Borgna, head of the Federation's Rome section, sponsor of the ceremony; Aldo Tortorella, an erudite journalist and member of Parliament, long on the Party's Central Committee; and Alberto Moravia, who would speak for Pasolini's friends and family and for all of Italy's lay culture, the skeptical, humanistic world outside the Church.

Moravia moved to the microphone: He did not need it, for the enormous crowd had fallen unusually silent. His face was tightly drawn, his collar was raised against the slight wind, a black sweater high up over a white shirt, making him resemble an old priest or— his architect father was Jewish—a rabbi. He concentrated only on the words, spitting them out in a rasping voice without any effort at oratorical flourish. He sounded impatient, even irritated, as he often was with his countrymen.

> It is unlikely that a man like Pasolini will be on this earth again soon. It is an irreparable loss, for his friends, for all Italians. Pier Paolo Pasolini's genius and simplicity were a rare thing, not easy to find.
>
> With him we have lost a constant testimony of the contradiction of our time, one who tried to provoke active and constructive reactions in the inert body of Italian society.

> As for his abnormality—that consisted in the courage always to tell the truth, and this had made him a precious element in our culture, an extraordinary poet. . . . The tragic and anguishing details of his death that still obsess us are the image of a country that must be profoundly altered. This is the last message that he left us with his disappearance.

Moravia wanted to set the record straight about Pasolini's place in Italian literature. He was neither a decadent poet nor one of Italy's hermeticist school that coped with Fascism by looking the other way, inward. Pasolini was a poet in the grand European tradition that celebrated the civic man, inheritor of a line that stretched through Ugo Foscolo and Leopardi back to Dante. As "Italy's most famous living writer" (as the press often tagged him), Moravia insisted that Pasolini was the single most important Italian poet of the second half of the century. He was not to be remembered as one of a cabal of sophisticates with undemocratic concerns, nor as a marginal figure because of his sexuality. On the contrary, he was to be honored as a prophet unloved in his own country, one with a message ignored at his hearers' peril. He was a public poet of his times who sang a critical, idealistic, embittered, and loving song of the people and their collective life. Honor was his due "because," Moravia said, "not many poets are born . . . only two or three to a century."

The body of Pier Paolo Pasolini was returned to his hometown of Casarsa in Friuli about two in the morning, Friday, November 7. Even at that hour, three thousand people were waiting in the streets. The coffin was placed for the night in the fourteenth-century church of San Rocco where the funeral would be held in the afternoon.

Mourners filed past the coffin all day, many signing a petition initiated by the town government demanding deeper investigation into the murder. Reporters estimated that fifteen thousand people crammed the streets. The local section of the PCI tacked on trees all around the chapel copies of his poem in *friulano* "Tornant al país" (Returning to my village):

> *Fantassuta, se i fatu*
> *sblanciada dongia il fòuc,*
> *coma una plantuta*
> *svampida tal tramònt?*
> *"Jo i impiji vecius stec i il fun al svuala scur*
> *disínt che tal me mond*
> *il vivi al è sigúr."*

*Ma a chel fòuc ch'al nulis*
*a mi mancia il rispír*
*e il vorès essi il vint*
*ch'al mòur tal país.*

Girl, what are you doing so pale near the fire,
like a little plant which loses color in the
sunset? "I am lighting the ancient fire which
will fly up darkly, saying that in my world,
living is safe." But that so fragrant
fire takes my breath away, and I want to be
the wind which dies in the village.

Father Davide Maria Toraldo, whose poetry Pasolini had praised in 1953, came from his religious community in Bergamo to officiate at the funeral.

About 5:30 in the afternoon, the cortège began its short walk from the church to the cemetery. The funeral flowers were carried ahead, followed by Susanna Pasolini supported by Graziella. They wound their way through the jam-packed streets to the cemetery gates at the end of a cypress-lined road. At the columbarium, Toraldo read from the Sermon on the Mount lines Pier Paolo had included in his *Gospel According to Matthew:*

> Blessed are ye, when men shall revile you and persecute you, and shall say all manner of evil against you falsely, for my sake. Rejoice, and be exceeding glad: for great is your reward in heaven: for so persecuted they the prophets who were before you.

# PART II

## 7

*There is first of all the question of origin, which often looms large*
*in individuals who are driven to be original.*
— *Erik Erikson*, **Life History and the Historical Moment**

# COLUS DI BATISTON

The clan of many families, all named Colus, had been living in the plain below the Alps at the northeastern fringe of the Italian peninsula since the Middle Ages. Records show them working the stony ground of Friuli (the forum Julii)—forum of the Juliuses, as in Julius Caesar—in the last years of the fifteenth century, when the Turks passed through on their march toward besieging Vienna, in 1499.

Pier Paolo Pasolini, twenty-two and fresh from Bologna University, wrote a play about the Turkish invasion of his mother's ancestral village, mixing events of the distant past with events of the Fascist occupation of 1944, which impinged directly on his own immediate family. The characters in *I Turcs tal Friul*—the play was written in *friulano*, not Italian—in all probability were his mother's forebears. The family includes two brothers, Pauli and Meni; Meni is killed defending his home and homeland.

On September 30, 1499, the play recounts: "A messenger brought dramatic news: the Turks had crossed the Isonzo and were advancing, destroying and burning all in their path; there are ten thousand on horseback and six hundred on foot." Some fled to the woods, others prayed, but Meni tried to organize a defense. The horizon takes flame and a chorus of Turks begins to sing. The mother, Lucia, climbs a tower and sees a band of youths running from the Turks, carrying with them the broken body of Meni. A dust storm comes up and the Turks retreat.

The father in the play, Giovanni, vows that if the town is saved, he will raise a church in thanksgiving. Pasolini has overlapped past and present, fact and fiction. For some reason, the Turks passed over the real Casarsa, and swept on to destroy over a hundred other hamlets. Instead of raising a church, thirty years later grateful Casarsesi commissioned a fresco for the house of worship they had. A stone was installed, recording that on September 7, 1529, Zuane [*friulano* for Gianni, that is, Giovanni] Coluso and Matia de Montico made the donation. There is every reason to believe Zuane Coluso was Pier Paolo's maternal ancestor.

Legend has it that the name of the town Casarsa is derived from *case arse*, "burnt houses." Proof has been elusive, but the usual, if unsubstantiated, explanation is that the name was born when the Turks did put the hamlet to the torch at another time. There had been a settlement at the site as early as the eighth century, when two Longobard brothers named Erfone and Marco divided up their patrimony around the river Tagliamento and ordered the woods to be cleared and fields planted. A warlike tribe called the Arimani were posted by the Longobards to keep guard on the settlements. Made safe from invasions from the east, farmers lived in town and worked their fields around it; they built giant houses of fieldstones stuccoed over, *fattorie* spacious enough to house not only a nuclear family and many collateral relations, but animals and food enough for both man and beast. Over the door of one such house, in what is now "downtown" Casarsa, there can still be seen the Colus emblem: a cartwheel, carved into a stone lintel. When the Apostolic Visitor, Monsignore Cesare de Nores, toured the diocese in 1584, he reported finding at

Casarsa a church "with six altars, 400 souls, 200 taking Communion and 200 not, and a fit priest."[1]

Some of the Colus clan probably died in the Turkish skirmishes, but enough of them and their progeny survived so that a certain Domenico Colus appears in the town records of September 9, 1810, born that day at Casarsa della Delizia. He is certainly Pier Paolo's great-grandfather, registered by the Napoleonic masters of the region as *bracciante* by occupation, a field hand who might have owned a few acres. He lived out his life in Casarsa and died there.

As recently as 1871, depressed agriculture had lowered Casarsa's counted souls to 3,097, or so report the careful records kept in the *municipio*. That was double the number at Domenico's birth, but the place was still not more than a village. By the latter part of the 1800s, Casarsa's population had risen to 8,500, but it fell to 6,000 and stayed there for the otherwise explosive fifty years in Italy between 1870 and the 1920s. The new kingdom's first small industrialization passed it by: Its routine was church, fields, marriage, childbirth, and death.

Save for the local barber (tripling as pharmacist and physician), and the priests, the Casarsese were peasants who minded their own business in their own language. They tried to stay out of trouble with the Austrians, tough taskmasters and serious tax collectors who came in 1797 at Napoleon's consent and stayed through World War I. People like the Coluses tried to avoid conscription, hoping to be left alone to till wheat in the uncooperative soil and gather persimmons in the foggy November. The women found solace in the Church and the men in *grappa*, the fiery narcotic distilled from grape skins. The *friuliani* are famous for this firewater, often taken at breakfast to warm the insides against a long winter's damp.

Such peasants as the Coluses were one step up from cattle, not consulted when it suited Napoleon to sign the Treaty of Campoformio after he had crossed the Tagliamento on March 16, 1797, effectively taking Friuli into his grip and out of that of the Republic of Venice.

The father of 1810's Domenico lived under the French, and Nico "the first" was in his prime, thirty-eight, when Casarsa and all of Friuli passed to the Austrians in 1848. The German-speaking bosses had constructed an extraordinary postal system, linking Venice and Verona in a day; it was something Domenico and his peers had little reason to use. Friuli was passed hand-to-hand. The foreigners who commanded kept to their language and knew the locals as servants and draftees; the peasants lived in ignorance and poverty, speaking not Italian but another tongue altogether, *il friulano*. Not so far from

Latin, it bears almost no resemblance to the dialect of Petrarch's Tuscany, which came to be modern Italian.

Domenico, Pier Paolo's great-grandfather, was almost certainly barely literate, although his granddaughter Susanna claimed he "wrote his will in verse." But he did not lack for an heir. At forty-four, he fathered a son also named Domenico, born at Casarsa, June 26, 1854.

Domenico junior lived until 1927, so two men named Domenico Colus, Pier Paolo's great-grandfather and grandfather, between them straddled a century. That first Domenico had married one Maria Polacco. She bore him six children in addition to the younger Domenico. Pier Paolo's friend Silvana Mauri Ottieri says he spoke about having "Slavic, and Jewish blood . . . from a woman an ancestor of his, a soldier under Napoleon, brought back from Eastern Europe." Perhaps it was true: *Polacco* means, literally, "Pole."

Inevitably, their young "Meni" had to face a life working the fields or find an alternative trade to better himself. So, even as the new Italian nation lived its first decade after Garibaldi's battles, he journeyed to the more prosperous, more advanced Piedmont where the House of Savoy kept an efficient economy and jewelbox court. There he apprenticed himself in the wine trade and learned the rudiments of distilling. This decision changed his life, and that of the family he made with the girl he met at Casale Monferrato, during his travels. This son of a mere *bracciante*, Pier Paolo's maternal grandfather, opened a *grappa* distillery, which made him one of the richest men in Casarsa, literate or not. He was remembered by his children for his elegant homburg, handlebar mustache, and beaver-collared top-coat. He looks down on their dining room still, in his sepia portrait photo hanging in Casarsa's via Guidalberto Pasolini, the street named for his slain grandson.

Domenico senior had been born into a Europe that still trembled at Napoleon's name. His son's life saw liberation from Austria, the unification of Italy under the Piedmontese monarchy, World War I, the arrival of Mussolini and the Blackshirts. But he did not see Casarsa change dramatically. Its main street stayed unpaved; the men worked their difficult fields, their wives attended to children and household duties, cooking cornmeal polenta over open hearths, the daughters married young, bore many children, and the cycle was repeated.

Life's trajectory moved from the baptismal font to a small community graveyard at the end of the main street, waiting at the foot of a cypress-lined avenue. No one looked at living as a matter of choos-

ing among alternatives and making oneself; one took the pattern that
awaited: serving in the army if called, working the land into premature age, if the bosses left one alone. Or there was emigration to
North or South America, a route so many took as to see 700,000
Friulians in Friuli today but 1.9 million in the rest of the world.
History was always something made by other people; even fairly well-
off small landholders like the Colussis participated in it only as it
happened to them.

So it was for all the family-clans in Casarsa, the dozen or so whose
names appear again and again in official records. Sometime in the
nineteenth century, many Friulians Italianized their names, adding
an *i* at the end, but little else changed. Page upon page mark the
births, marriages, and deaths of Querins and Fantins, Cesarins, Ca-
stellarins, Cinats, and Justuns. They are connected by bloodlines to
Fantinis and Cesarinis, just as Francescuts and Francescuttis spring
from the same gene pool. They were in Casarsa to fight the Turks, as
they were when Susanna Colussi, Domenico's daughter, was wooed
and wed by a soldier named Carlo Pasolini in 1921.

Susanna's mother, Marianna Giulia Zacco, was twenty when she
married thirty-two-year-old Domenico on April 9, 1887. She loved
music; they met in the foyer of a theater. He was known as a humorist
and liked proposing toasts in verse. They honeymooned in Mantua,
then returned to Casarsa, and he began the climb from the rural
proletariat into which he had been born to the urban middle class,
even to the *piccolo industriale* of the *grappa* trade.

But he was not an industrialist in the contemporary sense. He
simply erected a still in the courtyard of the house he built on Casarsa's main street, bought plums and pears from the farmers and
bottled liqueurs from their fermentation. He had no "brand name" to
speak of, certainly no distribution to retailers.

His outlet was a kind of café, a *taverna* that grew from the need
for a place to dispense his product. When they were old enough, his
daughters sold the *grappa* and local wines, like Pinot Grigio and
Merlot, over the counter, by the glass to the neighbors. Men came of
an afternoon to sit and play cards; those who could read the newspaper, especially those too old to be fighting the Austrians in World
War I.

The house that Domenico built stood five minutes from the train
station in one direction, in the other direction even closer to the sole
square, where the church stands.

In a wing at the back of the stuccoed two-story house, overhung
by a persimmon tree growing in its back garden, Domenico brewed

his product with the work of his own hands. In summer, he set up not more than four tables and chairs to go with them in the interior courtyard. Eventually, he called the serving area the Osteria al Giardinetto (the tavern in the little garden). *Osterie* (unlike *trattorie*) purvey only drink, no food; with Italy's prosperity the authentic ones have all but disappeared.

Upstairs the family lived, spread among rooms of the plain house painted rose. Meni's daughter, Enrichetta, the last to live there, says the whole place smelled of fruit *grappa*. From the courtyard echoed up to the bedrooms the voices of teamsters on the Venice-Trieste line, who spread the word that the hole-in-the-wall café was a good stopover for a coffee and a bottle of *acquavite* to carry away.

The little business was known by a generic name Premiata Distilleria a Vapore (prizewinning vapor-operated distillery), but no one recalls that it really won any awards. One was free to call a business as one chose. At its height, the Colussi *grapperia* bought only 250 *quintali* of wheat from local farmers, paying up to 17 lire for each. Domenico was never a market force, committed to buying a farmer's whole harvest; he paid the going price for raw materials and adjusted his production to his cash flow.

Within two years of their wedding, Giulia Zacco Colussi (as she was always known) suffered as many miscarriages. A man attentive to the possible utility of religious practice, Meni started crossing the Piazza Vittorio Emanuele on Sunday mornings, thirty yards to Mass. He went to pray that his wife would bear a child successfully to term; he was thirty-five and still not a father. So ardent was his desire for living offspring that he vowed to make an annual pilgrimage to Udine, to the Church of the Madonna delle Grazie, if he were so blessed.

In 1889 a son, Vincenzo, was born and soon spoiled. He was sent to a *collegio* in Conegliano run by priests and then to Udine; he was given just enough education to lose any interest in distilling *grappa* or settling for life in Casarsa. The town already had a schoolteacher, so Vincenzo took a salaried job with the railroad. This did not last long, and he took another post in nearby Villotta. Ever restless and indulged by Domenico—who always gave in to this first child and his sixth and last, also a boy—he proposed to emigrate.

In 1906 news reached Friuli of an earthquake and fire in San Francisco and easy money to be made in its aftermath. Construction workers were pouring into the town; carpenters earned four dollars a day while lawyers in New York earned less than half that. Vincenzo, seventeen, set sail for California and never returned. Months after his departure, a letter came from a friend, reporting that the boy had at first built fruit crates, then window frames for new houses to replace those leveled in the disaster. His parents had wept at the waste of his education, but they wept much more when a second letter reported that Vincenzo had taken sick or been in an accident (eighty years later, his sole surviving sister, Enrichetta, had forgotten the details). He died en route to a hospital and was buried in a grave no one of his family ever saw.

Meni's prayers were answered again and again, for Giulia bore five other children in the ten years after Vincenzo. In 1891 came a second child, a daughter named Susanna, first of a succession of girls. Then Chiarina, in 1893, who threw over her training as a seamstress to work in a hotel some relatives started in Benghazi and spent much of her life wandering the world. She finally returned to Casarsa, where she told her nephew Nico stories about camels; she is buried with her parents and siblings in the village cemetery. After Chiarina and Susanna came quiet Enrichetta. She later married Antonio Naldini from Ferrara, brought to Casarsa by the war. Enrichetta stayed with needlework, opened her own tailor's shop, and bore daughters named Franca and Anna—Pier Paolo's second cousin Graziella was a daughter of this Anna—and a son, who was naturally named Domenico. She passed her life in her parents' house in Casarsa, in old age a devout woman who said the rosary beneath her father's portrait.

After Enrichetta came Giannina, independent as a man. She never married and lived her entire life with her sister Enrichetta in their parents' house, teaching school at San Vito di Cadore a few kilometers away. She always rode a bicycle and became the beloved, sharp-tongued village schoolmistress, candid and strong. Until his death, she helped her father in the distillery. She, and not the sons Vincenzo and Gino, enjoyed the work.

Giulia must have hoped Susanna would not prove footloose like Vincenzo and Chiarina but would settle down nearby. She was so pretty, and knew it, with dark chestnut hair that fell in waves, high cheekbones, smooth and very white skin. She was bright too, trained to be a schoolteacher like Giannina. She was sent to the nuns at San Pietro al Natizone until age eleven when a *maestra* suggested she try for a scholarship to high school. She won and went by train every day to Udine until she graduated at eighteen. Domenico paid for Enrichetta to study there as well. But she suffered the special pain of adolescent sibling comparison. Susanna wrote an assignment called "A Fable: If I Were Queen," which the teachers praised and compared to her sister's, at Enrichetta's expense. The sisters' sons were to repeat the pattern.

Education was valued, but it was not essential, for when news of Vincenzo's death came about 1910, Enrichetta left the nuns' school and was apprenticed to a seamstress, as Chiarina had been. She lived in the house of her teacher in Pordenone for three years. About a year later, Susanna returned to Casarsa, qualified to teach elementary school, which she did at nearby Valvasone. The quicker-witted and the prettier, Susanna had discovered books and ideas and would not spend her life making other people's skirts and blouses for Communion Day and mending their torn jackets.

Life in the Colussi household proceeded calmly enough in the decade before World War I: Vincenzo was dead, Chiarina away in Africa, and the three unmarried girls lived at home. Enrichetta had her tailoring clients, Susanna and Giannina taught school. A matriarchy of peasant society was in place, women whom Silvana Mauri Ottieri, a frequent visitor to the house, called "preying mantises— the sort who consume first their husbands and then their sons."[2]

Like traditional men of his time, Domenico seems to have been determined to have as many sons as possible. So, at thirty-three, after four daughters in a row, Giulia bore him Luigi, always called Gino. Nothing was too good for him, even the sacrifice of sending him to the university in Milan to study science and engineering.

Gino's life intersected that of his nephew Pier Paolo in odd ways. Domenico was in his mid-forties when Gino was born, and he must have hoped his last child and only surviving son would take over the family business. But Gino had no interest in distilling, nor in his studies in Milan. He loved art and literature, antiques, clothing, dressing up, helping Enrichetta design garments for her clients. He left the Politecnico in 1914 but not before writing a comic review, favorably received in student circles, called "Foxtrot and Lemonade." He served briefly in the disastrous Royal Army and by 1922 was in Bologna, working at the Messaggerie Italiane, a nationwide periodical and book distribution agency.

Gino catalogued books by day and at night went out to enjoy the life of the big city. He was twenty-three and extremely handsome, with peaked eyebrows, a long narrow nose, and a firm but fine jaw. His raffish taste and come-hither looks appear in a black-and-white photo his sister Enrichetta kept hanging on a hall wall in Casarsa for more than fifty years: Gino with his head tossed back like Rudolf Valentino, a scarf tied in a knot around his neck, his chin held very high so that a dramatic shadow was cast by the photographer's light, accentuating his cheekbones.

About that time he must have caught the eye of a young German dentist come to Italy. Paul (Paolo) Weiss had traveled from Munich to Bologna's famous medical school, where certain techniques of his trade were even more advanced than in Germany. He enrolled at the university and took a second degree; the twenty-five-year-old Weiss lost his heart to Italy. Somehow, he met Gino Colussi and decided he wanted to stay. His handsome Italian friend was taken on, ostensibly to tutor him in the language—so the story was told to Domenico and Giulia. They helped each other: Gino needed a sophisticated and affluent friend, someone interested, as Weiss was, in the arts. Weiss needed a secretary and bookkeeper for his dental practice, an Italian to make sure bills went out, someone able to handle the hiring of nurses and to keep the office running smoothly.

The family tale is that Domenico lent Weiss money to open his first office and later helped Gino, by inheritance, to start a gift shop called La Piccola Galleria. It opened its doors in Bologna in 1927, the year Domenico died.

The arrangement soon included another young man, born in 1905 and so a few years younger than the other two, a Florentine, Arnaldo Cerchiai. Gino, Paolo, and Arnaldo became partners in business and in life. Gino did not just keep the office books and help run the shop. He wrote. In 1920, barely twenty-one years old, he paid a Bolognese typographer to print a sentimental D'Annunzian novel, *The Two Souls of Conte Sergio*. He followed with *Notturno a Santa Rosa* and in 1938 *Lot's Wife*. The novel addresses the phenomenon of large families whose several children are so distinct as to seem sprung from different sets of parents.

Gino and Weiss moved to Rome in 1930 and Gino ran the office. Arnaldo stayed in Bologna three more years, then closed the shop there and joined his friends. They reopened just off the via Veneto, in via Lazio, expanding the stock to include unique pieces from Murano, the island in the Venetian lagoon known for blown glass. Weiss' dental office was nearby, as was their collective apartment in the via della Porta Pinciana, an address *molto per bene*. At eighty-six, both his friends dead, Gino recalled Arnaldo as "without education, but with so much taste he could give lessons to others, able to correct their mistakes."

The Princess Barberini found her way to the little shop, as did the royal princesses Yolanda and Mafalda. The Prince Chigi found just the right gift at the stylish boutique, run by the two good-looking young men with such refined taste and decorous manners. Big spenders from the Order of Malta were customers. Dr. Weiss was also faring better than even he might have hoped. The great Guglielmo Marconi, the most distinguished Italian scientist since Galileo, came to have his teeth cared for. And so did the king himself.

But for all his airs, Gino was also a good son and made the long journey home to Casarsa as expected, sometimes with Weiss, who was treated as another son. But those visits became rare, and dwindled to nothing. During all Gino's years there, Giulia Zacco Colussi visited Rome only once. Weiss worked on her teeth, just as he paid for an expensive week-long stay in a fashionable clinic for Enrichetta's husband, Antonio Naldini, so heavily gassed in World War I that he remained an invalid thereafter, subject to violent trembling.

After World War II, Paolo Weiss closed his practice and retired to a commodious apartment in Piazza Vittorio, living out his days building his art collection and painting elegantly delineated still-lifes and portraits in a style very controlled, with the atmosphere of Gustav Klimt about them. When an exhibition was held of his work, Gino's nephew Pier Paolo wrote the catalogue. The doctor lived two years with Arnaldo, who finally moved in with Gino in via Fabio Massimo, in the district called Prati, near the Vatican.

Arnaldo and Gino closed the Piccola Galleria in 1969. They had no interest in seeing someone else operate their creation. Weiss died in 1973, after selling his collection of pictures at auction. Arnaldo lived on until 1978. After Pier Paolo's murder and the sale of the house in via Eufrate, cousin Graziella and her husband Vincenzo Cerami, once Pasolini's student, came to live with Gino, by now frail and in his eighties. He died in 1991, over ninety, and was buried in the Casarsa town cemetery, near his parents and all his sisters and brothers-in-law, near his troublesome nephew Pier Paolo.

Grandmother Giulia lived until near the end of the war, and died at seventy-eight. She too is buried in the Casarsa cemetery, sharing a tomb with her footloose daughter Chiarina. The same walled-in field holds Giannina, the only daughter to die a Colussi, as she was born. With Gino dead, that branch of the Coluses, called the Batiston (presumably "of the rod" or "of the stock") to distinguish them from other families of the clan, disappeared forever.

Enrichetta recalls that one day, sometime before World War I, "a rich man from Udine" stopped his car in front of the Pasolini house, lowered a window, and said to her and her younger sister, Susanna, "You two Colussi girls are the prettiest in all of Casarsa." Sixty years later, Enrichetta—who allowed herself to go gray and lose her figure, neither of which Susanna ever did—recalled her sister answered, "If you use *voi* [the plural "you"]—then you must not mean me." Innocently competitive and relentlessly coquettish, Susanna meant to be singular; she had no intention of waiting in the doorway forever.

But Susanna turned thirty before a young officer, posted by the war's demands to the nearby barracks, came to court. Enrichetta does not recall precisely how Susanna met Carlo Alberto Pasolini—"they might just have met in the street" she says—but what is certain is that the handsome artillery lieutenant fell madly in love with her shining eyes, her elegant figure, her fetching way of turning her head to one side, a head she adorned with a spit curl and the very best hats she could buy.

He claimed to be descended from a distinguished family, minor nobility from Ravenna. After not succeeding at much else, he settled on a military career, which suited his character perfectly. Obsessed with strength, with virility and status, almost a caricature of one set on the idea of being a man, his authoritarian personality responded to the new Facist regime that took power in August 1922. He was a supporter of that party's goals and agreed that a strong government was needed to keep order, control striking unionists, suppress the growing anarchy which swept Italy with the end of World War I.

The regime's bravura—songs and uniforms, love of titles and saluting—suited him. He insisted that everyone call him "colonel" after he had reached that rank, even his relatives and even when the war was lost and over. Often "colonel" was spoken as sarcasm among the Colussis when Carlo started to drink, and when he increasingly gave in to rage as the years passed.

By the time he was posted to the frontier town of Casarsa, he had served in Libya as early as 1915 and knew that he liked the life. He had no intention of changing course just because Mussolini was prime minister. On the contrary, the Fascists' talk of empire and rearmament and the honor due soldiers was exactly what the young officer had hoped for. He served the regime with enthusiasm.

He was swaggering and forceful; she was romantic, anxious to leave her father's house. They were soon engaged, but uncertainty about Carlo's future made them put off the wedding. The betrothal was too long for the young couple; in late 1914 or early 1915, Susanna became pregnant. But siring out of wedlock was unacceptable for a career officer with a promising future. With the help of the family doctor, whose certificate secured her leave from school, Susanna was hustled off to relatives near Mantua where a baby boy was born. They named him Carluccio, but he died three months later. He was never spoken of again, at least never in the presence of the siblings who followed him.

With war's end, the beautiful and spoiled Susanna and her dark-eyed fiancé could wed; she was thirty-one, he thirty, and she was pregnant again, seven months and showing. They went to church, but first to the *municipio* and stood before Mayor Gioachino Morello, who wore the red-white-and-green sash of his office. The wedding certificate in the town records is dated December 22, 1921.

The groom's widowed mother came to Casarsa for the event. The Colussis found Susanna's new mother-in-law unlikable—*antipatica;* she was haughty and made it understood that her son had married beneath him. She talked of her husband's family crest, of "lands and *palazzi,*" to put her in-laws in their social place; but no one ever saw the land or the palaces, and the explanation was that they had been lost through bad administration during Carlo Alberto's adolescence, thus forcing him into the honorable if not remunerative military life. What little remained from estate income was spent on Susanna. Her nephew Nico remembers his Uncle Carlo lavishing on his Aunt Susanna what seemed extravagant gifts of flowers and (later found to be worthless costume) jewelry.

Mother-in-law Giulia Drudi Pasolini might even have implied that Susanna had plotted pregnancy to force her son into marriage. In any case, she stayed in Casarsa a week, paid for the wedding luncheon, and was little heard from again. Family gossip was that she drank, that after she died, a mountain of empty Chianti bottles was found under her bed.[3]

Their second, but first surviving, son was born in Bologna, only fourteen weeks after the ceremony, on March 5, 1922. He was named Pier Paolo after his paternal great-uncle, a poet who had died at twenty but not without having been listed in the so-called Golden Album of the Italian nobility, a kind of Debrett's. A Roman wag who knew Pier Paolo in the sixties insists he sometimes wore shirts embroidered with a coronet on the breast, but this man is known for his extravagant tales.


The newlyweds went to live with Carlo Alberto's mother in Bologna; she could help with the new baby. Susanna's "baby brother," Gino, came to live with the new parents. But the stay in Bologna did not last; the Pasolinis were only to return to that city more than a decade later, when Pier Paolo enrolled in the best local high school. Officer Pasolini's career was proceeding well, and that meant frequent changes of post. In 1923 they were in Parma; by 1924 in Conegliano; by 1925 in Belluno.

It was at Belluno, I was a little more than three years old. About the boys who played in the public garden in front of our apartment building, what struck me more than anything were their legs, and of them the concave part at the back and inside of the knees, whose tendons stretched when they ran with a movement at once violent and elegant. I saw in those moving cords a symbol of the life I was yet to meet: they represented for me "being grown-up" in that running boy. Now I know it was a feeling that was acutely sensual. If I try, I can feel again that sensation . . . and the violence of desire. It was the sense of the unreachable, the carnal—a sensation for which a name did not yet exist. I invented it, it was *teta veleta*.

The adult Pasolini was fascinated by his own autobiography as source material, and to a degree his contemporaries sometimes found excessive. He claimed to have clear memories of his very first year; he said he recalled his grandmother's enormous bed in Bologna, enclosed within a wooden alcove, and from Parma, where he was only two, the name of a pet guinea pig.

In a diary entry of 1946, the so-called *Quaderni rossi* ("Red Note-books") only made public by his cousin Nico in 1986, he wrote a memory of 1925, when the family was living briefly in Belluno:

I recall in the kitchen the big table where my growth was measured and marked, and a big chest full of the fragments of my toys. I recall my parents' bedroom, I slept in a little bed at the foot of their giant wedding bed.

He re-created their bed and his own in his film *Oedipus Rex*, casting a handsome actor as the young Laius and Silvana Mangano as Jocasta.

On October 4, 1925, in Belluno, a brother was born, named Guidalberto. From the same diary:

The morning Guido was born, I was the first one awake, and I ran into the kitchen to see him, lying in a crib. I ran into my mother's room to tell her the news. For a long time, I gloried in being the first to see him.

Susanna's sisters came to take care of Pier Paolo in the last days of the pregnancy. One of the aunts told him that babies came from the sky.

After a few months, there we were in the kitchen, my mother and father, in a very cheerful mood. Here is the table, there the hearth and by it Guido's crib. "Mamma," I ask, "how are babies born?" She looked at me, laughing, and said "Out of the stomach of the mother." My father was smiling too. I listened to her answer as though it were a joke, ridiculous, unthinkable; I defended my dignity with great force. It isn't true, they come from the sky, I cry. They rushed to reassure me that I was correct. But I was shocked (if a word like shocked can be used for a child of three years old) by contact with an order of things too different.

Pasolini wrote that "in the first years of my life, my father was more important to me than my mother. He was a presence that was reassuring, strong. Then suddenly, when I was three, the conflict broke. From then on there was tension, anguishing, dramatic, tragic between him and me." In 1971 he recounted his earliest withdrawal from Carlo Alberto to Dacia Maraini, for an article she was writing for Italian *Vogue* about the childhoods of famous Italians.

He told her how he had become agitated as the birth of Guidalberto neared. "When my mother's labor began, I began to have a burning in the eyes. My father fixed me still on a kitchen table, opened my eyes with his finger and gave me drops. From that 'symbolic' moment I began not to love my father anymore."

The Freudian universe had not yet expanded into Italy; terms like *Oedipus complex* and *close-binding mother/distant father* never passed Susanna's ears or lips. She simply did what came naturally and that was to invest all her love in the boy-child who had come to replace the baby she had lost. After she, Carlo, and Pier Paolo were all dead, Susanna's nephew, Nico, wrote, "She was never in love with her husband."[3] With an inevitability he liked to call genetic, Pier Paolo became *le petit prince*, the *dauphin* to a Princess Susanna, herself too much enamored of youth, too romantic for her own good. From the very start, Susanna's attachment to Pier Paolo had the frantic edge of compensation. Her son would be sensitive, poetic, true to her, and as different from the mass as she felt herself to be. When he died, she told reporters that "Pier Paolo was always just as I wanted him to be."

The defenseless (a favorite word of Pasolini's in adulthood) child acceded utterly to his mother's powerful imprint. It took, not like a surface varnish but like a dye into the essence of his psyche, and stayed for life. They agreed early they would always spend their lives together. They conspired to shut the husband and father out of their circle.

Unable to show or share emotion, Carlo hid behind form: Under one heavy brow he wore a monocle; his uniform was always perfect; he kept his in-laws, the countrified Colussis, so many peasants, at arm's length. At one point his adoration of Mussolini's regime was such that he threatened to denounce to the authorities as a Communist the (baker) brother of his brother-in-law, Enrichetta's husband, Antonio Naldini.

Carlo Alberto did not demur when someone seeking to ingratiate himself even called him "Signor Conte." Honor was all; intimacy only for women. He suffered his beautiful wife's coolness in silence, followed by pent-up explosions that only served to push his wife and son further from him. He pouted and sometimes raged; she withdrew. She loved him, Naldini recalls, "as a duty, exactly like a peasant wife."

Susanna took refuge from her disappointment in Pier Paolo, made him not only the replacement for the boy she lost but for the husband in whom she was losing interest, and with whom she increasingly quarreled. Her transfer of love and attention from her husband to her boy went beyond the usual. If she realized it, she made no effort to redress the balance.

Susanna lavished Pier Paolo with praise and reinforcement. He worked to earn her approval, her happiness at his growing assiduousness in Latin and Italian studies. When Pier Paolo was just short of six, he returned from the first grade to show his mother the medal with a green ribbon he had won for being the best pupil in class. He had already begun to show a talent for drawing at four; his school papers, from the earliest grades, were selected by his teacher as the model for the class.

He later claimed to have written his first poem at age seven, in the third grade. He did so at Susanna's prompting; as an adult, he said he started to write "to have her love."

> It was my mother who showed me how poetry can be really written, not just something studied at school. Mysteriously, one day, she gave me a sonnet, which she had composed, in which she expressed her love for me (who knows by what strange sequence of rhymes, it ended with the words "of love for you I have a whole bunch." [". . . *di bene te ne voglio un sacco*".] A few days later, I wrote my first verses. . . .[4]

Already he displayed the triangled cheekbones from her side of the family, the flattened nose, thin lips, her look around the eyes, at once soft and alert.

As an adult, he wrote of his relationship with her:

> Whenever I'm asked to say something about my mother, to recall something about her, it is always the same image that comes to my mind. We are in Sacile, in the spring of 1929 or 1931; my mamma and I are walking along

a path in a field somewhat outside the town; we are alone, completely alone. Around us there are bushes, beginning to bud but still with the look of winter; the trees, too, are bare, and through the long line of black trunks we can see the blue mountains in the background. But the primroses are already out. The edges of the ditches are covered with them. This gives me an infinite joy that, even now as I speak of it, overwhelms me. I squeeze my mother's arm tightly (indeed we're walking arm-in-arm) and bury my cheek in the modest fur coat she's wearing: in that fur coat I smell the odor of spring, a mixture of cold and fragrance, of house and countryside. This odor of my mother's modest fur coat is the odor of my life.[5]

These feelings, which she unreservedly reciprocated, sustained them when they fled to Rome and she washed other people's floors. Later, after their years of travail, when he went to England and Turkey, Yemen and Nepal as director of international movie productions, he phoned her almost every day. And when he was in Rome, he never slept under any roof but hers.

In 1899, Sigmund Freud wrote in *The Interpretation of Dreams:*

There must be something which makes a voice within us ready to recognize the compelling force of destiny in the *Oedipus,* while we can dismiss as merely arbitrary such dispositions as are laid down in . . . other modern tragedies of destiny. And a factor of this kind is in fact involved in the story of King Oedipus. His story moves us only because it might have been ours— because the oracle laid the same curse upon us before our birth as upon him. It is the fate of us all, perhaps, to direct our first sexual impulse towards our mother and our first hatred and our first murderous wish against our father. Our dreams convince us that this is so. King Oedipus, who slew his father Laius and married his mother Jocasta, merely shows us the fulfillment of our own childhood wishes.[6]

Pasolini later read Freud intently. True to the classic psychoanalytic formulation, he could describe but not help himself; with chilling precision, he wrote about (and filmed) his own Oedipal complex. Instead of working to banish or subdue it, he fell in love with it. And if he and his neurosis were not lovers, they did cohabit happily enough.

Susanna's conviction of his innate superiority made him secure, and also free of the need for others' approval. Others mattered as means to his own goals, stepping-stones on his own path. But she also made him detached, what friends later found sometimes oddly cold, strikingly self-sufficient. He needed others for sex, publishing books, financing movies; but deepest love was only for her. As the decades passed, the combination of his life and his nurture became explosive. Instead of needing others' approbation to live, he almost came to live for their disapproval. No one's acceptance mattered but hers, and hers was never, ever to be withheld.

Pasolini freely acknowledged that, save for one vague incident in Rome muddled in his poetic reference, he never slept with a woman. Women fell in love with him when he was a boy, as a young man, and grown. Genuine friendship was possible, collaboration, intimacy of mind—these he had with several women: Silvana Mauri, Laura Betti, Dacia Maraini, Maria Callas, Elsa Morante—but not possessive, sexually jealous love, not melding and wanting only to be always with that other and propagate.

He never characterized his homosexuality as "chosen," nor as a "refusal" of "normality." He believed he had no decision in it: He lived the struggle between his parents, felt the touch and smelled the odor in Susanna's fur coat. This blended with the back of the boys' knees, their stance and swagger, and the matter was decided. Whatever else happened in his life, that would never change.

## 8

*A poet has to woo not only his own Muse but also Dame Philology, and, for the beginner, the latter is the more important. As a rule, the sign that a beginner has a genuine, original talent is that he is more interested in playing with words than in saying something original.*

—*W. H. Auden*, The Dyer's Hand

# A MODEL BOY

Italy had emerged from the bloodletting of World War I still agricultural, even feudal; it was fiercely regional, barely industrialized, and deeply religious, a robust urban anticlericalism notwithstanding. Class lines were very clear: The Pasolinis were somewhere toward the center of the social pyramid, well below the aristocracy and urban professionals, up from schoolmasters and small shopkeepers (even if these had more money), high above day laborers and peasants, at about the rank of second-tier city lawyers or academics.

Carlo Alberto's gambling debts were not yet out of hand, although even early in his marriage he did once wager away his entire paycheck. Years later, when he could not hope to help himself, his creditors threatened to take the furniture. In a favorite family story, Pier Paolo is supposed to have offered to dress in rags and go begging.

The career military family's constant change of address did not allow Pier Paolo durable friendships. His early years are a litany of changing homes: like the twenties, the thirties (his years from eight to eighteen) passed in a series of moves. After Parma came Conegliano and Belluno, then Sacile and Scandiano, all before he was fourteen, in 1936, before settling into high school,

> [At Sacile] I found my playmates grown-up, unrecognizable. I found Norma, Lavinia, Margherita, the Fatati brothers. I heard them talking about a certain *"taculin"* [dialect for *"taccuino,"* a change-purse]. Suddenly, I felt myself excluded . . . they spoke with great naturalness, using a confidential tone that I would never have known how to use. There was something slightly sinful and yet utterly normal in their manner which struck me . . . I felt myself permanently excluded.[1]

He was thrown upon himself, forced to be self-reliant. Carlo Alberto did not live in barracks, but returned to a comfortably furnished home every evening, even if only long enough to change clothes and leave for a card game, with much drink. He was satisfied that Susanna kept her figure, had her hair done in the latest bob, dressed elegantly, and took great care over her makeup. It was part of his *bella figura* that she reflect well on him.

Every value the husband held dear, the wife did not. He loved rank, cerermony, uniforms, titles, anthems, and medals, accepted truths, a good reputation, keeping up appearances. Susanna dismissed all that as empty, phony. He attended church because it was the thing done; she rejected it as bereft of spirituality. Her religion—or so it seemed to her son Pier Paolo—was the practice of altruism, and a natural, almost pantheistic faith born in a peasant-like trust.

Carlo adored the struttings and pronouncements of the new Fascist regime; she made no secret at her revulsion. They argued frequently, complete with pounding of fists on tables from him, tearful flights behind slammed bedroom doors from her. She parried his ponderousness with a distancing gaiety and nonchalance, only showing herself fierce and uncompromising where the interests of her sons were at stake. His sexual advances were rebuffed: Procreation done, his presence was tolerated.

In his "Red Notebooks," diaries of his mid-twenties, Pier Paolo recorded (and perhaps partially created) his earliest memories. One concerned a movie flier which his parents brought home one night, an announcement for the local movie house's coming attraction. The full-color illustration depicted a "young adventurer," presumably handsome and virile, caught in the paws of a tiger. Pier Paolo wrote: "He lay with his head thrown back, almost in a woman's position, defenceless, naked. Meanwhile, the animal was swallowing him, ferociously."

He wrote that seeing the image, "I was seized by that same feeling I have sensed when confronted with the young boys at Belluno, two years before. I felt a tremor inside me, like an abandonment. I started to want to be like that adventurer, eaten alive by a beast. From then on, before falling asleep I imagined myself in the midst of a forest, attacked by a tiger. I allow myself to be devoured by it . . . and then, naturally, because this was absurd, I devised a way of liberating myself and killing it." [2]

The fantasy is ambiguous, the dream both to be devoured because defenseless and to emerge victorious, slaying the sexual beast who has attacked him in an act as exciting to prey as to hunter. But he went further. Sometime after the adventurer-tiger fantasy (which would have been at about age eight to ten ("before puberty"), he found himself either "seeing or imagining" Christ naked on the cross, "barely covered by an odd strip of cloth around his flanks." Soon, thereafter,

> there flourished in my fantasy the desire to imitate Christ in his sacrifice for other men and to be condemned and killed despite being innocent. I saw myself hanging on the cross, nailed up. My thighs were scantily wrapped by that light strip and an immense crowd was watching me. My public martyrdom ended as a voluptuous image and slowly it emerged that I was nailed up completely naked. Overhead, above the heads of those present, so full of veneration with their eyes fixed on me—I felt [blank space] facing an enormous, turquoise sky. With my arms spread, the hands and feet nailed, I was utterly without defense, totally lost . . . sometimes I used to stretch out my arms against a gate or a tree, to imitate the Crucifixion; but I didn't stay too long in that audacious position. [3]

Perhaps some Catholic girls at their most impressionable age, when sexuality and intellect are both awakening, identify with Catherine of Siena or Teresa of Avila. Boys often are fascinated by the naked passivity of Christ, the figure weaker yet more powerful than any on earth. What made Pasolini different was that part of him froze here:

the fantasies of infancy were blocked, the identification with Christ remained. In almost all his films, when the turmoil of human sin and suffering becomes overwhelming, the camera pans upward, "over the heads of those present," and stares into the ambiguity of heaven, of what Paul Bowles called "the sheltering sky."

Sometime in the very cold winter of 1928–29, when seven-year-old Pier Paolo built a kind of igloo in the family courtyard, Carlo was arrested for debt. He had really gambled away the family furniture. To prevent its confiscation, they hid it in the town granary. Susanna returned to teaching, bicycling eighteen kilometers over frozen ground every day to the primary school in tiny Sesto alla Reghena.

Pier Paolo now spent his first and only full year at Casarsa, living in his extended family with its chatter in dialect, its rhythms of work and play, its jokes and nicknames, its enveloping intimacy. He attended the school with his cousin Franca Naldini.

The year made a profound impression: It became a model rooted in memory both conscious and unconscious of a peasant life that was pure and innocent—and most importantly—natural. He and his cousins played "in the kitchen corner . . . making necklaces out of coral." The freewheeling atmosphere of the Colussis was fresh air to a nervous boy made anxious by his father's constant state of tension. He assembled the feelings and later forged a linkage: on the one side Casarsa = life = purity = happiness = Susanna = the Friulian dialect of the peasantry. That was good, and on the enemy side urbanism = hypocrisy = moralism = Carlo Alberto = the standard Italian of the educated bourgeoisie. He found in Casarsa a standard for comparison, even an image of social perfection to carry with him when he went to Rome, and beyond: He was happy in the courtyard of the Colus clan house, where "outside there was the music of mosquitoes and of oleanders."

"Think of it!" the already self-conscious intellectual, keen on irony and word-play, exclaimed to Giuseppe Zigaina, when they met in 1946. "I live in Casarsa . . . Casarsa della Delizia" (Casarsa of the Delights). Savoring the exquisiteness of the split personality in the name ("delights" but "burnt houses") suited a boy also split, who already presented one face to the world and an altogether different one to himself.

With the end of 1929, the family moved again, to Sacile, a town at the border of Friuli and the Veneto. Cousin Naldini reports Pier Paolo began to fill a manuscript book with poetry and told his mother, "Mamma, when I get big I want to be a Navy captain and a poet." The notebook was lost during the family's moves during the war.

Pier Paolo entered the equivalent of third or fourth grade, but his teachers held him back because they found his Italian theme-paper "beginner's work." His father immediately withdrew him from the school, and the eight-year-old began to commute by train from home in Sacile to school in Conegliano. In 1957, he reminisced in an essay submitted to a writing competition held by the State railways:

> I awoke at five in the morning: and in November, December the weather is Friuli is no joke. They were frozen, black mornings, immense, from the Pian Cavallo to the sea. The wind blew over the mud and on the ugly, sleeping houses of the village. I saw an old *accelerato*, which went slowly toward Venice, one serving only office workers, factory workers, and students: but at that hour it was almost empty. I still feel moved and loved if I think about that train.
>
> There were days when, in the big, dark carriage, which trembled as it moved, I was alone: in a little corner, next to a window acid with smoke, not properly closed: and I watched the sun come up. It's true I had begun writing poetry several years before, when I was in the *terza elementare:* but there, at that hour, alone in the carriage looking at the borning sun there was time and means to confirm my innocent vocation, one which I considered almost a duty.[4]

Between 1933 and 1935, the Pasolinis lived in Cremona, and Pier Paolo, like the good son of a good family that he was, took fencing and violin lessons. At thirteen, he discovered literature. He read Giosuè Carducci, fell in love with Jules Verne, and, like many other boys, consumed the "Sandokan" tales churned out by Emilio Salgari. He also become enamored of the ancient myths. Years later, he spoke rhapsodically of discovering the story of the Shield of Achilles, in which Homer addresses the nature of representation, the relationship between reality and imagination. The precocious youth flourished within a humanistic curriculum virtually intact from a century before, one rooted in the classics, in rhetoric and composition. Of the three years in Cremona he wrote, "Those days which preceded the summer of '34 were among the most beautiful and glorious of my life."

In 1935, Hitler visited Mussolini for the first time. He wanted to know this dictator better, one so secure after a decade in power that he dared to proclaim, "Italians are best governed by police, and bands playing in the streets." Pier Paolo turned thirteen, and spent hours drawing, filling sheets of paper with birds and animals out of his reading of the classics. "There became clear to me the problem of representation as something powerful and primordial, exactly because it was pure. . . ."

"Pure" meant intact, uncontaminated by inevitable compromises forced by reality. One could make the world any way one chose, but the artist was an absolute, unfettered creator. The pubescent boy wondered, and wrote in his diary: ". . . if I were to draw a field, need I depict every blade of grass? I did not then understand that if I filled in an area with green pastel, I would render the mass of that field and that would be good enough for leaving the individual blades out." He "suffered" when he felt constrained to do the only thing he knew was just: Every blade of the field where God created Adam had to be drawn, and he drew them.

Every summer throughout Italy's generally successful thirties— the Duce made war, but somewhere else—Susanna and her boys returned to Casarsa. Aunt Enrichetta sewed clothes enough for the coming school year, and friendships suspended with the end of the previous summer were ardently resumed.

Guidalberto emerged as a normal boy: He loved hunting and found his friends among those whose greatest joy was stalking birds with simple buckshot rifles. Cousin Nico Naldini recalls a friend named Renato who had a woodshop. The boys built a sailboat and ran it on the canals between the fields. Pier Paolo graduated from a smaller to a larger bicycle and used it to explore endlessly, ever farther from home, to find Friuli for himself. He was a charter member of a band of boys who joined every afternoon for long outings.

In 1936, the year the League of Nations voted sanctions against Italy for attacking Ethiopia, senior officials in Rome endorsed Himmler's call for closer Italian collaboration with the Gestapo. The Duce's reference to Germany of only two years before as "a racist, lunatic asylum" were forgotten. By the Fuehrer's second visit, starting in Rome on May 6, 1938, the dictators' roles were reversed. The Italian was no longer giving instructions but was taking them; laws against the Jews came within the year. The last night of Hitler's visit, a huge crowd was assembled in the main square of Siena. Before the thir- teenth-century town hall, he and his hosts were entertained: Twelve hundred young people, backed by five thousand accordionists from all over Italy, danced the *saltarello*, the leaping-dance. Then Hitler went home, seen off at the Ostia station by King Victor Emanuele, who wore his uniform of First Marshal of the Empire. Mussolini wore the more meaningful getup, that of commandant general of the na- tional militia, the private army available to depose the king if needed. Everyone smiled for the newsreels, which were sped to the cinemas.

Pier Paolo would have seen them at his local movie house—youths his age dancing the *saltarello,* leaping into madness.

Bombast, oratory, and propaganda took the place of action. The press was completely a tool of the State, and the State stage-managed celebrations and public dramas enough to make the ancient bread-and-circuses seem but one long amateur night. Official policy encouraged martyrdom—the slogan "better one day as a lion than a hundred years as a sheep." At the now obligatory civil wedding ceremonies, Italian couples were told the man had two duties, that of husband and of soldier. A new law was passed in 1938 making military instruction obligatory from the age of eight to thirty-two. When the *sposo* went away *soldato,* he was given a medal in the name of the Duce: it read *"Si avanzo seguitemi, si indietreggo uccidetemi"* (if I go forward, follow me; if I retreat, kill me). After the "triumph" in Abyssinia, songs about its "heroes" were hits: "Ti saluto, vado in Abissinia" (Farewell, I am going to Abyssinia) and "Faccetta nera" (Little black face), a kind of Fascist anthem: "Little black face, beautiful Abyssinian / Wait and hope, the time is coming / When we shall be near you, we shall give you another Duce and another King."

Italy was living the age of kitsch.

By decade's end, everyone was a Fascist at least in name, or had made his peace with the system, or fallen silent, or been silenced. This Fascist universe (historians call it "the years of consensus") was the world into which Pier Paolo and his bicycling companions had been born, like fish swimming in a Fascist sea who never knew any other. His Aunt Enrichetta sewed the mandated white blouses and black skirts for the Casarsa section of the Fascist women's organization, le Donne Fasciste.

And Pier Paolo did as everyone else and joined Fascist-controlled clubs. One was the Casa del Soldato, a youth center offering organized soccer games. Some political indoctrination was inevitable and Pier Paolo was photographed in the uniform of the obligatory Fascist University Youth (GUF). One graduated to it after a membership from five to seven years in the Figlio della Lupa (Son of the She-wolf) corps. Before that came the Balilla corps (seven to fifteen years); each called for new uniforms every year. One could hardly appear in a fez of last year's color. Pier Paolo seems not to have made any special issue of it. It was in the nature of things; one went on with life's important callings—friends, soccer, literature.

From 1937, the Pasolinis settled in Bologna, renting an apartment in via Nosadella, in a quarter near the Porta Saragozza, which one

*Pasolini at the beach with friends, circa 1950s.* Photo: Courtesy of Piero Colussi

*Student Pasolini*
*(top, left) with*
*other members of*
*his soccer squad.*
Photo: Courtesy of
the author

*Susanna Colussi*
*at the time of her*
*marriage. Photo:*
Courtesy of the
author

*Guidalberto Pasolini,*
*partisan, in the Carnic*
*Alps above Casarsa, 1945.*
Photo: Courtesy of the author

*Pasolini,
Ninetto
Davoli, and
Maria Callas
during a visit
to Ninetto,
army draftee.*
Photo: Marli
Shamir

*Pasolini in
Grado, 1949.*
Photo: Giuseppe
Zigaina

*Maria Callas, Pasolini,
and Alberto Moravia in
Mali.* Photo: Marli Shamir

*Laura Betti and Pasolini.*
Photo: Elisabetta Catalano

*Pasolini and Giorgio Napolitano, PCI official, at the Festival of Unity, 1974.*
Photo: Sonia and Nando Danielli

*Pasolini at home, holding*
Le ceneri di Gramsci, *1969.*
*Photo: Bechetti*

*Pasolini in his house at Chia, near Viterbo, October 1975.* Photo: Dino Pedriali

*The graves of mother and son, Susanna Colussi Pasolini and Pier Paolo Pasolini, Casarsa.* Photo: Courtesy of the author

friend of the time has called "poor but elegant," opposite a printing shop. Susanna stayed here after Carlo Alberto went to the war, and Pier Paolo enrolled in the excellent Liceo Galvani and discovered Shakespeare and Dostoevsky.

"Every morning I went to find them at the school entrance, which even now I remember," he wrote years later. "Via Castiglione . . . the Liceo Galvani . . . I, at that moment, was the happiest boy in all of Italy." The rich kids played tennis at a private club, but lower-middle-class boys went to play soccer for whole afternoons—Pier Paolo, Fabio Mauri, Gianni Scalia, Renzo Renzi, mixing with the sons of bakers and construction workers who lived far from the city's elegant center. Their playing field was at the edge of town in the Prati di Caprara, toward what was then the semideserted Borgo Panigale. Sometimes they went to the tiny village of Casalecchio, now a suburb of Bologna, in the direction of the sanctuary of the Madonna of San Luca, perched on a hill over the city but connected to it with two miles of porticos built over a hundred years, to keep clerical processions dry.

Pier Paolo played what was then called the *terzino* (later, the left wing); he and his buddies dreamed of being equal to the Bologna professional *squadra*, which played in the grand new municipal stadium just inaugurated by the Duce.[5]

During Pier Paolo's 1938 school year, Mussolini took the fateful step of formal alliance with Hitler and visited Berlin. Amid the marches and the speeches, the pronouncements about Axis world domination and the brotherhood of all Germans and all Italians, very few saw it was the beginning of the end. But at the Galvani the year before, Pier Paolo heard Rimbaud's *Bateau Ivre* read in class by a teacher named Antonio Rinaldi. He embroidered his reaction with the years and made a kind of legend of that moment. With some hyperbole and some truth, he later claimed that the world of conformity to Fascism and literary convention broke apart when he heard the poem. Even discounting his urge to self-dramatization, it was an important moment in the mind of a young poet hungry for a modern model, looking for his own voice.

His examination results came back so excellent that he was able to skip a year, moving that much faster toward the university. The test of "classical maturity," the watershed separating those who would and those who would not proceed in school, was behind him. A summer of beach at Riccione and the usual Casarsa rhythm lay ahead: long bicycle rides into the countryside, where he had found the courage to stop and talk to boys working the fields, swimming in the

Tagliamento's eddied pools. He had other exams to face, so he took time to study under a stand of acacias in the open air. Bologna friends came to visit Casarsa, and a tranquil summer passed, the last peaceful one Europe would know for many years. With fall 1939, Pier Paolo, age seventeen, enrolled not in the army but (as the law allowed him) in the Faculty of Letters at the University of Bologna.

Pier Paolo's intellectual (and that meant career) options were limited, although he seems never to have seen them in that light. His father did not provide an acceptable model. As for Susanna, she approved of poetry but had no idea how men made careers of it. She knew that schoolteachers were respected and had job security. Pier Paolo's family offered him no male models: He had to invent himself. Those around him in adolescence were women.

Italy's school system under Fascism was distinctly layered: Bright students were spotted fast and directed early to the *liceo classico* or the *ginnasio*, whose curricula were anchored in Greek and Latin, history and Italian composition. Fascism did not loosen this nineteenth-century structure; on the contrary, it was reinforced. Foreign notions of progressive education and classroom democracy were strictly forbidden. Such ideas, as well as much of the rest of the world's work from 1922 to 1942, flooded Italy—and fast—only at war's end. No such end was in sight when twelve-year-old Pier Paolo was tracked in 1934.

As he proceeded, he found little latitude for experimentation. The American college smorgasbord of majors and electives was unknown. Italian universities knew nothing about Charles William Eliot's general-education innovations at Harvard; a student at Bologna simply "inscribed" himself in a faculty, studied a corpus of set material, wrote a thesis within that field, and that was that. Nineteen-year-olds came to think of themselves as chemists, not students taking a chemistry course. The margins were in finding the most interesting lecturers and reading on one's own. Lengthy, written examinations, set papers, when successfully completed, allowed the degree; one took them as one was ready. There was time for self-education (or not), with panic cramming toward the end. Later, Pasolini called much of the university "mediocre and Fascist"; but one was also left to make one's own mind, and he did. The system's hands-off style was elitist and self-contained, designed to produce a caste for a society in which holding a degree still meant something.

For Pier Paolo, instinct and influence coincided: He could do well that which he wanted to do. He had always been drawn to the figurative arts, almost as much as to literature. At the beginning in Bologna, he was an incipient art critic or art historian as much as a budding man of letters.

The literature and languages faculties were housed in a converted palace of tattered splendor on the north side of the via Luigi Zamboni, cutting through the heart of the ancient Romans' Bononia, a short walk from the two leaning towers Dante described and the Piazza Maggiore. The building had been the seat of the Poggi clan, whose heraldry was still to be seen over every window, a mound of six carved stones topped with an eagle. Up a grand staircase, and a turn to the right are the library's reading rooms—long tables of exquisite woods, inlaid with the initials of the university, under shaded lamps. Somehow an area of niches with nutwood-lined shelving on three sides had survived from the era of a gentleman's library into that of the mass-production State university. Alcove "H"—they bear letters, like London club reading rooms—houses the Italian literary classics: Pier Paolo, were he at Bologna now, would still find the Bolognese Carducci installed here, with Leopardi and Manzoni.

Pier Paolo reveled in the university's ability to pretend that the world at large did not exist or, if it did, that it counted for very little. He was a player who excelled within the system, taking immediately to Bologna's urban, self-conscious academic culture, one familiar with modern painting, given to film retrospectives and reading foreigners in their original language. Somehow, in the midst of Fascist conformity and resistance to ideas, the life of the mind flourished here. The formalities of loyalty were observed: All student publications, for example, passed before the eyes of a censor. And yet, discussion thrived under the very noses of political authorities who seemed not to have understood the subversion free discussion engenders. The understanding was much like that at Oxford, Cambridge, and the most prestigious universities everywhere: that governments come and go, but what happens in the academy is what really counts. The university predated the regime by almost nine hundred years and did not forget it. Fascism (a regime but never convincingly the State) could not be successfully challenged; but it was still only a recent arrival, layered for barely a decade over a way of life that had existed for centuries.

Pasolini attended lectures by poet Alfonso Gatto on the poetry of Hermeticism and soon joined his circle. He sat an exam on the provincial poets first and then attacked the reading list of the Hermeticists *en bloc*, starting with Giuseppe Ungaretti. His was the total immersion of one who lived for poetry—talked it, read it constantly, devoured lectures on the subject. He was studying to take vows in the secular religion of humanistic culture, a religion complete with liturgy and saints, schisms and sages. Looking back much later, he described himself at university as "not an apprentice but an initiate."

He also fell under the influence of the already legendary art historian, charismatic Roberto Longhi, holder of the chair in the history of art since 1934. Longhi was delivering ground-breaking lectures on Masaccio and Masolino; Pier Paolo attended in a state of what he called "febrile excitement." He saw, for the first time, the frescoes he later adoringly recorded on film. And the art historian also loved the movies: He was famous among his students for making a special trip to Paris to see Renoir's *Grand Illusion* and Chaplin's *The Great Dictator*, both banned in Italy. Pasolini encountered Longhi in the stalls of Bologna's Cinema Imperiale and decided that his teacher was one of the few truly great men he could ever hope to know.

Pasolini started a monograph, meant to become a degree thesis on modern painters, but as he explained to his friend Gianni Scalia, the school's bureaucracy required that he write on literature, since that was his declared major.

A decade later, Longhi's influential magazine *Paragone* first published Pier Paolo's work-in-progress on his first novel, as well as his first major poetry in Italian. The acolyte came to be his mentor's equal and friend; along with Longhi's friend the literary critic Gianfranco Contini, the art historian held a unique rank throughout Pasolini's life as revered maestro. Three decades later, the famous Pasolini declared that much as he admired the work of Roland Barthes, he would "give it all for a page of Longhi or Contini."

Under Longhi's guidance, Pasolini discovered the Italian cinema as it came into its own. In 1934 Mussolini had established the Direzione Generale per la Cinematografia, headed by Luigi Freddi, a strong supporter of Fascism. By the next year, a special fund to support film production was created at the Banca Nazionale del Lavoro. The same year film was added to the Venice arts festival, and on April 21, 1935, Mussolini himself came to inaugurate the great film production complex in Rome called Cinecittà, erected to replace the Cines studios that had burned. Cinecittà still stands where Mussolini put it; a quarter century after its opening by the Duce, Pasolini—like Fellini, Antonioni, Visconti, De Sica, and Rossellini— worked there.

No less than Count Galeazzo Ciano, the Duce's son-in-law,

was encouraging the GUF to set up Party-blessed film clubs. Pier
Paolo frequented the Bolognese chapter, the Cineguf. "There," he
wrote, "is where the first love for cinema started." On June 6, 1939,
the club presented (free to members), in via Castiglione, *Beau Brum-
mel* with John Barrymore and Mary Astor, double-billed with another
silent, of Laurel and Hardy. The only problem with the Cineguf was
that, under the racial laws of 1938, Jews were not allowed to join.
One evening the Jewish Gino Treves, son of one of the Treves publishing brothers, rose to speak in a discussion following a screening.
He was defended by his friends but was invited by the management
not to attend other evenings.

Even as war neared, university life was bliss. Pier Paolo became
captain of the Letters soccer squad, skied in winter, and threw himself into literary projects. In the nurturing air of Bologna, he attended
lectures by Vincenzo de Bartholomaeis on Romance philology and
became enraptured by the subject. Somehow this scholarship thrived
in the university even as Mussolini worked to stamp out regional
dialects. The regime's reasoning was that Italian unification and
strength demanded adherence to a single version of standard Italian.
A regionalism thousands of years in the making—one which saw a
Genoese unable to communicate with a Triestino, a Neopolitan in
another linguistic universe from a Torinese—seemed to threaten the
power of the centralized State. Mussolini knew well Metternich's dismissal of Italy a century before as merely "a geographical expression." The on-paper unification made fifty years before Fascism took
power had hardly begun to undo the regional loyalties that centuries
had made. The grandfathers of the Italians he now ruled had much
longer been citizens of the republics of Genoa, Siena, Florence, or
Venice, subjects of the kings of Naples or Sicily, the duchies of Savoy
or Milan. Convinced that the French and German authorities had
built modern states partly by enforcing linguistic hegemony, the regime frowned on publication in dialect while admitting the impossibility of stamping it out in daily speech.
    Pier Paolo's ear for the nuances of local speech had been developed
from childhood; with the concentration of an intelligent child without
television, he noted the varieties of *friulano* spoken on either side of
the river Tagliamento, the shadings into the Veneto dialect his mother
spoke, differences in expression in each of the towns where the family
lived.
    The university at Bologna allowed him to turn that enthusiasm

toward scholarship, and the ground was laid for his becoming a philologist-anthologist of regional poetry. And, in a subtle fashion, he also formed a commitment in the classroom to write in the language of the people he loved, the separate vocabulary of Friuli. He knew full well it was something learned, adopted, taken on as an observer from outside. Claims that he was a "poet of Friuli" have more to do with local pride than fact. His parents did not speak the language of the peasants of Casarsa: they were of a higher social class; after his birth, they were frequent and long-term visitors in Casarsa but visitors still. And when Susanna chose to speak in dialect (Carlo spoke only proper Italian), it was heavily inflected with the vocabulary and cadence of the adjacent Veneto, the far richer neighboring province to the west, which includes Vincenza and Verona, Treviso and Padua.

In 1940 the student cafeteria served substantially less meat than a decade earlier. Pier Paolo apparently thought little about it and often ate at home. That May, Holland and Belgium fell to Hitler and the Germans reached the English Channel, having crossed two hundred miles of France in seven days. Dunkirk fell on June 4 and church bells rang in celebration throughout Germany for three days. A week later, the French government deserted Paris for Vincennes, leaving it to Pétain's collaborators for four years. Mussolini now entered the war against France and Britain. The same month, university student Pier Paolo wrote his friend Franco Farolfi that he had received top scores in English literature and in philosophy. In the horrible winter of 1941, he wrote a friend about seeing Pirandello performed. His great excitement was discovering Beethoven; he heard the fourth, sixth, seventh and eighth symphonies on the radio, which was then increasingly given to broadcasting German music.

In retrospect, his career is extraordinary for the degree to which he succeeded in keeping true to the lifework he early made a calling. While he was for several years a columnist for newspapers, he never made his living solely as a full-time staff member of any publication. He did not—as other distinguished writers did (Italo Calvino and Cesare Pavese are two examples)—work for a publishing house. He was not a staff critic for anyone and ceased teaching school at the earliest opportunity. The thirty years of his lifework after university were almost exclusively an exercise in making a living at center stage, as the poet, novelist, film director, playwright, critic. From adolescence he was not within someone else's orbit but always the animator, the *protagonista*.

Aside from Carlo Alberto's talk of a distant ancestor-poet, no one in the family had dreamed of earning his way as an intellectual. Within ascertainable records and confirmable memory, no one on either side had made a living as an artist. Pier Paolo made the jump in a single generation from military man's son and farmer-brewer's grandson to artist, without passing through industrialists, professionals, professors, or managers. In this he was to find one more link with an immigrant pharmacist's daughter, the equally narcissistic and brilliantly self-made Maria Callas née Kalogeropoulos.

He recorded in his secret diary, kept locked in a drawer, "I read a book and a half a day." He melded his worlds, connecting life in the university with that of Casarsa. What he learned in the formal setting of study about the nature and development of Romance languages went with him to the summer swimming hole at Casarsa: Soon he not only enjoyed the evening outings with neighborhood peasant boys come to cool off from the fields but studied their speech. He listened with the ear of a scholar but intended—and this from the earliest recorded memories—to use it in the vocation, the *mestiere* of a poet.

Learning was a compartment in Italy, set apart from most people by a history that made it the stuff of courts and the Church. Scholarship was a profession for those few whose economic and social opportunities gave them access to it, only tenuously linked to any commitment to a generally educated public. Pasolini broke that mold by mixing levels, by taking the insights of scholarship and putting them to work in his art. Erudition did not make his poetry recondite. On the contrary, he avoided both the naïve (real or feigned) and the difficult when he turned to write. In this he was the Italian cousin of the Anglo-Saxons, such as Auden, Eliot, and Stevens, and far from the Continental tradition of literature as the Italian Hermeticists practiced it, incantations made by a cult for consumption by a caste.

On December 1, 1940, Pier Paolo "volunteered" in the university officer training corps. It did not seem an act done in the shadow of war, only something precautionary. Throughout 1940 and all of the next year, Hitler did the Axis' dirty work in Europe. Even the invasion of France and the Low Countries seemed somehow far away, the Alps so high. Italy's bailiwick and her spoils were to be in the Mediterranean; the Duce planned to cash in on the loot, thanks to his partner's hard work. Italian soldiers were to suppress the Balkans, the Greeks, and, easier yet, the Arabs in North Africa. Nothing to it, he decided; he worried, in fact, that there might be too few Italian casualties for the conquests to deliver on their full propaganda potential. It was inconceivable that the war would ever come to Italian soil. The Duce said so, and he was "always right."

Carlo Alberto must have been pleased that Pier Paolo enlisted as other eighteen-year-olds had done; Susanna worried. But he had not been carried away, had not left the university to sign on with the first volunteers carried away by Mussolini's speech from his Piazza Venezia balcony when the Americans declared war on Germany and Italy on December 11, 1941, four days after Pearl Harbor.

Pier Paolo kept on with his studies and stayed in Bologna. He and Luciano Serra, with their new friends Francesco Leonetti and Roberto Roversi were planning their own literary magazine, *Eredi* (Heirs). Its self-important program was nothing less than to document the continuity of the classical tradition into the work of Ungaretti, Eugenio Montale, and Vittorio Sereni, a continuity understood, between the lines, not to have been broken by Fascism.

Roversi—who spent the rest of his life in Bologna, owner of an antiquarian bookstore—has recalled:

> We were in the Margarita gardens, sitting in a just-cut field; out of the yellow splendor of the sun and the grass arose a dense perfume, so rural, of mown hay stacked and drying. Only a few people, a few women and girls walking here and there. We three sitting there (Leonetti, Pasolini and I) spoke of a magazine to make, which we wanted to make, which we *had* to make. The name already proposed was *Eredi*. We spoke cheerfully, with happiness brought from finally something important to do; at a decision which we had to see through, committing ourselves. We were impassioned. That smell and that feeling put their mark on me, incised themselves on my memory. A man passed on a bicycle, dressed in civilian clothes; slowly, looking around; did he need to speak with someone? He saw us, we looked at one another, he came close but did not stop; he spoke softly: "Hitler has invaded Russia." It was the twenty-second of June of '41 and we were, in that moment of our youth, completely outside the world.[6]

*Eredi* followed the formula made classic by a century of Italian small journals: contributions by the founders and their friends, positions taken on cultural politics and their inevitable ripostes, debates, a mix of erudition and polemic, an enthusiastic sense of "us" and "them." Pier Paolo was in his glory as editor, contributor, and critic.

He could regularly be found at the editors' unofficial hangout, the Cappelli bookstore. Official restrictions on paper were enforced: Italy then as now imports all it uses, and Allied sanctions were cutting into supply. So while publication of the first number was postponed, the four formed plans to publish a volume of verse with contributions from each, costs shared among them.

They spent hours discussing their project over chestnut cake and cheap Sardinian wine, and dreamed of being poets. Pasolini was the least self-ironical of all, determined that he and his friends should be laical monks of a kind, dedicated to something higher than others were. When his partners tired of planning and coping with administrative problems, he bolstered their morale. To act in poetry with high seriousness was the aim, even if it meant sacrifice.

He wrote a friend,

> It does not matter if the magazine comes out at some indeterminate date and one that is far off. So much the better for our preparation, our seriousness, our maturity if it comes out two years from now. Serra and I will be professors, and earning money; we will, all four of us, have personalities fifteen times more developed. Just think what two years' (even one) growth can mean to adolescent cultures like ours. Let's go ever deeper into the problems of contemporary Italian life, and we will know how to see clearer and deeper.[7]

In an exquisite bit of unconscious self-revelation, Pier Paolo reprimanded his friend, contributor Fabio Mauri, who sometimes skipped editorial meetings to go out with girls. "If girls can take the place of poetry for you," he told him, "it means poetry isn't much loved." He also wrote to bolster and to scold Serra: "Remember, for your friendship, I have sacrificed many others, and there are many acquaintances that I haven't followed up, for fear of getting sidetracked." He took commitment to literature as the measure of sincerity, its quotient of sacrifice periodically checked. Fidelity to the work always came first, people second. Later, when he was famous, he broke friendships over an idea or the quality of a book, cut off close contacts that had lasted decades because of disagreement over artistic policy.

He returned to Casarsa in the summer of 1941 with a program of intense study. He installed himself in a room of his own at the top of a ladder above his grandfather's *grappa* equipment storage, complete with bookshelves of his own making. A photo shows the happy, perfect (and scrubbed clean) bohemian, his jacket draped insouciantly over one shoulder, a glass of wine on his writing table beside a notebook, a contented smile on his face. He was the poet in his attic—his mother nearby and the world outside might just go to pieces without its mattering too much.

He wrote Serra in Bologna that July about a hailstorm "that recalls the millennia" and described how he and cousin Nico moved to save some baby ducklings in the orchard. "I laughed, but Nico was very worried."

He virtually churned out poetry in Italian and occasionally *friulano*, carefully marked and laid aside in a binder carefully labeled *Scartafaccio* (Notebook). He also drew, using green ink and ochre straight from the tube, using oily cellophane, the only paper available. He drew the neighborhood boys at play in the courtyards, men carrying their tools walking to the fields. He drew his grandmother and painted landscapes of the flat countryside in morning fog. He wrote to Roversi, describing the Tagliamento at full summer torrent as "white as a skeleton."

He was a summertime explorer of linguistic varieties: Friuli on the Casarsa side of the Tagliamento his domain, a bicycle his vehicle. "In western Friuli, especially Basso [the lowlands at the base of the Alps], it was possible in ten minutes by bicycle to pass from one linguistic area to another more archaic by fifty years, or a century, or even two centuries." He eavesdropped, feeling what he called "a kind of mystical act of love" for the speakers and their speech; the life around him, his ardor for the boys he met merged into adoration of their expression. Reality was in language, and by reproducing the loved words and their sequence he could appropriate the adored human universe they inhabitated. In making the boys' dialect his own, he made its speakers his:

> Once I had come into contact with dialect, it inevitably produced its effects, even if initially I adopted it for purposes that were only literary. As soon as I began to use it, I understood that it opened up something alive and real and it acted like a boomerang. It was through *friulano* that I came to understand, at least a little, the reality of the peasant world.[8]

The same process was to occur years later in Rome: The language of the so-called *sottoproletariato* gave entrée to their world. And it was the search for a world he could belong to, where he was accepted having chosen it, that animated him most.

On July 14, 1942, there issued at Pier Paolo's expense three hundred numbered copies (seventy-five set aside for critics) of *Poesie a Casarsa* (Poetry at Casarsa), under the imprint of the Libreria Antiquaria, the bookshop of Mario Landini in Bologna's Piazza San Domenico. Pasolini wrote in 1970, at age forty-eight, "I was exactly twenty years old; but the poetry drawn together there I had started to write three years earlier, in Casarsa, my mother's village, where we went every summer for a simple vacation with relatives, what the meager stipend of my military officer father allowed."

They were poems in Friulian dialect, characterized by "the prolonged hesitation between sense and sound [as Pasolini later characterized them] . . . and strongly favoring sound." Years later he dismissed his youthful work not only for lack of "sense." He called the collection "semantic expansion operated on sound pushed to the limit of transferring meaning into another linguistic domain, from which it returns gloriously indecipherable."

But the verses were not indecipherable. Rather, they were hymns of praise for a world he approached from the outside and embraced with a feeling he understood to be tenderness, almost religious humility. From the summer of 1941:

> *Fontana d'acqua del mio paese.*
> *Nessun'acqua è piu fresca che al mio paese.*
> *Fontana di rustica amore.*

> Fountain of water of my village.
> No water is fresher than that of my village.
> Fountain of rustic love.

Many years later, Pasolini claimed that he started writing in Friulian speech "of the right bank of the Tagliamento" with the word *rosada*, began with an experimental poem that gave way to one which was preserved and lines that called the evening "luminous" (*imbarlumida*). He was not afraid to refer to water not in a romantic pond but in a ditch. His second poem reads: *Sera imbarlumida, tal foscal / a cres l'aga* (Luminous evening, in the ditch / the water rises . . .).[9]

But he did something more than record words for the love of them. He constructed an ideal world of natural innocence—including lack of shame at natural erotic feeling—at the base of the "blue and unsullied foothills of the Alps,"[10] hills where bands of partisans of both Communist and of Christian Democratic persuasion, deserters, informers, mercenaries, and Nazis would soon go to massacre one another. In Casarsa, at the base of those foothills, Pasolini wrote "the Devil sinner . . . laughs in my eye" and wrote how he prayed in vain that "the bells" would "drive him away." The earliest published poems are suffused with identification with the suffering Christ and a longing for death, and they are also the voice of an ardent and very young poet who has force-fed himself on the French Decadents.

He did not use the verse only to confess himself. He used it to report to the world, making art out of nature. Pier Paolo wanted to be the bearer of poetry's polished glass. And he understood that the language he invented for his poetry was not one anyone spoke. On the last page of *Poesie a Casarsa*, he added a note:

> The Friulian *idio* [idiom] of these poems is not the genuine one, but the one gently intermingled with the language of the Veneto which is spoken on the right bank of the Tagliamento; furthermore, the force I have applied to it, to constrain it within poetic meter and diction, is not slight.

*Poesie a Casarsa* was a beginning so very modest that his literary career might have died there. The book might have sold a few copies to friends and family members, been remaindered and forgotten: thirty years later, the printer wrote him he still had a few copies in his storeroom, "collectors' items by now, I imagine." But his slim volume fell into the right hands. Gianfranco Contini, who was already one of Italy's most influential literary critics and whose power as career-maker would grow over several decades, offered his blessing. Pasolini recalled, "About two weeks after the book came out, I received a postcard from Gianfranco Contini, who told me that the book had pleased him so much that he was immediately reviewing it."

Contini was living in near-exile in the frontier town of Domodossola, teaching Romance philology at Fribourg in Switzerland. He used his academic post and access to the foreign press to espouse cultural diversity through use of dialects, a radical and risky line directly contrary to the Italian government's cultural intentions. Pasolini served Contini as a case-in-point, to show that young Italian poets were still writing in minor languages, for *friulano* is a separate language from Italian and itself divided into dialects.

Twenty years later, Contini recalled to Naldini that Mario Landini's Libreria Antiquaria was one of his sources for new books and new poets.

> One day in 1942, the postman delivered a packet with the lovely and old-fashioned handwriting of Mario Landini . . . which for the first time included a little book printed under his own imprimatur. I didn't know the author, Pier Paolo Pasolini, someone one could tell from his name to be of Ravenna origins, and I noted the language of the *Poetry at Casarsa* was *friulano* but "of this side of the water" ("*di cà da l'aga*"), thus an exception inside the exception.[11]

A distinguished Romance philologist, Contini knew *friulano* varied widely between "*di la*"—"over there" of the Tagliamento—the eastern, toward-Trieste side—and *"di cà"*—"over here," as measured in the minds of those who spoke it on the western banks, the Veneto side. Pasolini's exploration, in a poetry like none he had ever read, of the difference and subusages among villages was no less than food and drink to the scholar in Contini whose passion was all minor languages that were offshoots of Latin. He wrote that the little book was "the pure language of poetry," strong words when poetry was supposed to be written only in the pure Italian approved by the regime's Ministry of Public Instruction. It suited the critic as it did Pasolini that it was written in "an absolute language, non-existent in nature."

It was praise beyond Pier Paolo's wildest imagining:

> Who can describe my joy? I leapt and danced under the porticoes of Bologna; all the worldly satisfaction one can hope for from writing verses I had to the fullest that day in Bologna: from then on, it would have to be less.[12]

Contini's review appeared in the *Corriere del Ticino* in Lugano on April 24, 1943. That it was published not in Italy but in Switzerland—in its Italian-speaking canton, but exile territory nonetheless—seemed to Pier Paolo a personal affront made by a dying Fascist system.

Pasolini understood the praise was not for him alone and also that the critic was far more famous than the work he praised. He found himself misunderstood or, at least, lauded not precisely for the right reasons. Contini had turned the book into evidence with which to strike at the regime; Pier Paolo was only grateful at being noticed.

The blessing from this career-maker confirmed Pier Paolo's sense of purpose. He might have before him only the future of a country schoolteacher, but he was now published and favorably received by an important voice. At twenty, he had moved out in front of his friends in the field that mattered most to them all. They noticed with an inevitable mixture of pride and envy. Roversi wrote to Naldini, recalling those days:

> He had an extraordinary tranquility and facility in writing which never ceases to amaze me; and he started right away to excel, over those of us who also attempted it, in an extraordinary invention of *dialetto colorato* [painted, or tinged dialect] (as it seemed to me to be) . . . at a language that was sentimental but with so much contained modesty . . . as to make it new and different, that is new and original. . . .[13]

In January 1941, Carlo Alberto Pasolini, awarded the Colonial Order of the Star of Italy, was called up and left for transit to the African front. By the summer of 1942 he had been promoted to the rank of major, been decorated with the prestigious Silver Medallion and been taken prisoner by the British in Kenya. In the prisoner-of-war camp, the Fascist true believer received a copy of his son's book—its dedication was to him, but it was written in the dialect of his mother's world.

At home Pier Paolo had corrected the proofs of his first book during a three-week training course at Porretta Terme, an excursion for university men in the officers' training course. On the occasion of Hitler's 1938 visit to Florence, Pier Paolo and Mauri went there as part of a winning debating team. The young Germans and Italians camped in tents set up in a park; Mauri remembers Pasolini in high spirits, dancing up and down a flight of stairs in his *avanguardista* uniform, carrying a glass ball, mocking the martial music that came from loudspeakers. Then he went to Weimar, to the congress of the Nazi-organized "Ludi Juveniles"—a kind of Axis youth intellectual Olympics. Pier Paolo was sent in the Bologna GUF's delegation, joining the Hitlerjugend at the event meant to bring together the best of Nazism-Fascism's new generation. Pier Paolo wore the necessary black uniform (a photo exists, said to be taken "in front of Goethe's house at Weimar") and kept his own counsel.

In August 1942 Susanna and the boys returned to Casarsa, this time intending to stay there until war's end. The risk of bombings of the cities had grown, food was starting to be scarce, and in Casarsa a network of friends among the farmers ensured they would not starve. The same month, Pier Paolo began contributing to *Architrave*, a monthly magazine published by the Bologna GUF from January 1941 to June 1943, when Fascism began to unravel. His last article appeared after only five months' collaboration, a four-column essay entitled "Philology and Morality," which appeared the last day of 1942.

He captioned his prescient and self-revelatory declaration with a proverb from Paul Valéry, a motto to whose principle he remained loyal and whose elaboration he never abandoned: "The poet dedicates and consumes himself in defining and constructing a language within language." Warning that "murmuring voices" needed to be "calmed," the twenty-year-old *intellettuale impegnato* defined his ground and made a plea for a kind of historical consciousness:

> It seems to me that a certain intransigent moralism has become fashionable . . . with a lot of young esthetes turning into so many little Savonaro-

las . . . to those who go around talking about "we young people" and "our new generation," [I say they] ought to look a bit backward. . . . A morality and content are necessary, agreed . . . but we run the danger of *contenutismo*.[14]

That "content-ism" (for lack of a better term) he resisted was the theory that the work of art must be judged only by its social message, that style is secondary and even dangerous, in effect that art must serve ideology. Twenty years of silence had bred a mild hysteria in the young, a strident insistence that people take sides, show their colors. The outline of an ongoing debate between Pasolini and his opponent-comrades in the postwar hard-line Italian Left is already clear. He wrote, "Only by closing in on ourselves, and in the saddest human solitude, can we give ourselves the necessary vision, and that way help ourselves to formulate our own 'civilization'."[15]

Here already is prefigured his defense of art, not for art's sake but at least art not for politics' sake, a stance that would surround debates about his poetry and novels during the next two decades. The culture of the Left already forming underground was one that demanded that anti-Fascist—post-Fascist—art toe a line. Pasolini called for a different and riskier course: The artist must be free. He was already moving toward the position that the writer, by refusing to be a propagandist, even for the social order he desires, does not thereby become either an apologist for its enemies or a decadent aesthete. Pasolini's resistance to ideological pressure, even from his friends, has to be understood in context: He was living in a university where every professor (save for eleven nationwide) had kept his post only by swearing a loyalty oath to Fascism. All thought and all work were matters of State policy: The Duce had called for "a totalitarian concept of culture."

It is hardly surprising that observers mistook young Pasolini for an escapist of the Hermeticist stamp. The elitism of his vision is undeniable. When he writes "*to educate* [emphasis Pasolini's]—this will be the highest—and most humble—task entrusted to our generation," he has in mind a generation of intellectuals as avant-garde. And for the source and models for this new consciousness, what Pasolini calls its "moral and political base," he answers, ". . . a Contini, for example, who has taught us how to study a text philologically." Understanding that the end of the world into which he was born was near, he added, cryptically, ". . . the present conditions of the country are no more than the threshold of a profound . . . and most important examination of consciousness." This "examination" was also to be grounded in a return to a "*civiltà antica*"—an Italianism that survives even Fascism, waiting within "the shadow of the hearth, under the leaves of our orchards, and in the gestures which for centuries have not altered. . . ."

It was impossible that Pasolini continue writing under *Architrave*'s director, the Fascist operative Eugenio Facchini, who in the same issue called for unity with those who were "fighting and falling in the name of the King and the Duce, in other words, in the name of the nation." Instead, he joined the editorial board of a new undergraduate journal *Il setaccio* (The sieve).

*Il setaccio* did not try to confront problems of world war and peace, the economic order, the political future of Europe. Its essays and poetry addressed "the cultural problem," a phrase with specific density in Italy where the heritage of Croce and of several millennia before him made culture something no one could actually define but all agreed existed, a complex of attitudes and achievements some people had taken in and others not. This traditional notion was one the precocious youths of the magazine did not contest. For them, the issue was the content of culture after the war, culture as the matrix that sets the tone and orders civil life, something important, real, worthy of arduous discussing and defining.

So the undergraduate group wrote essays on the role of the intellectual, translated Baudelaire, commented on French writers like Georges Bresson, published their drawings and did everything adults did—arbiters of what was in and what was out—dispensing accolades and brickbats to established names like Pavese, Vittorini, Longhi.

One of the group said the magazine was only to give "that little private space for thinking, and for speaking freely." That modest claim does not do credit to the results. Pasolini and his friends were announcing a resistance to dogma at a time when resistance to dogma cost lives; theirs was a traditional position, in that it claimed to be free of politics, but in an Italy whose regime counted every Italian either as a friend to be rewarded (perhaps only to be left in peace) or as an enemy to be harmed.

From the beginning of Pasolini's involvement with the project, one can only be astounded at the laxity with which the authorities exercised their statutory right of censorship. In his article "I giovani, l'attesa" (Youth . . . the waiting period), he called for poets to be left in solitude and endowed with liberty to pursue whatever line of inquiry they chose. He may have argued that the "waiting" was for maturity, but readers may also have understood it to mean sitting on the sidelines until Fascism's collapse. By the third issue, January 1943, he reported on his visit to Florence and to the Fascist youth conference at Weimar. Six months before Mussolini's fall, he made the unorthodox argument that European youth were still connected to the traditions that predated the regime, that a line (which could safely only be called "humanist" not "democratic") ran throughout European life ". . . across García Lorca and Picasso." But the homosexual Federico García Lorca had been murdered by Franco's men, and Picasso was in French exile, in permanent protest against the Duce's Spanish ally. The censors either were lazy, ignorant of what the reference implied, or both.

Indirectly Pasolini argued that the nineteenth-century literary tradition had gone underground and was reemerging, intact and restated, almost as though Fascism had never happened. At twenty Pier Paolo declared himself a champion of a patient underground. While "waiting," youth's solution is the road taken by Joyce's Stephen Daedalus, trapped in an oppressive environment—"silence, cunning and internal exile." Readers were told the best way to keep European culture alive was ". . . to overcome obstacles by the force of love, not knock them down, but slide over and around them, as water does over the land."

The regime worked hard and, with success, to recruit intellectuals to its side. The director of the magazine, Giovanni Falzone, had made a name for himself with panegyrics to the so-called Fascist Era, the Duce's rewriting of history along the lines of the "thousand-year Reich." But now that the war was starting to go badly, Pasolini staked out another line. In "Last Discourse on the Intellectuals"—perhaps a pretentious title for one just celebrating his twenty-first birthday that month—he wrote "for me, 'intellectuals and the war' is not only an inadmissible phrase, but there is no connection at all between the terms." He wanted to be cut free from propaganda, and had decided that the only way not to be a part of the system was to be left out of its grasp completely. To argue that literature is independent from life was the only way to keep it from serving Fascist ideology: What reads today as escapism and a call for flight into the ivory tower was, in 1942 and 1943, a matter of separation as the only route to survival. His argument was a championship of Ungaretti and the other Hermetic poets on political grounds; in Pier Paolo's understanding, theirs was a form of passive resistance, a refusal to praise the regime—turning inward until the bad days passed, hurting it by not helping it.

He closed his essay-tract with a personal emotion, a vignette printed in parentheses. It was, again, to be read symbolically by those who understood. Its message is the same: Wait, be patient, keep working, for our time is coming. He merges personal feeling of an almost solipsistic intensity with nothing less than civic consciousness.

> (My mother and I are sitting in the room which first sheltered her infancy and then my own. And in this room, in the dark of the night, from a boy who has paused before our door, calling to a friend. And this call does not do as it did before, when I was a small boy, welling up nostalgia for the past, or vague tremors, but instead recalls with new pain the moment in which we are living now. It brings to life, for a moment, before my eyes the image of my father and of my dearest friend [Ermes Parini, who would die at the Russian front in 1943], whom the war has carried from me. It is two years since I have seen the first. And of the second I know nothing, and I spend my saddest hours imagining him, in Russia, wounded, missing, imprisoned . . . and I have here, in front of me, the suffering expression of my mother; and I long to express all this, but it is not possible: it is too alive, violent, painful.)[16]

The whole world was in the boy's body, and the sound that issued from it was the message of reality. Politics and personal sexuality form a continuum. In Pasolini, the connection is short and direct: The boy *was* the world and his call its voice, in a manner that can only be called primordial, at a level best understood as preconscious.

On July 25, 1943, the Grand Council of Fascism voted Mussolini out of power, disrupting far more than a university literary magazine. In the months following that fateful day, cats replaced beef at the butchers and the war came onto Italian soil. With Allied bombardment of Bologna ever more likely, Pier Paolo had to cut his studies short and flee, leaving his thesis incomplete. By the winter of 1942, Susanna had taken her boys and returned to the then relative safety of Casarsa della Delizia.

# 9

*Victory finds a hundred fathers, but defeat is an orphan.*
*—Count Galeazzo Ciano, Mussolini's son-in-law*

# FRIULIAN RAPTURE

Susanna and her sons found refuge in a part of the large clan house on via Risorgimento in Casarsa, unchanged since the days when her father, Domenico, built it for his *piemontese* bride. Nico Naldini, who was there, recalls that it was packed with furniture Carlo Alberto had ordered from a military carpenter, "exuberant flower-covered furniture, all lacquered black."

Pier Paolo—pedagogue wrote lessons in poetics to friends still in Bologna, explaining that every word was unique, that it was no good at all to think that "street" and "paving" were somehow interchangeable.

The _Setaccio_'s remaining numbers would have to be edited with his participation through the mail, just when Pier Paolo felt he was needed at Bologna to fight for the magazine's life. So, like a field commander cut off from his troops, he instructed his contemporaries, made so many minions. When Fabio Mauri failed to deliver copy by deadline, Pier Paolo lashed out, "I am very displeased: Your face comes to my memory but not colored with the lovely colors of trust and open affection. Why do you always disappoint me this way?"[1]

His "agents" in Bologna began to send news of ever more serious threats to close down publication unless the Fascist line were toed. In February 1943, Pier Paolo wrote Fabio Luca Cavazza, ". . . I am convinced we must not give in." The "educational mission of our generation" is what he holds dear, "and now that we have a means for attaining this—a drop in the ocean—why must we submit?" The way to handle the hard-liners, he advised, was to compromise "with nobility," give in now to return to fight another day, a strategy that ". . . cannot in any way impugn our dignity." They must, he wrote, be "like the water lying on the land, infiltrating slowly," be patient, as Italian culture must be patient to resist foreign domination.[2]

In March, he wrote the ever-loyal Cavazza: "If they do not want to publish _Il setaccio_ as we have established, and in every detail, let the Doctor [Falzone] know that I want nothing of mine to be published." Since Pier Paolo provided the bulk of every issue, and arranged for the rest, the threat was to kill the Bologna GUF's highbrow showpiece.

The same month, he received the magazine's fourth (February) number and declared himself pleased. ". . . I want to kiss everyone on the forehead," he wrote Cavazza, "and for you three or four more kisses for 'The end of Guerrino' [Cavazza's screenplay in this issue]. When did you read Freud? I congratulate you for your cinematic imagination."

As for his degree thesis on contemporary painters, that would have to be finished in his poet's garret, above his grandfather's _grappa_ works.

Near the kitchen's open fireplace, he installed shelves and in this central place of honor arranged his books; to young, hero-worshiping Nico, there seemed to be "thousands" of them. There he shelved the white-covered copies of the _Poesie a Casarsa_, come into the world the year before.

I had just reached twenty-one and only then made the move from Bologna to Casarsa. I recall the first days of February 1943. I dedicated myself to discovering that Casarsa which was mine, turning green again. I rediscovered the inflections of that language (not the Veneto dialect the family spoke)— I noted its open vowels, its sibilants which barely touched in a secret sense . . . inexpressible, hidden in all that world. . . . I went out in the early hours of the afternoon, putting the village far behind me, making long tours of the surrounding hamlets . . . I did not hesitate to risk some shame, to try anything to stop in my path one of those boys so pitilessly ignoring me, racing by on their bicycles or working amid the mulberrys or the interwoven vines. . . .[3]

He called these forays—his first acknowledged homosexual cruising—"secret and guilt-ridden." Raw with self-consciousness, he decided the boys he wanted now consciously avoided him; he was sure they worked as hard to avoid his eyes as he did to catch theirs. He wanted a chance to unleash his charm on them, an opening that would let him fast-forward through idle chat and acquaintanceship to intimacy. In 1963, when that world was far behind him, forever lost, he wrote lines in memory and *memoriam,* in a poem called "A Desperate Vitality."

And one after-lunch, or one evening, I ran,
screaming,
through the streets of Sunday, after the game,
to the old cemetery, there, beyond the railroad
tracks,
and performed, and repeated, till I bled,
the sweetest act of life,
I alone, on the little pile of earth,
the graves of two or three
Italian or German soldiers,
no names on the wood-plank crosses
—buried there since the other war.

And that night, amid my dry tears, the bleeding
bodies of those poor unknowns
dressed in olive drab

appeared in a cluster above my bed
where I was sleeping, naked and emptied,
to smear me with blood until the sun rose.[4]

When cruising came to nothing, he bicycled home at least with the boys' language and laughter in his ears. That speech, far more than the linguistics of dialects he had learned from philological books by Ascoli and D'Ancona at Bologna, went into the poems. He devoured the usages and "mis-usages," wrote them down, to use.

He later recalled, ". . . I never spoke it myself. I only learnt it after I had begun to write poetry in it. I learnt it as a sort of mystic act of love."

In *Il setaccio*'s final number appeared Pier Paolo's warm review of an exhibition of paintings in Udine, including those of a politically committed realist painter of about his own age named Giuseppe Zigaina, a real *friuliano*, a carpenter's son, born at Villa Vicentina.

Altogether, the editors put out six issues from November 1942 through May 1943, skipping April. Pasolini appeared in each at least twice, and occasionally with four contributions: say, an exhibition review, two poems and an essay. By then, he had about forty other poems written during 1941 and 1942, poems he planned to put into a volume called *I confini;* they appeared only after his death. From them:

> Burn, burn
> sun of my village, little desert flower.
> The years pass over you,
> and I also pass, with the shadows of the acacias
> with the turning of the sun, in this quiet day.[5]

In Casarsa, he met a refugee from the Balkan front, a contemporary named Pina Kalz. An accomplished musician, she entranced him with her playing of Janáček and then Bach's six violin sonatas. They staged theatricals in Susanna's kitchen, sketches in *friulano*. He wrote, "The hundreds of evenings we spent together from the summer of '43 to '45 when, with the end of the war, she returned to Yugoslavia, make me feel a special sort of desperation of the inexpressible. . . ."[6]

Sometime in the spring of 1946, he wrote a long confessional letter to Franco Farolfi in Parma. His friend had raised the issue of "emotional equilibrium," of what later came to be called "feeling at home in one's skin." Pasolini, at twenty-one, felt no such comforting integration:

> Every image from this earth, every human face, every ringing of bells knocks against my heart with an impact that is almost physical. I do not have a moment of calm, because I am always living thrown into the future: if I drink a glass of wine and laugh loudly with friends, I see myself drinking and I feel myself laugh, with an immense and sorrowful desperation, with a pre-

mature regret over what I do and enjoy, a continuously alive and sorrowful awareness of time.

But I am not ill and I am not crazy: I am normal and serene, not only in external gestures and behavior but also within me . . . probably I owe my salvation to my imagination, which knows how to find a concrete image for every feeling, or so it seems to me, capturing it and preventing them [the images] from whirling around unbraked in my brain.[7]

But all was not well, and far from it:

Everything which other men take as obvious and accept, for me are abstrusely and painfully open to question: my existence is one continuous shiver, a remorse, or nostalgia.

He wrote another friend at the same time, "The only philosophy which I find anywhere near to me is existentialism with its poetic . . . concept of *'angst.'* " He offered critical appraisal of a movie he had seen, contrasting the "innocence and rhetoric of the content . . . often silly" with the "originality of the technique, something poetic (almost all close-ups). . . ."

On June 4, he wrote Farolfi in the wake of reviews of *Poesie a Casarsa,* not only Contini's but one by Alfonso Gatto in the first issue of *Ruota* (Wheel), and another in the *Bollettino della Società Filologica Friulana* (Bulletin of the Friulian Philological Society) in Udine.

"It ought to be an extremely beautiful time for me, but instead I am extremely sad, suffering, disappointed. Why? Because our youth is over, [our] gestures [are] now set for life." He describes himself as "sitting, writing, tending toward DEATH." All of twenty-one, he exploded with remorse for "days gone, our school days." He sounded panicked: "I cannot live because I cannot manage to get used to the thought that there will come a time for me, a death.[8]

But within hours, even minutes, his mood changed or another facet of the several feelings he felt at once rose to the surface. He posted another letter the same day, to Luciano Serra:

I continue to work a great deal . . . and must confess that my imagination is very much matured in these last months, and I have come to a clarity of invention which strengthens me to live, and often excites me. I have invented an infinity of myths. I have created a legendary history about places which before never existed; I hope one day it will be seen to have some value. I have been invited to contribute poetry to the *Bulletin of the Friulian Philological Society*.[9]

He called it "the most exciting news" that Contini's review "will be republished in a university journal soon." While waiting for the radio news to come, with "ten minutes free" before going to swim in the Tagliamento, he wrote Serra,

> Serenity has taken on the shape of a girl from Valvasone, fat and handsome, somewhere between a magnolia flower and a St. Peter's apple. I kiss her and hold her tight every evening, and she asks nothing of me in exchange save to make her happy. [10]

But as if to give the lie to what may have been one, the letter's next paragraph introduced the real love of that summer, the first great reciprocated passion of his life: a boy named Bruno. It is he, not the "magnolia flower" of Valvasone, who obsessed him.

He and Bruno went together to the river for nude swimming. Once, they were caught in a violent storm, which Pier Paolo later wrote was "livid like an erect penis." He wrote how the tempest made the sky turn "black and yellow," how they stopped on a bridge to look at the swollen river. The letter closed with a vignette, the sort that calls for film: "Three, four wagons of gypsies, like us escaping the storm, which by now was howling with some shivering drops, made their way toward Codroipo. Inside a sky-blue wagon, a gypsy boy rings a full peal on a trumpet." [11]

Hitler by now understood that the Duce had lost control. He sensed Mussolini was trying to break free of his grip, and he had no intention of letting him go. He withdrew some troops from Russia to be ready to occupy Italy when Fascism collapsed. The Vatican, sensing a danger of Communist insurrection in Italy, proposed mediation. Feelers went out to the British in Lisbon, but they would accept only total capitulation. By May food was running out; the Duce spoke of abundance as some Italians were dying of hunger. He suggested using "execution squads" to keep Italians from revolt.

By June 11 the first Italian territory fell—the island of Pantelleria, which Mussolini had personally selected for fortification because it was "unassailable." When asked by the Cabinet what would happen next, he enigmatically replied that he had "several cards up his sleeve."

A month later the Allies had seized the beaches in Sicily and were moving inland. The Duce reminded all Fascists of their oath to die for him if necessary.

On July 16 he agreed that the Grand Council of Fascism might meet for the first time since 1939. The session was set for July 25. The "man sent by Providence" seemed oddly indifferent to events. Had he not described himself as "a cat that always lands on his feet"?

Those high summer weeks Pier Paolo roamed the outskirts of Casarsa on his bicycle; Allied bombers had not come this far north as yet. At nearby Feltre, Hitler gave Mussolini a dressing down, demanding that Italian forces be put under a German commander. The Duce buckled, could not quite follow what Hitler said (he refused a translator), remarked that perhaps they were both slightly mad. He seemed seized by mental paralysis. His disgusted chief of staff, General Ambrosio, resigned. Even as the dictators met, the Allies bombed the San Lorenzo quarter in Rome, arriving from the South. After his visit there, Pius XII (who had served many years as *nunzio* in Munich, where a street is named for him, Pacellistrasse) sent a telegram of protest to President Franklin D. Roosevelt. That was July 19. The king suggested that Mussolini ought to think of resignation. The Duce did not last the week.

Now, as the world collapsed around him, Pier Paolo was living in an Arcadia called Friuli:

> I went out on my bicycle in the first hours of the afternoon, and far from the village, making long tours around the surrounding hamlets: I was looking for love, for lust . . . with the ingenuousness of a city boy, I was looking for my "divine" presences, boys willing to sin, there, right where I would never find them . . . I passed and passed again, through Bannia, Fiume, Orcenico, Castions . . . continuously, invariably disappointed . . . running against a fatal impossibility.[12]

But the impossible happened, and the summer Fascism fell became the summer dedicated to Bruno. Pier Paolo wrote a thinly veiled account of their romance, a novella about his headlong infatuation with the peasant boy so unlike himself. He wrote it all down in his diary of 1947 and transmuted it slightly in a manuscript he hid. It was published only posthumously as the novella *Atti impuri* in 1982.

> He had the darkest black hair . . . and two eyes whose violet color only struck me later, a faded, colorless face, irregular and much burnt by the sun. A scar was quite visible on his lower lip. Even his half-nude chest, because covered only by a singlet . . . gave off a smell of dust and river water, I don't know, something which gave me a slight horror, all the more so because it was mixed with the smell of a "milit" [a cheap Army cigarette, a *"militare"*].

... I lay in wait for him endlessly: when I saw him appear with that walk of his, how shall I call it, a little animal-like (his right foot was a little out of whack), I felt faint. An entire complication of connections links me, with infinite tricks and subterfuges, to this boy. But finally, I was in luck. When the summer's heat really mounted, bringing back swimming season, I was able to see him whenever I wished. We used to go and swim in a gravel pit in the fields behind the cemetery; just after lunch a mob of boisterous kids invaded the shore of that watering hole, trampling the grass which gradually was worn away, leaving dirt. The interior disorder, lack of self-consciousness and lewdness of these sons of day-workers and field hands was extraordinary. There was one long, shameless laughter, a piling up of words that made no sense—something worthy of a pack of monkeys. When they left, the surrounding fields looked as though occupied by a band of gypsies. And they swam naked, even the ones past puberty; and often they would masturbate among themselves without even going to the trouble of going into the cornfields. Bruno was one of these, and although serious and sluggish, none the less powerful for that. His family must have been proletarians for generations, and one felt about him the deafness of an animal; he was violent, rude, and this is what made him a success among his peers.[13]

One day, at the height of that summer, Bruno arrived with a friend, intent on gathering grass to feed some pet rabbits surely intended for eating. Pier Paolo tagged along, noting between them "a certain understanding." "It was natural that friendly horseplay broke out," and that led to sexual intimacy "despite my limited skill."

In his diary, self-accusation overflowed. "But do I have to go into all this to someone? If this someone is myself, all right then, that I at least open with a small, golden key the door into my intimate self. My habits of feeling are too honest: I never wanted to be deceitful, in fact, the sensitive and generous boy I was for so many years, even [when] desperately lying."

Days passed, and they meet again at the gravel pit. This time Bruno is already naked and Pier Paolo wrote, in italics, ". . . and I could see, with a shiver of joy, that he was impatient for me to undo the knot of my undershorts." They met near the train tracks. But sometimes Bruno stood him up, disappeared for days. Pier Paolo was "crazy with jealousy" and—as though playing with him—Bruno would then reappear and go with him into the cornfield.

Pier Paolo's dream was to hold a "consenting body, in the wilds of nature": He wanted to make love in the open air, out of sight of others but with the frisson of danger of being discovered. Finally, Bruno agreed and they left the road and went into a field, bikes and clothes left behind. They embraced, but Bruno held back, was "mi-

serly." Pier Paolo records his disappointment and transforms it:
Bruno seems to disappear from his grasp "like the two sky-blue wagons of the gypsies" carried away on the wind.

In the poems entitled "The Religion of My Time," published in
1961—when everything had changed—he recalled those days.

> As a boy, I'd dream of these
>
> fresh sun-warmed breezes,
> forest fragments, Celtic oaks,
> shrubs and leafless blackberry
>
> bushes, red, ripening, nearly uprooted
> by the sunlit autumn—and the inlets
> of blindly deserted Northern rivers
>
> with their sharp smell of lichen,
> cool and naked like Easter's violets . . .
> Flesh was unchained then.
>
> And the sweetness that was
> in the day's color very nearly
> sweetened even that pain.
>
> Ragged young men, rough, erect,
> from barbarian families migrating
> endlessly through hushed forests
>
> and along the flooded plains
> consoled the solitude
> of my narrow bed, my road.
>
> History, the Church, a family's
> vicissitudes, are really
> just some naked perfumed sun
>
> warming a deserted vineyard, some rows
> of hay in corroded groves,
> a few houses stunned by the sound
>
> of bells . . . Young men of ancient times,
> truly living when their breasts
> filled up with spring in those more
>
> beautiful ages, were simultaneously
> dreams of sex and images drunk up
> out of the old paper of the poem
>
> which from volume to volume, in mute
> fevers of supreme newness
> —Shakespeare, Tommaseo, Carducci—

made all my nerves one tremor
. . .

And yet, Church, I came to you.
I was holding Pascal and *The Songs
of the Greek People* tightly in my hand,

ardent, as though the peasant mystery,
quiet and deaf in the summer of '43,
among the village, vines, and banks

of the Tagliamento, were at the center
of earth and heavens; and there,
my throat, heart, and belly torn

on the distant path to the quarries,
I was consuming the hours of the most
beautiful human time, my whole

day of youth, in loves whose
sweetness still makes me weep . . .[14]

The meeting of the Grand Council of Fascism on July 24 and 25
ended in a vote of nineteen against Mussolini, seven in favor; the
king was asked to find a policy to save Italy, restore powers to Parliament and the Grand Council as guaranteed by the constitution but
always flouted by the Leader. The Duce was not named, but the
message was clear. The diehards on the Council deeply resented what
they saw as his betrayal of Fascism, especially his persistent refusal
to consult them. During the meeting he was asked if he saw any
chance of victory at all or, if not, how peace would be made; he
offered no answer. During a break in deliberations, he suggested that
he was willing to let the king become commander-in-chief if matters
stopped there.

The meeting resumed after midnight. Mussolini suggested that he
had a secret weapon to solve the crisis but could not reveal it. Instead
of demanding a vote of confidence, which he might just then have
won, so confused were the participants, he let a motion go to vote
that would strip him of his power. He later explained that he felt
helpless, without willpower. He declined the suggestion that he arrest
the nineteen who voted against him and fell silent.

The next day he received the Japanese ambassador, all business
as usual. Some of the nineteen wanted to reverse their vote, but he
declined. He let it be known that a new list of ministers had been
drawn up: The "traitors," as he called them, would be punished.

The afternoon of July 26 he went to the Villa Ada to see the king, to explain that the council had voted a restoration of some of his powers. The monarch, he felt with reason, was utterly compromised now and could never survive the fall of the regime. He started to ramble but was interrupted by Vittorio Emanuele who said the war was lost and Marshal Badoglio would now take over as prime minister. Plans had been afoot for weeks within the secret police for the Duce's arrest, plans of which he was ignorant.

The king walked him out the front door into the waiting arms of police, who put him under arrest. As he was escorted into an ambulance, Mussolini was assured that his personal safety would be safeguarded.

All the paths to defend the Duce evaporated. Badoglio's face appeared on the front page of *Il popolo d'Italia;* senior party officials fell into line; the Fascist militia, with new German tanks, did not act to reinstate him, although they might easily have done so in the first hours or days. The regime, so noisy, ended with barely a whimper. The culture he made was poisoned on its own rhetoric, infantilism, and a self-destructive blend of inferiority complex and exhibitionism. When pushed, it proved hollow, paper-thin, and collapsed in a writhing mess of self-interests.

Mussolini even brought himself to write to Badoglio offering "every possible collaboration." The king vetoed a proposal for handing the Duce over to the Allies, to symbolize a new Italian tractability. His plan was to go on fighting, call up new troops, and at the same time contact the Allies to broker peace terms. The dynasty had moved, but very late, to defend itself; Vittorio Emanuele had three short years left before the Italians voted his family out of the country.

That night of July 25 Guido Pasolini daubed *"Viva la libertà"* on some walls in Casarsa. The police stopped him and were about to arrest him, which would have led to almost inevitable deportation to a German work camp, but Pier Paolo's fast talking saved the day.

Soon leaflets from partisan groups (there were many, splintered as were the Fascists) appeared in Bologna, then reached Casarsa: Pier Paolo read them avidly. They called on Italians to put down their arms and welcome an imminent Allied occupation.

In Fascism's collapse Pier Paolo saw a chance for Friuli to assert its independence. He sat down immediately to write a call to the people of the so-called Little Country (La Piccola Patria). He ran off three hundred copies of his flier on a machine in the Casa del Fascio itself. He stopped only long enough to shout with joy when the fall of Mussolini was read on the radio the morning of July 26. He had found his way to serve: to fight "with the arms of poetry" for Friulian political autonomy. He saw it as a matter of giving the honest men and women he loved their due.

With September the Germans invaded central and northern Italy, and Pier Paolo was called into service in the Italian army, now in fact an arm of the German command. He reported to Pisa on September 1. By the eighth he was at Livorno about to be sent into the field. That day Marshal Badoglio secretly surrendered Italian forces to the Allies.

In the course of what was to be Pier Paolo's very brief army life, Susanna came to visit him in barracks at Porretta. He reported the scene to a Bologna college friend: "Today my mother came to see me, and she has just left. Thinking of her gives me such a pangful pain of love; she cares for me too much, and I for her. I am a poet for her. She wrote me a letter the other day that made me burst out in tears."

Twenty-five years later he told the English journalist Oswald Stack:

> I'd done brief chapters on Carrà, De Pisis, and Morandi. What happened is that I took the text with me when I was called up in 1943. I was only in the Army a week when the armistice was announced [8 September]. I lost my thesis because it was in the barracks when we were taken prisoner—two Germans in a tank took our whole regiment prisoner. A friend and I, who were the least military sort in the outfit, then performed our first unwitting act of resistance: instead of surrendering our arms to the Germans, we threw them in a ditch and then, in a burst of machine-gun fire, dove in after them. We waited for the regiment to march off, and then made our escape. It was completely an instinctive and involuntary beginning to my resistance.[15]

The Germans were too busy separating collaborationist Italians from Partisans to worry about one more deserting twenty-one-year-old. Hitler moved against their former ally and sent troops to occupy Friuli. The battleground with the Allies was going to be Italian soil, not German if he could help it.

At Monte Cassino, Allied casualties between mid-January and the end of March totaled 52,130. In the north the two bridges over the Tagliamento became strategic targets; trains passed through Casarsa station every day, carrying Italians POWs to German concentration camps in Austria. Guidalberto Pasolini started building a cache of stolen German weapons.

On September 8 the puppet Italian government surrendered, putting its population savagely and helplessly between the fury of the retreating Germans and the advancing Allies. By month's end the bulk of the Italian army had been interned by the Germans.

On the twelfth a German commando unit landed on an isolated mountain peak in the Apennines and, without firing a shot, liberated Mussolini. Badoglio seems to have thought the Duce terminally ill with cancer, but Hitler's guest now visited the Fuehrer's headquarters on the Russian front and broadcast an appeal to all Italians to help him rid the country of the "traitors" (including his son-in-law Ciano) who had pushed him from office.

It took all the next year of civil war in Italy to drive the Germans and Mussolini loyalists out of the north. Now began the months of hand-to-hand combat in the streets, ambushes and revenge, atrocities of every kind on the ground while Allied bombers passed in waves overhead, their bombs shattering and pounding civilian and soldier, Italian and German alike. With German help, Mussolini was established at Salò, a village north of Milan on Lake Garda. Effectively a German prisoner now, he answered to the local commandant. In name only, he commanded the upper half of the peninsula, the invading Allies the southern.

Five members of the Grand Council (including Ciano) who voted against him were arrested, put before kangaroo courts, "tried," and sentenced to death by firing squad.

In a few months Italians were transformed from a civilian population that did not know conflict on their own soil into a people living in an armed camp, a German-occupied zone. Between the bombing of San Lorenzo on July 19, 1943, and the end of the following year, they were imprisoned by the Germans, shipped to camps, tortured, and terrorized. As they formed into a dozen tiny parties, often only armed bands, the country became the field on which Communists, anti-Communists, Fascists, Italians, and Germans fought.

In Friuli the Nazis commandeered all the bicycles, so Pier Paolo took to foot. One day he walked the few kilometers to Versuta, and there struck up a conversation with a peasant woman named Ernesta Bazzana. She was in her courtyard when the stranger approached and asked if he might rent a room from her. She needed the money, and there was something about the earnest visitor that overcame her natural resistance. A few days later he returned, dragging a cart full of books.

Versuta, only two kilometers from Casarsa, a last tiny hamlet at the edge of another village called San Giovanni di Casarsa, seemed safe from the bombs and the Germans. Pier Paolo loved the place from the start, finding people "even friendlier" than in Casarsa; the boys had "an ancient beauty" that conformed to the type he had fixed on: dark ringlets low on the forehead and an air of rebellion.

He was planning to open a school. He was one of the few college near-graduates in the area, and local schools as far away as Pordenone and Udine were closed. His friends would be the faculty, paid with butter, eggs, and flour. After his death, his aunt Giannina recalled how he refused to accept a duck some parents sent as payment for a child's schooling. "Imagine, these people are starving, and they sent us their duck," he told her.

His makeshift classroom would propagate Friulian pride, perhaps even plant the seeds of separatism. No license was necessary; no government office was functioning enough to issue or deny them. It was something for him to do while he waited for the war to end so he could finish his degree at Bologna.

His brother Guido talked all the time of joining the Partisans in the mountains.

In the middle of a field at the edge of the hamlet, an abandoned house became the school. It had two hallways on each of two floors, with rooms on either side. Here Pier Paolo and his five friends established themselves, using as titular head the name of the chaplain of San Giovanni, their legal cover to the authorities.

Children came from miles around: twenty-odd boys and girls, semi-literate farmhands and their sisters. Pier Paolo taught literature (including Dante) and history five hours a day, a Jewish refugee named Giovanna Bemporad offered Greek and English, sciences were taught by Cesare Bortotto, mathematics by Riccardo Castellani.

Amid the ever-more-frequent bombing raids, he felt that the days were "always serene, sweetly light."[16] It all seemed everyday and yet mythic to Pier Paolo. He was living a miasma of feelings, trying to understand who he was, why he was as he was.

By mid-November officials in Udine had wind of the school and let Pasolini know it had to close. It did, but immediately moved into the Pasolini family dining room, the students continuing their impassioned reading of Dante and Petrarch, Leopardi and Virgil, Wordsworth, Ungaretti, Machado, and Marlowe. They wanted to be poets themselves, for Pier Paolo's teaching mesmerized them.

But a school was not enough. There had to be a small magazine, a medium for disseminating ideas. A committee formed: cousins Pier Paolo and Nico, Bortotto, Bruno Bruni, the brothers Ovidio and Ermes Colussi, Fedele Ghirart, Pina Kalz, (Fede)Rico de Rocco, Virgilio Tramontin. With the seriousness of world leaders announcing an historic pact, they met and declared their (second) academy founded on

February 8, 1945, "at Versuta." They christened it The Academy of the Friulian Tongue.

Soon Pasolini, Bartotto, and Castellani had firm plans for *Il stroligut* (The astrologer). They meant it to be the written voice of those who lived on their side of the Tagliamento, equal to a respected journal of similar name published by the Udine Philological Society. The gentle presumption of the challenge amused them.

The magazine instantly became a forum for campaigning for Friulian postwar autonomy. Politics and culture were one; the connector was language. Pasolini and his friends agreed with Nietzsche without having read him: "A victorious language is nothing but a frequent (not even a regular) sign of successful conquest."[17]

*Stroligut*'s first issue appeared in August (*Auost* in Friulian) 1944 from the Primon printworks in San Vito—or, more precisely, "San Vit." The editors intended to publish in a language that would ". . . unite it [Friuli] . . . to Provence, Catalonia, the Grisons, Rumania and all the other Little Homelands [*Piccole Patrie*] of the Romance tongue."

Castellani contributed a short story and poems, and verse appeared by Bortotto; Nico printed a verse play and poems and Ovidio Colussi, short prose pieces.

Pier Paolo wrote a *memoria* of a spectacle—drama and recital— he staged with Pina Kalz, and he wrote political "polemic." In an unsigned preface plainly his, he made the case that western and central Friuli were distinct zones and peoples, and now the time had come for the right bank of the Tagliamento to offer its written literature as part of its own political life. Friuli's oral tradition—what its rural poor always had had—was not enough: It was not to be lost and certainly not dismissed as a minor dialect spoken by a few at the edge of a foreign border. The speakers of *friulano* must defend their identity, which depended on the life of their language. "We can count on its rustic and Christian purity," Pier Paolo claimed, with more hope than fact. The publication's editors insisted on presenting themselves as open to others not in their circle: ". . . our esthetic is not closed in on itself, being one of the heart and not only of the brain." All this from Friuli's adopted son—the son who had adopted Friuli—from an intellectual in love with a world that he had willed his own.

People began to notice this Pier Paolo Pasolini and to have opinions about him. Some saw nobility of a kind, a high-minded dedication to liberal goals by a natural leader. Some thought him an officious university boy, cultural carpetbagger, and self-promoting busybody. With as much fervor as the young Mussolini, he was determined to be *presente*—to count, to have weight in the scheme of human social life.

His stance for Friulian autonomy made more potential enemies than friends. Both the emerging Christian Democratic Party and those on the Left opposed regionalization and feared that in the war's aftermath this entity called Italy, barely glued together before the world war and Fascism traumatized it, would fly apart. As the battle heated toward war's end, Pier Paolo joined in his own way as combatant.

Always his own best publicist, he used *Il stroligut* to promote himself. In that premier issue's preface, written as war raged around him, he recounted how the magazine came to be and placed his own *Poesie a Casarsa* at the center of a movement as a crucial precedent. In a footnote, he provided his volume's publishing data and explained that "this little book stirred much interest among certain Italian critics (Contini, Gatto, Russo); while in Friuli there were certain reservations (and as to language alone, absolutely justified). All this is significant."

He set the terms for a public debate and, having built himself a platform, took the last word. The young man, *sue sponte*, identified a movement of historical significance in the fight for regional cultural autonomy and declared himself a significant player in it. His sense of historical selfhood, far more powerful than garden-variety narcissism and with origins more mysterious, did not so much carry him through life as drive him through it.

By the start of 1944 the war turned to nightmare. On January 11 at Verona, Italians loyal to Mussolini and acting with their German guardians shot Ciano and four other senior Fascists. The scene was filmed by the propaganda office: Mussolini read Ciano's last letters before forwarding them to his mother and his own daughter Edda Mussolini Ciano, the dead man's widow.

The Duce, visiting Hitler, was told by his master that Italian soldiers at the Russian front had been heard singing Communist songs. The humbled former ally asked that the Germans arm the million Italians in Germany; with them as invading force, he could stage a comeback. But the Nazis thought they could not trust such an army. Italians were best used as forced labor. The ranks of Italian Partisans, hiding in the mountains, grew as Italy's German-controlled government issued orders that all men were to report for service and that anyone helping fugitives was to be shot.

*   *   *

Guidalberto passed his high school exit exam in April. He wrote his father that he was "anguished" at holding a political line different from Carlo Alberto's, but the reality of occupied Italy was something the prisoner in Kenya could not imagine. "I am convinced that if you were here you would have no doubt what side to join," he wrote. He assured him that Pier Paolo "reins me in," but he [Guido] was often "carried away by emotion."

For some months the younger boy had been stealing arms from a German barracks storeroom, hiding them beneath the floorboards of his bedroom. More than once, he and his friends had helped themselves to rifles and ammunition from trains stopped at the Casarsa siding. Soon he dared more. With his friend Renato he raided the storeroom at a nearby airfield where the Germans based Junker 25 transports, stealing from under the noses of armed guards. Guido's war spoils worked their way through underground lines to the Partisans now active in the Carnic Alps—visible, blue, and snowcapped almost all year from Casarsa.

While Guido was living in the sphere of action, Pier Paolo saw the German bombers as a source of new words. He wrote a friend, "Do you know what a CA-313 is? A Macchi? Do you know what are longerons, spars, main frame members? ribs? landing flaps? I imagine not. I am completely immersed in the study of such things which, in case you do not know, have to do with aviation."

Should anything else have been expected from a boy who, at age nineteen, instructed his peers that ". . . a word, being a point, actually being one of a series of them that forms a line, a circumference, its value is specific. The poetic nucleus of a poem must, then, never be just a word, but a grouping of them."

By now law and order were breaking down everywhere. In the south around Naples, reports were that the contents of one of every three Allied supply ships in its port were stolen by audacious black marketeers. The Papal Legate's car was found to be running on stolen tires.[18] An effort to break the Mafia traffic in purloined penicillin ran headlong into the power of Vito Genovese, second-in-command to Lucky Luciano in New York and now in charge in the old country.

In an undated letter to Serra of February or March 1944, Pasolini wrote, "The war smells of shit."

In March the distinguished specialist in the literature of the Baroque, Professor Carlo Calcaterra, holder of the Chair of Italian Letters at Bologna, accepted Pasolini's proposal for a thesis on Giovanni

Pascoli's lyrics. Ever the errand boy, Serra was asked "if you please" to send "the best bibliography, the complete Pascoli opus and all major critical works about him." Pier Paolo wrote, "I hear Bologna was bombed again"; in Casarsa, air raids had put explosives "in the neighborhood, the airfield and so on."

On April 6 Klaus Barbie's Gestapo in Lyons arrested fifty-one Jews at the safehouse in Izieu, forty-four of them children between four and seventeen. One non-Jew was released and one Jew escaped; the rest died at Auschwitz.

Mussolini's Republic of Salò was collapsing; the so-called Adriatic Littoral was in revolt. Nico recalled, "In this period, Guido asked me to buy some paint, and with it he wrote 'Down with the Germans,' 'Down with Hitler' and 'Viva Mazzini' on the [town] walls. He was very brave. The stuff of heroes, destined to die young." [19]

In May street pamphlets calling for all-out resistance to the Germans and their Italian collaborators appeared on the streets of Casarsa. The police, loyal to the Badoglio regime, interrogated Pier Paolo, Pina Kalz, friends named Gastone and Luciana. They were intellectuals and so troublemakers, and were among the few in the region both articulate and brave enough to draft the text and secure passes to be out after the ten o'clock curfew.

On May 29 another reference to a close call, now in a note to Serra: ". . . we were accused of passing around those handbills, one of which I saw in the shop of my aunt [Enrichetta]. Understand, Luciano, of what a horribly humiliating thing they accuse me! We, who had laughed so hard and deplored the rhetoric of that manifesto!" [20]

Pasolini told Serra that the police apologized and even accused one another. But they soon regrouped. Guido was, in fact, author of the leaflets. The brothers each had his clique and Pier Paolo seems not to have known the identity of the author of the manifesto of deplorable "rhetoric."

The *carabinieri*, working with the Gestapo, came to the Pasolini house to arrest Guido. Grandmother Giulia knelt to plead for him. When it was clear that her entreaties had failed, she ran and brought a photo showing Carlo in Kenya with the commander of Italy's armies, Filiberto di Savoia, the Duke of Aosta himself, the Fuehrer's ally. Surely that would show the family's Fascist loyalties. But no—the Germans did not care at all about Italy's armies or its destiny.

The commander put a pistol in the boy's back, forcing him onto a truck. After a few days, he returned from Pordenone, having survived an interrogation and a beating. A few days later, Giulia died.

Pier Paolo drew her on her deathbed: He used a soft pencil to show her with a cloth tied under her jaw. He used the back of a sheet of writing paper whose words show through the sketched image.

Guido was spending time at Versuta, with contacts among the Resistance regiments. At the end of May he left for the blue hills north of Casarsa to join the Partisans. He carried a satchel of sandwiches, a dictionary that had been scooped out to hold a Beretta pistol and the *Canti orfici* (Orphic songs) of the homosexual poet Dino Campana.

Pier Paolo accompanied his brother to the station. The younger boy made a show of buying a ticket for Bologna while Renato (a friend) acquired one for Spilimbergo. In fact, Guido switched with Renato, changing trains for Pielungo in the mountains.

Long after Guido was dead, Pier Paolo wrote of that departure:

> It was a morning on which unawares
> a sea light dreamed on the eroded horizons;
> each blade of grass as though struggling to sprout
> was a thread of that huge and obscure splendor.
> We came in silence along the hidden embankment
> by the railroad, light and still warm
> from our last sleep together in the bare barn
> that had been our refuge amid the fields.
> Behind us Casarsa turned white and lifeless
> in the terror of Graziani's last edict;
> and, struck by the sun against the shadow of the
> mountains, the station stood empty;
> beyond the spare trunks of the mulberry trees and
> the brushwood,
> alone on the grassy tracks, the Spilimbergo train
> was waiting . . . In the white color of the air and
> earth, I watched him leave with his suitcase,
> in which a volume of Montale was jammed
> among the few clothes and his revolver.
> His jacket, which had been mine, a little tight
> at the shoulders, the boyish nape of his neck . . .
> I went back along the burning road . . .

Once in Partisan-held territory, Guido signed onto the Action Party and became a soldier in the Commando division of the Osoppo-Friuli brigade, a non-Communist, republican band of guerrillas. They wore green neckerchiefs to distinguish them from the Communist Partisans of the Garibaldi brigade, who wore red. He was nineteen. Guido left behind a girl he cared about, named Wilma; he told her she filled him with "a tremendous and desperate longing."

Guido stayed in the mountains until the following January, 1945. Life for Pier Paolo and Susanna—alone, together—went on, centered around letters smuggled past the Germans from Guido, others passed through British censors from Carlo Alberto.

Pier Paolo's feelings about his Partisan brother were complex. On the one hand, Guido was heroic; on the other, impetuous and foolhardy. Pier Paolo wrote Serra not long before, "What a lot of speeches you make about the guerrillas and the 'guerrilla wars.' I don't know whether to laugh or get angry. If you care so little about your own blood, save it for now, and if need be shed it for something better than a guerrilla war with those worthy Croats." That was exactly why Guido had gone to shed his.

The Allies reached Rome that June, and the city fell to General Mark Clark's army without the street-by-street resistance for which Mussolini had hoped. He had wanted the country fought for "inch by inch," damage to its people and artistic heritage be damned. Slowing the Allied advance would give the Germans time to perfect their V-series rockets.

In the meantime, he authorized creation of the "black brigades," straightforward terrorists whose atrocities even Graziani, the Fascist general, admitted were the worst of the war. Mussolini explicitly approved that women and children be shot, and with every murder of civilian hostages the ranks of the Partisans grew. He was willing to plunge Italy into an internecine bloodbath: By refusing prisoner-of-war status to nonregular army Partisans, he generated a civil war that raged in parallel to the Allied advance and in its midst.

As a precaution, Guido signed his letters "Amelia." He had his picture taken: In it, he leans one arm against a tree, looking into the distance. His thick hair is wavy, his cheeks still full with teenage baby fat; he wears shorts and a T-shirt and holds in the crook of his left arm an antiquated rifle with a heavy wooden stock.


Pier Paolo's sentimental education under Bruno's tutelage continued. Pina Kalz fell in love with him. He recorded in his diary that her love was for that "dead zone," which she wanted to explore, that part of him "behind the moral fullness, my accessibility, abandonments." One Sunday, before the usual soccer match, they went walking in the open fields; ". . . we were really suffering: I (at least on the surface) from boredom, she of desire." He was thinking "only of Bruno, and nothing about her." They wandered in silence, picked flowers, and held them between their teeth ("Oh God, I think that under one of those oak trees she combed my hair . . . and put a blossom in it") and when they went back to the other people "our relations were not cordial anymore."

He went to the hamlet where Bruno lived, hoping to see him. When he at first failed to appear, Pier Paolo wrung every exquisite note from his unhappiness. Bruno was useful even absent, helping Pier Paolo explore the terrain of his interior life.

When Bruno eventually appeared, following his sheep, he sauntered up, "his chest bare, a pair of greasy, coarse shorts covered his thighs and legs and two heavy clogs on his feet. With his uneven gait and burned, unlovable face, he drew near and squeezed my arm and then my flank, miraculously establishing that between us two there need be no more shame."

The more experienced but younger of the two led his partner to a sort of hidden cave near the tracks. The young poet noted that Bruno insisted on secrecy and was "pretty skilled" at finding places where he could "give vent to his libido." Unlike his quivering but attentive charge, Bruno was in no hurry: He paused to gather a nest full of eggs and lit a cigarette "allowing me to caress him." Pier Paolo reached for euphemism to describe sex with Bruno: "when we finally stretched out between two bushes, desire freed itself from his conscience; and I could almost know the fullness of abandon."[21]

Pier Paolo spent the spring waiting for Bruno, looking for him, lurking in the places he frequented. "I passed many hours in that desolation," he wrote, and finally the summer came and a return to life centered on swimming. Bruno turned up at the usual place, as did Pier Paolo. But now Pier Paolo's insistences were refused, his glance avoided. Pasolini took a copy of Tasso with him, and of Tommaseo—author of an anthology of Greek lyrics—and waited "in a very beautiful meadow encircled by vines and a trench that ran between the trees" for Bruno's mood to come around. He listened to "thousands of birds, singing on different scales," and waited for his changeable paramour to yield.

"Often I imagined that I heard a human voice in the midst of the birdsongs, and got up, trembling, on the absurd pretext that it was Bruno calling me." A year later he learned that Pina used to go there and look for him.

Aerial bombardments became daily occurrences. People gathered in panic in the piazza when the alarm sounded and then fled through alleyways into the open fields, trying to distance themselves from the roads and train station targets.

Susanna and Pier Paolo were ready. She had the jewels Carlo had given her. And in a leather satchel, Pier Paolo had his manuscript notebooks, including the latest work: his play *The Turks in Friuli* and his notes on Pascoli. He dated the play May 1944.

Susanna received a letter that summer from Guido:

> My thoughts return by some strange fixation to Pier Paolo; I have thought of him intensely even during the past few days . . . what is he doing? Why does he never write me? Sometimes I am obsessed with the idea that he thinks of me with a certain bitter irony it makes me shudder . . . it seems strange to me to be sitting here among friendly faces after such a long pilgrimage . . . I need winter stuff, sweaters, Balaclava, wool gloves, socks and another pair of heavy shoes (those I have are in a pitiful state). So: either you, or Giannina together with Pina must carry these things you know where as soon as possible! Pier Paolo must be calm about this—the trip for a woman poses no danger at all.[22]

By late September the Fascist squads threatened to execute anyone who did not enlist in their service. Air raids intensified and the Germans pillaged as they retreated from a siege of the town. The Pasolinis had put off definitive flight until the last possible moment: Now they hurried to Versuta to stay.

On September 10 a munitions dump exploded, reddening the sky over Casarsa until morning. Soon alarms were sounding every night, making people run from their beds into the fields, hoping the bombs would strike only the train depot at the center of town. The women, recalls Naldini, "often stood in the road and said the rosary" and Pier Paolo "carried Susanna—unable to run in her high heels—in his arms."

The next month Partisans killed two German soldiers, and reprisals began at once. Naldini recalls:

> A family, friends of ours, offered a refuge: crossing the courtyard of the farmhouse, one could arrive at the belltower of the [Casarsa] church. Pier Paolo carried with him a folder, leather-covered, with his manuscripts in it and the latest volume of a history of Italian literature.[23]

Nico followed and stayed with his cousin, who had climbed directly to the top of the tower. Forty years later the younger boy recalled staring down into the town square below and a small stretch of road that was visible.

> Pier Paolo was seated on a step and continued to annotate his history text. We spent two days and two nights in that belltower which, for a few hours,

shook from airshocks set in motion by an enormous bombardment of the bridge over the Tagliamento.[24]

During the course of several days Pier Paolo carried their goods the few miles to Versuta. Finally, when it seemed impossible to enter the town-center of Casarsa, some peasants came for what remained and hauled it in a wagon drawn by two oxen.

Just before going, Susanna and Pina Kalz undertook a dangerous journey into the mountains, to see Guido at Savorgano del Torre, above Tricesimo. Now he had taken the name Ermes, in memory of Ermes Parini, known to be dead on the Russian front. It was the last time Susanna saw her second son.

Now, at Versuta in time of war, Pier Paolo met the peasantry face to face. He studied them and wrote:

> At the age of fifteen, they are charming idols, bedecked with modesty, with tenderness, with a liveliness they cannot express, at eighteen their promising grace (but one without a future) which had straightened up their lives is already immobilized, and their touching timidity has taken on darker, more monotonous colors; there remains for them to gratify the curiosity of the flesh and this makes them even more vulnerable, more impassioned, but by twenty the fire is out.[25]

At night he sat in the stables with them, people who had never been to school, part of a world unchanged since the previous century. He drew them and listened to their language.

While Guido was somewhere in the mountains and Carlo Alberto a prisoner in Africa, Susanna and Pier Paolo were alone and inseparable. The locals took them to be fiancés, seeing them walk together holding hands every afternoon in the fields around the village.

In 1986 his cousin Nico for the first time published two letters Guido sent after Susanna's last visit: one to his mother; another to the brother for whom he had so much hero-worship and whose approval he so craved.

> Dearest *Cicciona*,
>
> Here I am at last with you with my notorious grin on my face. I have a sense of well-being and peace all over . . . I am, in fact, seated among dear people (whom you know and who covered me with such kindness, making me embarrassed since I've become so primitive and coarse) . . .
>
> If it were up to me—you must believe me—I'd write you every day—I have received Pier Paolo's letter. It really brought peace to my mind; I am very grateful to have it. The poetry really interpreted in an extraordinary way my state of mind and the feel of certain windy days lit by the sun; I was up

there, on one of the peaks, and the valley spread before me all the way to
the sea, to Istria and the villages (their roofs were red) swarming over the
green flatness (light, but still that green . . . ) I followed nervously the line
of the shingle-bed of the Tagliamento: At a certain point the countryside
grew dim in a faint and nebulous blue . . . there you were, perhaps thinking
of me. Pier Paolo should please write me again, when he has a chance,
giving me great joy.[26]

The letter to Pier Paolo explained the movements of the Partisans
and the conflicts among them. Some of the guerrillas were loyal to
Tito and worked for a Communist takeover of Friuli, intending that
after the war it pass to Yugoslavia by dint of their leadership and
control. Others, including Guido's brigade, were not sympathetic to
Yugoslav Communist designs for annexing Friuli.

Guido captured the deathly tension of that autumn in his letter to
Pier Paolo, smuggled to Casarsa:

> A Garibaldian commissar in Mernicco aimed a pistol at my head because I
> yelled in his face that he has no idea what it is to be "Free Men," and that
> he was arguing like a fascist federalist. Indeed in the Garibaldian ranks
> you're free to speak well of communism, otherwise you're treated as an
> "enemy of the proletariat"—no less!—or else an "idealist sucking the blood
> of the people"—what crap!
>
> We hold up our heads and declare that we're Italians and we're fighting for
> the Italian flag, not for "the red rag."[27]

He joined others to start a propaganda newspaper called *Quelli del
tricolore* (literally, "Those of the [Italian red-white-green] tri-colored
flag") to make the case for staying free of Tito's plans, those neither
Communist nor Fascist but for an independent Italian republic that
included territorial sovereignty for the northeast provinces like Friuli.
He asked Pier Paolo to contribute, "writing as one Italian to other
Italians." He wrote, "I understand perfectly that you probably have
neither the time nor desire." But, in case he did, Guido enclosed an
envelope that could be passed through underground channels via
Udine.

Guido wrote that on the anniversary of the Russian revolution,
November 7, the Slovenes celebrated with their Italian Communist
Party brothers-in-arms. Within sixty days, the zone near the contested Italian-Yugoslav border—hamlets with names that became notorious, like Prosenicco and Subit and Porzus—had become a civil
war's killing ground, one of the first battlefields of the hot, internecine
phase of the Cold War.

The winter passed in a battle of nerves and words of growing mistrust among Partisans, who—not sure whom to trust—fast decided to trust no one. The Ossopo Brigade was under the command of a man named Bolla; he used his troops (Guido among them) as bargaining chips in negotiations with the Nazis through the Bishop of Udine. Growing fear of betrayal and finally panic made the Communists decide to rid themselves of these troublesome Republican Partisans. The afternoon of February 7, 1945, Guido and other very young troops had taken positions at Porzus, high in the hills. The replacements they expected never showed up, having been captured and killed as "spies." Guido and thirteen others were taken, and the plan was to kill them after a summary kangaroo court before Garibaldi Partisan "judges."

First, a "political" meeting was called, and Guido shouted to his captors that "the only justice Communists knew was a bullet in the back of the head." At the trials held in Pisa and Brescia after the war, summoned to investigate the massacre that followed Guido's murder, witnesses testified that no one bothered to answer Guido's suicidal outburst.

Small groups of the Republican volunteers were taken out and shot during the following days. Guido, although wounded in the shoulder and the right arm, escaped and hid in a farmhouse of a woman named Libera Piani, who cared for him without asking questions. He was bleeding heavily. It was plain that he was just a boy, a teenager.

Two Garibaldians arrived, claiming that they would take him to the hospital. They dragged him from the house, and under arrest at the house of the head of the local cell of the National Liberation Committee, Guido lay almost dead from his wounds.

A third Garibaldi Partisan came, recognized Guido, and went for a bicycle. Again the Garibaldians claimed he would be carried to the hospital at Cormons; instead, he was taken to the place from which he had escaped.

Groundless rumors typical of the tone of life in the war zone in those months circulated among the population, accounts claiming that the martyrs had been beaten to death with hammers. Rather, Guido was forced to lie in the grave that had been dug for him and was shot. Years later, when the murders were a score to be settled as well as justice to be done, thirty-six defendants—among them local Communist leaders—were found guilty by a court sitting at Lucca. They received prison sentences but were absolved of treason.

The pain of Guido's murder only struck Pier Paolo in the spring, for official news of his death did not reach Casarsa until the end of

May. The silence from their Guido-Amelia-Ermes was broken by the news that his silence would be forever. After a memorial service in Udine, he was buried in the Casarsa cemetery on June 21, in a common grave with other victims of the incident, just inside the cemetery entrance, to the right of the portal.

Pier Paolo learned the news from another Partisan, when he was out walking with his cousin Annie near Versuta. Since Pier Paolo knew before Susanna, it was he who had to tell her.

On August 21, 1945, six months after the event and with the war officially over, Pier Paolo awakened from grief enough to write to Serra at Bologna of Guido's murder in the cold mountains the previous February 12. He recounted what the family understood had happened at Porzus, barely two months before the armistice

> I cannot write of it without crying, and all my thoughts come out as confused as my tears. At first, I could only feel a horror, a repulsion at living, and the sole, unexpected comfort was believing there is a destiny out there one cannot escape, and thus something humanly just. You recall Guido's enthusiasm, that's the phrase that keeps hammering inside me: He could not survive his enthusiasm.
>
> That boy was of a generosity, of a courage, an innocence one cannot believe. How much better he was than all of us: I see his image now, alive, with his hair, his eyes, his jacket and I feel myself seized by an anguish that is so unspeakable and inhuman. . . . I must be able to weep for him forever, without end, because only that would be a little bit equal to the immensity of the injustice which has befallen him. . . . The only thought which consoles me is that I am not immortal; that Guido did no more than go generously ahead of me by a few years to that end toward which I am headed.[28]

Pier Paolo told Serra what he knew about how Guido died. More details were to emerge in the inquests of 1948 and again in 1952. Pier Paolo went to both, to testify against those charged in the murders.

> On the 10th of September of 1943, he and a friend risked their lives several times by stealing arms from the Germans at the Casarsa airstrip; and so it went throughout the autumn of '44 . . . his friend Renato [Renato Lena], during one of these extremely dangerous undertakings lost a hand and an eye; but that didn't stop them; on the contrary, throughout the spring [of '44] during the night curfew they distributed propaganda leaflets and wrote on the walls (you can still see what he wrote on a fallen down house in Casarsa: "the hour is near"). And you, Luciano, remember when we were

arrested, and they accused me of writing that propaganda; it was Guido instead. From that time on we were under surveillance, continuous and exasperating. We often went to sleep at Versuta. But Guido had already decided, and for some time, that he was going to the mountains. And he left, at the end of May, without our being able to convince him to stay hidden at Versuta, as I have done now for a year.

I helped him leave, one early morning . . . they were the days of the greatest terror and the strictest surveillance . . . We said goodbye and kissed one another in a field behind the station; it was the last time I saw him.[29]

It seems Guido was offered a chance to switch sides and save himself. If he would join the pro-Tito forces, his life would be spared. He refused the offer. Over several days, he was threatened and cajoled; both he and a companion named D'Orlandi resisted. Pier Paolo wrote that they said "they wanted to fight for Italy and liberty and not for Tito and communism."

Guido had signed on with the Action Party; Pier Paolo claimed in 1970 that only he had prevented Guido from joining the Communists. Guido described his comrades in a letter to Pier Paolo as "very honest people, gentle and loyal . . . very much like Serra."

"His martyrdom must not pass unknown, Luciano." Serra was composing an essay entitled "Remembrance of Guido," which appeared on September 18 in the weekly edition of the Bolognese Action Party publication *Giustizia e libertà*. Pier Paolo admonished, "Try to write something . . . it would be an enormous joy also to our poor mother, who wants at all costs to have some reason why her son is dead. I cannot continue in this vein, because I feel too much anguish."[30]

Pier Paolo told Serra that he, too, has joined the Action Party, "pushed," "egged on" ("*spinto*") by Guido's example. But the little school had to go on, even the rehearsals of the little theatrical *I fanciulli e gli elfi* (The little children and the elves); but the country schoolmaster's political agenda had become radicalized.

The Academiuta di Lenza Furlana and its magazine offered both structure and platform for Pier Paolo's skills as polemicist and pedagogue. He thought poetry could change history by educating consciousness. He was sure that his passion was enough to find a public who would listen, be changed, and, in a vague sort of way, became not only molded into civic independence but even somehow individually saved from anonymity and exploitation.

He wrote of "establishing a culture where for centuries there had been little but songs in dialect, and foreign occupation. It would not be elitist, but instead a group absorbing the sounds and feelings of the common people." Such was the native, naïve Marxist in the making.

Pier Paolo's poems appeared in every number of *Il stroligut,* a corpus of new Friulian work in his invented-acquired dialect. Without grants, advisers, universities, foundations, or publisher, he made something from nothing. He had found a cause, a reason for making a poetry altogether different from the modest vision of Pietro Zorutti (1792–1867), still the ruling figure in Friulian verse.

Pier Paolo's disciples were ardent, but photos show in their faces a premature maturation, the sad-faced, forced adulthood of boys who were wearing the passed-down pants and jackets from older brothers gone to the front, where the junior offspring expected soon to follow.

His poetic output in *friulano* is found in the Academy's five thin volumes, stretching from the spring of 1944 through 1947. The first— *Stroligut di cà da l'aga* (roughly, The astrologer on this side of the water [the river Tagliamento]) bore its date in the still-mandatory Fascist style: April MCMXLIV (1944).

The scholar in Pier Paolo observed for his readers how different rural Friuli was from rich Piedmont, from the liturgically-laden world of nearby Aquileia, where the Roman garrison "City of the Eagle" gave way in the fourth century to the Christian Patriarchs.

*Il stroligut's* August 1945 ("No. 1") issue opened with a declaration signed "Guido Pasolini (Ermes)," entitled "The Martyr to the Living." Its author was Pier Paolo. Willing to put words into his dead brother's mouth, he was prepared—and within six months of Guido's murder—to remember him by using his memory for political ends. Pier Paolo composed a hymn to death and patriotism, punctuated with the threnody of one sacred word: "consciously":

> Consciously, I sought death after a brief youth, which also seemed eternal to me, as it was the only, irreplaceable one I was to have.
>
> Consciously, I renounced the joy of being in the world with myself, with my parents and brother and all of you . . .
>
> Consciously, I became a martyr after one year of struggle, of anguish, of suffering, of war; yet being valorous is nothing, nothing because it is not possible to compare all that is in life with the terrible silence of death.
>
> Now I, a martyr, turn to you, the living . . . It was my enthusiastic heart which carried me to this terrible sacrifice; and I accept, that way, my end.
>
> I turn to you to urge you not to forget the feelings which carried me toward death, and the ideals for which I have been martyred.
>
> Italy has not fallen, and I do not see her even touched by the events of these past few years of her history, because her greatness is something spiritual, and rises above all our miseries and those of others. It was for this

spiritual greatness that I died. And to him who has lost faith in the face of
the misery of the Patria, I say that never in her history has she been able
to count so many martyrs who glorify her. . . .

It is in this spiritual greatness of the Patria, in which I beg you to believe,
that you will find reflected and gathered together all the love which made
me die for you.[31]

Under the banner of "Absolute Friulianism, Romanic tradition,
inspiration of contemporary literature, liberty, fantasy," the youths
of the Academy gathered around Pasolini's charismatic leadership.
They met every Sunday afternoon in the little dining room at Versuta,
to read the poems they had written, to hear Pina play the violin and
Pier Paolo recite lines from *I tancredi* which appeared out of his
notebooks but never went into print.

Pasolini and Naldini looked back on these months, the winter of
1945, as filled with laughter, singing, "extreme gaiety." Later, in
retrospect, he called it "a kind of Arcadia."

Life was simple, "pure." Nico walked over from San Giovanni,
where his family had taken shelter in a mill. "He called with [a
volume of] Ungaretti under his arm." Ovidio Colussi and his brother
Ermes visited ("two boys who were sensible and open") as did the
painter Federico De Rocco from San Vito.

They met in Susanna's dining room until March 5, when aerial
bombardment virtually flattened the house. After that, the gatherings
were in a little shack, a half-decayed stucco farm building in the
middle of Versuta's corn fields. Pier Paolo spent hours painting in
oils and drawing in pencil and charcoal—the farm buildings, the
fields, the boys, working side by side with De Rocco.

Teacher and students rehearsed his "Little Children and the
Elves": Pier Paolo played the Bear, and the class was divided be-
tween the boys and the elves. It was an island of love and sanity, as
Italy imploded.

In that winter of 1944–1945, when lack of news from Guido began
to be worrisome—when Guido was dead, but his family did not yet
know it—Pier Paolo fell in love with Tonuti Spagnol. The diaries
call him "T." Later, in 1947, Pasolini wrote he could not recall
whether moonlit walks with T. were before or after May 1945 "but
they must have been before" since after would have been incompatible with grief.

Often they walked the two miles to San Giovanni, Pier Paolo's arm
on T.'s shoulder, the younger boy's head on Pasolini's. This position
seemed bliss to him: the leaning of the head on the shoulder—so

intimate, trusting. It became the sign of surrender to love in his novel of adolescent adoration *Amado mio,* written the next year.

He kept working. *Il stroligut* was now a full-scale literary magazine, astoundingly sophisticated for its time and place, complete with translations into *friulano* of Tommasseo, Wordsworth, Verlaine, Jiménez. The war was over, Fascism gone. The young intellectual was free to publish foreigners and dialects and let his free imagination roam without strictures and not in the service of the State.

About the same time, a little volume simply called *Poesie* appeared—105 copies—at Pier Paolo's expense, first of a series he wrote and printed until he left Fruili forever five years later. It closed with three love poems "to a boy from Versuta."

On November 11, he wrote his mother from Bologna, "Has Daddy [*il babbo*] arrived yet? . . . Who knows, maybe he's there with you now? How much I wanted us to wait for him together." Six days later, he reported to Susanna that he encountered his now released and repatriated father in Bologna's via Castiglione. "He was in Rome, at uncle's [Gino] and I sent an express letter to let him know I was here." The train line to Casarsa passes through Bologna, the central terminus for all central and northern Italy. "Think what enormous joy. And how much more that Daddy seems full of health and vigor, so young. Soon we'll all be together . . . Lots of kisses, little one, take courage."

Carlo Alberto added a few lines to the postcard, explaining that Pier Paolo wanted him to himself for a few days, so their arrival in Casarsa would only be November 23. Thus Carlo Alberto returned from war, both decorated for valor and broken.

Father and son passed almost a week alone together, to catch up on the years. They must have walked the porticoed sidewalks of Bologna, their talk overflowing: Guido, the bombardments, the war in Africa and prison camp, Pier Paolo's first book—would Carlo Alberto have mentioned its dedication?

They had to contemplate the collapse of the world Carlo loved, the only one Pier Paolo knew. Both were starting over: the son on the verge of his university degree in a country that needed to heal and reconstruct. His thesis on Pascoli was accepted and the degree in letters *magna cum laude* granted on November 26.

Carlo was entering into the last act of his life, one in which his role was on the sidelines. No one wanted a demobilized former Fascist officer, small-scale hero or not. His loss was Guido and an unhappy marriage, his consolation in drink. He could look forward to a modest but adequate pension and the respect the village would accord him, a decorated prisoner of war. He seemed much subdued, tamed both by his own experience as detainee and the death of Guido.

In 1970, Pier Paolo described the father who returned, "reduced by illness, poisoned by the collapse of Fascism in the country and of the Italian language in the family; destroyed, ferocious, a tyrant without power, made mad by bad wine, always more in love with my mother who never loved him back, now intent only on her grief."

His play in *friulano*, called *La monteana*, was booked to be performed, but technical difficulties intervened and it never appeared. At the end of October, he joined the "Association for Friulian Autonomy," a Udine-based group. The membership card was headed, with more hope than political likelihood, *Patrie dal Friul*. On the line calling for "occupation," Pier Paolo penned *"intellecuale."*

Joining this lead organization dedicated to Friulian rights did not mean Pier Paolo was meekly lining up with its agenda. As early as 1943, in *Il setaccio*, he unleashed a sharp attack on the clique of provincial scholars at Udine who appointed themselves keepers of the idea of "Friulianness":

> No one can boast that the Friulian capital is, culturally, an avant-garde center, with its emaciated and backward group of literati (who go around proclaiming on the "People of Friuli" their thin and confused notions) and with its old philological center [the Society of Philology], rigid in a tight traditionalism.[32]

Turned twenty-four in March 1946, Pier Paolo could now look forward to a respectable and secure career as a local schoolmaster. He held an excellent degree, something rare enough in schoolteachers in far Friuli, and even had classroom experience to his credit. He was known; finding a job should not prove difficult. He would assemble life's crucial elements, the *sistemazione*, be literally "systematized," with a secure government post with pension waiting and status in the community. He could pursue his poetry on the side, of course, when obligations to what would soon be his own family allowed. There was always Guido's death, but in other respects life was normal enough. The reunited Pasolinis waited at Versuta for their house on the main street in Casarsa to be rebuilt.

The public schools would soon reopen, spelling the end of the Academy: Those who could would return to proper State schools, the poorer ones to field work. As for plans for more poetry, for a life in letters one way or another, Pier Paolo had plenty.

He understood Casarsa was deep in the provinces, at the far edge of everything happening in literature that excited him. But people stayed put in those times of unemployment and even uncertain nourishment; he made no plans to depart.

He began in earnest to orchestrate his career as a poet. The little printing press in Casarsa was hired again to put out *I diarii*, a further collection of mostly pastoral poems in *friulano*. Eugenio Montale himself, not yet the Nobel Prize–winner but an influential journalist on the verge of becoming chief literary critic for the *Corriere della sera*, showed interest. He reprinted one poem from *I diarii* in the cultural review *Il mondo*, which he had helped found.

The Academy was renamed after Guido "who died, not yet twenty years old, in the mountains of Venezia Giulia, an example of disconsolate heroism, of mute enthusiasm."

Carlo, apparently convinced that Pier Paolo was on the way to a fine career in literature, ordered construction of a room adjacent to the Casarsa house, at ground level, space to be set aside for the Academiuta. It was at once a memorial to Guido and an investment in Pier Paolo. Years later, long after everyone else was dead, the last survivor of the Colussis, seamstress sister Enrichetta, rented it out, first to a lady for a cosmetics shop and later to a dry cleaner.[33]


With 1946, life sped up. April saw a first visit, by long train ride, to his mother's brother Gino in Rome, living a *mondain* life with his German dentist lover Paul Weiss—frequenting high society, knowing artists, writers, people of taste and influence, other homosexuals.

Plans now were also laid for a visit, at last, by Contini to Casarsa; it came to nothing. And Pier Paolo took up his diary, opening what he called the "Red Notebooks" (*Quaderni rossi*) by writing in capital letters "INVOLUNTARY PAGES (Novel)" and a date purposefully left incomplete—"23 May 19—."

The diaries take up three volumes, stretching from May 1946 through August 8, 1947. He wrote that it was a diary "which I write against my will (maybe this, and nothing else, is divine punishment)." It was his confessional; he had decided that a man of letters had to keep a book on himself, for self-study.

Selections were published by his cousin Nico in 1986:

> 24 May 1946. Noon sounds. Weak thunderbolts issue from low, grey clouds. How many times in my life have I found myself in conditions just like this.

My head aching from too much reading, my senses full of odors from the kitchen, the sky and the countryside stretched out around me under a heavy veil, without color. It is horrible: a thought passes through my mind like smoke: the title of a book on its creased cover [*Sagesse*], Sundays, friendship with certain young peasant boys. Does my life consist of these things? Luckily, it isn't possible to separate single facts from one another: much stays mixed up in that mystery which we call, in a hurry and only when faced with ourselves, "my existence," or, more simply, "I."[34]

A week later, he wrote about Tonuti, noting the boy's mouth had started to resemble that of his mother, that he was now almost sixteen. "It is more than one year since . . ." and he trails off. He records a daydream in which he is naked, lying by the riverside. He starts to yell, loudly, "*Fiori infuocati . . .*" [Flowers on fire] and starts to run. He begins to gather flowers. "Here is my poetics," and he starts to tear the petals and then mix their colors.

On June 2 he wrote, "I love life—pure life—nothing else." He wonders that the voices in the courtyard, heard from his attic room during rain, sound like "other worlds." He sees T., and hovers over his "innocence" which he likens to the sight of "the snow-topped mountains above the plain."[35]

Pier Paolo now forwarded to Contini, his best reader and certainly most respected, the new Friulian poems to be added to *Poesie a Casarsa* and the poems of a new book, *The Nightingale of the Catholic Church*, including the second part, "Il pianto della rosa," completed that year. Now he entered them in a poetry competition sponsored by a Lugano newspaper, *Libera stampa*; Contini was one of the judges.[36]

I loved too much: it was childish,
without irony, my sweet hope:
I did not concede the least respite
to my dreams, nor the least smile:
but they were the Origins. And my kisses,
not reciprocated, were capable
of distracting me from a certain death.
And the way of death was opened to me.

. . .

I travel again backward over my path:
devoid of you how sweet is the Paduan landscape,
without shadow of mirage!
The Livenza lets loose its green
roses, the Idria reflects unfragrant
violets, the sky without blue looks upon
the Casarsan ditches without infancy.
And the dinner knives tinkle in the New Years'

dinners in joyful neatness.
The May bug moans without echoes
to the sense of the hidden little boy.[37]

He turned to playwriting, also sending Contini his three-act *Il
cappellano*, with a request for judgment and help in getting it into
the proper hands. The manuscript changed title several times—*Storia
interiore, Venti secoli di gioia*—and finally was performed, only
in 1965, under the title *Nel '46!*

The Partito d'Azione, which Guido had joined, grown out of the
wartime anti-Fascist Giustizia e Libertà movement, was breaking
under postwar pressure. As though a chemical brew whose elements
separate under heat and pressure, the Action Party exploded: Its
conservatives moved right to call themselves Christian Democrats—
capitalist, pro-Vatican and pro-American—while its left wing
merged into the socialist and Communist parties. The polarization of
postwar Italy came to Friuli. Pier Paolo became a Communist.

But when he published a piece in the Udine daily *Libertà* (Dec.
31, 1946) which opened, "Being Communists ourselves . . . ,"[38] the
local PCI section quickly ran a notice that this Pasolini was not free
to speak for them, and was not even a card-carrying member. That
had to wait until the next year; he was fully signed up and active in
1947.

Already his independent *modus operandi* was clear: He had announced himself a Communist when he felt he fit his own definition,
not when a bureaucracy handed him a card. The gadfly already had
a bone to pick with the old-fashioned autonomists who chatted about
poetry to one another. Soon he went after the local Communists, whom
he intended to lead.

He was his own style of populist humanitarian. The class struggle
renewed with fresh ferocity in Friuli with war's end. The fight between
landowners and peasants for control of the region's poor terrain was
now filtered through the poet's sensibility. His political strategy, a
hard-nosed Marxist class analysis, was tempered with a quasi-erotic
nostalgia based on sensual imagery. Friuli's proletariat? That was
Tonuti in the courtyard, the women at the fireplace, the workers bent
over scythes in the flat fields below the blue mountains around Casarsa. It was romantic, occasionally impractical, but deeply felt and
accessible as needed when he sat down to express himself.

These poor were, in his mind, morally better than the bourgeoisie.
He later wrote, "My hatred for the bourgeoisie is not documentable
or discussable, it is what it is." He wanted no more to analyze and

tear it apart for study and reconstruction than to scrutinize his Oedipus complex. That, too, was what it was. And also eminently useful.

The intellectuals in deeply peasant Friuli knew one another, and the circles of writers, painters, and professors overlapped. Pier Paolo was now a part of that world, recognized as someone to be watched, paid attention to. But he had little use for his neighbors. He wrote that "it does not matter at all to me to have the approval and applause of that sad city which is Udine, nor of the rest of Friuli . . . it means nothing to me at all, the approval of the bourgeoisie of Udine." His ambitions, by his own account, were already larger and thus "difficult" to realize.

He appended a chronology of his work (with all the seriousness of one asked by the Swedish Academy for a résumé), specifying that the Libreria Antiquaria at Bologna had been first to publish him, that he had written two plays, one the unperformed *La monteana*, the other *I Turcs tal Friul*. He added that the first was still scheduled for performance, the other's stage future unclear.

A month later—the terrible 1945 drawing to a close—he wrote Franco de Gironcoli, one of those in the *Il stroligut* circle:

> As for my Friulian poetry, I am passing through a slight crisis of confidence; I think that here in Friuli . . . very few, even those animated by good will, possess the cultural awareness to appreciate exactly what I am doing. . . . All they see in my work is an elegant documentation of the present state of spoken Casarsese, or the possibility of some kind of renewal of Friulian literature in a manner that is "modern." They do not pick up the major fact, that my *friulano* (and yours) are languages without a history, uprooted from habits . . . absolute unto themselves.[39]

Ever more the secure, self-appointed arbiter of taste, he passed out bouquets and brickbats. The Udinese poet Mario Argante received a letter dated December 2, 1945, out of the blue. The entrepreneurial Pier Paolo had first sent him an unsolicited copy of *Il stroligut*, suggesting that even if it had not arrived, perhaps his correspondent had heard of it. Then, without the least apparent embarrassment at what might seem presumption, the young man offered praise for Argante's work. Would he perhaps send some unpublished work to Versuta, to let Pier Paolo even better know his poetry ("certainly superior to all the . . . Zorutti-ites who infest Friuli")? He linked his polite inquiry to a practical carrot: "If I find in it [your work] something which corresponds to my poetics, or in other words [fits in with] the taste of *Il stroligut*, I will be happy to print it in our next issue."

To another correspondent, he cited Novalis and Baudelaire, and explained, "I cannot work, at this point, for other than perfection." He stood back, with bravura:

> It is not for nothing, you see, that I am perhaps the only one in Italy, and I hope consistently, among those who write verse who does not imitate Montale, nor Saba, nor other minor figures (Betocchi, Penna, etc.), nor the French symbolists, nor the better romantics. . . .
>
> But I realize I have done what I did not want to do, almost made a discourse on my own poetry . . . I hope it is the first and last time. . . .
>
> So far as your book is concerned . . . I consider it an optimal preparation for a future novel.[40]

He not only meted out criticism and praise but took advantage of the latter when it came his way. An article hailing the very first issue of *Il stroligut* (August 1945), had opened doors for him at *Libertà*, in Udine; from earliest 1946, Pier Paolo was a regular contributor. A short story appeared in January and a poem entitled "The Death of Guido." March brought three more of his poems to the newspaper's pages, and two critical essays. By April 1946, *Il stroligut*'s second issue included a poem, a translation of Ungaretti into Friulian, and a theoretical essay on poetic language. The intelligentsia of Friuli had now all heard of this young man in Casarsa.

The new year invigorated him, as if that were needed. He wrote to Serra, calling him a "pig" for writing for others while failing to deliver a promised manuscript for the magazine:

> The other little reviews, yes, because they pay you. Well, all right, *Il stroligut* also will pay modestly. Think that my little magazine is literally the most beautiful thing in all Friuli and has a sure impact. To write for us will bring you far more benefit than writing article-ettes for the Jesuits.[41]

Still the useful whipping-boy, the long-dead Pietro Zorutti came under Pier Paolo's critical fire in a September article: He lambasted the provincialism of Friuli's leading man of letters and took to calling him "poor Zorutti." An effective and ruthless polemicist, Pier Paolo had mastered the *ad hominem* attack, even using a dead man as straw man.

Pier Paolo had his own path out to the larger world: It was Contini. In February he wrote his mentor (or so Pier Paolo had appointed him), reporting that he had sent an enlarged *Poesie a Casarsa* to the publisher Bompiani ("I am waiting . . ."), that the Italian poems gone to Montale were only at the poet-journalist's insistence ("otherwise I would not have had the courage"). He explained that the second number of *Il stroligut* printed *friulano* in an orthography of Pier Paolo's own invention, which he thought necessary only for this oral tradition. It was meant only to show that it could be done; he added, "in number 3, I'll return to the normal one." He mentioned the "true danger" in which he lived to be "an excessive solitude." "Please know how precious to me would be your advice, which I so fear that I do not deserve."

Contini answered (the letter is now lost), prompting one in turn from Pasolini in March. This time Pier Paolo poured out his heart, calling his solitude "voluntary," accusing himself of egotism. He refers, only in passing, to "an excessive habit for Proustian experiments." Perhaps he hoped Contini would ask for specifics. He did not.

In answer to Contini's curiosity about this "academy," which published so often and so well, Pier Paolo admitted, "The other members of the Academy *exist*, at least physically; but they are very young students from middle schools, save for one or two."[42]

Perhaps Contini would look over some of the writing of Pier Paolo's cousin Domenico Naldini and that of a friend Bortotto "if you have time?" He throws out an idea, that *Il stroligut* be reconstituted as a magazine of all the minor Romance languages, covering the zone described in a book by Cecco d' Ascoli, covering a linguistic curve drawn through the Swiss Engadine, the Ladino-speaking valleys of the border country, and into Friuli, places where the language has "a mountain fragrance."

"You are the only one who could edit such a magazine," he wrote Contini, assuring him that the material while "not vast is unknown, exciting." He offers this as "an idea I have had for several years, and which alone I could never realize. Now you tell me if it is so absurd."

In March he wrote Serra not only to reprimand him for holding up the magazine's printing with his tardiness (a "very beautiful essay" had not arrived) but to say he was living "between two deserts always more absolute." The solution was a change: On March 27 he begged off a meeting of the executive committee of the Friulian Philological Society because "tomorrow I depart for Rome." He took a few lines to describe the level of teaching of poetry in the region's schools: "ignorance on the part of the teachers, unawareness of the children."

Again the guest of Uncle Gino and Paolo Weiss, he sketched their world in a letter to Tonuti on April 3. The paintings he mentioned were part of Weiss's valuable collection, auctioned after his death:

> My dear Tonuti,
> Perhaps it would interest you to know where I write you from, where I am

right now: I am in a small room, full of shadow, in the midst of an infinitude of pictures hung on the walls: Madonnas, gentlemen, mangers, crucifixions, holy families all in violent and soft colors. The furniture is antique, and everything is old and valuable. There is a silence so tranquil and dreamlike that one feels to be in the midst of a meadow, in summer, after eating. But instead of cicadas one hears a far-away and faint concert of horns and whistles: it is the traffic of the capital, a street going where you cannot imagine.[43]

Later that year, in *Libertà,* he recounted a far less positive vision of urban life, perhaps not so much because of the place as the company:

I recall this from my very earliest time, a part of my life from which I remember little. I found myself in a place with my father. Then I started to feel a frightening beating of my heart; I jumped to my feet and turned around to look at the city: red, immense, deserted. I was seized by dizziness, and at the same time by an enormous calm. My vision was obscured, and everything presented itself to me with that mixture of extraordinary brightness and confusion that objects take on when you have just had the news of something terrible and irretrievable [*una sventura irreparabile*].

And then I understood I was dead; I understood that bridge, that house, that city I was not seeing with my eyes. And there was also music, a sad and high music that brought on the images.

Contini was planning a trip to Venice and suggested he might be able to stop in Casarsa. Pier Paolo explained: "Among the fallen-down houses you will see ours, and that is why we camp out in a peasant farmhouse in the middle of the fields. If you decide to come this way, in the midst of all this misery, perhaps you will find two pleasant things: the little room where our Academy meets and the *tagliatelle* my father makes, a most hospitable Romagnolo . . . As a result of all these inconveniences, I fear that the joy of your visit would be all mine and not yours."

In a postscript he mentioned that cousin Nico—"the translator of Jiménez"—is also an avid Contini fan. He also suggested that in case this sidetrip proved inconvenient, he, Pier Paolo, would be able to meet Contini in Rome, Bologna, or Parma. "These would be the cities where I can go anytime." That would allow him to commune with his *maestro* without subjecting the experience to Carlo Alberto, *tagliatelle* and all.

But Contini did not visit Casarsa that June, nor in July. Finally, in August, Pier Paolo went by bus to the Val d'Aosta, in the far northwest of Italy, to be with the very ill Fabio Mauri. Pier Paolo wrote Cavazza that the ride was spent with "two fools" and a hunch-back who sat down "with his hump right in my chest."

From there, he contacted Contini, writing: "It is not a pleasure visit, on the contrary a real sacrifice." But "Wednesday or Thursday I depart again and can come to Domodossola: may I hope to find you there? . . . I'll come by your house at about ten." They had been corresponding for five years.

Decades later Contini recalled,

> I do not think I have ever been present at such an outpouring of shyness: so much so that at a certain moment, to lift the heaviness of the conversation (we were at my place in the country) I suggested we go to explore the neighborhood, now much deteriorated ecologically, but then still uncorrupted.[44]

At home in nature Pier Paolo finally relaxed, and their conversation flowed.

In another *Libertà* piece, dated November 6, 1946, Pasolini framed his interest in "the Friulian question" such that the coming political map-drawing would be dictated by culture, not the reverse. His evidence (and, in his eyes, proof) was inevitably linguistic: "It is enough to board a train (for instance, the one that goes through Casarsa at seven in the morning) and compare the students and clerks from Pordenone and those from Casarsa, and especially with those from Codroipo and Basilinao."[45]

Language, he argued, was the key to an almost anthropological system of politics: "Sentimentally and irrationally, we . . . feel that Friuli is not the Veneto. . . ."

On January 26, 1947, he wrote again in *Libertà* on "Friulian Aspirations": The Communist Party was a way of "transforming prehistory into history, nature into consciousness." It was the needed mechanism for making culture political. Or better, for putting politics at the service of culture.

If the "committed intellectual" was as welcome in the Communist Party as it claimed, then he was ready. If the Party favored populism and the regeneration of local pride, he was willing to join forces. If he were naïve in failing to see the drive toward conformity and orthodoxy in the Party, then it was the foolishness of the idealist, the illusion of ardor.

The matter became moot with the DC landslide victory in 1948 and its political hegemony through the fifties and sixties. Only in 1963 were five "special regions" created: Sicily, Sardinia, the Val d'Aosta, the Trentino-Alto Adige, and something called "The Autonomous Region of Friuli-Venezia Giulia." Casarsa was within the province of Pordenone; Friuli's capital—Trieste.

He befriended other poets in the region: Dino Menichini, the writers Sergio Maldini, Elio Bertolini. With Zigaina, he began making long bicycle tours to deliver speeches on freedom and liberty in town squares. The poet and the PCI-committed painter bicycled at night on country roads to Cordenons, outside Pordenone, to address Communist rallies. They stayed friends for life.

Pasolini soon was reviewing Zigaina's exhibitions and Zigaina was making illustrations for Pier Paolo's poems. At the close of 1946, he finished *Atti impuri,* the unpublishable story of his love for T.

On November 21 he wrote in the second of his "Red Notebooks":

> Time has passed and I am still here at Versuta, day after day, always more amazed to see my specific case confirmed in the general rule.

Restless and feeling isolated, he wrote:

> Today is the festival of Saint John: a gloomy and ill-starred holiday. And now that it is night I find myself alone in my room, desperate, without the strength to think of myself, to move or to weep, because in my desperation there is no more purity, no more innocence. I have found myself too often in this condition . . . now I am a desert completely explored; there is no way to save me. I am all consciousness.[46]

The inevitable explosion was only a matter of time.

His articles paid him little or nothing, but they had quickly legitimized his as a voice to be reckoned with. By the next year he was appearing frequently and polemically in the Friuli autonomy group's periodical. He was deeply impatient with the local literary scene, which he found self-satisfied and uninformed. He had to reach farther afield, and he applied a prodigious energy to selling himself and ideas. He would go to Rome, to Uncle Gino, to see if he could make the connections in the literary circles there that would provide a forum bigger than the "little country" of Friuli. Visiting Rome, yes, but there was no talk of moving there.

# 10

*The battlefield of Chaeronea was covered with the bodies of lovers
lying in pairs.*

         —*Lawrence Durrell*, **The Greek Islands**

# THE PARTY'S FOOT SOLDIER
# IN THE GARDEN OF ALCINA

Helping the now apparently mad Fabio Mauri and his distraught sister
Silvana allowed Pasolini to meet Contini at last. The late summer
saw him in the Italian Alps, where Fabio's parents had sent their son
in hopes that, in the peace and beauty of the place, his mania would
pass. But during Pier Paolo's visit to Champoluc—all rocks and
glaciers in the upper valley of the river Evançon, not far from the
Matterhorn—Fabio woke in the middle of the night. Running in the
snow in only his underwear, he hid in a grotto until morning. "I

could see Pier Paolo and a painter named Bobo Piccoli pass below, looking for me," Mauri recalled forty years later, but he kept silent and they returned to base, frantic. The youth, obsessed with religious visions, emerged the next day, and an ambulance returned him to a clinic.

In her anxiety Silvana hugged her friend. "He stiffened, and I think he realized he had to tell me the truth." He left the next day, to call on Contini, and immediately thereafter wrote Silvana a lovingly supportive letter. "I believe you must resign yourself to the thought that Fabio has lost his reason, that is, that he is ill; but immediately following this thought you must have another: that he will be well."

By October Pasolini was back in Rome.

From the capital he reported to Tonuti on October 25: "I have gotten to know people, not works of art. I have met some writers and literary people here, and these encounters bear no resemblance at all to meeting Michelangelo or Piero della Francesca." He also mentioned "the intellectual and social life which, sadly, at Versuta is unattainable." On the strength of Contini's introduction, he met the recognized writer and literary entrepreneur Giorgio Bassani.

At a trattoria called Dino's, he also met literary arbiter Emilio Cecchi, whom he had read at sixteen. Like Paolo Weiss, a "discreet" homosexual of the judgmental stamp, Cecchi (then forty) was an accomplished journalist, literary critic, Anglophile, and the highly praised author of three volumes of essays that Contini called "a cross between Montaigne and Charles Lamb."

He apparently did not mention to Tonuti or to anyone else what Silvana recalled more than forty years after a dinner at which she joined Pier Paolo, Weiss, and Cecchi, "They ignored us completely, as though Pier Paolo and I were not even there. But we laughed it off."

Pier Paolo did recount for Tonuti the discovery of another Rome, the one tourists do not see, one not much mentioned. It was, literally, a descent into a world he would spend much of the rest of his life exploring and reporting:

> Something quite powerful happened to me yesterday. While I was standing on one of the Tiber bridges, waiting for friends (it was night), there came to me the idea of descending the staircase which carried one down to water level. I did it as quickly as I thought of it, and found myself on a patch of mud and sand. It was very dark; I could make out the arches of the bridge over my head and, along the river's length, could make out lamps, an infinite number of lamps. I was about twenty meters below the level of the city and

> its din came muffled to me, as from another world. I really never thought
> that in the heart of a metropolis it was enough to descend a staircase to enter
> the most absolute solitude. . . .
>
> But the strangeness was this, that I did not feel myself near the Tiber of
> today but that of two thousand years before, and I thought I saw, with
> hallucinatory precision, Horatius Cocles swimming across.[1]

He closed with an early glimpse of the love-and-hate relationship
he would always have with the city: "Here people live too much in
the brain and not enough in the heart: The only feeling people have
here is the ambition for a better house, and, in general, greed for
pleasure and money."

He wrote Silvana, asking "scientific" news of Fabio and dodged
her request that he be "true." He explained that that was difficult
for him in letters, that seeing her live, he would be better able to
"be pardoned certain hateful compromises between absolute frankness and a half sincerity." He wished her "very well" but was not
yet able to confess the truth of himself. Instead, like the actor who
knows how the play will end, he left that day to come in its turn,
watching with calm as his nature and that of the world around him
moved toward the confrontation he understood was inevitable.

Back in Casarsa, to celebrate the end of 1946, he published on
its last day "Valid Opinions on Friulian Autonomy," codifying feelings in the air that would lead to the founding of the Popular Movement for Friulian Autonomy the following January. With 1947 poetics
and politics were merging.

By the start of that year, the seams in anti-Fascist unity had burst
and the Communist Party—returned to legitimacy from the illegality
to which Mussolini had banished it—staked its own claims. The
Committee of National Liberation had collapsed, and the Communists
had their own identity and line on every issue. Palmiro Togliatti
returned from his wartime exile in the Soviet Union to head a PCI
intent on becoming a mainstream opposition party, if far from being
in power.

Regional autonomy was out: Now even the organized Left favored
national cohesion. The PCI leadership wanted Rome to be stronger
than the provincial administrations they were sure would stay in the
hands of the DC. They dreamed of someday running a unified country
through a parliamentary and cabinet majority. They did not welcome
a strong Friuli, with its own local, feudalistic power brokers, any
more than a strong Lombardy, Piedmont, Sicily. The Christian Democrats took the opposite side, viewing in the crotchety, stiff-necked
Friulians a solid bulwark against the east.

By an independent route Pier Paolo came to agree with the Christian Democrats' position, the pro-autonomy one, but he wanted it to be espoused by his PCI. He argued that the best buffer against Slavic expansion was a Friuli "conscious of itself, electrified by the dignity conferred on it by right of its clearly differentiated language, customs, and economy." That argument did not prevail. Power blocs in Rome mattered more than the political agendas of poets in the provinces.

As he was expounding his vision for postwar Friuli from Casarsa, he opened an active correspondence with contacts made in Rome. To Ennio de' Concini, editor of the *Fiera letteraria:*

> I hope that your cordiality did not explode completely at one time at the moment of our encounter, but rather that there remains a residual sufficient to accept this letter.

With the guts and bravura of a precocious undergraduate, he offered his new editor a glimpse into his unique mode of sight and expression, recycling as any artist does.

> I must confess that during my brief stay in Rome, the only person I came to know (or rather to recognize) was Horatius Cocles: I saw him swimming across the Tiber, near the Cavour Bridge.[2]

But the letter was about business. "Seeing and considering that the poetry which has appeared until now in the *Fiera* are not masterworks," by way of remedy he forwarded three poems from his *Diarii* series; perhaps De' Concini would consider them? By the end of the following year he was contributing essays on no less a figure than Saint-Beuve. A pattern was set: Pier Paolo's self-assured self-promotion, supported by on-time, bravura delivery.

Back in Casarsa, he drew a great deal and painted. He wrote the catalogue for an exhibition of Paolo Weiss' paintings; Gino and Weiss had the booklet printed under the imprimatur of their gift shop, Editore Piccola Galleria, Roma. It was that easy to be a publisher, just by claiming the name. He wrote a poem called "Europa," and the next year he entered it in competition for the Cesena poetry prize, hoping Montale's presence on the jury would help him (it did not). He also produced another small volume of poems—its imprint his own Academy—entitled *I pianti:* twenty epigraphs on the theme of his grandmother (*nonna*) Giulia's death.

\*    \*    \*

Two years' political struggle separated the plebiscite on the monarchy and the ruthless parliamentary campaign of 1948, Italy's first vote in more than twenty years and its referendum on the Cold War. Now Pier Paolo, a signed-up comrade of the PCI, moved to attack the "establishment" Friulian autonomists as pitiful, ineffectual, rearguard romantics. Viscerally committed to Friulian autonomy, he threw himself into that battle as a way to be a man among men, to bond within community, to overcome his "deserts" and solitude.

But he was an odd political operative, always too romantic. Writing Gianfranco d'Aronco, secretary of the Autonomists' movement, to explain why he missed a meeting, he offered, "At this moment (it might seen gratuitous to you) the bells of San Giovanni are ringing, out of my blue windows I see the mountains and I imagine the sea. Nature is with us, dear D'Aronco."[3]

"Inspiration of Contemporaries" appeared in the *Fiera* in March but only after Pier Paolo wrote his editor to chide him for being long-silent. This was to be a constant friction over the decades and the hundreds of articles in dozens of magazines and newspapers: Pasolini, the ardent contributor, absolutely committed to his writing and publication as an almost sacred duty to educate, versus businessmen-publishers with priorities other than a campaign for their readers' moral salvation and maintenance of a Pasolini platform.

His Gramscian role as vanguard intellectual, bringer of consciousness to the people, seemed clear, and made its demands. He wrote Giovanna Bemporad on January 20, 1947:

> The people are foolish, vile, confused; but there is in them an aspiration, an inferiority complex which can be seen as the residue of an abstract goodness; this is worthwhile, and must not be overlooked by those of us with consciousness.[4]

He urged her to step outside herself, not to find her only solace in poetry. As for his prediction of her answer, that her self-involvement is inevitable and that "the other is always infinitely less important than the I"—this will not do. "It is others who make history." He is determined somehow to be with them in that, to have community, to find brotherhood.

Pasolini, twenty-six and living in Casarsa, was perfectly in step with bigger places and greater themes. A new kind of intellectual was coming to birth across Europe: the "engaged man," *l'homme engagé*. Camus' *La peste* appeared in 1947 and was immediately translated into Italian. Elio Vittorini had joined the Communist Party and was bringing out his magazine *Il politecnico* in Milan. It printed Steinbeck and Saroyan—Leftists even in America!—whose names were on everyone's lips: It seemed that the man of thought and of action could be one; the split between them so ingrained in Italy since the Middle Ages might be healed.

The solution to Pier Paolo's terrible secret was to dissolve his obsessive narcissism into political action; the antidote to Poetry was History. Had not Field Marshal Sir Harold Alexander announced that with war's end Italy was already rehabilitated? Pier Paolo wanted to be at the heart of the generation that made Italy over, and this time the right way, through an idealistic Marxism brought to fruition in the Italian Communist Party. He knew nothing about Stalin's purges. Hungary in 1956 and Czechoslovakia in 1968 were in the future, undreamed of.

The civil war that divided Italy from 1943 through the Armistice also purged a widely shared sense of shame. Italians understood that the regime had gone wrong, but it had been their regime, one they had perhaps not chosen in full awareness but had acquiesced to as the years passed. They understood now that throughout its long life, especially after 1936, they were almost all either enthusiastic or indifferent, but certainly not in active opposition. Mussolini had skillfully exploited the traditional values of Italian life, used local conflicts and power structures, cashed in on fears, reinforced prejudices, and meted out rewards and punishments in such a way that Fascism seemed normal. Their dictatorship had been just that— theirs, home-grown, and their Duce a local boy whom they accepted so long as he made good.

Large numbers emerged from the war convinced that, save for the fatal error of allying with Germany instead of the Allies, the Duce had not been so bad. Some radicals suffered, a few homosexuals, some Jews. This conservative wing of Italian opinion found a home in the many parties on the Right. Within months of the Armistice, Occupation authorities had officially recognized sixty political parties around Naples alone, from monarchist to Bolshevik.

Italy, officially at peace in 1947, was deeply divided: Forty percent voted to keep the king; another sizable minority argued that only they, the Communists, had captured and killed Mussolini and fought the Nazis. In some regions, the Christian Democrats were no more than the old-style front of landowners, industrialists, and clergy; in other areas they were very liberal, blending into the socialists. Liberty brought confusion.

\*   \*   \*

The politician Pasolini did not drive out the poet.

From the wizened heights of his mid-twenties, he wrote Contini, remarking that he has a "tender spot" for the poems of *The Nightingale*, "which represents me at twenty-one and still a virgin," infused with "peasant Christianity" not without "sweet and equivocal sources of heresy." Desperate for the love and approval of an intellectual equal, an older male he could respect, he closed a note to Contini of late January, "I salute you cordially, and, may I say this, with affection, Your Pier Paolo Pasolini."

Contini's response must have seemed, literally, water in the desert. It brought Pier Paolo to a most un-Friulian effusive candor.

> I must confess to you that your letter gave me a moment of cherished joy. By now I owe you so much: you have a decisive role . . . My terror is at not being able to touch delicately enough the apparatus of this friendship, for me something difficult exactly because perhaps too much wanted.[5]

Contini had found a publisher for *The Nightingale*. Pier Paolo also asked, "would [he] do this favor?" Let [Carles] Cardó know that the renamed *Il stroligut* would be out "in a month and a half or two" reconstituted as *Quaderno romanzo*, complete with an anthology of Catalan poetry? This collection called *Fiore di poeti catalani* [Flowers from the Catalan poets] appeared in June, in the third issue of the *Quaderno* (Notebook), proudly described as one of the "Publications of the Academy." And while he is at it, could Contini ask Cardó to contribute an essay on Catalonia, "including discussion of the problem of Friulian autonomy," which Pier Paolo thought analogous?

He had kept a charge account at the Cappelli bookstore in Bologna. Would Cavazza please acquire and forward copies of the magazines *Il ponte*, *Letteratura*, *L'indagine*, *Società*, and *Psychoanalysis*, the last "if it still comes out"?

The week after his twenty-fifth birthday he was preparing a lecture on poetry for the Popular University of Udine, soliciting an essay from Serra for the *Notebook* and studying for a philosophy final exam he had still not taken at Bologna. The next month brought a review of *The Nightingale* in the *Fiera* by the already respected poet Giorgio Caproni and a request to De' Concini—living, as Pier Paolo wrote him, "amidst the perfume of Roman stones"—that he alone choose a book for Pier Paolo's next review. "Here, in the middle of the fields, we do not gather the subtleties necessary for the choosing of books to review."

In his private "Red Notebooks" he took stock.

I am twenty-five . . . but I continue to be an adolescent . . . If my eternal adolescence is a sickness, it is a slight enough one. The hateful side of this is its reverse, that is my contemporary oldness. In other words, the avidity with which, like a kid, I devour the hours dedicated to my existence, while carrying with me a tender and glistening baggage of youth carried into a situation of precocious experience and thus of indifference . . .

We are in 1947: this was the year in which *nature* lost its value for me. Now I am sitting on the shingle-bed of the Tagliamento for the *n*th time; here are the veins of sand running along the endless perspectives of gravel which, climbing upward toward a horizon tinted with a gloomy blue, go to lick the sky . . . None of this is mysterious enough to seduce me anymore: it is as though I had drawn the shapes a thousand times, enough to do so with my eyes closed.

It seemed that he would always live in Casarsa, always be the poet at the periphery. His depression fixed on his relationship with Tonuti.

Everything between me and him happened under the sign of guilt: it is three years since I first saw him on the bridge over the Viersa, two years and a half since, in that [blank] farmhouse, he gave in to me, more than a year since I dared to say that this love was over. Notwithstanding that, I have not lifted a finger to resolve things, to have a moment of chastity which might end up predominating. . . .

He thinks it is love for the boy that keeps him in Casarsa:

That body which walked alongside me, those fields flooded with light, that moon so violent and remote . . . my altruism to T. was simply gratitude . . . He, in fact—what an incredible thing—loved me; it was not a love that was conscious and sensual, but it was at least a sentiment different from the others . . . he is the sole reason I renounced everything, and stayed, spending my days in a village of ten houses.[6]

Silvana came to spend Carnival in Versuta. Almost forty years later she recalled to Nico Naldini:

I took icy trains to reach Casarsa, twelve, twenty hours from Milan. I go off in a field of grass frozen solid, and then in the hot kitchen of his mother at Versuta, two brandies by the fire. By day, drunk with happiness, silly, we raced along the frozen banks of the Tagliamento to get to some tiny parish movie house nearby, or frantically danced (we were tireless and virtuoso dancers) the tango, polkas and the fox-trot at country dances, or we went to follow the processions of the peasants for Carnival (a girl dressed up like a boy, chatting with . . . a boy dressed like a girl), disquieting masks, [going] from house to house to drink wine and eat polenta . . .

> His (Pier Paolo's) homosexuality was still a sweet game among boys, he
> had a little red notebook in his pocket and we played at tearing it away. But
> his face would sometimes suddenly seem devastated with anxiety, following
> the movements of the sweet peasant boys, the young "saplings," as we called
> them among ourselves, the opposite of the "king-trunks" who were like the
> black, gnarled mulberry trees, the black and old peasants.[7]

She was not gone from Casarsa two hours on February 19 when he
wrote to her. He asked that she imagine him in a room with "the
rustle of Carlo Alberto reading his copy of the local *Gazzettino*." He
tells her that he will stay awake until at least ten or eleven, "to keep
you company during your journey home." He writes he is there with
her, in the truck she insisted on hitching a ride in back to Milan: "I
am keeping that Silvana company," she whom he credits, "I do not
know how," with "reawakening the young man in me." Lest he appear
too ardent, sending confusing signals, he retreats: His profession of
intimacy is lightened—"perhaps I'm sleepy," he suggests.

When De' Concini asked why he had not been sent a copy of *The
Nightingale* or *I pianti*, Pier Paolo ever so gently let him know that
he had not wanted to seem to be looking for a review:

> But now that I see you like the book for itself, and not because of me, I am
> very happy to send you a copy—and with a dedication, something I never
> did for anyone before . . . Do not be stunned at these complexes: think that
> I am northern, provincial and "childish." You know, for that review, I
> thought I'd do "Diavolo in corpo" by Radiguet. Would that be alright? I'll
> be in Rome the 15th and 16th, staying with my friend Silvana Mauri, niece
> of Bompiani. I hope we can see one another sometime.[8]

Before the trip to Rome, he had to sit one philosophy exam in
Bologna. On March 10 he returned to find waiting letters and a package from Silvana—a large, illustrated book on German theater, a
thank-you for the Carnival stay. He wrote her:

> Let's talk about Rome. I'll certainly arrive Wednesday the 19th [of March
> 1947] and depart April 2 . . . so I urge you not to arrive later than the 20th!
> Look, I'm sure there will be "divine" days . . . like those at Versuta . . . in
> any case, you will be my *cicerone* (as I am at Versuta)![9]

He reminisces about their time together in such a way that Silvana
might have thought something else could come into their relationship.
Meanwhile, her brother Fabio was largely recovered, scoring a top
mark in an esthetics exam at the university. Giovanna Bemporad,

whom he visited in Bologna, had begun to show eccentric tendencies. He reports to Silvana: "She even wears socks which are usually masculine . . . I think I found her in a state of involution."

During this Roman visit he saw more of Giorgio Bassani. Six years Pier Paolo's senior, Bassani had moved to the capital from his native Ferrara in 1943. Already a published poet, he was collaborating with the American-born Princess Marguerite Caetani on *Botteghe oscure*, a magazine they hoped would relaunch Italy as a cosmopolitan center.

Bassani was established, and he recognized Pasolini's potential. He offered the first of many good turns he did the younger man at crucial moments over the years: to try to find him a real publisher for his poetry, not the local Casarsa print shop and "Academy" imprint, not Contini's ideas; something concrete, which so far had come to nothing.

No wonder Pier Paolo felt half-man, half-boy at twenty-five: In Rome reputable people spoke seriously of finding him a legitimate publisher; at home in Casarsa, Carlo Alberto opened and read his mail.

One day, Carlo Alberto read not only his son's mail but the "Red Notebooks," learning everything they offered about Tonuti, about all the boys. Pasolini, looking back, forgave "the Colonel" as lacking the "moral preparation" to cope with what Pier Paolo called "this enormous disappointment in regard to me." But even that yielded before his sense of selfhood, a "unique sense of destiny" that made him return to the Notebooks—to confess all—even after the integrity of their privacy had been violated. He analyzed his feelings and returned the verdict: no remorse, no guilt, no search for redemption as the world defined it.

From Rome he sent Maldini in Udine the schedule of his week; it reads like Cinderella come to the ball of postwar Roman culture, warming up for the dance:

> Friday, the editor Falqui
> Saturday afternoon, De' Concini
> Saturday evening, a salon with the famous surrealist
>     painter De Chirico present
> Sunday another party, [Giorgio] Caproni present
> Monday, Fabio Mauri arrives; a party at the Saffi
>     household
> Tuesday, his [Fabio's] sister Silvana comes from Milan.[10]

That week he learned that his poem in *friulano* "Vea" (*Veglia*, in Italian), "Vigil," won the All'angelo prize in Venice (awarded by a hotel and restaurant of that name)—40,000 lire and newspaper mentions.

By April 8 he was back in "my Casarsese atmosphere" after a train ride full of church bells and the song of "hundreds of clappers." When the train stopped at Sacile, he experienced an "unpleasant daydream from childhood" associated with the town. At Pordenone, a solitary bell rang. "That bell was accusing me," he wrote Silvana.

He steeled himself for whatever would come, accepting his own nature, even with anguish:

> Adult? Never—never, like existence
> which does not ripen—remaining always green,
> from one splendid day to another—
> and I can only remain faithful
> to the stupendous monotony of the mysterious.
> That is why, in happiness,
> I never let myself go—that is
> why in the anxiety of my guilt
> I never reached a true remorse.
> Equal, always equal with the unexpressed,
> at the origin of that which I am.[11]

The *Fiera* published his *Piccola antologia friulana* on May 22, complete with critical notes, further confirming his rank as a scholarly specialist in the poetry of dialect. The same month he gave himself space in the third issue of the *Notebook* to address "the poetic background" to the Friulian autonomy debates. He also contributed an essay to an anthology of poetry in dialect, edited by the important critic Enrico Falqui and printed by Mondadori.

In June, after three years at Versuta, the Pasolinis and Naldinis had moved back into the spacious three-story house in Casarsa. The room Carlo Alberto had made for the Academy was inaugurated on June 16, dedicated to showing film classics, holding meetings and readings. Pier Paolo wrote Naldini that he expected the Philological Society, seeing competition, to send over a "big torpedo."

A glass-topped display case was installed to exhibit the just-printed third issue of the *Quaderno romanzo*, dedicated to the Catalans. That October and November saw Pier Paolo publish an art review in *Lotta e lavoro,* a short story about the village of Valvasone, outside Casarsa, in the *Messaggero veneto,* other occasional pieces in *Il mattino del popolo* of Udine. He knew the *Messaggero veneto*— "a reactionary newspaper"—to be the voice of the Christian Democrats, and in July he wrote a friend to explain that he did it only for the money, which he had trouble collecting. That September he contributed a short story, called "The Colors of Sunday," and ended his collaboration.

Starting with October and extending through the following year, he contributed regularly to *Il mattino del popolo,* a better publication and with a more upscale readership. Already his frequent art exhibition reviews had spotlighted *pastiche*—the mixing of materials and of levels of expression, high and low—as the technique that drew him most.

In June he published the essay "An Autonomous Friuli" under the pseudonym "Erasmo Colus," a name he used again six months later in *Il mattino del popolo* to sign a piece about his school in far-off Bassa Friuli.

In July he sent Contini "Ciants di un muart," "which I wrote with you in mind as sole reader." Pasolini hoped to see it in print, but publication came only in 1954, in a volume called *La meglio gioventù,* joined with other poems in friulano not written until the next decade.

He confided to the critic that turning twenty-five saw him "in an ugly period." As for the reasons—what Contini called Pier Paolo's "complexes"—the young man replied that "the affection which links me to them is by now an uncurable disease: mortal." He knows "something is wrong" with him, that his obsession with adolescents brings pain, and that he is wed to that pain—in love with fatality. His "complexes," in his own words, are something more than merely habitual.

His prognosis is brutal. Whether he wants to hear it or not, Contini is now told. Pasolini explains that he is the bearer of *"una malattia inguaribile: mortale"* ("an incurable disease: mortal"), the sort of which one dies. He suggests that the fantasy has come to him to go to Venice and *really* die, "as in Mann's book."[12]

Such confessions were, typically, bracketed in an otherwise cheerful letter. Would Contini assist in retrieving a copy of *Nightingale* from the jury that had failed to return it? "Bassani has promised to speak about it to the Astrolabe [publishing house]," with an eye to publication, and Pier Paolo needs the version with updates and insertions. He asks whether, in case it is printed, Contini would accept a dedication "*A Gianfranco Contini con sottile amor de lonh*"—"to Gianfranco Contini, with subtle love from far away"?

The summer of 1947: Nico and Pier Paolo on bicycle outings to *sagre*, village festivals in honor of the local saint's name day. For dancing, wooden planks laid on the fields, light bulbs strung around its perimeter and criss-crossed overhead. Factory-made bulbs were still not to be found, so someone took paint and daubed clear ones, low-voltage, postwar austerity material. The new American music the soldiers brought with them was played by a local band: fox-trots, something called "boogie-woogie," and mazurkas, tunes descended in Friuli from its shared roots with Yugoslavia in Austro-Hungary's gypsy music.

Naldini has recalled:

> After the dancing, which had proceeded with a very sweet tension with very sweet girls, a few of us sat around the tables in the open air drinking while the country night sky cleared. They were the nights when, returning home, with the cold which heightened the effect of the wine, we [a group of boys including Nico and Pier Paolo] did those "mechanical movements" which made us laugh so. . . .
>
> One evening in a village at the lower end of the Tagliamento, a place called Malafiesta—it was already autumn—we were invited by a new friend to come and warm up his new kitchen where a cricket sang in the fireplace. On the way back, eating up the twenty-five kilometers of country and deserted villages, Pier Paolo joked that we would never again be so happy and that we ought to go down to the banks of the river and cut our veins.[13]

He mentioned to Contini in August that he was considering sending *Pagine involontarie* (literally, "Unwilling pages") to the Lugano newspaper *Libera stampa*'s literary prize competition. The novel he planned was to be culled from the "Red Notebooks," merged with parts of the Tonuti story.

But on further consideration he thought better of it and submitted the *I diarii* poems in Italian. The closest he came to printing the confessional novel in his lifetime was *Amado mio*, truncated to short-story length, published in *Il mattino del popolo* on December 11, 1947. *Amado mio* did not appear complete and in book form until 1982, seven years after its author's death, thirty-five after it was written.

*I diarii* did not win a prize, but juror Contini anonymously offered a breathtakingly astute comment:

> It is an admirable fact how Pasolini, dominated by narcissism, even by what the clinicians refer to technically as infantilism, has come progressively to

make this his constant theme, one which would seem not to offer many resources, but in successive approximations offered in various literary modes, poetry in dialect, poetic prose, epigraphs, dramas, technically rich lyrics in particular: from Pascoli to the *crepuscolari* [the school of "twilight" poets] to Saba, and to Penna has found abundance of a not unusual vein.[14]

The politics of regional separatism heated up that summer. The issue had to be sorted out before Italians went to the polls the following April. The opposition made its case that an independent Friuli would starve, that autonomy was, at the least, premature. Pier Paolo wrote a "fairly well-fed and pungent" piece for *Libertà*, which failed to print it.

He was undaunted; his tactic was to ask D'Aronco, as secretary of the Autonomist League, for a list of names and addresses. Pier Paolo would send fifteen parliamentary "honorables" and regional politicians copies of the latest *Quaderno romanzo*. Surely its article "Autonomous Friuli" would sway them. Thus did the poet-professor imagine the workings of politics. The autonomists never stood a chance. While they were busy haggling over the bylaws of their group, the Christian Democrats consolidated ties with the politically astute and active Church.

Silvana wrote in August, reporting a relapse in Fabio and again complaining of Pier Paolo's mysterious silences, his hurting distance. On the fifteenth he answered that the upset he had felt in the past was gone and that "serenity" had returned because he was writing in his "Red Notebooks" "the ferociously private facts about my life, intimate things, the inconfessability of which made me act in a way with you that was so unvirile, so dishonest."

From our very first meetings, you understood there was, behind my friendship, something more but *not too different*; a sympathy which was even tenderness. Remember something more, Silvana, and then you will finally have understood: See us two again in that restaurant in Piazza Vittorio [in Rome], in front of the *calzoni* and recall the heat with which I defended your girl friend, a homosexual. For pity's sake, Silvana, do not become alarmed at this last word: Think that the reality is not in that, but in me and that I am, overall, compensated by my joy, by my joy and curiosity and love for life. All this is to be useful to you in only one respect: to explain to you some of my restraint, my lack of understanding, some of my tentativeness and false innocence which perhaps (I say perhaps) hurt you. . . .

Now, Silvana, willing or not, you have entered the tiny circle of my vital confidence, in the small room of my "I"; and now I can direct toward you all the goodwill I want to, without feeling the confusion of a child caught in the act . . . remember that, at bottom, this letter means nothing: I am in fact the same as you saw in Bologna, in Macugnaga, here, in Rome . . . when can we meet? Yes, at last, we can speak, speak of it until we are crazy. Oh how you must have hated that Pier Paolo who lied to you with his silences, standing in front of the chimneypiece in Macugnaga, while you put your fingers in hot water, seized by the vitality of your words! This will not happen again.[15]

Almost forty years later Silvana, long since married to the writer and editor Ottiero Ottieri, wrote Pasolini's cousin Nico:

How did it happen that I, a middle-class girl, without dialect, without peasant roots, heterosexual, and he, by then completely caught up in the poetry of Casarsa, maternal, inexpert in the world, afraid of people he did not know, always contrite at his "unknown interior," with his strong, brilliant mentality, of a studious student, homosexual, came to follow one another for our lifetimes, wrote to one another, told stories, met, when it seems hardly possible and inside his life there was always more which separated him from mine, [he] frantic with work, with a thousand other encounters, with persecutions and provocations? Re-reading his letters, now I understand. Beside his mother, the sole love of his life, but a fixed figure and symbolic, crystallized in the childhood and out from which he always projected an infantile innocence, I was the place of his "vital confidence," the red thread of total acceptance.[16]

She was not the only one to whom he wanted to confess. A few days after this letter he wrote Contini, enclosing the preface to *Pagine involontarie*. The preface is a long apology for "a perhaps indiscreet sincerity." Contini's reaction is unknown, but the rest of the book went back in the drawer for the rest of Pasolini's life.

In October Contini published a critical essay, "Project for a Portrait of Niccolò Tommaseo," in the *Fiera letteraria*. Tommaseo (1802–74) was the author of a pioneering work on poetry in dialect, *Popular Songs of the Tuscans, Corsicans, Illyrians, and Greeks*, published in 1841–1842: It is the volume Pasolini carried to the Tagliamento, squeezed under his arm, to read while awaiting Bruno.

Contini, in rediscovering the philologist, provided Pasolini with a model not only for his project for turning *Il stroligut* into a magazine of Romance literature, but more. When Pasolini himself became a critical anthologist of Italian poetry in dialect, he worked with Tommaseo literally and figuratively at his side. No wonder he wrote Contini that he had read his study "in bed, but had to get up to keep my heart from beating so hard, and walk up and down in the room."

On the seventh of that month, he made this entry into his red-covered diary:

> Last night some boys from Versuta, my friends, came twice to get me, and not finding me went ahead without me to Rosa. I was at the Casarsa station to see off two friends, the poet Menichini and the painter Zigaina, who had come to spend Sunday with me.
>
> I dined quickly, rinsed off the dust and went down to the courtyard where T. and Alfredo, forgotten by their buddies, were waiting for me. We left together for the festival at Rosa. I was in one of my joyous states, when I put myself into a world that seems made specially for me, the metallic night with a moon which undid the darkness with its pink liquids, the long street vibrating under the whiteness of dust—I spoke joyously with T.[17]

Tonuti described his feelings at seeing the stalls of the sweets-makers who came every year to town for the festival of the Madonna in San Giovanni. Pier Paolo asked why he didn't write a poem? "He was confused, and answered, I think: 'I am not capable, it doesn't work for me.' But I reassured him, telling him that after myself and my cousin [Nico] he was the best poet in Friuli. We all laughed; I hope T. understood that I was telling the pure truth."[18]

Pier Paolo was exhilarated at the crowd, for like the crowds in the Roman slums and, later, in Morocco and Yemen, it let him lose himself for a while and shake off the sense of separateness. He noted the platform, dancing and whirling around, the boys sitting together at the sidelines, taking it all in, excitement in their eyes. "There, mixed in with the crowd, but alone, I saw a boy, whom I barely noticed, the first time he passed by, dancing. At the second pass, he conquered me. I would have said he was a foreigner, a Roman or (my unbridled imagination) one from Syracuse."[19]

Pier Paolo watched while the boy took a seat, waited until a friend at his side moved on, and approached the "one from Syracuse." Now the boy felt threatened, although Pier Paolo's interpretation is all based on gesture, silence.

About this time he wrote in his "Red Notebooks":

> I am tired of being so very exceptional, out of the rules: all right, my liberty I have found, I know what it is and where it is; I know, and could have said so from the age of fifteen, even more . . . In the development of my individuality, of my diversity, I was precocious; it did not happen to me to cry out, like Gide, one day "I am different from the others"; I always knew it.[20]

He decided he could not question anymore or seek acceptance or "authorization." Instead, he determined to live and let the "horrible horizontality of life" resolve his doubts within living itself. He wrote: "I close all this, for I have passed, after a brief visit to Calvary, out of the orchard of infamy into the garden of Alcina, and find that there I am well."[21]

In Ariosto's *Orlando Furioso,* Alcina is carnal pleasure personified, a kind of sorceress who makes love in her garden of enchantment and then turns her paramours into beasts, stones, trees.

Pier Paolo began almost nightly outings in search of boys, sometimes with cousin Nico but usually alone. They went as far as Codroipo and to the movies at Castions. Pier Paolo was excited at the frisson of boys and girls looking at one another; he spoke frequently of the boys' hair, for him the seat of all sexuality. Intimate with Nico because of their shared secret, he talked about the boy he'd seen at a dance, named Angelo, and how he wanted to help him become a painter.

That fall, he was hired as the combination language and literature teacher in the middle school at Valvasone, a country dependency of the main school at Pordenone. He made the daily ride of six kilometers round trip by bicycle in the company of a fellow teacher, Sergio Vacher.

Years later his co-worker recalled spending long hours with him every day, utterly unaware of his "tendencies" although struck by the way Pasolini spoke of homosexuality as something quite normal.[22]

The principal was a progressive, sensitive man named Natale de Zotti; he spotted in Pasolini a natural teacher. A *maestro mirabile*, he called him, one ready and able to manage a classroom with unheard-of student participation, open experimentalism, along lines of the newly influential Carleton Washburne and John Dewey. Pasolini taught Italian literature and grammar, and he coached soccer. According to poet Andrea Zanzotto:

> Pasolini made a small garden in the courtyard of the school and taught the Latin names of the plants; he drew posters with colored figures . . . and invented fables like that of the monster *Userum,* so that the children would have a good time learning the endings of the substantives of the second declention, *-us, -er, -um.*[23]

As usual, he was devoted to his students and they obviously so to him. A photo shows him posed before the school's front door: he, handsome, meticulously dressed, serious to the point of fierceness; they in hand-me-downs from older brothers, short pants showing wear, scuffed shoes.

Decades later, two of his students published a "Souvenir of Pasolini":

> It was early in October of that long-ago 1947. In the lower classes of the middle school of Valvasone there entered a young teacher; he called everyone to order and introduced himself: he was the professor of letters and he was named Pier Paolo Pasolini.
>
> We thought he could not be rich, because every day, in the dark and the bad weather, he did twelve kilometers on a bicycle from nearby Casarsa, where he lived and where he returned for lunch.
>
> That modest bicycle was his trusty companion for all of the two years he stayed with us, even when one saw around the first motorcycles and the first scooters. For those two years, we were the richest and luckiest students in all of Friuli. Slowly, step by step, he led us onto the vast steppes with Anton Chekhov, full of solitude and of sadness. He made us know . . . the tragic world, brimming with the humanity of Verga's Sicily. With him we crossed the Atlantic to pause, touched and thoughtful, in the little cemetery in Spoon River, and then we went down to the Deep South of the United States to warm ourselves with Negro spirituals. He made us love Ungaretti, Saba, Montale, Sandro Penna, Cardarelli, Quasimodo and many other poets who, back then, were not the Nobel prizewinners they were to be, who did not even appear in the school anthologies which were all full of Leopardi, Carducci, Pascoli, D'Annunzio.
>
> He was a marvelous reader, and we remained for hours at a time entranced, hearing him. He taught us to recite, to paint, to play soccer.[24]

With 1947 the good maestro of Valvasone took out official, card-carrying membership in the minuscule PCI cell at San Giovanni di Casarsa: its members could gather in one small room. The younger men sat around listening to old Communists talk, men who, before Fascism, had dared to occupy the local landowners' fields, to be driven out by police after a few hours. They had seen hope in a Popular Front that was moving across Europe, bringing socialism; young people, in France and in Holland, in Italy and in England, were consumed with eagerness for something to happen, something better than the system that had thrown Europe twice in this century into war.

That dream had collapsed in world war, and now the PCI seemed the only possibility, the Action Party having evaporated, the Autonomists incapable of more than shoptalk among themselves. San Giovanni was more radical than nearby Casarsa; here, and even more so at San Vito a mile away, were poor field hands, tenant farmers, and even some factory workers. Casarsa was dominated by small land-holders of ardent Catholic faith and concomitant conservative politics.

To Pier Paolo the situation in the plains around Casarsa was clear: the Communists stood for the have-nots, the ordinary people exploited for centuries, the speakers of the dialects he loved, the fathers and brothers of the boys he loved. The rich were the Christian Democrats, allied with the Church: They were the former Fascists suddenly be-come democrats, the sort approved of by Carlo Alberto. And they were hypocritical practitioners of a religion that labeled him a sinner bound for hell.

In 1971 he addressed those who wondered how he had brought himself to join the party of those who had conducted the massacre at Porzus. For decades, remarks had appeared like those of *Il secolo d'Italia* in 1960: "Pasolini, Marxist writer, took up the ideas and defends the system of those who massacred his brother."

But Pier Paolo had decided that Guido had been the victim of an historical accident, a tragic but unique case:

> I think there can be no Communist who would disapprove of the actions of the partisan Guido Pasolini. I am proud of him, of his generosity, of his passion, which compel me to follow the path I do. That his death occurred as it did, in a complex situation that is difficult to judge, causes me no hesitation. It only goes to confirm in me the conviction that nothing is simple, nothing happens without change and suffering, and that what counts above all is critical lucidity which destroys words and conventions and goes to the bottom of things, inside their secret and inalienable truth.[25]

The idea that struck intellectuals of Pasolini's generation with the power of a gunshot was that their work was also a form of labor, their contribution socially useful and not simply diversion, decoration, and entertainment. It was an idea Visconti brought back from France, the vision Pasolini found in the field hands of San Vito, one explained in Marx and Italian theorists Piero Gobetti and above all Antonio Gramsci.

Crucial to legitimizing politically atheistic Marxism in the Catholic Mediterranean was the Resistance: In that struggle, the Left argued, it had proved itself to be patriotic, nationalistic, trustworthy. Here Pasolini's personal drama intersected with history. Communists had murdered his brother, and yet their party—if it stayed true to its humanistic roots in the early Marx (whom he knew only superficially but had read)—offered the sole consistent hope for decency and a just civilization in a country that had passed too fast from feudalism to Fascism, from one set of Bourbons and henchmen to another.

Pier Paolo had never read Lenin or seen a reliable press report on life in the Soviet Union. He knew little of dialectical materialism, the dictatorship of the proletariat, and nothing at all of Stalin's Gulag. He knew that the Italian home-grown version of Gramscian Communism was nativist, populist, seemed democratic and—above all—was willing to do something new, break out of business as usual. He fused his love of the peasantry, or at least the ecstatic estheticism that loved the idea of the downtrodden, with this Gramscian national Communism. Out of a mix of local cultural aspiration, idealism, and substantial anguish came his commitment to the Communist Party of the immediate postwar years and its program.

He expected that Party to be loyal to the humanitarian ideals expressed in the prison writings of Antonio Gramsci, and when he thought it strayed, he reprimanded it.

In 1926 Mussolini had trumped up charges against Gramsci, a member of Parliament, and put him before a so-called Special Tribunal for the Defense of the State. The kangaroo court did its work. By the time he came to sentencing in June 1928, he had been in detention eighteen months and was in declining health.

Only in 1933, in response to a public international outcry, was he moved to a private clinic, still behind bars. Just as the order for his provisional release was signed, he died in April 1937. Mussolini, smart enough to respect a worthy adversary, had said, "We must prevent his brain from functioning for twenty years."

Instead, the imprisoned man produced thirty-three "notebooks," some two thousand pages of history and theory. When his "Intellectuals and the Organization of Culture," written in his prison cell, was first printed in 1949, it marked a revolution among Italians. He offered artists and thinkers a role that was not that of propagandist but a respected slot in the ranks with the proletariat, not just adornments at modern courts and Church.

Pasolini was so committed to this vision after the war that when contemporaries spoke of art for art's sake, he answered with such seemingly populist preachings that they accused him of "neo-Zhanovianism," named after the art-only-for-the-State socialist realism of Stalin's heavy-handed minister of culture. The "classic" Pasolini was already—even while still in Friuli—here in all his "difficulty": When the Fascist state tried to enlist art in its service, he used *Il setaccio* to argue for freedom of thought. After the war, when intellectuals were almost all on the Left and working to be more committed and more conformist-than-thou, again he took the individualistic line. He was, at once, as noisome to the Right as to the Left, to the Left as to the Right. In passionately divided Italy, being in between—the gadfly, the balance wheel—is a most vulnerable place to be. As conformity of the Left became the style of "enlightened" opinion, Pasolini reacted by refusal. He would join the Communists, yes, but would feel free to lecture them on human rights, the evils of party discipline; to the most doctrinaire among them, this poetic fellow in San Giovanni di Casarsa must have seemed too awfully spiritual (if not something worse) to be a reliable comrade.

The great powers debated the Truman Doctrine and a triumphant Christian Democracy toyed with land reform. In almost forgotten San Giovanni di Casarsa, residents awoke on Saturday mornings to find wall placards, hand-daubed posters, glued to the walls of the village's Renaissance loggia, next to the church. They were often in both *friulano* and Italian, and written with a noticeable skill of language and style. As the Allies were debating partitioning Greece and Berlin was being divided, Pier Paolo took wax crayon to wrapping paper to argue with the statesmen.[26]

A typical placard, one neatly lettered onto an oversize page, read:

> The satisfactions of a fool.
>
> Two men were talking in the courtyard of a house. One said it was better not to get involved in politics and let the world go on as it had to since it had always been this way and always would be, the bosses always existed and always would, and so on and so forth.
>
> The other lost patience and said, "We communists don't think like that. One shouldn't let oneself be led by the nose by those who have done so thus far. It's time to put a stop to it!"
>
> And the first answered, "At least we have freedom." And the other: "What freedom? To die of hunger?" And the first, "And why not? I may be dying of hunger but I can go to De Gasperi and tell him "you are an idiot." 
>
> Replied the communist: "These are the satisfactions of a fool."[27]

He discovered himself to be "a political man . . . without my having realized it," and threw himself into full realization of the role. To the rather grim comrades huddled close for reassurance in the Christian Democratic northeast, this too-articulate fellow traveler was something of a loose cannon. He went around talking of what "we Communists" ought to believe, as though, even without card-carrying membership for a year, he had been appointed their spokesman. He did not even check with them before writing his placards for the church loggia. And he came into the Party for his own reasons, which he stated years later: "What made me a Communist was the Friulian farm-workers' struggle against the owners of the large estates and farms immediately after the war."[28]

Versuta, paradise to Pier Paolo, proved a nightmare for Carlo Alberto. He returned from his Kenya POW camp to the kitchen, keeping house while his wife and son taught school. He brought back in his suitcase Pier Paolo's *Poesie a Casarsa*, in the dialect he dismissed and with the dedication the poet dismissed in 1966 as "made out of conformity."

He was hurt that Susanna kept her physical distance and Pier Paolo distanced him with silence. As for the neighbors, they were simply beneath him, as were his own in-laws with whom he lived at close quarters.

Increasingly, "the Colonel" found it best to lose himself in a liter of white wine at the local *taverna*. At night, under the wine's influence and the burden he felt at life's betrayals, he raged, pounded his fists, shouting until more than once Susanna fled the house or ran crying into the bedroom, locking the door behind her.

Pier Paolo once went so far as to summon a psychiatrist from Udine: Carlo Alberto literally threw him out.

In January 1948 Pier Paolo wrote Serra: "[I am] almost seized by an avid, Dionysian happiness—save that I am always worried about the physical, and even more the psychological, condition of my father."[29]

By August he commented to Serra, "Believe me, there are no words to describe certain situations which come about in our house during my father's moments of crisis."[30]

That month he began regular and soon frequent contributions to the Venetian *Il mattino del popolo*: His short stories, art criticism, ideological essays (like "The Two Proletariats" in the May issue) appeared throughout that year. Carlo was proud: His son's name in print represented both income and, above all, status. Teaching at Valvasone provided what Pier Paolo called "substantial amusement," and publishing an outlet for deeply felt convictions.

Evenings went to "the usual life of obsessive joys," and there were "radiant Sundays." His life was full, if split: a public one of participation, commitment, and growing public leadership, a private one mounted on a time bomb.

Naldini has recalled, "We never used the word 'homosexuality' until Pier Paolo one day told me he had discovered it a few years before. It seems a schoolmate had told him about Oscar Wilde, who had written a love letter to a boy and ended up in jail." Cousin Nico, so often the lesser in family comparisons to Pier Paolo, also recalls of those first years after the war, "I was jealous of him. I had a lot of friends and we would play together in the courtyard of the house. After about the age of ten, some of them became very handsome and I loved them from afar. Pier Paolo, instead, secretly kissed them."[31]

The feelings and behavior had no name, other than *amicizia*, friendship. Decades after the world did have names, and Pasolini was well known for his homosexuality, even Tonuti denied that his friend was homosexual.

Europe's boundaries were still fluid in 1947: Many (including the U.S. State Department) thought Italy and, later, Greece might have joined either NATO or the Comintern. Eastern Europe—right up to Italy's border, a tram ride from downtown Trieste—had disappeared behind what Churchill dubbed the Iron Curtain. The most important reading in Washington was George Kennan's article (signed "X") in *Foreign Affairs* magazine, calling for "containment" of the Soviets. The West was not prepared to see the landings in Sicily and Anzio, the slaughter of the U.S. Thirty-sixth Infantry Division, and the huge Allied casualties at Monte Cassino serve to liberate Italy from the Germans only to pass it to Communist Italians in Moscow's service. The Cold War was born before the end of the hot one: Free Polish troops finally took hill 593 at Monte Cassino, but the very day the Abbey fell, Stalin took Poland.

The battle lines quickly set: Italy was either to have a capitalist U.S.-oriented, conservative regime looking to the Holy See on matters of public morality or a government of the Left, presumably dominated by Communists, suspected of taking cues from Moscow. The stakes were the highest possible for 45 million people crammed into an area smaller, and less arable, than California.

At a memorial ceremony for Guido and the others killed at Porzus, Pier Paolo rose to speak. He called them martyrs and said that they had "an incorruptible goodness." Then he attacked the peace treaty

Italy was asked to sign, one he thought unjust because Italy would lose part of its territory. He said, too, there was also spirituality—even in Communists—and argued that this humanity was inherent "even in the worst of men."

The De Gasperi administration had issued the necessary decrees for land reform as early as the end of 1945, but so powerful was the opposition, so divisive the subject, that implementation had not started two years later. The Allied administration and the centrist-Right coalition cabinet agreed that agricultural reform, perhaps even forced land distribution, were necessary to revive the economy. On the industrial side where the minority of Italians made their living, production at war's end was at 23 percent of its 1938 level. The government decreed a restructuring of the distribution of the proceeds from crop sales: it gave 55 percent to the sharecropper, 40 percent to the landowner, and 5 percent into a fund for agricultural stock-piles. It was dubbed the *Lodo* [meaning "award" or "arbitration"] *de Gasperi*. As expected, the holders of large estates vowed to fight what they perceived as pure Communism: in Tuscany, they simply refused to obey. In Friuli, where people keep emotions pent up until explosion, matters were even worse.

The law also called, in a general fashion, for the unemployed (now grown to alarming numbers) to be hired. In Friuli, with high unemployment, two years had been long enough to wait. On the morning of January 7, 1948, summoned by the parties of the Left and labor unions, three thousand people gathered in San Vito and began to agitate. The landlords offered to hire 120 unemployed men and pay 4 percent compensation for land improvements provided by the government. The local labor council demanded that 600 be hired and compensation be paid at 50 percent. Negotiations began and faltered; a court in Udine decided that the government orders only covered a fifth of Friuli, and large areas would receive negligible benefits. Soon workers struck their own deals with official agricultural agencies; it looked as though more workers would be hired than originally agreed to by the owners' association.

Then, on January 28, a committee representing the workers went to confront the owners of an estate at Rota, just outside Casarsa. No one answered; they entered and were furious to find the absentee landlords away and only a cat and a dog to greet them. Suddenly the police appeared in force, backed by the army. A few demonstrators helped themselves to *il padrone*'s precious sugar, which they ate with their bare hands straight from the larder. By January 30, officials had been sent from Udine: the crowd had swollen to five thousand.

All the fears of a Red Terror's seizure of private property seemed concrete in a hundred screaming women who drove off the police with scratches and kicks. Barricades went up, an occupation began, and quickly the administrators of the estate agreed to the demands and the police withdrew. It was a tiny incident in a faraway province, but of enormous symbolic potential, charged with emotion.

Subsequent demonstrations occurred in Cordovado, and this time the police beat some demonstrators. The occupation of the Villa Rota at San Vito led to legal charges; thirty were tried, twenty-two convicted of matters such as theft (they had broken into the house), the taking of a shirt, an old pair of socks.

Pier Paolo had watched the scuffles from the village piazza, and talked—rather as an investigative reporter—to the participants between waves. They were the boys he knew, today wearing red kerchiefs tied around their necks. Pier Paolo took it as the stuff for a novel. He first called the work-in-progress *The Days of the Lodo de Gasperi*, then *La meglio gioventù* (The better youth) and finally *Il sogno di una cosa* (The dream of something). His friend Franco Fortini had cited the phrase in January 1962; Pasolini wrote and asked for the source. Fortini, researching in his *Marx, Engels, Lasalle: Works* of 1914 ("dirtied and burned by the bombardment of '43"), found the line in a September 1843 letter of the twenty-five-year-old Marx to Ruge from Kreuznach, discussing the making of a new magazine:

> Our motto must therefore be: reform of consciousness not by means of dogmas but through the analysis of consciousness which is not clear to itself or presents itself in religious or political forms. It will then be clear that the world has for long had a dream of something. . . .[32]

Pier Paolo embroidered the facts of that day into a narrative with invented characters and dialogue never said, or at least imperfectly recalled. He made a docudrama, a nonfiction novel, long before the terms were current. And it was pessimistic: The dream always remains a dream. In the retelling of the events, as in life, the workers' revolution fails.

With the uprising as background, Pasolini told the story of several boys, protagonists named Nini Enfant and Mario ("Milio") Bortolus (who had "eyes that looked like blue crystal") and Eligio Pereisson ("burning eyes . . . like two pieces of glass"). When they met,

> It was from that moment that they loved each other. Now, after the first words, a kind of enthusiasm, of warmth, began to come into their talk that

made everything beautiful: the idea of going to drink a glass, which was the
most commonplace one they could have had at that moment, felt amazing to
them . . . they laughed as if they were laughing between themselves for
very special reasons, while the young people around them had to listen in
wonder.[33]

After the fair, they bicycled to Eligio's house, ate polenta, drank
more, and talked. "When the flask was finished Milio and Nini took
leave of Eligio. He accompanied them to the door of the courtyard.
'Goodbye, Eligio!' shouted Nini, 'goodbye, keep well.' But when they
had taken a few steps, he turned back. 'No—I want to give you a
kiss,' he said. 'Come here!' Eligio laughed and offered his cheek.
'No, on the mouth, damn it,' said Nini, 'we must kiss on the mouth.'
They kissed, mimicking two lovers. 'Goodbye, Eligio,' the two of
them shouted as they rode off on their bicycles."[34]

The "revolution" consisted in the boys Nini, Milio, Eligio, and
Jacu who entered the mansions of the absentee landlord counts of
Spilimbergo and "sat on the velvet armchairs" and after that relieved
the cellars of "sacks of sugar and flour for which their poor mothers
in Ligugnana and Rosa blessed them."[35]

But the police came in an armored car from Pordenone and the
"boys of the [Communist] Pioneers inside the villa from being besieg-
ers became besieged." The ironclad vehicle, one of Interior Minister
Mario Scelba's *celere*, knocked down a wall and was only kept from
advancing by the village women who lay down in front of it, shouting
at the police, "Go on, go on, if you have the courage, sons of dogs."
The estate administrator accepted the workers' conditions, "then each
one pedaled lightheartedly home because of the famous victory."

When a riot began, "suddenly there appeared, coming down the
Avenue of Remembrance from Casarsa four or five army trucks full
of soldiers." The local Section boss "pushed his cap back on his
head" and called the retreat. The uprising was over; the "dream of
something" was to remain only that.

Deeply disillusioned that the newly free and republican Italy's
government sent police against them, some of the boys decided to
emigrate. Only in Yugoslavia, they thought, would their socialist
dream come true. But no sooner did they cross the border than they
were imprisoned and then made into virtual slave laborers. Eligio's
health broken by tuberculosis, they returned to Friuli: "We've seen
some bad times at home, but we never dreamed of hunger like this."

Pasolini found the narrative did not come as easily as poetry. He
labored on the manuscript throughout 1948 and 1949, interviewing

participants and others. Every detail he could wring from the real Peresson (Pasolini renamed him only slightly) went into the book. And the real Archimede Bortolus, who had emigrated to a Swiss village, returned to find Pier Paolo importuning him to write a résumé of his experience, down to details like "a fine little tarred road surrounded by fruit-trees" at Cressier. It became a chapter five, about "Milio's" misadventures in the Swiss village of Salvenach.

The neo-realistic chronicle of the struggle against the rich left room for a lovingly detailed rendition of place by the elegiac Pasolini. When the door of the workers' clubhouse is left open, "a rectangle of melancholy yellow light sizzled on the mud." When one of the peasant girls tries on a new red dress, it "was almost dazzling" and when a boy, now grown up enough to work in the Mangiarotti factory, hovered in hopes of meeting her, it was in the midst of "frozen fields, which were almost black in spite of the last flaming beams of the sunset way across the plain."

The boys' lives are Pier Paolo's life: trips to the riverside, dancing on Sunday, pissing together into a ditch ("giving it water," they called it), an occasional tragedy. Interwoven into the plots of the 1948 and 1949 drafts, "duly varnished" (as he later wrote) for publication— but omitted in the finally printed version of 1962—are the stories of a priest who organized programs for kids after school and a militant Communist woman, a young intellectual presumably based on Pina Kalz and/or Giovanna Bemporad—one who writes Sunday wall posters calling on the peasantry to make revolution, mounting her work in the public square on behalf of the PCI cell to which she belongs.

Pier Paolo assigned the teacher-priest a homosexual passion for one of his students; to Renata the militant (in the first draft, Renato) he gives political idealism and a complicated relationship with the priest, based on their commitment to the need for faith in one or the other of Italy's two religions, the Roman Catholic or the Marxist.

In his first drafts, Pasolini's Renata and the priest are wooden, symbolic cutouts. He eliminated them in the final draft, as well as extraordinary passages like the one in which Don Paolo discovers the public urinals: The priest discovers that men gather to urinate against a marble slab, partly concealed from view, private and yet public, a place of anonymous meeting where furtive glances and pretended indifference fool no one.

Don Paolo is—like his creator—an idealistic teacher, who contends that "only he who loves can teach." He must give of himself but carefully; he must attend to the nuances, attentive to the line between exciting a student's affection and slipping into sexuality.

> I've noticed how much better the youngsters of the people are than those of
> the bourgeoisie. They are better because purer to themselves, and they are
> the victims . . . while the young people of the bourgeoisie, in getting older,
> will improve, their minds strengthened against decay and regression, those
> of the people, as adults, will become increasingly nonentities.

But research and writing of the book were interrupted: The months
between the San Vito incident in January and the April 18 general
election demanded his attention for making speeches in village
squares, writing wall posters, encouraging the faithful, and recruiting
new adherents. The spring was given over to political militancy.

Activist Pasolini grew frustrated with the MFP (Movimento Popolare Friulano). When a special insert about the group appeared in
the biweekly newspaper *Patrie del Friul,* he wrote D'Aronco, "Naturally, I don't like it." He took the occasion (February 25) as excuse
to resign from membership.

About that same time he wrote to Silvana, "The doctors say my
father is paranoid." He used the same term to describe Carlo Alberto
in a letter to Contini.

What could not be tolerated by a reading public was the manuscript
Pier Paolo finished now, in secret: *Amado mio,* the long story that
grew out of the "Red Notebook" entries of 1947 and before. It consisted of seventy-five type-written pages, four chapters, single-
spaced, and was headed "An unfinished novel."

*Amado mio* is a "coming-out" *Bildungsroman,* a barely disguised
confession of the love of a provincial schoolmaster for one of his male
students, set against a background of wartime shortages, the smell
of mud, the sound of enemy aircraft, the bravura and hysteria of "love
among the ruins." Written in a highly charged poetic prose, it follows
a first-person narrator—a Latin teacher in a country middle school—
as he tries to conjugate verbs and decline nouns amid Allied attacks,
Nazi bombardments, and reprisals.

The narrator, Desiderio, is in love with a thinly disguised Tonuti,
but the adoration is, like Pier Paolo's, not a source of contentment
but "an invisible monster." The plot turns on the teacher's effort to
elicit love in return from the boy. The narrator–Pier Paolo recalls
exactly how it was on a Sunday morning when some of his students
stopped by his house after Mass, how he was seated on a windowsill,
"wearing a green jacket over my shoulders" and spotted the boy
[Tonuti] "with his little boy's socks, his blousy shirt, his golden and
pale complexion, those eyes. . . ."

*Amado mio* was the escape valve for Pier Paolo's longing for Tonuti, a place to pour out on paper his desire for boys, to name the ache of not freely and openly acting on his nature. He made himself into Desiderio, "his name is desire itself," in love with a younger boy; Desiderio is rejected, then granted a kiss, then rejected again.

A courtship ensues: The desired boy kisses, then runs, seductive as Thomas Mann's Tadzio. Finally, the boy refuses and Desiderio lives his dejection. The story seems to end there, as a homosexual tale presumably ought—with failure, the older "corruptor" rebuffed. But Pasolini merely paused at the downturn, on the way to a happier ending. The boys go to an open-air country cinema on the Venetian laguna at Caorle, where a makeshift film screen is a sheet stretched between trees under the stars, beneath a benevolent sky, such a sky as Pier Paolo wanted to believe smiles on all forms of love.

Desiderio is "a single aching wound" as the film comes on: Gilda. Made in 1946 and set in that year, it was released the year Pasolini wrote, 1949. (The book is set in May 1946.) The star of "the most beautiful film Desiderio had ever seen" is Rita Hayworth. She croons a ballad called "Amado mio." She is sultry and alluring, and her midriff shows.

The images on the screen transform the younger boy's feelings and turn Desiderio's despair into hope.

> Before the image of Gilda something wondrously shared enveloped all the spectators. The music of *"Amado mio"* was devastating. So much so that obscene remarks shouted across the audience—"Watch out your buttons don't pop!" and "How many times you gonna do it tonight?"—seemed to merge in a rhythm in which time seemed finally to be assuaged, to grant a respite with no happy ending.[36]

His descriptions are exact: Hayworth's breasts are of a certain kind, the unexpected analogy, her gaze is both ironically called "near-sighted" and morally labeled "cold and tender," something at once "mysterious" and "stupid." Hayworth is giant Woman, literally filling the screen. The camp dialogue of a plot set in wartime Buenos Aires culminates when Hayworth, the pampered but frustrated wife, breaks out. In rebellion against convention, she seizes the floor of her husband's nightclub and launches a sultry rendition of "Put the Blame on Mame."

Hayworth-Gilda shimmies a bit, steps around the floor, tosses her mane, and moves her very white shoulders inside her lustrous gown. As sexy as any postwar film figure to appear in Italy, she is both Madonna and whore as she removes her two long gloves very slowly, tossing them to the crowd. By the time she has finished her song, she is still dressed and yet seems disrobed.

Gilda served to excite the younger boy, the target Tonuti. After her striptease, he can hardly be blamed if, confused and aroused, he accepts release where he can find it. By film's end Desiderio is "rewarded": His beloved whispers "tonight." Out of the lyricism of Pasolini's factual description comes this corny ending. The incidents and feelings in the novella come almost straight from the "Red Notebooks"; Desiderio's birthday is, like Pier Paolo's, March 5; he, too, has a brother killed in the war, named Guido. The story's protagonist is one of the students who meet in a building in the fields, sometimes in the open air; the teacher instructs his class in the Friulian popular *villotte* and rehearses them for performance.

He creates a character called Dina, transparently based on Pina Kalz. She falls in love with Desiderio, understands his fixation on his students, and warns against it. She wants, as the narrator explains with some surprise at the futility of her errand, "to save me." They discuss the matter, and she withdraws (just as Pina did, returning to Yugoslavia forever).

Pasolini sometimes wrote as though with a pen dipped in self-hatred and remorse. The boys are "angels" and he "a sole devil" among them; Desiderio also imagines boys calling after him, "Shameful, shameful," and he feels all eyes are on him.

And there is the book's cinematic touch:

> That March was cold, restless. In the market there was a merry-go-round and some shacks thrown up temporarily for the village's saint's day. Evening fell. In an atmosphere that suggested a coming storm, I wanted to go and look at this squalid event . . . I recall all this with a specific and painful spasm (which then transformed itself into a false and hysteric joy) at finding myself in the midst of so many charming and distracted boys.

Sunday is the worst day, "with all its boredom we know," for then he walks about and sees those he craves staring at him "with insolent irony." The protagonist, mirror of his maker, is also certain that a boy with blond hair whom he met on the way to San Lorenzo plans to tell someone how he had been offered something "obscene, unnameable, forbidden." There is danger of being exposed, his secret revealed, brought to public shame.

# 11

*I am a teacher of behavior.*

*—Bertolt Brecht*

*. . . in the midst of the Aeneases who carry their Anchises on their backs, I pass from one shore to another, alone, hating these invisible parents astride their sons for all their life.*

*—Jean-Paul Sartre,* Les mots

# SAINT SABINA'S DAY IN RAMUSCELLO

As Pier Paolo turned twenty-four in 1946, Toscanini returned from exile and reopened La Scala. The Nuremberg trials convened to pass the justice of the victors on twenty-one of the vanquished. Italians started using "Am-lire" ("Am" for "Allied Military"), Occupation-issued paper money with Roosevelt's Four Freedoms listed on the back (in English only); they brought always less on the black market, where prices by 1946 and 1947 reached eleven times their prewar level. On June 2, 1946, a still shell-shocked populace voted Umberto

II (dubbed the May King) off his throne. Forty years later he still refused to abdicate and the Italians refused to bury him with his ancestors in the Pantheon.

What counted most in January 1947 was the visit by coalition Prime Minister Alcide de Gasperi to Washington: He returned with a reconstruction loan pledge of $100 million. It seemed that the Americans would literally keep Italy from starving—a condition Britain faced that winter.

The grant did not come without a price. De Gasperi had to promise that Communists and socialists in his Cabinet would go. So the six-party coalition of December 1945 shifted sharply to the Right. Committee of National Liberation officials, often Communists, were replaced. By May they were thrown out, and hardly a finger was raised in protest. The commission charged with imposing sanctions against Fascists was disbanded. It seemed a fact that the newly made Republic could not staff a bureaucracy, newspaper, a courtroom, a faculty, or the military without people connected to the old regime. Both the dyed-in-the-wool and those who simply did what they had no choice but to do—all were spared a purge.

The war had killed 35 million Europeans (20 million of them Russians), destroyed half the Continent's cereal production, reduced coal supplies to 40 percent of prewar levels, and created 20 million displaced persons, practically nomads foraging for food. In the Harvard commencement address of June 5, 1947, Secretary of State George Marshall proposed the aid plan that bore his name. The American reconstruction of Europe—at a price of $12 billion—would, he argued, prevent the entire continent's joining the ten countries and 100 million people that had already disappeared into the Soviet empire since the war's end. By reconstructing European infrastructure, the United States would not only keep the Soviets out but, more immediately, weaken the growing threat of takeover by indigenous Communist parties, of which the two largest were in France and Italy.

Even before the massive infusions of the Marshall Plan, about $2 billion in aid flowed into Italy between 1943 and 1947. Italians were not left without knowing to whom they should be grateful.

One of Italy's best brains in public service, Finance Minister Luigi Einaudi—the anti-Fascist, liberal economist later to become President of the Republic—intervened to halt inflation and support the collapsing lira. But his laissez-faire policy, while effective, allowed the large monopolies to prosper at the expense of the mass of the population. The recovery that came was dramatically uneven: Hoarders and speculators thrived, merchants and landless tenant farmers did not see their condition improved. The De Gasperi coalition seemed too weak to intimidate the strong and too willing to take the stringent measures needed to bring stability without penalizing the weak. The black market flourished because the Cabinet feared the political repercussions of rationing.

Tough choices, the price of losing the war, became clearer in July 1948 when, a mere two months after adoption of the Marshall Plan, Stalin sealed off Berlin, and the blockage led to an airlift. War seemed so likely that Marshall wondered whether the United States ought not to make a preemptive strike against Leningrad.

When the Marshall Plan Conference was convened in Paris, Pier Paolo returned to his placards on the loggia wall in San Giovanni, explaining that the meeting was only an American effort to divide Europe, to weaken Moscow. He, like almost all Italian Communists, saw the drive to enlist European participation as nothing more than the building of an anti-Soviet alliance. The Soviets had been valiant allies against the Germans. Besides, they were Europeans—the Russians—somehow not quite as foreign and faraway as the Americans. He headlined his poster:

THE DOVE OF PEACE FLIES TO PARIS

It is useless and silly kidding oneself: The Americans are playing for keeps. They really want war [with the Soviet Union]. Along with the Americans, all the capitalists of the world really want war. The rich want war against the poor.

We the poor had better not kid ourselves, the rich do everything to prevent our fighting for our rights. In the face of a threat of another horrible war, a white dove is rising and flapping its two wings in the sky over Europe. This dove is the desire for peace of some 600 million workers.[1]

But unlike the Soviets, who declined the invitation, Italy did join with fifteen other countries in the Plan, even though division on the wisdom of doing so effectively wrecked the De Gasperi government. By the end of 1947, it was tottering and new elections were called for the following April.

An interim parliament, called the Constituent Assembly, was convened in order to write and enact a new Constitution. It did so in January 1948 without strife: the Christian Democrats held 35 seats in the house; a combination of the socialists with 21 and the Communists with 19 seats could have outvoted the conservatives. But the parties on the Left chose not to unite to push for sweeping economic reforms. They distrusted each other more than they did the Right.

To almost everyone's amazement, PCI chief Palmiro Togliatti even backed the passage of Article 7, which integrated Mussolini's Concordat of 1929 into the new supreme law, giving the Church a privileged position in public education. He addressed the Assembly on March 25, 1947, announcing where the atheist PCI stood on the role of the Roman Catholic Church in the future of Italy.

> The colleagues of *Democrazia Cristiana* sometimes talk as if considering themselves the only defenders of the freedom of religious conscience of the Catholic masses. I do not think that any left-wing party would want to leave to them the exclusive right to its function.
>
> In our party too there exists, and I believe they are the majority of our members, Catholic citizens, and we are asserters and defenders of the freedom of religious conscience. It is true that we defend this freedom in the manner of a democratic, modern progressive, communist party, if you wish; but, at any rate, we defend it.
>
> We do not leave to you the exclusive right to this function . . . we are facing political and economic problems that are accumulating and getting tangled with each other. In this situation, we need religious peace, and we cannot let it be disturbed by any means.

So the Communists split from the socialists and voted for Article 7. "Gradualism" and "legitimization" were the watchwords; the revolution was declared dead by those who were supposed to lead it. Togliatti, with characteristic tortured prose, remarked of the document he accepted, "It is not a Socialist constitution but represents . . . a transition period in which there exists a struggle for an economic regime in which there exist economic forces that tend to spill over into each other."[2]

The fate of Trieste was decided in Rome: Tito's claims were disposed of by a four-power "committee of experts" who set the boundary. Communists in Friuli claimed that the British and Americans had sold off their great and good Italian "ally" in a settlement which saw substantial numbers of ethnic and linguistic Italians handed over to Yugoslavia. Little Friuli was a pawn in a superpower game: It looked as if it might even be traded to Austria in exchange for certain border power stations that served Genoa and Turin.

Italy had to accede to American wishes whatever they turned out to be. The war's totaling of accounts charged the impoverished Republic to make good in reparations the damage Fascism had done: $5 million to Albania, $25 million to Ethiopia, $100 million to Russia, $105 million to Greece, $125 million to Yugoslavia. The Americans would pay, of course, and add it to the debit side of Italy's national account. Meanwhile, the American army lingered on in Italy—not called one of occupation as in Japan but effectively present until the autumn of 1947. Even Togliatti understood that Italy depended on American goodwill, not only for its security but for its very survival. Had not Lenin said that timing was all, that the leadership must choose the right moment to strike? This was plainly not that moment.

When the Americans presented the peace treaty, even the anti-Fascist philosopher Benedetto Croce denounced it. The price Fascism had exacted from Italians seemed to count for nothing; it ignored the struggles of the last months of the war when Italians were caught between battling armies, neither army on its own soil. But the Constituent Assembly ratified it, price tag, concessions, and all, and it went as part of the package with Italy's delegation to the Marshall Plan Conference. The deal went forward: Within two years, the "rehabilitated" Italy joined NATO. All was forgiven, just so the legalized Left was kept far from the levers of power.

The Christian Democrats were beneficiaries of this Allied realism but so was Togliatti, who accepted a portfolio as Minister of Justice and supervised the granting of amnesties. It was not unheard of even for formerly card-carrying Fascists now to become card-carrying Communists. The Italian capacity for survival—for "arranging oneself"—moved to the front; so-called "contradictions" that might have convulsed other people were managed. Memories were shortened, and the country held together.

But on a local level, some Left-wing trade unions acted on their own. The General Confederation of Labor (CGIL) was headed by Communists who had an agenda more radical than the Party's. They organized strikes against the taking of the aid, inspired from the sidelines by the Soviet Union, which loudly refused to participate in the Paris talks. The police were called in and the Communist deputies in Parliament objected. And that is all that came of it.

By the start of 1948 everyone understood that April's elections represented the major referendum on Italy's future. The Cold War, which had already heated up when almost 7 million Communist (or Communist-affiliated) trade unionists in France had gone on strike, was now to be fought at the Italian polls. In February a coup in Prague brought a Red government to Czechoslovakia, and the Marshall Plan passed the anxious U.S. Congress soon after. Within six weeks, the U.S. Department of State announced that all economic aid to Italy would cease if the Left won the coming vote. Americans of Italian origin were urged to write their relatives in the old country, encouraging them to vote for the Christian Democrats.

Italy had to understand that turning against Washington would have its price. The diplomatic nicety that a free Italy was now one of Europe's centers of power, to be treated like war allies France and Britain, rang hollow and fooled no one.

Fewer than half a million cars were owned by a population of more than 45 million. Only 225,000 were enrolled in universities; 10 percent of all Italians (probably more) could not read or write. One Christian Democratic poster came right to the point: "You cannot put the topping on pasta with the speeches of Togliatti. That's why intelligent people vote for De Gasperi who got free flour from America for spaghetti, and the fixings too."

The Church made sure the coming vote was set in other terms as well: Was Italy for God or the Antichrist? Priests spoke plainly from the pulpit against the PCI and its candidates. Even Cardinal Spellman, in faraway but ever-present New York, raised money to defeat the Reds. On February 10, 1948, Pius XII went on the radio to declare the elections nothing less than a holy crusade, a confrontation between God and Satan. The founders of the legalized neo-Fascist party, the Movimento Sociale Italiano (MSI), could meet within the walls of convents and monasteries; Communists were excommunicable atheists, by their own admission. One Father Lombardi, commonly billed as "God's microphone," easily mixed arguments against "Stalinist materialism" with appeals to primordial fears of hellfire. He issued a radio appeal, picked up by parish church halls up and down the Peninsula, that "the Italy of Saint Francis, of Saints Clare and Catherine, of Saint Bernard, the Italy of Saint Pius V . . . once again stand up. Once again, history is watching you and from you awaits the watchword." Pilgrimages "for the Virgin" were organized: Villagers took to the open roads to carry the message that God had moved them "to forbid that there prevail the enemies of God"— the socialists and Communists. A young satirist named Giovanni Guareschi, eventually to become a national institution, told people, "In the secrecy of the voting booth, God sees you. Stalin does not."

There was relief from all the ideology: A sixteen-year-old bakery worker named Lucia Bosè was crowned "Miss Italy 1947" in a contest sponsored by a perfume company. They thought it better publicity for selling their product than the slogan of 1939: "Five thousand lire for a smile." The runners-up included Gina Lollobrigida and Silvana Mangano. Giuseppe de Santis was directing *Bitter Rice*, about proletarian rice workers and the corruption of American values. It starred beauty Mangano, in a very tight sweater.

The full-color magazines were full of Dior's "new look"—more fabric, high hemlines. When a contessa named Pia Bellentani killed her lover at a society party at Villa d'Este, the story ran for weeks. Gandhi was assassinated in India, and the State of Israel was born. As the voting approached, matters seemed to calm and improve. President Einaudi announced a rise in industrial production.

For their part, the Communists could only insist that they were Christians as well. Pasolini again instructed the good citizens of San Giovanni di Casarsa from the loggia wall:

> Black souls. What is this political policy that the priests are carrying out against us poor people? They're the ones who ought to think as we do; it seems to us that our feelings are Christian enough. Christian Democrats are amazed if the Communists go to Mass, when instead the Communists might be more amazed in seeing the Christian Democrats at Mass—with their souls as black as coal.[3]

The Church declared 1948 "the year of miracles." There appeared everywhere images of the Madonna—weeping, bloody, lifting up before her eyes the old and babies. Communists were accused of lacking *timore di Dio*, "fear of God." When trainloads of relief goods arrived from America, the stations were decked out with bunting and flags— the Italian and the Stars and Stripes.

The Communists also banged the drum of patriotism. They put a picture of Garibaldi at the center of their red star and "guaranteed" that their program was "Peace, Work, Liberty, Justice." But such abstractions were to be no match for the Virgin's crusaders and the American threat—transmitted to compromised politicians—that those ships full of grain and coal, eggs and butter, could easily stop docking at Italian ports.

Voices that strove to calm the hysteria were outshouted. Pietro Nenni, head of the socialists, was ignored. He argued in vain,

> The elections are not for or against Christ, not for or against America, not for or against Russia, but for better administration, for the nationalization of industrial complexes, for agricultural reform. The other themes have nothing to do with it; the Church has nothing to do with it.

The Left sailed on into defeat. Their announcements listed the number of days until the election as the days remaining until "a new liberty will come to Italy." They were sadly disappointed.

On April 18, 1948, the DC won 48.5 percent of the vote, more than thirteen points higher than their success of two years before. The Popular Front fell from 40 percent to 31 percent, about 8 million ballots. Christian Democracy did especially well in the Veneto and

Friuli. His strength in Parliament allowed De Gasperi to resist both Vatican pressure for an all-Catholic government and American pressure to outlaw both the Communist and Socialist parties. Now a full range of parties flourished or at least were allowed, from far Left to the MSI.

In San Giovanni, with the battle against American anti-Communism lost and Italy signed on for the Marshall Plan six weeks later, Pasolini admonished from his placards,

> Italy has adhered to the Atlantic Treaty. This means that Italy has agreed to a war pact against Russia. The entire Italian working class knows what this means: it means that the rich of the world have united against the poor of the world. Workers of San Giovanni, even if you voted for De Gasperi, try now to moderate what he is doing [he now switched from blue ink to red: They are betraying you. They want to make you fight and die for your bosses.[4]

Another day he delivered a lesson in European history with a twist. Penned in large block letters, with underscoring of the blue-inked text in red, he listed:

> 1896: war
> 1911: war
> 1915: war
> 1935: war
> 1936: war
> 1939: war
>
> What government wanted these wars? Capitalistic government. It is capitalism that wants war. Now, capitalism wants to start another war. And against whom? Against Russia. Why Russia? Because Russia is the cradle of socialism. The Christian Democrats, enslaved to capitalism with their religious campaign, have understood that to make Russia and socialism hated is to lay the foundation for a new war: a war of the rich against the poor.[5]

This was tough talk, even dangerous, in an isolated, rural hamlet where the police chief, the schoolmaster, and the priest still commanded deference from the people, and in turn all three deferred to the landlords.

Pier Paolo's brush and box of pigments were ready to put the best face on the disaster. For the occasion of the international socialist Day of Labor, May 1, he pressed on, despite the debacle of two weeks before.

> A great day today: Today is the celebration of socialism; the red banner
> waves gloriously. Let us not forget that it is in the name of this banner that
> for more than a century the redemption of the working classes has been
> realized and there has been progress in the world. Everything that is good
> and human that has been achieved in this century is thanks to socialism.
>
> Workers, do not forget it: without socialism, you would still be slaves. . . .[6]

He closed by calling for "a day of struggle by the working classes."

During the debate over the Atlantic Treaty, PCI General Secretary
Togliatti had risen on the floor of Parliament and threatened revolt.
He said the Communists' response to the Americans' "imperialistic
war" would be a workers' uprising. His words found a fast answer in
one newspaper whose editor suggested Togliatti "would be not only
metaphorically nailed to the wall: before the Republic would allow
his treason."

On July 4 a student from Catania named Antonio Pallante took up
the comment. Togliatti had risen to leave the Chamber of Deputies,
as was normal during extended debates, and headed for Rome's best
ice-cream parlor, Giolitti's in the via Uffici del Vicario. As he
emerged, Pallante shot him at close range, hitting Togliatti in the
nape of the neck and in the back, the bullet lodging in a lung.

Emergency surgery at the Policlinico lasted more than two hours.
Togliatti's wife was flown from Turin in a private plane provided by
the managing director of Fiat, but the gesture availed him nothing:
Within hours, the Fiat workers locked him and sixteen members of
the board of directors in their offices and flew the red flag from the
Mirafiori factory roof.

Work stopped at a thousand factories across the country. In front
of Milan's Duomo, demonstrators held signs that read, THE INDUS-
TRIALISTS SHOT TOGLIATTI. In Rome cobblestones were torn up and
thrown at the Celere, Interior Minister Mario Scelba's crack new
police units. The headquarters of the MSI was sacked by demonstrators in Genoa, and five armed military carriers were overturned.

Sporadic violence broke out all over: A leader of the owners' agricultural association was murdered in Siena; the bridge over the
lagoon linking Venice to the mainland was occupied by workers trying
to block access by troops sent from Pordenone and Padua. Workers
and political operatives occupied the central telephone stations linking north and south; they had to be assaulted for the stations to be
retaken by the police. Several were wounded and a commander was
stabbed to death.

By July 17 workers had complete control of Genoa and the Ligurian coast from Sarzana to Ventimiglia at the French border. It seemed like the Paris Commune of 1870 again. On the third day of their control, the police were sent in and three were killed, two wounded. In all, more than twenty people died during a week of violence.

Togliatti emerged from a coma and, with the panache that makes for exquisite legend, asked his secretary how Italy's favorite cyclist had fared in the Tour de France (he won it). He was still in shock, but the condition passed and on July 15 he talked with his doctor in Latin. (Even Communists had a classical education under the old regime.) The next day he was declared out of danger and a two-week recuperation period was predicted. Carried in a window-shaded Soviet Zis put at his disposal by that country's embassy in Rome, he left the hospital on July 31 to recover at a lakeside. By the end of September he had returned to the capital, greeted by a crowd of half a million.

The government moved quickly to "normalize" events, now that Togliatti was out of danger. The result? Now it was plain that Minister Scelba, who prided himself on being called Minister for Police, was prepared to use the large internal army of the national police force to suppress the activities of Left-wing politicians and their supporters, without too much concern for the line between legitimate political dissent and crime.

Scelba had American "advisers" to help coordinate his effort; after the election of April 18, not to take any chances, an extra 20,000 men were added to his Celere. By mid-July, when Togliatti was shot, Scelba commanded 200 new armed vehicles, 40,000 Celere overall, 30,000 reservists, 180,000 men between *carabinieri* and the Guardie di Finanza, and behind them, if needed, the army. When the post-attack strikes began, Scelba had acted fast: He surrounded the Roman electrical stations, understanding that if the Communists knocked out the lights, the first night in the dark would bring panic. When the first three days of Togliatti's coma passed, Scelba moved to see that every act of politically inspired vandalism was punished to the maximum; those singled out as militants were to have prison terms. Pallante was locked up in Regina Coeli for thirteen years and eight months—a term reduced to nine years, of which he served only part before disappearing into total obscurity, without the thanks he had expected from the Right. Life returned to normal; Italian Communism was not ready to overturn the applecart.

Overall, out of the Togliatti affair and the troubles following it, some 7,000 people were meted out judicial sentences. From 1948 to 1953—Scelba's years as Interior Minister, before rising to succeed

De Gasperi in the Prime Ministership—62 workers (45 of them signed-up Communists) died in encounters with the police, 3,126 were wounded, of whom—by their own declaration—2,367 were Communist Party members.

Scelba thought it necessary and proper that there be a continuity in the style of public discipline between Fascism and the new republic. He made no secret of his hatred of intellectuals and imposed on his vast department a petit bourgeois mentality, which made sure that any prefect separated from his wife or found guilty of concubinage or adultery would lose his job. It took some years, but his path and Pasolini's inevitably crossed.

The PCI's handling of the aftermath of the attempt on Togliatti proved a disaster for the Left. They crumbled in Parliament, even condoning a proviso that spontaneous strikes be squelched. By refusing to lead, they created a gap between the Party's top officials and its rank-and-file that never healed. The obvious gap between a still revolutionary rhetoric but an accommodationist politics-as-usual called their leadership into question, engendering a cynicism that grew to undermine the PCI when Hungary was invaded in 1956, Czechoslovakia in 1968, and the students revolted that year.

Party doctrine plainly called for class warfare leading to the dictatorship of the proletariat. The theory was that the top leadership would be an avant-garde and lead the rank-and-file to revolution, and only when they thought the time was right. Self-motivated insurrections, questioning from below, wildcat strikes were not welcomed.

But industrial workers at the core of the Party had an altogether different experience, one formed in the war. In the three days after Togliatti was shot, these now-Communist veterans seemed to get out of control. The Party bosses leaned on the unions and the rank-and-file was sent back to work. The PCI leaders, it appeared, feared losing dominance over the Party more than they feared a Christian Democratic regime with which they could do business, one that allowed for a secure, comfortable opposition with its spheres of influence left intact. After twenty months of partisan warfare against Fascism and the Germans—fought in alliance with the Soviet Union after all—the workers felt their leadership had betrayed them.

The Italian Communists on the factory floor and in the fields were left twirling in the wind: If they wanted to make revolution, they were on their own. The leadership of the 1948 strikes were the men who had hidden in the woods to take potshots at the Germans, who had mined the bridges, who had seen their fellow Partisans captured and shoved against a wall to be shot by the Germans and their Italian collaborators. They thought the end of the war meant fundamental change in Italian social and economic life and that the PCI would lead them there. After the attempt on Togliatti, they found themselves occupying the factories but facing Scelba's soldiers with no support from the Party leadership. Hotheads were not free to push the leadership faster than it wanted to go. In fact, an order went out within Party channels to "severely punish those who take initiatives not approved . . . contrary to the Party's line and in that way play the game of, and act in the interests of, the enemy." Orders went out from the top: Let the revolt peak and fizzle.

The Party "base" ought to have expected this betrayal. Togliatti had already gone on record as saying, "The Partisans in the north of Italy demobilized peacefully . . . they ask only the privilege of working harder than anyone else, to set an example, to show once again that the workers and the peasants of Italy represent the best of the Italian population."

Such a man was not going to turn the former Partisans against the legally elected, even conservative, State. Stalin, who knew Togliatti well, described his long-time guest and ally: "a lawyer, a professor . . . he will never make a revolution."[7]

The year of its electoral debacle, the PCI commissioned member Luchino Visconti to go to Sicily and record the misery of fishermen there, to make a documentary that would inspire outrage. He meant to make a trilogy: fishermen, peasants, and miners. Shot without script, *La terra trema* created a scandal at the Venice Film Festival: Was this to be the art of a happier postwar Italy, nonactors depicting grimy lives without hope? A thoroughgoing esthete, Visconti's remark about his Sicilian characters could have come straight from Pasolini: "Their noble faces, framed in their black kerchiefs, have the grace of a portrait by Leonardo. . . . These Sicilians," he told the press about his cast, "hit upon poetic *trouvailles* that no one could ever have discovered by remaining behind a desk. They behaved exactly as they did in real life."

In September Pier Paolo's teaching contract was renewed for the academic year 1948–49 (he sat exams in Latin and Italian letters in Padua), and he was given new responsibilities—to create a kind of "experimental" school out of his class at Valvasone.

Now Carlo Alberto's increasingly violent rages alternated with depressions so deep that doctors were again brought in. Pier Paolo wrote Serra:

> The "paranoid syndrome" of my father makes our family's life a hell, and it is a problem without solution; I really don't know how it will end. Believe me, there are no words to express certain situations which are created at home during my father's moments of crisis.[8]

In February 1949 Pasolini was honored with an invitation to the first congress of the Communist federation—the regional authority—at Pordenone. When the gathering's official bulletin appeared in March, it printed a piece by Pasolini on culture: "Does a new and progressive culture exist? This is the first question which would be posed to me by a worker or a peasant: but the question is premature."[9]

He claimed that the bourgeois education even of writers who challenged the system held them back as creators, if not as critics. "There already exists a literature of denunciation," he wrote, but it was written in the language of the middle class. After citing Eliot and Joyce, he turned to veiled autobiography:

> Let's be clear: nothing could be more hoped for than that there be born to our world of letters a Proust, with all his pathological psychology; but a Proust who transformed his own life into the frame of an aristocratic society as did the author of the *Recherche* is, by now, anachronistic and inconceivable.[10]

He argued that the intellectual must now "renounce," must "carry out that introspective, interior, diaristic examination which is, in fact, the vital exercise of the man of thought . . . without which it is impossible to be an artist." The words sound like a new Hermeticism, but the source was intensely personal only as a route to the explicitly public, even political. And yet—and here was the difference from the escapists—the artist must not flee the world but must be "in his work, more objective and more, let us say even this, Christian." Pasolini, artist, took the stance (and before a gathering of PCI stalwarts) that turning inward and facing outward were not incompatible choices. However personal and self-involved he may seem, he was engaged in an exercise of understanding (and aiding, for art was also to teach) mankind by ever better understanding the one man he needed to know best, himself.

And what of the conformity that came with Party loyalty? He temporized but not to the point of self-betrayal: "Loyalty and political commitment end up by working as the powerful reagent of the literary consciousness." The artist will be "a loyal comrade in politics," but "the Communist *letterato* must be completely free to do as he likes in literature."

That month, he wrote Silvana that he was much occupied with meetings, conferences, his wall placards, and polemics with neighborhood priests who "condemn me from the pulpit."

"For me," he wrote her, "believing in Communism is a great thing." As usual during these years, he confessed to her as to no other:

> My sickness consists in *not changing* [emphasis Pasolini's], you understand, right? And if therefore there is in me some change, it is purely superficial, and has to do with a moral degeneration (but on that we have to have a different discussion) . . . I have lost a lot of scruples and a lot of timidity; I have learned, for example, how to make love without love and without regrets. . . . "To become unhappy is a duty" (Gide), this has been the sole duty of my life, and I have gone about it with obstinacy, the torment and the ill will which "duty" demands. What a miserable thing your friend is, huh Silvana? . . . I live delicious subterfuges, perfectly happy to be hidden.[11]

He wrote Serra about the same time, "I do not share your ideas about [Sandro] Penna and [André] Gide, whom I admire unconditionally." Penna—whose lyrics on the love of young boys are as candid as a pederastic Catullus; Gide—the champion of homosexuals and Communists.

He was also writing criticism: an article on the poet of Romagna dialect Antonio Guerra, for the *Progresso d'Italia*, which never appeared; another, called "Literary Conversation," for the same newspaper, which did. But his poetry was not being accepted by editors; *Atti impuri, Amado mio,* and *Sogno* were all stalled. He continued to send Contini manuscripts.

Poet Vittorio Sereni (who later translated William Carlos Williams) asked him to collaborate on the magazine *La rassegna d'Italia*. Pier Paolo responded that "having drawers filled with prose and poetry of which I am the only reader, I now face the problem of choice. I pass six months at a time without meeting anyone with whom to discuss poetry. . . ."

The poet Giacinto Spagnoletti asked him to send poems in Italian from which he could chose for an anthology he was assembling. Meanwhile, Pasolini paid for the printing of five hundred copies of *Dov'è la mia patria?* (Where is my country?), work of the previous year. It was intended for *friulani*, who could not easily read Italian (the poems are translated at the foot of each page), the poetic equivalent of his political posters, all part of his strategy for cultural consciousness-building in Friuli. His friend Giuseppe Zigaina drew thirteen plates in charcoal: "Men at the River," "Workers on Strike," "Workers Exiting a Factory," "An Injured Worker Working." They are abstracted but plainly recognizable, drawn to a political purpose by an artist with a profound ideological commitment.

The poems describe angels in heaven as "sons of the Rich with books under their arms, singing drunkards' songs." Its message is clear: Those who struggled against the Germans must now struggle against the exploitations of the Italians who seek to profiteer. In "El testament Coran" (1944), a small epic about the war, the poem's protagonist recounts Guido's arrest and what Pier Paolo saw. It is written in the vernacular Pier Paolo heard along the banks of the Pacher, a rivulet running near the villages of Cordovado and Bagnarola. He swam here and made notes on what he heard—expressions written nowhere else. They also made their way into this poem and the lyrics in *Quadri friulani* (Friulian pictures), first entered in the "Red Notebooks" and finally printed in Rome in 1951 under the title *I parlanti*. From "El testament Coran":

> In mièth de la platha un muàrt
> ta na potha de sanc glath.
> Tal paese desert come un mar
> quatro todescs a me àn ciapàt
> e thigànt rugoio a me àn menàt
> ta un camio fer in ta l'umbrìa.
> Dopo tre dis a me àn piciàt
> in tal moràr de l'osteria.
>
> Lassi in reditàt la me imàdin
> ta la cosientha dai siòrs.
> I vuòj vuòiti, i àbith ch'a nasin
> dei me tamari sudòurs.
> Coi todescs no ài vut timòur
> de tradì la me dovenetha.
> Viva il coragiu, el dolòur
> e la nothentha dei puarèth!

In prose translation:

> In the middle of the piazza was a dead man, lying in a pool of frozen blood.
> In the midst of the village, still as the sea, four Germans shouting in anger

dragged me to a truck parked in the shade. After three days, they hanged
me from the mulberry tree by the tavern. I leave as inheritance my image
in the conscience of the rich. Empty eyes, the clothes which stink of my
uncouth sweating. With the Germans, I had no fear of betraying my youth.
So, long live the courage, the sadness and the innocence of the poor!

The summer of 1949 was not happy. As Nico Naldini has recalled,
"One day, Pier Paolo—who was superstitious—pointed out a dead
cat to me that was lying on the road, and he said it was the image of
our summer. His political activity had already engendered hostility . . . we heard warnings, vague intimations of blackmail. Pier
Paolo was perceived as a turncoat to his background by the Christian
Democrats of Udine." The political opposition had picked up rumors
about Pier Paolo: His sexuality was "known about." Those unhappy
to have been his political target realized they held ammunition to put
at least one troublesome local Communist agitator out of commission.
Only the right occasion was needed.

Pier Paolo heard some comments directly; others were reported. It
seemed only to excite him into taking more chances, or perhaps he
simply chose not to fight Fate. He acted as though one who wanted,
and at almost any cost, to get out of what had become a too-small
Friuli, claustrophobic Casarsa, an impasse at home where Carlo Alberto had sunk into vindictive fixations, and a literary confinement
in dialect and political issues of only the most local importance. In
July he described his life to Gianfranco Contini as

> made crazy, between extreme ugliness (father paranoid, mother heart-
> rending, a dog's life in a school, a life of people who are stupid and perfid-
> ious, political hatred and conspiracy of silence) and an extreme happiness,
> which you know where and how to diagnose.[12]

The storm broke at a place called Ramuscello, a bunching of
houses in the fields, a fraction of the tiny town of Cordovado. It was
during the village festival for Saint Sabina on September 30, 1949.
During the dance, held on a wooden platform built in the fields, Pier
Paolo encountered a boy he already knew. He and three others
seemed willing to go into the fields, and so the four went—as they
may have before—to masturbate. One boy was fifteen, two of the
others were sixteen, and the last was fourteen.

Three weeks after the events, on October 22, a complaint was filed
with the *carabinieri* station at Cordovado: charges—"corruption of
minors" and "obscene acts in a public place," violation of penal code
sections 521 and 530. In the stilted prose of a provincial police

report: "It has come to the awareness of Brigadier Luigi Scognamiglio of San Vito al Tagliamento, on duty the tenth of this month, from an informant that in the district of Ramuscello there has been verified a scandal, to wit four minor male youths who masturbated an individual." The police investigation among "impartial persons of good faith" revealed that the boys had publicly claimed to have "*menato l'uccello a*" Pier Paolo Pasolini," literally "yanked the bird" of the *professore*.

The fifteen-year-old was interrogated. He said that he and the others were approached at the festival for Saint Sabina and that Pasolini "offered sweets and then invited them to go into the countryside." The official declaration:

> Arrived there, Pasolini began to kiss [a boy], putting his tongue in his mouth and massaging his member and then, taking down his own trousers, exposed his own member and agitated it to the state of *lussuria* and, satisfied, paid the boy 100 lire. This transpired within the presence of the other three.
>
> The interrogation of [another boy] was no less immoral than that of [the first one].[13]

Two of the boys also claimed to have received the same payment.

One of the sixteen-year-olds also reported that Pasolini had arrived in Cordovado another evening, by bicycle, and invited the boy to the cinema, "offering to pay for the ticket, but the boy, knowing the illness from which Pasolini suffered, declined the invitation and sought to keep away from him." This boy emphasized that he had done nothing with Pasolini but that he knew the others had. His name was stricken from the proceedings.

The report continues: "Despite invitations to do so, the parents of the boys have not come to the [police] station, explainable by the wave of shame which the boys have caused to inundate their families."

There was nothing to do but hope that no one would press formal charges. A lawyer was retained, one Bruno Brusini (in *friulano*, Bruno Brusin).[14] More than three decades later, Nico recalled that it was their pragmatic Aunt Giannina who took it upon herself to call on the boys' families and suggest—ever so gently—that perhaps some payment of money would satisfy the parents' sense of damage enough so as not to testify, not to add criminal sanction to the price Pier Paolo had already paid and would still yet pay? If the parents acting for their minor sons would drop the matter, odds were fair the public authorities would feel satisfied that Pasolini was no longer a threat to the established order. Giannina went with Brusin to offer each set of parents 100,000 lire.[15]

Meanwhile, Nico went to see a man named Giovan Battista Caron, once head of the *liceo classico* in Udine from which Naldini had graduated, now a newly elected Christian Democratic deputy. Caron had warned that trouble was brewing and now made an offer: the Christian Democrats were willing to cover up the whole matter if Pier Paolo would give up politics. They did not ask that he join their party, only that he be quiet. According to Naldini's recollection, Caron was willing to approach the local bishop, to ask if he would suggest that the parish priest also call on the parents to convince them to forget the whole business. Nico carried the offer to Pier Paolo, who rejected it.

In a long letter to Fabio Luca Cavazza a week later, Nico wrote:

> Pier Paolo had a lot of enemies among the Christian Democrats because of his political activity, and they kept the ball in the air and did everything they could to be sure this business . . . of no importance would provoke a scandal to ruin him for life. All that has happened: they have demonstrated a diabolical ability.[16]

The Casarsa branch of the Territorial Legion of the *carabinieri* of Padua interrogated Pier Paolo in Cordovado. According to their report, he "admitted committing the immoral acts harmful to the boys cited above and offered as justification having exaggerated that evening in the drinking of wine and having wanted to attempt an erotic experiment of literary origin and character, stimulated by reading of a novel on a homosexual subject by Gite [*sic*]." He went further, specifying that he had chosen those boys because they seemed *meno educati*, "less polished," than others. Officer Scognamiglio, with station commander Bortolo Menegetto countersigning, closed his report with the observation, "In Casarsa, he [Pasolini] enjoys little esteem because suspected of committing immoral acts." Because of "general indignation" in the community and Pasolini's work as a teacher, it was deemed opportune to send copies of the report to the Prefect at San Vito for use in prosecution, as well as to higher-ups within the police.

News of the denunciation quickly reached DC headquarters in Udine and was passed to the newspapers. On October 28 notices appeared in all the dailies, some more detailed than others. The *Messaggero veneto*, which Pier Paolo so loathed, ran the headline "A Serious Charge Against a Man of Letters"; it suggested that motivation had been because the professor was "excited by recent reading." Newsboys concentrated on Casarsa, where they posted themselves in the piazza only yards from the Pasolini house, often passing and shouting under the family windows. The *Gazzettino*, Carlo Alberto's paper, announced the same day: "Professor Charged With Immorality."

On October 29, well before even preliminary legal proceedings, let alone trial, the PCI regional federation at Udine met in extraordinary session and voted Pier Paolo's immediate expulsion from the Party. Guilt and innocence were irrelevant; it was of no consequence that no charges had been brought, no evidence heard, no adjudication made. Charges and bad publicity for the Party were enough to justify expelling him on grounds of "moral unfitness," *indignità morale*. The Party official who went to some trouble to expedite the matter and wrote the expulsion notice printed that same day in *L'unità* was Ferdinando Mautino. This notice appeared in the national editions of the PCI official daily:

> We take as our starting point the bringing of a serious disciplinary action against the poet Pier Paolo Pasolini in order once again to denounce the deleterious influence of certain ideological and philosophical currents coming from Gide, Sartre and other decadent poets and literati, who seek to present themselves as progressives but in reality bring together the most harmful aspects of bourgeois degeneration.[17]

Sartre, for his troubles at reforming the Left from within, had been branded "a typing hyena" by Stalin's Soviet Union. On June 9, 1950, Togliatti—writing under the pseudonym Rodeigo di Castiglia—suggested that Gide should not write about the relationship between the parties and the classes but "occupy himself with pederasty, of which he is a specialist, and stop [addressing] other matters of which he knows nothing."

Homosexuals (including dissident intellectuals, and Pasolini was both) were beyond the puritanical pale of the "new Party" PCI, dedicated to "proletarian morality," even more intolerant than it had been of lax Fascism. This Communist Party, already on the defensive against charges of atheism and loyalty to Moscow, would have gone to far greater lengths than the expulsion of a minor official like Pasolini to demonstrate itself more traditional than the traditionalists, most patriotic of patriots, citizens like any other. Only more honest, better.

Christian Democrats and Communists had agreed that the traditional family was the right form of life. The Minister of Agriculture in 1948, Giuseppe Medici, declared that the peasant woman must be

> not only the companion of a man who works but must divide the duties of family maintenance: It is her job to sustain that complex of creative energies which makes the family all of society writ small, a society which within its own frame resolves its economic problems and thus fulfills its social duties.[18]

Togliatti agreed. "We want to make of the family not only a center of solidarity but a center of the battle against moral corruption." A good Communist was like a good Christian Democrat when it came to private life, and perhaps as Catholic.

Following his bad press and Party expulsion, the regional educational authorities moved fast. He was immediately stripped of his teaching post, a position promising tenure, which he could otherwise have counted on for life. No appeals were available, hearings unknown. All that in the course of forty-eight hours.

He was convinced that the regional Christian Democrats had worked with the local priest and the police to destroy him. But they had not set a trap; rather, they watched and waited for him to do what they assumed he would do and then made the most of it.

On October 31 Pier Paolo wrote Mautino, calling him by the name he had used as a hero of the Resistance:

> Dear Carlino,
> About three months ago, as perhaps you know, I was blackmailed by a priest: either I deserted Communism or my scholastic career would be ruined. I answered this priest as he deserved, with an intelligent lady acting as intermediary [perhaps Degan]. A month ago, an "honorable" [Parliamentary deputy] DC friend of Nico let me know, very indirectly, that the Christian Democrats were preparing my ruin: for pure *"odium theologicum"* [theological hatred]—those were his words—like hyenas they were waiting for the scandal which some rumors had foretold. In fact, no sooner had the maneuver at Ramuscello occurred, always for *odium theologicum* (otherwise it would have been treated like an unimportant matter, any old experience which could happen to anyone in the sense of it being a completely interior issue), probably the Marshal of the Carabinieri executed orders given him by the DC, letting its directors in on the story, and they in turn made the scandal explode in the [provincial administration] and in the press.
> Yesterday morning, my mother was losing her mind, my father is in an indescribable state: I heard him cry and groan all night. I am without work, that is to say, reduced to begging. All this simply because *I am a Communist*. I am not surprised at the diabolical perfidy of the Christian Democrats; I am

amazed at your inhumanity: understand well that to speak of ideological deviation is idiocy. Despite all of you, I remain and will remain a Communist in the truest sense of the word. But what am I speaking of, I who at this moment am without a future. Until this morning, I held to the idea of sacrificing myself and my career out of loyalty to an ideal; now I have nothing to lean on. Someone else in my place would kill himself; tragically, I must live for my mother's sake. I urge you to work with clarity and with passion; I tried to do so. For this I betrayed my class and that which you call my bourgeois education; now those betrayed have vindicated themselves in the most shocking and overwhelming manner. And I am left alone with the mortal pain of my father and my mother.
I embrace you,
Pier Paolo[19]

Mautino did not answer the letter. But he held it for twenty-eight years, as he did the conviction that he was correct, and released it to the press after Pasolini's death.

Pasolini's lawyer went to work. The court of first instance found that he and the boys were in a place "hidden from view by a small wood." Thus, it was not an obscene act "in a public place." As for the "corruption of minors" charge, the fifteen-year-old declined (or rather his parents did) to bring charges. The trial court sentenced Pasolini and two of the boys to three months in jail, suspended pending appeal, plus costs. This rather mild judicial result hardly mattered: Pasolini was publicly condemned as a corruptor of minors, out of the Party and out of a job. This sentence came down on December 28, 1950.

As allowed by Italian procedure, an appeal was filed in Pordenone a week before the first sentence was formally entered in the chancellery records on January 5, 1951. The appellate verdict went into greater detail. After causing two of the boys to masturbate him, Pasolini (the official report explains) brought himself to ejaculation and then, "his lust not satisfied," approached a third boy "who had been present at the disgusting scene," kissed him on the mouth, "introducing his tongue," and "invited him to masturbate him, which the boy refused to do."

These are the facts in their crude reality, according to the declarations of the boys to the *carabinieri* at Cordovado and to the Prefect at San Vito al Tagliamento, facts amply and cynically confessed by Pasolini, who thought to excuse himself by reference to recent reading of a novel on a homosexual theme by Gide, and even dared to say that by committing said acts he was completing the education of said boys. . . .[20]

On January 22, 1951, the Pordenone appeals court held that the lower tribunal had erred in not proceeding against the accused for obscene acts just because one boy had declined to bring charges. They held that the public authorities could proceed in their own right because the corruption-of-minors act charged was "objectively and subjectively linked" to that of obscene acts in public. The appellate verdict held that the sixteen-year-old's majority meant Pasolini was chargeable only with the "libidinous act" vis-à-vis a fifteen-year-old; it condemned Pasolini (free subject to appeal) for acts with that fifteen-year-old alone, with instructions to the district attorney to seek to initiate charges arising from Pasolini's conduct with the fourteen-year-old.

Pasolini's new lawyer, one Mario Belli, took the case to technical grounds: The place where the encounter took place was not a public one but was under the shelter of bushes in a field that was private property. Further, a "wall" of densely growing bushes and a copse (a *boschetto*) of acacia trees blocked it from view. A farmhouse nearby turned only a windowless wall toward the group. As for the acts of "corruption," "the law punishes insofar as actions arrive at reality and concreteness"; it was claimed that no "crime," as defined by law, had been committed, presumably because no sexual act was consummated; what Pasolini had done with the boys was no more (and no more illegal) than that which boys that age frequently did among themselves.

Only on April 8, 1952, did a three-judge panel absolve Pasolini along with two of the boys of "obscene acts," for lack of evidence. Pasolini was absolved of "corruption of minors" with a sixteen-year-old because the latter was not a minor at the time of the acts; and proceedings were dropped in connection with a minor for lack of a formal complaint. Contrary to the first court, a second appellate court held that without his complaint, no proceedings were allowed. Only then did the prosecuting attorney renounce his right to appeal to the Italian supreme court.

Even before the initial verdict of January 1950 Pier Paolo had left Friuli for good. When the final sentence was rendered, he had been gone from his once-Arcadia more than two years.


When the story first broke, many of his friends fell silent. Some later claimed to have learned the truth about their friend only with that morning's paper. More than one vicious, anonymous letter and notes with satiric barbs were shoved under the family's door. The writer

Paolo Volponi came and was amazed that the entire town seemed, in an instant, to turn against one whom before they had "considered a little prophet." Carlo Alberto raved, blamed Susanna for what "her" son—"your homosexual son," he is supposed to have said—had done. She took to her bed for an entire day, and Pier Paolo lay at her side while they talked it through.

Much later, as though continuing that intimate conversation, he addressed her in a poem. He begs her to see past her naïveté, and to forgive him:

> Didn't you understand that the world
> of which I am the blind
> and loving son
> was not your son's
> joyous possession,
> soft with dreams, armed
> with goodness—but an ancient
> land of others that to life
> imparts the anxiety of exile?

Some of the schoolboys of Casarsa stayed loyal, as did colleague Teresina Degan. A committed Party leader of impeccable credentials, she had objected long and loudly at the way Mautino railroaded Pier Paolo's expulsion. She lodged formal complaints that a quorum had not been present, that debate had not met the PCI ruling committee's own procedures. She was alone, the sole woman in the leadership, and ignored.

On November 10 Pasolini wrote her:

> It was a perfect piece of work, minutely and fearfully timed: we have a lot to learn from them. As for me, I am condemnable for an innocence which is really indecent. Perhaps it is late to learn, but the seven or eight friends who remain with me tell me I am young and can start over. What a lovely consolation! There was a moment when I could rid myself of the dunghill of bourgeois hatred, but now I feel renewed—and if I have ever had a vitality, I feel it now upon me like a new garment. What you say, calling me a defender of the working class, is now a fixed point in my thinking and, do not fear, nothing will change it.[21]

He spent most of the following three months in Friuli, and mostly at home. On December 31 he wrote Farolfi:

I have lost my teaching post because of a scandal in Friuli following on a denunciation made against me for corruption of minors . . . the Christian Democrats and the Fascists of Udine took advantage of the occasion to cut me in half, and they did it with a repugnant cynicism and skill. But we will speak of that another time.

Today is the last day of the year: I have nothing before me, I am un-employed; absolutely without any type of work, my father in the physical and psychological condition which you know. A suicidal atmosphere. I am working doggedly on a novel [*Sogno*], in which I put all my hopes, including practical ones; I know these are insane hopes, and yet somehow they satisfy me. In these conditions, naturally I cannot come to Parma. Who knows, now, when we will see one another again, and that displeases me very much since I always have wished you very well.[22]

On January 27, 1950, Pier Paolo wrote a last letter from Casarsa to his sole female confidente, Silvana Mauri:

Since my last letter, my situation has changed very much for the worse, to the extent that a worsening is even imaginable. My father, seized by one of his usual crises, of nastiness and craziness, by now I don't know [which], has for the umpteenth time threatened to leave us and made some agreement to sell all the furniture. You cannot imagine what this has done to my mother. I cannot stand any more seeing her suffer in this inhuman and unspeakable way. I have decided to take her—even tomorrow—to Rome, unknown to my father, to entrust her to my uncle [Gino]; I cannot stay in Rome because my uncle has made it clear that he cannot keep me there, but I hope matters will be different for my mother. From Rome I do not know where I'll go, maybe Florence . . . If you want to write me something, my address for at least a few days will be: care of Gino Colussi, via Porta Pinciana 34, Rome. After that, I do not know what I will do or where I will go; my life is at a turning point that is more than decisive. I hope that somewhere in the world will be a little work, even the most humble, for me; they say one does not die of hunger. Thus, at the dawn of my adventure, I send you my most affectionate regards, and also to your family.[23]

According to Nico Naldini, at five in the morning on January 28, Susanna and Pier Paolo rose and left the house where Carlo Alberto slept, without good-byes. They "fled, as in a novel"; so Pasolini described it in 1970, looking back over twenty years.

They walked to the train station. They had what they could carry in suitcases, and Susanna her phony jewels. Pier Paolo carried two manuscripts: *The Nightingale*, poems written from 1943 through 1949, and the novel about the uprising at San Vito, *La meglio gioventù*.

Nico saw them off. Thirty years later, when they were all dead—Guido and Carlo Alberto, Pier Paolo and Susanna—the cousin recalled: "Susanna seemed a young girl, leaving on her first journey, walking that street, held by the arm by Pier Paolo. Everything that had happened in the recent past seemed almost erased from her face and the future not to worry her; there would be, at least, a life to live together with her son."[24]

*In Rome, from the Fifties to today, August 1966,*
*I've done nothing but suffer and work voraciously.*
*After that unemployed year and the end of life*
*I taught in a small private school*
*for twenty-seven dollars a month.*
*In the meantime my father rejoined us*
*and we never spoke of our flight,*
*mine and mother's.*
*It was a common occurrence, a transfer in two stages.*
*We lived in a house without a roof, without plaster,*
*a poor people's house at the city's far edge, next to a jail.*
*A dustbowl in summer, a swamp in winter—*
*But it was Italy, naked and swarming Italy,*
*with its boys, its women,*
*its smell of jasmine and poor soup,*
*sunsets on the fields of Aniene, piles of trash—*
*and as for me, my poetry-dreams intact.*
*In poetry, a solution to everything.*
*It seemed to me that Italy, its description and destiny,*
*depended on what I wrote about it,*
*in lines infused with immediate reality,*
*no longer nostalgic,*
*as if I had earned it with my sweat—*
*never mind that I on certain days*
*didn't have a hundred lire for a shave.*
*My frugal figure, though unstable and crazy,*
*was at that moment in many ways*
*like the people I lived with:*
*in this we were true brothers, at least equals—*
*And thus could I, I believed, deeply understand them—*
    *—Pier Paolo Pasolini, "But It Was a Naked and Swarming Italy"*

# "AT THE CITY'S FAR EDGE"

Uncle Gino, "my sweet uncle/who gave me a little of his blood," paid for Pier Paolo to lodge in the spare room of a policeman and his family in a poor section in the heart of the city, near the Portico d'Ottavia. It was in the Piazza Costaguti, in the Jewish ghetto by the Tiber, the quarter where tourists would later venture in search of Italian-Jewish food specialties.

Pier Paolo was without work and remained so for two years. In 1966 an internationally famous film director, he wrote:

> I lived like someone would [who was] condemned to death always with that *worry*, like something borne—dishonor, unemployment, misery. My mother was reduced for a time to being a servant. But I do not recover from this evil. Because I am a petit bourgeois and I do not know how to smile like Mozart . . .

In the first months he did not call on his few Roman literary friends, at least not the heterosexual ones like Giorgio Bassani. He discovered Rome alone, as though for the first time in its history. Susanna, retained as housemaid and governess in the family of an architect, met her surviving son in the afternoon and together they walked her employers' child in a pram.

Pier Paolo did not settle his mother and move on to Milan or Florence as he had expected. He stayed in Piazza Costaguti until his father joined them in the summer of 1951, almost eighteen months after mother and son had left Casarsa.

Then the three of them moved to a house far from the center, one "without a roof" near the Ponte Mammolo, in a district called Rebibbia after the high-security prison at its center. The rent was 13,000 lire a month, half what Pier Paolo later earned as a schoolteacher. It was, by chance, standing on land once owned by Silvana Mauri's family. It was here, he recalled, "in my Rebibbia house in the poor, outlying slums I began—my true, real 'poetic work.' "

Without money or a clear future, he was now also free of the past. He no longer needed to live a double life or to worry that his secret would come out. He need not even dread, as he often did, shaming his mother. They had been through all that and they had survived. In this new place with new people, he could begin again, as himself. His relief at this was more than enough to balance discouragement. He appeared to have cut the cord to Friuli fast and clean, the way he did friendships. The shadows remained, of course, but they were the stuff for poetry.

What he called "a violent load of vitality" saved him. While he lived in a rented room (without "a hundred lire for a shave"), the Vatican declared a Holy Year, crowding the city with pilgrims come to hear old Pius XII proclaim the dogma of Mary's bodily assumption. Street urchins polished their pickpocketing skills and the Christian Democratic regime repeated that everything would be all right as long as dissent was stilled and Italian families worked hard.

Pier Paolo thrived in another parallel and underground world of his own making. He pulled out his folders and returned to work on *Atti impuri* and *Amado mio*, resuming his correspondence with the boys in San Vito. For two years he lived off his mother's earnings, his father's tiny pension, handouts from his uncle Gino. He labored at his poems and the three novels as if under contract to publishers, although none had shown any concrete interest.

By night he sought boys everywhere, especially along the river. He discovered them with the same ardor as an ethnologist who, after years in the library of some European university, meets "his tribe" face to face. By May, only four months in the city, he had published an article on the street speech of the native-born Romans. Far more than an accent, but less a full-blown language than *friulano, romanesco* had its own phrases and colorful blasphemy with variations by neighborhood. Romans were still born and died in the same district, as immobile in the city as Italians between regions: the people of Trastevere spoke differently from those of Monteverde, the rich of Parioli were as distinguishable from the poor of the slums as Kensington was from the East End, Sutton Place from the South Bronx.

Pier Paolo's special terrain, seized almost with proprietary vigilance—he called it "almost obsessive"—was the universe of Rome's poor and the criminal, of the bottom of the social scale—those without status, hope, or pretension, living at the frayed margins of a society whose social fabric is carefully stitched. He was, in effect, a tourist, come from the bourgeoisie "slumming" but no less sincere for that. Rome, he wrote in a kind of ecstasy, was "bloody with absolute novelty." His was the reality of

> all these amorphous children whom it seems impossible somehow or other to count, to extract from chaos and from that infinite series of random acts that escape any conceivable statistics and which only a poet, to his misfortune, is in a position to grasp in their unimaginable entirety.[1]

And he discovered easy sex: the pissoirs of the Lungotevere, the cruising grounds of the Janiculum, and the Ciriola boathouse (now gone without a trace), where soldiers and mechanics, shop clerks and petty thieves, went to swim and to dance with girls or one another.

The Ciriola barge, tied up beneath the Castel Sant'Angelo, its corroded planking fading a paler blue in every Roman summer, figured in his first film a decade later. The boathouse too stepped into the symbolic, affective place once held by the Pacher, his swimming hole in Friuli, did so as seamlessly as the Tiber did the Tagliamento. The accents of Trastevere and Testaccio—the slurred indolence of Roman street talk—took over from those of Friuli. He wrote, in undisguised glee to Silvana Mauri, that he lived "a life all of muscle, turned inside like a glove, absolutely without sentimentalism, among human organisms so sensual as to be almost mechanical."


At midcentury, the face of classical Renaissance and Baroque Rome had been transformed (arguably disfigured) by Fascism. And yet it was also unchanged, a provincial metropolis of many villages, in which the rhythms of family life, the social pecking order, and ease of daily interaction were more intact than in industrial cities in the north, to say nothing of the rest of Europe. It was sleepy, slightly backward, as inefficient as the bureaucrats who populated it; as Hollywood soon discovered, it was also "charming" and "characteristic," full of "local color." The noble families were poised for marrying American heiresses, the trades and skills—gilders and ironmongers, upholsterers and tailors—largely intact. Cars were relatively few; horses could still be found for drayage. Skirts were tight at the waist and flared out, and men wore baggy pants and often hats. Dress betrayed class in the era before jeans: Workers dressed their role, in singlets and rough fabric; middle-class men wore white shirts; and proper women never went out without hats equipped with veils and gloves coordinated with their shoes.

The Pope rarely traveled beyond his summer residence at Castel Gandolfo; divorce was rare, though less so than abortion; men went home for long lunches their wives or cooks prepared; grandparents were not sent to nursing homes unless so sick that the nuns had to care for them. Homosexuals stuck to careers in the Church, design, the bureaucracies, and hairdressing, and found one another at soirées, along the Tiber, and at the back balconies of movie houses. It was a world of hierarchy, clear roles, and received opinions. It seemed quickly resettled, in the years after the war; it was, in fact, on the verge of explosion.

Something revolutionary was occurring; it was at its height in Pasolini's first years in Rome, a radical mutation in the population of the city and its character. Peasants from all over the Roman countryside, from the Abruzzi, outlying Lazio, and farther south, came to find work. The postwar provinces—bombed, without capital or housing, impoverished—started to empty out. The immigrants moved together, re-creating their villages at the edge of the city, first with corrugated metal and flattened cans, then masonry blocks, a bit of cement. They found menial jobs or none at all. Their shantytowns were called *borgate*, fast-growing slums that no one could manage or control. Running water was problematic, postal service chancy, and electricity often unheard of. The city government had neither money nor will nor manpower to upgrade them into satisfactory places to live: The *borgata* expanded into Italy's version of the Latin American *favela* and long before African slum-cities like Lagos made news in the West.

Pier Paolo lived in and sought out this Rome, a city whose economic "boom" was still almost a decade away. Released from twenty years of the Fascist fog and ten years of wartime anxiety, deprivation, and death, Italians wanted nylons and a job, more meat, a new coat, and the promise that things would improve. They also wanted to know what they had missed in those lost years and what was happening in the world beyond their long-closed borders. New magazines like *Epoca* fed these yearnings with images of happiness and starlets, and of a consumerist paradise as clean and optimistic as ever was to be found in the pages of America's *Life*, *Epoca*'s unabashed model and ideal. But Pier Paolo set out to chronicle the world *Epoca* ignored, even avoided, and he touched this world like water on hot oil.

In a series of short stories, he let the invisible poor, sometimes nasty, Roman nonpersons express themselves in what he saw as their dignity, an "authenticity" that was itself alone beauty. He wrote "Squarci di notti romane" and other stories: "Il briondomoro," "Gas," and "Giubileo"—all packed like neo-realist films with the faces and bodies, voices and adventures of the street boys he both loved and studied in what was a single, merged act of mind and feeling. The lyrics about village fountains and peasants returning from the fields of Friuli as the Angelus sounded disappeared. Instead, as though a city fire hydrant had sprung open, he emerged as his own kind of lyrical naturalist.

Although he tried different lines of work during his first months in Rome—an extra at Cinecittà, private tutor, proofreader, even bookseller at a street stall—it made sense for him to turn to journalism, where he had experience. Apparently impervious to discouragement, he constantly approached newspapers with story ideas and was not too choosy about whom he worked for. As an excommunicant of the PCI, however, he did not approach *L'unità* or any of the Party's other publications; years later Franco Fortini said, "Between 1950 and 1955, the only people who helped Pasolini in Rome were the Catholics."[2] In 1950 he sold nine articles to *Il quotidiano*, a newspaper published under auspices of the Curia of the Roman Catholic Church. One was a version of a chapter of *Amado mio* entitled "Adriatic Adventures"; another, a collection of poems in the dialect of Trastevere called "Romanesco 1950"; a third, a report about the crude conditions of life in the Roman periphery. Papers like *Il popolo di*

*Roma* and *La libertà d'Italia,* allied with the Left wing of the Christian Democrats, were also willing to commission occasional articles. *Il popolo* printed his piece on Sandro Penna, and the following March his comments on books "piled up over a week": "out of all this reading, certainly more fortuitous than fortunate," the only one that "was really rewarding" was "the great Belli," the poet of Trastevere, of Roman dialect and plebeian life. In March 1950 he published in *La libertà* a review of Leonardo Sciascia, a "regional" writer who would become Sicily's greatest writer since Pirandello; and in June "Ragazzo and Trastevere," which he presented as "an anthropological study." "For myself, I would like to be able to know through what mechanism of his heart Trastevere lives within him, shapeless, throbbing, sluggish. Where does Trastevere end and the boy begin?"

These bits of freelance work took him all over the city by bus and tram, putting him in contact with people the likes of whom he had never known before. His was a real Rome, not the superficially picturesque one of the Trevi Fountain and the Spanish Steps or the urban *Cavalleria rusticana* movie set of Audrey Hepburn's *Roman Holiday*. Poor and teeming and yet (by later standards) safe, Rome seemed a giant arena constructed of baroque façades and peopled from the paintings of Caravaggio and Guido Reni, where cherubs walked the streets and were willing to talk, or something more, just for the fun of it. A cigarette offered or asked for was enough to open the floodgates of reticence.

It was Gramsci who wanted intellectuals to make their work address "the soul of the people." From his prison cell, he had called for "a people's literature." What better than the people's dialects, first *friulano,* then *romanesco?* Pasolini's people were not the industrial proletariat, fast becoming petit bourgeois, but several steps lower, the underclass of Italy's untouchables. He found in them the outcasts to whom Christ ministered; Marxism (not to be confused with the PCI) and Christianity (not to be confused with the Church) were not at odds but met in contact with this *sottoproletariato,* in his sympathy and passion for the human soul, and desire for the bodies that housed it.

Pasolini's self-made ideology crossed Gramsci with primitive Christianity. Everyday life was itself sacred; every person, in the expression of his innate selfhood without regard to bourgeois values, was holy. He saw the scavengers and hustlers of the *borgate* literally as "fourteen-year-old Christs." Their unexamined private lives were without sin, as was his, whether engaging with them in sex or not. Any institution of Church or State that stood between them and self-realization was the enemy. Commitment to them, and to their anarchy, gave Pasolini a route out of *Künstlerschuld* ("artist-guilt"). The good boy who had shone at school had found a route to rebellion that coincided exactly with his artistic goals; self-expression in art and self-actualization in life—here, and at last, in Rome, compounded like chemical affinities.

Thanks to his particular reading of Gramsci, he lost any fear that literature (and he) were useless. Art could serve without becoming propaganda. Showing people as they were—letting them express themselves as directly as possible in their own language (and later in film) with their own actions and practically without words—redeemed him from decadent estheticism.

The city seized him (in his word) "viscerally": The result was an extraordinary formula coming from the defender of consciousness—"this Rome, so present and near that only someone who lives it in full unconsciousness is capable of expressing it."

He believed that the sole difference between him and the boys was this one factor he could not alter: They lived their lives "unconsciously," with the enviable moral indifference of plants or animals. He lived his "desperately," with the consciousness of the well-educated middle class, always aware of the past. In his mind and in his "viscera," the slum's boys merged with their streets, noises, buildings, the trees, the Tiber into a living magma that pulsed. He saw a boy standing on a street corner and saw him "supple as a dove [who] moves inside his clothes like the stem of a carnation in a vase."

His adjectives for the chaos and power of the city spilled out in clashingly expressionistic pairs, indifferent to mere logic. The sun was at once "frothy and shining"; the boys' hair waved "friendly and softly." The world was like the Modenese *carbone dolce* candy—sugar made to look like a lump of coal—a phantasmagoria.

His practical situation seemed hardly to have mattered: His first months in Rome passed in exultation. Within six months of his arrival, he wrote a long exclamation, set in the story "Roman Nights"—as confessional as the diary poems, as explicit and powerful as a film, a prose painting in action.

> Think, if you will, of the Isola Tiburtina. lit by reflectors the color of ink or mint candy wrappers. Coldly reddish, in the middle of the desecrated darkness of the river, which has become a spectacle, a stage set, the glory of the municipality of Rome, an iridescent and tissue-paper attraction. Think, if you will, of the bus, that softly passes and heavily over the bridge. And of the thousands of unknown souls spreading out toward the Ghetto, toward Campo dei Fiori.

Around the pale blue and white pissoir is the ganglion, still outwardly healthy, clean, disinfected, normal and anonymous. Then you glimpse two or three torsos in idle positions, legs planted on the ground or bent with the bottoms of the feet against the parapet, resembling the legs of statues: pointlessly with an immensity of time to waste. The Outer Line trams, the Monteverde-Bainizza, go by but these torsos and legs remain. The expectation of a customer rises in their eyes like a bubble of water: they are eyes crudely veiled in black and yellow, black pupils under blond eyelashes, blond complexions blackened by the sun—duck's ass haircuts, waves frozen in their heat. Those looks—pretended distraction—the lethal high-tension current that leaps the gap, and from which they seem remote, as from another element. Squeezed into those eyes, amassed and concentrated, are layers of a Rome without antiquity, modern, ordinary, tattered and of an actuality that burns like a blowtorch at dizzying speed . . . Coming from those strata of Rome, which lie inside them like muscles, they breathe the air of the hot nights, so compact and serene that their honor is saved, pure and spotless, like that of horses.[3]

Save for the radically bohemian Sandro Penna, among the very first whom Pier Paolo sought out, no one in 1950 saw Rome this way. Penna came close to making a living from writing, or at least managed to live without any other regular work. He never taught, never held a regular job of any kind; he survived, unwashed in garbaged rooms, by trading poems for paintings, which he then sold, as he did ballpoint pens or anything else, to make ends meet. He was indifferent to fame, hated the telephone, and ignored publishers, who were left baffled by his attitude, which remained the same even when they offered him money. He literally lived for his circle of boys, seeking them out every evening. He became Pasolini's guide, a still-pagan Virgil leading an ardent Dante into the circles of the world where bodies were given, or shared for a trifle.

Penna's poems had first appeared in 1932, fostered by Umberto Saba, who for years had received manuscripts from a man he had never met. A collection appeared in 1939 and another in 1950, called *Appunti;* in September of that year Pier Paolo published a glowing review of the volume in *Il popolo di Roma*.

The two poets, whom so many found "difficult," hit it off immediately. They even had a competition, part serious and part running joke, to see who could "do" the most boys in the least time. They frequented the Ciriola: Penna heavy-lidded and chain-smoking, Pasolini all angular, scrubbed, silent yet eager.

\*　　\*　　\*

In a poem of 1964 Pier Paolo described the rhythm of his first Roman years:

> I work all day like a monk
> and at night wander around like an alleycat
> looking for love . . . I'll propose to the Church that I
> be made a saint.[4]

What lay behind the rhythm is best revealed in the correspondence he maintained with old friends. On February 10 he wrote Silvana at length, the Ramuscello scandal still raw:

> Ever since arriving in Rome, I need only sit down at the typewriter and I start to tremble and do not know what to think: Words seem to have lost their meaning. I can only tell you that the ambiguous life—as you well call it—which I led at Casarsa, I will continue to lead it here in Rome. And if you think about the etymological origin of the word ambiguous you will see that life cannot be other than that for someone living a double existence.
>
> I did not have an upbringing or a past you could call religious or moralistic, to appearances; but for many years I was one of those one calls the consolation of his parents, a model son, an ideal scholar . . . Excuse me— I only wanted to say it will not always be possible for me to speak with modesty about myself; rather it will often be necessary to pillory myself, because I don't want to trick anyone anymore—as, at base, I tricked you and other friends who now speak about an old Pier Paolo, or a Pier Paolo to be made over. . . .
>
> I think, speaking of this, that I want to live in Rome, precisely because there will that way be neither an old nor a new Pier Paolo.
>
> Someone normal can resign himself—what a terrible word—to chastity, to missed chances: but in me the difficulty of loving has made the need to love obsessive.[5]

He calls his "condition" something "chronic, incurable." The result is that when he sees "a boy seated on a wall," he is seized by a "desperation" and lets trams go by for hours in the hope of meeting him, "to my disgrace and remorse."

> But, then you ask me whether what happened to me—punishment, as you rightly call it—served me for nothing. Yes, it served me, but not to change me nor even less to set me free: it served me to understand that I had touched bottom, that that experience was exhausted and I could start from the beginning without making the same mistakes; I freed myself from my evil, fossilized perversion of reserve, I feel lighter and the libido is a cross but not a weight dragging me to the bottom.[6]

He reread what he had written to this point, said it made him unhappy, and continued:

> This last crisis in my life, an exterior crisis, which is the rendition of an interior one which I put off day by day, has reestablished, or so I hope, a certain equilibrium. There are moments when life is open like a fan, where you can see everything, and then it becomes fragile, insecure, too vast. Try and see this totality in my statements and my confessions. My future will certainly not be that of a university professor: by now there is upon me the sign of Rimbaud or Campana and also of Wilde, whether I want it or not, whether others accept it or not. It is a discomforting thing, annoying and inadmissable, but that is how it is: and I, like you, do *not resign myself*.
> 
> . . . I have suffered the sufferable, but I have never accepted my sin, I have never come to terms with my nature and I am not even used to it.
> 
> . . . My homosexuality was something more, outside, had nothing to do with me. But I always saw it as something next to me, like an enemy, never feeling it inside me. Only in this last year have I let myself go a bit. . . .[7]

He tells Silvana that she is "the only woman I could have loved"; but to understand that impossibility, he suggests she read *La porte étroite* (*Strait Is the Gate*).

She responded two weeks later, mentioning, in parentheses, that she would be married that April to writer Ottiero Ottieri.

He also wrote to her about his work. He reported to her the next day that "the novels which I am writing are three. Don't be shocked, in these last months, I have done nothing but write, even ten hours a day."[8] And he reminded her of his "Red Notebooks." Those are "diaries of my love for Tonuti," he tells her, "started in '46, when it [his love] was already at an end, . . . and I continued writing until '48: There was already then a little volume of about a hundred pages." His recent return to the manuscripts has been to "objectify" them, change true names to fictional ones, and "give less confession and more liberty of invention." During the first months of 1950 the work had grown to two connected but separate texts—*Atti impuri* and *Amado mio*, "of 200 to 250 pages, only two or three chapters missing." He wrote her, "The protagonist of *Amado mio* resembles me less than that of *Atti impuri*; and more than that, he is quite different from me in character . . . the action takes place a little bit in Friuli, a bit in Rome, the Rome of the neighborhood movie houses, of Trastevere, of construction sites and the via del Tritone."[9]

He described *Sogno* (still under the working name *La meglio gioventù*) as "very different from the other two, and very complex." It was, he explained, a cross between Varga and Proust, inspired by the tone of Vasco Pratolini's *Cronache di poveri amanti,* a best-selling novel in 1947. "I've now written more than half the book: I had planned to finish it before leaving Casarsa. But instead, here I am, unable to find a clear period for writing . . . in case the capacity to write does return to me, which one would you suggest I finish?"[10]

Pier Paolo's lifeline to Casarsa was cousin Nico, and it was to him that a series of letters went requesting—commanding—errands. When Carlo Alberto wrote to reaffirm his decision to sell all the furniture and perhaps everything else in their Casarsa home, it was to Nico that Pier Paolo wrote, asking him to "save my books." "Put some in Aunt Giannina's kitchen and some in your room," he instructed. He adds that Nico should save his notebooks, the manuscripts found "in the desk drawer," the notebooks of *Atti impuri,* tucked into the bookcases.

Nico was also ordered to take some of his philosophy books ("the ones published by Laterza") and "make some excuse to go to Padua and sell them for three or four thousand lire." He needed money to go out with the boys he met, to buy pizza, coffees. "Send it [the proceeds] by money order, not certified mail." He mentioned meeting the brother of the star of the film *Sotto il sole di Roma* (Under the sun of Rome, 1948), telling his cousin: "[He is] seventeen years old, much handsomer, [than his brother] . . . [and has] become my friend. We met last night through the interventions of some god." Courtship costs; he needed to make at least a minimum of *bella figura.* Ever his ally, his Aunt Giannina sent him 300,000 lire. He thanked her via Nico, also charging him to express gratitude to the DC deputy Caron, who had tried to soften the scandal, without success.

A flash of Pier Paolo's daily life emerges in a March note to Nico. He asked that he go and retrieve a collection of his poems in *friulano* from a magazine editor in Udine. When Nico failed to move quickly, Pasolini chastised him:

> I need them for *Botteghe oscure* . . . try to imagine the shocking conditions in which I live: for the last ten days I've been going every morning to uncle's place to see if there is any mail; nothing, no one writes to me any more. I spend the rest of the day dying of dejection. By now I have pretty well reached the outer limits of desperation.[11]

By late February his poems were somewhere within Mondadori's bureaucracy, and he began to lose hope. He wrote Sereni: "I yield in the face of a pair of shoelaces that need tying, imagine when faced with the Gordian knot of Mondadori." He felt overwhelmed in the face of "the bureaucratic-administrative moment."

At his "outer limits," Giorgio Bassani stepped in. He spoke with his friend and employer, the Principessa Caetani, of *Botteghe oscure;* would she take on Pier Paolo as private librarian? She declined, with the feeble excuse that he was too young.

Nico was again sent on a survival errand, this time to offer a Bartolini watercolor for sale to their painter friend De Rocco. "If you get 10,000 instead of 25,000, that's also all right." Again, Nico, it seems, was slow to react. Pier Paolo wrote: "Forgive the peremptory tone, but with the deaf one needs to shout."

Later that spring he wrote his cousin-confidant:

> The trauma-Rome is wearing off: there remains the acute, intolerable desire to be a millionaire. It has been a long time since I've had a word from aunt Giannina: greet her and kiss her for me. I have recently written your mother about two *salamis,* a half kilo of butter and a dressing-gown [which presumably she was asked to sew]: isn't she doing anything about it?[12]

In June, he wrote Nico:

> I am becoming a Roman, not knowing how to spit out a word in Veneto or Friulian and I say *li mortacci tua* [untranslatable Roman curse, roughly, "the same curses upon you" crossed with "up yours"]. I swim in the Tiber, and so far as regards human and poetic "episodes" which happen to me, multiply by a hundred those that occurred in Friuli.[13]

By the spring of his first year in Rome, matters literary, if not financial, improved. At the end of May, Giacinto Spagnoletti wrote to say that he, Attilio Bertolucci, and Carlo Bo had chosen five of Pier Paolo's Friulian poems for the first issue of a new magazine, *Quaderno della Fenice* (literally, The Phoenix Notebook) to be issued twice a year from the publishers Guanda. "The magazine will be sent you . . . let me know if we have chosen well. If not, the fault is mine."

On August 22 he wrote Susanna at Ferrara, where she had gone as live-in housemaid and companion. He reported spending "all afternoon at the Tiber with Penna, and also the evening I pass with him, in endless discussions." A week later he wrote her again to say he had been awarded second prize in the "Catholic-People's Calendar" competition—50,000 lire for the *friulano* lyric "El testament Coran":

> Are you pleased? I took pleasure in it especially for you, and for the positive influence it will have on Daddy (even if temporary). It is a nice victory because, since the winner was predestined, I won second place on pure merit, as the jury held unanimously.[14]

The Ramuscello case was due for trial in September, making a Casarsa visit necessary. He had trouble sleeping and Susanna worried. He wrote her: "Don't be concerned. Penna gave me some earwax (imagine if we had known about that at Casarsa!) thanks to which, in the morning, immersed in the deepest, visceral silence I can sleep as late as I wish. . . ."[15]

Pier Paolo sent Susanna, still in the country, a photo of himself. She wrote him about it:

> How happy I am to have you. Every so often, even frequently, I stop and open my purse and kiss you and return to my work refreshed. The expression on your face is perfect. At first, it seemed too serious, but then looking harder one makes out your enigmatic smile, which is the loveliest thing one can see in a face, the expression not only of your genius, but also of your generosity of spirit. Don't laugh: I express myself as I can.[16]

In late September he received another honorable mention, this time from the Soave prize committee; within weeks the editor-critic Carlo Muscetta asked Pier Paolo for the Friulian poems to propose to his employer, the publisher Einaudi. But this project, too, came to nothing; the book, bearing the title *La meglio gioventù*, appeared from the Florentine house of Sansoni only in 1954.

On October 4 Susanna wrote him another postcard:

> Today is Guido's birthday. Who knows if anyone will remember and go to take flowers. Do you remember how for his birthday he wanted strudel with new apples and raisins? Do you recall how just now six years ago you hid in the belltower of Casarsa, hidden because the Germans were out looking to seize men? What horrible, painful days! And yet Guido was with us, and we were happy. . . .[17]

Three days later he wrote to reassure her:

> Don't worry about the flowers: how can you imagine anyone will forget that the 4th is his birthday? Other things, instead, Germans etc., must be forgotten, dearest fatty, they must be forgotten. I kiss you and embrace you with infinite tenderness, Your Pier Paolo[18]

By year's end he had completed another poetic "diary," this one entitled *Roma, 1950*. It was published a decade later, in 1960, by the small Milanese firm of Gianni Scheiwiller. By then Pasolini was one of Italy's most famous poets, a best-selling novelist, respected critic, figure of public notoriety, and about to take up the movie camera.

Pier Paolo spent New Year's Eve 1951 in comfortable, homosexual, Veneto-Friulian company with his cousin Nico and the writer Giovanni Comisso of Treviso. The details are lost, but somehow late in the day a group—whom Naldini has called "a band of drunken boys"—stole Pier Paolo's wallet. It is not too much to imagine that the three, or Pier Paolo alone, came on to the boys, who played along and then took their revenge on the *frocio*.

What matters more is what happened next. During police interrogations, Pasolini found himself in a holding cell, the complainer become, if not the officially accused, then treated as a criminal. It was a small matter but did not seem so to Pier Paolo.

He felt himself "persecuted, exiled, and vilified." The adjectives are Contini's in a letter of solace, but Pier Paolo accepted them as accurate. Not yet thirty, he had decided that he was being punished by the State, persecuted by the PCI, deserted by many friends—for what he had not chosen to be. The decades brought more incidents—attacks, trumped-up charges, legal proceedings, evidence enough to seem not proof of paranoia but confirmation of a rightly reasoned theory.

By July 1951 Carlo Alberto Pasolini joined his wife and son in Rome and the family settled in the Rebibbia house at via Giovanni Tagliere, 3. It was a badly built, illegally thrown-up stucco shack beyond the city's zoning laws. Silvana Mauri Ottieri remembers going there by taxi and being shocked at how far it was from the center, how far down an unpaved road. Susanna and Carlo shared one of its two rooms; Pier Paolo's was the other.

The career officer on a fixed pension of shrinking value, his wife in love with her clothes and cosmetics, and their son—who had been the star at Bologna's Faculty of Letters and was a published poet—now lived in a slum, "a dustbowl in summer, a swamp in winter." There Carlo Alberto sat in the kitchen, "filling the space with the hugeness that dead bodies have," Pasolini wrote. Hours passed as he stared into space, elbows on the kitchen table, fists sunk into his cheeks in deep depression.

The solution he found was ironic even if inevitable: He became Pier Paolo's secretary, watching the papers in order to clip whatever articles of his son's appeared, running to the stationer, to the post office. He was always there when friends called and collared them, insisting shamelessly on recounting Pier Paolo's latest encouraging chat with an editor, what progress was coming in a career he could not otherwise share.

From here, Pier Paolo continued to spur Nico (as best he could) to collect payment from one Mario Verderi, who had rented the little room in Casarsa used by the Academiuta. The rent had still not been paid in August, and Pier Paolo wrote again, now asking a special favor. Nico was to go to certain municipal officials in Casarsa and be sure they understood that Carlo Alberto, even though father of the scandalous pederast, was someone important:

> Do a favor for my father (who continues to be all right): say, at your first opportunity, to Suor Banchi [a nun]—for propaganda—and to Emilio Fillelo and Dr. Berlese—that my father won the Silver Medal for military valor "in action" [*sul campo;* "in the field." Not behind a desk]. (If you can, let this be known also at City Hall to Francescutti; it matters a lot to my father that he know this).[19]

Carlo Alberto, who would return to Casarsa only to be buried, wanted it understood by those who counted that he might have left for Rome, but not in personal disgrace.

Pier Paolo's way into the essence of humanity was its speech. He later told his publisher, Livio Garzanti, that he could not write about the *borgata* without using its expressions, shocking though they might be to good society: "The slangs spoken in a dialect were absolutely necessary to write . . . it is they which give me the happiness necessary to understand and describe my characters." Years later, he explained ". . . when I arrived in Rome, I started to use the dialect of the Roman subproletariat in an objective manner (as opposed to the "poetic" in Friuli), to obtain the most exact description of the world I had before me."

Among the first results that pleased him enough to survive as a chapter of a growing novel was the short story "Il ferrobedò" (a corruption of *ferro beton*—"reinforced concrete"). It is like nothing else written in those years, a precursor of the most revolutionary book of the decade, Carlo Emilio Gadda's 1957 *Quer pasticciaccio brutto de via Merulana*, which singlehandedly legitimized dialect in "serious" prose.

The similarity is not coincidental. Pasolini studied engineer-novelist Gadda during his isolation in wartime Casarsa; in 1954 he wrote an essay that dubbed Gadda "an object . . . of veneration."[20]

Years later Contini recalled one wag dubbed Pasolini one of "the little nephews of the engineer."[21]

"Il ferrobedò" is a brilliant evocation, immediate as film, of the boys who hang at the edges of the Società Ferro Beton factory and depot in the heart of the slum called Donna Olimpia. That neighborhood, hardly a world of bourgeois nicety or of "Catholic morality," is what Pasolini called "the matrix" in which his hero, a boy named Riccetto, lives. It is 1945, the Germans are retreating, and the population has found the nerve to loot.

Pier Paolo introduces his protagonist *in medias res,* in an act of petty thievery, speaking and behaving as literature's heroes were not expected to do in 1951:

> Over there the Ferrobedò was like an immense courtyard, a walled-in field sunk in a valley, as big as a town square or a cattle market. On one side were the rows of wooden dwellings, on the other the warehouses. Riccetto traveled the length of the Ferrobedò with the yelling crowd and stopped in front of one of the houses. But there were four Germans who kept them from going in. Beside the door was an overturned table. Riccetto shouldered it and ran toward the gateway. Just outside he bumped into a boy who said, "What you doing?" "I'm taking it home, what do you think?" said Riccetto. "Come on with me, stupid, we can get better stuff than that."[22]

Riccetto robs a blind man; he and his pals throw gravel at a prostitute he spots in the bushes "with a Negro":

> With her breasts half out of her dress, the whore got up in a spitting rage and started to scream at them. "Ah, shut up!" yelled Riccetto, making a megaphone with his hands. "Your ass is sucking wind, you dirty no-good bitch!" But at that moment the Negro sprang to his feet like a wild man, and holding up his pants with one hand and brandishing a knife in the other, began to run after them. Riccetto and Marcello ran out from among the bushes, shouting for help, toward the high bank and the path that led over it. When they got to the top, they dared to look back for a moment, and they saw the Negro down below, waving the knife in the air and yelling. Riccetto and Marcello went on running, and looking at each other, they laughed and laughed.[23]

The gangs of boys in Donna Olimpia lived by their wits amid cracked high-rises in an endless din of street noise in a world they called *monezza* ("trash"). And that is what Pasolini described; better yet, he let the boys describe it in their own words. The task he set for himself was nothing less than to paint Italy's postwar portrait "without nostalgia." The place names that replaced those of Friuli—places he said "a bourgeois cannot even imagine"—were now Borgo Pio, San Lorenzo, the *borgata* of Pietralatra, Tiburtino III: He put them on the map of Italian fiction and in the country's consciousness.

Many thought he was only indulging in the "sublime of the base," living an intellectual's pretentious *nostalgie de la boue*. But Pasolini was far too taken by his drives for something so superficial as that, and far too able to exploit his unconscious consciously. The *borgata* acted as a magnet pulling on the most fundamental part of him. Its reality was not something only sociological but moral, esthetic, and erotic together. Writing of the place and its people was not just a work of the imagination but the only way to possess it, to make it even more real than it was. Writing would make it survive time as he, the boys, and the place could not.

"Il ferrobedò" first appeared in the June 1951 issue of *Paragone*, the literary edition of the arts and culture magazine edited by Roberto Longhi, Pasolini's mentor at Bologna, and his wife Anna Banti. *Paragone* was regular reading for poet Attilio Bertolucci; he read the story and remembered it. As a consultant to his fellow *parmigiano*, the publisher Guanda, he soon brought the house the idea for Pier Paolo to assemble an anthology of poetry in dialect. Bertolucci also worked as scout for the young Livio Garzanti; his assignment was to help the house build a winning list of new writers. It took, though, until April 1953 for the crucial connection to be made—Pasolini to Garzanti through Bertolucci—but when it was, Pier Paolo's Bologna *maestro* Longhi's act of editorial appreciation in printing "Il ferrobedò" lay indispensably at its heart.

Meanwhile, Pier Paolo continued to approach the editors of dailies, seeking freelance article work. In August he went to Puglia in the deep south; his reportage appeared as "Visions of the South; Letters from a Train" in *Il quotidiano*.

By the latter half of 1951, a steady output of work—all that he chased down, most badly paid—reveals an extraordinary versatility: *Botteghe oscure*'s eighth issue made room for *I parlanti*, Friulian work written in '48; *La fiera letteraria* ran a piece on the poet Danilo Dolci in September, and the same month *Il popolo di Roma* printed an opinion piece on "writing in the schools."

With an ease that stunned his contemporaries (and engendered more than a little envy), he moved from poetry to criticism, from feature reporting to short stories. Two *novelle* from 1951 (collected

in book form only in 1965) are *Testaccio* (more accurately, "Studies on the Life of Testaccio") and *Notte sull'ES* (A night on the tram).
From the latter:

> The rocks, the stones, the roofs, the pavements, the tufa, the cornices, the mortar have fused into a single crust, the crust of an architecture fixed for centuries, in this very same place, with these curves, these corners, these walls and perspectives, in such a way as to have replaced a rural nature the memory of which has been completely lost—they have fused into the pure appearance of a city (the absolute city that is Trastevere). . . .
>
> They have been fused as into a hardness of bone, which has thus arrested forever, within the confines of our history (so vast and uncertain in its unfolding, so elementary once it has passed), houses, streets, and churches already crumbling to dust.[24]

Into this metahistorical Trastevere he introduces Rafele, aged nine, "made of elastic, of stone. The hair falling over his forehead and eyes, in which there is no particular expression . . . extraordinarily beautiful, perhaps just because it is alone and nothing but his hair."

He is spotted by a notary who looks at him a certain way, saying nothing. Rafele understands; his face shows "the subtle shadings of complicity." The boy follows: Is he "corrupted"?

> They walk along the deserted embankment toward Regina Coeli, pissoirs alternating with the hard, metallic trunks of the winter chestnut trees. Rafele barely responds to the notary's kind questions, for childhood makes him deaf to everything that is not directly useful, conventional (getting jerked off like older boys, then money). The same ferment, to be noted in his way of walking, as though on scorched feet, a little ashamed, of his dry, statuette-like belly, keeps whirling to be resolved on the spot, with the complete novelty of his buttons being slipped out of their buttonholes, and the offer of his little gift, already hard as a cobblestone, a chestnut twig; it happens at the bottom of a stairwell wet with rain and urine, oozing with liquid mud, on a patch of sticky grass under the dripping bridge, almost level with the current of the Tiber . . . The clash—unnoticed, sunk in the opaque distance between them: Rafele's hurry, and the other's desire to keep going endlessly. The boy is then silent, as like two thieves they descend the stairs; indeed, he is almost about to cry. He is afraid that the notary will leave without giving him anything. He doesn't have the courage to ask him for money, and therefore his chin is almost trembling, and a furious, frowning shadow forms in the arch of his eyebrows, and in his mouth. But the notary thrusts three hundred-lire bills at him; he then tries to say an affectionate good-bye, but Rafele, sticking the money in his pocket, runs down toward Ponte Sisto

without even looking him in the face, such is the distance between the old age of the notary and his own childhood.[25]

In "Studies on the Life of Testaccio," Pasolini again reported the world of boys in loving detail: their "magnificent" slingshots and their stance toward an indifferent reality:

> In every act or undertaking there is an undercurrent of irony: nothing must be done seriously, and therefore each one of their passions (fishing, killing lizards) slides on an ironic base, and makes them hostile, ambiguous. This is part of the street-smart philosophy of the quarter, where it is necessary not to be different. They are ever competing with each other in boredom, the possibility of being able to do without others, the immediate capacity for catching others red-handed in credulity, faith, commitment—in naïveté.[26]

The Testaccio slum-quarter is rendered as a set of film-script directions:

> Panoramic opening—from above, as in some French film classic, René Clair—: Porta Portese, the Juvenile Reformatory—of a solid, discolored Roman baroque—high, deserted Tiber embankments. But this in passing: the camera will immediately focus on the Testaccio side. Ponte Testaccio. Bare shore, of a poisonous green, above the water of the Tiber, still swollen from the winter flooding. Long, yellowish block of five- or six-story houses, early twentieth century, with a northern, seaside look. Asphalt of the streets near the river.
> Distant and misty view of the Porto area, of the gasworks.[27]

An "ordinary" rainstorm in the city becomes the occasion for a prose that is part poem, part film clip:

> Evening descends on Testaccio like a storm; through the network of streets around the piazza with its gardens, you hear the iron shutters of stores being lowered with a sudden crash; the shadows of children run with bottles of milk, and the delivery boys launch their tricycles at full speed amid the confusion of people who rush home as though they were actually fleeing a sudden downpour of rain. The air is more dirty and turbid than dark; the headlights of a car, already burning, gleam harshly at a curve on the still clear and daytime pavement. It looks as though a wind charged with odors and humidity is rattling windows and glass doors, shaking the dead saplings in the park, and putting the whole quarter in a state of alarm; instead it is the calm hour of supper descending.[28]

As 1951 wound down, he finally gained some substantial recognition: His poem "Picasso" appeared in the November issue of *Bottegheoscure*. He was inspired by the Picasso of the dove of peace, the Left-wing artist.

But Pasolini took issue with Picasso's choice of exile. He wrote, of course and as usual, of himself:

> It is by remaining
> inside the inferno with a cold
> determination to understand it, that one seeks
> salvation.[29]

In December he delivered his first radio talk for the cultural channel of the RAI (the Italian State radio-television system). It was entitled "Popular Poetry and Mass Culture" and went well enough. And yet no regular work.

Finally, in December, a break. He could not teach in the State schools, having been dismissed under a cloud, but, for longer hours and less pay, a post might be found in a private school. Vittorio Clemente, known for his verse in dialect, put in a word, and Pier Paolo found himself at year's end taken on the teaching staff of a private middle school (optimistically called the Francesco Petrarca School in via Appia Pignatelli), far out of town at Ciampino, near the civil airfield of the same name. The routine was similar to that in Friuli, save that the kids were tough city types instead of pliable peasants. He earned 300,000 lire a month, which he passed to Susanna to maintain the three of them.

As he had in Valvasone, he drilled his students in Dante but also asked that they bring from home songs, rhymes, sayings, and proverbs to discuss in class. He wanted them to see these as literature too, as also worthwhile.

At last, after two years in the capital, he had work. And a publishing assignment: He was to assemble for Guanda a small anthology of the most important poetry in Italian dialects, to appear under Bertolucci's general supervision. Translations into Italian would appear at page-bottom, with cocredit as selector, and a signed preface, by Pier Paolo. He was not asked to produce the anthology alone but was assigned a collaborator.

The commute from Ponte Mammolo to Ciampino took three and a half hours a day. As best he could on several buses, he read every poem of significance in Italy's dozen-plus distinct dialects written

since the start of the century. In "The Tears of the Excavator," written
in 1956, he documented this life:

> Poor as a cat in the Coliseum,
> I lived in a slum of dust clouds
> and limestone, far from the city,
>
> far from countryside, squeezed each day
> onto a wheezing bus;
> and every trip back and forth
>
> was a Calvary of sweat and anxiety—
> long walks in the heat's haze,
> long dusks in front of my papers
> heaped on the table, among muddy streets,
> low walls, small whitewashed
> windowless shacks that had curtains for doors . . .[30]

He returned to memories of his second Roman year again in 1961,
when so much had changed. The poem is entitled "Ricordi di miseria"
(Memories of misery).

> How much life has been taken from me,
> sadly unemployed for years,
> a dazed victim of obsessive hopes.
> How much life,
> having to run in hungry crowds every morning
> from a poor house lost at the edge of town
> to a poor school on another periphery:
> work accepted only by one in desperate straits
> to whom every form of existence is hostile.
>
> Ah, the old seven o'clock bus
> stopped at the end of the Rebibbia line
> between two hovels and a small skyscraper,
> alone in freezing chill or sultry heat . . .
>
> Those faces of everyday passengers
> as if out on a pass from sad barracks,
> dignified and serious,
> with the feigned vivacity of the bourgeoisie
> masking the age-old fear
> of the honest poor.[31]

During these months he wrote *L'Appennino* (The Apennines). It
appeared at the end of 1952, again in *Paragone*.

At year's end he wrote Tonuti in response to a letter from the boy, one which had been full of news about skiing, work, and a fall from a new motorcycle:

> [My life] is enormous, neutral, an impasto of violence both good and evil: it resembles Rome a little . . . I am working like a dog to finish a short story which I have to have done within the month, and the rest besides.
>
> For now, I want to tell you one thing: you were the most beautiful time of my life. Because of this, not only can I never forget you, but on the contrary will always have you always in my deepest memory, like a reason for living.[32]

# 13

*Oh Rome! my country! city of the soul!*
*The orphans of the heart must turn to thee*
*lone mother of dead empires.*
*and control in their shut breasts*
*their petty misery.*
*What are our woes and sufferance?*
*Come and see*
*the cypress, hear the owl, and plod your way*
*O'er steps of broken thrones*
*and temples. Ye!*
*Whose agonies are evils of a day*
*A world is at our feet*
*As fragile as our clay.*

          **—Byron, Childe Harold, IV, LXXVIII**

# IN REBIBBIA EXILE

Pier Paolo wrote a friend in 1952, "I shall never assimilate." He doubted that he could imcorporate the rough, extroverted style of Romans. But he might also have been describing something far broader. His life was spent eluding categories and cultivating ever more powerful enemies. His program, gradually developed in response to what life brought him, was not simply in declining to assimilate but was becoming a great refusal.

He had come to Rome with some recognition preceding him, in

literary circles, and begun a slow and methodical climb in its often petty society, cliques quite as provincial as those of Udine, populated by writers often claiming to be divided along ideological lines but principally warring for the attention of publishers and too few readers.

Editors, always approached through intermediaries and to be handled with extreme deference, routinely failed to respond to inquiries even when solicited; phone calls regularly went unreturned; initial enthusiasms were left to cool. One way to get attention was to win a prize, and that was best done by cultivating the jury before a competition and those who were prospective jurors at all times. Someone trying to make a name as a poet had constantly to forge alliances, to seek to do and collect favors, to garner notice.

Pasolini's correspondence during his first five years in Rome is littered with complaints about checks "in the mail," promises not kept, leads that evaporated. Occasional acts of quasi-disinterested generosity—those of Bassani, Bertolucci, and especially Contini—stand out as exceptions. Only one with Pasolini's staggering energy and massive tenacity could have kept at it: Also, he knew he had no alternative. And he was every bit as determined to be noticed and successful as those with the power to help him sometimes seemed impervious to his blandishments.

And he did assimilate. He played the game of reputation-making with skill and to the hilt.

When Giacinto Spagnoletti's school text on twentieth-century poets appeared, so did a rift in their friendship, which returned—much exacerbated—a decade later. After warm letters and mutual praise, somehow Spagnoletti delivered to his publisher a collection of poetry in dialect up to and through living writers but excluding Pasolini. A series of letters flew between them in March. Pier Paolo was hurt and angry, claiming that he could understand excluding his Italian verse, but not to include a single one of his Friulian poems was inexplicable. And, worse, Mario dell'Arco had been included—the coeditor Guanda had imposed for the Bertolucci-midwifed anthology—someone Pasolini came to feel took more than half the credit for doing well under half the work.

Spagnoletti passed the blame to editors within the publishing house; Pasolini refused the explanation. After a month Pasolini asked that they speak of it no more. He insisted, "I still consider you guilty" but added that "blame is . . . soon fused into a cordial light which your image emanates when I think about it." In later years he would leave off the icing. Softening his tone but without withdrawing his accusation, he suggested, "I've a million ways to excuse you: first of all your critical liberty [to choose and exclude from the anthology as he saw fit], then my lack of faith in myself, and all the circumstances. . . ." [1]

But he still needed the well-connected Spagnoletti's help. Soon after their flare-up, he wrote to ask if he might let the judge of a competition know that the submitted pseudonymous piece on Ungaretti (entitled "The Poet and God") was Pasolini's, something he had worked at intermittently since 1948. The prize was called Le quattro arti; Pier Paolo ended up sharing the critical essay category with two others. He excused himself to Spagnoletti for the politicking, but "one who works five or six hours a day for twenty-one thousand lire a month" (he explained) might be forgiven it. Any income helped: Unlike public institutions, the Ciampino school paid when in session, not during the summer.

The magazine *Paragone* also published books, a literary list of its own: By April, they had agreed to bring out *La meglio gioventù*. In Rome, far from the real Friuli, Pasolini would finally be able to see in print his evocation of its world, one now infused with the imagined presence of a nonexistent Provence. But somehow the project failed to materialize.

That month he asked Fabio Luca Cavazza to learn what he could about a new collection of Friulian verse issuing in Udine. Pier Paolo had submitted two poems to "a certain shit named Rino Borghello," only to have them returned, because one was "too long" and the other "too late." I "know my chickens up there," Pasolini wrote, their "insensitivity . . . and imbecility." While he "couldn't care less," Carlo Alberto thought such a thing "without my name on it is intolerable . . . he's made himself sick over it . . . So I have to see where things stand. Also to put things in order with that shit when I go to Udine: either to greet him or cover him with contempt."

Every town of any size and many companies thought a small monetary prize to culture a sure sign of their modernity, their proof positive of supporting *civiltà* and getting space in the newspapers free. Taranto, at the heel of the Italian boot, had such a competition. Entry called for a manuscript, envelopes, and stamps: Carlo Alberto saw to the mechanics. In May, Pier Paolo won Taranto's award for a short story about the Mezzogiorno, "Terracina-Operetta Marina"; his vocation seemed to be maturing.

He contributed to the magazine of the RAI (the State radio and television network) and appeared in Mario dell'Arco's magazine *Orazio*, dedicated to dialects.

And he wrote a prefatory note to *Il fiore della poesia romanesca*, a collection of poetry in Roman dialect by Belli, Pascarella, Trilussa, and Dell'Arco, edited by Leonardo Sciascia and published in 1953. Pasolini is erudite but also shows himself as the autodidact as bore. Instead of the vividly concrete prose of the short stories and the novel-in-the-works, his critical voice here is clogged and prolix, slow to clear itself before speaking; the opening sentence of the preface alone numbers 169 words.

And yet amid the name-dropping and its stretching for credentials, a unique vision appears. He links the poetry of dialect—as the language of the plebs found in Rome's distinct neighborhoods—to the films of the time, those "of Emmer and Castellani." The written word and the filmed human who speaks and moves are simply two equally accessible media to him, not ends (not Literature and Cinema) but means to render reality. Already Pasolini the visual artist pulls at the constraints of language and reaches for pictures as the better way to reproduce life. He wrote: "One cannot think about Belli without 'seeing' Trastevere, not simply 'thinking about' Trastevere." He managed to discuss the first three poets and mention Dell'Arco once, in the last line referring to his "play of intelligence." A few years later he wrote his friend Biagio Marin in Trieste that he had "definitively broken" with Dell'Arco, whom he called "an *arriviste*, hypocrite and dishonest. . . ."

Save for the Ciampino school's inroads on his time, he was now a career man of letters, increasingly if sporadically respected and sought out by others who were the same. He was working in earnest on a novel, originally to be called *Ferrobedò*, like the story: a panorama of the *borgata* and its boys but with a plot calling for more space than a short story. It consumed him and countless, unregretted hours went to collecting anecdotes, eavesdropping, engaging boys in conversation to see how they would turn a phrase, react to a hypothetical situation he posed. It would be two years until it was finished under the title *Ragazzi di vita*, but working on it gave him faith again that he could still write with passion, and well.

In June he wrote "Rome and Belli" for the daily *Diario di Roma*, a soft-scholarly look at the most famous poet of the city's poor, the one whose epigrams were part of the urban folklore and whose statue marked the unofficial entrance to Trastevere, by the Ponte Garibaldi. Pasolini devoured Rome and the Romans like a scientist starved for data, a processing plant ravenous for input:

> Poor, joyous fourteen-year-old Christs,
> the boys from Donna Olimpia
> can toss their whole day away,

passionately misbelieving,
lucidly confused
drawn by their nearly animal

hearts' poor impulses toward
the morning joys of Villa Sciarra
and the Janiculum, joys of students, nurses,

young girls, toward the clamor their
friends make, which the pale sub absorbs
in a sickly halo of grass and air . . .

Mornings of pure life! When the soul
hears no other calls
than those of the sweet chaos

of daily good and evil
They live it, abandoned
by all, free in their human fervor,

to which they were lightly born, because poor,
because sons of the poor,
resigned to their destiny and yet

always ready for new adventures
of the dream, which, descending from
the heights of the world, sets them innocently

in motion, and to which, corrupted, they sell
themselves, though no one pays them; tattered
and elegant in the marvellous manner of Romans,

they wander into the well-to-do
neighborhoods of people who live the dream. . . .²

He found the *borgata*'s boys "tattered and elegant in the marvelous
manner of Romans" living confirmations, encountered every day,
that the capital was where he must stay. Here he could make a career
as a writer, perhaps enter the world of film. He understood that
something like a new golden age of postwar Italian cinema was coming, a wave he could perhaps ride. It counted that here he was freed
from the "ambiguity" of Friuli. That dealings were difficult was to be
expected. Contrary to his repeated claims, he did adapt to the city,
and fast, coming to be as much at home there as anywhere.

He wrote Spagnoletti during the summer of 1952: "You know how
Rome is! All vice and sun, crust and light: a populace possessed by
the joy of living, exhibitionism and contagious sensuality, spilling
over into the outskirts . . . I am lost in the midst of it.³

In July, he wrote Silvana about a certain Cristoforo. He had started chatting with him in the grounds of the large park at the city's center —Villa Borghese—on the evening of the Strega Prize–giving:

> His father died (I think in the war), then in '48 his mother (for whom, it seems, he has great affection) remarried . . . the new husband completely ignored [him]. Now he has no family and no home: every so often he works as an electrician, and when he has earned something sleeps at a landlady's, but she throws him out when he has no money. Thus he passes three-fourths of the year in the open air, in the sense that he has no roof but sleeps and eats in the Villa Borghese or under one of the Tiber bridges. You understand what misery can force on one: I know, for example, that he once robbed a Swiss pilgrim of his suitcase, which allowed him to live for five or six months without further stealing. He is an earthenware vase among iron ones. There, in the Villa Borghese among real thieves, real delinquents.

He tells Silvana, "I know plenty of thieves, etc., who are happy," but this boy was not like that.

> This one really touched my heart. Imagine that he let me know that his principal torment (that very hot afternoon of the Strega) was not to have soap to wash himself. (Think of his wardrobe, Silvana, a pullover, a pair of socks and a pair of shoes: that's all he has. He washes his clothes himself, in the Tiber, waiting nude until his things dry.)

He decided that she did not need to hear more of the

> thousand episodes of his life which I could recount for you, but to someone who lives fully a bourgeois life, the necessary facts are lacking to understand the truth of certain situations which they learn of only from news reports . . . from which every flavor of the truth is lacking.
>
> But I do not love (forgive me if I speak so plainly) this boy: sexually he does not interest me: I am interested in his case, and I do not know what to do to get him out of his shocking state, that of someone who awakens and in the first light of Villa Borghese says to himself, "Today, if I do not rob or find some invert, I do not eat."[4]

He wondered if Silvana could get the boy a place in the therapeutic "village" where her brother Fabio lived. But soon he wrote her again: Cristoforo had disappeared.

He continued his literary politicking, as he worked on his anthology of dialect poetry. He wrote Serra, still in "extremely civilized" Bologna, wondering if he might find out if his essay on Ungaretti, which had won the Quattro arte prize, would finally be published in a journal edited by Professor Calcaterra. Serra ought to contact Calcaterra, but go gently, remembering that Calcaterra also sat on the jury of the Modena poetry prize for which Pier Paolo planned to compete. A poem, once written, could be submitted repeatedly to different juries, recycled, make money more than once and all for the small trouble and expense of the posting: "You will find all this business about prizes absurd: and so do I: ridiculous and undignified. But one lives from it . . . You know that, teaching in a private school, one is not paid during the summer and so how to make ends meet?"[5]

When, in August he learned that Catholic poet Carlo Betocchi planned to compete for the Udine prize, a large purse for lyric poetry and for organ music, Pasolini wrote to warn him of petty provincial politics, but urged him to try anyway. He offered to write letters to accompany Betocchi's poems ("something not necessary if the jury is composed of 'prepared' people"). "I think that in Friuli they would be well satisfied to have you the winner: it is true that they are of an unimaginable ignorance, that of contemporary poets they know only Ungaretti and Montale and *by name alone,* but I have already thought through how to make you known to the public."[6]

Pier Paolo would arrange that Dino Menichini at the *Messaggero veneto* write about the poet and would—"forgive the cynicism"—cite Betocchi's "Catholic origins." He soon wrote Betocchi that the other names of jurors had been released and "in Friuli a scandal has broken" around rumors of jurors' votes bought, of the prizewinner decided well in advance. He enjoyed such politics and came to be good at it by doing it; he candidly called the process manipulation.

When the poet Giacomo Noventa sought to withdraw from the dialects anthology because the definitive edition of his poems was coming out at the same time—and he had agreed with his publishers not to compete with it—Pier Paolo cajoled, encouraged, fought to keep him in: "A note at the bottom of a page [in the Anthology] would be enough to explain things . . . you are too important a poet to fear variations [on your work] . . ."[7]

Nico was included in the anthology, and Tonuti Spagnol named. In early December Pier Paolo wrote Tonuti explaining that he was present "because I hope you will continue to write Friulian verse, in all simplicity and modesty, as you have done until now. . . . I want to get more of your poetry (for example, I saw a lovely one of yours in *Il stroligut* last year [now edited by Naldini and others in Casarsa]). Have you much more of military service [at Lucca] to go? What will you do then?"

Cousin Nico was told his inclusion was an "investment" in future performance, and not to rest content with such recognition. "Work, and study for the university," he was instructed from Rome. When he asked advice on a thesis topic, Pasolini explained, "The poetry in dialect which emerged in the 1300s were the Friulian, the Genoese, Umbrian, Sicilian and Venetian . . ."[8]

Naldini, he suggests, could write a critical essay and edit a selection of regional verse. "It could be the basis for a future anthology for Guanda we two could do together." He soon forwarded some of Nico's poems to Sciascia in Palermo, proposing them for publication in his magazine *Galleria.*

Nico, treated both as equal and batboy, was to send to Rome everything of Pier Paolo's written in Friulian that was still in Casarsa. Meanwhile, Dell'Arco had launched *Il belli*, which, Pier Paolo wrote a correspondent, was an "exquisite magazine . . . fifteen fixed collaborators who, instead of being paid, must be the financiers: two thousand lire an issue, every two months (it seems)." He wrote Nico, who was somehow to help finance and participate:

> I am not very enthusiastic about it: but on the other hand it is necessary to have an outlet, a little outlet of our own for the polemics which will buoy up the anthology. I know you don't have two thousand lire a month: but we can go to uncle Gino, with whom, for you, I will also speak; after all, two thousand lire is a miserable sum.[9]

During the next two years he contributed to *Il belli* a multipart "Pamphlet in Dialect" spread over four numbers, poetry in Friulian and a "Homage to Giotto." In 1954 the magazine disappeared into the vast warehouse of Italian little magazines of short but brilliant life. Pasolini was not sorry to see it die; in January 1953 he told Naldini he thought it "fairly ugly," the result of "that pig Dell'Arco wanting to do it all alone."[10]

In the autumn of 1952 he savored the novel sweetness of being "fought over." Both *Paragone* and his Bologna friend Luciano Anceschi wanted his prizewinning essay on Ungaretti. He had promised it to Anceschi, editor of important anthologies in 1943, 1952, and 1953, so he wrote on October 4 to Pier Bigongiari of *Paragone:* While he "valued that magazine above all others," would they, this time, accept instead a critical piece on Caproni? They did, and it appeared in December 1952, along with his long poem *L'Appennino.*

Throughout the winter of 1952–53, his life had been a taxing pendulum: up at seven to travel to Ciampino for a full day's labor, home at three to dive into the mountain of poems to be read, evaluated, and selected for the anthology. He maintained a correspondence with every poet in the book, assembling bio-bibliographical notes without editorial assistance of any sort save for Carlo Alberto. It was a one-man production, created from the whole cloth of energy and labor, from conception to lining up reviews upon publication.

*Poesie dialettale del Novecento*'s title page listed Pasolini as second of the work's two editors. But he wrote one friend that "the book was made completely by me (also in the manual sense)." That Dell'Arco had any credit at all was, he explained to Serra, "purely nominal . . . due to previous engagements Guanda had" with him.

No sooner was it in the bookstores than Montale's praise appeared in the *Corriere della sera* of January 15: "Only a young poet could have brought to fruition a project of this kind with such sure instinct. . . ."

Montale was far above the reach of Pier Paolo's lobbying: no recommendations here, no putting in a good word as with a provincial poetry jury.

When the influential critic Enrico Falqui reviewed *Poesie dialettale* in March, expressing reservations, Pier Paolo responded at length. His letter-rebuttal is both *ad hominem* and self-revelatory. Falqui seems "disappointed"; but, asks Pasolini, is that disappointment not really with poetry in dialect—which he defends as meriting study like his—as "with every work in the world"?

> It may be only my impression: but I see in you, in your manner of speech, of writing, of feeling, a kind of resentment, of boredom or annoyance at what is happening around you: and you are perfectly right, in a certain sense, and to a certain point. We live in an atrocious world, evil because stupid. . . . But is criticism possible . . . even for one who acts from an impure locus like a newspaper . . . without love? All cold and closed in a defensive stance and ready for a too-bitter debate, is it not too disdainful to be constructive?[11]

He accused Falqui of "bad faith" and "irony," and going out of his way to attack certain Left-wing poets included in the book.

Inevitably, there came a sequel. A month later Pier Paolo wrote again, explaining that, "I explain myself, again, by letter because you, orally, intimidate me, put me in a state of almost aphasia. . . ."

Falqui had criticized the book for giving too much attention to the Friulian school, and he wondered whether the Academiuta deserved the "historic importance" Pier Paolo seemed to give it. In effect, he accused the book's maker of being too self-promoting. Pier Paolo responded with a page count: "Friulians 25 pages, Neapolitans

60. . . ." He also responded that he, Pasolini, did not serve himself well, "especially if you read the entire work overall, and not [his own] six or seven selected poems."

In a sense Pier Paolo had the last word this time. Falqui published his collected criticism in 1955, including his review of Pasolini's anthology, under the title *Novecento letterario;* Pier Paolo then reviewed it in the pages of *Letteratura.* Such was the dance of Italian letters: the same few partners in a small room.

Within weeks after *Poesie dialettale*'s publication, Guanda proposed he produce a second such collection, to be called *Poesie popolare.*

At first Pier Paolo hesitated. He wrote Spagnoletti, "Maybe they are not wrong from either the commercial or cultural point of view but I am not too enthusiastic, because I would have to do it with an [academic] specialist, given the vastness of the material." [12]

He preferred to bring out a Pascoli collection, but Mondadori, holder of the rights, would concede to Guanda's use of only "thirty or forty poems." "Now someone has to approach them through friendly channels and convince them that to generate interest and strong discussions around Pascoli is also in their interest." Could Spagnoletti help? He could not, and Pasolini dropped the idea: "I withdraw, with great sadness, from the idea of a Pascoli anthology," he wrote Spagnoletti. Guanda's proposal seemed better the more he thought about it: "If all the regional anonymous poetries are like those I already know . . . a delicious book could come out of it."

But after his experience with Dell'Arco—"who, unfortunately, is not an imbecile"—Pier Paolo wanted no part of a collaborator, and there would be none. This collection appeared in 1955—all his, as the *Canzoniere italiano.* Still a standard work on Italian regional popular verse, it was dedicated "to my brother Guido, who fell in '45 in the mountains of Venezia Giulia, for a new life for the Italian people." It is far more than a reprint of assembled regional poetry. Its extended preface is a small book of distinguished research and analysis providing a critical history of the field, its bibliography a region-by-region synthesis of scholarship definitive enough to merit a paperback edition (not by Guanda but by Pier Paolo's later house, Garzanti) in two volumes, in 1972, almost two decades after its first appearance. And, inevitably, reissuance, by Garzanti, in 1993.

A whirlwind of work opened 1953. His Friulian collection *Tal cour di un frut* was published now, with a lengthy introduction in which he summarized his thinking of many years on the use of dialect in poetry. Publisher Luigi Ciceri was left to line up local reviews: "I want nothing to do with those people or those newspapers." As for critics outside Friuli, Pasolini wrote, "I'll take care of that using the copies you send me." And he did: In October, Spagnoletti spoke on the poems on the RAI's radio program "Literary Landingplace."

With February he began a regular collaboration in a new illustrated weekly called *Giovedi* (Thursday), edited by Giancarlo Vigorelli. It was soon agreed that he would write an article per week on poetry, the choice strictly his. In April *Giovedi* published his panegyric to a poet-friend he much admired, entitled "The Ecstasies of Betocchi." After its appearance, the Florentine wrote him, "I believe you have written the most beautiful article I have ever read about my poetry." In June the magazine printed Pasolini's piece on the great nineteenth-century novelist Alessandro Manzoni.

He was writing also for the *Fiera* now and several small but influential literary journals, such as *Il caffè* and *Il belli*. And he was within the circle of those well received at *Paragone*. Reviewing was part of his vocation of public pedagogy; and the truth as he saw it was always to be told, friendship notwithstanding. When Elio Bartolini's novel *Due ponti a Caracas*[13] appeared, Pier Paolo wrote Nico on April 23, 1953, putting into action a hierarchy of values that persisted throughout his life, putting friendship after his convictions, whatever the cost: "I liked the novel very little, not to say not at all (sadly): and now it is painful for me to write to Elio because I cannot do other than tell him the truth."[14] The review was what he called "a kick in the face, as they say in Rome."

But while he was an acute and uncompromising reader of accomplished friends, he kept an extraordinary tenderness for others. On May 21 the pulp magazine *Oggi* ran a story about Cesare Padovani, a boy of fifteen, living in Nogara near Verona. He had been born with a brain lesion that paralyzed his mouth, right arm, and legs. Despite this, he taught himself to write with his left hand, wrote poetry, and drew. The article prompted a letter from Pasolini to the teenager, opening a correspondence that would last twenty years:

> Excuse me if I intervene like this, unknown and uninvited, in your literary life. I have just finished reading (by chance, because I never read this stuff) an article about you in *Oggi:* something pathetic overall, to say the truth, and a bit humiliating for you. You are trying to be unreachable by the evil of such people who, to increase the circulation of their paper, are capable of doing anything, even (in your case) making indelicate inroads into an interior life, profiting from the fact that boys have interior lives . . . I wanted

to be in touch with you only because I see in this ill-famed article that you write poetry in dialect. This interests me enormously. . . .[15]

With 1953 Pier Paolo's "vocation" was already beyond simple classification, and it was fast becoming more so. The poet of the "little country" of Friuli had addressed the dialects of all Italy, established a critical voice, a corpus of incisive journalism, built a record as entrepreneur on behalf of other writers he valued and went to great lengths to encourage. And he had in his desk a novel to make him seem most Roman of the Romans, its most powerful new native voice.

He was occupied with several important projects. His poem "*L'umile Italia*" was printed the following April in *Paragone*, and survived his frequent, ruthless prunings to appear in later collections. It narrated not just autobiography (there was always that) but the life of Italy past and future, the whole reality of nature and humanity in that place, as though seen from above. He was invited to publish in *Itinerari*, a new Genoese magazine, and he did so "gladly"; his "Canzonette" appeared in its July-August issue. And there was talk of an ongoing publication of small volumes of poetry to be called *Quarta generazione*, and that too started well. Nine poems appeared in 1954, also printed in the cultural magazine called *L'approdo*, based in Turin.

He was now ensured a readership somewhere for almost everything he produced: the postwar explosion of small magazines dedicated to new writing coincided perfectly with his frenetic output. But he could not yet afford to stop teaching: The anthology had paid a flat-fee pittance and the articles brought in only pin money.

And yet he was known to writers, part of the prestigious circle of *Botteghe oscure*, the recognized crème de la crème of literary cliques. And he exulted in his life. More than twenty years later the writer Uberto Paolo Quintavalle—cast to play in *Salò*—recalled meeting Pasolini in 1953. "He wanted everyone to know that he frequented the toughest sorts of characters and was not physically intimidated by them. He would bend his arm to stiffen his biceps and say, 'Touch it, touch it, feel what a muscle I've got, feel how strong I am.' "[16]

To celebrate his small but palpable success and to gather material for the second anthology, Pier Paolo made a brief journey to Naples. He reported to Nico, "what stuff . . . !" Here was raw humanity (the boys), dialect, a popular culture apparently untainted by bourgeois "civilization" and its hypocrisy. "I'm going back in two weeks. The South, the South."

He submitted his lengthy preface to his (and Dell'Arco's) Guanda anthology for an award in the criticism category of the prestigious Viareggio-Savinio prize. He wrote a member of the jury, Luigi Russo, to explain that it had been the publisher's idea, "for commercial reasons I share," but he wanted to apologize that the entry arrived so late. Such gentle public relations notwithstanding, no prize.

Back in Rome he wrote Nico in Casarsa. "I don't want to seem the moralist, but I have really come to the conviction that the pleasure which is most intense and sincere is that which one feels after having worked: The entire day, and thus all of life, is filled."

As for himself, save for a brief vacation with Sandro Penna, "amid grandiose Tiberine panoramas," he was "engulfed by work . . . the anthology, the articles for *Giovedi*, new commitments to *Paragone*, two or three pieces for the radio (among them a short story, which is driving me crazy), and now there has appeared the chance to collaborate on a screenplay with [Carlo Emilio] Gadda based on the short stories of Bandello. . . ." It proved a dead end. Such was the life of those who lived by their wits in Rome's culture industry.

Apparently without missing a step, he turned to the Pordenone competition and in July submitted the short story "Lied," set in Friuli. He called it "marginal but acceptable" and took second prize of thirty thousand lire, not the top award's hundred thousand, "which would suit me." "Better this than nothing," he wrote his father from Casarsa; the same note specified which poems Carlo was to type, what phone calls he should make on his son's behalf—one to Caproni, another to get an editor's address.

*L'Appennino* was now translated "well enough" by William Weaver, a young American starting a career that would make him the preeminent postwar translator of Italian into English. It appeared in an avant-garde New York magazine called *Folder*, in an issue bearing a silkscreen cover by the painter Grace Hartigan.[17] Pier Paolo was thirty-plus, and now on his way.

By October Pasolini-matchmaker had put Leonetti and Bassani together, leading to the Bolognese writer being asked to contribute to *Botteghe*. He wrote Leonetti, "Since the invitation [to contribute] is always valid, together with poetry you could send them also one or two short stories, even long ones if you have them."[18]

With year's end he wrote to his rediscovered friend in Bologna, "Only last night, at dinner, raising his arm to the heavens, Bassani exclaimed, 'I have read Leonetti! Excellent! He is the best of those in Bologna . . . and so forth.' "

But literary power-brokering was not so simple. By the following February he had to tell Leonetti that "the Princess" had found Leonetti's poems "unpleasing." "You understand that this is, properly interpreted, a compliment, but certainly publication would have been preferable . . . Bassani feels very badly, as do I. But Bassani is also an editor at *Paragone,* and tomorrow night we see [its managing editor Anna] Banti . . ."[19]

Along with avid literary wheeling and dealing, he kept working on his novel about the boys of Rome. He told one correspondent the first week of January 1954: "I hope to publish within this year." It was, he said, not only almost finished but "absolutely clear in my head."

On November 6 he wrote Leonetti that they ought to leave for their planned trip to Sicily—part work (Sciascia's conference), part tourism and good talk. By month's end he sent Sciascia, for his *Galleria,* a typescript of the RAI radio talk "Popular Poetry and Mass Culture" he was to give the next month (December 28), as well as some of Nico's poems and "what I believe are the last poems in *friulano.*" He was a Roman now, and Rome was his symbolic universe.

The day after New Year's 1954 Pasolini sent Sereni in Milan *Il canto popolare,* poems in Italian written in 1952 and 1953. He explained that it had taken him so long partly because "I needed to make citations to certain popular verses, Piedmontese and Sicilian, from books only found at the National [Library], and the National was closed; now that it is open, those books are out on loan."[20]

He suggested Zigaina be commissioned to make illustrations, and he provided a list of the eleven persons he wanted sent free copies: "Longhi, [his wife, Anna] Banti, Contini, Leonetti, Marin, Ungaretti, Ottieri, Penna, Gadda, Vigorelli, Zigaina."

This watershed year of 1954 brought another, more credible chance to write for the cinema: Giorgio Bassani again weighed in with a crucial connection. Mario Soldati was shooting *La donna del fiume* (Woman of the river) in the valleys of the Comacchio, yet another Carlo Ponti production about the war, based on a short story by Gambini. It was a vehicle for the new challenger to Gina Lollobrigida: a Neapolitan twenty-four-year-old beauty named Sophia Loren, who married her producer two years later.

Scripts were collaborative efforts, and Bassani, who had worked with Soldati in 1953 on *La provinciale* (The wayward wife) was to be chief writer, but free to hire others as needed; by the time the film was released, five people besides Pier Paolo received screenwriting credit.

Some low-life characters figured in Soldati's story and in the treatment based on it by Moravia and writer Ennio Flaiano. But the elegant Bassani, chronicler of Ferrara's Jewish *haute bourgeoisie,* could not imagine what such people would actually say nor how they would say it. He called Pasolini for that. In early March they left by car for the north, to visit Bassani's Ferrara and inspect the locations in the rich wetlands of the Venetian Lagoon.

By his own account, on the journey north the older writer studied Pasolini with the same intensity that Pier Paolo studied the boys of the *borgata*. The comparatively straitlaced Bassani could not help but notice how Pier Paolo always talked to the boys pumping gas and was always willing to take aboard a hitchhiking soldier. Pier Paolo, who liked Bassani, might have taken some pleasure in shocking him: Prompted by his companion's questions, he explained with gusto what "cruising" entailed.

Bassani remembered, and later created a thinly fictionalized Pasolini in the person of the homosexual "Dr. Athos Fadigati, the well-known professional man from Ferrara," protagonist of the novella *The Gold-rimmed Spectacles* (1958). But Fadigati is an embarrassment to his social equals because he takes the young, handsome Deliliers to the beach at Riccione. He makes something of a fool of himself, driving "a red Alfa Romeo 1750 two-seater, very sporty looking," precisely the car Pasolini later owned.

Bassani was always careful later to point up the differences between his inspiration and his character. With the inevitable fate of *invertiti*, Fadigati confronts alone "the terrible emptiness of the days." Bassani repeated the stereotype: the older man, mistreated by his adored (but unadoring) younger love object. Pasolini, on the contrary, was described by all who knew him as "tough," "masculine," "virile"—so much so that his soft voice came as a surprise. And bursting with life, with *vitalità*. No "emptiness of the days" here.

The world of films and scripts was all well and good, but certainly it was not going to interfere with making literature. Pasolini took the film work, he said, "for lucre"; he had been so long desperate for money that he set aside his novel to do *La donna del fiume*, slowing the book's completion. As of March 1954 he still had no plan to quit the school at Ciampino.

Later, he wrote:

> The work of a writer for the cinema can be very beautiful, in fact, in abstract form, I consider it very beautiful. But sadly one works amidst ignorant, stupid people who do not know what they want. The screenwriter ought not even know a production exists . . . he ought to work with the director and that's it . . .[21]

"Ignorant, stupid people" or not, only *La donna del fiume* and subsequent film-writing jobs paid for Susanna and Carlo Alberto's liberation from Rebibbia. During March he moved them into "a delicious and dignified place," a proper middle-class apartment in Monteverde Nuovo, a respectable quarter, via Fonteiana, 86, apartment 26. "My father could finally occupy himself with a [household] move which gave him satisfaction . . . the pleasure of commanding, of vanity, of bourgeois decorum."

Carlo Alberto offered his own practical reasons for welcoming the upgrade: "It is," he said, "a place where the trash is picked up regularly."

Gadda lived in the same block; and, perhaps best of all, the flat was near the via di Donna Olympia, where the *ragazzi di vita* were living out the book he was writing. The writer Paolo Volponi came to visit, and if it was a Sunday, he accompanied Pier Paolo to the *borgata*. "He was looking for names and gestures which served him for his first novel."

Giorgio Caproni visited via Fonteiana, and saw Pier Paolo writing poems on an ancient typewriter, "a true and proper museum piece." Leonardo Sciascia also recalls seeing "a tiny [Olivetti] Lettera 22, on a table in the corner of a big, empty room." Susanna sat patiently, happy just to be nearby. She later recalled: "He used to stop and read me a little now and then, written on pages no bigger than notebook paper." He once told Caproni never to mail a letter save in Rome's historic center. One wanted to be in the center, have that as postmark; one had to be a player, someone *presente*.

His world continued to explode. In June the entire corpus of his Friulian poems, now entitled *La meglio gioventù: Friulian poems, 1941–1953*, was published by the Florentine house Sansoni under the aegis of *Paragone*. He called it "a moment of exceptional importance for me": at last, a summary of more than a decade's work, what he saw as his closed, complete, and poetically successful Friulian period. The dedication was to Contini. Decades later he said, "It . . . should be considered my first published work."

He wrote Sciascia again in October, explaining that *L'Appennino* was about to be published in America. Could *Galleria* perhaps use something else? He offered his book "stagnating at Mondadori for three years." It was in several sections: "The Nightingale of the Catholic Church," "Diaries (1943–47)," and "Lingua." He added that all the poetry, especially the part called "Diaries," had appeared "a little chaotically" in magazines, but this was a chance to bring them all together.

When Sciascia's edition of *Dal diario (1945–1947)* appeared, Pier Paolo wrote his always loyal, soft-spoken friend:

> The booklets are delightful! . . . only Bassani, with whom I am working, has seen it thus far: and he was struck by the dignity and taste of the little thing. So much so that I had a little idea: why not publish, in the next group of narrators, the extremely beautiful short story of Bassani's called "The Last Years of Clelia Trotti" which appeared in *Paragone* number 52? [22]

In early August *La meglio gioventù* shared the Carducci Prize with poems by Paolo Volponi. Pier Paolo wrote Sereni, "As for the Carducci Prize which [Carlo] Bo [a member of the prize jury] spoke with you about, it was something not very pleasant, which I accepted only out of urgent, hateful need of the 150 thousand." Volponi remembers Pasolini sent his check to Carlo Alberto. The publisher Mondadori threw a party for the winners and made a great show at the prize-giving at Marina de Pietrasanta, with remarks to the effect that he "must" publish this Pasolini. Pasolini wrote, "As for Mondadori, I don't give much weight [literally, not much *spago*, "string"] to his theatrical gesture . . . but naturally, I accepted [to show him work] just as I accepted the . . . prize. I cannot do otherwise. . . ." [23]

The publisher was suddenly interested in work from a poet who had already offered work but had been ignored. Pier Paolo's response was withering disdain: "as though these things did not exist four or five years ago, eagerly put forward by the undersigned [PPP] who submitted them for a reading."


That summer he went for a long road trip with Bassani: "Florence, Arrezzo, Assisi, Perugia, Todi, Spoleto . . . in the footprints of Giotto and of Piero [della Francesca] . . . I am returned feeling stronger," he wrote Marin in Trieste, "and I hope to return to work . . . otherwise our sin makes no sense, is hell on earth." What he saw went into the poems. With the fall, after what he called a "shameful summer from the creative point of view," he reapplied himself. He returned to *Ragazzi* and to producing new poems, and in December the journey through Tuscany and Umbria bore its first fruit in "Homage to Giotto," published in *Il belli*. Later he published a long poem, made in these months, under the title *La richezza*. It was first printed by Antonello Trombadori in *Il contemporaneo* on August 31, 1957, and in book form in 1961. But by then Pasolini was recognized as among the preeminent poets of his generation.

In October school resumed . . . he wrote, "Calvary recommences."
He went to great lengths to attend a conference in Trieste to speak
on "dialect and its literary problem" to the "Club of Culture and the
Arts." But planning was needed, so as to miss as few days as possible
of paid classroom time.

"Harassed by need for money," he asked Sereni about the possibility of writing a piece about "Friulian houses."

On November 30 he wrote about *Ragazzi* in the making:

> The novel will have nine chapters [it emerged with eight] of which 1, 4, and
> 6 ["Swimming in the Aniene"] are complete; 2, 5, 7, and 8 are written but
> have to be set right and completed, 2 and the last need to be done. Knowing
> myself (and I am not lazy) and the nature of the work, I believe I need about
> five or six months, given that this month I can work less since I must
> complete other things.[24]

In December he wrote Contini, asking for a telephone call of recommendation. He had taught three years at Ciampino and was now
anxious to pursue a lead for a post within the staff of the national
Encyclopedia. Much maneuvering was needed: Pier Paolo had a
friend who worked there, who would speak with a certain Migliorini,
the man he asked Contini to call. In parallel, a contact in Friuli,
Senator Tessitori, had spoken with the president of the Encyclopedia
(Ferrabino) and an insider named Petrocchi had spoken to the director (Bosco), who had declared himself "willing to take me on." Now,
to Contini, because "a finger is needed to push the button . . . a
word by Migliorini, who, it seems, is coming to Rome tomorrow to
speak with Ferrabino or Bosco."[25]

As always, Contini delivered; Pasolini went to see Bosco, who
"while staying in generalities, gave me some hopes." Pasolini never
worked at the national Encyclopedia.

# 14

*It is this feeling of being trapped within the inflexible limits of national inclinations which gives Italian life, under the brilliant and vivacious surface, its fundamentally bitter, disenchanted, melancholic quality.*

—**Luigi Barzini, The Italians**

# *ANNI MIRABILI:*
## *Ragazzi di vita, Officina, Le ceneri di Gramsci*

In the spring of 1954, Giorgio Bassani came to the door of his friend Attilio Bertolucci in the via delle Quattro Fontane, bearing in tow a visibly shy young man. Pasolini was already known by reputation to Bertolucci, then forty-three: It was his passionate business to know who was up-and-coming in Italian letters.

Pier Paolo came to the encounter with the imprimatur of Contini and the further credential that the demanding Bassani had taken him into *Botteghe oscure*'s selective circle, to keep company with Elsa

Morante, Sandro Penna, Bassani himself, and other "first-class merchandise" (as Pasolini wrote), *anglo-sassoni* like "R. Duncan . . . T.
Capote."[1]

Pasolini knew Bertolucci's work well: Three years before he had
reviewed the volume of verse *La capanna indiana* in *Il giornale* of
Naples. The book had won the Viareggio Prize for poetry that year;
Pasolini wrote that its publication put its author "in the first position,
exemplary"[2] of his generation, the one ahead of his own.

Decades later, Bertolucci remembered his visitor as "very soft-
spoken" but elegantly dressed in "a white sweater with birds on it."
Following that meeting, he made a connection that was to prove fateful: Bertolucci was a consultant to Livio Garzanti, who had received
the old Treves publishing firm (once the house of D'Annunzio and
Pirandello) as a graduation gift from his father, Aldo, who was less
than enthusiastic about his son Livio's plans to make a career in
philosophy. Bertolucci was the younger Garzanti's talent scout, and
when Livio asked for suggestions for possible new authors, Bertolucci
showed him the previous October's *Paragone*, with the short story *"Il
ferrobedò."* Garzanti read it overnight and the next day asked for a
meeting with its author. Pasolini had already discussed with editor
Anna Banti the prospect of making the story into a chapter of a novel
for *Paragone*'s book imprint. And he had signed an option for the
same purpose with Mondadori.

Garzanti wrote Pasolini, who answered on November 27, 1954:

> *Gentilissimo Dottore,*
>
> Your letter, unexpected, was more to me than a surprise, a great joy. I really
> never thought my piece in *Paragone* could somehow reach you. The novel,
> of which that piece constitutes chapter IV, is in effect almost completed,
> while another, its twin, is in the works, in rough draft. I am working in-
> tensely, and have been for some time. Naturally, I would be most happy to
> be in contact with you. I hope, in fact, to see you soon, here in Rome.
> Please accept, in the meantime, most cordial greetings from your most de-
> voted,
>
> Pier Paolo Pasolini[3]

But then nothing happened: No offer had been made, no contract
signed. Pier Paolo worked at the book when he could. Months passed.
Garzanti asked Bertolucci what had happened to Pasolini, who
seemed to have disappeared. Pasolini wrote the publisher to explain
his situation, without asking outright for the obvious financial solution:

> I do not have time . . . to work. You know that for a salary of twenty-five
> thousand lire a month I go and teach in Ciampino, leaving at seven in the
> morning and returning at two, soaked through with exhaustion? To live, I
> must pay attention to contributions to magazines: and on top of that I have
> a mountain of proofs on my desk: this has to do with an anthology of popular
> poetry which I am doing for Guanda, very complicated and highly demand-
> ing. You understand in these conditions that for now I cannot work for
> myself: that which I want most. The eternal complaint.[4]

To break the logjam, young publisher and young author finally met
the following April in Garzanti's Roman hotel room. Garzanti listened
to Pasolini's ideas: The novel would be about the Roman underclass,
a journey through some days in the life of the boys who lived, hand-
to-mouth, on the streets. It would rely heavily on dialect, Pasolini
explained, and not seem pretty to some. Garzanti offered to double
Pasolini's schoolteacher earnings—an advance of 50,000 lire, two
months' Ciampino wages—but the chapters had to keep coming. The
book completed, Garzanti would look it over with an eye to publication.

Everything seemed to happen at once, or rather the seeds Pasolini
had planted all sprouted together.

On November 15 he sent Garzanti a three-page, single-spaced
typewritten letter spelling out the plot of *Ragazzi di vita* in detail,
with a chapter-by-chapter synopsis. He explained the "narrative arc"
of the novel:

> Postwar Rome, the chaos full of hope that came in the first days after Lib-
> eration and the reaction of '50–'51. It is a precise arc which corresponds to
> the passage of the protagonist and his friends (Riccetto, Alduccio, etc.) from
> infancy into first youth: or further (and here the coincidence is perfect) from
> the heroic and amoral era into that prosaic and immoral. To render "prosaic
> and immoral" the life of these boys (which the Fascist war had made grow
> up as savages: illiterate and delinquent) one has the society which reacts to
> their vitality yet again in an authoritarian manner: imposing its moral ide-
> ology.[5]

Everything Pasolini had learned of the Roman subproletariat would
be in it: the postwar world's betrayal of the ideals of the Resistance
and the safe universe of Christian Democracy's Italian fifties as the
victorious enemy of vitality, of amoral boyhood, of innocence. In the
plan to Garzanti for *Ragazzi di vita* he laid out the theme on which
he worked variations for the next twenty years.

> Note that I, as the narrator, do not interfere. As I never denounce directly
> the Fascist responsibility for those concentration camps which are the Roman
> *borgate*, or the present responsibility of the government which has done
> nothing to solve the problem. Everything is implicit in the congeries: exter-
> nally chaotic, internally ordered, of the facts.[6]

Two weeks later he wrote an evidently nervous Garzanti that the
use of dialect and slang was, in fact, necessary. "It is these which
give me the joy necessary to understand and describe my characters . . . "; yes, he would "correct" the manuscript when the book
was published, that is, practice self-censorship as suggested by his
publisher. But not too much. He insisted: "The useful ones will stay
(even if they are a bit obscure): here style and commerce enter into
polemics [with one another]. . . ."

He had promised to deliver his manuscript on April 15; on April
13 he did so. "If it were for myself alone," he wrote Biagio Marin in
Trieste, "I would live the life of Dino Campana." But he wrote Garzanti:

> Here, punctually, is the novel. The copy I send you is a bit disorderly with
> corrections but this is certainly no time to retype the whole thing yet again
> . . . about thirty words are underlined, which indicates that they are to be
> improved or corrected and not put into the galleys. I have been working like
> a beast, as you can imagine: now I don't know anything about my work, I
> am neither content nor discontent, I am simply exhausted. I hope with all
> my heart that you are not displeased: not least of all for the gratitude I owe
> you. As for the swear words, as you can see, I used a lot of dots: I could
> (naturally with reluctance) do more of that, if you think it advisable. The
> expressions in slang seem to me almost all understandable or intuitable: and
> if at some point they are not understood or intuited, it does not matter,
> because they only serve for some color, an exclamation, which slide past
> without harming the overall clarity, or so I believe.[7]

A month later it was back in his hands. Garzanti thought cuts were
needed; his reading of the proofs—and that of some booksellers—
suggested scandal. Pasolini complied but wrote his Bolognese friends
that he was cutting the book because of Garzanti's "moral scruples."
He wrote Silvana Mauri Ottieri that "Garzanti showed himself to be truly
ungenerous."[8] To Sereni he explained that he had "to correct and to
castrate." In two days, on May 11, he sent the modified version back
to his publisher, writing, "As you can see, I put dots in the place of
all the *brutte parole* [literally, "ugly words"—slang and off-color
expressions] and cut some sequences, for example an entire episode

involving a prostitute in chapter seven." But, he said, "After counsel from all my friends and out of intimate conviction" he was not willing to cut the scene of the "*frocio.*" Have faith," he told Garzanti, "if it does not reach the sales level of [Goffredo] Parise [*Il prete bello*, 1954], it will be a much-discussed novel and thus read not only by the good-taste types (*buongustai*). . . ." He reminded Garzanti that he now had resigned from the school at Ciampino. "I am without work, and my sole thread of hope is this novel. . . . We have had experiences both pro and contra: always violent. It will be an emotional adventure."[9]

Apparently not expecting much, Garzanti ordered a very modest first printing. When it reached the stores the novel's dust jacket depicted three boys close-up, their faces filling the space—one face was blue, another yellow, and one orange. Like a giant mask, almost African, the orange-faced *ragazzo di borgata* holds a cigarette to his smiling lips; a mass of wavy black hair falls to his beetle-brow and his collar is turned up in the manner of James Dean. His eyes are black and stare directly at the viewer; behind him the Tiber is yellow and St. Peter's dome is blue in the distance. Pasolini's Bolognese friends sent a bottle of Châteauneuf-du-Pape in celebration.[10] That, at least, was some consolation after he had passed "one of the ugliest periods in my life."[11]

Reviews came gradually; sales were as modest as expected, nothing more. By July, partly thanks to the small size of the first printing, it went into reprint. On July 2 Pasolini wrote Garzanti, thanking him for a copy of the second edition:

> I am already working on the second book (a provisional title, but already announced to some types from the [news] agency "Italia," *Una vita violenta* [A violent life] (which could also be *Death of a ragazzo di vita*) less happy perhaps but more concentrated in the narrative on one character. I read with displeasure the rancorous and ugly little piece by [Emilio] Cecchi [a review in *Corriere della sera*, June 28]: everyone considers it unjust, and among them [scholar and critic Giacomo] Debenedetti has told Cecchi so. In any case, on Monday will be a debate [about *Ragazzi*] at the Circolo del libro [literally, the Book Club] . . . and I trust Cecchi's piece will be buried.[12]

He wrote Garzanti, saying that Cecchi's opinion seemed to be helping sales. "Please thank Cecchi for that."

About the same time as some of the *buongustai* were (as he had predicted) drawing back from *Ragazzi*'s candor, a young boy (*un giovincello*) came running up to Pasolini in the Piazza San Silvestro, shouting, " '*A Pá, A Pá,*' all content" and proceeded to repeat the episodes he liked best. Pasolini passed the episode on to Garzanti: "And then, light and expert as the Romans are, without too much fuss, his job done, he went away, utterly happy." [13]

At the beginning of July, when all seemed well and the book was selling, Pasolini started work on his second filmscript (again with Bassani), *Il prigioniero della montagna* (The prisoner of the mountain), directed by Luis Trenker, whose work he admired. On July 4 he wrote William Weaver in Virginia, hoping that the translator's plan for publisher Alfred A. Knopf's American edition of *Ragazzi* would proceed, despite what Weaver called "the enormous difficulties which an American translator must face." That, too, stalled; the New York house wanted Weaver's reassurance that the author was not too "bohemian."

Pasolini welcomed the screenwriting work that continued to come his way. He wrote that the film world observed "the law of the jungle" but it was a way out of poverty. He told an interviewer in 1975: "At twenty-six, when I wrote my first novel, I didn't have enough money to go to the barber." When Garzanti wrote, unhappy at the delayed delivery of the second novel, Pasolini explained he had to work for the movies: "Could I have lived," he wrote in September, "since this past January with [only] the two hundred thousand lire which the novel provided me?"

Furthermore, even though his contract called for his being paid 10 percent of the 1,000 lire cover price on the first 3,500 copies and 13 percent above that, his royalty check seemed short. By August—his accounting queries unanswered—he wrote to his publisher:

> You cannot play mute and I cannot play deaf when we speak and hear perfectly well . . . while a year ago, 100 thousand *lire* would have been like a treasure to me, now having completed a film and starting another, it [the money] can also not be so important. But what matters to me is you: to whom I owe gratitude and who—despite a character not exactly smooth and sweet—I like very much. [14]

By December 2 he wrote Nico that with year's end he would have "a million and a half in the bank . . . two or three cinema projects which are circulating. If all goes well, maybe this spring I can buy an apartment of three rooms. And maybe I can send you a little money every month, on condition that you agree to take your [university] degree." [15]

The Roman film world was very small, and word of a good scriptwriter spread fast; by September Pasolini announced his imminent departure for Indochina, to write a film for director Alberto Lattuada based on the novel *Il soleil au ventre* by French novelist Jean Hougron. But, after a month's work on what he called "a very difficult script," the plan "to follow Loren's rear-end as a glorified goal"[16] came to nothing.

What mattered more were his dreams for *Ragazzi di vita*. He clipped every review and assiduously wrote personally to thank those who went into print to praise it.

On July 21 a bomb went off, causing a publicity fallout that made the book far more discussed than even Pasolini dared hope and "an emotional adventure" beyond even his prediction. A public prosecutor, acting on direct orders from the office for "spectacle and literary property" of the President of the Council of Ministers, filed a legal action against the novel for "public obscenity." Rumor had it that the action had been initiated at the request of the Minister of the Interior, Fernando Tambroni. Attilio Bertolucci told Pasolini the news; Pier Paolo later wrote a poem about that moment, called "Récit": "But it was more human, Attilio, a human injustice / that before wounding me it passed first by you. . . ."

Article 21 of the 1948 constitution prohibited publications and entertainments "contrary to good morals." Once charges were filed and pending trial, the book was ordered removed from the stores, as the Fascist-made Code of Civil Procedure, inherited and left virtually intact by the Republic, provided. Summonses were issued against both author and publisher based on the book's "pornographic content." Unacceptable language had been found on pages 47, 48, 101, 130, 174, 227, 231, and 242—words like "fart" and "cocksucker" were apparently contrary to the law. The court convened in January the next year but had to adjourn when it emerged that the judges had not yet read the book. Ten months passed.

Better publicity could not have been bought at any price. Promoted by Ungaretti and Carlo Bo, the novel took fourth place among the five finalists for the 1955 Strega Prize. Pasolini wrote a friend that the winner, his friend Giovanni Comisso [for *Un gatto attraversa la strada*, literally, A cat crosses the road] "didn't need the money." But *Ragazzi* did win the Colombi-Guidotti Prize at Parma from a jury presided over by the prestigious Giuseppe de Robertis that included Gadda, Bertolucci, and poet Carlo Cassola; it was partly meant as their rebuke to the Viareggio Prize jury, which had awarded *Ragazzi* a pointed second place. If and when the novel was vindicated at law, it would return to the bookstores bearing a paper band announcing the honors bestowed on it by some of Italy's intellectuals of acknowledged probity and social acceptability. The case became a fight for freedom of expression under Christian Democracy.

Reading the novel more than thirty years later, one can only wonder at the hysteria in Italy in 1955. As its would-be censors knew, the book was plainly not pornographic: "Cock" appears as constantly as it does in Roman slang, and there are scenes in which boys sell themselves to pederasts in the balconies of Roman cinemas, equally true to life. *Ragazzi*'s fundamental unacceptability lay in its graphic description of life in the Roman underclass, not simply sex and street talk. That was too much: The face of Italy had to be heavily made-up; it made a *brutta figura* for Italians to write of such things as poverty and social marginalization; it was bad public policy to let other Italians read about them.

Here was a book from a reputable house that suggested some people were being left out of Italy's new "prosperity," living as precariously under democracy as they had under Fascism. Pasolini's characters lived happily—"vitally"—outside the laws of the Church and the State. It was scandalous that they lacked goals, order, loyalties.

Bourgeois Italy pretended that it was, at last, about to shake off its provincialism, molt into another reality, more modern, more European. Into this atmosphere of transition and the anxiety brought by instability, Pasolini brought his new heroes, who belied the optimism. His "hero," Riccetto, and his friends were outlaws, society's outcasts, adolescents already living dead-end lives. Their very existence was inconvenient, inappropriate, annoying. In life they could be ignored by avoiding their neighborhoods. But the book, sold in all the best bookstores, shoved the terrible truth under the public's nose. Such compellingly written bad news was something like treasonous, its messenger was most unwelcome.

At novel's opening, readers meet Riccetto, "who was going to make his first Communion," but instead of a "little soldier of Jesus," he decides he'll go "running around down by the Tiber, trying to make a pickup." Two great institutions of society and the State—Church and school—fail to impede him from a life of petty crime. The day the novel opens, the "asphalt was shimmering in the heat," and Riccetto quickly skips out on his Communion to join a mob about to break into the Ferrobedò company warehouse to steal. His is a universe of permanent free time and the search for easy money; he is the Roman version of the Neapolitan *snaguzzi*, boys discarded by their parents and left to fend for themselves. He lives not in a world of abundant Italian cuisine, a solicitous mother, and freshly ironed sheets, but amid "the smell of garbage stewing in the sun." Inevitably, he learns about sex from a prostitute.

Pasolini's poker-faced prose, utterly without sentimentality or self-pity, refuses to soft-pedal: Riccetto is plainly drawn from life, and it is plain that what he says and does happens every day just over the brow of the Aventine Hill dotted with middle-class villas, "down where Testaccio steamed along the Tiber's edge," and even within yards of the Vatican.

The very air of Riccetto's Rome is violent. The city is "burning in the sun" when the boys reach the Tiber, under air "as taut as a drumhead." Not the romantic stuff of legend, the Tiber is "yellow as if it were casting up all the garbage it was freighted with." Human garbage—discarded humanity, people it has generated and now refuse-ed—is drawn to garbage.

Riccetto's friends are not the sweet innocents of Friuli. They bear names like Wise Guy, Tar Baby, and Fats, their hair hosts lice, and they shout "Fuck you" just to weigh in with their presence. For no reason, Riccetto saves a drowning swallow. His friend Marcello thought, "It was nice watching it drown. But Riccetto dried it out and let it free . . . five minutes later it was wheeling among its companions above the Tiber, and Riccetto couldn't tell it from the others."

This scene is one Pasolini transferred intact from a story he had written in 1950 called "The Little Swallow of the Pacher." Rather than Rome and the Tiber, it is set in Friuli along the greater and lesser Pacher rivers. For his novel four years later Pasolini kept the drowning swallow incident, simply translated the dialogue from the dialect of Friuli into the slang of *romanesco* and changed the proper and place names.

Like *Amado mio*, *Ragazzi* is set in 1946, when the Allies were still occupying a hungry capital from which the Germans had unceremoniously departed. The Donna Olimpia housing project where Riccetto lives with his mother is one thrown up by Mussolini's regime, housing for the workers. Festooned with Fascist emblems outside, within it offers "a single room . . . with four beds at the four corners of the walls, which weren't even walls but partitions." No one has privacy: Survival, to say nothing of self-respect, could be won only outside such a place—on the streets.

Without growth from reflection on his experience, Riccetto passes from adventure to misadventure. He falls in with a cardshark, "who incidentally came from Salerno." The smooth-talking, sexy *meridionali* who fascinated taciturn Pasolini later reappeared in *Accattone*, filmed in 1960. One is sketched here in full for the first time:

> They were two sports, and they had plenty to tell each other about life in Rome and Naples, about the Italians and the Americans; each listening respectfully to the other and appearing to believe every word of it, but at the same time giving each other little underhand digs whenever they could, and at the back of their minds each thinking the other was an idiot, satisfied when he spoke himself but annoyed when it was his turn to listen.[17]

Pasolini, the now experienced scriptwriter, puts his narrative immediately on his reader's mind-screen. When the southerner speaks, seeking to "snow" Riccetto, he drinks. Soon "his face seemed rubbed away: it looked like a piece of scorched meat, with its half-closed eyes lit with an intense light that came from God knows where, and thick lips that hung down and stuck together." The same lips—as though literally transcribed—appear on Gennaio, the old king cuckolded by his young wife in *The Canterbury Tales*, in 1972.

As they leave the *trattoria*, the con artist "conscientiously" goes through some fairly difficult maneuvers: "He sneezes, blows his nose through thumb and forefinger, and pisses." The Christian Democratic government found such characters ones that Italian readers could do without. Riccetto works to hold his own in banter, passing along stories Pier Paolo picked up in his wanderings and encounters, including one about "Polack GIs" who set two prostitutes on fire with gasoline.

An Italy of returned normalcy, even glamour, was not supposed to produce boys who ate from garbage heaps.

> A toothless man, coal-black stubble covering his jaws, which were white from the morning wind, and two eyes that made him look like a suffering Christ gleaming like a dog's or a drunk's even at four in the morning, said to Riccetto, "Go ahead." Riccetto didn't need to be told twice, and while the garbage men grinned, bending over the cans full of congealed garbage, saying, "Go ahead, there's nice greasy stuff here to eat," and "Take advantage of it, sonny, there's a feast waiting for you here," he paid no attention to them and took hold of the other board, which was sticking out of the truck, and with his colleague he set to work enthusiastically, rolling the cans of garbage into the truck and emptying them. . . .
>
> Riccetto and the other boy were left alone at the garbage dump, the bottom of the quarry below them and the cracked fields all around. They sat down, one at the top of the heap and one at the bottom, and began to search among the refuse.[18]

Two years before *Ragazzi,* in a scholarly and as usual autobiographical preface to Sciascia's *romanesco* anthology, Pier Paolo had
written of Rome's "population lazy and choleric, ironic and bloody,
sensual and without tenderness . . . habituated to every compromise,
hardened, vicious and thus capable for a *capriccio o una bella azione*
of risking thirty years in Regina Coeli." Now they sprang to speaking
life.

What shocked many was that the world of *Ragazzi di vita* showed
so little compassion, so little *pietà;* the boys who populated Pasolini's
streets were as mean as the world that made them. The novel closes
as Riccetto watches, helpless, as one of his buddies drowns in the
Tiber. His reaction is only to remark to no one in particular that it
would "be better to beat it out of here." He cannot afford to mourn
and does not stop to do so, offers no hint of remorse or of reformation.
He moves on like a bird in a flock, one of whose number is shot from
the sky while the others fly on.

Garzanti hired a first-class lawyer, Professor Giacomo Delitala. At
his request, Pier Paolo prepared a "package" of favorable reviews by
such critics as Contini, Bertolucci, and De Robertis. Garzanti wanted
him to line up critics Contini, Alfredo Schiaffini, and poet Giuseppe
Ungaretti as defense witnesses. He wrote Contini: "And here I am,
more pierced than a Saint Sebastian. Have you two days, the fourth
and fifth of July, to throw away? . . . I do not dare insist, but limit
myself to fulfilling my obligation to Garzanti." [19] He wrote that he had
now lived "five months with this wearisome fever"; not for himself
("it does not matter to me"), but "for my mother and father" he feared
"ending in San Vittore [prison]." Contini could not come but wrote
assuring him that a copy of his comments on the novel printed in
*Letteratura*[20] would do just as well.

Meanwhile, work proceeded on the second novel "with love but
also with fear and mistrust." When Garzanti's money arrived late
again, he wrote on September 28: "You understand that in these
conditions one works with ill will, and lets oneself go at every temptation, often cinematographic: economically I live in a state of insecurity and of orgasm, try to understand this: I live day-by-day, and
if the cinema offers me some possibilities, how can I refuse it?" Two
days later he wrote to say he now had "more than a hundred pages"
done, had passed "a happy week." With May, he was writing dialogue
for Fellini's new project, called *Le notti di Cabiria.*

The trial of *Ragazzi di vita* at long last convened on July 4, 1956.

It was the very day of the vote for the Strega Prize, the worst possible time to rely on the presence of the literati. Because Delitala expected the writer—not just the writing—was going to be judged, at his request, Pasolini arranged for a copy of the Ramuscello incident's acquitting sentence to be sent to him from Friuli.

Alberto Moravia wrote in defense of *Ragazzi*, and the respected Giuseppe Ungaretti told the court that the novel contained "religious values." The renowned poet said:

> It is the job of the novelist to present reality as it is. . . . Pier Paolo Pasolini is the most gifted writer whom we have in Italy today. Everything he does— novel, criticism, poetry—is proof of an extremely serious commitment and offers results which ought to honor anyone.[21]

Unimpeachable Carlo Bo took the stand, testifying in a similar vein, that *Ragazzi* "has a great religious value because it proffers pity for the poor and the disinherited. I found nothing whatsoever obscene in the novel. The dialogue is that of boys who speak; the author felt the need to express them as they are, in reality." The judges were convinced.

Pasolini addressed his judges, when they finally stopped postponing and his chance to defend himself arrived:

> I did not mean to write a novel, in the classic sense of the word. I only wanted to write a book. The book is a reportage, a testimony of the life I lived in a Roman neighborhood for two years. I sought to make a documentary. The language in Roman dialect was stylistically necessary. When I anthropomorphized a bitch, a she-dog, I wanted to say that many times the boys, sadly, live like animals. In the title *Ragazzi di vita*, I wanted to communicate ragazzi di *malavita* . . . I have tried to think with the mentality of the boys . . . I intended to present with perfect veracity one of Rome's most desolate zones.[22]

The words could have come from Flaubert, charged with "offending public morals" with *Madame Bovary* immediately after its publication in the *Revue de Paris* in 1856–57.

Under pressure of prestigious firepower (testimonials were also submitted by Contini, De Robertis, and Schiaffini), the judges conceded. Its point made, the government let the prosecutor retreat, saying, "The matter does not constitute a crime." The verdict acquitted both author and publisher and praised the "climate of calm dignity" surrounding the proceedings.

In its sentence of acquittal the tribunal even praised the book's "pages of authentic lyricism." The case closed, copies of the novel that had been in government warehouses for a year returned to the stores, where demand was overwhelming. By August, one month after the trial, Pasolini was sending Garzanti a marked-up copy for purposes of the new edition now needed.[23] At the same time he asked for an accounting of his income so as to budget for a ten-day trip to the mountains with Susanna, not well and in need of a cure.

The highest office in the land had stooped to make Pasolini famous, notorious far beyond the circle of poetry readers and literary critics. He was now newsworthy and stayed that for the next twenty years.

In Italy, where culture is politics by other means, the Communist Party had to take a position on the novel. Among one vocal faction, the same values that saw Pasolini summarily expelled in 1949 still ruled; under attack, their position had hardened. Togliatti's Central Committee was still locked in orthodoxy in 1955, sleeping the last hours of the Stalinist dream just before being rudely awakened by the invasion of Hungary.

If the Church rejected the book because its characters never repent their sins, the Party—in perfect mirror fashion—rejected it because they failed to pick up their membership card at their local section house. On September 9, a few months after the novel's appearance, Carlo Salinari, a leading PCI cultural spokesman and recognized authority on the literature of realism, laid down the Party's line on the book. Writing in *Il contemporaneo*, he rejected Pasolini's use of dialect as "regionalistic," ironically the very charge used by Fascism to suppress any noncentralizing tendencies. By a special twist of logic, he dubbed the use of Roman slang as "not national" and therefore "not populist." He faulted the novel for "clouded inspiration"; the work was deficient because it grew out of Pasolini's "narcissistic" literary sensibility. What was needed was literature that served the Party's moral cause—with the right "perspective," not offering only ambiguity and suspended judgments. He wrote, "Pasolini seems to have chosen as his theme the Roman subproletariat, but the real content of his morbid interest is the dirty, the base, the unseemly and the murky. . . ."[24]

Others joined in to accuse Pasolini of artistic carpetbagging: He did not come from the *borgate* himself, so what was this identification with its inhabitants save sexually motivated slumming? Again, the issue he had faced in Friuli reared its head. How could he write in

the dialects of *friulano,* his exasperated opponents argued, when his
family spoke proper Italian at home? How dare he, not sprung from
Trastevere and Testaccio, use their language? The issue seems absurd today, but then, fueled by envy, it came from intellectuals who
sensed in their midst a class traitor, one prepared to betray and to
outdo them. This was an artist unsettling to scholars, on whose terrain
he trespassed, and a scholar who made artists feel inadequate.

The PCI agreed with the government that the *borgata* was simply
not a proper subject for literature, and Pasolini evidently not the sort
of man to give moral lessons to anyone. As inquiries came from
French (Gallimard was one) and German (Herbig was one) publishers
seeking translation rights, leading Italian Communist critics were
charging him with "estheticism"—a code word encompassing not
only homosexuality but every sort of moral softness. In August, Pasolini wrote Garzanti:

> The other day, [Antonello] Trombadori called me to his office at [the Com-
> munist weekly] *Il contemporaneo* to offer his personal apologies for the ar-
> ticles written by his comrades and to declare himself an admirer of the book.
> I really do not know what to think. But, to tell you the truth, all this matters
> very little to me, given the staggering superficiality of its judges.[25]

The critique of the man through the work echoes the response to
Whitman. In November 1855 a reviewer of *Leaves of Grass* concluded
with an apology for "entering such a mass of stupid filth," explaining
that "[t]he records of crime show that many monsters have gone on in
impunity, because the exposure of their vileness was attended with
too great indelicacy—*Peccatum illud horribile, inter Christianos non
nominandum*—" 'that horrible sin not named among Christians.' "[26]
The water was necessarily bad because it came from a poisoned well:
Like Whitman, Pasolini—in so many words—was homosexual.

One of the comrades for whom Trombadori apologized was his
uncle, Gaetano Trombadori. In the Roman edition of *L'unità* of August 11 he wrote that the book's "language, the words," are what
most "spring to the eyes," "The narrative proceeds on two, parallel
linguistic levels. The 'spoken' is all dialect and slang. On the narrative line, instead, dominates a rich, literary language, with bits of
slang and dialect scattered through it. The spoken comes all from
the protagonists; the narration all from the writer."[27]

The critic, with all the sanction of appearing in the official PCI
daily, suggested the two levels interact well, and took exception to
those who argued that the higher level and the lower failed to fuse.

Trombadori cited precedents, "from Verga to Céline to Carlo Emilio Gadda."

The "problem" he sees is not any of that "but another." "The book can please and not" because the narrative is "a succession of things and events, each closed within itself, not connecting. One who has read one chapter could say he has read them all." Pasolini's episodic presentation suggests the boys live without form, that one event in their lives fails to have anything to do—neither cause nor effect— with purpose or plans. The critic complains that the book's eight chapters depict activities of the boys that are all, in essence, alike; nothing changed but the locales, from the river Aniene to Trastevere to Villa Borghese.

Rather than accept the book as documentary, the Party's critics took it as fiction, as unacceptable invention. But even a book that claimed to be fiction could not be allowed to portray a boy like Riccetto, who never betrays the slightest consciousness that his life is part of the class conflict leading to the inevitable victory and dictatorship of the proletariat and restructuring of life along Marxist-Leninist doctrinal lines.

What the reviewer missed is that Pasolini knew perfectly well what effect he was creating. To use Pasolini's distinction, *Ragazzi* offers reality instead of realism, an apparently unedited recording without the form imposed by art. As he pointed out to a friend who wondered that there was no "development," such a thing was impossible without "consciousness," which his characters—on purpose—lacked. To him the *borgata*'s inhabitants really were outside of history, which belonged to a middle class that worshiped time and believed in progress. In this, Pasolini has hidden his technique too well for his own good: What appears an inability to construct a narrative that builds to some point was instead a calculated decision to show the lives of the boys in all their mediocrity, repetition, aimlessness, and even boredom. His book is episodic and without "progress" because its subjects' lives are exactly that as well.

His boys simply live, unthinking and cruel as animals, expecting only to grow older. They seek neither wordly acceptance nor enlightenment, neither repentance nor redemption. Their beauty and their worth, in Pasolini's eyes, were measured on a scale quite other than that of the PCI. In fact, that others found them legally and morally reprehensible only enhanced his conviction of their higher form of innocence. Dubbed by the Salinari wing of the PCI a "romantic reactionary," Pasolini forgave his beloved characters all. His empathy was no less real—but rather increased—because inexplicable to those unequipped to share it.

He found himself labeled "pornographic" and "a corruptor" by the Right. The MSI's daily *Il secolo d'Italia* found in him a *bête noire* to serve as whipping boy for decades. The ultra-conservative *Il borghese* ran cartoons depicting him as the *poeta della porcata*—"poet of the pigsty," rhyming *"poeta della porcata"* with *"poeta della borgata."*

In the midst of his mauling by the media, Pasolini found a handful of intellectuals who read him in an altogether different light. Contini appreciated Pasolini as the conveyor of a poetic tradition of dialect, now moved into narrative. Bassani understood him to be the voice of a culture intact but threatened. A few critics noted the book's extraordinary vocabulary: The Roman sky was "suffused with an artificial, candied light," and trees were "tubercular." Amid the profanity of the boys' speech and the dead-end chaos of their lives, a sun out of van Gogh was "cooking the fields," which at other moments were "so parched by the sun that they were as bare as in winter."

This vision had impact on an influential few who saw the poet in the novelist and the moviemaker in the poet; but to the general public Pasolini was presented as that admitted homosexual hauled up on obscenity charges and nothing more. He was a source of scandal, someone one had heard about in a not-so-savory context. The popular press decided his life was as interesting as his work and made of him the stuff of *cronaca;* he had been accused of pornography by the State and to many was probably guilty because charged. His entry into fame coincided with this image.

The trial of *Ragazzi* was the first of thirty-three legal actions brought against his writing and films in twenty years. His name and scandal were from now on inseparable; they grew together. The "avowed" homosexual—who outraged the Church one minute and the PCI the next, who became rich from films he disavowed, who condemned the student protesters in 1968 and sided with the proletarian police—was finally the maker of *Salò* and "inevitably" slain between that film's making and its release. For some time it had only been a matter of time.

During the preparation of *Ragazzi* for publication, Francesco Leonetti had written from Bologna, the first contact in the dozen years since the days of *Eredi* and *Il setaccio*. Pier Paolo responded that, taken "with the feeling of the years," he wept. Soon a visit was on: Leonetti and Roversi would come to Rome and old times be relived. He wrote, "I have a riverful of things to say, about you, about us, about that unforgettable and too important Bologna time. . . ."[28]

On October 18 Leonetti wrote: "This is the moment to make a magazine. This project, as you might have predicted, is in common with Roversi. In fact, over the past years, more and more he put it forward and I said no." But contacts, nothing sure, were made with various publishers, intrigued at the idea of a "literary appendix." "The magazine was something certain (definite, clear, even if not secure) for me when Roversi . . . said to me, 'I will not move, one cannot move, without Pasolini.' " Leonetti suggested it had to be about poetry, poetics, and poetry criticism and rarely other subjects, something for people (as they were) about thirty years old, and a real collaboration. Could Pier Paolo afford it, financially and otherwise?

On October 20 Pier Paolo answered, listing his many obligations: "I am full of commitments up to my scalp . . . notwithstanding which, I am with you and Roversi: ready to work without holding back, with you. Is there anything to doubt?"

Leonetti wrote, explaining that they had made no headway in lining up financing. Pasolini expressed regret but not too much: "I am very sorry. It could have been a beautiful thing, a period of our lives. . . . In the meantime, let's write one another and try to get together: come down here to Rome!" Then Leonetti fired back that all had changed: The new magazine's first issue would appear the following February, if Pasolini would join them: "Without you we will not make it go." They wanted it to appear once every two months in large format, sixteen pages in two columns. Pier Paolo was needed to produce a poem for the first issue. The proposed title was *Il quartiere* (literally, The quarter, as in The neighborhood); Pasolini, responding, thought it too reminiscent of *Il mulino* (The mill), which already existed. They would settle on a name together.[29]

In February, no first issue was ready; Pasolini wrote his partners exhorting that they had to have "our ideas clear . . . only with a real reason [for a magazine] and an honest one does a formula come, and only with a formula, success." He hastened to add that he meant "success" not in the "vulgar" sense but "etymologically," reaching a goal.[30] By the end of that month a list of possible titles was circulated: discussions began on whether to have footnotes, what typeface was right, what the regular features ought to be. Letterhead was printed. On March 2 Pasolini wrote poet Vittorio Sereni in Milan: "The magazine is born . . . you know our intentions are very serious, that we intend to inaugurate a revision, always within our subjective and objective limitations, of the literary world in which we have lived . . . will you commit yourself to contribute?"[31]

The same day Pasolini wrote Franco Fortini (also in Milan) to explain that their mutual friend Sereni would soon be approaching

him about writing for the new publication. Fortini had been editor of
Elio Vittorini's *Politecnico* from 1945 to 1947 and a founder of *Ragionamenti*, a magazine at least partly translated into French by Roland Barthes in exchange for articles from the Freud project *Arguments*. His credentials as an enlightened, if highly argumentative,
intellectual of the Left were substantial. But the honeymoon was
short-lived.

Pasolini suggested they call it *Secondo Novecento* (literally, Second
half of the twentieth century), but that spring he discovered the title
was already in use elsewhere. Maybe they could call it *Il Carducci* in
honor of Bologna's greatest poet? By mid-March the choice was between *Officina* and *Laboratorio*; they settled on the former, partly in
homage to Longhi, intellectual Bologna's patron saint, whose great
art-historical study of 1934 was entitled *Officina ferrarese*. *Officina*
means "workshop," or "atelier," and captured the sense of process
they were after. In May 1955 the first issue of *Officina* appeared (forty
pages, editorial offices on via Rizzoli, Bologna), edited by its founding
trio: Francesco Leonetti, Roberto Roversi, and Pasolini. Practical
details of printing and circulation were seen to by the chief salesman
at the Cappelli bookstore, Otello Masetti, to whom young Pasolini
had gone for advice on whatever was new and worthwhile reading
during the war years at university. Every magazine was required to
list a *direttore responsabile*, even if only a figurehead; Masetti, listed
in the official register of journalists, served the purpose. The printer
was paid and deficits absorbed out of the unreliable profits of Roversi's antiquarian bookstore, the Palmaverde in via Castiglione.

Roversi—compact, intense, committed to literature as a way of
understanding, and even of remaking the world—was concerned that
Italian intellectuals born in the years after the first war had not taken
the time, nor shown the courage, to address their Fascist upbringing.
That generation (Roversi born in 1923, Serra 1920, Leonetti 1924,
Pasolini 1922) came to maturity under a regime that did not so much
censure or censor new ideas as ignore them. Mussolini's dictatorship
had exercised control by imposing silence: No attention was paid to
anything from above the Alps. What was not welcomed simply did
not exist. No trials were held drawing attention to books thought
suitable for banning; few tiresome writers were escorted to the border;
many were sent to internal exile, unable to publish, but none were
shot. A warm, suffocating, and even soft blanket had settled over
Italy for twenty years. Roversi wanted *Officina* to say so. It infuriated
him that suddenly no one was a Fascist anymore or had ever been
one.

It was he who proposed to Leonetti that they make a magazine "of the mid-century"; they did not care particularly that it have a large circulation or make money. It did neither. What mattered was that they and others they brought in, like Pasolini, have a platform.

*Officina* started out as did *Il setaccio*, a passion shared by friends who thought it was amusing, after dinner, to send a postcard of praise to Montale, to Gadda, to Ungaretti. They planned articles and discussed politics and the ill fortunes of the Bologna soccer squad; at the start, there was much lightness, a casual feeling. But the magazine grew into an important voice at the center of Italian intellectual debates over neo-realism, dedicated to forging a new position vis-à-vis Soviet naturalism. The place of the new Gramscian intellectual in postwar Italy was still up for definition, and the issue seemed to matter more than ever before. All history and literature demanded restudy, reexamination in light of the "clearer understanding" this generation felt it had arrived at with pain, only after passing through the crucible of Fascism. Culture was not to be take for granted but consciously made over, with only the worthwhile retained. The editors were proud to be pedagogues and fought among themselves with the ferocious self-righteousness of idealists. After all, Gramsci had written that "education is the greatest problem of class."

In the issue marking the end of *Officina*'s first year—Number 6, April 1956—Pasolini's contribution was the magazine's position paper on the times and the publication's place in it. He recalled how as university students making *Eredi* more than a decade before, he and his *compagni* had

> nothing more than our literary passion. In contrast to the young people of today, we had no alternatives: we found ourselves in a world that was unique and complete, at least so far as our consciousness was concerned. We lived side-by-side the ironclad regime of Fascism and the institutionalized style of Hermeticism.[32]

The universe he looked back on was one without any form of political liberty. "We did not know that such a thing as anti-Fascism existed (that was only a matter of a few months away; we were only adolescents) and the aversion to Fascism which we felt exhibited itself in absurd, idealistic moralistic demands." He reminisced that he and his friends "read Croce in chemistry class," and he described Fascist society as "a pyramid . . . with the exquisiteness of elites going one step ahead of the masses who followed ever behind, behind but upward." He and his friends were sheltered from a "hidden world, one that was ignored, [where] there were people dying in prison because they had a different ideology, or many different ones." Then, with the fall of the regime, "Everything fell apart."

The great difference the decade after the war had brought was that the rein on intellectual freedom seemed to come now from a legal Left, as intent on smothering debate as the Right had been, the Right whose intolerant values had supposedly been vanquished with the war.

What Pasolini wanted for *Officina* was the same as he had argued for *Eredi:* freedom from the cultural line of the political parties. His idea was set out in his article on "the position" as though his colleagues shared it: "Here we will limit ourselves to reject any simplified position, anything too set in its ways . . . we are a periscope that works on a horizontal plane, open to the immense horizon of phenomena."

With Budapest on the horizon, Pasolini urged his readers to avoid any hard line. He is a Communist, he says, but disloyal to the Comintern. He dismissed what had come euphemistically to be called "perspective" in the arts as a cover for party allegiance, rigid ideology. With almost reckless independence for the times, Pasolini bucked the chic dominance of the Left just as—when he was a university student more than a decade before—he had argued the claims of independent art against the hegemony of the Right. In fact, the PCI leadership confirmed his worst fears and failed to stand up to Moscow until the Prague spring of 1968.

*Officina* posed a challenge to the most traditional notions of culture, and yet it was not at the cutting edge of the new world just being born around it. As Paolo Volponi understood, the magazine's matrix was that of "preindustrial culture," its view of literature "craftsmanlike" if not elitist, certainly not awake to the mass media or publishing as an industry. He believed the magazine his mentor made "never felt the problems of . . . the world of the economy and of labor."[33]

Volponi was unusual, for he had worked in the Olivetti typewriter works in Ivrea and was among the very few writers who knew "a factory physically—how wide it was, how long, how it was to be inside, how it was lit, what workbenches were like and the famous assembly line and the mass of workers, who at the sound of a siren went out and inside the factory, how they were dressed and what they carried in their hands." Most of those who published works of serious quality in Italy came straight out of the university and a tradition utterly out of touch with much of human reality. Volponi wrote of *Officina,* looking back:

Literature then was like this: it has something of the old, monkish climate about it, uncertain, coercive, provincial but not any more linked with that knot of real rapport with the provinces—that was the culture of Italy in those postwar years. Even if some activity began, some contact with international culture, we were very unsure of our capacity; our ability in understanding other languages was very limited. In our group—and I include myself [as he could have Pasolini as well]—the only one who could read a newspaper in English was perhaps Moravia, no one else.[34]

*Officina* had been officially dubbed with the subhead "a twice-monthly publication of poetry," and printed a steady stream of new verse. But there was also room for analytic essays, sometimes long and complex studies like those of Franco Fortini, invited to join the group because (as Scalia recalls) "we needed a certain kind of Marxist."

It soon seemed to Fortini that he was joining what he later called a group of "innocents," purely "literary types" far from the seemingly advanced circles of engineers and sociologists he knew, people who spoke the new language of industry and technology. In cultural analysis as well, Fortini felt himself to be at the cutting edge: He spoke easily about Theodor W. Adorno and Walter Benjamin, then known to very limited circles in Italy.

Leonetti, more than the others, saw the magazine as the working heart of an effective movement, something partway between culture and politics. He was attentive to letters written and retained, to keeping minutes of editorial meetings, to making the magazine the visible expression of something not yet born but that would be even more than just a magazine. Pasolini, more than the others, took *Officina* as a way to dispense largesse, promoting Roman friends, pushing careers with all the ardor and thoroughness that he had Nico and Tonuti in Friuli.

From the first of its two series, *Officina* lacked only Moravia (who did publish some notes on levels of language in the second series); otherwise, its roster was a virtually complete pantheon of the names dominating Italian literary culture at midcentury: Giorgio Bassani, Attilio Bertolucci, Giorgio Caproni, Carlo Emilio Gadda, Vittorio Sereni, Cesare Garboli, Paolo Volponi. Starting early in 1957, Italo Calvino took Gadda's place, publishing *I giovani del Po* in installments. Pasolini told his collaborators: "It is not a masterpiece but a good Calvino . . . if we publish all of it, fine; if not, let's be patient."[35]

This was difficult: Pasolini lived in Rome, had film work. So sometimes they met there, and on other occasions he met his collaborators when passing from Rome to Milan to see Garzanti. They stayed in touch, all of them editing manuscripts, each working to keep the pages open for his favorite outside contributors.

It mattered not at all that *Officina*'s distribution was never more than a thousand copies. As many were given away as sold. Its scrutiny of "generic Marxism" in an Italy at a crossroads made it talked about far more than the circulation suggests; influence was its business, and it thrived that way, as one of the voices at the very center of a crucial debate about culture and society.

With Angelo Romanò, Pier Paolo wrote a series of essays arguing for freeing Italy's poetic tradition from the shackles of Fascism. He rejected Hermeticism for its lack of communication and willed isolation.

Pasolini—Gramscian intellectual, Gramscian poet—wanted his modernism grounded in tradition. After *Officina*'s death, Roversi told an interviewer from *L'unità* that the goal had been "to correct Croce with Gramsci," to leaven Italian classical idealism with a nationalist but humanist Marx—all without being sucked into the PCI's intellectual vacuum cleaner. The program was, in effect and before it had a name, a cultural Eurocommunism.

*Officina* grappled with the great themes: To the extent that its editors made a "movement" and had a single argument, it was that literature was still valid and must not refer only to itself. Writers of poetry and fiction were supposed to interact with the world, not flee from it. *Impegno* (commitment) counted, but to what? They agreed the old answers were not sufficient. They split on where to go next from where they found themselves. Pasolini could only name the goal. It was, he wrote in retrospect, to "define what was the new type of intellectual at the moment when the spirit of the historic Resistance was ending. . . ."[36]

The polarization that events in Poland and Hungary brought to the Italian Communists in 1956 made ventures like *Officina* seem almost pathetic. Historical materialism had turned into an orthodoxy backed by troops firing real bullets at common people; the PCI's long claim to be keeper of the heritage of the Resistance—what Pasolini called its "red rag of hope"—was severely challenged from both without and within. When Polish workers rose to install the liberal Gomulka, many Italian comrades asked why it was that the PCI leadership was not prepared to distance itself from Moscow after it proclaimed all such liberalization "counterrevolutionary" but rather insisted that the Poles were incited only by American *agents provocateurs*. When Soviet tanks rolled into Budapest, the questions became louder and more insistent.

At the PCI congress in December 1956 a delegate from Messina dared to state the problem: "No one can deny the fact that in southern Italy hundreds of thousands of peasants and workers have come to us because of their enthusiastic faith in the infallibility of Stalin's directives . . . we must explain to them . . . that Stalin was wrong."

The Communist leadership of the CGIL union openly defied the Party Directorate, siding with the Hungarian insurrectionists. Every handful of Italian intellectuals seemed to have its own printing press, issuing manifestoes attacking the PCI's official line. Throughout the country, litmus-test petitions circulated, and signing or not signing them broke friendships. Within a few months the Party lost 300,000 members.

Bending to pressure, General Secretary Togliatti announced that the Soviet Union and its Communist Party were no longer "the guiding State" and "the guiding Party." Now the PCI would be linked to Moscow only by "common goals and common ideals," not more. No sooner did he say so than the Central Committee in Moscow met and declared that "independent roads" to socialism were unacceptable. Rather, there existed "basic laws applicable to all countries embarking on a socialist course." The message was meant to be read not only in Warsaw and Budapest but in Paris and Rome.

At this, the PCI's greatest crisis since the debacle of 1948, Pasolini decided to stay in the Party and fight from inside. He wrote to Franco Fortini: "I confess to you I have not signed any of the petitions which have been raining down in Italy but I would gladly have put my signature to your supplement called 'The Facts on Hungary' [*Fatti d'Ungheria;* in *Ragionamenti,* of which Fortini was editor]." [37]

But he did weigh in with an epigram that seemed to good Party comrades meant to kick them when they were down:

> . . . Your pain
> at no longer being in the front lines
> would be purer, if in the hour
> in which the error, even if pure, is overcome
> you had the strength to call yourself guilty.

He put salt in the wound:

> You wanted your life to be
> a struggle. And now here it is on a blind
>
> siding, here the red banners
> droop without wind . . . [38]

He demanded the PCI's bosses publicly admit their mistake about the Stalinist dream in art and in politics, recant and then retrench to serve the people "in its heart," not just in doctrinal pronouncement. He wrote, "You shouldn't try to deny the reality of any of your moments of crisis, change of mind and discomfort." He wrote the PCI stalwart, and editor of *Il contemporaneo* (where Salinari published), Antonello Trombadori:

> It's no longer a matter of doing the usual auto-criticism, discounted ahead of time. The matter is much more serious and important, and I say this to you not as an opponent but as a friend. And friends sometimes say things much more violently than an opponent, as you know. . . . Have you followed *Officina?* Have you followed my writings, in prose and in verse?[39]

In the verse, he scourged the atheistic politicians of the PCI, and—to the amazement with annoyance of many—in terms of religion, "It is to error/that I urge you, to religious/terror . . ."[40]

Pasolini's friendship with Alberto Moravia fascinated them both, partly because of its unlikeliness: The older writer was worldly, cynical, an apostate Jew intrigued by travel and women. He seemed a curious colleague and champion of a mystical Catholic, renegade Marxist homosexual.

Moravia's common-law wife, Elsa Morante, shared something perhaps even deeper with Pasolini: Both left a large margin for a quasi-religious mystery in life, and a passion about writing that some thought even deeper than Moravia's. Pier Paolo found in her a woman who was both intellectual equal and spiritual soul mate; without the prospect of sex, they could indulge their sometimes abrasive commitment to complete openness, a lust for frankness at any price. It was a trait for which each became famous, and one which finally cost them their friendship.

In the autumn of 1955, when the storm over *Ragazzi di vita* was at full gale and he was at work on its sequel, Pasolini took *la Morante* his poem, called *Le ceneri di Gramsci* (The ashes of Gramsci). Together with the poet Alberto Carocci, Moravia was editor of *Nuovi argomenti,* a voice of the "independent Left" aimed at finding a way out of simpleminded anti-Communism without disappearing into the Party's orbit. Carocci refused to print it, since the magazine's policy was to stick to prose. But Moravia insisted and the long poem appeared in the issue of Fall 1955–Spring 1956.

In March 1956 Pasolini explained to Garzanti that he was late sending the poems because of "an urgent article for *Officina*." Culture career-making took much of his time: He promoted a young poet named Mario D'Amico (who signed himself Mario Diacono) to Sciascia for *Galleria*, and then suggested that he write on the *Canzoniere* for Mario Boselli's magazine *Nuova corrente* in Genoa, where his own piece on Virgilio Giotti was slated to appear. He wrote to thank Sciascia for a copy of his *Le parrocchie di Regalpetra*, writing that reading it gave him "a real, powerful and moving sense of fraternity. How rare are hearts like yours. . . ."[41] He wrote "*carissimo Tonuti*" that he was "content" at news of the youth's forthcoming marriage.

His own "new" novel dragged on, with protestations to Garzanti that "it is all clear in my mind, even down to certain small details." He had the first chapter written, the second roughed out. On February 28, 1956, Garzanti wrote (nudged, he admitted, by Bertolucci) to guarantee forty thousand lire a month, starting immediately.

A few months later Pasolini again wrote his publisher, promising to send the full volume of poetry, named *Le ceneri di Gramsci* after its title poem, "within fifteen days: Please be careful with it, I beg you. It cannot have the sales of a novel, but, within the limits of a volume of verse, it can have a good success." Garzanti was silent; Pasolini, in the middle, even sent his publisher a letter from Mondadori about an option for a book of poems Pasolini had signed with that house. He apparently hoped this would spur Garzanti to commitment. Pasolini asked that Garzanti definitively claim the project, even orally, and guarantee that he would "really interest himself" in the volume. He wrote Garzanti, "as a friend": "Now you must tell me what to do." He wanted the problem he had made—of multiple contracts for the same work —to vanish, so he could write

> in peace, without other worries (as in the last ten days) which keep me from writing a single line. Besides all this, I have not received "the monthly": why? Is this an oversight or a decision on your part? Counting on your money, I have done nothing to earn this month, and so I find myself in a nice fix [*un bell impiccio*]. Add to this worries about the trial [of *Ragazzi*, to hang fire another two years] and you can imagine the state of mind in which I live.[42]

The "solution" finally agreed upon, the stratagem to call off Mondadori: a back-dated letter Pasolini produced, one "confirming our agreement of December 1953 [pre-Mondadori]" for delivery "by next

October" of the poetry collection. Arnoldo Mondadori apparently let the matter drop.

Only on March 18, 1957, were the verses in Garzanti's hand.

> Here is the manuscript for *Le ceneri di Gramsci*, please excuse its being a few days late: but I have been struggling furiously against some verses which did not line up. I send it as is, here and there corrected and uncertain: I would add that the last words —about ten or so—I'll correct on the galleys. I urge you, act quickly, because with the first of May I have to be away (outside of Italy) for a bit.[43]

A week after sending the manuscript, he wrote: "I am passing anguishing days . . . waiting for the book. For its appearance I want to come up to Milan and oversee a bit its distribution to the press, dedications and so on. When would you suggest I do that?"

*Le ceneri di Gramsci* appeared on June 6. Pasolini was in Milan for its official release, and went after to Ivrea to pass a weekend with Volponi, including a long-planned attendance by the two fans at a Sunday soccer match.

He concentrated everything he knew and felt in the eleven poems written between 1951 and 1956: anger and lament for the disastrous postwar life (it seemed a premature death) of the ideals of the Resistance, the confrontation between what the generation born into Fascism had dreamed for and what the first postwar years brought. Here was his chance to fly over Italy's landscape, moving through the human comedy like Dante, integrating social history and personal feeling, his own confessions and anguishes and Italian national biography. *Le ceneri* was the occasion for his particular voice that perfectly melded intensely subjective confession and public oratory.

The volume immediately struck a chord not only among those who followed poetry but far beyond. Its threnody for lost hopes was quickly recognized as a kind of Italian "Howl," the summation of where Italy stood just then. Calvino wrote, hailing it as "extraordinary . . . one of the most important facts of Italian postwar literature and certainly the most important in the field of poetry." He put in a dig: "*Il contemporaneo* lets it pass without a word . . . I am convinced that with *Le ceneri di Gramsci* there opens a new epoch in Italian poetry." He added that he, too, disliked *Ragazzi*, for "reasons of 'position' . . . I think it is a minor work of Pasolini's, that the real Pasolini is a poet and critic, one of the strongest of the new generation and in the camp of the 'Left.' " Salinari answered Calvino: He also called *Le ceneri* "a real literary event" but held his ground on the issue of "perspectivism."

On July 27 Garzanti wrote his author, "Your book is selling well. It's just that I was foolish enough to publish only fifteen hundred copies. I've now ordered it to be reprinted because it's sold out these past few days."


In the title poem, the poet visits Gramsci's Roman grave at the Cimitero degli Inglese (the so-called Protestant cemetery). The thinker whom Mussolini feared and silenced lies in "extraneous earth," surrounded by English aristocrats and parsons; he who forged the consciousness of Pasolini's generation now rests in a forgotten corner. Like Keats gazing upon the Grecian urn, Pasolini looks at the tombstone and addresses it, and something beyond it: "Patrician ennui surrounds you," he tells his silent listener,

> And the only sound that reaches you
> is the faded hammer blow on an anvil
> from the workshops of Testaccio, drowsy
>
> in the evening, with its shacks of poverty, its
> naked piles of tin cans and scrap iron, where
> singing,
> leering, an apprentice is
> ending his day, while the last raindrops fall.[44]

Something is wrong in the place which ought to offer peace. Like a symphonic overture, the poem opens with the strains of nature itself unsettled and so denying the respect and tranquility due the dead. The sky and sun (which Pasolini always brought into play, whether in words or on film) are violent; nature (as almost always in his work) is unnatural. The world is not right with itself:

> It isn't May-like, this impure air
> which darkens the foreigners' dark
> garden still more, then dazzles it
>
> with blinding sunlight . . . this foam-streaked
> sky above the ocher roof terraces which
> in vast semi-circle veil
>
> Tiber's curb and Latium's cobalt mountains . . .

With no less than Dante as model, Pasolini draws all of Italy into his matrix of disquieting in-betweenness. He telescopes on several levels: The high style of the ancient epic begins the poem, a call (as though Milton summoning the Muse in *Paradise Lost*) to an invisible presence, the specter of Gramsci that lives in the "ancient walls." But the atmosphere is contaminated: Not only is the timbre of antiquity heard but "naked piles of tin cans and scrap iron." The refuse of modern Rome serves him as bronze helmets and shields did Homer: Pasolini-the-*pasticheur*, working under "the sign of contamination," forces the high and low together, the sacred and the profane. As in life, he pushes existence into jarring confrontation and registers the effect of what he has made. Just as Riccetto is as worthy as Romeo, so even the sound of a tired workman in the rain of a slum can reach the ears of the great Gramsci.

The stage has been set for the poet to confront his prophet in an atmosphere both turbid and portentous. May is not supposed to be like this in Rome, and the already dark cemetery is surrealistic—both darker then brighter than normal. The sky arches over all: The graveyard and its tenants and the roofs and beyond them all of Italy. The Tiber's curves are invoked, as though by the ancient bard: "Latium's cobalt mountains" are present in the all-seeing eye and ear of the teller.

Pasolini now proclaims what is wrong:

> Inside the ancient walls
> the autumnal May diffuses a deathly
> peace, disquieting like our destinies, and holds
> the world's dismay,
> the finish of the decade that saw
> the profound, naïve struggle to make
> life over collapse in ruins.

The very air suggests the betrayal of the dream for which Guido had died: the failure of the Left, and of all Italians, to hold together and realize the vision of a more just postwar society. Gramsci has failed, or been betrayed; capital and Church have returned to power. The decade since the war's end has been "a deathly peace, disquieting," trapping Italians in a spring that did not become summer. A "naïve" decade has ended in an "autumnal May"; a time that ought to have led to summer instead has come to be a spiritual winter of dashed dreams.

The second stanza addresses temporality: The bones of "princes and pederasts" lie together here, in a Rome "impious" in its piety, caught "exhausted" between two worlds. The times are those of "the truce in which we don't exist."

> Choices, allegiances . . .
> By now their only sound is this bleak
>
> noble garden's, where the deceit that
> diminished life stubbornly persists in death.

The poet refocuses on Gramsci, at whose grave must be laid the shattered dream:

> There you lie, banished, listed with severe
> non-Catholic elegance, among the foreign
> dead: the ashes of Gramsci . . . between hope
> and my old distrust, I approach you,
> chancing upon the thinned-out greenhouse, before
>
> your tomb, before your spirit, still alive
> down here among the free. (Or it's
> something else, perhaps more ecstatic, even
>
> humbler: an intoxicated, adolescent
> symbiosis of sex and death . . .)
> And in this land where your passion never
>
> rested, I feel how wrong
> —here, among the quiet of these graves—
> and yet how right—in our unquiet
>
> fate—you were, as you drafted your final
> pages in the days of your murder.

The carving on Gramsci's tombstone does not commemorate his work; nothing is inscribed there of his place as founder of what became Europe's most potent Communist party. Rather his stone's "non-Catholic elegance" consists only in austerely listing "Antonio Gramsci, 1891–1937."

The poet must state where he stands, literally and figuratively, in relation to his fallen hero. His "old distrust" grows from his expulsion, the bitterness at Ferdinando Mautino and the Udine Central Committee, the apostles who betrayed. Pasolini must confess to Gramsci, berate and love him, announce his passionate presence:

> And here am I . . . poor, dressed in
> clothes that the poor admire in store

windows for their crude splendors
and that filthy back streets and tram
benches (which daze my day)

have faded; while, less and less often, these
moments come to me to interrupt my torment
of staying alive; and if I happen

to love the world, it's a naïve
violent sensual love, just as I
hated it when I was a confused

adolescent and bourgeois evils
wounded my bourgeois self . . .

The poet—"poor"—his soul laid bare, asks Gramsci: Is it not right that he—Pasolini, Gramsci's moral child—hate those who hold the keys to the kingdom of earth? His "almost mystical contempt" for those with power is visceral, but he cannot devise a program for change, cannot leap from poetry to politics. All that is possible is for Pasolini to identify with the pushed-out, the marginal and unwanted. But his intellectual awareness ("consciousness") is at war with his feelings:

Yet without your rigor
. . . I survive because

I do not choose. I live in the non-will
of the dead postwar years: loving
the world I hate, scorning it, lost

in its wretchedness—in an obscure scandal
of consciousness . . .

Already he understands what charges will be drawn against him: that the poet's absurdity is the only stand to take in a corrupted world. What matters and is to be cherished, even in the face of ridicule, is to embrace his crisis and celebrate his split allegiance.

The long poem's symphony mounts to crescendo, to a summary statement of Pasolini's very essence. His mind shares the Marxist dream with other men, yet his deepest selfhood is different from theirs and keeps him from brotherhood with them. That is "the absurd scandal of consciousness" he has come to confess at Gramsci's tomb:

The scandal of contradicting myself, of being
with you and against you; with you in my heart,
in light, but against you in the dark viscera;

traitor to my paternal state
—in my thoughts, in the shadows of action—
I know I am attached to it, in the heat

of the instincts and aesthetic passion;
attracted to a proletarian life
that preceded you; for me it is a religion,

its joy, not its millennial
struggle; its nature, not its
consciousness.

Pasolini now conjures Shelley, drowned off the Ligurian coast at Lerici in July 1822, buried in a once forgotten corner of Rome, now an intersection of heavily trafficked streets. The choice is apt: the Anglo-Saxon Romantic, the poet of Mutability, the radical utopian who fell in love with Italy and died with a copy of Keats' *Lamia* in his pocket. Pasolini uses history as does Cavafy, whose work he could not then have known. Shelley's conjured shade fuses with a hallucination of Italy, molting:

. . . Ah, how
I understand, silent in the wind's wet

humming, here where Rome is silent,
among wearily agitated cypresses,
next to you, Spirit whose inscription calls out

*Shelley* . . . How I understand the vortex
of feelings, the capricious fate (Grecian
in the aristocratic Northern traveler's

heart) which swallowed him in the dazzling
turquoise Tyrrhenian Sea; the carnal
joy of adventure, aesthetic

and boyish—while prostrate Italy,
as though inside the belly of an enormous
cicada, bursts open with white coastlines

in Latium brushed here and there with veiled
swarms of baroque pines and delicate
yellow glades of heather, where a young

Roman peasant dozes, penis swollen
among his rags, a Goethean dream . . . Coastlines
in Maremma darkened by stupendous pools

of adders' tongues, in which the hazel bush
is sharply etched, along footpaths the shepherd
unknowingly fills to the brim with his youth.

Pasolini now tours Italy as though from the air, and the sights and
sounds put him inside something much larger than political commitment (even to Gramsci) can explain or dominate:

Landsliding coastlines convulsed as though by

a panic of fragrance on the steep, languid
Riviera, where sun struggles with breeze
to confer supreme suavity upon the sea's

oils . . . And everywhere the boundless
percussion instrument of sex and light
buzzes joyfully: so used is Italy to it

she doesn't even tremble, as though
dead in her life; fervently,
young men with tan sweaty faces

shout the name of their comrade, from
hundreds of ports, among the Riviera's
people, in backyard cardoon gardens,

on small filthy beaches . . .

Will you ask me, unadorned dead man,
to abandon this desperate
passion to be in the world?

His cathartic confession that does not offer resolution now made,
the poet departs.

I'm leaving, leaving you in the evening
which though sad descends so sweetly
for us the living, as its waxen light

curdles in the twilit neighborhood.
and stirs it, makes it everywhere larger,
emptier, and in the distance, rekindles it

with yearning life, which, using harsh
rumbling trams and human shouts
in dialect, performs a faintly heard, absolute

concert.

The poet leaves behind the ashes of Gramsci to plunge back into the city, whose place-names he intones as though that of a loved one:

> The streetlamps have awakened, studding
> via Zabaglia, via Franklin, the entire
> Testaccio, naked with its lurid
>
> hill, the streets along the Tiber, and across
> the river, the black backdrop that Monteverde
> amasses then disperses invisibly into the sky . . .

The poem-sonata closes on the strains of a word-picture of the hated-loved world, rendered surreal, a "corporeal collective presence" in which the poet longs to live, to remain. His confession—and in Pasolini that also means confrontation—is now done:

> . . . It's nearly suppertime;
>
> the quarter's few buses shine with clusters
> of workers clinging to their doors, while
> bunches of soldiers stroll, not hurrying,
>
> toward the hill, which conceals amid rotten
> excavations and dry mounds of garbage
> the shadowy nests of whores waiting
>
> angrily atop that aphrodisiac
> filth; and not far off, near illegal shacks
> next to the Mount or surrounded
>
> by buildings that are nearly worlds, boys
> light as rags play in the breeze,
> no longer cold, of springtime, burning with
>
> juvenile thoughtlessness, dark adolescents
> whistle their native Roman night of May
> along the sidewalks of the evening
>
> feast; and garages' rolling shutters
> roar down joyously when the dark
> has made the evening serene, and among
>
> the plane trees in Piazza Testaccio,
> the wind, dying with shivers of storms,
> is good and sweet, though grazing the coarse hairs
>
> and tufa of the slaughterhouses, it gets
> soaked in rotten blood and everywhere
> agitates the refuse and odor of poverty.

At poem's end, poet and Italy are one; its quandary and his are one:

> It is a dim hum, life, and those lost
> in it serenely lose it, if their
> hearts are filled with it. Here they are,
>
> the wretched enjoying the evening. And potent
> in them, the defenseless, through them, the myth
> is reborn . . . But I with the conscious heart
>
> of one who can live only in history,
> will I ever again be able to act with pure passion
> when I know our history is over?

Another long poem (dated 1956) appeared in the *Ceneri* volume. Entitled *Il pianto della scavatrice* (The tears of the excavator), again it puts the poet "in the foreground," and the political life of Italy "behind." Pasolini's estheticism, and it is even narcissism, infuses this ode to Rome and to what six years living there had done to change him.

> Stupendous, miserable city,
> you taught me what men learn
> joyously and ferociously as children,
>
> those little things in which we
> discover life's grandeur in peace:
> going tough and ready into crowded
>
> streets without addressing another man
> without trembling, not ashamed
> to check the change counted
>
> by the lazy fingers of the conductor
> sweating along passing facades
> in the eternal red of summer;
>
> to defend myself, to attack, to have
> the world before my eyes and not
> just in my heart, to understand
>
> that few know the passions
> in which I've lived; that they're
> not brotherly to me, and yet they are
>
> my brothers because they have
> passions of men
> who, joyous, unknowing, whole,

live experiences
unknown to me. Stupendous, miserable
city, you made me

experience that unknown
life, you made me discover
what the world was for everyone.[45]

The poem recounts his "calvary of sweat and anxiety," traversing
the city "on a wheezing bus" to teach at Ciampino. But that experience serves as paradigm for the universal, not simple solipsism: "A
soul within me, not just mine, / a little soul in that boundless world, /
was growing, fed by the joy / of one who loves, though his love is
unrequited."

Neither his friends nor his enemies needed to conjecture about his
private life. He put it on the page for all to know:

And everything filled with light because of this
love.
It was perhaps still a young boy's heroic love,

and yet matured by experience
born at the foot of history.
I was in the center of the world, in that

world of sad Bedouin slum towns
and yellow prairies chafed
by a relentless wind

from the warm sea of Fiumicino
or the countryside, where the city
disintegrated among the hovels, in that world

which could be dominated only by
the penitentiary, square ocher
specter in the ocher haze

pierced by a thousand identical
rows of barred windows, amid
ancient fields and drowsy farmhouses.

His first Roman days in the Rebibbia quarter past, he could "walk
home [to the ] . . . Janiculum." "Here's Villa Pamphili, and in the
light / quietly reflected on new / walls, the street where I live."

It is there that he spies "an excavator," a *deus ex machina*, a figure
who appears with the perfect and necessary illogic of Hamlet's grave-
digger. He is the indispensable agent so that the poet may reflect,

> Why does just grief invade me, facing
> these tools scattered in the mud,
> in front of this red warning flag
>
> hanging from a sawhorse in that corner
> where the night seems saddest?
> Why, facing this faded shade of blood,
>
> does my conscience so blindly resist
> and hide, as if obsessed by
> a remorse that deeply saddens it?

History is "finished," both Italy's in general and its Communists' dream in particular. The blood of its Resistance martyrs has faded and the "red warning flag" hangs where it is darkest and the night "saddest." Pasolini returns to his hard-won bourgeois home, undresses "in one of via Fonteiana's / thousand rooms where people sleep," and remorse again overwhelms him:

> Why is there within me the same sense
> of days forever unfulfilled
> that fills the dead firmament, under which
>
> this excavator rests, turned white by night?
> . . . Ah, days at Rebibbia
> which I thought lost in a light
>
> of need and which I know now were so free!

He has lost the freedom of the poor and unknown, and his loss of innocence has been his country's too. He has changed: The bitter wisdom of the postwar experience means that "The world was becoming the subject / no longer of mystery but of history / Marx or Gobetti, Gramsci or Croce, / were alive in my experience."

What has happened to him and everyone else? A disillusionment as the decade since war's end took a direction he had not foreseen and could not forfend:

> The subject matter of a decade's obscure
> vocation changed, when I gave all I had
> to clarify what seemed the ideal image
>
> for an ideal generation;
> on every page, in every line I
> wrote during the Rebibbia exile,

there was that passion, assumption,
gratitude. The few
friends who came to see me,

new in my new state
of old work, old misery,

on those forgotten mornings
and evenings near the Penitentiary,
saw me bathed in a living light;
a meek, violent revolutionary

in my heart and language. A man was flowering.

The stanzas of "Excavator" are also a medical chart of Pasolini's soul. The attacks on *Ragazzi* and expulsion from Friuli, the distance from his father and brother, Susanna's strangulating love, the shattered dream of the Soviet utopia, his need to keep busy, frenetically so, and perhaps even the root of his sadomasochism, these overlap and collide with explosive power in the poem:

A bit of peace is enough to reveal
inside the heart an anxiety
clear as the floor of the sea on a day

bright with sunlight. You recognize
without feeling it, its pain,
there, in your bed, your chest, thighs,

feet abandoned, like someone
crucified—or like Noah
drunk, dreaming, naïvely oblivious

of his derisive sons, so strong,
so pure, laughing over him . . .
Now the daylight's all over you,

in the room, like a sleeping lion.

The "daylight" is the real world, the social universe, that calls for political justice, reform, even revolution. It is "daylight" that signals what the mind knows, the consciousness, and it is this daylight which is at war with the "dark viscera." Pasolini's mystical and yet public *via crucis* suggests an Augustine at war with himself in the days of the Cold War:

By which roads does the heart come to
its full perfection, even in this
mix of pain and bliss?

A bit of peace . . . And in you reawake
the war, and God. The passions
are only slightly pacified, the fresh wound's

barely healed, when you spend
the soul, which seemed already fully spent
in dream actions ending in

nothing . . . Now the old
lion, stirred by hope,
reeking of vodka, from his offended

Russia, Khrushchev swears to the world—
*now you realize you are dreaming.*
All your passions, all your interior

torment, all your naïve
shame at not living—
in your feelings—at that point

where the world renews itself,
seems to burn in the happy August of peace.

That "point where the world renews itself" is, for him, the dependable solace of masturbation.

Yet that new breath of wind

pushes you back to where all
winds subside; and there, you, tumor
which renews itself, you find once more

the old crucible of love,
the senses, terror, joy.
And there in that drowsiness is the light . . .

in that innocence that a baby
or animal or ingenuous libertine has
is true purity . . . the most heroic fury is

in that escape, the most godly
feeling in that base human act
consummated in morning sleep.

As the sun mounts the sky, "a sudden human scream is born" and Pasolini's focus turns from himself to all of Italy in that year. The poem becomes lament, a keening prayer *urbi et orbi*, as universal as the papal Christmas greeting:

The scream is the old excavator's,
tortured by months and years
of morning sweat—accompanied

by silent swarms of stonecutters; but it's also the freshly
convulsed earth's, or, within the narrower

limits of the modern horizon,
the whole neighborhood's . . . It is the city's,
plunged into a festive brilliance

—it is the world's. The crying is for
what ends and begins again—what was
grass and open space and has become

waxy white courtyards
enclosed within a resentful decorum;
what was almost an old fairground

of bright plaster slanting in the sun
and has become a new block, swarming
in an order made of stifled grief.

The postwar, modern world is something horrible: its order "stifled grief." The poet's "conscious heart" understands the impossibility of stopping history; even the Communist Party is too weak for that.

The crying is for what changes, even if
to become something better. The light
of the future doesn't cease for even an instant

to wound us: it is here to
brand us in all our daily deeds
with anxiety even in this confidence

that gives us life, in the Gobettian impulse
toward these workers, who silently raise, in this
neighborhood of the other human vanguard

their red rag of hope.

Pasolini and Garzanti agreed the poet would appear at the publisher's office at about five o'clock on June 6, the day slated for the book's publication: "I hope to find the book ready: I confess that I am very anxious, because I put too much store in this book."[46] On June 12 he wrote from Rome that he was "happy, with my book in front" of him. Discussions were under way for translation of *Ragazzi*

into French—"the translator wrote to me and she seems to be intelligent enough and capable." The French publisher Correa issued *Les
ragazzi* in 1959, after Pasolini withdrew support for proceeding with
Gallimard.[47]

Friends, including actor Laurent Terzieff and a French screenwriter with whom he was working on the script of *La notte brava*, had
alerted him that the street-slang in that house's proposed translation
had come out as "the language of an old lady." "This stuns me; I
care very much about the French market."[48]

George L. Picard, representing *Harper's*, was interested in the
American rights to the novel—would Garzanti please pursue that? A
Brazilian publisher wanted to translate the work.

A month later he wrote Garzanti to mention that *Le ceneri di Gramsci* was not "reaching the critics." Twenty-four hours later he wrote,
"Here in Rome, people are complaining that they cannot find it in
the bookstores (especially, it seems, at Bocca's): Is it because the
copies were sold or not yet arrived?" As for Mondadori, Pasolini
alerted Garzanti that the publisher "wants to take the Viareggio away
from me and give it . . . to himself."[49] Mondadori's lawyer was in
touch with Garzanti, who had to buy the rights from the other house.
He wrote Pasolini on July 23: "With Mondadori, money to avoid a
suit . . . your books already cost me more in legal fees than author's
royalties. Your work is worth it, but I hope that this sort of thing
does not repeat itself in the future."[50] Pasolini answered immediately, writing that he did not feel guilty: "I always did what you told
me to do, which is what I shall continue to do."

On July 26 he left for Moscow, sent by the PCI magazine *Vie nuove*
to report on a youth festival at the Lenin Stadium. He wrote, "Moscow
is an immense Garbatella, a mixture then of Liberty [the Italian term
for "Art Nouveau"] and twentieth-century." It reminded him of "the
provincial cities of the north: Vicenza, Treviso or Udine. Moscow is
a city of peasants. . . ."

As Debenedetti had predicted, *Le ceneri di Gramsci* shared the
important (and much-publicized) 1957 Viareggio Prize for Poetry with
Arnoldo Mondadori's *Quasi una vicenda* and Sandro Penna's collected
poems. On August 26 Pier Paolo drove to Viareggio, to collect his
prize money (a million lire, which he immediately sent to Carlo), in
his first car—a Fiat 600 given him by Fellini during the making of
*Le notti di Cabiria*.[51]

In June 1957 he came under fierce attack. Gruppo 63's spokesman
poet Edoardo Sanguineti (who congratulated him by writing that he
hoped "we will continue to argue") and other poets of a school

Pasolini had dubbed "neo-experimentalism" issued an anthology that Pasolini condemned as "wrong" because it was indifferent to history, was too self-referring, and too closed off from society. Their stance seemed to be Hermeticism revived in other terms: a retreat from engagement into private reference, private solace. As for their formal experiments and forays into concrete poetry—the group was determined to be internationalist, looking toward New York and Paris—Pasolini reacted as did Capote (another classical modernist) to Kerouac. Confronted by the success and apparent challenge of *On the Road* (Kerouac appeared on Steve Allen's TV program), Capote quipped, "That's not writing. That's typewriting."

Sanguineti, riding a wave of press attention as the latest in the never-ending stream of *enfants terribles*, fought back. His barbs struck home, especially when he accused Pasolini of being the one who was too subjective, and the one "who alone is beautiful and who insists on running the whole show."

It was the first, small skirmish of worse to come. Pasolini kept writing and publishing poetry but began to sound embittered by the reaction of the newer generation, furious and then contemptuous at the small-mindedness of the literary scene, frustrated at the inevitably small audience attracted by the making of poems and the writing about them. Already even in the explosion of his fame as a poet, it soured. The ground was laid, even with *Ashes'* success, for the move to film—to a poetry off the page.

In August he sent *Il contemporaneo's* Trombadori "La ricchezza," partly written as early as 1955. Now it was in three parts, which he described:

> The first part is the description of my *private* misery and private desire to be rich. The second part is the description of the misery of a population (like that of the sub-proletariat), the Roman one, and its desperate, traitorous, influenced-by-the-bourgeoisie (RAI, TV, illustrated magazines) wish to be rich. The third part is a lament for the missing solution (my interior one), and the lack of a social solution possible for the nation in the immediate postwar period.[52]

The second part, with references to Piero della Francesca (and the poet's fantasy of owning one of his works) grew out of the trip through Umbria made with Bassani.

With October he was working at a new poem; he called it "A un ragazzo" (To a boy), with dedication to his friend Bertolucci's son, Bernardo. He addressed the precocious youth who wanted to know everything of his elders. But the interlocutor, the "*tu*," transmogrifies, and Bernardo becomes the dead Guido:

> I saw you disappear with your little suitcase,
> where inside a book of Montale's was tight
>
> amid the few clothes, your little revolver,
> with that white color of the air and the earth.
>
> The shoulders a little tight inside the jacket
> which had been mine, the youthful nape . . .

And then, returned to Bernardo or perhaps to himself as the *giovinetto*, he closed:

> *Ah, cio che tu vuoi sapere, giovinetto,*
> *finira non chiesto, si perdera non detto.*
>
> (Ah, what you want to know, young man,
> will end unasked, lost in the unsaid.)[53]

Poetry was not at all. About the same time, he wrote a one-act comedy-monologue called *Un pesciolino*, meant to be performed by the Teatro dei Sartiri in Rome; it never ran. He returned to a play he had started in 1946 as *Il cappellano*, now reworked as *Nel '46*. And he went to work on an occasional basis for *Vie nuove*, reviewing favorably (but with reservations) *L'isola di Arturo* (Arturo's island) by his friend Elsa Morante.

*Officina*'s success, but especially Pasolini's greater one, was the magazine's undoing. By 1957 he was deep in film work and his partners were anxious to find a publisher to take on the magazine's printing and distribution. After flirtation with several, especially Longanesi, a deal was struck with Valentino Bompiani: A new series would start, with black cover with cream lettering (as dictated by the publisher's graphic designer), printing and distribution by that publisher (he was also Moravia's). The "new" *Officina*'s editorial secretary would be Bompiani's nephew Fabio Mauri. And the editorial board would expand to six: in alphabetical order (as listed), Fortini, Leonetti, Pasolini, Romanò, Roversi, Scalia.

But some wanted the quarrelsome Fortini expelled; he offered to leave, calling editorial meetings "atrocious . . . the stuff of making ulcers." Somehow a first issue appeared, dated March-April 1959. There was even optimistic talk of issuing a series of "small volumes of *Officina*," books under the magazine's imprint.

In the first issue of the "new series" (in the "Testi" section) Attilio Bertolucci published "Piccola ode a Roma" (A little ode to Rome), dedicated to Pasolini and as much about him as about the metropolis.

> *Tu eri viva alle nove della mattina,*
> *Come un uomo o una donna o un ragazzo che lavorando*
> *E non dormando tardi, hanno gli occhi*
> *Freschi attenti all'opera assegnata. . . .*
>
> (You were awake at nine in the morning,
> like a man or a woman or a boy who works
> And does not sleep late, who have their
> eyes fresh on the assigned task. . . .)[54]

Then came Pier Paolo's seventeen epigrams on contemporary people and events. He had written Roversi the previous November, "I am putting right also my ugly epigrams, searching to render them less ugly." [55] He also warned Leonetti and Roversi that the series of pithy tidbits "terrorized" him: "Before making an official consignment [to the magazine's other five editors collectively], I want to make a private one to you two, to have a way to discard, correct, or even renounce [them]." He told Fortini (in the course of critiquing his colleague's essay "Against the idea of a modern lyricism" as without "verve"), "my epigrams are still here, in a moment of powerful hate by their author against them."

In early December he sent them, "full of dread" (*tremebondo*) suggesting that all the editors could meet over Christmas when he, Moravia, and Morante made a tour of Emilia. But Leonetti wrote assurances that he and Roversi thought the epigrams "full of your passion, which literally, I love." Their sole advice was to substitute "canker" for "cancer" in one epigram called "A un monte." Instead, Pasolini eliminated the entire epigram from the group.

As though in provocation, or so it seemed to the offended, he entitled the cycle *Umiliato e offeso* (Humiliated and insulted). They were to signal the abrupt end of *Officina*, even in the very days when Pasolini wrote his colleagues that the cover of the magazine's coming third series ought to be "leather-colored." [56]

The longest epigram was a page and a half, others (like the fourth) two lines. In one dedicated to "Some Little Potentates," he assured "the editors and directors" of the *"rotocalchi"* (the illustrated magazines) that they would "go to the deepest part of that Hell in which you do not believe."

The sixth was dedicated "To Certain Radicals": He blasted members of that spin-off of the Liberal Party as intelligent *arrivistes* whose "English clothes" and "French one-liners" made them substitute "reason for pity" and kept them "from knowing who you are: conscious servants of the average and of capital." [57]

And he addressed one "To Myself."

> *In questo mondo colpevole, che solo compra e*
> *disprezza,*
> *il piu colpevole son io, inaridito dall'amarezza.*
>
> (In this guilty world, which only buys and despises,
> the most guilty am I, parched by bitterness. [58]

He entitled the last and longest of the cycle *A un Papa* (To a pope), an epigram on the death of Pius XII. Its closing lines, directed straight at Pius, were to prove *Officina*'s death sentence:

> No one asked you to pardon Marx! an immense
>     wave breaking from millennia of life
> separated you from him, from his religion:
>     but in your religion don't they speak of mercy?
> Thousands of people under your pontificate,
>     before your eyes, lived in stalls and pigsties.
> You knew it: to sin does not mean to do evil;
>     not to do good, that's what it means to sin. . . .
> How much good you could have done! And you did not do it
>     there has never been a greater sinner than you. [59]

*Officina*'s secretary, Fabio Mauri, had not read the epigram ("I would have stopped it," he said thirty years after) before forwarding copy to Paolo Benedetti, the Catholic convert from Judaism who was Bompiani's editorial director in Milan. Naldini, also in retrospect, has claimed the publisher's lawyer vetted the material and found it acceptable. Somehow it had slipped through.

The elegant Bompiani was up for membership in the Circolo Romano della Caccia (the Hunting Club of Rome), an ultraconservative retreat (modeled on the Parisian Jockey Club, in its turn on the London clubs) for the so-called black aristocracy, those Roman nobles who held titles from the Vatican. The Club called him to task, accusing him of blasphemy for publishing such words; he was dropped. Furious, Bompiani summarily severed his connection with *Officina*, writing Leonetti that it was he who was "humiliated and offended." Roversi, who could ill afford it, was left with the printer's bill for the already produced second issue of the second series.

But the matter did not stop there. The press had picked up the story, and soon Mauri was visiting the (unofficially but essentially Vatican-controlled) Banco Ambrosiano and the Banco di Santo Spirito, with the hope that they would not take those subtle but effective actions that would end with the calling in of their long-standing, long-term loans to his uncle's publishing business. "I went from one senior Jesuit to another, aggressively arguing that my uncle ought not to be blamed for an epigram which appeared in a small magazine he happened to print. I remember seeing a Jesuit who lowered his voice when he came to the point and tapped on a giant table. When I finally got him to say, 'All right, reassure your uncle,' I could barely hear him. Only the echo of the drumbeat of his fingers."

And did not Pasolini care that he had done such harm to the family of his friends Silvana and Fabio? Mauri thinks not, but not out of calculus or callousness: "He just had nothing in between; he had no middle measures. He did these things as though they were normal, as though he lacked an arm. 'When he was bad, he was very, very bad but when he was good he was an angel.' "

In 1974 Pasolini looked back with some dissatisfaction at his *Officina* experience.

> What is irritating and unsatisfactory about *Officina* is its naïveté, which is also to its credit. Its inability to foresee imminent neocapitalism and the rebirth of Fascism is humiliating for its editors . . . in *Officina* there was neither disobedience nor extremism; there was the calmness of reason in the act of rebuilding. But it was not true calm, or rather it was an unjustified calm. . . .[60]

In November Roversi wrote Fortini: "Free yourself from the Pasolini complex and its fortunes. Find your own that will be yours, not his, not ours." Pasolini's troubles with Bompiani (and with his colleagues—Romanò said he was offended by the Pius XII epigram, while Scalia called it "religious") were not the only reasons for *Officina*'s demise. Relations between old friends Leonetti and Roversi also came to crisis. Leonetti published a book of poetry called *La cantica*, and one of *prosa d'arte* (roughly, *belles lettres*) and a novel.

On the flyleaf, Leonetti wrote of himself that he, apparently alone, "founded with Pier Paolo Pasolini the magazine *Officina.*" All efforts at peace-making with Roversi failed: The two never spoke again.

Relations were strained all around: between Roversi and Leonetti and also between the two of them and Fortini. By the end of 1958 the parties, no longer on speaking terms, turned to Pasolini to make peace. He wrote Fortini that "perhaps there is something objectively difficult in your character (not for me, I believe, but for everyone else who has a relationship with you)." And yet, he wrote, it was "impossible to proceed" without Fortini's "desperate critical intelligence." His insufficient solution was that Fortini would stay away from editorial meetings and send his writing to Rome: Pasolini would play mediator, passing it on to Bologna.[61]

It was too little and too late. As early as January 1957 the Bolognese accused Pasolini of neglecting the magazine in favor of the cinema, a charge he vehemently denied. By April 1959, at the height of the storm over the papal epigram, Pasolini chided Leonetti that his "certain moralism" was an annoyance (*rompe un po' le scatole*): Yes, he agreed, their magazine could somehow be what Leonetti called a "guide to ethical conduct," but "in thought and action . . . not in the field of ethics." His friends were falling prey to the classic division: moralists vs. decadents. Pasolini wanted to straddle these categories, to redefine them. Fortini, deeply angry with all his coeditors, accused Pasolini of "a double game"—apparent loyalty to the group's high ideals (which included being read by the right few) and driving ambition played out in Rome, in the cinema.

The second series, Number 2 (May–June 1959) was too far along to be stopped, but it was to be the last *Officina;* by then, Bompiani's name was gone from the cover, and the editors were not listed inside. Scalia wrote on "La letteratura di partito" (The literature of parties). Roversi provided an article on "Il linguaggio della destra" (The language of the Right), Leonetti one called "Le poesie come cultura" (Poetry as culture), and Pasolini convinced Moravia to write "Aforismi linguistici" (literally, Linguistic aphorisms)—a series of brief aperçus on writing, separated by asterisks. Pasolini called his essay "Marxisants": he contended the Communist Party had to become "the party of the poor" and yet not impose populism on art. The writer "in this period of transition"—when neo-capitalism was showing itself also enlightened, and old-style (Stalinist) Communism was in crisis—had to confront a society that seemed at once to call for optimism and yet be on the verge of "its greatest crisis." "I believe a world so complex and so rich has never before confronted the writer as writer."[62]

The final number's *discorso critico* went to Fortini: His was the longest piece— on the Hungarian Marxist critic Lukács and his place in Italy. It was equal to all the other contributions' lengths combined. The once-happy group was so thin-skinned by this point that Fortini, Roversi, and Leonetti proposed that the essay be printed intact, with only a small end-note explicitly denying that all six agreed with its content. But the "Gramscians" (including Pasolini) thought Lukács (and Fortini) too dogmatic and wanted the piece severely truncated. After much acrimony, the note was not added and Fortini's last ten lines—in a piece of four pages, single-spaced— failed to appear.

He was furious; he called it "a real and proper censorship" that "changed the sense" of his entire work; thirty years later he still accused his former colleagues of acting in bad faith. On May 31 he resigned in fury. Scalia was not sure that Fortini did not (at his partners' explanation and request) cut the omitted lines himself to fit the print run to avoid forcing the making of an entire new page, in effect four sides.[63]

With *Officina* dead, Leonetti and Roversi joined Vittorini and Calvino's magazine *Il menabò* (literally, The rough layout, as in a graphic artist's dummy), launched in the spring of 1958; in a sense, it proved a continuation of *Officina*. Roversi also worked to start a magazine of his own, which he did in April 1961—*Rendiconti* (it ceased publication only in 1977). Romanò was increasingly committed to a career in radio, and then in State television.

Pasolini too was ready to move on. Khrushchev had delivered his "secret speech" on Stalin at the Twentieth Party Congress, and although its contents were not known, revisionism was in the air. Kennedy was coming to power and John XXIII forging what seemed to be a permanent liberalization in the Church. *Officina* was too small a spade with which to move mountains.

In January 1958—well before the papal epigram scandal broke— Pier Paolo wrote Nico, "I don't know if *Officina* will continue: It is starting to be a burden on me, and I really want to work for myself, that is for my novels."[64] And yet, feelers were put out to Einaudi (through Calvino) and Mondadori, to take the place of Bompiani. As late as July the next year, Pasolini wrote Roversi that the hoped-for series printed and distributed by Einaudi had to have "a decidedly ideological platform"; he even suggested returning to the original three editors, the other three as "fixed collaborators—this would simplify everything."[65] It was not to be.

In the summer of 1975 a compendium of *Officina*'s articles covering the fourteen issues between 1955 and 1959 appeared, prefaced by a scholarly analysis. Pasolini attended the anthology's launch at a Roman bookshop. Asked to reminisce, he said, "What has become clear to me in this past quarter hour is that *Officina* is gone from my life. Not only do I not remember it any more, but I can say it does not have the least importance for me. It has been carried away in the passing of history."[66]

# 15

*We are in the time of wolves, it is useless to play little lambs.*
*—Pier Paolo Pasolini,* Lettere, II *(1955–1975)*

# LACHRYMOSA:
# *A VIOLENT LIFE*

At least so far as Italy's literary world was concerned, Pier Paolo had arrived. Carlo Alberto had lived to see his firstborn both the honored poet of *Le ceneri di Gramsci* and best-selling novelist of *Ragazzi di vita*. But his satisfactions did not eliminate his need for the anesthesia of drink. Even as his doctors warned him against even a spoonful, he persisted in downing two liters of raw red stuff a day.

"I came home just in time to see him die," Pier Paolo wrote.[1] Carlo Alberto succumbed on December 19, 1958, to extreme cirrhosis of the liver and the exhaustion of one who had tilted at windmills too long. "He had no wish to recover, he would not listen to us, to me and my mother, because he despised us." The next day Pasolini wrote Fortini, "His body is still here at home; we leave tomorrow for Casarsa and his funeral and so you can imagine the state in which I find myself."

In 1966, confined to bed with bleeding ulcers, Pasolini had a chance to rethink his relationship with his father. He was writing plays then about fathers and sons; *Teorema* was to be the seventh. He told the English journalist Oswald Stack:

> He had a very difficult relationship with my mother. I only understand this now, but he probably loved her too much, and then perhaps this was not reciprocated fully, which kept him in a state of violent tension . . . I always thought I hated my father, but recently when I was writing my latest verse play, *Affabulazione*, which deals with the relationship between a father and a son, I realized that basically a great deal of my erotic and emotional life depends not on hatred for my father but on love of him . . . I don't know— at least that's how I've reconstructed things.[2]

He was always willing to melodramatize his relationship with Susanna. He described her as "beautiful and light, with the lineaments of a . . . miniature."[3] Cousin Nico says Carlo was "sturdy, with bushy eyebrows and a thick nape like von Stroheim," and so quick to vent his frustration at Susanna's coldness in rages over "a glass out of place, a towel not washed, food too salty and so on."

Even late in Carlo's days—in the summer of 1955, when he was in evident, irreversible decline and Pier Paolo's life was on clearly ascendant course—the son kept the father at arm's length. On July 28, three months after the publication of *Ragazzi di vita*, Pier Paolo wrote him a businesslike letter from Ortisei, where he had gone to write the script of *The Prisoner of the Mountain*:

> I received two or three of your letters (naturally, too, the sweaters), clippings and a very beautiful letter from Contini. I hope that in the meantime you have received my express letter and have done what I have urged. But there's no reason to think not . . . Lots of kisses.[4]

Substantially more trouble, and affection, went into a letter of the same time to Susanna:

> Sweetest *pitinicia* [*friulano* for the Italian *pollastrella*—"little hen," mean- ing a simple young woman]

I received your delightful letter the same day that I sent you mine: and I think that even this one will cross paths with another of yours. But let's be patient: it's not as though we don't have plenty to communicate . . . I do not yet see the hour of our reunion, and this situation of being apart seems to me monstrous: it is so ridiculous that I do not succeed even in grappling with the idea of it. The work is finishing: I hope, at the latest, to be in Casarsa on Thursday. Lots and lots of kisses (also to the babies).[5]

After Carlo Alberto's death, he wrote Leonetti:

His last days, he had a face that called out for pity. "Don't you see that I am dying?" he seemed to be saying to me. And I continued being hard and evasive with him. He wanted to die, he did not take care of himself, he had nothing left in the world, except for his gloomy anguish, his hate, his need to be someone else, to love and to be loved.[6]

On the face of Carlo's tomb in Casarsa's town cemetery is mounted a photo of him in uniform, set in an oval frame on the stone which closes the end of his columbarium. The lettering names him as "Colonel" just above his birth and death dates, and lists his "Silver Medal for Military and Civil Valor."

He did not live to see Pier Paolo taken up by the chic intellectual set, a mix of literati and café society, movie people and critics, a self-conscious coterie that kept close tabs on entrance to their circle. In the frenzied Roman way, they frequented certain *trattorie* and not others, scrutinized the vagaries of one another's careers and followed the curve of reputations with the intensity of generals plotting battlefield stratagems.

Enzo Siciliano, a literary critic on the staff of *Nuovi argomenti*, has chronicled the *giro* of the Roman literary "set": Bassani, Penna, Goffredo Parise, Bertolucci, Morante, and Pasolini. To their periodic dinners, each would often bring some new literary protégé to be launched; Pier Paolo brought boys he met.

In winter, they usually ate at the Campana in via della Campana, or at the Bolognese in the Piazza del Popolo, also at the Carbonara in Campo dei Fiori, and in Trastevere, at Pastarello's or Carlo's. In summer, their favorite place was a trattoria on the via Appia Antica, a stone's throw from the Porta San Sebastiani, outside the walls. Outdoors, under a makeshift roof, some benches and a few rough wooden planks had been set up; the railroad, the Rome-Genoa line, ran close by. The friends call the place "*i trenini*" ("the trains"), and they went there especially to eat *fettucine* and lamb cutlets *alla scottadito* (literally "à la burned finger").[7]

With the years, those places they frequented that survived "the boom" became famous because they had eaten there. But all this was without the hard, commercial edge of a Harry's Bar, without the Hemingway hype, without the self-consciousness of the thirties' Algonquin or the self-promoting Elaine's of the seventies. The atmosphere was less panicked, more like the San Remo bar and Cedar Tavern of Frank O'Hara and Larry Rivers in America's fifties.

Everyone seemed to understand that the fifties ended an era as much as a decade. As these years of restlessness and disappointment wound down, a couturier named Emilio Schubert held sway at the Café de Paris on the via Veneto. In a Roman club called "un night" (the word was as foreign as the style, and as borrowed), visiting Jayne Mansfield nearly fell out of her dress and into the arms of waiting *paparazzi*. Fellini was lining up his cast for *La dolce vita*. History was going to be made: Anita Ekberg (in strapless gown) with Marcello Mastroianni in the Trevi Fountain. Rome had become "Hollywood on the Tiber" now that the whole world had discovered neo-realism through Rossellini, De Sica, and Visconti. The major American studios found Cinecittà an economical location, and the actors flocked: Sophia Loren (she had her own Rolls by 1961), Gina Lollobrigida, Ava Gardner, Tony Franciosa, Rod Steiger, and Walter Chiari, and right behind them the flashbulbs.

As though to balance his friend Elsa Morante's intellectual intensity, Pier Paolo now invested in two other friendships with women. One was with the actress Elsa de Giorgi: theatrical, famous for her roles in the "white telephone" movies of the thirties, she carried champagne with her and talked in a grand, amusingly affected manner about literature. Pier Paolo occasionally sought her out and accepted her invitations to dinners; they stayed in touch intermittently until the end, when he cast her in his last film, *Salò*.

In 1958 he met Laura Betti (born Maura Trombetti), probably introduced by their mutual friend, writer Goffredo Parise, although Fabio Mauri (who had known her in her native Bologna since she was ten and he fifteen) claims the presentation came from him. Argumentative to the point of violence, the actress and cabaret singer was already legendary for her infatuations and public fits of rage. Sitting in the front row at a play, she issued insults at the top of her lungs; she berated waiters and train conductors for no apparent reason, screamed at reporters. She knew "everyone," and the press took to calling her *la giaguara* ("the Jaguar") and counted on her for good copy.

A reliably quotable and sure-fire photogenic couple, she and Pier Paolo were tailor-made for the weekly tabloids and gossip columns: he, the "avowed" homosexual, she in dramatic clothes, platinum blond straight hair, and as likely to kick a reporter as to ask him in for supper in her Bolognese kitchen. One never knew what she would do or he would say, and this intrigued both the press and Pasolini. She took to calling him "my husband," relishing the chance to *épater la bourgeoisie;* she fearlessly attacked anyone who did not meet her quixotic standards or seemed unfriendly to Pier Paolo.

Her salon was staged in an apartment at via del Montoro, 4, around a corner from the Palazzo Farnese. The street is only a block long, nestled between the via de Monserrato and via dei Cappellari, packed with *palazzi* which receive with equal grace (or indifference) a lumberyard, a motorcycle repair shop, antique restorers, and elegant apartments, all within structures whose giant doorways are topped with the eight-pointed star of Pope Alexander VII. The sixties saw her keep a kind of open house, where segments of society mixed in a way stratified Rome never allowed elsewhere. She presided over a madcap household full of interesting people who were in various states of rebellion, willing to be welcomed and ordered about by her husky (chain-smoking) voice.

When Pier Paolo seemed too interested in other women friends, like the actresses Adriana Asti, de Giorgi, and later Callas, Laura made a scene. "One thing he knew for sure," she said after his death, "that I was there forever; even if I would have been like a dog or a cat. That was something solid." She imposed herself on his life, and he let her do so. "I made him understand that everything must be seen from the angle of the grotesque . . . I helped him go into life, real life. . . .[8] He once wrote that she was "a heroine . . . and an excellent cook." She made him a room of his own, upstairs from her apartment. After he was murdered, she kept it as it was: the letter *P* on the bell downstairs his only visible Roman monument.

He stayed in touch with Silvana Mauri Ottieri, living in Milan. Once he asked that her husband, Ottiero Ottieri, secure La Scala tickets for Aunt Giannina, who would come by train from Casarsa. Silvana Ottieri: "She wanted to see *La traviata* or *La bohème* but was disappointed because the day she came there was a première of Britten. Arrived at Milan station, she was almost immediately robbed. I recall she wore heavy, wool socks, a Scottish plaid shirt and a sweater with reindeer on it. Pier Paolo laughed and insisted I repeat for him again and again the story of the reindeer sweater." Another time Silvana went with him to Tivoli, to an official lunch in honor of visiting Soviet writers. "He spotted a shepherd and disappeared for an hour." A starlet was seated nearby. "Don't you want to touch her?" Silvana wrote on a menu. He wrote back: "You know I can't. Why don't you?"

The film-writing that kept him from finishing his second novel, *Una vita violenta*, paid well when it was to be had. In December 1956, when the young poet and later novelist Massimo Ferretti wrote asking help in becoming a film actor, Pasolini answered:

> The cinema, in which you seek insanely to trust, is in full crisis: while in 1954 some 160 films were made, this year there have been in the works eight or ten . . . famous directors are going around looking for work. That I am working is pure chance: once the job I am doing is done, there is the void. . . .[9]

An Indochina film project fell through, so did a collaboration with Bassani for writing a script based on Giovanni Testori's *Il dio di Rosario*. But Fellini was satisfied with the "local color" Pasolini had brought to the scene of "Divine Love" and other low-life dialogue for *Le notti di Cabiria* (he was credited as "collaborator for the dialogue"); so he hired him again, to work with Sergio Citti on lines for his new movie's orgy sequence. His contribution was not enough to rate a credit as co-maker of the "subject and script" of *La dolce vita* with Fellini, Ennio Flaiano, and Tullio Pinelli.

With 1957, Pasolini's foothold in the cinema strengthened considerably. He worked a bit on an American film (to be shot in Friuli) based on Hemingway's *A Farewell to Arms*, starring a doe-eyed Jennifer Jones (then Mrs. David O. Selznick) and a very young Rock Hudson. Volponi teased him, "I hear you're working for Selznick, Huston . . . one day I'll come to ring at the gates of your villa."

Working on *Le notti di Cabiria*, Pasolini had come to know Mauro Bolognini, a director with tastes quite as exquisite as Visconti's and as fascinated by his difference from Pasolini (despite their common homosexuality) as Pasolini was with him. In the small, even claustrophobic, world of Roman filmmaking, everyone finally knew everyone else.

A year younger than Pasolini, Bolognini had studied architecture and set design and worked as assistant to French directors Yves

Allegret and Jean Delannoy before making his first film in 1953. In a career spanning a quarter century, he turned out dozens of commercially successful movies but arguably his collaborations with Pasolini proved his most important. Their first project together was the script for *Marisa la civetta;* Pasolini started work on the script in August 1956. It appeared, produced by the young Carlo Ponti, in 1957, the same year as *Le notti di Cabiria,* the film on which he was working at the same time. By then, Pasolini was the notorious author of *Ragazzi di vita,* and his known name lent some bankability to a project.

Work led to more of the same. He scripted the voice-over for *Grigio* (Grey), a short documentary on Rome's stray dogs, made by the still almost unknown Ermanno Olmi. That year Franco Rosi, who like Bolognini and Pasolini was productive well into the seventies, shot *Morte di un amico* (Death of a friend) from Pasolini's idea, although he shared "subject" credit with three others. The critics liked the film; Warner Brothers distributed.

In rapid succession in 1957 Pasolini had three successes writing scripts for Bolognini's direction. *La notte brava,* a joint Italian-French production, also came from Pasolini's idea—about life in the *borgata;* screen credit for "subject and script" this time was his alone. One of the movie's toughs, Ruggeretto (Pasolini described it as a film "about *ragazzi di vita* and whores"), was played by French actor Laurent Terzieff:[10] Pasolini remembered him and cast him the following year in *Accattone,* and in 1968 he played the wise Centaur in *Medea.*

When Bolognini was ready to film Vitaliano Brancati's highly successful novel *Il bell'Antonio* (From a Roman balcony) in 1960 a cast and crew were assembled whose names reechoed for decades after. The lead was a very young Marcello Mastroianni; opposite him, a beauty queen from the Italian colony in Tunis, who had only a few minor film credits behind her, named Claudia Cardinale. Stage actress Rina Morelli—to become legendary for her 1965 performance in Visconti's production of *The Cherry Orchard*—played a major supporting role. Armando Nannuzzi was director of photography and Piero Tosi—who worked for every important Italian director, including Pasolini—designed the costumes.

Most importantly, on this film Pier Paolo met the executive producer, a young, red-headed businessman with ideals named Alfredo Bini, an entrepreneur willing to take risks and empower those who earned his faith.

Pier Paolo took up the film assignments, again interrupting work on the novel, now promised to Garzanti for March. On January 21, 1957, he wrote his publisher,

> Naturally, my displeasure is greater than yours that the novel will not be ready by spring. I am about at the half-way point (150 pages) and in two months it is impossible to finish it . . . It displeases me that you should think me indifferent to myself, to you, to our commitments. On the contrary, I think of nothing else, and with that excess of passion which, sigh, distinguishes me.[11]

Garzanti had cut off his monthly stipend, so Pasolini continued, "Now I have an unclear period before me: I must find some other way to make the forty thousand a month. And I so wish that 'other way' was between us. . . ."[12]

He added, "I believe I have an excellent probability of winning the prize for poetry [for *Le ceneri*] at Viareggio."

Ten days later:

> I repeat myself: I have much more displeasure than you that *Una vita violenta* is not finished. It is a thorn in my heart which pains continuously. But you absolutely must not believe that the book will not be completed; only my death could prevent that . . . but I do not write like Moravia [every morning, seven days a week, anywhere], my impulses are different, and occasionally, irrational. . . ."[13]

In December 1956 the PCI-controlled weekly *Vie nuove* had sent him to Holland and Belgium, to report on the conditions of Italian coalminers working there. Valentino Bompiani had finally agreed to start the new series of *Officina* the coming June; the same month, Bolognini's *Giovani mariti* (Young marrieds) was released, with Pier Paolo credited as one of its four writers.

Without money from Garzanti, he had to take on other script work; the book would be finished when it was finished. "I have obligations toward my mother and father; do you think forty thousand a month could have been sufficient? Do you think one can live without a minimum of security, month after month?" It seems Bolognini was interested in making a film of *Ragazzi*; Pasolini told Garzanti, "This will relaunch the book and let you recoup the money you have given me this year."

In September 1958 he made a second trip to Moscow, this time to a conference of Italian and Soviet poets. That month he again reassured Garzanti: "Chance has it that I return to my work at a moment when my false work [in films] is disgusting me, on account of the

run-ins I have had with Ghenzi and Ponti. Working for myself, out
of my private necessity and private joy, gives me a marvellous sense
of liberation and balance. I hope this continues for the coming
months."[14]

His money problems persisted. He proposed that Garzanti pay him
150 thousand a month for more months rather than 200 thousand for
fewer. He reminded him that royalties of 130 thousand were overdue,
for *Ceneri*. On November 6 he wrote, explaining that while September
and October's checks had come the first of the month, nothing had
yet appeared for November. If it did not come until month's end, he
would be "without a *lira* (excuse the *brutalità romanesca* . . . )." He
added, "I am proceeding magnificently with the novel and, what
counts for more, regularly. But I have got to be tranquil and without
financial worries, in order to work." In December 1957 Trombadori
solicited a chapter to print in *Il contemporaneo*. He returned the first
pages Pasolini sent as too much like *Ragazzi di vita* and asked for
something "which will not give too much embarrassment . . . [of the
kind that is] 'political.' " The book's eventual third chapter, "Night
in the City of God," appeared in the Communist-affiliated publication's October–November 1958 issue.

One scene:

> Shitter meanwhile felt like eating a few olives. He addressed the hick curtly:
> "Give me a hundred lire's worth." he said, putting his hand in the pocket
> of his overcoat. The hick pretended he hadn't heard. Shitter grimaced at
> him. "A hundred lire's worth," he repeated.
>
> Then the seller said, "Gimme the money first." Shitter stared at him
> again, patiently. "Now look . . . " he said affably, "a hundred lire's worth."
> "Money first," the man repeated stubbornly, since God knows how many
> times he'd been cheated, poor bastard.
>
> A kind of charge seemed to run through Shitter, who raised one foot,
> grinding his teeth, preparing to give the bucket a kick. "Now I'm gonna give
> this bucket a kick, right into the middle of the square, so go fuck yasself!"
> he shouted. "Come on, gimme those olives!" The man, resigned by now,
> ready even to be hanged perhaps, still held out stubbornly: "No, no, I wanna
> see the money," he said.
>
> Shitter was silent, looking at him. Slowly his face swelled, his mouth
> tightened, rose toward his nostrils, his eyes popped. All the muscles of his
> face were trembling, as if he were changing skin. He seemed uncertain
> whether to abandon himself to convulsions of rage and kick that stupid face
> in front of him, or else burst out laughing.
>
> "Hey, what is this?" he said in the end, almost in a low voice. "Did you
> take a good look at me? I'll smash the hundred lire in your mouth!"
>
> With this, he took two or three hundred-lire notes from his pocket, se-

lected one, plunged it suddenly into the water, and with a slap that could be heard in all the surrounding streets, plastered it against the man's face. Then, without even looking at him. still trembling, he went to his friends, who were in a circle, watching and laughing. Coletta patted him on the shoulder, then said to them all: "Let's go!" moving at the head of the band, his face looking like it was painted on a banner, towards Ponte Rotto.

They all went off swaggering, some this way, some that.[15]

Pasolini wrote Garzanti, "I am in a very happy moment with the novel: if it continues this way, at the end of March I will give it to you. I write five or six pages a day, and am filled with it, I flow novel from every pore. . . ."[16]

The following January, 1959, he declined Giacinto Spagnoletti's invitation to collaborate on an anthology of Italian poetry for the period 1909–1959. "I have to consign the novel in February: I do not even have time to breathe: it has become the dominating thought, unique and exclusive. I cannot even imagine thinking of another one. [What] you ask of me is too demanding to be done with the left hand. . . ."[17]

Pier Paolo delivered *Una vita violenta* that March. The very week he sent it to Garzanti, he answered a letter from competing publisher Giulio Einaudi:

> Your letter gave me great joy: I can tell you that since boyhood (my first book, from schooldays, was Montale's *Occasioni*) I have always dreamt of seeing my poetry issue from your house: Calvino must also have said as much. I hope now to put together the book desired. The only obstacle, and rather serious, is Garzanti, to whom I have commitments: I do not know whether he would let me go to another publisher, even with a book of poems and essays. He has regretted, recriminating and fretting, at having given me permission for *Nightingale*, at Longanesi.[18]

When *Una vita violenta* finally reached bookstores that May, not surprisingly it bore a dedication not to Livio Garzanti but "to Carlo Bo and Giuseppe Ungaretti, my witnesses in the trial of *Ragazzi di vita*" and acknowledged in an Author's Note, "With true gratitude, Sergio Citti."

It is, again, a picaresque tale of slum boys at the physical and moral margins of society, living by their wits, surrounded by human and material "refuse," prostitution of both sexes, explosive with

Roman slang and unbridled energy. In England the novel was billed as "the underbelly of *La dolce vita*."

Its focus is a *ragazzo di vita* named Tommaso Puzzilli. In January 1961, in the course of reviewing Moravia's *La noia*, Pasolini focused on the contrast between his friend's narrative strategy and his own, adding, "Please excuse the immodesty of the parallel, but it serves me to think about this." Moravia, he argued, did not enter into his character, at least not in the same way as he does. To make Tommaso "speak, live, concretely exist, I withdraw into him, to the point of a *mimesis* which is almost a physical identification. . . ." [19] Had not Flaubert said, "Madame Bovary, c'est moi"?

Again, Garzanti insisted on cuts. A scene set in a movie house especially worried the publisher, who called it "dangerously suggestive from a judicial point of view." When Pasolini complied, Garzanti wrote him, "I am very, very grateful for your accepting our suggestions. I do not believe it has taken anything away from the value of your work and the fact that I now feel fully calm allows me to launch your book as it deserves." [20]

After what Pasolini called his "self-censorship," the sequence in the red-light moviehouse was made to read:

> The little queen next to Tommaso was smoking, his elbow on the arm of the seat, his hand high and limp, the cigarette between two fingers. Tommaso looked at him, and the faggot also turned his eyes on Tommaso.
>
> The lights went down again. Immediately, Tommaso widened his legs, moving his left leg closer to his neighbor's: he sat there, waiting. He remained still, like a cat watching a dock, on the rickety seat. . . .
>
> The fag wasn't moving yet. Tommaso watched him, angrily. Whaddya waiting for, shithead? he thought to himself. He changed his position, slamming his back against the seat, almost breaking it, and giving another blow with his knee, almost breaking the back of the seat in front of him . . . The queen, at all that movement, had begun to look down. And so they went on for about ten minutes. Tommaso had stretched his legs wide and had slid his ass so far down on the seat that a little farther and he would have fallen to the floor, which was covered with spit, peanut shells and maybe some piss, too, for good measure. . . .
>
> Adjusting himself angrily in his seat, every now and then he nudged his neighbor who kept looking at the boy ahead of them but was also lowering his eyes more often on Tommaso. He nudged him hard, like you hit a closed door . . . So whadda we gonna do? Tommaso was thinking, almost aloud. The character next to him must have said to himself, finally: Well, let's get rid of him! And, all of a sudden, he stretched out his hand.
>
> When, in no time, he had finished, Tommasino, content, buttoned up again, without haste.

Then he raised his head and looked towards the character at his side.

The other kid paid no attention: now he was seized by a great interest in the movie. Tommaso watched him for a few minutes, his forehead wrinkled, his eyes dazed, and his mouth drawn in a grimace that, all peaceably, meant to say, "You really like this picture, eh?"

Then abruptly, he gave him a nudge.

The queen, stirred, looked at him as if he had forgotten all about him, and sat still for a moment. Then just as Tommasino was raising his hand to rub thumb and index finger together, as if he had a little ball of snot between them, the queen said: "Oh, yes, sorry, eh?" He spoke hastily and politely.

Tommaso then became good-natured: "Sort of forgot, didn't you?"

"Yeah," the queen said, with a little shake of his head, wriggling all over, as he rummaged in one of his pants pockets. He pulled out a hundred *lire*.[21]

Tommaso demands more and gets three hundred. Then he pulls a switchblade, and two hundred lire more emerge from a shoe.

Tommaso took the two hundred *lire* and put it in his pocket too. "The other shoe," he said. The queen obeyed him, muttering: "There's nothing there." In fact there was nothing in the other shoe. Tommasino put the knife back in his pocket, coughed a little, looked around, then got up and went straight towards the exit.[22]

Outside, "There was too much confusion, too much racket. Via Nazionale was a snakepit, and at every traffic light the bus was held up for half an hour: so it took a long time to reach the fountain in Piazza Esedra and the station."

The novel opens as cinematically as was to be expected from a working screenwriter. Carlo Emilio Gadda had already zeroed in on Pasolini's prose style: "When *Ragazzi di vita* appeared, he called it "a sound track."

Tommaso, Lello, Zucabbo, and the other boys who lived in the little shanty-village in the via dei Monti di Pietralata, were, as usual after lunch, in front of the school at least half an hour early.

But some other little snotnoses from the neighborhood were already there, playing with a penknife in the mud. Tommaso, Lello and their bunch crouched around the players to watch, satchels dragging on the ground. Two or three more boys showed up, with a ball, and they all threw their books on a mound and ran behind the school, to the open lot that counted as the main square of the slum.[23]

Tommaso's life in the lower depths of Rome includes robbing and beating a gas-station attendant, snatching handbags from prostitutes, and stealing a priest's chickens. One critic said *Ragazzi* was set in "a suburb of Hell," but *Una vita violenta* was worse. In one episode, Tommaso sets a friend's hand, which has been smashed under a tram, and aids in a robbery. That done, they take their victim for a drive and when they get out, Tommaso pins his arms while the others work him over until blood comes from an eyelid and he throws up. The police nab Tommaso when he pulls a knife on someone who threatens to ruin the serenade he has planned for his girl friend.

Once out of jail, the hero and his family move to a new housing project. He goes straight, gets a job, flirts with the ideal of a respectable life, even of becoming a Christian Democrat. Caught in a flood in his neighborhood, he becomes tubercular and is committed to a clinic. To be sure he had all the details correctly, Pasolini announced a visit to the Forlanini sanatorium where, he told Garzanti, "As luck would have it, I have a friend from Parma who is a young doctor."[24] A strike by hospital workers shows Pasolini's hero what Communism is, and he joins up. Slowly and only when it can serve him, Tommaso (unlike Riccetto) moves from class hatred to class struggle. He does so haltingly, passing from indifference to the PCI via Fascism and the parish house. Gradually, and on his own terms, he comes to choose another conformity and (it seems) responsibility, arriving at what Moravia called a non-Marxist Communism, an ideology "populist and romantic . . . fundamentally sentimental, in the sense of existential, creatural, irrational."

A hemorrhage finishes off Tommaso.

Pasolini later explained that these "contradictory stages"—leading to Tommaso's Communism—were possible because "*Una vita violenta* was born in the fifties before the Stalinist crisis [although published later], when hope, in the prospective shape it took with the Resistance and immediately after the war, was still alive, was a real fact. . . ."[25] Tommaso joins the movement cynically, out of self-interest, not ardor. He is both someone not given a chance by the world and also someone too venal and stupid to profit from anything that might happen by. And yet we are sorry for him; Tommaso is heroic despite himself. As for the Communist Party he finally joins, Pasolini depicted its comrade-operatives dividing the loot from stealing raffle tickets and then turning smoothly to organizing a political rally. Tommaso in hospital is useful and, therefore, finally of interest to them.

> The men from the Party came to see him, too; they had already agreed that if Tommaso died they would name the Pietralata section after him because

of his brave deed that he was now paying for so dearly. All worn, in bad shape himself, Lello came with them too, and Zucabbo, fresh as an apple that's just fallen off the tree, fat-faced under his dyed curls.

The only other news Tommaso had about the neighborhood was that a cabinet member had paid it a visit, seeing the bed of dried mud that covered it. He had made the usual promises, and meanwhile, those who were homeless had been parceled out among some convents, some schools, where there were already other people from the shacks.[26]

Convinced he is dying, Tommaso's friends start to weep at his bedside:

"What the fuck're you crying for? If anybody's gotta cry around here, it's me," Tommaso said.

"You're not dying, are you?"

Their eyes glistened in their crooks' faces, burned by the sun and by hunger. Lello and Zucabbo kept standing there, not moving.

"Fuckoff!" Tommaso said. "Instead of staying around here and keeping me company, go outside and screw around. It's Sunday!" He turned his face away and didn't say any more.

But as far as dying went, he decided he was going to die in his own bed at home; and, in fact, it was easy for them to get permission to take him away now. It was a fine day, mild, late September with the sun shining in the sky without a spot in it, and people talking, singing along the streets, in the new buildings.

When Tommaso was back in his bed, he almost felt he was a little better. After all, they still hadn't come to anoint him; for an hour or so the cough stopped, and he even asked his mother for some of that marsala Irene had brought him. But then, when night came, he felt worse all the time: he had another fit, coughing blood, coughing, coughing, unable to catch his breath, and it was goodbye Tommaso.[27]

Insight coincides only with death; Pasolini's protagonist comes to consciousness only when he has no future.

Pasolini had hopes for *Una vita violenta* in the Viareggio Prize prose category. He wrote Garzanti: "Everyone tells me that they will give it to me; I want to do something. Copies must be sent to the secretariat and to the jurors. And one must take soundings . . . Maybe you, as publisher, can make some move? This is the first time I ask you anything of this kind: I am quite confused and ashamed. But I would so like to have it, this Viareggio . . ."[28]

He was not above personally campaigning for the award (everyone did), and he let it be known that he expected his friends to help. He began writing contacts like Vittorio Sereni in Milan, Alessandro

Bonsanti in Florence, soliciting their votes. When some of those he had counted on for support kept silent, he was angry and let it be known.

Pasolini's friends rallied around the new novel. On June 9, 1959, Calvino wrote, "I have read it all. It is extremely beautiful. It makes a clear break from all our other books. All (or almost all) that I want in a book is in it. It is a book I would like to have written myself (with everything it has in it there, but differently) and which perhaps I will never write, but I am content that it has been written . . . it marks a qualitative leap up from *Ragazzi di vita* (itself lovely as a lyric poem). . . ."[29]

The Strega Prize for prose went to Lampedusa's *Il gattopardo* (The leopard), "discovered" by Bassani and published by Feltrinelli. *Una vita violenta* took third.

At the end of August he found his novel in competition with Moravia's *Nuovi racconti romani* (New Roman stories) for the Viareggio for prose. Moravia withdrew to leave the field to his friend, only to find the prize given to Marino Moretti. He wrote, "A prize given to Pasolini would have signified courage and been useful to all of Italian literature."[30] Pasolini, openly disappointed, hailed the winner: "Perhaps it is true what some say, that he ought to have won thirty years ago, but better late than never."[31] Garzanti wrote to console him over the missed prize: "To date, the book has sold 20,000 copies . . . as for the impact of the Prize on your financial problems, with the month of September [1959] I am raising your monthly [payment] to 200,000 lire.[32]

Carlo Alberto's death left Pier Paolo, at last, alone with Susanna. On June 25, a month after *Una vita violenta*'s publication and at the height of his efforts to win the Strega, he moved her into an apartment at number 45, via Giacinto Carini, in the same building where the Bertoluccis lived in the tranquil, bourgeois, and leafy district of Monte Verde Vecchio.

Life seemed smooth. But, in his poetry, Susanna joined him in failure and persecution; she alone could always be relied upon—her love alone was unconditional. He assumes that perfection and a kind of peace will unite them, but only in death. Until then, life is and was expected to remain "implacable pain." Within the year, he wrote:

> By now, at every hour, everything is for her,
> the child

for me, her son, it is finished, and forever;
nothing remains but to hope that the end
will really come to extinguish the implacable
pain of awaiting it. Soon we will be
together, in that barren meadow filled

with gray stones . . .

. . . .

Soon
we too, sweet survivor, will be

lost at the bottom of that cool
plot of earth: but ours won't be
a stillness, for mingled in it too much

will be a life that has had no goal.
We'll have a sad and difficult silence,
a painful sleep, one that won't bring

softness and peace, but nostalgia and reproof. . . .[33]

Tommaso's novel may have been, in part, Pasolini's effort to return to the Party's good graces; he did declare, "My intention was to write a socialist novel." In that, he failed. The PCI's culture critics did not approve the novel's depiction of the protagonist nor appreciate Pasolini's portraiture of its operatives. In October 1959 he wrote the critic Mario Visani: "You belong to that group of persons to whom now I give greatest trust: the Christian Democrats of the left, of the extreme left."

Pasolini was almost literally driven into the arms of the opposition. In January 1960 Senator Mario Montagnana—member of the Party's Central Committee, Togliatti's brother-in-law—addressed a letter to the director of *Rinascita,* the Party's cultural monthly and Togliatti's personal fiefdom. His words were widely taken as the PCI's official reaction to *Una vita violenta* and its author:

> Pasolini reserves the vulgarities, the dirty words, for the world of the poor. One gets the impression that Pasolini does not like poor people, that he despises in general the inhabitants of the Roman shantytowns [*borgate*], and despises our party even more. The hero, Tommasino, is in reality a juvenile delinquent of the worst kind: thief, robber, pederast.[34]

Such Communists as this Tommaso (and by inference his creator), the PCI could do without:

> The description of the Communist cell and of its secretary (a half-delinquent) and of the gathering of its members, is absolutely to be rejected with

> scorn . . .he (Tommaso) becomes a card-holder of the Communist Party. He needs a few hundred *lire* . . . he enters an infamous cinema . . . he moves near someone known to be a pederast, and allows himself to be masturbated by such a one and is given five hundred *lire*. Is this not enough to make one indignant?[35]

Luckily, Montagnana's was far from being the only voice within the splintered ranks of the PCI's "house intellectuals." Pasolini had his admirers and defenders even there. The next month, another PCI senator, Edoardo d'Onofrio (from the Roman slums himself, then head of the Party's Roman Federation and member of the city's ruling *giunta*) wrote the magazine, "I believe that one of the reasons that induces some of our comrades to make an incorrect evaluation of Pier Paolo Pasolini's novel *Una vita violenta* derives largely from the fact that they do not know the political and social importance of the presence in Rome of the numerous subproletariat."[36]

He credits Pasolini for not hiding the truth in "order to spare the Party" and urges his comrades to read the novel before rejecting it.

Pasolini's response to those whose attacks were not simply personal, who charged that Tommaso's world was unrealistically sealed off from another, broader reality, was this:

> When I was writing and talking about the lumpenproletariat I was wholly in that world, I couldn't cast glances toward what was outside of it since in that case I would have lost my coherence, my vigor, the integrity of that world, and I would have opened fissures in that particular style; I would have cracked its compactness. I wouldn't want, however, for someone to fall into the opposite excess, that is to consider the lumpenproletarian world as one that is completely finished. And this actually has happened in the last few years: as a matter of fact everybody, bourgeois critics and even Communists themselves, had convinced themselves that the lumpenproletarian world did not exist any more. And what was I to do with these twenty million lumpenproletarians? Put them in a concentration camp and destroy them in gas chambers? The attitude toward the lumpenproletariat was almost racist, as if they were people belonging to a world that did not exist any more; they were considered a closed book while, poor devils, they continued to exist. . . .[37]

With mid-June, Pasolini left for the south, on assignment from the Milanese magazine *Successo*, commissioned to write three articles reporting on conditions as he found them by following the coast from Trieste to Ventimiglia, clockwise—first south, then north. It was, in his mind, something modest: "a very small, stenographic *Reisebilder* in which I never went below the first [layer of] skin."[38] But it paid well, which justified declining an invitation from Laura's lawyer father to speak at a conference sponsored by the "political and cultural association La Consulta in Bologna."

The first part appeared on July 4, with two more articles spaced a month apart, August 4 and September 5. No sooner had the first appeared than suit was filed by Vincenzo Mancuso, a Christian Democratic city councilman of Cutro, a tiny village ten miles inland from Crotone in Calabria. He claimed to be infuriated at the "dishonor" Pasolini had brought on the hamlet, and before the Milanese, of all people. Pasolini had written:

> It is really a village of outlaws, as one sees in certain western films. Here are the outlaws' women, here are the outlaws' children. One feels oneself outside the law, or if not the law, the culture of our world, at another level. In the smiles of the young men returning to their cruel work, there is a quiver of too much license, almost of madness.

In one article of the series, *La lunga strada di sabbia* (The long road of sand), he described young girls playing on the beach near Taranto: "I see the little girls, so little, black like little worms but already a little blown up and also, perhaps because maybe adolescent with black eyes, smokey, mysterious and insipid."[39]

The legal complaint was no more (nor less) than an effective publicity stunt: Italian law does not provide remedies for defamation of an entire village. Released to the press, it read, in part, "An African tribe's women: that, for Pasolini, is what are the beautiful women of hard-working Taranto, port for our Navy and seat of our famous shipyards."

Local pride was hurt, or so it was alleged; but local politics, reflecting national confrontations, was really in play. Here was a university man from the north, where all the wealth was, one who had the ear of people who counted, attacking the poor Mezzogiorno where people lived like beasts. A "Special Fund for Development of the South" was in the air, but the money had not started flowing, nor the scandals it engendered when it did. Calabria was tired of being depicted as part of the Third World, and its fierce conservatives saw a chance to take a potshot at someone deemed personally vulnerable. They also wanted to belittle the Communist politicians who had come to power in the nearby city of Crotone. Why, they suggested, did the PCI officials not rise to the defense of local honor?

When he called Cutro a place "not of this world" but "on another level" and "beyond the law," it was too much. The reputation, the honor, decorum and dignity of the hard-working population of Cutro have been gravely offended . . . "the yellow dunes," another African term Pasolini uses, are punctuated by hundreds and hundreds of lovely little houses, many-colored, gay, erected by the Reform Agency where the hard-working people of the south, of Calabria, of Cutro, loyal to the Biblical imperative, earn their bread by the sweat of their brow and do not write articles against their own brothers, against Italians.[40]

The local press smelled a story and began to refer to Pasolini as "this gentleman of little learning" and "this degenerate Italian."

The local author of one article addressed him: "You know, Pasolini, that your city [they took him to be Milanese since *Successo* was published there] is morally on the same level as Paris? At sixteen, the young girl of your city, as white and as fine as you may wish, is no more a virgin."

As for his suggestion that some of the people of the region are not hardworking, "He would do well, he who has never known the harshness of labor, to be submerged in rivers of daily sweat like the peasant of Cutro finds on dry tufts of land."[41]

One newspaper editorial hinted rather ominously that violence against the person of Pasolini should not be unexpected.

The polemics hardened when an unimpeachable jury of Carlo Emilio Gadda, Alberto Moravia, Giuseppe Ungaretti, and Giorgio Bassani (with Giacomo Debenedetti in charge) awarded *Una vita violenta* the City of Crotone Prize. When Pasolini went south to collect it (Crotone is a few kilometers from Cutro) a group of Christian Democrats, with neo-Fascist assistance, caused an uproar at the Ariston Theater, passing out leaflets against the prize and its winner. He was in the midst of political battles only partly of his making; Crotone had a Communist administration and wanted to send a message about culture to its conservative, Christian Democratic neighbors. Pasolini was, again, as in Friuli, caught up as a symbol, a lightning rod useful to forces not of his making.

The Christian Democratic newspaper *Il popolo* took the bait. It editorialized: "The Communists of Crotone have betrayed Calabria." The farce mounted when the prefect of the province and the appeals court for Catanzaro absented themselves from the prize ceremony. The prefect had searched in vain for some legal pretext for denying the prize to "the Communist Pasolini"; he filed a lawsuit to have the prize annulled, but it was dismissed. In response, the local Communist youth corps assembled an honor guard to accompany the poet, to ensure his safety during the presentation ceremony. Rumor became legend: It was said that the phalanx of handsome young men who accompanied the controversial writer to the award ceremony were tied to him with bonds of excessive affection.

The prize was given. By then, the rank of the Cutro region's PCI, once confined to peasants, had been swollen with intellectuals and students newly signed on. At the next election, the DC was thrown out, and a municipal government of Communists was installed.

*Una vita violenta* was written, Pasolini later explained with some elasticity toward chronology, "right after the events in Hungary." He, Pasolini, felt something was needed to suggest an alternative to a Stalinist Marxism that had failed. Rather than abandon it, as many militants had after Hungary, Pasolini decided to fight to change the PCI from within, an unwelcome comrade but a comrade nonetheless. He invested his fight with the nostalgia for his lost, mythic past, the one that had to be revived to save the future. So, for decades, and despite its comrades, "he roamed about the 'temple' of this party, profane and perpetually faithful."

At the same time as Pasolini was alienating those in the PCI who might have supported him, he came under further attack from a new and redoubtable adversary. The Party's lukewarm praise of *Una vita violenta* had exposed him as a man without the crucial protection of friends in high places: In May, Catholic Action moved. The league filed a formal, legal "denunciation" of *Una vita violenta*, its complaint allowable under the loosely drafted provision of the penal code that permitted any defamed party—even one not meeting the Anglo-American requirements for "standing"—to move against an offensive publication.

The proceedings were entrusted to a Dr. Spagnuolo, who, in turn, passed the matter to Alessandro Cutolo, a psychologist and professor who took on the job of analyzing the book during February and March 1960 for a fee of 78,000 lire.

He reported that the novel's language was "very crude, very offensive," something not for family consumption but "artistically objective because it accurately rendered the world of the *borgata* as it was." Cutolo suggested that the penal action be dropped, and Catholic Action did so on March 14, 1963. Three years passed; Pasolini "won," but his bad reputation was made with many Italians who thought accusation by a reputable organization like Catholic Action tantamount to guilt.

With the scandalous success of *Una vita violenta* (it was eventually translated into a dozen languages), publishers saw him in a new light. People were interested to know what else this Pasolini had written. The small Milanese house of Gianni Scheiwiller printed *Roma 1950, diario,* and *Sonetto primaverile* (fourteen sonnets), written in 1950 and 1953 respectively. The list of the poet's work now included two novels of which everyone had heard something.

Pasolini was a success, but each success brought attacks, defamation, and what he perceived to be egregious misunderstanding. Each battle left him a little more scarred and ever more suspicious. The large-circulation tabloid *Oggi* wrote, "People are always talking about Pasolini, with furor and rage . . . he is, obviously, a bachelor." Gradually, a new usage entered Italian: "a Pasolini" became synonymous with "a fag," "a pervert." The press, sometimes quite consciously but usually selecting the facts for a framework that made him "more newsworthy," found the homosexuality-scandal angle irresistible. Pasolini was the author of the *Ragazzi di vita,* who could be identified as a *ragazzo di vita* himself; it sufficed that he was the author of *Una vita violenta* for rendering, by innuendo, that his own life was violent. The time-honored biographical fallacy took on new life. Pier Paolo bought a white Alfa coupé and the tabloid press kept an eye out for it in dubious neighborhoods.

By the first years of the sixties, he found himself in a fatal coupling with the popular press: His name sold newspapers and magazines, while they served him for getting at least some of his ideas across, for providing the notice he wanted. He was news, even if the frame was one of hatred, persecution, and homophobia. The connection looped back, and the arrangement fed on itself: He was scandalous and, infuriated at the depiction of himself, provided further scandal.

Pier Paolo turned to scriptwriting *La lunga notte del '43,* based on a short story by Bassani, directed by Florestano Vancini. In a fury of productivity, he was at the same time correcting the proofs on a collection of his essays in literary criticism (to be called *Passione e ideologia*), polishing the novella *Il rio della grana,* and starting two other novels, their working titles *Storia burina* and *La mortaccia.*

He found a new forum, aided by friends on the liberal wing of the PCI. In June 1960 he was invited to write a regular column for the Party weekly, *Vie nuove.* He was promised freedom of subject and expression: Sometimes he would review books or films, on other occasions answer letters from readers, at other times remark on whatever interested him at the time. He dedicated his article of November

26 to answering the new wave of censorship introduced by the Trombi government.

> I have said above that the cinema can be, and in part is, outside the strict control of the State (and when I say "State" I mean, a little freely, that atrocious, clerical-fascistic entity which is bureaucratically, and formally, Italy): so the State wants to dominate it. Producers are the opposite of heroes, and instead of stopping making money, they would stop making films, or they would make them the way the State and Mr. Trombi wishes them to be. Completely idiotic. . . .
>
> The great mass of Italians do not possess the critical tools to resist this action of the State; frequently, one is dealing with illiterates, with people who live in a cultural world truly medieval. There's no need to be shocked at their ingenuousness. That is, overall, something positive. Those who are truly scary are the "innocent" of the Trombi type (if they are ingenuous, I want to believe it) because their ingenuousness presupposes a culture that is provincial, hypocritical, mistaken to its roots.[42]

That Italian authorities fought such a hard, retreating action on the censorship issue is not surprising. The world was changing with dizzying speed: Within months, Castro had toppled Battista and brought Communism within ninety miles of Miami; Khrushchev visited America and debated Richard Nixon at a home appliances show; De Gaulle took charge of the Fifth Republic and began dismantling France's empire in North Africa. The transformation of the Italian economy seemed sometimes within the government's control, at other times careening without brakes. Some had even started arguing for legalizing divorce; rock and roll was arriving; kids answered back.

On the night of June 29, 1960, Pasolini was driving at about one in the morning on the corso Vittorio Emanuele. He heard a commotion coming from a side street, turned, and spotted a scuffle. His version stated that he then heard shouts of his name—"Pa"—from two street boys he recognized. They approached and asked for a ride, and Pasolini took them in. They went for a spin and ended up in a bad district, on the ever-so-evocatively named via di Panico, where a fistfight was in progress. The street had long been known for *malavita;* in 1949 screenwriter Cesare Zavattini used it in *Bicycle Thieves* for his hero's encounter with the nasty urban poor.

One of the boys recognized a man locked in battle with a half-naked woman. "That's the Baron, I know him," the boy declared.

"Let's get him out of here." Pasolini, who knew nothing of the background of events, took him in and drove away.

At seven the next morning of June 30 police called in via G. Carini, arresting him for "removing the instigator of a public disorder from the scene of a crime." Immediately, reports appeared in the newspapers under giant headlines, four and five columns wide, with photo. The angle: that Pasolini, *ragazzo di vita* in life as well as art, was again living out what he had written. The trial convened on November 16, 1961; he was charged with aiding and abetting.

Serious newspapers like Turin's *La stampa* dedicated extensive space—and for more than one day— to the case. The matter dragged on until July 1963, when an appeals court dismissed the charges. Pasolini was deemed to have been unwise, gullible, foolish, but not criminal. The charges were dropped for "insufficiency of evidence."

The theme of life-imitates-art was too good to pass up: When the judge asked what Pasolini was doing in a bad neighborhood very late at night, he answered, "I was taking a drive to gather impressions to use as background for a literary work I had to write." It was not perhaps the whole truth, nor untrue; in any case, it made for excellent copy.

Only ten days later on July 10 Pasolini drove along the seafront at Anzio beach. The place was a likely one for meeting boys, and in the heat of a high summer's afternoon, he stopped his car and walked to a seawall, where people leaned over to watch fishing boats bobbing below. A week later, when what happened next had become a matter of police record, this version of events appeared in the Roman daily *Il tempo*:

> Last Sunday, at about two in the afternoon, the author of *Ragazzi di vita* and *Una vita violenta*, driving his Giuietta, arrived at the seafront at Anzio, and parked there to walk out toward the pier. He was wearing a pair of light-colored blue jeans, a striped polo shirt and hid his eyes beyond two black lenses. At a certain point, having reached the parapet between the seafront and some restaurants, he encountered two boys of about twelve or thirteen years old, leaning over the balustrade, talking together. He approached them slowly and asked them some questions of no significance. The ice was broken, and in the course of a few minutes Pasolini had started a discussion which, judging from gestures and approaches was more than cordial and lasted more than twenty minutes, until the writer went into a restaurant for lunch.
>
> Made curious by the strange reaction provoked in the boys by the writer's questions, two professionals who had followed the discussion without hearing any of it, approached the boys and asked what it was that they had talked

*Giuseppe Pelosi,*
*November 2, 1975.* Photo:
Corriere della sera

*Pelosi and his lawyer,
Rocco Mangia, entering
the Rome Juvenile Court,
early spring, 1976.* Photo:
*Mauro Ruspantini, Master Photo*

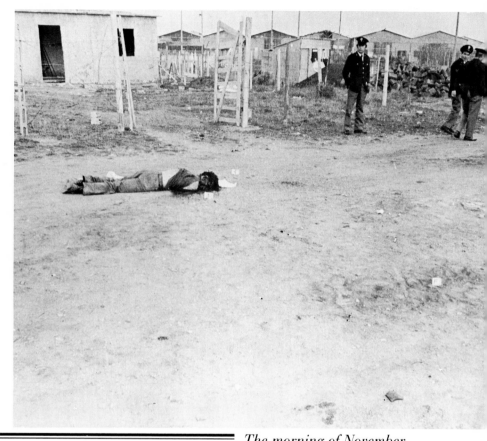

*The morning of November 2, 1975, Ostia. Photo: Mario d'Ilio,* Il messaggero

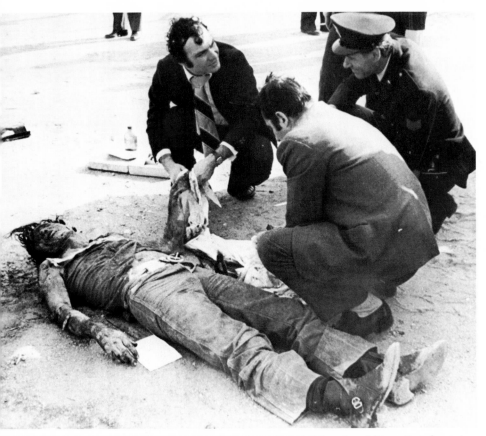

*The dead Pasolini found—*
*the worst image of all.*
Photo: AP/Wide World Photos

*Al Biondo Tevere restaurant, where Pasolini and Pelosi ate together, en route to the Idroscalo di Ostia.* Photo: Dino Pedriali

*The crowd's farewell at the PCI's farewell ceremony in the Campo dei Fiori, Rome, November 5, 1975.*

*Photo:* Paese sera

An FGCI (Rome Communist Youth Federation) poster announcing Pasolini's funeral, which was defaced by the Jesuit priest Arturo della Vedova. Schifo ("disgusting"); blasphemo ("blasphemer"); coprolalo ("goat-buggerer"); Partito C...Italiano [Partito Cazzo Italiano] ("Italian Cock Party"). *Photo: Mario d'Ilio,* Il messaggero about. At first, the boys didn't want to say, and drew away. But later, they admitted that the writer had asked them how old the boys were that were messing about on a boat nearby, and then expressed an appreciation which the boys could not refer to without blushing. Understanding what this was all about, the two professionals called for help from the police.[43]

Other versions that emerged were far less circumspect. In one, Pasolini asked how old the boys in the boat were, and the two on the quai said that they guessed "twelve or thirteen." Pasolini was then supposed to have remarked, "They must have little cocks. How about yours?" causing the two to laugh nervously and move away.

In another version, Pasolini is supposed to have remarked that they were young "but might still have nice cocks."

As for the "two professionals," one was Costanzo Costantini from *Il messaggero* and the other Alfredo Passarelli from *Il tempo*. *Il tempo*'s report was coy: "The boys [queried by the journalists] said he [Pasolini] expressed an appreciation for two boys diving from a boat in the port to which the [questioned] boys could not refer without blushing." And as for their insistence in questioning the boys, interrogation in court revealed they offered each a hundred lire if they would "tell all they knew."

A case of entrapment or not, headlines announced "Another Embarrassing Denunciation of Pasolini." The public prosecutor for the Anzio region forwarded the case of "attempted corruption of minors" to Rome, urging that it be merged with the via Panico action; four days later the Roman prosecutor's office sent it back. By December the authorities halted proceedings for "not arriving at the level of a crime."[44]

The via di Panico trial did not go well. The trial court found Pasolini guilty of aiding and abetting in the first degree; an appeal was filed in November 1961 that dragged until acquittal only in 1963. By then several other and more clamorous trials were under way, growing out of Pasolini's films, writings, and private life.

His treatment at the hands of the national dailies seemed coddling compared to that of the far Right. As early as 1959 the publication *Iniziativa* (without naming but plainly identifying him) referred to those who "put a knife in the ribs of society, and even have the temerity to be considered great artists." G. de Rosa, a Jesuit, wrote in *Civiltà cattolica* in October 1961 that Pasolini—"failed poet"— "ought to think a moment before he calls others 'corrupted' . . . because he himself is no master of morality." The MSI's *Il secolo d'Italia* referred to him as "a man . . . in quotation marks." He was branded as one "not to be taken seriously," "seeking publicity," and "homophilic" in the same breath. Proof of his infamy came in the street produce markets, where sweet anise (*finocchio*) came to be called "*pasolini*." This time "a fruit" gave his name unwittingly to a vegetable: *finocchio* had long been one of the many well-known slang terms for "homosexual."

From 1960 the neo-Fascist press had a new weapon. That year the Russian Soviet Republic adopted article 112 into its penal code: imprisonment for five years "for sexual relations between men." Soon comments appeared to the effect that "if Pasolini went to the Soviet Union, they'd put him in a labor camp." The PCI's external opposition and internal hard-liners found much use in this. Why, they asked, did the Italian Communists—who claimed to be so upright—continue to count this plainly immoral Pasolini among their number? The more famous he became the more his expressions of militant Communism were an embarrassment.

A campaign seemed to have existed to drive a wedge between Pasolini and the PCI. In the fall of 1960 imitation Pasolini poems were sent to the newspapers, and one false epigram (critical of the Socialists) even made its way past the editors of *L'unità*. Pasolini went into print to deny its authorship.

Pasolini systematically transformed the food of negativity into the nourishment of scorn: He dedicated himself to his announced goal—"intellectual clarity." He would examine all of reality, condemn without dread of anyone, proclaim his jeremiad whatever its price. He seems to have crossed an invisible line about that year, into the freedom a condemned man feels to speak without fear.

Pasolini as a kind of poetic Ché Guevara was born with the new decade. His merging with a clearly defined persona, which only partly reflected his person, had roots in both pride and rage. It was a useful conceit but went deeper than pose, and yet left him febrile with fatigue and frustrated into a smileless mask, soon victim of a bleeding ulcer. Sartre said of Baudelaire's pride that it "exhausts itself in the very act of asserting itself." The description fits the adult Pasolini, eventually at war with both friend and foe—with all who misunderstood.

It is too simple to think the role of permanent gadfly made him unhappy. On the contrary, he exulted in what Heine called *Maskenfreiheit*, "the freedom conferred by masks." What confused and angered many was that, as his worldly success grew (more than theirs), so flowered his anger and disaffection. The visible evidence of his lust for contradiction was abundant and always increasing: In the mid-1970s he went on television to argue for banning television. He emerged as a distinguished university graduate who argued for the abolition of compulsory education, as the open homosexual against abortion. Challenged for his inconsistencies and resented for his refusal to lie back and enjoy the success others would have found sufficient, he dug in his heels.

After 1960 he kept writing poetry and criticism. But he entered a new phase, addressing a public far more vast than those who read. His worldwide public became the audience seated before the giant black page of the movie screen, reading another language far beyond the confines of Italian.

# PART III

# 16

*Unlike literary language, cinema does not evoke reality; it does not copy reality, like painting, and it does not mime reality, like theater. Cinema reproduces reality.*
    —*Pier Paolo Pasolini,* Empirismo eretica *(Heretical empiricism)*

# *ACCATTONE*

Everything seemed possible in the Italian cinema in 1960. Visconti's angry but bankable, melodramatic *Rocco and His Brothers* shared a public with Fellini's fantasies and the new angst-dramas like Antonioni's *La notte*. Radically different from films like *La dolce vita* and *L'avventura* seemed to be making a revolution in Italy equal to that of the French New Wave. Pasolini was fascinated by them: They were modes of representing reality perhaps more profoundly and forcefully than even the best written language allowed. That boy who had been intrigued at how solid green, painted, could "stand for a meadow," understood the power of the screen image. Somehow poetry paled, not just because it was for the few and he wanted an audience of many.

Markets overseas—especially in America—were opening as never before. By 1959 an "art film" like *La dolce vita* was earning huge profits. From 1958 to 1969 Italian production rose steadily from 141 films to 246, while the number of American films distributed in Italy fell from 233 in 1958 to a low of 127 in 1967.[1] A second "Golden Age" was dawning at Cinecittà. As one historian has written, "For a brief and exciting moment, it seemed that Cinecittà and via Veneto would challenge Hollywood and Beverly Hills."

A key figure was now emerging in European cinema: a man who did it all—writing, casting, directing, and editing. The day of the *auteur* had come, and Italians adopted the French word in a gulp. Pier Paolo had served his apprenticeship well and was now the right man in the right place at the right time. He declared later, "I had to be, at every moment, the author of my own work."

In January of the new decade, he declined an invitation to write a piece of literary criticism for his friend Luciano Anceschi, founder of the Bologna-based literary magazine *Il verri*. Film work was more pressing, even if still as helper to someone else. He explained,

> I have to recount, in a manner that is technically exact, the Roman stories of Moravia [for Bolognini's *La giornata balorda*]; I have to recount, again, in a new style, for the director Brusati, *Una vita violenta* [the project did not come to completion]; I am finishing with *La lunga notte del '43* by Bassani [written with Bassani and the director], for the director [Florestano] Vancini; and I am writing a "treatment" . . . for a film which I will make as director, *La commare secca*.[2]

By that frantic year's end Pasolini had his name on thirteen scripts, several verifiable successes enhancing the reputation of Bolognini. He told a reporter who visited the set where Bolognini was directing *La giornata balorda:* "In three months I will debut as a director." He explained he was writing a script of his own, that he would soon direct a film himself. He had in mind *La commare secca*, not *Accattone*.

Another project in the works was *La ragazza in vetrina* (The girl in a window), based on his visit to the Italian miners in Belgium and Holland. Rodolfo Sonigo had produced a treatment, based on Pasolini's short story about an Italian who goes to work in the Belgian coal mines. Fed up, he comes above ground and takes a train to Amsterdam, where he meets another miner, also desperate, who tells him about the prostitutes who sit in the windows of Amsterdam's red-light district. The first miner passes a happy weekend on the beach with a girl he has bought, spending all his hard-earned money. After two frantic days he returns with her to Amsterdam and boards a train to go back from where he has come. The film closes with the elevator that carries him descending below ground, a light extinguished. Again, neither Church nor Party intervened to make a happy ending.

Pasolini was enthusiastic about the project and wrote a script "on spec." That done, both producer (Emanuele Cassuto) and director (Luciano Emmer) were found; it was released in 1961, the same year as Pasolini's debut as *auteur* in his own right.

By this time his claim to a director's chair was quite as credible as that of Michelangelo Antonioni, founder of a magazine of film criticism, or that of Federico Fellini himself—cartoonist turned journalist. Luchino Visconti came from the legitimate stage, Vittorio de Sica had been an actor. In fact, the completely cinema-based types were the exception; the industry was populated with writers following the example of D'Annunzio—Bassani, Mario Soldati, and many more. Film (not movies) in Italy was not yet an industry but one more art form, a means of expression. The underpinnings were those of a craft, its output a myriad of free-standing small projects (studios like Titanus and Ponti were the exception); the money came from all sorts of individual capitalist-enthusiasts, *impresari* as in the London or New York theater or the world of Italian opera in the nineteenth century. Only in gigantic and over-specialized America would Pasolini's passage into cinema seem extraordinary.

Later, when challenged by reporters who doubted his calling because it came late (he was now thirty-eight), he said, "I had always thought of making films. Before the war, I had thought of going to Rome to attend the Centro Sperimentale, if I could. [The war intervened and] . . . the old idea of making films came to a standstill and disappeared.[3]

Pasolini had built an odd, wary friendship with Fellini during the writing and shooting of *Nights of Cabiria*, one enlarged when Pasolini wrote the low-life scenes for *La dolce vita*. He went to see the far more established "man of the cinema" about his idea. After the success of *La dolce vita*, Fellini had decided that *auteurs*, he first among them, ought to share in the wealth they were bringing producers. He was going to be his own financier (or, at least, his own packager of bank and "angel" financing), using his own money and that of publisher Angelo Rizzoli to start. The company they formed was called "Federiz"—an amalgam of *Federi*co and *Rizz*oli. Their plan was not only to produce Fellini's films but to underwrite some of the new projects that seemed to be surfacing in Rome every day.

In a preface to the published edition of what became his first directed script, Pasolini claimed to have written most of the story as early as 1944. Fellini proffered backing enough to pay for a few days' shooting. Pier Paolo wrote in a kind of diary that he was so excited he did not sleep for three nights. It did not seem all that risky: He had asked for an extraordinarily small amount of money to pay his troupe of all nonactors. A reasonable return seemed likely: The man had a track record as a scriptwriter and notoriety enough to generate interest. It ought to make for box office for the fledgling production company.

Pier Paolo called his film *Accattone,* a slang term encompassing street urchin, bum, down-and-out, ne'er-do-well. An *accattone* was not simply a petty criminal but a dropout, someone marginal more than shiftless, one who perhaps traffics in stolen goods: not quite a thug, as much *clochard* as brigand. That Pier Paolo had hardly stood behind a camera seemed of no importance to him or his backers. He admitted in print that he had no idea what the term "panorama" meant in film use; he was certain it made no difference. By now he had been paid to analyze cinema as a paid critic, and he made a success as a screenwriter after mastering a vivid prose style full of faces, sounds, and things rendered three-dimensionally. His short stories of the fifties were deeply cinematic, studded with master shots and close-ups and nothing in between—literary equivalent to Godard's films of a decade later. Without forcing, they (like much of the poetry) "fade to black," "dissolve" between scenes, "jump-cut," and are peopled with characters who talk credible lines and behave vividly.

He was prepared to use what he had absorbed since the days of the parish cinemas of Friuli: films of a beloved Dreyer and Mizoguchi, Eisenstein and Chaplin. He remembered what he learned after bicycling long distances on dark country roads to see Rossellini's first masterpieces. In 1964 he told a gathering of film students at the national film school of the Centro Sperimentale, "It has been an entire lifetime that I have been thinking about the cinema."

His thoughts led to a restricted, instantly recognizable and forceful palette: long shots for groups, close-ups *(primi piani)* on faces, where he believed the soul of a person was written. In technical terms, he was never fancy. Later, when budgets allowed it, even his special effects were supposed to look "phony," illustrating the "art" in "artifice."

Pier Paolo chose his friend Franco Citti to star, not because he was a fine actor but because he was not. In Pasolini's view he did not just act the antihero Vittorio (Accattone); he "was" Vittorio. Pasolini knew this and recognized his character in Citti's character, from the moment they met. Pasolini wanted his nonprofessional (even unprofessional) actors to come right off the *borgate* streets of Torpignattara and Pigneto. They were not expected to act but to be themselves, and thus stand for ideas, much like Visconti's Acitrezza fishermen of a dozen years before. The last thing the viewer was to look for was the polished, professional quality of the performance. He was unabashedly willing to simplify his actor-personalities into symbols; rather than "the person inside the actor" directed to "emerge," Pasolini wanted living puppets. They were to be equivalents of words aligned in a poem, means to ends.

So *Accattone* was born an anachronism. In 1960 the hit on both sides of the Atlantic was Laurence Harvey in *Romeo and Juliet,* complete with an Italian supporting cast speaking fractured Elizabethan English. Pasolini's first movie was, in this sense, the original neo-realistic school's last hurrah.

Without exception, in more than a dozen films spanning the next fifteen years, *his* filmed people remained profoundly secondary, no more important (sometimes less) than the landscapes in which they moved, or the music—on both of which he sometimes seemed to lavish more attention. Later, famous, he told a gathering of film students: "I have an almost ideological esthetic preference for nonprofessional actors who themselves are shreds of reality as is a landscape, a sky, the sun, a donkey passing along the road. They're all elements which I manipulate and turn into whatever I want. . . ."[4]

When he came to cast Maria Callas as Medea, she was to stand for unbridled nature gone mad when hemmed in by civilization. He did not ask the century's most famous soprano to sing a single note. Silvana Mangano in *Teorema* was to stand for all unfulfilled *bourgeoises,* "waiting for something to happen." No wonder he found fables to his liking, stories where characters are unidimensional symbols acting out meanings. And is that not the very heart of *Salò,* the Marquis de Sade's story of the 120 days—a plot without real characters, only types?

\* \* \*

*Accattone*'s picaresque plot recounts the mishaps of Vittorio, a permanently unemployed figure of a Roman slum, a *povero cristo* who lives off the earnings of a prostitute named (perhaps too pointedly) Maddalena. His principal calling is hanging out with friends, each a "type" with a street moniker like "The Onion." His wife, Nannina (played by journalist Adele Cambria), hovers in the background, always dark-eyed from lack of sleep and clung to by several dirty children. She somehow manages to be sure Vittorio goes forth in a freshly laundered and pressed shirt or in an up-to-date white sweater (nothing a manual laborer would wear), his preened chest displaying the necessary and appropriate gold chains. He is the Latin *macho* man, a cock-of-the-walk riding for a fall.

He and his buddies (all chronically out of work but determined never to be in search of it) wander the Rome of shiny new cars and *benessere* like so many all-but-invisible visitors from a foreign planet; they are in, but not of, the postwar recovery.

One day—just for the hell of it and a bet of a thousand lire—the *ragazzi* challenge Vittorio to dive off the Ponte Sant'Angelo into the Tiber. If the impact doesn't kill him, the sewage will. But *bella figura* (a *capriccio*, a *bell' azione*) gets more than its due among such have-nots. He rises from their table on the Ciriola boathouse, climbs to the balustrade's edge. Asked what should be his epitaph, he laughs and shouts: "Try it to believe it."

Pasolini frames Citti (in grainy black-and-white) as one more angel on Bernini's bridge line-up. German publisher Klaus Piper, visiting Rome to meet the author he had translated and published in Munich, recalls visiting the set and being struck by Pasolini's insistence that the scene be played again and again, until the picture in his mind corresponded precisely to what the camera could see.

So Vittorio dives. Cut to boys singing as they swim, laughing and playing in the mud of the river bank: a page from *Una vita violenta*, filmed.

Maddalena is victimized by some Neapolitans (again the heavies, dubbed by actors from Eduardo de Filippo's troupe), in revenge for Accattone's having stool-pigeoned to the police about one of their friends. Now Pasolini rings all the bells of his love of dialects and regional types. The muscular Neapolitan thugs smile sweetly, have sex with her first, then beat her ruthlessly (the scene of four muscular types slapping the defenseless woman is chilling) and leave her in a field. He cast his friend (a real actress) Adriana Asti (later married, briefly, to a recovered Fabio Mauri) as a street-toughened hooker with a giant patent-leather handbag. She has a soft spot for Maddalena but keeps a keen eye on her own clientele. And what shall she be called? *Amore*, of course.

Maddalena's continuing loyalty saves Accattone in the subsequent police sweep and line-up. But his mistreatment of her brings arguments to the point of fists with her brother and father, who brawl with him in the dirt outside their *casa abusiva*. Their struggle is against a soundtrack of Bach—the banal framed as sacred. Four years later Pasolini told students at the Roman film school that this had "a certain grossness" and yet was "very justifiable." It was no less worthy of being called art than a *Seicento* painting of Jacob wrestling with the angel.

Pasolini hardly presents pimp Vittorio as admirable: At one point he steals and hocks the christening chains from around his small son's neck, whispering in the child's ear, "Your father is a bastard. Be a good boy."

Love without family responsibilities appears to Vittorio in the form of Stella (literally, "Star"). Like a guiding star, she seems to have come from another world, yet she is mired in this one. Her father died in the war, her mother was a whore, and she ekes out a living endlessly washing old bottles in a garbage dump. Pasolini told interviewer Jean Duflot this was his "private homage to [painter] Morandi"—famous for his still-lifes of bottles. Her home is a shack, but her spirit is surrealistically pure. Beautifully played by Franca Pasut, she is both ingenuous and voluptuous, an innocent amid cynics, at once shy and open, a slightly pudgy Italian Marilyn. She is anything but "melodramatically sentimental," as the consistently hostile *Vita* magazine[5] labeled her. If she is too good to be true, she is in that no more than any other dream, acknowledged to be a dream, of innocence and redemption.

Accattone asks her name.

> "Stella. And yours?"
> "Vittorio. But you seem so sweet? Are you from Rome?"
> "Yes."
> "Strange."

Vittorio at least remembers innocence, recognizes it when he sees it, and is drawn to it. But he is so corrupted that he quickly degrades her in the act of trying to make her his ticket out of a daily hell. He buys her clothing and dresses her like a doll, with a new dress and new shoes. She is genuinely moved and he responds to her tenderness. Desperate for self-esteem, he says, "Don't call me Vittorio. There are plenty of them but only one Accattone." They kiss.

He puts Stella out to sell herself. On her first encounter, she starts to cry and her client forces her from his car and leaves her on the outskirts of the city. To save her walking the length of the via Appia Antica, Accattone commandeers a motorcycle and goes to fetch her.

Revolted at his own behavior, he determines to find work, even bearing the taunts of his buddies, who act like a Greek chorus from their café seats, deriding his determination to go straight: "You have off the first of May, but for us every day is a holiday." He spends one day at manual labor. Unaccustomed to lifting iron tubing all day in the sun, he passes out.

That night he dreams a dream Pasolini said he heard from Sergio Citti: He is following a funeral cortège and comes upon the Neapolitans who had beaten Maddalena. They are all dead, lying naked and barely covered with dirt. The unreal procession passes—a Buñuelian moment—heading for the cemetery. In 1980 Contini wrote that Pasolini's *Accattone* light reminded him of the Spanish master's Mexican-era films, like *Los olvidados* [The young and the damned, 1950], which he believed Pasolini had even bettered.[7]

Vittorio follows the procession and inquires who has died. "Oh, Accattone is dead." He leaps over the graveyard wall to find himself in open country, where a grave-digger (a return of the poem's "excavator") is at work. Vittorio asks that he dig a little to one side so that he might be buried in the sun.

With indisputable inevitability (such is his universe) Accattone the next day returns to what he does best, a life of petty crime. Together with his buddy Balilla (played by Mario Cipriani, a mason by training, whom Pasolini had met the year before on the set of Lizzani's *Il gobbo del quarticciolo*), he plots the theft of some whole *prosciutti* from a vendor's delivery truck. As they escape with their booty hidden under the refuse of a pushcart, they are discovered and the *carabinieri* appear. Accattone has almost gotten away with it. But there is no hope for him: Like Riccetto and Tommaso, he is born doomed.

He runs, grabs a motorcycle, and speeds off, leaving his friends in the hands of the law. We hear a scream of brakes, a canned soundtrack crash. The camera follows the police and their now-shackled charges as they run to see what has happened. Vittorio has lost control of the motorcycle, sideswiped a truck and now lies in the street (Pasolini filmed the scene at the Ponte del Mattatoio), his head bashed against a curbstone.

Pasolini placed the camera on the ground, looking up at the faces Accattone sees. Balilla, handcuffed, crosses himself. Vittorio-Citti murmurs, *"Ma, io sto bene"* ("But I'm fine"), and dies. No confession, no extreme unction, no absolution. Accattone is punished and dies without seeking salvation. His is a life wasted in the living and apparently unredeemed at its ending. The world has no need for the likes of him.

Pasolini was again telling the public bad news it did not want to hear. That year Italians got Sophia Loren in *Two Women*, which opens with the bombing of San Lorenzo on July 25, 1943. The Americans gave her an Academy Award for that performance. *Accattone* was something subversive. Did Pasolini imagine people wanted an unvarnished look at the fate of Rome's *borgatari*, what he called "a Rome dead without ever having lived"?

*Accattone* was like the early "poor" Visconti of *Ossessione* (before the costume dramas) or the Rossellini of *Roma, città aperta* (Rome, open city) (1945), but different, blacker. Vittorio's struggle up and out fails; he dies against a curbstone, a petty thief who does not move one bit up the social scale. It is the tale of a man who writhes and fails.

The elegance of a refined cinematic technique had no place in this vision. He had in mind, or so he said, "the frescoes of Masaccio": so the camera stayed still on characters' faces a long time, it panned slowly, it approached almost always from the front. He later explained, "I always conceive the background like the background of a painting, like a stage set, and for this reason I always attack it frontally. . . ." With slight change, that remained his style for a decade. It earned him the hostility of lovers of film technique for its own sake, who mistook a conscious artistic choice for lack of knowing better.

Traditional film critics took the work as a kind of cultural insult, a slap in the face. That Vittorio's squalid misadventures proceed against a background of Bach suggested that this bum's story had something epic about it, worthy of noble, liturgical music. The juxtaposition was a contamination of art: precisely what Pasolini intended. In 1967 he told the magazine *Bianco e nero* (Black and white):

> In *Accattone*, I wanted to represent the degradation and humble human condition of a person who lives in the mud and dust of the Roman *borgata*. I felt, I knew, that inside this degradation was something sacred, something

religious in the vague sense of the word, and thus this adjective "sacred," and I added to that with music. I said, therefore, that the degradation of Accattone is, yes, a degradation, but in some fashion a sacred degradation, and Bach served me to communicate this, my intention, to the broad public.

The story of *Accattone* was, he wrote, that of "one summer, that of the Tambroni government," which tottered under attacks from the far Right. "One summer is nothing compared to a century," he said four years later, "but it's a lot in the life of an author who exhausts his activity in the span of a few years."

> At that time, in that place, a subproletarian like Accattone had no hope save in "a superstitious catholicism of a pagan" . . . there was no other solution available to him as there is not for an enormous number of people similar to him . . . With Tommasino I provided a drama, with Accattone a tragedy: a tragedy without hope, because I hope few will be the spectators who see some significance of hope in the sign of the cross with which the film ends.[6]

The filming, which he later called "the most wonderful days of my life" was begun beneath the brooding presence of Fellini, a director of radically different sensibility. The first phase, through October 1960, was exciting: It was Pier Paolo's first time behind a camera, his actors' first time in front of one. His teacher was the Roman-born Tonino delli Colli, who stayed with him for more than a dozen films thereafter; he was the director of photography who taught the new director what lenses did. Pasolini passed what he called "marvelous days" in the company of his enthusiastic cast and crew, including his neighbor in via Giacinto Carini, nineteen-year-old Bernardo Bertolucci.

More than a decade younger, Attilio Bertolucci's son was far more a child of the cinema. Taken on by Pier Paolo to assist on the set and learn what he could, he later recalled to a journalist from *Cahiers du cinéma*, a magazine that took Pasolini seriously from the start:

> We left via Carini every morning at about 8, going toward the *borgata* called Maranella, the Pigneto and all the other places which, seamed together, made that unity that were the places of *Accattone*, a pre-psychological, pre-historical, pre-dialectical, pre-political hero. Pier Paolo drove an Alfa Romeo [the red model 1750] . . . and I sat next to him. As we proceeded he told me his dreams of the night before and he elaborated them, along with the pace of the street signs, with the maniacal precision of one who understands his own disorder and tries to compensate for it with an obsessive observation of the rules of the road.[7]

But *Accattone* started was almost never finished. Producer Fellini was to be shown the first week's rushes: Only then would the production proceed with full budgeting. But, after a long silence, he (whom Pasolini was to call "the Great Mystifier") took one look at two scenes, 150 meters of film shot in the via Fanfulla di Lodi of the Prenestini district and the via Formia in Torpignattara, and dropped out. No, he wanted no part of the project, and his objections were not simply matters of taste. Pasolini's camera work was crude, the angles not polished, the lighting rudimentary. Fellini was already the master craftsman of the closed set, the controlled environment of studio work, keen on special effects and sophisticated illusion.

Pasolini's acknowledged model was Carl Dreyer's 1928 *Passion of Joan of Arc*, a work with nothing "magic" about it—no Fellini escapism—but one of the most profoundly religious films ever made. Pasolini, who saw it in his early twenties, took from it what he called "a norm of absolute simplicity of expression." He also said that film "has influenced me by giving me the sense of the close-up, the sense of figurative severity . . . it's been one of my cinematographic and visual models."[8]

By comparison with Fellini's interests at the time, *Accattone* was a rehash of neo-realism's films of fifteen years before, old-fashioned in its bleak quasi-documentary quality. Fellini expressed regret that he did not like Pasolini's work, and knew that other producers like the young Tonino Cervi and Sandro Jacovoni had toyed with producing Pasolini's first film and only moved on when Federiz came forward.

Fellini's reaction unraveled their friendship forever. Summoned to Federiz's office in the via della Croce, Pasolini heard that the two scenes he had shot and edited himself on an old Moviola "had not convinced." Pasolini countered that the actors were inexperienced, as was he. Almost daring the moviemaking moguls—even without a track record to support the bravura—he stiffened his resolve. Given a chance to shoot the scenes again, he explained, he would change nothing. He later wrote that Fellini, "like a grand and elegant bishop," changed the subject. What about the costs and the possible returns? No matter that the entire production budget was a paltry 40 million lire. (*La dolce vita* brought in 2,000 million lire on first release.) No, Federiz would not underwrite Pasolini's directorial debut.

On December 3 he wrote to his *Vie nuove* readers about another novel-in-progress, called *La mortaccia*. It was to be the story of a *ragazza di vita*, a prostitute named Teresa who descends into Hell and recounts it as she sees it, "a fusion between her language—the romanesco of the *malavita*," Pasolini explained, "and mine as narrator, literary Italian."[9] She meets Christian Democratic ministers in Hell, Stalin, thieves, Neapolitans and Milanese. "My operation will be comic and satiric . . . what interests me is to use the Dantean *Inferno* to arrive at a judgment, historically objective, a diagnosis that is exact in Marxist terms, of our society." A part of the novel was published unfinished (in *Alì dagli occhi azzurri (1950–1965)*[10]; the rest has never appeared.

December 1960 and January 1961 seemed "empty"; *Accattone* was in suspension. He worked at a translation of *Antigone* (for Vittorio Gassman) and the poems for the coming volume of verse, *La religione del mio tempo* (The religion of my time). It appeared the following May, in his words, expressing "the crisis of the sixties . . . the neocapitalist siren on one hand, the revolution ending on the other: and the void, the terrible existential void which was a consequence."

His state of mind at decade's close sounds in *The Religion of My Time*, published under the shadow of the attack on *Una vita violenta*. The poem's language lends itself to printing in a newspaper or magazine; it reads as he argued poetry should—"like prose"—accessible to all, a provocation directed to all.

> Everything is painful to me: these people
>
> who supinely follow every summons
> by which their masters wish to summon them,
> heedlessly adopting the most disgraceful
>
> habits of predestined victims;
> the gray of their clothes in the gray
> streets;
> their gray gestures on which seem stamped
>
> the conspiracy of silence over the evil that
> invades them; their swarming around an illusory
> prosperity, like a flock around a little
> fodder;
>
> the regularity of their tides, whereby which
> throngs
> and deserts alternate in the streets,
> regulated by the obsessed and anonymous
> ebb and flow of stale necessities. . . .[11]

Those who felt themselves targets of these lines did not forgive their author just because his critique could boast a long ancestry of Italian self-criticism. No one remembered that their beloved Rossini had said "Thank God for the Spaniards . . . If there were no Spaniards the Italians would be the last people in Europe." [12]

The book was dedicated to Elsa Morante; it comprised poems written between 1955 and July 1960. The title poem, which had appeared in *Officina*'s twelfth issue (April 1958), casts poet as prophet and his tale as a lament:

> Thus when I look into the souls
> of the ranks of living individuals
> of my time, close to me or not too far away,
>
> I see that of the countless possible
> sacrileges
> that every natural religion
> can specify, the one that remains
>
> always, in everyone, is cowardice . . .
> It is this cowardice that makes man irreligious. . . .[13]

The times had hardened far beyond what Leonetti's Fabian-style reasonableness could survive and the "mysterious mornings of Bologna, / Casarsa, arching, perfect as roses" were buried, gone with "an earlier hour of my life. . . ." The happiness of that time and place, of "the silent smells of fire, for joyful / misery to be heard all around, / for the Angelus to sound" was now dead. He looked back on it after the decade of the fifties in Rome, and wrote, "It was a brief passion."

One of the "new epigrams" was "Ai letterati contemporanei" (To my literary contemporaries):

> I see you: you're there, we go on being friends,
>     happy to see you and greet each other, in some café,
> in the houses of ironical Roman ladies . . .
>     But our greetings, our smiles, our mutual passions,
>     are gestures in a no man's land: a *waste land* [in English]
>         for you: a margin for me, between one history and another.
>     We can no longer really agree: it makes me tremble
>         but it is in us that the world is enemy to the world.[14]

And he took a swipe at those who had undone *Officina*, giving himself the last word; the twelfth "new epigram" was "To the Prince [Urbano] Barberini" whom he called "a dead cadaver" (a phrase he said he took from Belli). And the thirteenth was "To the Nobles of

the Hunting Club": "You never existed, you old papal sheep: / now
you exist somewhat because Pasolini / exists a little."[15]

As for Valentino Bompiani himself, his good friends Silvana and
Fabio's uncle

> Everything which they defend is pure evil.
>> They are so blind and so greedy that they
> know no hope.
> Fascism is the true, latest novelty, the
> authentic
>> light of this country, in a world which
> still proceeds.[16]

In the last of the fourteen "new" epigrams, he addressed the recently dead John XXIII (*A uno Spirito*, To a spirit). "Only because
you are dead, I could talk to you as a man: / otherwise your laws
would have prevented me." He tells the "Spirit" that "only in this
absurd state" does "death reign . . . but I am not dead, and I shall
speak."[17]

He left for India with Moravia before New Year's Day 1961. They
were gone six weeks; as was his custom, Moravia reported his impressions in a series of articles in the *Corriere della sera*. Elsa Morante
joined them for part of the trip. She and Moravia separated that year,
after twenty-five years together, and Moravia (then fifty-five) set up a
household with the writer Dacia Maraini, several decades his junior.

Pasolini the traveler absorbed and took notes. They went from
Bombay to New Delhi and Malabar; in Calcutta they met Mother
Teresa in what Pasolini called "a misery which takes your breath
away . . . she resembles in an amazing way a famous Santa Anna of
Michelangelo. . . ."[18]

Between February 26 and March 23, 1961, he too published his
Indian impressions, in six articles in the daily *Il giorno*. The next
year he and Moravia each expanded his articles into a book with titles
to fit their temperaments: Moravia's was *An Idea of India*, Pasolini's
*The Smell of India*. He wrote that "while Moravia went to sleep" he
went walking alone because only that way, "lost, mute, on foot, do
I succeed in discovering things." Zigaina has said Pasolini told him,
"smiling": "[In India] I went to a fortune-teller and he told me I will
be killed by three boys." In February "willing, happy, curious as
monkeys," they went to Kenya; they returned there together two years
later.

In the meantime, Bolognini had intervened with his excellent connections throughout the Roman film industry. He contacted producer Alfredo Bini, who agreed to finance *Accattone*. The budget was set at 80 million lire, less than one-third the average cost of an Italian production that year. Bini, through his ARCO Film, put up half.

Shooting started again with March 1961. Bini's arrival was a tremendous stroke of good fortune for both men: The producer was enthusiastic, artistic, but level-headed about money. Neither wanted the other's job: Bini did not want to be a film director any more than Pasolini cared for business. The producer gave his author-director absolute freedom to choose the actors, the locations, write the script he wanted without interference. Bini was savvy enough to recognize the commercial value of the notorious Pasolini—the scandalous homosexual, lover of teenage boys, accused breaklaw, poet of *Ceneri*, of the banned *Ragazzi* and scandalous *Una vita violenta*. He also seemed to appreciate his director on artistic grounds and shared Pasolini's distaste for conventional film beauty and stars. Bini was prepared to take *Accattone* to market as Pasolini made it.

They were to collaborate for almost a decade: Bini produced every one of Pasolini's movies through *Oedipus rex* in 1967. Inevitably, when their rapport soured, Pier Paolo came to write about his relationship with "my contemporary from Gorizia / red-haired, hands in his pockets / heavy as a paratrooper after mess hall. . . ." Pasolini expected loyalty, and those who disappointed were exiled.

Pier Paolo made sure that he owned the screenplay's publication rights. Free to make a deal with Rizzoli for its publication, he did; he apologized to Garzanti, claimed his "hands were tied," and offered to make a short story from the film, something which "is for you."

On July 1, 1961, he wrote in *Vie nuove:*

> It was in fact yesterday that I went to choose the sites for shooting the last frames of *Accattone*. Outside Rome, out toward the valleys and mountains of central Latium, to be precise between Subiaco and Olevano, but it was above all around Olevano that I concentrated, so much like a place painted by Corot. I remember his light and smoky mountains . . . I had to choose a mountain which, in a dream of Accattone—toward the end of the film, not long before his death—he envisions . . . paradise. Accattone does not just die, but he goes to paradise. But you will say: that's the limit! Not only after the "conversion" of Tommasino [protagonist of *Una vita violenta*], now P.P.P. gives us a film . . . with catholicism par excellence. And you would be right to be scandalized if it were that way.[19]

On August 31, *Accattone* was shown at the 22nd Venice Festival, where *Last Year at Marienbad* won first prize but lukewarm press.

Gadda, Parise, Moravia, and Guido Piovene participated in the ritual press conference in the Hotel Excelsior. Pasolini entered the Palazzo di Cinema accompanied by what *Vita* magazine called "a nice group of *ragazzi di vita* who flayed their hands clapping and also a violent sea of catcalls and objections."[20] Many critics declared the film's realism "excessive," the language of his *borgatari* shocking, something "socially" pornographic. But one magazine reported that summer, "Cinemas showing the film in Rome are as full every evening as an egg." *Vita*'s staff reviewer suggested that the attention only came because of its official condemnation: "otherwise, it is in effect a work of modest importance."[21] The magazine opined that "[the world] of Pasolini is, after all, a one-way world, where hope never flowers nor a sentiment capable of giving a sense of human dignity." As for the reason why its characters are trapped in their dead-end lives: It was their own lack of "moral force." That the Roman dialect would be "understood with difficulty in the rest of Italy" was deemed a shortcoming; Elsa Morante and Adele Cambria's appearances were dismissed as "intellectuals' solidarity" and the effect of black-and-white" was "suffocating but suggestive." On the cultural Right, Pasolini's vision of what he later called "the sacrality of the authentic" fell on deaf ears.

In retrospect, such reactions seem something from another world. But they had influence and were backed with enforcement. The film waited until November 9 for the indispensable ministerial approval of its release. But the Government decided that a new law, to take effect in 1962, in this case alone had to be anticipated by a year: Normally, certain films were banned to those under sixteen.

By special order of the censors, all posters advertising *Accattone* had a special notice pasted on them: "Specially prohibited to those under 18." Bini could not have done better himself. Inevitably, the special ban drew ever larger crowds to the cinema Barberini, the movie palace built by Roberto Rossellini's contractor father in the old days of Mussolini's construction boom.

*Accattone* opened commercially on November 22, 1961, just four days after the trial court of first instance absolved Pasolini from any wrongdoing in the via di Panico incident. The very widely read weekly of no intellectual pretension called *Oggi* (Today) previewed *Accattone* for its readers and warned them it was "one more film about human garbage."

He was a man who made news. He had, after all, been charged at law with helping a fugitive from justice escape the scene of his crime, a scene stepped from the script of *Accattone*. The papers had made that front-page news, large-type headlines; tough Roman districts were now described as "the restless *ambiente* of Pasolini."

He had been in the audience at the Cinema Reale in Trastevere when *La lunga notte del '43* was shown; his name on screen, as scriptwriter, brought what he called a murmur "with just enough malice and irony to bring a terror of lynching to my heart."[22] The film was already the subject of special Government notice, singled out for censorship under a new, tough law. In characteristic fashion he turned even this ugly experience to good use. As though making of his life the stuff for legend, the raw material for polemic at whatever the cost, he wrote two pages of commentary and reflection on the "incident" of the "murmuring" in Trastevere, published in *Il giorno* on November 6, 1960. If he were to be victim of a lynching, he would make sure it was a public one. That way it would be a lesson, and teach. His friend Biago Marin wrote, "Be careful, surely they are lying in wait. Strange stories are circulating about you, all of them tending to defamation. Be careful, Pier Paolo."[23]

At the Barberini premiere, a group of young men from a neo-Fascist club called *Nuova Europa* forced their way inside, assaulted spectators, set off stink bombs and threw ink bottles at the screen. Not without wit, they threw rotten anise, *finocchio*, at the screen. They did not assault Pasolini: That came later.

For half an hour the theater was thrown into pandemonium. At the second showing, Rome's intellectuals and film community turned out in solidarity. Visconti embraced Pasolini in the lobby, and Pier Paolo told reporters, "If the Fascists have it out for me, let them come to my house."

What a handful of teenage Fascist toughs, drunk on romantic notions of "making a statement" to "show that pervert," produced was a short spell of chaos in one movie house and a lot of publicity useful to Bini. But the State's official censors took the little protest to full term, giving birth to a censorship that saw the film removed from every screen in Italy. The Ministry's watchdogs, not paid to do more, stopped with the simplistically documentable evidence: The script was littered with swear words, seemed to idealize (at least not condemn) a social no-good, and served up a presentation of prostitutes without moralizing.

When *Accattone* was pulled from the cinemas, liberal newspapermen like Mino Argentieri, howled. "Maybe we can close an eye at a little comic film; maybe we can look the other way when there is a stripper," he wrote, but to condemn Pasolini was to fall in line with the strictures of nothing less than "a clerical regime." The critic called for "a firm opposition," needed to protect films like this, ones he designated "artistically accomplished."

Moravia went further in his review in *L'espresso* on October 1. He suggested that "Pasolini's novels were an unconsicous preparation for the cinema." He argued that Pasolini had, at last, to give up the attenuated power of language's metaphor for pictures, for the images "which cannot be other than direct and immediate."

Only a year had passed since Mario Montagnan had used the pages of *Rinascita* effectively to drum Pasolini out of the ranks of artists acceptable to the Party.

Memories were fresh of *Una vita violenta,* in which Pasolini's creature seemed to resemble his creator too closely for comfort: "Tommasino, the protagonist, is in reality a young delinquent of the worst sort: a thief, a robber, a pederast. . . ." It mattered that *Accattone*'s premiere also came barely a year after Catholic Action had filed its legal denunciation of the second novel. A consultant to the court had written that while the book was not so obscene as to require penal action, "[it] . . . was certainly not one to be left to be passed around freely within a family." Then *Accattone.*

Moravia tried to calm the waters:

> The entire film centers around this extremely beautiful personage, profoundly felt, exquisitely presented in all his complexity. Accattone is many things at once: he is Roman secular skepticism, the relic of a society still rustic and artisan-based; but he is above all the expression of . . . an unconscious will to suicide.[24]

His opinion, not in a small-circulation journal but in a national weekly, carried weight. Pasolini perhaps could not be so easily dismissed when Moravia, by now the godfather of Italian letters, called him "a serious director, solid, tenacious, intelligent and poetic, who works on every image as he works on every word."

More than a decade later, Pasolini told an English interviewer, "Public opinion turned against me because of some sort of undefinable racist hate which, like all racism, is irrational. They just could not accept *Accattone* and all its subproletarian characters."[25]

Even more effectively than with written language, film let Pasolini approach reproducing reality without the distortions of intermediaries. The goal was nothing less than to bridge the gap between nature and art. It was obviously a medium better suited for such an ambitious goal than words, words some people knew and others did not.

Through praxis, he had begun edging toward a theory, five years in the making, of a "cinema of poetry" (as opposed to a cinema of consumption) that used images—and the least possible amount of dialogue—as a universal "language of reality." Because he saw life with the same poetry and as religiously as had the boy in Friuli, the task was to invent for himself—as though inventing the cinema again and all alone—a film technique that communicated that sensibility. Occasionally, the results seem forced, too self-conscious, excessively "stylized." But when Pasolini's vision was effectively transferred through the eye of the Arriflex he carried on his shoulder, the result was a cinema as powerful as the best of neo-realism, with a poetic quality that leavens its gritty, documentary tone.

About this time, he told one of the seemingly countless interviewers who asked whether he was deserting literature, "The desire to express myself through the cinema comes from my need to use a new medium, a technique for renewal. It also signifies a desire to escape from the obsessive . . . finally, it will let me live, finally, in accord with my philosophy." [26]

Had he not successfully made the move to cinema (the historian's counter-factual proposition), what could he have expected? By 1960 he was more famous as a poet than his friends Roversi and Leonetti; he could easily have made a career as an editor, for example. Had he stayed with poetry, more prizes would have come his way. He would certainly have been in that circle of "men of culture" *(uomini di cultura)*, intellectuals known by the company they keep and the line they take, men (and a few women) who live by their writing. He would have held a visiting professorship in an American faculty, perhaps even lived to see dissertations written about his work.

Had he stayed with the written word, producing novels, essays, travel writing, he would always be given space on the expanding cultural pages of the newspapers and been called on (like Moravia) for his opinion when a quote was needed even on a topic far beyond his expertise.

Italy has room for polymaths, and believes in "genius": he would have debated with the linguists one day, edited an anthology and written a book review the next, given papers, overseen translations of his work. Both poet Eugenio Montale and screenwriter Cesare Zavattini painted, and were treated as respectable amateurs in the medium. That, too, was open to him—an old age of interviews, round tables, and the palate of colors he loved. Had he separated his life and his work even a little, he might, like all the Colus clan, have lived very long, like Susanna who died at over ninety, five years after her first-born's murder.

*     *     *

In the months leading up to *Accattone*, he had set to the commissioned translation of Aeschylus' *Oresteia*. In December 1959 he promised actor-director Vittorio Gassman the first part of *Agamemnon*, "within the first two weeks of January," to be followed by the others, spaced a month apart. His version, which he admitted was done in haste, treats the forces of violence—the irrational Erinyes—as the psychoanalytic unconscious. They must be repressed, just as conscious reason must hold the unconscious at bay. He wrote from a preexisting Italian version, checking against English, French, and the Greek. Some critics found it flat, too essayistic; others claimed that he overemphasized the place of the Furies as against, for example, the encounter between Orestes and Electra or the drama of Clytemnestra.

He was present when Gassman's Turin-based Teatro Popolare Italiano performed his Aeschylus in the Greek amphitheater at Syracuse on May 19 (Einaudi published the text—to his annoyance, without sending him galleys—with critical notes on the production); the company was interested in his writing something for them to do at the Spoleto Festival. Even staging *Ragazzi di vita* "with music, songs, and choreography" was suggested, "a kind of Italian *Three-Penny Opera*." When the subject reopened, with carte blanche offered him, he begged off, "terribly unsure, I have never written for the theater (save in prehistoric times) and do not know how." But by then he was immersed in *Accattone*.

But quite another platform than the theater occupied him during the period of *Accattone*, and for several years afterward. Editor Maria Antonietta Macciocchi, in charge of the PCI weekly magazine *Vie nuove* (New pathways) had offered him a column—"Dialogues with Pasolini." The Party was wide enough even for him. Or so it seemed. Macciocchi wrote years later she did not know the famous author of the *Ceneri* had been expelled in 1949 for *"indignità morale."*[31] Her own expulsion for ideological deviance (a lay excommunication) came in 1977.

To enlist him, *Vie nuove* sent its art and later cinema critic, the perfect agent to act as buffer between Pasolini and Party cultural hard-liners. "He did not need much convincing," recalls Antonello Trombadori. Macciocchi has written:

> He came into the editorial office wearing tight blue-jeans and a big leather belt with studs, shirt open at the neckbelt, a bit of the air of a rascal

completed in contrast to his gentleness and timidity, with the hesitation of a well-educated boy.[27]

He explained to his new readers:

> As usual, Signora Macciocchi has won. I am working on three film scripts, I am preparing a film of which I will be director, I am correcting a volume of essays of six hundred pages, I am organizing a novel in which, by now, I have invested everything, I am writing verses and articles, as the inter-mittences and obsessions of this vocation allow: as they say, I haven't time to breathe. I am on the verge of exhaustion: because to all this one must add the constant struggle, a daily one, against the offensives of Fascists and clerics. . . . But Signora Macciocchi has overcome every difficulty, came straight to my house, and directly touched my heart. She put to me, almost as a sweet duty, a "correspondence" with the readers of *Vie Nuove:* surely I could find one hour a week. I have accepted. But I do not really know yet what it is that I have accepted . . . I hope it will be useful and vital.

In her welcoming essay, Macciocchi denied that media fascination with Pasolini's private life ("where he passes the evening, with what singer [presumably Betti] or what diva") had anything to do with his invitation. On the other hand, she could not resist a vignette.

> Last year [May 1959], in a village lost in eastern Sicily, in Scicli, where we went with a group of journalists to visit the *cavernicoli* [grottoes, at Chiafura], I recall with amazement how a group of young people, intellectuals and salaried people, waited for him in the middle of the sunny village square: they knew Pasolini not only for his novels but for the magazine *Officina*, his short-stories in *Paragone*, even an article of his that appeared in the *Fiera letteraria*.

Pasolini wrote his impressions for a local group, the V. Brancati Circolo di Cultura (literally, culture club): they hailed the visit of the *uomini* (and one *donna*) *di cultura* and welcomed their denunciation of living conditions—hundreds lived in the caves. He found himself surrounded by people whose dialect was so intact, "become absolute only there," that at first he barely understood; but " 'the clic' was made." The young club members even knew an article of his from two years before, even made jokes about the Circolo Romano della Caccia incident. He passed the day with boys still in school, active in the sponsoring group. And he wrote about them: Bartolomeo Amenta "wearing glasses like some shoemakers wear"; Peppino Carrabba, "bursting with youth and happiness inside his clothes"; Giovanni Rossino, "a little, bearlike philosopher." He noticed, "television practically does not exist here: thus in Sicily, in daily customs and discussions, in the smallest interests, there is a different tone from the rest of Italy, infinitely more ancient [*piu antico*], and true, and also much more modern."

He participated in a *strapieno* ("packed") debate in the town hall. Pasolini said: " 'The Sicilian people no longer are ashamed of their misery' seems to me could be the slogan of our meeting; it intends to go out from this misery." He told them that there were caves like those they knew "two hundred meters from the Vatican where the Pope lives":

> I came to the grottoes of Scicli well immunized by my daily experience in Rome. My impression therefore has not been traumatic, violent . . . what really struck me . . . are the positive elements, of movement and of consciousness. Rarely in my life has it happened that I find myself speaking with people like you, so alive, so honest.

The same reception met him at Syracuse and Ragusa, to say nothing of "overflowing" halls in Tivoli, Ancona, Salerno, Terni, and in Rome when he participated in "public debates on *La dolce vita* or *Una vita violenta*."

Back in Rome, the editor and her prize contributor were stopping at a café outside her office in via Sicilia: "I asked him about Italian cultural life. He became my sole teacher *(unico maestro)*. He spoke softly, discreetly. . . ."

His column of correspondence called for answering letters addressed to him at the publication's office, but as he saw fit; he was at liberty to range beyond their queries to comment on whatever interested him. What interested him was challenging Communist moralism in those days of Stalinist intolerance.

His first *Vie nuove* "dialogue with readers" appeared before *Accattone* in May 1960—the last, five years later, on September 30, 1965. In between, he addressed De Gaulle and the "repressions of the Tambroni government," took a stand against censorship, analyzed the new films of Antonioni and what "neo-capitalism" and "well-being" brought in their wake.

At thirty-eight he had the stature and name recognition to do what Wilde did on his tour of the British provinces after his return from a triumphant American tour. Pasolini had a slot, like that given the old Auden, ensconced in the St. Aldate's Coffee House opposite Christ Church in Oxford, a place from which the poet-sage dispensed wisdom, without appointment, most afternoons.

*       *       *

Pasolini began his column when charges were pending against *La giornata balorda,* the film he wrote for Bolognini.

From one of his very first columns, that of June 25, 1960, he asserted the artist's independence of his backers. When one Paolo Boccaletti of Modena wrote to ask why it was that a wave of "moral hypocrisy" seemed to be building, a new prudery even on the Left, Pasolini answered,

> Your impressions are correct. There is a kind of *prudery* [emphasis Pasolini's] in the Italian Communist press: from time to time, certain articles in *Unità* seem to have been written with that prohibitory anguish of an old spinster. And even *Vie nuove* (let us say it, brutally), let's not kid ourselves. . . .

Nipping, if not outright biting the hand that fed him, Pasolini pushed the editors of the magazine hard for five years, sometimes almost daring them to fire him and make of him an example of the worst attitudes he ascribed to Party hacks. Macciocchi was his champion, staunchly defending him to the higher-ups who, more than once, had had enough. Within the first year, Mario Montagnan proclaimed to the PCI's central committee, "It is not possible that the prose of that homosexual Pasolini be read in the houses of the proletariat, of their families. Let's get this pederast out of *Vie nuove*." [28] Macciocchi resisted and even defied the Party's General Secretary by refusing to give space to a "re-valuation" of D'Annunzio, one which Togliatti thought would be useful among voters in the conservative Veneto.

But when Macciocchi was forced out and her successor asked Pasolini to resign, he did so "without hesitation," explaining to readers that he had broken off "because of illness." [29] Once again, he acted in what was also self-interest but might more usefully be understood as the ruthlessness of one with a program in mind, one in which individual people are means, not ends. Fabio Mauri noticed this when he and actress Adriana Asti in vain sought his comfort when their marriage (Pasolini had been a witness) faltered (they were divorced in 1957). "He stepped back from human events, *staccato* [detached], almost like God who cannot intervene but only watches as matters take their destined course." [30]

His *Vie nuove* "dialogue" of July 9, 1960, is typical of the column's style: A reader in Ventimiglia wrote to ask whether socialist opinion had not been too hard on Pasternak, then just died. Pasolini answered with a lesson in the history of ideas: He wrote that Marxism's "great mistake" was in confusing all irrationality with that which came out of late-nineteenth-century European decadence. In arguing for "rationality above all," he contended the Left had fallen into prudery, wrongly rejecting all fantasy and imagination as "reactionary." Rethinking the place of *decadentismo* ("decadence") as a historical movement ought, he instructed, to free Marxism in general (and Italian Communism in particular) from hypocrisy and intolerance. The Ventimiglia correspondent was not heard from again.

For evidence in any argument, he always turned to whatever else he was working on at the time. Just then, it was the translation for Gassmann:

> I would like to discuss an example which is perhaps a bit pedantic. Have you read the *Oresteia* by Aeschylus? I have recently been occupied with it, to translate it. The content of the *Oresteia* is essentially political: about the substitution of a democratic state—even if very crudely democratic—by a state that is tyrannical and archaic. The culmination of the tragedy comes at the moment when the goddess Athena (Reason: born out of the brain of her father: without the experiences that are uterine, maternal, irrational) summons an assembly of citizens who govern through voting. But the tragedy does not end there. After Athena's intervention, the Erynides—unbridled, archaic, instinctive, out of nature—also survive: and they too are gods, they are immortal. They cannot be eliminated, they cannot be killed. They must be transformed while leaving their irrationality intact: mutated, that is, from Curse-makers into Blessing-Givers. Italian Marxists have not, I repeat, posed themselves this problem: and neither have—so far as I can tell—the Russians.[31]

Never was cultural analysis more wed to everyday life, nor more self-revelatory; Pasolini found himself in everything, and everything flowed back to his selfhood. For him, the ancient playwright codified human realities, those deep-seated characteristics of man that predate politics. These are tied to the "uterine experience"—to Susanna, to whom all loyalty went—and were "irrational," the material of dreams and poetry. Fighting for the place of the irrational in politics (that is, in rationality) was fighting for himself and for her, for his commitment to her and thus his most profound identity. But he was going to fight without losing what the ancient Greeks called *sophrosyne* (self-control).

He went further, linking politics to art, as Plato had. Artists (he among them) will be unruly for the governors because they can never hone to the discipline of the merely political. They (and he, by inference) answer to Athena, giving the due they must even to her enemies. Pasolini's relationship to social reality will necessarily be restless, rough-edged, so long as the forces that ignore the rights of the "immortal" gods of irrationality are not allowed their sphere of influence. By comparison with the playing field on which he was moving, and the stakes he felt at issue, the occasionally noisome (but inevitable) victimization of a too-outspoken homosexual by passing politicos was child's play. His task was to confront it with stoicism, and plot his next attack—that was his destiny.

He wrote:

> In Italy, the moment is probably still premature: the intervention of Athena has not yet come. In Russia, there was that moment [the Revolution of 1917]: what is missing still is the appendix to that intervention: that is the transformation of Curses into Blessings (the desperate irrationalism and anarchical bourgeois into an irrationalism . . . that is new).[32]

He was never to abandon this theme. The mysterious visitor in *Teorema* is this irrational god, this Dionysius of the post-Revolution. The Trilogy (1971–74) based in fable appealed to him because what he called "archaic" societies—those societies preliterate, preindustrial, without sexual inhibition or class manipulation—had the wisdom (not to be confused with science or progress) to give the Eumenides their due. The worlds of the *Decameron* and *Canterbury Tales* and *Thousand and One Nights* had not lost touch with the irrational, not fallen into "conventionality, conformism, standardization," which he saw growing at an alarming rate in Italy in the summer of 1960. That they existed only in his creation hardly mattered: If the artist cannot create, God-like, what distinguishes him from other men?

A twenty-year-old in a Cremona TB clinic wrote to ask what to read, what was the best "system of study"? Pasolini suggested two anthologies ("De Sanctis and, for the moderns, Sapegno") but first offered nostalgia for his own youth, when he "had time to read":

> What days! I passed hours and hours at the Portico of Death [Il portico della morte] in Bologna, where they sold used books, reading titles, leafing through pages and indices. I was fifteen [enrolled at the Galvani high school] and until then had only read adventure books, and then somehow Dostoevsky's *The Idiot* came into my hands, and it was a revelation. I read all of Dostoevsky, and then Tolstoy: and then the tragedies of Shakespeare. Only about

> a year or two later I discovered modern poetry . . . I read Montale . . . and
> Ungaretti: they were revelation number two.[33]

He offered this gilded memory of the idyllic leisurely self-education of a son of the middle class despite his reader's explanation that
he is "the son of workers" who "asked for help from publishers by
asking for used books, but . . . received nothing"

> I set myself to read, like someone desperate, the contemporary poets, who
> were then the Hermeticists: and then I proceeded to the Symbolists, espe-
> cially Rimbaud. And, naturally, I continued voraciously to read the narrators
> of the nineteenth century: the Russians, the English, the French.[34]

Another reader wrote asking why he, "a son of the well-off," chose
Communism? Pier Paolo explained: "My father, it is true, was very
rich as a young man" but when he himself was born, Carlo Alberto
was "a simple infantry lieutenant and lived off his (miserable) stipend." He explained that his grandmother called Mussolini *Il culatta*
[roughly, "Big Butt"]—the sort of invented slang Pier Paolo called
"worthy of Carlo Emilio Gadda."[35]

He explains that it "was the direct experience of the problems of
others which radically transformed my problems—that's why I always
sense in the origins of Communism in a middle-class person an ethical instinct, something almost evangelical."

During the course of writing the column in *Vie nuove*, word trickled
back to him that perhaps he sometimes wrote over the heads of his
worker readers, addressed concerns not real to them in a language
they did not share. But sometimes his readers upped the ante, demanding sophisticated responses to complex questions. Such a case
was Andrea Resta of Naples, who asked him to address "realism and
neo-realism," the "relationship between realism and language" and
between language (official, standard Italian) and dialects. Pier Paolo
rose, and with gusto, to the challenge: It was another chance to join
the debates born in Friuli, the battle over language as ideological
tool, as expression of power. He could once again take to the battlefield of critical theory, as he had in *Il stroligut* and *Officina:*

> I think that an Italian realist writer cannot ignore the division of Italian
> society into two social classes: the middle class which uses a slovenly Italian,
> something merely instrumental and from television . . . and the popular
> classes which use the various dialects."[36]

The writer is free to move between levels and even invent words, just so that he does so consciously: "Do not consider realism a formal fact but an ideological one. . . ." The representation of "reality" need not depict only the reality of the ascendant bourgeoisie. Alternative realities exist, not inferior ones but different ones, which are almost always ignored or repressed. Treating the social origins of the writer counts, as does admitting that the middle-class definition of what is real and important is only one definition among others. History is not to be limited to tales of the winners, who steal it for themselves; literature is not only about the "haves."

Underlying these columns was an argument with Carlo Salinari because their debate was important, and about a problem which would not die: It was the Manichaean question—was all good on one side, all bad on the other?

In his book *Preludio e fine del realismo in Italia* (Prelude and end of reality in Italy), Salinari claimed that *Ragazzi di vita* was "founded on equivocations," especially those of language.[37] The Communist critic was convinced that at the book's base was not "*romanesco* in all its complexity and richness" but only slang of an unrepresentative criminal underworld. For him, Pasolini's expressions—put in the mouths of the *borgatari*—were only an "apparent realism," in fact, "hiding a literary taste that is typically formalist and decadent." Salinari considered the novel bad art because "The dominant element is . . . stench, this physical and moral filth [in which its characters live]. . . . It is easy to hide under a false realism the turbid inspiration." The world Pasolini displayed, in effect, was sick because he is.

And yet, when *Le ceneri di Gramsci* appeared, Salinari lauded it as "the first book of poetry of the new generation that is really important . . . and which represents, in the present year without a doubt the literary event of greatest importance."[38]

In 1959 he praised *Una vita violenta* because it marked "the relaunching of the personality, that is an attempt to give back to the person that organicity which was destroyed by Decadent literature." He was satisfied that now "the ideological axis which sustains the structure of the novel is . . . oriented toward socialism." But his and the PCI's line on slang and dialects remained unchanged: "Today dialect is for the most part surmounted . . . as a reflection of a conception of the world"; instead, what is in the "*classi popolari*" is "national consciousness" and the "breaking up of regional limits." Salinari and Pasolini could make peace but would never agree.

Like Salinari, Pasolini also believed in an ethical role for literature. But it took him to the opposite pole, to praise an unofficial
school of "Roman realists": Moravia and Cassola, Bassani and Morante. His is a "school" of favorites—those postwar writers who do
not accept things as they are, who argue for a wider vision of life
than found in "acceptable" letters. These names listed in the *Vie
nuove* column recapitulate his roll call of honor announced in the late
spring of 1960, at a debate convened on the occasion of the now
controversial giving of the Strega, the prestigious literary prize
founded in 1947 and funded by the family that produces a yellow
liqueur.

Pasolini's Strega participation came in the form of a verse epistle,
read at the Open Gate theater in Rome on June 27, 1960, a part of
the debate over who should win. He had "presented" (sponsored)
Calvino's *Il cavaliere inesistente*, faced off against Carlo Cassola's *La
ragazza di Bube*, good commercial material that lent itself to film
treatment starring Cardinale (in the U.S., *Bebo's Girl*) in 1963.

Once again Pasolini set the agenda to which others had to respond.
Knowing full well it would cause a scandal, he read from typed sheets
(the first line in English) the poem later published as *"In morte del
realismo"* (On the death of realism): *"Friends, Romans, countrymen,
lend me your ears! /* I come to bury Italian realism / not to praise
it . . ."*[39]

He did not finish reading all he had written. Nevertheless, as they
left, Calvino laughingly told Pasolini that his attack on Cassola had
cost Calvino "at least a hundred votes."[40]

Some people thought Pier Paolo only taking petty revenge on the
intellectuals who, a year before, had passed over *Una vita violenta*
to honor *The Leopard*. Others thought he opened a major debate on
the future of the realist tradition at the edge of what seemed sure to
be a decade of experiment. In his poem-address, he seized the critical
high ground, the role of awarding the praise and demerits—a kind
of Italian Edmund Wilson, whose books *The Forties* and *The Fifties*
were to American criticism what Pasolini's essay collection called
*Passions and Ideology* (1960) was to Italy. Both men were willing to
total the columns, render an accounting of where literature stood and
be teacher to their cultures. Pasolini—standing live before his peers
and competitors—singled out, as though for a jury's ribbons (or honorable mentions) "Gadda's *Pasticciaccio* . . . Moravia's fine and ruthless diagnoses . . . Levi's gentle sociology"; he named the "golden

story" by Bassani—the novella *The Golden Spectacles,* published in
1958—and the work of his close friend Elsa Morante, whose novel
*Arturo's Island* appeared in 1957. "And it leaves you Calvino. His
prose / French rather than Tuscan, / his imagination more Voltairean
than / homegrown . . ."[41]

A commitment to action, to the active role of intellectuals in politics, took him to Reggio Emilia in mid-July 1960 to speak at a
congress whose theme was "The Anti-Fascist Union of Intellectuals
for the Renewal of Italian Society." It was, in fact, late in the day's
battle and almost an act of nostalgia: The victory of conservative
politics was complete in 1960, restiveness among unions placated,
the student movement still unknown. Pasolini, along with Trombadori, addressed the gathering, and wrote in *Vie nuove* how impressed
he was at the "rational rigor, critical and methodological, of the young
people." In his essay of July 30 Pasolini said his "hair stood on end"
to think of how different the world was at that meeting from his
universe at the same age. In his youth, he wrote:

> All around us, there triumphed the blackest Fascism, without hope, [what
> passed for] information was . . . rhetorical nonsense: There was nothing-
> ness. The effort we had to make to emerge from that nothingness, from that
> monstrous condition, now seems to me to be miraculous: to manage to read
> Croce and Rimbaud, hidden (that's how we began) was a special case, meant
> taking a risk.[42]

What moved him about the youth leadership at Reggio was that
"at their backs, the young people of today have the experience of the
Resistance . . . that is why the young workers have so much power
of enthusiasm and the young intellectuals so much critical and rational rigor: It is the Resistance yielding its fruits."

Some people began to be annoyed at Pasolini's use of the Resistance. In fact, conservative elements of Italian society—mostly Christian Democratic—were losing patience with the PCI's effort to
appropriate the Resistance as their historical monopoly. A sense was
growing in some quarters that people like Pasolini were too quick to
seize on a falsified version—a myth of the Resistance—as proof
positive of their civic stature, too quickly moving over the complex
picture that was Italy in civil war, in collaboration and in accom-
modation, before and after the arrival of the Allies.

What Pasolini did not mention, for his readers all knew it, was
that the congress he addressed in Reggio Emilia had been called as
a protest against government crack-downs. The Tambroni govern-

ment, to outdiscipline that of Mario Scelba, had instituted mass arrests of suspected troublemakers on the Left. Demonstrations in the streets of Reggio and Genova had ended in police opening fire. Pasolini wrote that "the Italian police has acted like a foreign army," that a recording of the streetfight showed "salvo after salvo, with nothing able to stop it, as though a game, as though . . . a diversion [*un divertimento*]."

When 1968 hit Italy, he changed his position, but now—at decade's end—he wrote that "between the laborers and the police there is a leap of quality, a difference of nationality." Thanks to "the work of Scelba and Tambroni" the police are a "heavy corpus, decisive, politically oriented and conscious." In *Vie nuove* he repeated the accusation of Renzo Trionfera, "a journalist certainly not Marxist, writing in *L'europeo*," that the police are "directly linked to the Vatican." By October he referred in his column to "the alliance of Tambroni with the Fascists, protected by the police and blessed by the Vatican."[43]

By midsummer 1960 reaction to the excesses of his administration drove Tambroni from office; the exclusively Christian Democratic Cabinet fell in a chorus of attacks, among which must be counted Pasolini's, who labeled it "paternalistic and fascistic." The ground was beginning to be laid for the "historic compromise" of Christian Democracy with Italian socialism—the so-called "opening to the Left"—made by Aldo Moro in 1963.

Pasolini turned his *Vie nuove* space to local fights. The "solution" the Roman city government offered to cope with internal immigration was to refuse issuance of residency permits. Without such documents, one cannot work in Italy, cannot rent housing. Asked his opinion, he wrote, "In fact, the *borgate*, willed into being by the Fascists and consecrated by the Christian Democrats, are truly and really concentration camps."[44]

In mid-article, having launched an apparently political attack, he turned to art. The job of the artist, a matter that obsessed him, was to do something about such conditions as in the slums, "posing the problem, make it the object of indignation—that is not enough. One must work . . ." like the unionists, who are "real saints."

He demanded that artists throw themselves into the struggle. The film then on everyone's lips was Visconti's latest, so Pasolini offered an excursus to illustrate how art can serve the struggle for social justice: "I just saw last night *Rocco and His Brothers* [starring Alain Delon] . . . the directing, as usual, is splendid, the story, especially in the second half deeply moving. . . ."

And yet Visconti—the homosexual artistocrat, descendant of the

seigneurs of Milan—is found wanting. "Psychological depth" is lacking, Pasolini claims, the depth Visconti achieved in *La terra trema*.
"I would have asked of Visconti a greater courage to delve deeper
into the psychology: that which makes things complicated, facts contradictory, events difficult: and that never yields spectacle." Those
who accused Pasolini of being "obscure" met his answer: He dismissed "spectacle" as the lowest form of film, only a diversion, a
squandering of a powerful tool wrongly put in the service of merely
making money, of "forgetfulness"—in Pasolinian parlance the opposite of consciousness. So, in a single article (October 1, 1960), he
blasted both the mayor of Rome and a film director at the height of
his fame and power.

It is to his credit as polemicist that he understood that the status
of the thing criticized rubs off on its critic. For Pasolini—his first
film still in the works—to criticize Visconti, a recognized master of
the form for already two decades, served (among other ends) to make
Pasolini important. There is something royal about one who is taken
seriously as a critic of the king.

While his enemies accused him of craving attention, he also sometimes complained at its growing price. When a reader from Vicenza
wrote to ask how Brigitte Bardot could possibly contemplate suicide
(as the news reported), when she was "someone who had everything
from life," he had his chance.

> Don't think for a moment that the middle-class journalist cares at all for the
> truth: to be in some way honest; that is to be personal. He completely
> depersonalizes himself, to allow himself to speak to a hypothetical public,
> one which he naturally considers right-thinking but idiotic, normal but fe-
> rocious, uncensored but vile.[45]

In retrospect, he seems to be rehearsing an idea he later applied
to Marilyn Monroe and Maria Callas. Bardot's life, he wrote, had
been "mystified by others." She was a victim of the "myth of celebrity." The press, he claimed, created a completely false personality,
acting out of "sadistic cynicism" according to "inhuman rules." Reporters were people for whom terms like "respect, gratitude, seriousness, pity" had no meaning. In 1960 it was a new way of looking
at things:

> I, in a manner that is certainly very limited compared to B.B., have had a
> bit of success these past few years and I know what this means: I understand
> perfectly well the suicidal thoughts of this young woman. I know what it

means to be looked at like some rare beast . . . to be continually, systematically falsified, rudely manipulated so as to "make news."[46]

With the new decade, Trombi went into action, a one-man Italian
functional equal to "Shifty" Hays of the notorious Hays Office. The
State's new censorship campaign moved against Visconti, against
Francesco Rosi, against much that time proved to be the best of the
new cinema. Pasolini threw himself into the struggle, seeking to define the terms of the debate:

> Too often a great mistake is made in discussions about censorship: that of
> putting the debate in the terms proposed by the censors: that is of the
> moralistic-sexual. Instead it is quite otherwise: one must completely ignore
> their hypocritical pretext, and see what should be obvious to a child, that
> censorship is a political issue, with sex as a simple and shameless pretext.[47]

The "great political parties of the Left" (as he lumped together
Communists, socialists, and fractional groups) ought to admit this.
They should discard their prudishness—born, as he explained, out
of confusing bourgeois decadence with true, post-Revolutionary freedom of the body—and take the lead. In December 1960 he proposed
that the PCI interest itself in cinema, even to undertake movie production "as they have magazines and newspapers."

He went further. The Party as film producer would not be enough:
"The distributors, in general, are much more reactionary and tied to
clerical interests than even the producers (among whom are some
people fairly without prejudice and courageous) [an apparent reference to Alfredo Bini]."[48]

The "democratic parties" must have a chain of their own theaters,
similar to those the Church ran through parish halls. This, he suggests is "something a little difficult to achieve." But only that way,
he argued, could the hypocrisy surrounding censorship be defeated.

Simultaneous with his 1960 "dialogues" in *Vie nuove*, he also
worked briefly as film critic for *Reporter*, a weekly magazine of "news
and customs" directed by Adriano Bolzoni. Between the last week of
1959 and mid-March 1960 he wrote eleven essays, including profiles
of directors and reflections on the medium.

He protested that too few quality first-run films were being seen
in Italy; he reflected on his own work as a screenwriter for Bolognini
(which he found was satisfactory over all) and again raised the issue
of his unhappiness at his experience with Franco Rosi's *Death of a
Friend*.

He was already thinking about Anna Magnani, two years before casting her as star of his second film. In print he wondered why her form of humor, her earthy Roman womanhood, traveled successfully across the Atlantic—she won an Oscar in 1956 for *The Rose Tattoo*— while the great comic Alberto Sordi remained strictly a home-market phenomenon. His *Reporter* articles, somehow too serious and too rich for their setting, wondered out loud about catholicity in films, about the nature of laughter in movies.

And he generalized, even pontificated: "Cinema is not something that exists autonomously," he wrote, "an entity unto itself; it is culture, it is society, and it is history itself which conditions it." In gross terms, this view is simply the standard line. Coming at a time when Italian cinema was becoming obsessed with "purity" and self-quotation—fascinated with light, form, and color—once again Pasolini's stance was nonconforming, the harder rather than the easier road to popularity.

He wrote about American movies, with perhaps predictable incomprehension. *Some Like It Hot* (arrived a year after U.S. release), left "a bitter taste in the mouth." Apparently Jack Lemmon and Tony Curtis in drag failed to amuse him.

Occasionally, the readers talked back. On January 12, 1960, a letter appeared (in the magazine's second issue) from one who wondered why *Reporter* had to give space to a "writer of swear words." His connection to the public also faltered when he published an article he later called "exquisitely political" against the powers that were. He did not help his publisher's prospects: *Reporter* lasted a single year after Pasolini stopped publishing there, its pioneering mix of movie gossip and tales of the House of Savoy in exile taken up, expanded, and improved upon by mass publishers with deeper pockets.

In March he went to Milan and Turin with Moravia for lecture-debates on "The Novel, Language and Dialect," sponsored by Left-affiliated ACI, the Associazione Culturale Italiano. He postponed visiting the literature students of a friend at Pavia but raced to Ravenna for a poetry reading and then returned to Rome "working in the train," as he told his host.

*Vie nuove* now functioned as diary-notebook, offering a way to multiply his public effect: He would, for example, deliver a talk on the novel, then return to Rome to write about what the audience said, what he thought further. Thus he expanded his ideas—sometimes retracted, always refined.

He worked at home in the morning. Susanna made sure no telephone calls interrupted those hours and that he was left with the tape-recorder into which he dictated his column, his polemics, against a background of Bach or Vivaldi on the phonograph. He produced almost feverishly, at a staggering pace.

The attention his enormous output brought made enemies, not only friends and admirers. On October 20 *Vita* condemned even as it understood: "The volume *Passione e ideologia* by Pier Paolo Pasolini has been received with an uncommon and unexpected chill. The reasons are many, starting with the excessive clamor surrounding his gestures as a *ragazzo di vita,* increasingly identifying himself more and more with his characters."

The book of critical essays on the writing of his time opened with two "panoramic studies" that solidified his stature as a scholar of Italian poetry in dialect. One reviewed the output of this century; the other literally moved systematically down the Peninsula, offering both a history of studies in the field and his own research. The essays are heavily footnoted, classic literary history, substantial evidence for those who claim that here Pasolini showed himself a unique case among his contemporaries of the artist-as-scholar. In the last months of his life, he opened correspondence with publisher Giulio Einaudi about returning to the field; a research assistant was hired to collect new material in, and about, the dialects, so that Pasolini could write another such study. He wanted to take up where he had left off twenty years before, with *Poesie dialettale del Novecento* (Twentieth-century Italian poetry in dialect) and the *Canzoniere italiano; antologia della poesie popolare* (Italian poems: an anthology of popular poetry).

The collection's second part—"From Pascoli to the Neo-Experimentalists"—brought together his essays on Italian poetry and prose of the years 1951–1958, the work of "his" generation: He now published his 1952 essay on the poet Clemente, who wrote in Abruzzese; on Ciresse, who wrote in the dialect of the Molise; on Bertolucci and Caproni, Leonetti and Betocchi. He surveyed what he called *nostra geografia letteraria* (our literary geography), a poet and prose narrator on his fellow writers, almost always his friends. The "world of literary culture" sat around one table in his mind, its chairs held by those he saw and talked with, thought about, and wrote of every day. They are all here, in the docket: Moravia, Morante, Banti, Longhi, Contini, Bertolucci, Penna, Leonetti, Roversi, Fortini, Gadda, Betocchi, Zanzotto, Bassani, the critics he admired—Citati, De Robertis, Debenedetti.

By December 1956 he was so well connected as to be able to open a piece (on the state of Italian verse at mid-decade): "Several evenings ago, Gadda . . . timid and full of goodwill, asked me, 'If one wanted to come up to date with poetry, let's say, how many volumes, more or less, do you think one would have to get hold of?' " Years later he was still analyzing Gadda's work, trying to explain why it was—professionally, as a writer—that "I had, and have, a great love for Gadda." [49]

Respectfully enough in *Passione e ideologia* (the writer and critic had to have both passion and ideology, he argued), Pasolini confronts his elders. As for his contemporaries and juniors, having first instructed them just as thirty years before—"One should never sacrifice one word for another"—now as then he was their partisan promoter. The loving schoolmaster, bonded with his students in the passionate search for what he called sincerity and others called poetry, fought the world to make it appreciate his charges.

Unlike his late book reviews of 1972–1974, his "I" is kept controlled here; religion and psychoanalysis came to saturate his critical work only a decade later, along with a certain cultivated exhibitionism and taste for provocation.

Seen within the long arc of his criticism, the book's tone is calm, what one critic called "a unique moment, to be considered exceptional" of "equilibrium between participation and historicity." Pasolini is not yet the militant for whom literature is only one means for making politics, not yet the writer unashamed to put himself always at center stage. It was in the course of the new decade just dawned that he moved into opposition *(contro corrente)* to the two fundamental crises of Italian culture: the so-called *neoavanguardia* and *il '68*. [50]

# 17

*I love life so ferociously, so desperately, that it cannot come out well: I mean the physical facts of life, the sun, the grass, youth: and it is a vice much more terrible than cocaine, costs me nothing and exists in boundless supply, without limits: and I devour, I devour . . . how it will end, I do not know. . . .*

—*Pier Paolo Pasolini*, Lettere, II (1955–1975)

# *MAMMA ROMA,* THE GOLDEN BULLET OF BERNARDINO DE SANTIS, BLASPHEMY

After several postponements, Pasolini's via di Panico trial opened November 16, 1961—the same week as *Accattone.* How useful it was for the press version of life-imitates-art when he told the judge, "I was taking a drive to gather impressions about a neighborhood that I decided to use as background for a literary work I had to write." He insisted on telling the truth about himself, whatever the cost— just as he had warned Silvana Mauri he would do. It hardly mattered that in July 1963 an appellate court absolved him absolutely, holding that not only had no crime been committed but no brawl had occurred. Once again the verdict of "insufficient evidence" was enough to constitute guilt in the less meticulous tribunal of public opinion.

He wrote in his *Vie nuove* column:

> This is an evil which gives him whom it strikes a deep pain [or sadness, *un profondo dolore*]: it gives a sense of a world of total incomprehension, in which it is useless to speak, become passionate, discuss; it gives one a sense of a society in which in order to survive, one cannot but be evil . . . answer evil [*cattiveria*] with evil . . . Certainly that [price] which I must pay is especially heavy, and sometimes it gives me a real sense of desperation. . . .[1]

The last thing Pasolini now needed was more trouble.

On November 18 he was at work with his friend Sergio Citti on the script for a second film, to be called *Mamma Roma*. The two spent the morning working at the house of Elsa de Giorgi at San Felice Circeo, south of Rome. After lunch Pasolini called a break, put a tan jacket over his shoulders, and drove off alone toward the sand dunes of Sabaudia. Citti did not ask his friend where he was headed; in the quarter decade of their friendship, such things and silence about them were understood.

The version of the boy whom Pasolini met, Bernardino de Santis, was that a man had entered the modest bar attached to the gas station where he was working at about three-thirty, ordered and drunk a Coca-Cola, and started asking "strange questions." In the police report he filed the next day[2] De Santis swore under oath that the visitor had first slowly drawn on black gloves, then pulled out a black pistol, and loaded it with "a bullet made of gold." "If you move, I'll shoot you," he is supposed to have said. De Santis also swore that the man locked the door, closed the shutters of a glass door, and held the gun to his throat.

Then, the boy told the police that the stranger tried to force open a drawer of the cash register with his left hand. Before he could steal the two thousand lire inside, De Santis grabbed a knife off the bar and struck the man's hand. Zorro-like, the assailant said, "We two shall meet again," then fled.

Continuing, he claimed that when he saw Pasolini's Alfa Giulietta on a street in San Felice the next day, he "decided" this was the man who had threatened him, and he went to the police.

The atmosphere that surrounded Pasolini was such that no one laughed at the nineteen-year-old's official *denuncia*. On the contrary, a warrant was issued, and Pasolini's house and car were searched on November 22. In response to police questioning, Pier Paolo said he had entered the bar, drunk a Coke, and asked some questions to which he got scant answers. Right after, he returned to San Felice Circeo.

As always, the poet wrote his version of the events. He had gone driving "in the dry sun" and come to "a house standing alone in the sun."

> There was inside a grim boy.
> wearing, I seem to recall, a smock, his hair
> long like a woman's,
> his skin pale and taut, a certain mad innocence in
> his eyes like a stubborn saint, like a son who
> wants to be equal to his worthy mother.

He claims to have sensed that De Santis was unbalanced, even to the point of delusion:

> In practice, I saw at once, a poor lunatic,
> whose ignorance gave him traditional certainties,
> transforming his cadaverous neurosis into the
> rigor
> of an obedient son identified with the fathers.
> What's your name, what do you do, do you go dancing,
> have you a girl friend,
> do you earn enough money,
> these were the subjects with which I drew back
> like a dry fish
> from the first impulse of my old afternoon siesta
> lust.[3]

The press lapped it up, not bothering with boring questions such as "Did Pasolini possess a gun?" or "Did De Santis have a history of mental illness?" On November 30 Rome's *Il tempo* headlined: "Sensational Inquiry by the *Carabinieri* into a Disquieting Episode" and "Pier Paolo Pasolini Detained for Attempted Robbery of a Gas Station Attendant" and (in subhead) "The Writer Accused of the Crime by a Worker Has Denied the Charge But Admitted to Other Details—But the Inquiry Concluded with Binding Him Over to the Judicial Authorities."

Unable to resist the temptation, the paper ran with its story a still from *Il gobbo* (The hunchback of Rome), a 1960 potboiler in which

Pier Paolo, as a joke shared with his friend director Carlo Lizzani, played the bit-part of a Mexican bandit named Leandro 'er Monaco (roughly, Leander the monk). Pier Paolo appeared in the movie's poster—and in *Il tempo*—wearing a shirt open to the waist over a strap-shouldered undershirt, a heavy medallion around his neck, an equally heavy ring on his left hand and a massive bracelet bearing some sort of charm or amulet. Two women lurk behind him, wary and frightened. A young man stands to one side, glancing at Pasolini sideways, awed at the toughness of his gang leader's stance. Pasolini wears a kerchief and black gloves; his stare is menacing and he brandishes a machine gun.

*Il tempo*'s account passed along De Santis' version as fact. "Pasolini's strange carryings-on are beginning to be tiresome," its editors wrote. "Upstanding people . . . ask themselves how it is possible to allow free circulation to people who have demonstrated utmost contempt for common morality and law." The far-Right *Il borghese* asked, "Why is Pasolini still free and at large?"

One enterprising rag found a photo of Pasolini pumping gas at a Paris station. It appeared over the caption: "The gas station attendant is smiling at the photographer: maybe he doesn't know anything about his customer."

The press on the Left responded: Surely such charges against anyone else would have been dropped at the prosecutor's level. Why in the world would the Right-wing press think one with "the vulgar symbol of his wealth, his Giulietta" would try to steal two thousand lire? It was absurd to think he toted any weapon more dangerous than his portable Olivetti, or even to imagine that he knew how to load a pistol. Was this not one more example of an unholy alliance between the conservative press and the judiciary out to hound the enemies of the Christian Democrats' regime?

The Communist weekly *Rinascita*, always careful to temper its praise of his work with concerns about his lack of ideological conformity, wrote that Pasolini was subject to "real persecution." It allowed that he seemed this time really to be the victim of an atmosphere of "the shameful two-faced nature of bourgeois morality." By raising the debate to the level of ideology, they avoided having to address the truth or falsehood of the charges.

Pasolini was then a candidate for the Etna-Taormina poetry prize. His name was withdrawn, according to the publication *La notte*, after a raging battle among the jurors, because he was "a personality of the *cronaca nera*" [the "black chronicles" of the press], the reports of crime and scandal.

The MSI put its daily on the case. *Il secolo d'Italia* labeled Pasolini a "pornographer" working "to lower the country to the state where it is ripe for a takeover by the social Communists." That same evening a band of young toughs, mostly MSI members, assaulted the audience at the Quattro Fontane cinema where Paolo Heusch's film based on *Una vita violenta* was showing.

For seven months, "the Circeo holdup," as it was called, made copy. It seemed the time to put Pasolini definitively in his place. Lawyers for the prosecution found money to hire a professor of psychology at the University of Rome, Aldo Semerari. His report, "Psychiatric Notes . . . on the Writer Pier Paolo Pasolini" was dated June 21, 1962, and released a few days before sentencing.

Pasolini's chief lawyer, Francesco Carnelutti, did not object to Semerari's "study" being put into evidence. But the court refused to allow it; the doctor had never seen the subject. So, the unidentified promoters of the document went directly to public opinion. An underlined heading virtually begged that the press run the plant: "International Medical Press [*Stampa Internazionale Medica*]. Documentation for all editors-in-chief: reserved, not for publication."

Across three single-space type-written pages of so-called psychiatric notes, Semerari wonders why it is that a successful writer and film director would go to so much risk for two thousand lire. He answers that Pasolini shows the symptoms of "a developing pathological process, or at least an alteration in the congenital or acquired personality." But something more, he is "an instinctual psychopath, he is a sexual deviant, a homophile in the most absolute sense of the word." Pasolini has been accused of an insane act.

Unrestrained by civil libertarianism and not bothered with even the briefest encounter with Pasolini (Semerari was paid to work from news clippings and gossip), the psychiatrist sailed ahead. Pasolini is homosexual—itself "a mental infirmity"; his present crime is simply an inevitable symptom. Exhibitionist because a Communist, Communist because crazy, crazy because homosexual, and thus criminal.

> Well, then, if we analyze the criminal act with which Pasolini is charged in light of these considerations, we shall come to ask ourselves . . . at least apparently, is this not a case of a behavioral disturbance provoked by a pathological cause?[4]

Having read the file on the mutual masturbation in the fields at Ramuscello in 1949, Dr. Semerari was ready for diagnosis: Pasolini suffered "skeptophilia"—properly termed "scopophilia"—sexual pleasure derived from looking, voyeurism. The subject was, he continued, "a highly insecure and suggestible personality." The conclusion: "There is at issue here a socially dangerous person."[5] That Italian summer, Semerari's blithe references to "behavioral disturbances caused by pathological causes" were taken seriously, at least by a substantial portion of the most popular press, which passed the stuff along to readers unchallenged.

The circus ran its course: Photos of Pasolini wearing a white suit in the defendant's chair at Latina appeared in all the newspapers. De Santis' lawyer demanded that the records from Ramuscello be entered in the transcript. He also asked that *Una vita violenta* be read into the record: Three gas station holdups are recounted in its pages. A second lawyer for the prosecution, Valerio Veronese, moved that documents from Pasolini's trials for the Anzio incident and via di Panico be entered as part of the record.

The presiding magistrate asked Pasolini, "Why did you ask so many questions of De Santis?" The answer, again: "Because I was thinking about making a movie in that place, and these are the sorts of questions I always ask people to see their reactions." He asked the accusing boy: "Perhaps Pasolini made some proposition of which you were ashamed?" "No, he made no sexual suggestions, not of any type." Slowly, it emerged that De Santis resented being queried about his girl friend and his motorcycle, and had invented the rest.

That week Pasolini wrote in his *Vie nuove* column, "Nothing is more contrary to my nature than is violence," and continued:

> The only serious analysis to come to, the one made with friends, is this: the middle-class Italian is utterly without psychological insight. His psychology is one of miracle . . . one needs only hear the curses pronounced by Bernardo de Santis' lawyers about my "psychology." False, ridiculous, product of a culture malodorous as an old copy of the *Domenica del corriere* [a lowbrow Sunday supplement]. I describe violence, thus I must be violent. Look at this, one ought to redden even at the mere stating of such nonsense . . . Because a middle-class Italian does not possess, on his own, the tools needed to understand a soul: all of this has been told him, imposed, suggested, consecrated. From the first, he renounces his right to come to an autonomous judgment; any exterior judgment, one not even proved, only suspected, overturns his previously arrived at opinion . . . nothing at all suffices: in my case, a madman who says I acted like a nut.[6]

The sentence avoided the issue of what happened between the two. Its hypothesis: Pasolini was thinking about a movie and had simulated a robbery to see how someone involved in it would react. The tribunal reduced the charge of attempted robbery with a weapon to "threatening with a firearm."[7] Its sentence: two weeks in jail for robbery and five days more for illegally carrying a pistol (never found), and a ten thousand lire fine for failing to register the gun; sentence suspended, pending appeals.

The matter dragged on another six years. After a first appeal, the case went to Italy's Supreme Court. In 1968 Pasolini was not acquitted unconditionally but absolved on only technical grounds— once again, as before and after, "insufficiency of evidence."

In March 1965 Pasolini published some lines about the incident in *L'espresso:* "One day, a crazy man accused me of having robbed (with black gloves and cap; golden bullets in the pistol). . . ." Incensed, De Santis sued for defamation, setting off a new round of legal actions and press coverage. Only on January 31, 1967, did a court definitively dismiss the case. Association with Pasolini, no matter how trumped up, was a guaranteed vehicle into the press, a moment's limelight.

After the initial sentence, Moravia wrote:

> The judges realized that what De Santis was saying was pure madness, but they wanted to deliver a verdict of condemnation anyway, for the simple reason that Pier Paolo is a homosexual. In Italy there is no article of the legal code that views homosexuality as a crime. Therefore, they have contrived a loophole. It's a bizarre loophole, but for them it's enough.[8]

Years later De Santis ended up in a lunatic asylum. The damage was done: Pasolini was not only fair game but the favored target, a lightning rod in the battles over freedom of expression and civil liberties being waged between Left and Right. Following the trial, RAI (the DC-controlled State television system) summarily cut Pasolini from the series "Encounters with Poets" on the grounds that they could not interview someone against whom legal actions were pending. The Holy Office had taken under advisement whether Pasolini's works ought to be placed on the Index.

Sometime that year he completed a long poem entitled "Reality." All the fury he felt in the docket, where he remained silent and answered diplomatically, emerged.

Of his Latina judges:

> Ah, I don't know how to hate: and so I know
> I can't describe them with the ferocity necessary

to poetry. I'll speak only with pity of that
Calabrian face, with features both of
a child and a skull, who uses dialect

with the humble, scholastic language of the
grand . . .
who was listening carefully, humanely
and meanwhile, within his unspoken, unspeakable

interior forums, was hatching his plan
of the timid whom fear makes ruthless.
At his side are two other easily recognizable
faces,

faces from the street or a crowded bar,
weak, barely healthy faces of
the prematurely old, the jaundiced,

the bourgeois from whom no salt tears pour,
though not at all ignoble, no,
not at all lacking human features,

in the pungent black of their eyes, in the pallor
of foreheads tortured by the first
ferocious signs of aging . . . A fourth envoy of the
Lord

—married, surely; surely protected by a circle
of respectable colleagues in his provincial
town—curdled in the sigh of someone

with a bad stomach or weak heart—was sitting
alone on an isolated bench, as though preparing
for a premeditated engagement.

He turned to the State's prosecutor:

And in front of these, the champion: who sold
himself body and soul to the devil.
Classic character! I'd seen his face

some months earlier, and it had looked different:
the peasant face of a coarse young
man, balding, colorless,

but with a professional dignity.
Now a blush was deforming him,
like an old red scab

on his skin. The depraved light
in his eyes was that of the guilty.
His hate for what I stood for was hate

for the object of that guilt, that is,
hate for his conscience.
He wasn't dishonest enough. His imagination

wasn't big enough to conceive of an experience
of ignorance and blackmail.

The jeremiad to his condemners continued:

. . . To you it will be said:
"You don't count, you're the symbols
of millions of men, of a society."

And it—not you, its automatons—condemns me.
Well then, I'm content to be a monster. . . .

You, men of form—humble because
mediocre, obsequious because afraid—
you are people: let us consummate, you and I,

our relationship—in you, of arid hate,
in me, of knowledge. But about the society
of which you are the inexpressive rhapsodists.

I have something quite different to say: not as a
Marxist
anymore, or, perhaps yes for this moment only
—since the rapture of the Authors

of the Apocalypse is mythified
in a timeless fire: My loves—
I'll shout—are a terrible weapon;

why don't I use it? Nothing's more terrible
than being different. Exposed every moment
—shouted ceaselessly—incessant

exception—madness unrestrained
like a fire—contradiction
in which all justice is desecrated.

"Oh, blacks, Jews, poor hosts
of the marked and different, born from
innocent wombs into sterile

springtimes, of worms and serpents,
horrendous without their knowing, condemned
to be atrociously meek, childishly violent,

hate! tear apart the world of well-born men!
Only a bloodbath can save the world
from its bourgeois dreams, certain

to make it more and more unreal!
Only a revolution that slaughters
these dead men can deconsecrate their evil!"

This is what a prophet would shout who doesn't
have
the strength to kill a fly—whose strength
lies in his degrading difference.

Only when this has been said, or shouted,
will my fate be able to free itself,
and begin my discourse on reality. . . ."[9]

The hysteria engendered by the series of trials in these years worked as "open sesame" for a lunatic fringe waiting just offstage. In February 1962 a former Christian Democratic deputy from the south named Salvatore Pagliuca filed suit for defamation. One of the characters in *Accattone*—"with sparkling teeth, like a ferocious wolf"—is named Pagliuca. The ex-*onorevole* charged that the thief, pimp, and layabout (who bore his name) was "a person of the low-life [*malavita*], an exploiting thief of prostitutes and head of a group of ne'er-do-wells. . . ."[10]

Convinced his friends and constituents might think the screen character modeled on himself, the real Pagliuca demanded a change in the soundtrack so as to eliminate his name, and compensation. A court heard him out: The sixty-seven-year-old lawyer (the character in the film is plainly well under thirty) furnished letters sent him by prominent politicians, explained that he was a veteran of the First World War, the widowered father of eleven children. He allowed as how Pasolini's private life was best not discussed "out of generosity." Pagliuca claimed his bid for the Senate in 1963 was unsuccessful because of the ridicule Pasolini had knowingly heaped on him, that many had come to his defense: "numerous telegrams sent from all parts of Italy and abroad from personalities in the worlds of politics, the military, education, religion, intellectual circles, in addition to others from poor workers emigrated to the United States, Argentina, Canada, Switzerland, Norway, Sweden, France, Greece, and so on."

He further sought damages for diabetes he contended was brought on by seeing the film *Accattone*. His complaint alleged, "The projection of *Accattone* and the press propaganda in Italy and abroad so upset him and prostrated him to such a point that he became the victim of a nervous disorder and neglected both his professional affairs and his family."

In February 1965 the court declined to order moral damages. That the surname is a common one in certain parts of central and southern Italy (twenty-one in the Naples telephone directory, twenty-five in Rome) did not matter: Despite a holding that "no possibility exists" of confusing the film's character with the plaintiff, Bini was nevertheless ordered to excise the name from the soundtrack and pay compensatory damages.

Three months later a Roman named Di Marco decided he too had been the model for a young thug in *Ragazzi di vita*. He ultimately withdrew his nuisance suit, but editorals appeared defending his position. Why, they asked, could Pasolini not make his art without disturbing the lives of upstanding citizens?

As always, Susanna (who loved without condition) was the reason for going on. He tried to shield her from the news, maintain life as it had always been for the two of them. In 1959—before the triple blows of the via di Panico, Anzio, and Circeo trials—in an appendix to the poem "The Religion of My Time," entitled "A Light," he wrote:

> The house is filled with her frail
> childlike limbs and her labors;
> even at night, as she weeps, dry weeping
>
> covers everything; and such a terrible ancient
> pity grips my heart, returning home,
> I could scream, I could take my life.
>
> Everything all around her ferociously dies
> but the good within her doesn't die
> and she doesn't know how much her humble love
> —poor sweet little bones I love—
> by comparison makes me almost die
> of grief and shame, how much her
>
> anguish'ed gestures, her sighing
> in the silence of our kitchen,
> can make me seem impure and cowardly . . .[11]

The only solution was in death, when he and Susanna would be buried at Casarsa, "together . . . in that poor meadow crowded with gray stones."

In fact, a waterpump at the Casarsa burying ground provides water for those who come bearing flowers. The poet's reverie took him there, with Susanna, to visit Guido's grave.

> Butterflies and other insects swarm
> till late September, the season
> when we go back there where passion

keeps alive the other son's
bones in icy peacetime;
every afternoon she comes

to arrange her flowers, while all around her
all is still, and one senses only her grief;
she cleans the stone he sleeps anxiously under,

then goes away, and in the silence that walls
and furrows immediately retrieve

  . . .

            . . . Soon
we too, sweet survivor, will be

lost at the bottom of this
cool plot of land. . . .[12]

Charged with a little, in poetry Pasolini confessed to everything. Asked to recant and repent a bit, he seized the chance to summon all his forty years into a docket of his own fashioning. He was indeed guilty, but innocent, and judged by a wrathful taskmaster the likes of which an Italian judiciary could never imagine.

Oh practical end of my poetry!
Because of you I can't overcome
the naiveté that shrivels my prestige;

because of you, my tongue cracks with
anxiety, which I have to smother with talk.
I search my heart only for what's there.

To this I'm reduced: when I write
poetry, it's to defend myself, to fight,
compromising myself, renouncing

all my ancient dignity; thus my defenseless
elegaic heart / comes
to shame me; and tired, though alive,

my words reveal the fantasy
of the son who'll never be the father . . .
Meanwhile, one by one, I lost my poet

comrades with their naked wind-dried faces,
sacred goats like stern-faced
Po Valley fathers, in whose thin

ranks only pure relations of
passion and thought matter.
Carried along by the obscure events

of my life! Oh, to start again from scratch!
Alone like a cadaver in his grave!

His judges could never understand:

. . .

In reality I'm the boy, they're
the adults. I who by excess of my presence

have never crossed the border between love
for life and life . . .
I gloomy with love, and all around me, the chorus

of the happy, for whom reality's a friend.[13]

. . . .

He fought back by living and working. *Mamma Roma* would have
the success denied *Accattone* thanks to Anna Magnani, a faded star
but a draw still, known since her role as Pina, the woman shot by
the Nazis in Rossellini's *Roma, città aperta* in 1945. Again, the
*borgata,* and again people were taken off the street and cast this time
in a tighter plot.

Magnani had been in the audience at the Venice premiere of *Accattone* and immediately afterward told Bini that she wanted to work
with that director, whoever he was. Despite her troubles (or thanks
to their widespread publicity), her name was automatic box office.
For two years she had turned down every script proposed to her; she
wanted to work with artists, not just cinema professionals. Pasolini
immediately started thinking about a character he could build around
her. The story was ready in three weeks and shooting started on
April 9, 1962.

Pasolini kept a diary during filming, something that would have
suited his attitude even without having been told a market would
welcome such a document. Rizzoli published it as an extended addition to the book of the script. When a day's filming was frustrated
by bad weather, Pasolini wrote about his technique, a self-analysis
of style.

I think that the most serious defect of film criticism is its lacking of a taste
for philology.

Its fault lies in its being

all sensibility, with a tossed-in idealism, long ago left behind in the university and outside it as well by twenty or thirty years.[14]

He wants the soft, emotive criticism to toughen its terms of discourse. He is annoyed at film analysis that treats the medium as "mythic, never historic." And the Marxists, in love with history, are too "schematic." He wrote that the critics of *Accattone* "all failed" because they do not have "a philological penentration of the script as poetry," despite the fact that much of what was written was "often intelligent, very beautiful, very insightful." In the absence of such a critical framework, he would soon invent one.

His own remarks on filmmaking reveal a talent of excruciating self-consciousness, a mind divided between creator and critic, not at all a "naïf" behind the camera. Where, he wondered "out loud" were the critics who cared about what mattered to him?

> *Accattone* does not offer many technical usages commonly found . . . there never is a frame, whether a close-up or otherwise, in which you see someone from the rear or from the side; you never see anyone walk on the scene and then exit it; there is never any use of the dolly [he first uses it in *Mamma Roma*] . . . with its sinuous movements . . . impressionistic. Close-ups of profiles are extremely rare and when they exist, they are in motion. And along these lines there is an infinity of other technical details of this sort. Now, for all this there is an explanation. But an explanation presupposes some sort of analytic framework, a philological framework.
>
> For me, all these characteristics which I have listed so quickly are due to the fact that my cinematic taste does not have its origins in cinema but in the figurative. That which I carry in my head as vision, as a visual field, are the frescoes of Masaccio and of Giotto—the painters I love most along with certain mannerists (for example, Pontormo).[15]

*Mamma Roma*'s subject is survival and fighting back rather than defeat and resignation. Magnani plays the sort of character called "indomitable," she is absolutely self-sacrificing and obsessed. Her *borgata*'s Mother Courage not so much resents the rich as ignores them. Her proletarian life is a defiance of bourgeois morality, centered on a single goal: to make a better life than she has had for her son, Ettore, the boy she mothered by a pimp named Carmine. The issue: Will social reality allow her to push him up and out of the universe into which he has been born? Is there "progress" for the marginal?

A whore by profession, she gives that up to make a proper home for the teenager of sixteen whom she has worked to bring out of the slum of Guidonia. She takes up working at a fruit and vegetable stand in the open-air market; the scene of her cries to customers is the classic Magnani role, verging on cliché.

Ettore was played by a boy—not an actor—named Ettore Garofolo. Pasolini wrote, "I found him the other night and it was beautiful, like finding the last verse, the most important, of a poem, like finding a perfect rhyme."[16]

Mamma Roma's triumph in achieving a "respectable life" comes with a new apartment in a public housing high-rise. She wants him to live among *i signori* (gentlefolk) not in districts like Ponte Mammolo and Rebibbia. She brings Ettore to their new, hard-won home like a prince to his palace. Leaving all embarrassment at Oedipal feeling where it belongs—with the repressed middle class—mother and son dance a tango to a record, played on the new player she has bought him. As they dance (for Pasolini repeatedly the image of pure felicity), her face reflects total happiness, as though stolen from a cruel reality that happened to look away only for a moment. It cannot last. Lest the scene be too serious, Pasolini lets Magnani lose her footing: Mother and son fall on the floor, laughing. Slapstick pushes sentimental tenderness even higher, to pathos.

Everything seems to be improving until pimp Carmine (Franco Citti) appears and demands 200,000 lire as the price of keeping Mamma Roma's secret from her son. Meanwhile, Ettore meets Bruna (played by Silvana Corsini—Maddalena in *Accattone*). But "Mamma" disapproves; the girl's origins are too humble. "Besides," she says, "at your age the only woman you need is your mother." Ettore is drawn to the life of the *ragazzi di vita* and starts to go bad. He sells his mother's tango records in the marketplace and buys his girl friend a chain with a medallion of the Madonna.

Frantic, "Mamma" Magnani turns to the traditional source of wisdom, a local priest (played by Paolo Volponi) who lectures her on the duties of motherhood. He offers to help Ettore get work as a mechanic, but the boy has no training. Bruna betrays him and goes off with another *ragazzo*.

Mamma hatches a plot to force Ettore into the sort of "clean work" she wants for him. With fellow hooker Biancafiore (literally, "white flower") she entraps a restaurant owner into a compromising situation: Down to his underwear, he succumbs to their blackmail. If he will hire her son to work in his pizzeria; in exchange, his wife need never know of that evening's peccadillo. Magnani turns the hypocritical morality of the restaurateur on its head: His petit bourgeois morality will help her catapult her son out of the proletariat and into the class to which her buffoon victim belongs.

With her street earnings, she buys Ettore what he wants most in the world, a motorcycle, and he takes her for a ride. The two of them laugh like children: Mother and son are alone, together, and happy. With Biancafiore, she spies on his first day at work and is ecstatic seeing him in a white apron, serving pizzas. To watch unseen, she lurks outside, out of sight lest her giant black leather handbag—the prostitute's constant companion—embarrass him. She literally cheers him on as she weeps tears of joy, beams the full-wattage Magnani smile.

But the Furies always collect their due: Carmine appears, demanding she give up her market pushcart and resume life on the streets. They argue, Magnani draws a knife and threatens to kill him, which forces him to leave.

Despite all her efforts, Ettore is drawn to the excitement of petty crime. She announces, with all the yearning of the *petite bourgeoisie* that looks upward for its models: "I don't want him to be some sort of comrade." She offers to give him money, but he rejects it, and her, saying, "I earn my own." Like Tommaso (also perhaps "punished" in the same way, inevitably) he falls ill. We see him in the bed of a prison hospital, where he has been charged with stealing another patient's radio.

Desperate for money, "Mamma Roma" returns to plying her trade, but the words of her priest, calling her to responsibility, echo in her mind. Pasolini does not make the Church ridiculous, and although the priest is rather pedantic and dry, his message is not lampooned. On the contrary, because Mamma Roma tries to follow his counsel, she appears more noble, a heroine; Pasolini condemns her not to farce but to tragedy.

She sells herself for Ettore's "better life," but he throws it away. Despite her efforts, both mother and son are dragged down by forces they cannot control. Pasolini delivers Gramscian "national-popular" cinema, and unashamedly so.

When Ettore learns the truth about his mother (the agent who innocently but inevitably transmits it, as in Greek drama, is Bruna), he throws himself into crime. Traumatized by the confrontation with what he sees as hypocrisy, Ettore destroys what his mother has built: himself. Carmine, played as unleavened evil, has the last laugh.

If *Accattone* is Pasolini's *borgata* as a sealed, airless, and airtight system whose inhabitants must die when their values collapse on contact with a harsher, outside reality, then *Mamma Roma* is its coda: Any of the subproletarian people who try to struggle up and out will be pulled, or pushed, back and under. Accattone never imagines a way out; for Mamma Roma, that road exists but has been mined by "the system," whose front-man is Carmine.

Ettore ends up delirious, strapped to his hospital bed. His situation was predictable from the start, but Pasolini builds the tragedy so skillfully that the stolen radio seems as ghastly a misstep of Fate as Friar Lawrence's mistaking Juliet's poison for an innocent sleeping potion. Only his death and his mother's grief will bring catharsis. The closing action transpires against a background of Vivaldi, which Pasolini called "much more Italian [than Bach] . . . based on popular music, and so the contamination is much less violent and shocking." [17]

Ettore in hospital is laid out as though on a cross. Pasolini trains the camera on his feet, the body rendered in extreme foreshortening. The critics, alerted to Pasolini's art-historical proclivities, pointed out the similarity between these frames and Mantegna's painting *The Dead Christ* in the Pinacoteca di Brera, Milan: feet forward, body ashen, laid on a table. Pasolini claimed to be disgusted at the simplistic understanding given his figurative "quotation." That October he publicly addressed Roberto Longhi, to whom he had dedicated the film, in his *Vie nuove* column:

> Ah Longhi, step in, explain how it is not enough to put a foreshortened figure in the foreground and talk about the influence of Mantegna! But don't these critics have eyes? Don't they see that basic black and white and how strongly it evokes a *chiaroscuro* in that gray cell where Ettore (white T-shirt, dark face) is laid out . . . really inspired by painters working several decades before Mantegna? [18]

So much for critics who dared to praise him with insufficient erudition. As though unable not to remind everyone that he is the brightest boy in the class, he insists that being properly understood is more important than being liked.

Ettore calls for his mother, who has no idea where he is. He dies alone in prison, without Tommaso's facile deathbed conversion to ideology. For Accattone, death was liberation; for Ettore (as for Tommaso) it is condemnation. Pasolini's message is unvarnished: Only a poor kid from the wrong neighborhood could find himself in an Italian jail awaiting trial and end up dead. When people from a peasant culture are uprooted and come into the culture of the bourgeois city— a place they cannot enter or understand and where they are neither welcome nor at home—they die.

Magnani spends the night Ettore dies worrying and talks to herself as she breakfasts on bread and milk. She is behind her vegetable stand in the market when news reaches her that Ettore has died in prison hospital. At the news she launches an animal howl: Crying "Ettore, Ettore," she first "falls into the arms of the two people who have brought her the news" and then "like a crazy woman, starts running through the streets." According to Pasolini's script, she runs from the market, which "appears dark, like a stormy sea" into "dazzling sunlight, like a crazed horse."

Reaching her apartment in the Cecafumo project, a place (like Rebibbia) neither city nor country, she races to the room where she had danced with Ettore. She tears open the cupboards, grabbing the clothes she had bought him, symbols of her hope for his social integration and rise. Screaming, she presses them to her breast. Suddenly, she leaps up and races for the window and starts to throw herself out. Pasolini's camera is waiting outside, looking in that window so that she fills the frame, staring at the audience. Her friends (including actor Piero Morgia, whom Pasolini had used in *Accattone*) pin back her arms. "Finally, her cry bursts out . . . unexpected, useless, heart-rending."

The script as written but not shot called for her to bellow at the window, "*I responsabili! I responsabili!*" She wants not only mourning but justice. Someone is to blame. But the political angle was cut, leaving her final scream one of generic grief without an object to call to accounting. Pasolini kept it in the book version, published in July 1962.

So the film closes, the script noting, "Under her window, Rome stretches out, its buildings and its fields all smoky, opening immense and indifferent under the sun." [19]

The sun is patron-boss *(padrone)* and father *(padre)* of all in Pasolini's poetry, perhaps also patriarch Carlo Alberto. The sun sees all that the son does; it watches "indifferent" to suffering.


Nervousness in both director and star was inevitable; he had to match or beat the success of *Accattone* and she was in a difficult effort at comeback. Magnani was known as *la belva* ("the beast"), a wild animal on the set, determined to be boss. The press raised such a cry about inevitable clashes that she felt it necessary to issue a statement to the effect that she was sure that everything would go forward on the best of all possible terms, "since I have already arrived at a perfect understanding of the character I am to play with the writer-director." She announced that between her and Pier Paolo, there was "a relationship of cordiality and friendship the likes of which always happens between intelligent people who understand one another."

His shooting diary recounts an early (still happy) encounter with his leading lady. Magnani was waiting in one of the apartments the production had rented to serve as Mamma Roma's Cecafumo home:

> She wants to know if she can shoot the last scene—the one of the cry from the window—without a wig. [For the streetwalker scenes, she donned a bouffant hairpiece.] She wants it to be completely "her face." That's all she wanted to ask me. And she did it with a manner so childlike, so tentative that I was moved. She had understood perfectly my desire to have her seen genuinely this way—almost without make-up, her inner and true true face, in the moment the most tragic and sad of the film.
>
> This is a small example of how, after only a single day, and not more, of crisis, relations between me and Magnani went forward smoothly, clearly, with trust. The mutual incomprehension lasted two or three hours, not more. . . .
>
> I admit that the way I conceive of acting, even though I want it to be absolutely real, or rather realistic to the bottom, to the point of exasperation even—mine is completely contrary to every form of acting naturalism. I have no interest in so-called spontaneity, so-called naturalness; I am interested in pulling together, and then uniting, the phases of the feelings of the characters in their culminating moments, without those intermediate passages which require, and this is the point, spontaneity and naturalness. I am asking Magnani, who is used to sculpting her characters like a maker of monuments, of equestrian statues, to work instead like a jeweler, to say each line one at a time as though each were a tiny bit of gold. . . . This was, at first, embarrassing to me—who knows how to film in no other way—as it was to *la Magnani*, who was forced to compress into brief shots her impulse that would otherwise have expanded into a complete scene.

Later, when the film was finished, he was less enthusiastic about his star. He decided that his vision of the character had not been transmitted to *la Magnani*. Her fame had come by acting the one role the public wanted: herself. "She was not Mamma Roma," he wrote, "but she played it." He came to decide she was an actress and, as bad, of the wrong class:

> I wanted to explain the ambiguity of proletarian life with a superstructure over it of the *petite bourgeoisie*. This did not really come across, because Anna Magnani is a woman who was born and has lived the life of the *petite bourgeoisie* and then of an actress. . . .[20]

As his rapport with Magnani faltered, the newspapers were also reporting the "golden bullet" incident. He was nervous, not elated as he had been the first time out. "Circumstances" were preventing him from realizing his vision.

Franco Citti, who played the pimp Carmine, was arrested during the shooting and incarcerated in the *borgata* of Gordiani, northwest of Rome. The production was halted; costs mounted until his release. Bini decided both Citti and his character Carmine were expendable. He argued that the pimp could be a perceived threat, referred to but not seen and left at that.

Forced to choose between real *borgataro* Citti and businessman Bini, Pasolini chose Citti. He argued that his friend reminded him of a character in a story he had thought to write years before, one in which the hero has to fight a giant serpent.

> Franco Citti is one of those men who have to fight the giant serpent. His enormous vitality forces him into a constant battle against himself, toward a kind of life that is special, exceptional, out of the norm—something I perfectly well can understand. It is the fight against this vitality which those who fight only against a very small amount of vitality condemn. The nice people who pass their evenings in front of the television watching the ever so nicely ambiguous smiles of the presenters of the programs . . . are those who confront in themselves a vitality not much bigger than a worm, and so for them it is easy to condemn those who lose hours and hours of their days fighting against the sweet violence of temptation.

A film-diary entry:

> The idea of being without Franco Citti, that is without my new protagonist Carmine, in this moment has something shocking *("spaventoso")* about it. It is as though I had written pages of a novel or poetry and—while I was asleep or occupied with something else—a mob of people, vulgar, filthy, without awareness, ferocious, full of dismal militaristic ecstasy or that of students, were to come into my study and throw around my files, rummage around in my manuscripts, take pages and stamp on them, rip them apart, throw them away.[21]

Citti-Carmine remained. Unhappy with Magnani, Pasolini moved to raise Carmine to equal status, from secondary rank to male lead. In his scripted (but un-shot) version, Carmine tries to return to live with Mamma Roma, and when she moves to throw him out, he attacks her. They struggle to the point that he holds a knife to her neck. That was thought to be too strong, too real and was cut.

Producer and director encountered other problems. Critics on the Right had knocked *Accattone* for failing to present a picture of the progressing, healing Italy of the economic miracle then coming into sight. On the Left, hard-liners wondered about Citti's character (Vittorio) as they had with Tommaso: Why did this man live such a hell without coming to consciousness? Why did he act as though he were a helpless cog with a run of bad luck rather than seek the solidarity of the revolutionary workers to fight off the exploitation of the bourgeoisie? Where was the ideologically correct class analysis? What would they make of *Mamma Roma;* to the point, how is she going to take the death of Ettore? Pasolini's willingness to cut "The responsible!" suggested he was willing to compromise, that whatever ideology he talked, he accepted the "compromises" of commercial filmmaking. When she stares from her window, it is not to spit accusation at the guilty but rather (as he explained in the shooting diary) with "a silent stare between these two worlds so far apart, uncommunicating as though two different planets."

After the film's release, having undercut its strategy in the book, he hedged (or so purists thought) even further. He told *Filmcritica:*

> The theme of responsibility has three phases: individual responsibility, responsibility of an immediate environment and that of society. In the screenplay, all this was more explicit: naturally, later, when one is working, when one takes one's ideas and images into the concreteness of expression, certain things burn up, others alter. Thus the film is always something different from the screenplay.[22]

About 10:30 A.M. on May 3, unable to shoot because of rain, he wrote a reverie in his *Mamma Roma* diary:

> In the middle of this passage, in the morning sun, there was the sight of fields, completely covered with green: at one point which I would not be able to pick exactly, along the Appia Pignatelli, there was a wall completely covered in the densest green, completely interwoven, almost black but bathed in sunlight, with the violence of counterlight in such a way that every single leaf, in the middle of all this black, glistened as though it were made of metal. Above this wall there was another wall, in its turn covered with a vegetation equally dense, but because it was sloping, it was invested with another type of light such that there, all the leaves seemed to be metal.
>
> And above this wall covered with scintillating leaves, here is the top of a little wood, in another green, illuminated by another kind of light—smoky, foggy, dreamy.
>
> These layers of green, one laid on top of the other, each lit up in a different way, made me suddenly recall a spring from long ago when, in a light this unripened and a gathering of elements this ardent, I went with my family on an outing . . . of my very early youth . . . organized by my mother and my aunt exactly at the same hour, but in a countryside completely

different, a countryside of the Veneto, of the Venetan flatlands—precisely between Sacile to the foot of Monte Cavallo. We arrived in the midst of a sunshine very much like that of this morning. Hungry, we ate on the grass a sandwich the taste of which I have on my palate even now . . . we drank the orange drink which we bought in a village which for me was the capital of the world, far away now as though it were Africa . . . and in all this memory, brought on by the sight of the green hills along the Appia, there came into my mind my mother.

And I thought about this episode as one of the episodes of my mother's life, of the poor life of my mother; the precision, the concreteness, the neatness, the poverty, the absoluteness of tiny details which slowly, slowly added up to a life, and it mysteriously upset me. I found myself in a glade of Acqua Santa along the Appia Nuova, standing before an infinity of splendid green spread out everywhere, with tears on my eyes.[23]

Arriving at location, he finds "everything undone: the troupe spread all over by the rain, the marketplace all confused, gray, dripping."

Nothing is to be done. I feel a sense of anguish: the same one, exactly, that I feel when I see *Accattone* shown in re-runs, cut-up, violated, offered to a public that is unpredictable and paying no attention. This is the ephemera of the cinema; working in the cinema one has forebodings only of transitoriness and defeat.[24]

From the first, Magnani had complained that he was "always interrupting" her. His answer was along lines of "But, Anna, you are a great actress. Why do you need long scenes? You have no need for exaggerated effects. It is enough to frame your face and the goal is reached."

On a rainy, early May morning—he recorded the encounter and date meticulously—director and *diva* met to sort out their troubles. In his version—the only one later told—Pasolini manages both to give Magnani her due and to make her seem ridiculous:

I sense in the air a momentous encounter. There is the problem of the shots we made yesterday, pieces of the film which, for different reasons, upset both of us.

I: "Let's talk about that scene, Anna. That scene in which you laugh and ask your son, 'Isn't it lovely, this motor scooter I bought for you? Is it what you wanted?' That laugh. Talk to me about that laugh."

Anna: "That laugh. You know better than I do that to render that laugh in the spirit you intended for it, it can be executed in so many different ways. It can come before [the words], it can come after, it can come early or late.

"I am something extremely fragile. There was a moment when we started shooting the scene and you shouted 'Laugh. Laugh, Anna' and I made an idiotic laugh. It seems to me that my laugh in that scene is false, and since it did not come to me spontaneously—I think you agree with me on that—well, you made me lose the balance of the rest of the line. I acted badly, yes, acted badly, and since they say I am a used-up actress, an old she-wolf . . .

I: "On the question of whether the scene went badly, on that we are agreed. But what I want to bring to your attention, not exactly in relation to this scene but in relation to others, is this: when I say something like 'Laugh, laugh' while you are speaking lines, my breaking in like that from outside, is a kind of injection of expressivity, it is a habit which I acquired from when I directed actors just taken off the street, people I had to jolt like that just when they expected it least, almost as a trick. Now you must please understand and forgive my interventions and take them for what they are, only a habit."

Anna: "But of course, and that's why we talk about it with so much gentleness and friendship. I understand that you have worked with actors that you take and mold like so much raw material. They, even though they have their native intelligence, are robots in your hands. Now, I am not a robot, I have had your script in my hands for some three months, I have read it at least four times, I have analyzed it down to the smallest states of mind, its most important, its most subtle.

"Now, as an actress (no, I hate being called that) as the instinctive animal that I am, I put myself immediately inside this character. Thus automatically—and it is all to your credit, to the credit of your screenplay—I will function just fine.

"There's a kind of struggle going on now, inside of me, to make you happy. On the one hand, I feel as though I must function as you want even with my interpretive skills as they are, and on the other I see that not always do our visions of how to interpret your character coincide: thus I lost my balance; thus I am not either a good actress (I would be with luck, God willing) nor an obedient robot." [25]

They strike a deal: She will try to shoot scenes in his short bursts, and he will explain more and treat her as she sees herself, as a "conscious actress." Having recounted the scene off-screen—a diary about a film, equal in its dialogue's importance to that filmed—he "pulls back" to his lens. He closes the scene called "director and actress confront one another" in a mélange of description and reflection:

Against the sharp, lung-like colors of the houses at Cecafume—big buildings one just like another arranged asymetrically, the sky of the Aqueducts—it rains with an underhanded abundance. (There's a little too much desire to agree in the discussion between me and Anna.) Beneath the apartment windows of workers' dwellings, the market street shines in a sinister way, with its stalls undone, thousands of sawhorse legs turned on end and soaked. (The worse side of Anna's poetics is romantic and naturalistic; mine, on its worst side, is exquisite and mannerist.) I search for plasticity, above all the plasticity of image, on the road Masaccio never forgot; his proud contrast of light and dark, his white and black—or on that road, if one will, of the archaic, in a strange combination of subtlety and grossness. I cannot be impressionistic. I like the depths, not the passage. One cannot imagine an altarpiece with figures in motion. I hate the fact that figures move. Thus none of my scenes ever starts with "a field," or with an empty countryside. There will always be, even if very small, some people. Very small for only a moment, because right away I shout to the loyal Delli Colli to put on the seventy-five [millimeter lens] and suddenly we are at full figure: a face in detail . . . Anna is romantic: she sees the figure in a landscape, the figure in motion, immersed among things as in an impressionistic sketch, one hopes of the force of a Renoir: shadow and light in motion, on the figure and on the landscape, the silhouette which moves against a dark background, foreshortened—never frontal—along the banks of a river, rippling water, little woods of the luncheon on the grass . . . It is raining because God is sending it. At bottom, to make movies is a question of sun.[26]

At the end of August director and star were all smiles at the Twenty-third International Film Festival in the Venetian Lido; they made the expected joint appearances and accommodated photographers by touring the city together by gondola. The critics saw the film as the generally successful encounter of an Italian living institution and one of its most intriguing cultural personalities. But Italians were developing a taste for entertainment, and *Mamma Roma* was not a commercial success. Its box office was 168 million lire, about half the gross of Antonioni's "difficult" *L'eclisse* (The eclipse) the same year.

The critics blamed Magnani, accusing her of "overacting." She defended herself: "In Italy, there is a strange system. If a film goes badly, everyone blames the actress. They forget that I am not one of those professionals who does anything, but that I succeed only when I am free to do what I like, like a writer writing or a painter painting."

Pasolini tactfully explained that it was all his fault for expecting of his leading player what he ought not to have expected.

At a certain point, I thought that the Magnani of *Roma, città aperta* could pass wholly into my reality, but this did not happen and because Anna

Magnani remained effectively within her own consciousness as an actress, her own independence as such, and rightly so. It was my mistake to think I could take her completely into my hands and destroy her. It was absurd and inhuman of me even to think such a thing; and, in fact, *Mamma Roma* shows these limitations. But let us understand one another well: I consider Anna Magnani to be a great actress, and if I were to make *Mamma Roma* again, I would probably choose her.[27]

On August 31, 1962, acting on an order from his superior, the local lieutenant colonel of the *carabinieri* filed a complaint against *Mamma Roma* as "offensive to good morals" and "contrary to the community sense of morality because of obscene content, contrary to public decency." The words "piss" and "shit" are spoken, and the sound of farting is heard. The officer's claim also specified that actor Citti had "legal precedents at the tribunal of Rome." It was the first time a film honored with showing at the Venice Festival had ever been denounced even at its premiere.

But five days later, a magistrate threw the charges out. Pasolini said he felt "hauled before these kings . . . like a minstrel who, if he fails the password, is condemned to death." Ordine Nuovo, a self-proclaimed Fascist group, had its signal. Posters appeared on Venice's streets *"Basta con gli apostoli del fango"* (Enough of the apostles of mud). Without naming Pasolini, it referred to those who wanted "to destroy all values" out of their interest in a "world which exists only in their aborted mentalities and . . . social pathology." In large type, the posters declare: "Let us Block the Way of that 'Culture' which is the Avant-garde of Communism." The poster listed the enemy in block letters—all caps—most important first: "INVERTS. PROSTITUTES. PIMPS. HOOLIGANS. RAPISTS."

Pasolini wrote: "It is clear that something unjust is happening. something elusive, as in all self-respecting Kafkaesque situations."[28] To be sure no one missed the posters' point, some members of the neo-Fascist groups Avanguardia Nazionale and Giovane Italia attacked Pasolini in the lobby of the Quattro Fontane cinema in Rome, coincidentally located adjacent to the national seat of the neo-Fascist M.S.I. It was one in the morning of Saturday, September 22.

As *Mamma Roma* ended, a youth named Flavio Campo lunged toward Pasolini, shouting, "In the name of the nation's youth, I tell you that you are disgusting!" By his own confession and subsequent police report, he slapped Pasolini; according to some newspapers, he kicked him. Pasolini's friends, Franco Citti and Piero Morgia, came to his defense and about five more members of Avanguardia Nazionale joined in. It made for a small riot, all caught by waiting photographers. The police broke it up after substantial shouting, insults, fists thrown. All concerned were booked at the local station.

Pasolini's version of the incident contradicts that of all the eyewitnesses and is altogether different. He claimed that what he called "a rather emaciated young man, to tell the truth" shouted something.

> I lost my patience (I regret it) and hit him and knocked him down . . . I don't know what the newspapers that reported the incident thought they were doing by turning it around (accompanying their story with false photographs) in such a way that I became the one who got hit.[29]

Three weeks later, the day after the court dismissed charges against *Mamma Roma,* he wrote in the "dialogue" of his *Vie nuove* space:

> The public part of my life . . . all that part of myself that does not belong to me, and has become like a mask at the Nuovo Teatro dell'Arte—[is] a monster that must be what the public wants it to be. I seek to fight, Don Quixote-like, against this fate that takes me out of myself, which renders me some sort of automaton for the illustrated magazines, and which ends up by reflecting back on me, like an illness. But it seems to me nothing can be done about it.
>
> Success, as regards one's moral and emotional life, is something horrible, and that's all there is to it. . . . at certain moments in the day, merely the sight of a newsstand is enough to make me sick.[30]

Tommaso, Accattone, and Ettore all die. In 1968 Pasolini answered journalist Oswald Stack's question about death and the irrational in *Mamma Roma:*

> Death determines life, I feel it and I have also written it in a recent essay ["La paura del naturalismo"—"Fear of naturalism"—*Nuovi argomenti,* first series, No. 6], where I liken death to the editing of a film. Once life is finished it acquires a sense [the Italian Pasolini uses is *senso,* in English translatable both as "sense," as in "logical sense," and "significance"]; until that point, it has no meaning; its significance is suspended and thus ambiguous. In any case, to be sincere I must add that for me, death is important only if it is not justified or rationalized by reason. For me, death is the maximum of epicness and myth. When I'm talking to you about my tendency towards the sacred and the mythic and the epic, I should say that this can only be completely satisfied by the act of death, which seems to me the most mystic and epic aspect there is—all this, however, at the level of pure irrationalism.[31]

* * *

In February 1962 producer Roberto Amoroso had what seemed a good idea. People were interested in the new *auteur* directors: why not deliver a sampler, string together four shorts by four new names. He wanted to call it *La vita e bella* (literally, Life is beautiful).

In May Pasolini submitted a treatment called *La ricotta*—the name for an inexpensive, soft, white cheese, a staple of the Romans' diet. Amoroso took virtually "one look" and backed out, telling reporters it was "a collection of offensive indecencies objectionable to [his] moral sense and to that of the entire public." *Lo specchio* leaped to back Amoroso, saluting him for not "tossing into the air millions to allow Pasolini to pursue his polemics with the Church, the Italian middle class, capitalists, angels and saints." They dredged up, yet again, the "epigram on Pius XII, which cost the publisher Bompiani admission to the Circolo della Caccia."[32] In October, Amoroso filed suit for breach of contract, demanding damages of 60 million lire; he had paid one million out of a total writing and directing fee set at eight.

Bini stepped in. He kept together the quartet of directors, and proposed a title made from their names: *Ro*ssellini (the "Ro" of his name would serve), *Go*dard ("go"), *Pa*solini ("pa") and Ugo *G*regoretti (g). The episodic film in four parts would be called *Rogopag*. Pasolini wrote: "I found myself with a script ready when Bini asked me if I'd do the film for him. But he'd already decided to do an episode film. So that was that. I didn't have any contact with Rossellini or the others at all, I just knew they were doing episodes as well."[33]

Pasolini offered cinema about cinema, well in advance of that genre's vogue. His thirty-five-minute episode was shot that autumn in the Roman countryside—out the via Appia Antica, near the Acqua Santa acqueduct where prostitutes, *ragazzi di vita*, and the occasional shepherd found shelter in grottoes.

Pasolini opened his segment with two quotations from the *Gospel*, and his own statement.

> It is not difficult to predict for this my story some judgments which will be opinionated, ambiguous, scandalized. Well, all right, then I want to declare that however one takes *La ricotta*, the story of the Passion is for me the greatest story every told and the texts which recount that story the most sublime ever written.

That displayed for a moment, he cut fast to two men dancing the twist in front of the site of the Crucifixion. The dance was considered as shocking in Italy as in America, where the film *Don't Knock the Twist* had appeared the year before, the song "Duke of Earl" on its soundtrack.

The audience was kicked in the teeth by the picture, perhaps harder for having just been reassured by Pasolini's pious statement of praise for the Gospel: contamination through contrast.

*La ricotta* is a movie within a movie, recounting the mishaps of shooting a single scene. Some actors are playing out a crucifixion— the Crucifixion—for a potboiler on the life of Christ, the sort of film in vogue at the time. Their pettiness, cruelty, and the tragedy of their least honored make the story line. It is the sacredness of even the banal, the holiness in the lowest of humanity which ties together Pasolini's message. Pasolini pulled out his art-historical erudition: at one point, he switches into color for a still shot of Rosso Fiorentino's *Deposition from the Cross* of 1521. It was posed by the film-within-a-film's players; we know they are venal, ordinary people, until they fall silent in the quotation from sacred art, in *tableau vivant*.

To make certain that sacred art is not treated with too much respect, he desecrates ("contaminates") that as well. A boy carrying a clapboard used to mark takes saunters in front of the Deposition tableau. The viewer is reminded that even this holy image is also just the stuff of cinema's manipulation, part of a commercial story. One of the characters, supposed to call "Maria, Maria" to the grieving Virgin, is distracted by an "angel" (played by Ettore Garofolo), who loses his footing. She repeatedly fluffs her line. One of the Moors, in perfect Pontormo costume, moves when he should be still. From off-screen, someone hollers, "Tell the black guy to get back in place." A bearded prophet picks his nose; the actor playing Christ breaks up in laughter. So much for the sacred.

Within this intellectualized frame of commentary on art, cinema, and religion, Pasolini vented his rage. The character playing the Christ stand-in is a down-and-out named Stracci (literally, Rags) played by Mario Cipriani, the hoodlum Balilla in *Accattone*. His speech patterns are those of a Roman truckdriver who finds himself somehow cast as a bit player. He is without artistic pretensions; rather, he is one more *povero cristo* obsessed with the search for enough to eat.

He scrounges box lunches for his family, who appear on the set— dressed shabbily, looking like the poor the Gospels defend—just when the holiest of images is being reconstructed. Somehow the promise of Christ Crucified has been undermined completely by its encounter with the vulgarity, disappointment, and mean-spiritedness of this world. The moral atmosphere of the movie set is purgatorial, a profoundly godless place, where cynical stagehands holler phrases like "Leave them nailed up there." To entertain the bored crew at their lunch break, a voluptuous actress—whose role in the film we watch being made is, naturally, the Magdalene—performs a lewd bump-and-grind striptease to the background blast of a car radio.

While she performs and the crew egg her on with whoops and catcalls, Stracci is nailed to a cross. He blinks at the sun beating down on him, as Pasolini would say, "indifferently." Lowered between takes, Stracci has a "vision," in fact, delirium brought on by lack of food. He imagines that the entire troupe appears in the cave where he has hidden some *ricotta*. He wakes to find they taunt him as he lies on the cross, throwing food just out of reach; finally, someone stuffs a salami sandwich in his mouth and Stracci devours it without dignity, like a beast. So much for the torments and agonies of the Son of God.

Now the producer visits the set with his friends. Pasolini scathingly parodies the titles granted by the Christian Democratic regime to its cronies: the hangers-on call the gross mogul Commendatore. A gaggle of sycophantic journalists is in tow, and the usual Roman ladies in furs: among them, Pasolini cast Elsa dè Giorgi and literary critic Enzo Siciliana. To amuse them, to make them feel "part of the production," Stracci must be nailed up again.

Pasolini's stage directions say, "Flashbulbs go off; a lot of handshaking takes place." A brass band plays "Sempre libera" (a moment worthy of Fellini); the thunder-making machine rolls.

The two-bit actor steals another's lunchpail only to have the food devoured by the spoiled lapdog of a visiting *diva*, played in dark glasses and caricatured bitchiness by Laura Betti, who repeatedly calls the film's director "Darling" in English. Stracci cannot even get the better of the dog. It hurts him more than he it—when he finds his meal eaten, he cries. Stracci, who humiliates himself to feed his family and who never utters a harsh word or complains, is to be the sacrifice.

Finally, Stracci gets enough to eat. In fact, he devours so much *ricotta* that, just after he starts his line "When I am in my Father's house," he passes out. The cross is raised nonetheless (nothing can get in the way of the production: time is money) and "Calvary" is filmed. On the Roman periphery's bare and miserable hills, Stracci hangs on a cross, facing the brutal skyline of the Roman postwar's jerry-built apartment blocks.

Orson Welles, whom Pasolini had cast as director of the film-within-a-film, calls "Action" three times and the assistant director prompts Stracci with the words of the Gospel: "When shall I be in the Kingdom of Heaven. . . ." Everyone waits. "Action," Welles shouts and then again, now annoyed. Pasolini's stage directions read: "But Stracci's head hangs down like a ham [a *prosciutto*], immobile."

Someone in the troupe says, "He must not feel well," another "Who knows?" and a third sees the truth. Stracci—one of society's expendable men, a butt of jokes, taunted by his fellow actors—to everyone's amazement has died on the cross. Someone climbs the ladder to check, and the camera trains on the crowd below, looking up: "We see Stracci's head, dropped, on the cross, against moving clouds."

Pasolini's powerful rebuke had a shocking effect; Moravia called it "brilliant . . . astonishing and at the same time profound."[34] The poet-polemicist, known to his friends for being mild-mannered and soft-spoken, had gone for Italy's religious jugular, putting up for debate the question of the Church on earth: Where was sanctity and redemption when men like Stracci were allowed to live miserable lives? The *Officina* epigram "To a Pope" had been only an opening salvo.

The hilarious, "blasphemous" movie set was presided over by Welles (from a folding chair he never leaves); Pasolini told Bini he wanted someone "who looked like Fellini." Pasolini and the American wunderkind saw eye-to-eye on some important matters: Welles, a most European-ized of Americans, had once remarked, "Italy is full of actors, fifty million in fact, and they are almost all good; there are only a few bad ones, and they are on the stage and in the films." Pasolini agreed. "I chose him for what he did: a director, an intellectual, a personality with something like that which emerges in *La ricotta*."[35]

Fat and forbidding in a dark coat, with the dark rings under his eyes (like the ones Pasolini's poem attributed to Fellini), Welles carries a giant cigar throughout his time on screen and his manner is, at best, haughty and languid. Welles spoke his lines in English; Giorgio Bassani dubbed them into Italian.

Save for one grand setpiece, the director-playing-a-director remains silent throughout the film, only occasionally issuing orders like "the crown, get the crown"—for the Crown of Thorns, stored in a pasta box. His most extended lines are a dialogue with an unctuous journalist, played to parody perfection by Vittorio La Paglia, who had acted the restaurateur Pellissier, blackmailed by Magnani into hiring her son in *Mamma Roma*.

Pasolini gave full vent to his Furies, picking up where the rancor of the poem "Reality" left off. He put enough words in Welles' mouth to outrage powerful parties on every side, and ensure the film trouble. His script:

> (The journalist approaches [Welles, whom he must interview] with a face that looks like bread dipped in milk, like a baby asking its mother "pretty please" to give it some milk, or a whore asking a tip from a customer. He raises his finger [to signal his request for Welles' attention])
>
> Tegliesera: "Excuse me?"
>
> (The director notices him, coldly)
>     "I am Pedoti, from *Tegliesera*."
>
> Director (coldly, indifferently):
>     "Speak, speak."
>
> (Tegliesera widens his ugly mouth, like a good fellow.)
>
> Tegliesera (soaked in a smile): "I would like a brief interview, if you would permit it?"
>
> Director (looking him up and down, as if he were not there): "But not more than four questions."
>
> (Tegliesera giggles some more, servile enough to be an object of contempt.) Tegliesera: "Aaaah! . . . thank you, thank you. The first would be: "What do you seek to express in this new work?"
>
> (The director lowers his eyes, concentrates and when he raises them, says dryly):
>
> Director: "My profound, intimate, archaic Catholicism."
>
> Tegliesera (after noting the answer, mumbling avid satisfaction all the while): "And . . . what do you think of Italian society?"
>
> (Exhausted, but with ice-cold sureness), the Director:
> "The most illiterate common people and the most ignorant bourgeoisie of Europe."
>
> Tegliesera: ". . . and . . . what do you think about death?"
>
> Director (losing his temper, but always with the look of one worn out, bored) ". . . as a Marxist, it is a fact which I do not take into consideration."
>
> Tegliesera: "Fourth and last question: what is your opinion of the writer-director Pier Paolo Pasolini?"

Director (feeling inspiration): "He dances."

He thinks a little more, deeply concentrating, but he finds no more than that ineffable phrase, so he repeats it:
Director: "He dances."

Tegliesera (ashamed, full of flattery): ". . . aaah, thank you, thank you . . . my congratulations, good-bye.

(He turns his back, bent over like a courtier exiting from the court of the Sun King, or a corporal before his superior, when the Director, as if waking from a dream, calls him back.

Director: "Hey."

(Tegliesera turns around, thunderstruck. And the director picks up a book which he has nearby, reluctantly opens it and starts reading, hoarsely:)
" 'I am a force from the Past . . .' "

(He raises his head and looks about as though he were myopic or looking into harsh sunlight, at his interlocutor)
Director:
"It is poetry. In the first part, the poet has described certain antique ruins . . . about which no one understands anything anymore, just 'history and style of . . .' " (he sniggers, who knows why) "and certain horrendous modern constructions which, instead, everyone understands (he sniggers again). Then he attacks, like this: (he starts to read again)

" 'I am a force out of the Past.
Only in tradition do I find my love
I come from the ruins, from the Churches,
from the altarpieces and the hamlets
forgotten on the Apennines and the foothills of the Alps,
where the brothers lived.
I wander the Tuscolana like a madman
out on the Appia like a dog without a master.
I look at the sunsets, the mornings over Rome
over the Ciociaria, over the earth
like the first acts of Afterhistory
at which I am present only in the role of registrar
at the extreme edge of some epoch, buried.
He is monstrous, he who is born out of the
viscera of a dead woman. And I, adult fetus,
go around, more modern than any modern,
looking for brothers who are no more.' "

(He raises his eyes to look at Tegliesera, [who is] gathered up in a respectful stupor)
Director: "Did you understand anything?"

Tegliesera: "Uh."

Director: "Write, write what I say: you understood nothing at all, because you are an average men. Isn't that right?"

Tegliesera: ". . . uh, sure . . ."

Director (triumphantly, with a timid disdain): "—you are proud of it: proud to be an average man. That's what your bosses want. Don't you know what the average man is? He is a monster. A dangerous delinquent. Conformist! Colonialist! Racist! Slave-maker!"

Tegliesera (taking notes)
". . . ah, ah, ah . . ."

Director:
"Does your heart bother you?"

Tegliesera:
"—no, I was just making the sign of the horns [against the evil eye]"

Director:
"That's a pity, because if you were to drop dead right here in front of me, it would be a good bit for the launching of the movie. In any case, you don't exist. Capital does not consider existent the laborer, except insofar as he is useful for production. And the producer of my movie is also the boss at your newspaper . . . Good-bye."

(The journalist stays put, crushed: he does not know if the interview is over or not. But the Director has definitely turned his back. And so, with a last servile smile plastered on his face, the journalist departs.)[36]

Asked why he rendered the journalist so viciously, Pasolini told a reporter:

> I never completely despise anyone. It is not in my nature, which is always trying to have glimpses inside, and respect in everyone the mysterious, deeper aspect. That which anyone *really* is is something mysterious and profound. The profound and mysterious part of that man [the journalist Tegliesera] is not that he always allows himself to be duped, which is true of many people, especially the disingenuous, the sweet of character; his deepest and truest characteristic is his vulgarity, which is basically innocent because he does not know himself. He is only a poor guy who issues forth with vulgarity at every pore. I don't think he's bad or anything else: he's a coward and profoundly vulgar, but innocently so. This is his real quality which I used in both films [*Accattone* and *La ricotta*].[37]

Perhaps never has such a short film, made on such a small budget, so quickly brought down such a storm of protest on its creator. At virtually the same time, Fellini was making *Eight and a Half*, with a grotesque producer referred to as "a famous capitalist from Milan" and an American who asks "What is the connection between Catholicism and Marxism?" and "Is Italy fundamentally a Catholic country?" But Italian officialdom let Fellini (who had brought international acclaim to Italian cinema) pass. After all, his film's closing message was "I didn't know it's all right to accept you and to love you. How simple it is . . . Life is a holiday, let's enjoy it together"— words impossible to imagine from Pasolini.

No clowns from him. Rather than reassure and send his viewers home smiling, *La ricotta* spit in Italy's face his distaste for the cultural mediocrity of his countrymen and a demand that the Christian creed live up to its promise. His strategy—to make holiness an issue through acts of desecration—backfired in every way. The Director-Welles' irony was read literally; even Pasolini's making fun of himself was misinterpreted.

For Welles to condemn the "average man" as "a dangerous criminal" and label Italians as "illiterate masses" made enemies on both Left and Right. Traditional Catholics were outraged when Welles referred to his "profound, intimate, archaic Catholicism"; mainline Marxists were furious at Pasolini's suggestion that their ideology lacked any spiritual dimension, had nothing to offer on the question of human transitoriness.

In the last days of Pius XII's lingering influence, before John XXIII's actions seemed to rewrite and liberalize all the rules, a public prosecutor felt safe in moving against the film. On the day of its release to an apparently indifferent public, *La ricotta* was seized by police in Rome's "Corso" cinema. They acted on an order secured by Giuseppe di Gennaro, an assistant district attorney for Rome. The charge: "insulting the religion of the State," a violation of Penal Code section 402. *Vilipendio* was then charged: contempt, disparagement, scorn, defamation, abuse—of the religion that the Lateran Pact of 1929, and Italy's 1948 constitution, had declared the official faith of the Italian people.

It did not matter that the faculty of the Pontifical Gregorian University in Rome did not think the film blasphemous, or that the Vatican censorship commission had not declared it "excluded for all." What counted was that Pasolini was, again, a symbol: He had created a *cause célèbre*, one also useful to liberals and intellectuals who rose to his defense, charging an unholy collusion between the Vatican and Christian Democracy acting to strangle freedom of thought because they felt themselves on the defensive. Those in power—spanning sections of the press and the State (that is, Christian Democratic) film distribution and the financing bureaucracy—seemed determined to keep order by enforcing the most traditional Catholic morality, lest the economic miracle come derailed.

As the State marshaled its legal apparatus to defend the Church from "blasphemy," the Centro Cattolico Cinematografico attacked the film as offering "the threadbare framework of protesting Marxism." Recently enacted legislation allowed judicial authorities to seize films for "offense to good manners": Pasolini became the famous test case; and together with his film, Buñuel's *Viridiana* was also charged.

Liberal Catholics were in an especially tough spot: They did not want to seem to approve of Pasolini and yet wanted to defend freedom of expression and the Church's increasingly powerful tolerant wing. They saw a worrisome reaction already setting in to the first reforms of John XXIII's Second Vatican Council. General elections were slated for April 1963 and "permissiveness" was on the public's mind.

Conservatives found a rallying cry in the stand taken by Di Gennaro, a self-proclaimed lover of cinema who had written some screenplays and television documentaries. Fancying himself a film critic, he allowed that Pasolini's work had "too many concepts, too much use of symbols."

He told the court (and assembled reporters waiting outside): "I am confident that your verdict will reawaken the dead and recall to life and dignity those churchgoing Catholics who have abdicated their culture for fear of being accused of conformism . . . let Catholics beware of carrying the Trojan horse of Pasolini into the city of God." [38] Surely no one would defend a man whose Christ-figure dies on the cross of indigestion.

During interrogation, Di Gennaro asked whether Pasolini thought Stracci "has the sense of transcendence of God?" Pier Paolo answered, "Certainly." In his summing up, knowing his listeners would know what he meant by code words, Di Gennaro labeled the accused, "a superman of eccentric tastes and feelings." [39]

The prosecutor brought a moviola into court for the first time ever, better to illustrate his case, training himself on its use so as to operate it without a technician's help. Photos that appeared in the newspapers showed the judges, serious-faced, gathered around the machine, staring intently at its tiny screen. Pasolini stands among them, his expression impenetrable behind dark glasses. The judges saw Stracci hiccup on the cross.

The time was ripe for Italy's two faiths—the Church and its lay image, the secular Left—to come to confrontation. Di Gennaro virtually dared the tribunal to absolve Pasolini, arguing that to acquit him would be a condemnation of his, Di Gennaro's, actions. He declaimed, "It will not do not to realize that in this trial there are two accused parties: Pier Paolo Pasolini and myself."[40] Both men could not have right on their side, not in the polarized atmosphere of Italy that year where hard lines were drawn and anyone who was not a friend was an enemy.

The two-day hearing was a dress rehearsal for the debates on abortion and divorce to come and for all the debates of the sixties and seventies in which Italy worked through her transition from one sort of society into another. Pasolini's drive to desecrate yielded radiographic results: In telling what he saw "inside," as it were, he scandalized. Fury was unleashed on the messenger for telling unwelcome, hateful truths. As a young man, he had "warned" Silvana Mauri that he felt driven to tell the truth as he saw it, regardless of the price. That truth included self-revelation in public, a bitterly ironic amalgam of confession and exposé.

Any observer daring to interpret Pasolini's motivations has to beat Pasolini himself to the punch. He told a critic from the magazine *Cinema e film:*

> The world seems to me to be nothing other than a combination of fathers and mothers toward whom I have complete respect, a respect that is veneration, and (also) of a need to violate that adoring respect through desecrations that are violent and scandalous as well.

Di Gennaro, who went on to a career on the bench, also appealed to the vanity of a magistracy under attack for partiality. He proclaimed, "Your condemnation will have a pedagogic value which will extend beyond the person of the accused, you will teach [respect for judges] with it. . . ."

More than a decade later, only five months before his death, Pasolini reinvoked the trauma of *La ricotta*'s trial and his loathing for Di Gennaro: In his last open "letter to Gennariello":

> Now in my memory no one is more reactionary than this Di Gennaro. His concluding speech against my film was so deeply reactionary in religious terms that—as the numerous intellectuals and journalists who heard it can testify—it came close to Grand Guignol and the ridiculous, not to mention vulgarity. It was the oral masterpiece of the clerico-Fascism of the fifties (the trial took place in 1963).[41]

Di Gennaro asked for the maximum term allowed by the still-in-force Rocco Code of 1930: one year's imprisonment, without possibility of parole. On March 7, 1963, the court handed down a forty-four-page opinion, holding Pasolini "guilty of the crime with which he is charged" and sentenced him to four months in prison. Several years later Pasolini commented:

> I still can't say exactly why they tried me at all, but it was a terrible period for me. I was slandered week after week, and for two or three years I lived under a kind of unimaginable persecution. However, I can't really say why all this happened, unless as an expression of public opinion. . . .[42]

The next day socialist leader Pietro Nenni wrote, "Dear Pasolini, your condemnation is the index of how far we are yet from an awareness of the rights of art. . . ." His friend, critic Pietro Citati, wrote asking, "Is it not possible that you could manage to quit the cinema—and the public which follows it—and return to being the writer and critic which, first of all, you are?"[43]

March 1963 saw one more, the last, change of residence—this time to EUR, Esposizione Universale di Roma. The fairgrounds that became a suburb, which Mussolini built just outside Rome, lies about twenty minutes' drive from Piazza Venezia. It offered Susanna quiet streets with trees, little traffic, and fresh air. It was all for her, a place in which she could feel comfort and safety, in which to serve guests coffee with her own hands.

About this time he wrote "La ricerca di una casa" (The search for a house): "I go in search of the house of my burial, / making the rounds of the city like an inmate / of an asylum or rest home / out on a pass, with my face deformed / by fever, dry white skin and beard."[44]

He found a row-house villa in via Eufrate (the Duce had named the quarter's streets for the world's rivers), at number 9, a several-story structure cheek-by-jowl with others but with a small internal courtyard where Susanna could garden. The balustrade faced the unseen sea at Ostia and at night the dome of the Facist-built Basilica of Saints Peter and Paul shone in the distance. It was, he admitted, the height of middle-class comfort. It didn't matter what anyone thought; the only goal was Susanna's happiness. She was now past seventy, but her hair kept a coppery chestnut, at Pier Paolo's insistence.

Uncle Gino chose some substantial pieces of overwrought furniture, which cohabited with souvenirs from Pier Paolo's increasing travels. The effect was not Roman opulence—nor even studied good taste. What mattered to him was a worktable and bookcases in a study of his own, and in his bedroom a Zigaina hanging over his single bed.

By May they had moved in: Pier Paolo, Susanna and Graziella Chiarcossi (his Aunt Enrichetta's granddaughter, thus Pier Paolo's second cousin), come from Friuli some months before to enroll at the University of Rome. She helped Susanna keep house and provided company for her when Pier Paolo was away.

The late spring following the *La ricotta* sentence, the PCI went into the national electoral campaign bearing the banner of anti-censorship. In Rome, at the Cinema Palladium in the *popolare* quarter Pasolini called *La Garbante* (in fact, Garbatella), the Party organized a public debate on the theme of "Who Is Suffocating Liberty of Expression?"

Pasolini, Antonello Trombadori, and a PCI Senate candidate named Tommaso Morgia (secretary of a Rome labor council, no relation to the actor Piero) were joined by Tommaso Carlo Levi and Federico Fellini. The former called the *Ricotta* verdict against Pasolini an attack on "the fundamental freedoms felt by the modern spirit . . . and both the letter and spirit of our constitution and the rights of man expressed in the UN Charter . . ."; Fellini, aiming rather lower and elsewhere, said the condemnation was "incredible, unacceptable, a source of anguish . . . it seems the best spirits are always blocked by the obtuse . . . those people are putting him [Pasolini] in a condition to express in his coming film on the *Gospel* exactly what is the sadness of not being understood." For Trombadori, a Communist Parliamentary deputy from 1968 to 1983, such solidarity as shown that evening toward Pasolini proved that "the PCI appreciated him . . . whatever they may have thought of him in their most private hearts."[45]

Pasolini told an interviewer from *L'unità*, "The situation of sacrificial lamb is certainly not the best for making calm judgments."

Appeals were filed and on May 6, a full year after the first sentence (his incarceration postponed pending appeal), a higher court held "the act does not constitute a crime." Early in 1967 Italy's Supreme Court held that "the offense has been annulled through amnesty."

But censorship had carried the day. Under pressure Pasolini had agreed to cut a single scene from *Accattone*, "because it was too long."[46] *Mamma Roma* appeared as he had written it, but only later as a book. He explained, "The changes in the published script I made two or three years after I shot the film, for literary reasons. When I read through the script later I didn't like it—from a literary standpoint—so I changed it." [47]

*La ricotta* was even less lucky. It was released to circulation but only on court-ordered conditions: The silencer would be applied to the sound track whenever certain "blasphemous" lines were spoken; the striptease was cut, as were the three calls for "the Crown," for which Di Gennaro had claimed Pasolini must be guilty of "lack of respect." Instead of "get the crucifixes out of here," the line would read "on to the other scene." Instead of "Cuckolded!" the actor would say, "What a pity."

In the published version, Welles says, "Poor Stracci! He had to die. It was his only way of telling us that he, too, was alive." Pasolini agreed to change this line (he called it "a little thing")—the price for freeing the negatives from the government's sealed warehouses— to read "Poor Stracci. Dropping dead was his only way of making revolution." Six years later, rather lamely, Pasolini told Stack, "It wasn't a succcess because, as you know, if a film doesn't come out at the right time, it has had it." [48]

Pasolini published his version of the script—not the expurgated version released to theaters—in November 1965, part of a collection of work written over fifteen years, including the film he never made, *La mortaccia*. He called the volume *Alì dagli occhi azzuri* (Alì with the blue eyes), a title suggested by Sartre.

Greater damage was done than to *La ricotta*'s script. When Susanna heard of the first verdict, she became hysterical and fainted. Pier Paolo summoned Moravia and somehow managed to reach Di Gennaro by phone at his home. On this occasion, so rare his friends spoke of it for years afterward, his mask fell. The Pasolini famous in the Roman film world for never cursing—no theatrics in a world of gossips, one-upmanship, and entourages—shouted at his prosecutor. For harming Susanna. Somehow a photographer was present and recorded Pasolini yelling into the phone.

If he was going to be condemned for "blasphemy," then the only solution was to make the most religious film ever.


While shooting *La ricotta*, Pier Paolo met Giovanni ("Ninetto") Davoli. The boy had the day off work and was hanging around the set, visiting his brother, who worked there as a carpenter. Born October 11, 1948, Ninetto was fourteen, the youngest of five brothers. Pasolini had turned forty that March.

Ninetto (he was never called anything else) had a mop of intense, shiny, dark ringlets, eyes that seemed to laugh even in repose and twinkle when he laughed, something he did as often as Pasolini did rarely. He saw life as a gift, not a *via crucis*; without pretensions of any kind, he treated the famous, rich, and powerful as he did anyone else. What counted was life and loyalty.

Pier Paolo wrote about Ninetto, "Everything about him has a magical air . . . an endless reserve of happiness." Soon Ninetto was part of Pier Paolo's informal entourage: A photo of those first years then shows him at Susanna's family-style lunch table—Pier Paolo with Franco Citti, Ettore Garofolo, and Ninetto, so many *ragazzi*, gathered at their friend's place. Susanna stands at the table's edge, paused in the act of serving food or clearing plates. Pasolini looks serious but content; the boys seem excited, happy.

Pasolini soon mythologized his love, this son of Calabrian immigrants to Rome. Ninetto joined and emblemized the golden circle of boys who did not grow up, for whom life was always a game and joy. These lines from 1965 were published as an "Avvertenza" (Notice) at the end of the short stories from 1950 to 1965 collected in *Ali dagli occhi azzuri:*

> Look, here into the orchestra comes a madman, with
> soft
> and merry eyes.
> Dressed like the Beatles.
> While great thoughts and great actions
> are implied in the relation of these rich people
> to the film spectacle,
> made for him *too*, he, twirling one thin finger
> like a merry-go-round horse,
> writes his name "Ninetto"
> on the back of the velvet seat (under a little
> long-eared nape associated with rules of behavior
> and the idea of the free bourgeoisie).
> Ninetto is a herald
> and overcoming (with a sweet laugh
> that blazes from his whole being
> as in a Muslim or a Hindu)
> his shyness,
> he introduces himself as in an Areopagus
> to speak of the Perisans.
> The Persians, he says, are massing on the frontiers.
> But millions and millions of them have already

peacefully immigrated,
they are here, waiting for the No. 12, the No. 13,
the No. 409 tram
of the Stefer line. What beautiful Persians!
God has sketched them, in their youth,
like the Muslims or the Hindus:
they have the short lineaments of animals,
gaunt cheekbones, flattened or upturned little
noses,
long long eyelashes, curly hair. . . .

Their leader is called:
Alì of the Blue Eyes.[49]

# 18

*Italians do not write or think about their customs, as if they
thought such studies were not useful to them.*
—*Giacomo Leopardi*

*Christ, in his time, was an intellectual, thus his friends were intellec-
tuals, as mine are now.*
—*Pier Paolo Pasolini*, Il vangelo secondo Matteo

# THE CINEMA OF IDEOLOGY:
## *RAGE, LOVE MEETINGS,* AND *THE GOSPEL*

In September 1962—three years after the coronation of a son of
Bergamo, Angelo Giuseppe Roncalli, as Pope John XXIII—Pasolini
visited a Franciscan study center at Assisi, called Pro Civitate Cristiana. Founded by Don Giovanni Rossi in 1939, the center's reformist
impulse had received the blessing of the new pontiff, a childhood
friend of Rossi's: In his assignment letter of November 1959 John
charged the scholar-priests with "leading society back to the principles of the Gospels" by forging links to the non-Catholic world
through interaction with those who made its culture. It was under-

stood that this meant dialogue with Marxists, even Italian Communists, whom the previous pope had threatened with excommunication.

The Curia's own Ecumenical Council had officially stated that the mass media "if properly used" could contribute "enormous benefits . . . to the human family." Films, it was held, could function as had "the so-called Bible of the Poor—that is, as had large frescoes, sculptures, and, in short, all of sacred art." So the study center, simply known as Cittadella, began hosting seminars with film directors, writers, and producers, each encounter lasting several days.

One of their most ambitious had as its theme: "Cinema as a spiritual force in the present," and Pasolini, invited in the past but now accepting for the first time, attended. The seminar concluded, he found himself what he called "unable to leave."[1] The roads out of the city were gridlocked with traffic, at least until the pope, who happened to be visiting at the same time, departed in his train for Rome. Effectively trapped in his room, one furnished (as they all were) with a copy of the Gospels (something he later wrote his religious colleagues was "your delightful and diabolical calculation!"), Pasolini started to read.

"I read them straight through," he wrote his hosts soon after, "after some twenty years . . . as though a novel . . . and there came to me, among other things, the idea of making a film . . . the idea . . . threw in the shade all the other ideas for work I had in my head, it weakened and devitalized them. And it alone remained, alive and thriving within me. . . ."[2]

Now he was even busier than usual. *Mamma Roma* had been written in two weeks; and he planned another novel, *Il rio della grana*—to become the third part of a "Roman trilogy" with *Ragazzi di vita* and *Una vita violenta*. It was to be the story of a boy named Pietro, "pure, ingenuous," who comes from the depressed countryside to Rome "in the days when Pius XII dies and the new one is elected." The narrative would focus on his encounter with his new environment, one which challenged his "*Meridionale* religious moralism" at every turn. The novel was never completed; there were movies to be made.

In February 1963 he wrote Don Lucio Caruso of the Cittadella's Ufficio Cinema, knowing it would reach Caruso's boss Rossi:

> My idea is this: to follow, point for point, the "gospel according to Saint Matthew," without making any script and without any reduction. I will faithfully translate, in images, without omission to or deletion from the story. Even the dialogue must be strictly that of Saint Matthew, without even a line of explanation or feeder lines: because no images or words inserted can ever be of the poetic height of the text. It is this poetic height which, with

some anxiety, inspires me, I want to make a work of poetry. Not a religious
work in the current sense of the term nor a work of ideology. In words both
simple and poor: I do not believe that Christ was the Son of God, because
I am not a believer—at least not consciously. But I believe Christ to be
divine and I believe there was in him a humanity so great, rigorous and
ideal as to go beyond the common terms of humanity.[3]

Rossi thought it was a momentary enthusiasm and would pass, but
Pasolini insisted, the Cittadella could hardly refuse. John XXIII had
written in the encyclical *Pacem in Terris:* "True, the philosophic
formula [of Communism] does not change. . . . But who can deny the
possible existence of good and commendable elements in these programs?"

Pasolini wrote the leadership at Assisi: "I would like it if my film
could be shown on Easter Sunday in all the parish cinemas in Italy
and the world." He asked for "assistance and support" so that his
"poetic inspiration" would not "run up against" their "sensitivity as
believers." A Cittadella biblical scholar named Don Andrea Carraro
was seconded as his consultant; through him Pasolini met the influential Padre Grasso at the Gregorian University, who wrote, "I have
seen in you a good man, in search of values able to give sense to
life."

But there were risks. Pasolini wrote Bini on May 12, 1963, that
he understood "All this once again calls my whole career as a writer
dangerously into question. . . . But it would be a fine thing if, loving
the Christ of Matthew as I do with all my heart, I should then be
afraid to call something into question."[4] A few days later he wrote
Carraro asking for brief descriptions of what each of the Apostles
would have looked like—"a few lines on each would be enough." He
was going in search of actors off the street.

Caruso and Carraro were to accompany Pasolini to the Holy Land,
to scout locations. The Israel and Jordan they visited were at war.
Between June 27 and July 11, 1963, the unlikely entourage dutifully
visited Galilee, Jordan, Damascus, Bethlehem, and (in Jerusalem)
the Garden of Gethsemane, in company with a small team of technicians. Their little caravan of station wagons included a cameraman
Bini sent along. The result was *Sopraluoghi in Palestina,* a fifty-five-
minute documentary of Pasolini and his Cittadella colleagues visiting
and discussing locations mentioned by the Evangelist.

At one point in the film, Caruso asked Pasolini what he thought
of the sites they had visited. And did Pasolini think they could be
used in the film? He answered that the Holy Land had been "a practical disappointment. But corresponding with this . . . an esthetic

revelation." He had been put off that "after a few hours driving" from arrival at Tel Aviv there appeared "reforestation works, modern agriculture, light industry." Israel was too modern to play its ancient self. And not only was its built world disappointing. So were the people. Pasolini: "I realized it was all no use—that was after a few hours driving."[5]

The Italian Mezzogiorno was the natural site for the biblical film, in the same way as nonactors were the natural choice to play in it. Pasolini believed, and in 1964 he had some grounds for it, that "a Southern Italian peasant . . . is still living in a magical culture where miracles are real like the culture in which Matthew wrote. . . ."[6]

Out of the Holy Land journey came the poem "Southern Dawn," published the following year in the volume *Poesia in forma di rosa* (Poetry in the form of a rose):

> I was walking near the hotel in the evening
> when four or five boys appeared
> on the field's tiger fur,
> with no cliff, ditch, vegetation
> to take cover from the possible bullets—for
> Israel was there, on the same tiger fur
> specked with cement-block houses, useless
> walls, like all slums.
> I happened on them at that absurd point
> far from street, hotel, border. It was one
> of countless such
> friendships, which last an evening
> then torture the rest of your life.

He and his companions talked:

> till night came (already one was embracing
> me,
> saying now he hated me, now, no, he loved
> me,
> loved me) they told me everything about
> themselves,
> every simple thing. These were gods
> or sons of gods, mysteriously shooting because
> of a hate that would push them down from
> the hills like bloodthirsty bridegrooms upon
> the invading *kibbutzim* on the other side of
> Jerusalem. . . .[7]

The sexual rite was repeated, as it was in the next years on every location from Jordan to Morocco to Turkey to Nepal, life in what he called "secret valleys of lust / sadistic, masochistic. . . ." That was before the collapse of the world, before the boys "bit by bit / have become stone monuments / thronging my solitude by the thousands."

Financing *The Gospel* was proving difficult; furthermore, the Cittadella was not going to be rushed. In December 1963 Pasolini left for a third long journey to Africa: Kenya, Ghana, Nigeria, Guinea— traveling with Bini, Moravia, and Dacia Maraini. He said the trip of two years earlier had been by chance, but now he wanted to make a film set there. He found what he called "an immense reserve of subproletarians . . . even prehistoric, coming into contact with . . . neo-capitalism."[8] He decided, before turning to the *Gospel*, to recount the confrontation between European and indigenous cultures; he had a script ready, because he always was far into his next project before the preceding one was complete.

He called it *Il padre selvaggio* (The savage—or wild—father). At its base lay the conviction that racism was far more than rejecting the legal equality of others. It went to the existential center of people: "As though the presence of other destinies were a threat to our own. Or rendered them vain by suggesting other ways of being in the sun, amid the houses, along the dry rivers, between the walls, etc."

French actor Serge Reggiani was chosen to play the single white role, that of a European schoolteacher who confronts his African students' growing consciousness of colonialism and determination to resist it. Pasolini imagined the progressive schoolteacher "between eighteen and thirty . . . a little bit the beatnik found in some European capitals, a little bit the young intellectual of the Left, all brain."

The lead would be played by a black African whose character, named Davidson, is the son of a tribal chief. The message: that even an anticonformist European's idea of "free Africa" is wrong; when independence comes, the Africans are unprepared and colonialism gives way to war. After many travails, Davidson returns to his village, where his father is concerned not about United Nations troops but about ancient rivalry with a neighboring tribe. Davidson completely throws off the teaching of his English schoolmaster because it is not enough to erase generations of his own preexisting culture. He reaffirms—Pasolini said he would be like a hero in ancient literature, who comes to insight through a series of challenges—" 'the religion' of Africa."

But Bini, rather than enthusiastic about *Padre selvaggio*, was furious about the trouble he thought Pasolini could have avoided with *La ricotta*. The film's unctuous journalist, savaged by Welles, was called Pedoti—too close for comfort to Pedote, a well-known State prosecutor whose questioning during the *La ricotta* trial had been especially nasty. It was the Salvatore Pagliuca business, which had cost Bini money, replayed. Bini's recollection:

> We had never discussed the name of this character and I don't recall now, more than twenty years later, what it was. But nothing special. Then, after the last cut was done and we had gone home—Pasolini to his house, I to mine—he seems to have gone back to the studio and somehow inserted the name of Pedoti, a too-small change from the name of the prosecutor. . . .[9]

The producer claims to have only learned of it at the showing of the film: "I called him into my office and we came to blows . . . I slapped him a few times." What is certain is some 300 million lire went down the drain when an enraged magistracy ordered *La ricotta* into a sealed warehouse for four months. Bini has written that "only a great deal of effort" saw him recover his costs on a production he held among Pasolini's very best.

While the two men persevered still to do their best work together, Bini refused to gamble on *Il padre*. As he often did, Pasolini took the last word, in a poem. He entitled it *E l'Africa?* (And Africa?); it is dated January 30, 1963, but was published fifteen years later, as preface to the screenplay never shot. "The pain I had—and which I seek to express in these ingenuous verses of 'And Africa?'—still burns painfully. I dedicate the screenplay of *Il padre selvaggio* to the prosecuting attorney of the trial [of *La ricotta*, Di Gennaro] and the judge who condemned me." Of Bini, he wrote:

> His yellow and red face, blurred
> in the print, high, in its smooth,
> round chin, low: with half-whiskers
> red, cruel, in profile, like
> a middle-aged *Landknecht*,
> come down from Lands with spired roofs and
> frozen rivers . . .
> It was this face,
> that, behind a table of rustic taste,
> for big bureaucrats,
> gazed at me with its blue but classic eyes,
> while outside atomic bombs exploded

in the jaundiced sky of an afternoon
of twenty years ago.
Then it began—swollen
with hysterics, and red
like a foreskin of blood—
to reproach me, to call me crazy . . .
And I . . . innocent, offended . . . I listened,
once again mixing in my throat of a youth
dressed
by his mother,
tears and remonstrances: uselessly! He
practical man, was right:
I had spent too much money for useless
refinements,
and, also, I had touched the sore points of
the great,
innocent, too, in their glorious private
life.
. . . in the meantime, his face split in two:
actually, for a few moments,
he was someone else, who appeared at a
doorsill,
not far from the table, in the light
of that ancient afternoon of a yellowed war.
It was him, the true boss . . .
But that other one, there, who by osmosis
had emerged from Bini's thorax, was my father.
The father not mentioned, not remembered
since December 'fifty-nine, the year in
which
he died.
Now he was there, almost benevolent boss:
but suddenly he was once again my Gorizian
contemporary . . .[10]

Pasolini reluctantly "forgot" the African film and turned to the
*Gospel,* his *Il Vangelo secondo Matteo.* At various times between
February and May he traveled to Assisi to do research in the Citta-
della's library and to ask advice of its priests.

Alfredo Bini claimed to have a purpose in working with Pasolini,
nothing less than a "project . . . to put to the test Italian social customs about love and sex, about politics and religion. The program

was that, a plan for making change." He proposed a film about Lazarus but agreed to widen the possibilities (and difficulties) when Pasolini suggested an entire Gospel. The producer remained sanguine, even long-suffering, once noting without rancor, "It's funny that the only one of the Gospels that does not include the story of Lazarus is Matthew's." Pasolini explained that he chose that version because it was "the most epic of all, being the most archaic, that closest to the mentality of the Hebrew people."

Bini's problems were substantial; underwriters were hardly lining up to finance the work. Throughout the eight films by Pasolini that he produced, Bini's personal risk never fell below 50 percent. For almost two years, starting in 1963, Bini made the rounds of bankers and distributors, trying to launch *Il Vangelo*. The heads of five banks turned him down; no one in Italy wanted to pay for a film about Christ by the notorious Pasolini.

Bini, who later said of those productions of the sixties, "I wanted to revolutionize everything," discovered that working with Pasolini "was like going to bed with a leper." When the State-controlled Banca Nazionale del Lavoro finally conceded a partial underwriting, it was on express condition that the film pass the censorship board. Distributors kept their distance, to wait and see.

The Cittadella's cooperation was crucial. In May they received Pasolini's first draft of the script. Caruso wrote back to Bini:

> I have read . . . straight through in a sitting. It is extremely beautiful! My first impression is one of stupor: is it possible that the author is that same Pasolini of which certain newspapers say such terrible things? Not only does it show the strictest adherence to the words of the sacred text, not only does it show the strictest adherence to ethical and dogmatic orthodoxy, but we have here a work whose execution is far above the usual.
>
> . . . Everything now depends on Pasolini, on his faith. Will Pasolini be able to keep lit behind him the great flame of faith? To make a film about Jesus, one needs first of all to believe in Jesus, otherwise what would come out is a work that is cold and academic.
>
> The situation as it is now is that we have received from Dott. Pasolini notable reassurances and an excellent script: all that seems to me to bode well.[11]

But after he read the final script in November, Caruso suggested changes and Pasolini compromised: The Magdalen was easily removed—she is barely mentioned in Matthew; no particular military should be recognizable in the garb of soldiers who would wear helmets out of Giotto's Arena Chapel fresco cycle; phrases which end with a swear word were shortened to exclude it; a reference to "priests" was changed to "mystics"; some off-color jokes coming from the populace were eliminated.

Pasolini wrote Assisi to reassure: "I criticize this society in the name of values which are substantially religious. And this is the theme of my film." He begged them: "I want to make a sincere film, one without vulgarity. You must grant me your advice on the completed work. . . . You have seen my work, my self, my mother: You must be sure of your judgment of me. I know I am a difficult and discomforting friend; but do not throw me overboard, judging me by a work not yet done! . . . It requires little of you to help me: a little faith, a little patience and above all letting me have a list of those concrete points which scandalize you."

The Cittadella proceeded, and for its trouble was attacked. *Il secolo d'Italia* editorialized that the film was "the triumph of calculation over faith" and that the devil had used the Cittadella: "Christ has not come to [the Film Festival at] Venice. He is stricken for the umpteenth time. And before dawn spreads over the Laguna, He will have been betrayed even by those who claim to profess Him." The article was reprinted even in the *Tribuna Italia* in faraway São Paolo.

The Cittadella remained calm but firm.

> To all who tell us that Pasolini is not only an unbeliever but a sinner as well, we humbly reply that, even if true, this does not seem to us any reason to shut the door in his face and deny him the help he has asked us for. Jesus loved everyone, but had a preference for publicans, sinners, thieves, even poor creatures who had fallen even into the most anguishing moral misery . . . Jesus died to help everyone, to save everyone . . .[12]

But the full-blown storm over the release of *The Gospel According to Matthew* was almost two full years away. Pasolini had two other, small film projects in the works, while Bini looked for money to shoot the Cittadella-blessed script.

*La rabbia* (literally, "Rage") was not simply a timely film for him to make, but necessary. Ever since *Le ceneri di Gramsci*, he had a reputation as a "civil poet," one with a scathing and yet lyrical perspective on the world. In cinema, too, why not let him manipulate the images of the events of his time directly, in a documentary telling history as he thought it ought to be told? Giorgio Bassani and Renato

Guttuso signed on to do the voice-overs. His script was a long prose-poem with history (History as Pasolini wrote of it) playing itself.

Pasolini described the project to Carlo di Carlo (his assistant director starting with *Mamma Roma*) as "a polemical and ideological essay on the events of the past few years." Di Carlo recorded in his diary that *La rabbia* was

> a poetic text expressed through images, with rage built in. The rage of Pasolini. His rage against the middle-class world, against barbarism, against intolerance, against prejudice and "I'm all right-ness." Against the power that was then inveighing against him in a persecuting way. *La rabbia* was a protest film in many aspects ahead of its time.[13]

As always, Pasolini's private trajectory had its public, commercial uses. Producer Gastone Ferrante publicly acknowledged that he wanted to play Pasolini off against a conservative director, each creating half of a two-part film. His notion was to have the two comment on world history: Pasolini from the Left and Giovanni Guareschi from the Right. Two notorious figures, face to face.

By April 1963 the publicity started to appear: "Guareschi against Pasolini. Pasolini against Guareschi. Not since the time of Binda and Guerra [famous bicyclists] has there been such an exciting rivalry in Italy."

Pier Paolo claimed that he was not prepared to share a billing he believed would go to legitimize the Right-wing Guareschi by association. "I do not wish to contribute . . . even as an antagonist, to the diffusion of such ideas [as Guareschi's] among the young. . . ."

Much later, in 1968, he told an interviewer:

> I did my episode, thinking that was all there was to it, but when I'd finished the producer decided he wanted to have a commercial hit and so he had the brilliant idea of getting another episode with a commentary from the other side of the political system. However, the person he chose, Guareschi, was unacceptable. So there was some trouble with the producer, and anyway, the film was a flop because people weren't interested in such highly political material.[14]

Pasolini proceeded with his own work, hoping it would see release. Out of the ninety thousand meters of newsreel from a series called *Mondo libero*, he selected those scenes and frames to piece together along the narrative line of his script. Guareschi, working out of the same raw footage, worked at another editing machine "about ten yards away." Di Carlo recalled, "We caught a glimpse of his mustache only now and then, because he and Pasolini did not even greet one another [in the corridor of a rented apartment in Viale Liegi] in passing."

Out of the mountain of images, Pasolini constructed a kind of narrative, sometimes connecting one image to another by analogy, at other times by opposition. As he explained a few years later, "My criterion was, let's say, a Marxist denunciation of the society of the time, and what was happening in it."[15] His canvas was nothing less than the whole world's history, 1956–1963.

*La rabbia*'s opening frames show an atomic bomb's explosion (presumably those of early November 1 and 8, 1956)—herald of the new age, although the first Soviet atomic blast had been on August 29, 1949 and the first hydrogen blast in the summer of 1953. Then came a fast cut to street fighting in Rome and Madrid, brought on by the Soviet invasion of Hungary. The million questions raised by such juxtaposition are left unanswered.

Until the murder of Aldo Moro, nothing marked a watershed in Italian political life more than the 1964 death of Palmiro Togliatti. Two million people crowded the Piazza San Giovanni: Pasolini spliced contemporary footage of that scene into his film. The longtime Socialist head, Pietro Nenni, can be seen in the cortège and Sandro Pertini, later President of the Republic. Other newsreel footage: De Gaulle, against the sound of gunfire. The liberator of France is not depicted as the presiding eminence of French peace but as the warrior-dictator responsible for the bloodbath of Algeria.[16]

Projecting scenes of the Congo in 1961, then much in the news, Pasolini took a clear line: As we see Patrice Lumumba, the voice-over declaims, "A new problem is born in the world: it is called color." Corpses on the streets of Havana appear, visual music to the spoken text: "Now Cuba is in the world." Frames of the work of George Grosz and Ben Shahn give way in rapid succession to a gallery of the leaders of a then coming-to-independence Third World: Nehru, Nasser, Bourghiba, Sukarno.

Now Cuba: "To die in Cuba is like dying in Naples," the voice-over intones. And then—returning to the issue of racism—"The only color is the color of man."

Pasolini shifts the scene to Italy, where jarring images in violent proximity are meant to unsettle the viewer. On the surface, all is *benessere*: Ava Gardner, at the peak of her renown, lands at an airport and is received like royalty. Sophia Loren visits a village eel festival and charms the cheerful peasants. Frames of Louis Armstrong, be-

loved in Italy; then frames of skulls. *La rabbia,* so amateurish in
technical execution twenty-five years later, is sometimes as jejeune
as an idealistic boy without caution or calculation announcing his
first loves and first anger born of disappointment.

Pasolini cuts to a Fiat factory, where a worker explains that the
union leadership has been "bought off." The voice-over likens him
to "a desperate, loyal dog."

> You see these? Severe men, in double-breasted suits, elegant, who take off
> and land in airplanes, run about in powerful automobiles, sit at grandiose
> desks like thrones, who met in solemn hemicycles, in chairs splendid and
> severe: these men with faces of dogs or of saints, of hyenas or eagles, these
> are the bosses.
>
> And, you see these? Humble men dressed in rags or in clothes mass-
> produced, miserable, who go and come on vomitous, squalid streets, who
> pass hour after hour at jobs without hope, who gather together humbly in
> stadiums or diners, in miserable huts or tragic skyscrapers: These men, with
> faces equal to those of the dead without features and without light save for
> that of life, these are the slaves.[17]

As the screen fills with pictures of Eisenhower acclaimed at the
1956 Republican convention in Chicago and Elizabeth II in coronation, Bassani intones a theme dear to Pasolini, one that runs from
*Le ceneri di Gramsci* to the end.

> We find ourselves at the start of what will probably be the ugliest epoch in
> the history of man: the epoch of industrial alienation . . . When the classical
> world is exhausted, when all the peasants and all the craftsmen have died,
> when industry has made the cycle of production unstoppable, then will our
> history be over.

Pasolini moves on. Pius XII, "the aristocratic Pope," dies. We
see footage of his funeral and of John XXIII's coronation—blessings
from a sedan chair, waving ostrich fans. And the director offers a
public tribute, and advice, to the man to whom he would soon dedicate his *Gospel:*

> The new Pope in his sweet and mysterious turtle smile, seemed to have
> understood that he must be the pastor to the most miserable: [to] fishermen
> for sharks, shepherds for hyenas, hunters after vultures, planters of thistles
> because theirs is the antique world and they drag themselves forward through
> the centuries with the history of our greatness.

Now to life in a Russian village, peasant dancing, shots of Lenin in thought, visitors to a Soviet museum. War in Algeria, the liberation of Oran. Like poetic punctuation, another A-bomb explosion, and . . . America.

Of all the sequences he assembled, Pasolini later claimed to like best the one he dedicated to Marilyn Monroe. Already as much an icon in Italy as in America (she had won the *Davide di Donatello* award for best foreign actress in 1958), she allowed Pasolini what he later called "the only bit [of the film] that is worth keeping."[18] He felt that he understood her. He calls her "shameless because passive / indecent out of obedience," with a beauty "that she always held back, like a smile amid tears." Of her death, he wrote in his script that she "unexpectedly disappears, like a golden dove." His elegant *addio:* "Out of the stupid ancient world and the ferocious modern world, all that remains is beauty, and you—you carried it with you like an obedient smile." He inserted footage of her funeral, and then abruptly shifted. Again, the atomic mushroom.

Russian music and the launch of the cosmonauts. With the fast cuts of a music video two decades before its time, Pasolini's editing threw on screen the Soviet space launch, Pontormo's "Deposition," Picasso. Then a mass reception in Red Square, honoring cosmonaut Hermann Titov [the second man in space after Gagarin's 1961 flight], bussed on both cheeks by Khrushchev, even a young Brezhnev visible amid the assembled Poliburo brass. Bassani speaks Pasolini's lines into the mouth of the smiling Soviet hero, seen talking to a Soviet general in a grainy newsreel that imparts a sense of the unreal and faraway:

> I return from the cosmos, comrades,
> and my first duty is to tell you
> that the mission I have completed
> is a new mission of men.
>
> My humble technician's experience
> concentrates now that which will be yours,
> which will be that of your enemies,
> that of the political chiefs
> and that of the poets.
>
> Flight makes all men equal
> brothers in altitude.
>
> And this is the second matter I must tell
> you:

> that up there, comrades,
> everyone was my brother,
> bourgeois and worker,
> intellectual and subproletarian,
> Russians and Americans.
>
> Our flight has reopened
> deeper wounds in the crust of the earth:
> and that this, the third thing I had to tell
> you
> comrades and enemies,
> political bosses and poets.

At this point, Pasolini's written script diverges from the filmed version. The dark-toned first draft—the one cut—read:

> My last and greatest duty
> is finally to tell you, returning to earth
> from the cosmos,
> that it is not here, not here that
> it matters to be brothers
> out of some optical illusion or vain sentiment,
> but there, on the road to the future
> where there are opening in the skies
> multiplying, the ancient, bloody paths of
> the earth.

The film could not end on such a pessimistic, even black vision of the horrors of human history (as Pasolini increasingly saw the past, repeating itself), replicated into the future and into space.

Instead, *La rabbia* closed with the cosmonaut's poem as a call to do better. It leaves a glimmer of hope:

> The ways of the heavens must be ways of fraternity,
> and of peace: to tell you this is
> my last and greatest duty.
> Because, comrades and enemies,
> political men and poets,
> the Revolution needs only one way,
> the one inside the souls of those who
> leave to the past the old, bloody roads of
> the earth.

The film circulated in Italy all of five days: two each in Rome and Milan, a day in Florence, and then disappeared into the archives of the Cinetecca Nazionale. Warner's, the distributors, used the excuse of "racist material" in Guareschi's half to remove the entire film from circulation everywhere and for good. Pasolini wanted to forget it: "Anyway the film was a flop because people weren't interested in such highly political material." [19]

*La rabbia* done, Pasolini turned to another poetic excursus on film. Bini was still unable to line up financing for *The Gospel According to Matthew,* and Pasolini told his *Vie nuove* readers: "I have been passing terrible days, days of anxiety . . . I put myelf into a grinder to do the impossible documentary on sex, in a state of terror, because if we do not succeed in making *Il Vangelo,* for external reasons, I do not know what to do with my life at this point. But let's hope this is only a gloomy perception." Having addressed politics and religion, there remained for him the other leg of life's fundamental triad—love and sex.

Assisi was alarmed; they were lending their name to a collaboration with Pasolini and now he was making a new film explicitly about sex? Pier Paolo wrote to reassure Caruso:

> My film-inquest will not only be without any of those elements of eroticism or scandal (in the simple sense of the word) of which I am accused: but it will be a severe film, and absolutely rigorous and concede nothing, nothing at all to any public or superficiality . . . I must still finish shooting it . . . I do promise that as soon as it is finished I will show it to you, before anyone else, to you and your colleagues at *Pro Civitate.* This is absolutely my duty, given the collaboration so dear, sincere, and truly Christian which you have given me already on this *Gospel.*

He even gave them a veto, offering, if they disapproved, to "put it in the can, waiting for *Vangelo* to come out first." And "If it pleases so-so, such that with making some changes, it might go ahead all right, I would make these changes, which we would discuss together. May I add before my signature 'in faith'?"

His "impossible documentary on sex" had, by his own description, "absolutely no success at all in Italy. It came out in a few 'art' cinemas, and I don't think it ever went abroad because it did so badly in Italy . . . it was only cinephiles and sociologists who went to see it." [20]

In this *Comizi d'amore*—shot between August and November 1963—he met the Italians face-to-face and they him: microphone in hand, cameraman just to one side, interviewing them in his own soft voice about intimate matters of feeling. He seemed at home in the role of interviewer, for the goal was the only one his life pursued— that of pedagogy—and the subject was dear to him, the many ways of loving. On film, he is mild-mannered but tenacious, almost self-effacing in aura and yet insistent that his interlocutors confront his direct and candid questions.

The film has a sweetness about it, as though shot in sepia. Pasolini was a gentle inquisitor, pressing ever so lightly on his subjects, urging them to explore their prejudices. A sweetness hangs over the answers: often full of incomprehension, sometimes simple hatred, they emerge from a country just awakening—and knowing it is late— to the very loud noise of this century. In 1963 Italians had not often been asked on film (or any other way in public: press polls were in their infancy) what they thought about divorce and sexuality. For him to travel north and south, city and country, and up and down the class scale was still something fresh. Save for the intellectuals, people seemed excited that a camera had appeared; some giggled, others pontificated, all but a few were self-conscious and nervous.

Those least upset at the encounter were also those least upset at the facts of life: the peasants in the deep south, the rural proletarians without expectations of middle-class propriety or its repression. Just as Pasolini had claimed all along, the poor were frank and forthcoming; the higher the class, the greater the palpable denial of sexuality joined with a willingness to impose intolerance of it in others.

The ninety-eight-minute production—its working title was *Cento paia di buoi,* (A hundred pairs of oxen)—had a simple premise: Pasolini would approach intellectuals and soldiers, schoolgirls and farmers, and ask them questions. It turned out not to be so simple. As finally produced, the encounters with "ordinary people" were interspersed with round-table comments by a two-man panel consisting of Italy's pop psychoanalyst Cesare Musatti and Alberto Moravia, the novelist of sex *par excellence.* At several points the scene cuts to them as they dissect what has just been seen, and offer their on-the-spot analyses in response to Pasolini's questions. While their job was presumably to provide the insights of higher science and of culture, the duo's comments are fascinating independent of their merits, both because they reveal a nation's "enlightened opinion" in transition and because Pasolini's two *éminences grises* were somehow positioned "outside" of Italy, somewhere else. Their sophistication, their "consciousness" separates ("alienates," in Marxist terms) them from the others seen on screen, who are "just themselves." They are, Pasolini explains, "authorities."

Even before the credits, we are launched into an encounter with Italian "actuality," a kind of "You Are There: Palermo, 1963." A man—unidentified as Pasolini but hardly needing introduction—approaches a group of boys in the Sicilian capital and asks, "How were you born?"

Their answers, full of laughter and charm, range from babies found under flowerpots to "the stork goes to Jesus and gets a baby and then brings it here to Palermo." Pasolini then cuts to an artisan's workshop in Florence where a woman explains, rather pathetically, that it is not her place to discuss such things, but she hopes her twelve-year-old son will not grow up to be a homosexual. Ignorance, thanks to obfuscation and prudery imposed by sexism, is already on the agenda.

Next he visits a holiday beach: As he interviews two girls, their friends and strangers crowd around to share in the excitement. One man, in swimming trunks, explains that fatherhood is the goal of all and anyone not obeying its natural law is something unspeakable. Pasolini, in thoroughly professional journalistic style, asks open-ended questions that draw this subject's narrow-mindedness into full self-revelation. He does not comment; that is left to Musatti and Moravia.

He visits the Emilian ("between Bologna and Ferrara") countryside, Italy's breadbasket. Farmers dressed for work stop to talk, leaning on pitchforks, and do so frankly and without false modesty. A farm family's mother, her head wrapped in a kerchief more reminiscent of prewar Poland than of the new industrial Italy, takes the lead. She is pleased that in matters of the heart and the body her daughter has more choice than she had at the same age.

Ever the sports fan, Pasolini then sought out members of the Bologna soccer team during a break in practice, focusing on especially good-looking players who are especially tongue-tied: They are virile, but their physical prowess has hamstrung their candor about intimacy.

He returns three times to his round table. His friend Moravia (considered a scandalous personality quite apart from his friendship with Pasolini) says he thinks everything will turn out for the best, that it is a good thing for taboos to be put into the open. Practicing psychiatrist Musatti is less optimistic: He says people will not really open up and share their opinions and feelings on film and, if pressed, will lie.

Next stop: the Lido, Venice's chic beach. Waiting under an umbrella-ed table are journalists Oriana Fallaci and Camilla Cederna in beachwear. He asks what they think about the relation between the sexes, dutifully recording their not-too-original observation that the role of women changes with class and region. Fallaci says certain workers in Milan are "on another planet."

The film visits a small Sicilian village, where three young women explain how little has changed: Virginity is expected; courtships have their rituals. The men are supposed to be ardent, the women in need of shelter until an arranged marriage, itself a sacrament the breaking of which is grounds for justifiable homicide. An eighteen-year-old talks about the need to elope, sole way to be free of social obligations.

Pasolini asks what they thought of the law outlawing houses of prostitution (*bordelli*—in slang, *casini*), enacted by parliament on September 20, 1958; it was the *Legge Merlin*, named for its proponent, Senator Lina Merlin, a Socialist imprisoned five years by the Fascist regime. Arguing that only Francoist Spain equaled Italy in backwardness, she overcame not only laws that governed the operations of the legalized houses of prostitution—accepted as necessary escape valves—but something invisible and more entrenched: *la viscosità italiana* (literally, "Italian viscosity"), the resistance to change no matter how merited.

Having addressed courtship, marriage, and birth, Pasolini moved to bring homosexuality to the fore. He approached Giuseppe Ungaretti as the famous, old poet, fully clad in a business suit, reclined in a beach chair. His oracle-like pronouncement: "Civilization is in fact against nature, and men have some unnaturality about them." Both poets leave it for the viewer to sort out whether this means that homosexuality is uncivilized (that is, bad) or natural (as opposed to civilized) and thus good. Giuseppe Ravegnani, Eugenio Montale, and Susanna Colussi Pasolini were also inteviewed but were cut in editing.

One of the most effective scenes was shot in a Milanese public ballroom. As the music plays and dancers move in the background, Pasolini stops two girls. No, they have never heard the terms "masochism" or "sadism." But, yes, "There are men who are women." He asks what the term "sexual deviancy" means. One girl says she has no idea.

Pasolini insisted until he got his response: The girl says she hopes never to be involved in such a *disgrazia* as homosexuality (it means both "misfortune," as in an accident, and "disgrace"), and that should any child of hers "be born that way," she hoped it would "outgrow it." "Being born that way" was Pasolini's understanding of the phenomenon as well: He believed it strictly genetic, something like hair or eye color that ran in families. To friends, he cited his cousin Nico and Susanna's siblings—his Aunt Giannina and Uncle Gino—as proof.

Embarrassed at the subject-matter, one girl giggles and says, "When I marry, let's hope all goes well." Her friend, suddenly serious, says that if she should happen to have a homosexual child, she would "take care of it, too, since it is also something sent by God."

In a Catanzaro bar, a group of young bucks allow that while homosexuality is something to be treated "rationally," it still is "disgusting." A train conductor (holder of a secure and well-paid unionized public service job) says that he is scandalized at the existence of sexual deviation; three well-dressed businessmen in a first-class compartment agree. While one dances around the issue, comically hemming and hawing, another visibly puffs himself up with indignation to proclaim that "as a family man," he is "repulsed" by such a thing. Given enough rope, his representatives of "modern" Italy cheerfully hang themselves.

Now Pasolini cuts to Moravia, who explains that to be "scandalized" is a sign of insecurity and that when confronted with the so-called scandalous, people fear losing their own identity. Of himself, Moravia offers, "I am never scandalized, save only by stupidity and never even that. To understand is not to be scandalized—he who is shocked by diversity is he who sees in it something threatening. The Pharisees were scandalized. Christ never."

Musatti suggests that conservatism is instinctual and "we fear our own instincts."

Returned to a seaside resort, Pasolini talks with a man who says that "marriage is the pillar on which we build the family, and thus all of society." He is not only content but exudes obliviousness— even callousness. One middle-aged woman says, "Women ought not to have as much liberty as men."

As though craving relief, Pasolini stops a young woman who speaks forthrightly on every subject posed. Grateful and relieved, Pasolini finally intervenes to tell her "only girls like you have clear ideas."

Most of the answers he gleans are so formulaic that Pasolini returns to ask Moravia why the middle class has "left a vacuum" and seems incapable of genuine response. The writer explains that "to answer [your questions] is to legitimize taboos and to look inside oneself." Pasolini remarks, with what must have been appreciated as calculated understatement, that sexual intolerance, ignorance, and the double standard seem to be thriving in the midst of Italy's touted economic boom. All was confusion and hypocrisy.

In his film's closing sequence, Pasolini-documentarist gave scope

to Pasolini-lyricist. He films a wedding, an ordinary wedding and
normal people—not rich, not too poor—so typical as to be invisible.
The preparations of the bride and groom, their families and friends,
are lovingly chronicled in montage style. Pasolini cuts from one scene
to another, building toward the ceremony: it is life but, because art,
now even richer. Everything in the film has built to this point: the
union of two creatures whose innocence and happiness the poet cel-
ebrates and defends.

Pasolini makes his camera dwell long and slowly on the principals.
His lens caresses the boy and the girl and their mothers and fathers
against no dialogue; only an Elvis Presley song. Then as the wedding
proceeds (Pasolini cast his young cousin, Graziella, as the bride),
Pasolini's voice sounds in the background, slowly reading a poem
with the repeating cadence, "Tonino and Graziella are marrying."
His melancholy verses are full of hope, exhorting them to love and
maturity; the poet wishes for the couple that their love expand with
the consciousness of what love means, and he wishes them "the
triumph of reason over instinct." He incants:

> Every right is cruel
> and they, exercising the right
> to be what their fathers and mothers were,
> only confirm
> dear as they are to life
> the gaiety and innocence of life.
>   . . .
> Let the wish for Tonino and Graziella be
> this:
> "To your love, let there be added awareness
> of your love."

Pasolini does not ridicule the couple's obedience to social expectations nor their willingness to repeat the clichéd ceremony. Neither
arch nor preachy, he delivers the wedding scene as the defiant coda
to the preceding footage so full of misunderstanding, blindness, and
hatred. The wedding is sacred, he seems to be saying, not because
of religion but because it marks human communality—like eating
together and dancing, two recurrent motifs in his films. It is religious
only because humanity alone is divine, without need of churches or
Church.

*Comizi d'amore* (released in the United States under the awkward
title *Love Meetings*) premiered at a film festival in Locarno and re-

turned to Italy with little success. Pasolini's explanation for why it "failed":

> The public saw itself reflected too faithfully. The ideological and social world that Italians live in only becomes meaningful to someone who is outside it; all people saw in it was their own everyday life reproduced . . . the average Italian, with no deep awareness of the world, no real social consciousness, does not realize what's going on. He feels immersed in the film like in everyday life.[21]

In later films, Pasolini did not allow that immersion but rather choose the alternative. The film was to be self-evidently an artifact, its story just that, told by a storyteller to listeners and viewers. His path through his particular naturalism was leading to self-confessed mythology: to the *Gospel, Oedipus, Teorema, Medea, Decameron, Canterbury Tales, Thousand and One Nights*—even *Salò*.

*The Gospel According to Saint Matthew* was to be the summation, in classical and theological terms the *summa*, both of sensibility and of scandal. The poet of *The Nightingale of the Catholic Church*, who had identified with Christ in masochistic ecstasy, whose anger at the Church was also that of a disappointed lover, now took his turn to give answer to the blasphemer.

In turning to Matthew's Gospel, Pasolini and Bini calculated they could afford to buck the Italian and worldwide tide in cinema; distributors were always ready for a biblical epic, which is what some must have imagined Pasolini would produce. Undoing expectations and overturning the reigning style now fixed his image as contrariness; as if there had even been any doubt, from *Gospel* onward he became the paradigm of the artist-in-opposition.

Pasolini made the story of Christ's birth, work, and death in black-and-white with nonactors, no great beauties, little makeup, and a pastiche sound track without original compositions. His settings were the bare hills of deep Calabria, a landscape plainly indicating *miseria* to his Italian viewers. No ancient colonnades, no chiseled Charlton Heston-style face would mouth a scriptwriter's version of the life of Christ set against sets and costumes of Roman decadence. Every word said on screen would come directly from Matthew's text. But the film was to be seen as "by analogy . . . I was not interested in exactitude. I was interested in everything but that."[22] As he had promised, the "pornographer," "blasphemer," and "pervert" even submitted his shooting script for approval to the priests at the Cittadella.

Timing was all. Pasolini was acutely aware that the recent liberal shift in the Vatican, tailor-made for him, might not last. He told one interviewer:

> I had good relations with Don Giovanni Rossi and the others from the Pro Civitate Cristiana organization and some other people from the Catholic left . . . but everything was made easier by the advent of Pope John XXIII who objectively revolutionized the situation. If Pius XII had lived another three or four years I'd never have been able to make *The Gospel*.[23]

What Pasolini called an "objective revolution" that John effected was going to take root in the radical vision of the film. If even an "Accattone" is touched by the divine, and Ettore is a *povero Cristo* splayed on his prison hospital table in imitation of Christ, and Stracci literally worthy of crucifixion, then the reverse was also true: as there was God in man, so too there is a violently human man in God.

The Christ of Pasolini's *Gospel* was like none ever filmed in Italy before: both hard and soft, both victim and the violent scourge of the moneychangers in the temple, perplexed and perplexing. It is true that Pasolini took the stuff of his life to make his art. But he also transformed autobiography into myth and found in myth the stuff to render his autobiography cogent. Debate raged around the question of whether the work was that of a "practicing Catholic": The drive to categorize Pasolini and appropriate him to one camp or another seemed to demand such simplification. As always, he broke apart the categories. His goal—and it was absolutely conscious, calculated— was a systematic redefinition of the definitions; the individual films were part of a unitary grand design—so many poems in one long book—a lifelong project dedicated to a fundamental revision of values at the level of system, not of symptoms.

Faced with the complexity of the Christian message in an Italy that made politics of religion and a religion of politics, Pasolini's insistence on intricacy and contradiction was deeply disturbing. In 1968 he addressd the core of his creative motivation:

> Maybe I didn't realize this myself until a month ago when I saw it [*Vangelo*] again after a gap of two or three years. It's not a practicing Catholic's work, it seems to me an unpleasant and terrible work [in the sense of terror-giving], at certain points outright ambiguous and disconcerting, particularly the fig- ure of Christ. . . . Nothing I have ever done more fitted to me myself than the Gospel . . . my tendency always to see something sacred and mythic

and epic in everything, even the most simple, humdrum and banal objects and events. . . . I also realized that the Christ figure is all mine, because of the terrible ambiguity there is in him.[24]

He attributed the outcry around the film to its "disconcerting and scandalous novelty" explainable because, he said, "Nobody in Italy reads the Gospel." "I asked every single person I knew and only three or four at most had read the Gospel . . . no one expected a Christ like that, because no one had read Matthew's Gospel. . . ."[25]

Pasolini was as ambiguous about religion as he made the personality of his Christ about his own divinity. The Pier Paolo of the afterwar years had looked at "those fathers and sons living / the evenings of Casarsa" and seen "the church of my adolescent love, / dead deep in the centuries, lived / only in the old dolorous odor / of the fields."

With time, he came to declare,

> Woe to him who doesn't know
> this Christian faith is bourgeois,
> in every privilege, every rendering,
> every servitude; that sin is
> only a crime against offended
> daily certitude, is hated because of
> fear and sterility; that the Church
> is the merciless heart of the State.[26]

The charges repeatedly brought against him burned away his love of the institutional Church, leaving something behind. He responded to one of his *Vie nuove* readers, who had written in, claiming to have been "shocked" that a comrade would make a film of apparent use to the enemy, "I don't have inside me that internal resistance against religion which inhibits a Marxist who had been really a bourgeois Catholic." Fighting on both fronts, he explained to his atheistic fellow traveler that even Gramsci had allowed that "the religious idea does not constitute a reason for division in the working class, just as it does not constitute a reason for division in the bourgeois class. . . ."

He painstakingly explained:

> You know that every discrimination is ahistorical and inhuman. There is nothing more ridiculously wrong-headed than racism. Now, on the part of the Communists toward the priests, and the priests toward the Communists, there is a kind of "racist" stance . . . but do you imagine that Pope John is scandalized or indignant in the face of the eight million Communist voters in Italy? I do not think so.[27]

The story of Christ, as Pasolini chose to tell it, would rob the priests of their "monopoly of the Good," and let him still be able to call himself "not very Catholic." The script let him externalize his own feelings of persecution in identification with Christ, and by inference rebuke the Church. And yet it served for exploring a deeply held religious conviction that Christ was relevant. The apparent contradiction that so shocked observers was anything but contradictory or shocking to him:

> An atheistic philosophy is not the only possible philosophy of Marxism—especially since it is true that the Marxist base among workers was always, in its majority, believers, and also at the higher reaches [of the PCI] there have been many Catholic Marxists. And it is a current and typical fact of contemporary Marxism to include many elements within it of the bourgeois and irrational culture, elaborating them in a way that is complex and original.[28]

He cast the biblical personages straight out of his own circle: the poet and critic Enzo Siciliano was Simon of Canaan, his old friend Francesco Leonetti was Herod II, writer Natalia Ginzburg donned hopsacking to play Mary of Bethany, and her husband in life played her husband in Scripture. The poet Alfonso Gatto played the apostle Andrew. Writer Giorgio Caproni agreed to play Joseph of Arimathea ("He even offered 700,000 lire. A good sum for those times"[29]) but ill health prevented his going past the trial shooting.

Elsa Morante's nephew, Giacomo, played the Apostle John; her brother Marcello was Joseph, cast opposite a young Mary played by a girl taken off the streets of a poor Calabrian town Pasolini visited on location search. Joseph is prematurely balding, she beetle-browed and plain.

Ninetto was given "the tiny part of a shepherd boy," what Pasolini afterward called "a kind of screen test." To play the aging mother of God, the Mary of Nazareth who views the sacrifice of her son at Golgotha: Susanna Colussi Pasolini, daughter of Domenico of Casarsa delle Delizie.

The "ambiguous" Christ—Pasolini's description—was to be "an intellectual in a world of the poor available for revolution." Pier Paolo wrote, "I have an idea of Christ that is almost inexpressible. He could be almost anyone, and in fact I looked for him everywhere. I looked for him in Israel, in Sicily, in Rome, in Milan . . . I thought of the Russian poets, the American. Perhaps I am looking for him among the poets . . . I felt the only real possibility would be to use a poet. . . ." One candidate was Jack Kerouac, "And then I discovered that the photograph of Kerouac was ten or fifteen years out of date. . . ." Nico Naldini says his cousin also approached the Spanish poet Luis Goytisolo and Allen Ginsberg.[30] Pasolini also wrote to Yevgeny Yevtushenko in Moscow:

> You don't know it: but I have been thinking about you for a year . . . I want you to play the part of Christ in my film on the *Gospel According to Matthew*. All this implies I do not know myself either.
>
> Where did this idea come from? You perhaps know that I, not being a director . . . a serious one, do not look for my interpreters among actors: until now, for my subproletarian films, I have found them, as we say in Italy "on the street."
>
> For Christ, a "man off the street" will not suffice: to the innocent expressivity of nature must be added the light of reason. And so, I thought of poets. And thinking of poets, I thought first of you.
>
> The whole world will think it strange that I chose for Christ you of all people, a Communist. But am I not perhaps a Communist? The conceptual reasons for my work are quite complex. But I will simplify them all by passing along the first frame of my film: "This film seeks to contribute, to the modest measure allowed a film, to the world toward peace in the world begun by Nikita Khrushchev, Pope John, and John Kennedy."
>
> I do not want to add other explanation and more imploring. This is an idea which pleases or does not, in and of itself. In the meantime, read the Gospel according to Matthew!
>
> I embrace you affectionately, with great hope, your
>
> Pier Paolo Pasolini[31]

Beneath the active surface, the project was still far from sure. That March, Pasolini wrote an editor at Einaudi, who had suggested a new project: "Within the next two weeks, the decision will be made whether to make *Vangelo* or not: if I do not do it, I will have much free time, and given the success of *Il vantone*, I could also attempt [a translation of Molière's] *Tartuffe*. Could you let me have a definitive yes or no in the next two weeks?"[32]

Just then, Pasolini had an unexpected visitor at his home in EUR. An enthusiastic Catalan economics student named Enrique Irazoqui had decided to try to meet the author of *Ragazzi di vita*, which he had read in Spanish translation.[33] Pasolini later claimed the decision to cast the youth—who had never acted before and never did so after—was "a sudden inspiration involving psychological factors, a way of seeing people."

> I came back to the house and found this young Spaniard waiting to see me, and as soon as I saw him, even before we had started talking, I said, "Excuse

me, but would you act in one of my films?"—even before I knew who he was or anything. He was a serious person, and so he said no. But then I gradually won him round.[34]

Irazoqui, son of a Basque father and Jewish mother, was thin, stoop-shouldered, heavy-browed: anything but the muscular Christ of Michelangelo. He was the closest Pasolini could come to the Christ he described to a reporter from the *Gazzettino* of Venice the previous February: "the son of a German Jew and a mother from the Caucasus."

The Spaniard looked to be a Christ as preoccupied thinker, the sort to act out a mental passion that would be "a violent summons to the bourgeoisie that has stupidly thrown itself toward the destruction of man."

He reported in *Vie nuove* his thoughts as he worked to film and edit his story of Christ. In April he began shooting, finishing by summer's end. With October, he wrote his "Dialogue" readers:

> The atheism of a militant Communist is the essence of religion compared to the cynicism of a capitalist: in the first, one can always find those moments of idealism, of desperation, of psychological violence, of conscious will, of faith—which are elements, even degraded, of religion—in the second one finds only Mammon.[35]

The film's Christ is the enemy of the Pharisees, the man of absolute pity and terrible rage, the spokesman and advocate of the poor of Galilee, the ancestors of the poor of Friuli, the predecessors of the peasants of the Mezzogiorno who step from their lives onto the film of 1964. Pasolini told students at the Centro Sperimentale di Cinematografia, "Misery is always, in its most intimate characteristic, epic . . . this, my way of seeing the world of the poor, of the subproletariat, has consequences, I believe . . . in the very style of my films."

Filming proceeded amid intense press attention. For Jerusalem he used Matera, capital of the notoriously backward province of Basilicata, deep at the base of the peninsula's boot. A wild and bare region called I Sassi (literally, "Rocks") offered the landscape for the Garden of Gethsemane. The peasants of Lucania served as the Nazarenes who applauded the arrival of Jesus. Barile in Puglia became Bethlehem, and the desert where Christ walks with the Apostles Pasolini found ready to hand in the isolated, impoverished Calabrian countryside, which he chose because he found it "intact through the centuries." To film the temptations of the devil, the troupe moved to the slopes of Mount Etna.

Setting the story of the Son of God against the literal background of contemporary Italy was only what the beloved painters Pasolini had studied under Longhi had always done. Had not Cima of Conegliano (commissioned in 1494 to paint Christ's Baptism for the Venetian Church of San Giovanni in Bragora) placed his models in the landscape a few kilometers from his Veneto home? His painted hills, behind the sacramental pool, are visible still between Belluno and Feltre. Every precedent in Italian art permitted Pasolini's John to baptize Christ in the Chia river outside Viterbo, north of Rome "standing in for the Jordan." It was in Italy's pictorial tradition that he found the posture of the sleeping soldiers at the Resurrection, the decapitated children in the massacre of the innocents.

He knew what he wanted for the crucial Sermon on the Mount sequences, scenes whose first version so upset Don Giovanni Caruso that he wrote Pasolini asking that it be cut from the screenplay. It had to be something to "reprove modern man . . . for his gray orgy of cynicism, irony, practical brutality, compromise, conformism." At first he filmed the scene near Tivoli, amid its olive trees and along the roads. Later, he decided more close-ups of Irazoqui-Christ's face were needed and these he shot indoors. The studio work, like so much else in Pasolini's films, was "primitive" by Hollywood standards: One can almost see the technicians changing the lights and hear the sound machines being operated. Such considerations mattered not the least for this, his "cinema of poetry," still unnamed.

Altogether, he shot a hundred thousand meters of film, enough for almost three hours viewing time, and then, as always, created his movie in the cutting and editing room. The final work is full of long (sometimes seemingly interminable) close-ups on faces, slow pans, and formal set-pieces like Christ's baptism. This, the film's first scene, was filmed in upper Lazio, its composition unabashedly followed Leonardo's painting of the subject. At times, the film proceeds for long stretches completely without dialogue.

Within the safety of a loyal-to-the-text chronological order, Pasolini's *Gospel* progresses from the announcement of the coming birth of Christ through his childhood, baptism, the expulsion of the moneychangers, debates with the Sanhedrin, to Calvary—closing with the Crucifixion, deposition, and discovery of the stone rolled away from the mouth of the Sepulchre. Looking back, he was characteristically unsatisfied, and referred to his Christ as "at times . . . almost embarrassing, as well as being enigmatic." "The miracles of

the loaves and the fishes and Christ walking on the water are disgusting pietism," he said—but only in 1968. "The jump from these
kinds of holy picture scenes to the passionate violence of his politics
and his preaching is so great that the Christ figure in the film is
bound to produce a strong sense of unease in the audience."[36]

If Catholics, as he saw it, came out of the film "a bit shaken up,
feeling that I have made Christ bad," so was Pasolini deeply in
crisis—about what should be the stylistic approach to his narrative.
What he called the "reverential" style of *Accattone* now seemed "gild-
ing the lily . . . it came out rhetoric . . ."

> I got discouraged and was about to give the whole thing up, and then when
> I was shooting the baptism scene near Viterbo [between Orto and Viterbo]
> I threw over all my technical preconceptions. I started using the zoom, I
> used new camera movements, new frames which were not reverential but
> almost documentary . . . the style in the *Gospel* . . . combines . . . an al-
> most classic severity with moments that are almost Godardian—e.g., the
> two trials of Christ shot like cinema verité. The same contrast between the
> styles of *Accattone* and *The Gospel* comes out in the references to painting:
> in *Accattone* there is only one figurative element—Masaccio, perhaps deep
> down Giotto and Romanesque sculpture as well . . . whereas in *Gospel* there
> are numerous different sources—Piero della Francesca in the Pharisees'
> clothes, Byzantine painting (Christ's face like a Rouault) . . . Recently
> [1968] I saw an exhibition of Rouault's work with some paintings of Christ
> where he had exactly the same face as my Christ.[37]

He began to use a 300mm lens, producing two effects: "that of
flattening," to give the pictorial plane "of the fifteenth and sixteenth
centuries" and also the "actuality of a documentary."[38] With substantial help from director of photography Tonino delli Colli, he had
progressed beyond "the consistent and extremely simple style" of
*Accattone:*

> The first time I saw the [entire] film, just after I'd finished it, I thought it
> did have stylistic unity, and this surprised me; and then I realized this was
> because I probably do believe after all. The stylistic unity is only my own
> unconscious religiousness, which came out and gave the film its unity.

The script—with occasional "old-fashioned" leaps through bits of
text printed on screen—was true to Pasolini's promise to the Cittadella: not a word is not found in Matthew. The music, which Elsa
Morante helped him select, was mostly Bach, with Webern, Russian
revolutionary songs, original music by Luis E. Bacalov, and the re-

cently released *Missa Luba* from the Congo. As background for the Massacre of the Innocents, he used the same Prokofiev that Eisenstein had used in 1938 in *Alexandr Nevsky*. Pasolini's chosen background for the Baptism of Christ: the American black spiritual "Sometimes I Feel Like a Motherless Child" and Mozart.

As expected, Christ is a revolutionary. One interviewer took issue and challenged that Matthew does not read as Pasolini rendered him.

> Many people consider him [Matthew] the most counterrevolutionary of the Evangelists: that his main point was to convince the Jews to back Christ, who was a moderate, against the religious Pharisees who were the religious leaders of a national liberation struggle.

By way of answer, Pasolini took what must have seemed a necessary refuge in generalization and the rights of poetry:

> I was not interested in reconstructing the whole situation exactly. It is the feeling of the Gospel as a whole when you first read it that is revolutionary. Christ going around Palestine is really a revolutionary whirlwind: someone who walks up to a couple of people and says, "Drop your nets and follow me" is a total revolutionary. Subsequently, of course, you may go into it more thoroughly, historically and textually, but the first reading is profoundly revolutionary.[39]

After a summer spent editing, he released *Gospel* for showing at the Twenty-fifth International Film Festival in Venice on September 4, 1964. Moravia and Maraini returned from vacation in Yugoslavia to be there. Except for his consultants at the Cittadella, no one had seen the film.

Except, as the law required, the censors. On August 8 Dott. Prof. Commendatore Alberto Albani-Barbieri, a member of the official censorship commission, wrote in response to Don Giovanni Rossi's letter commending the film: "I have seen *Il Vangelo* and think it is a work worthy of praise, both for its artistic dignity and for the height of its inspiration, [which is] worthy of the Text."

At the Festival's Palace of Cinema, Pasolini met with whistles, followed by tossed tomatoes and raw eggs. Those responsible were (again) identified as members of Ordine Nuovo, Circolo Giovanile Azzuro, Gruppo Universitario San Marco, and Associazione Italo Iberica. They threw leaflets outside; inside the theater, they tossed more eggs and spitballs at both screen and audience, assaulted a journalist, Bassani, and the painter Renato Guttuso, well known as a Communist. The local police contingent had been tripled, already making the premiere good news copy: Intellectuals and the rich in tuxedos and evening gowns were photographed marching between a police cordon under TV lights, lining up to see a film about Christ by Pasolini. Several young men moved to assault him; police intervened, arresting a few. The scene lasted about ten minutes until the lights were dimmed.

The Festival over, Pasolini left for a vacation wth Ninetto. Returned to Rome, he wrote Laura an angry letter: She had made such a scene on the telephone when Ninetto made her wait that Pasolini had hung up on her. She had, he wrote, interrupted with "a brutal aggression, cold, absurd" the tranquility of a rest in which, "finally—maybe for the first time in my life—I felt the world a friend . . . Ninetto, swimming, [had] shouted 'how beautiful life is!' "

Film critic Tullio Kezich reported that the whistles at Venice had been drowned out by the "ovation which the public gave the poet of *Le ceneri di Gramsci*."[40] Pasolini wrote to thank him for the piece. But when Goffredo Fofi reviewed *Il Vangelo* negatively in the Left-militant *Quaderni piacentini*,[41] Pasolini addressed a scathing letter (with others to follow) to the magazine's director, Piergiorgio (brother of the film director, Marco) Bellocchio: "It is a judgment which is not a judgment, but rather an observation which becomes one through the moralism which is typical of your *Quaderni*, and which is very traditional, very typical of the Italian petite bourgeoisie. Now you have found new subjects and new terminology to practice it: but it is still the same."[42]

He accused Bellocchio of being, in effect, no better than "an editor of [the rabid Right's magazine] *Il borghese*, of searching for "moralistic, ideological pretexts to divert [attention from] the scandal you feel faced with me, [one] consistent with the generalized psychosis."

Franco Fortini, a collaborator and adviser to the *Quaderni*'s editors, joined the fray. He signed his open letter to Pasolini "your friend."

> I urge you to be humble . . . You enjoy the invective of this Jesus too much. It cannot (nor can I) help you . . . I don't know if you'll understand the intention of this letter, I bear you a grudge, because your public life shows the signs of ugly and also clumsy calculation; I am angry because of the objective (i.e., counterrevolutionary) evil that your public aspect has helped to create; I have the hope that you may contradict yourself to the point of wanting to contradict yourself no longer . . . it is not enough, dear Pierpaolo, to scorn adulation; one must not deserve it.[43]

The matter exhausted itself in an orgy of epistolary bravura, insults, threats of lawsuits, and counterthreats.

Two years later Pasolini (not one to fail to punish foe or reward friend) jabbed again at *Quaderni piacentini*, calling it a place "where a group of the best, worst Marxist critics have taken refuge: *beatnik* Stalinism."

The Venice Festival awarded *Gospel* a Special Jury Prize, but the Golden Lion of first place went to Antonioni's *Red Desert*. Pasolini wrote in *Vie nuove:* "It seemed to me an extremely beautiful film."[44]

Bini organized a private screening for a group of prelates (he later claimed "a thousand bishops and cardinals") then meeting in Rome for a *"Corso di Studi Cristiani,"* a study program organized on the occasion of the Council, still acting under the liberal spirit that survived into the early days of Paul VI's pontificate. Arrangements were made and confirmed that *Il Vangelo* would be screened within the Vatican's own auditorium in the via della Conciliazione.

Nervous lest anything go wrong, the producer went several hours early to the site and found it locked, dark and sealed. "Work in Progress" signs had gone up overnight. "I think someone in the Vatican panicked," he recalled many years later, "and just decided at the last minute that showing the film there, to the gathered "Princes of the Church," was too risky. So I got together a fleet of thirty taxis and ferried them to the Cinema Ariston in Piazza Cavour. When the dedication "to the dear, joyful, familiar shadow . . ." ["*Alla cara, lieta, familiare ombra* . . .] of John XXIII came on the screen,[45] Bini claims his guests "applauded exactly twenty minutes." In due course, the group issued a statement calling the film "profoundly Christian."

Soon after, a jury of the Office Catholique Internationale du Cinema (OCIC)—presided over by a Peruvian bishop—awarded *Il Vangelo* its highest prize, the first ever to so honor an Italian production. The citation read in part: "The author—without renouncing his own ideology—has faithfully translated, with a simplicy and a human density sometimes moving, the social message of the Gospel—in particular the love for the poor and oppressed—sufficiently respecting the divine dimension of Christ." The papal private secretary requested a private screening of the film for the Holy Father.[46] It was no small satisfaction for the producer of *La ricotta*, in which prosecutor Di Gennaro had claimed that the scene of Stracci-Christ's cries of anguish on the cross were caused by the pleasure of masturbation at the sight of the lewd stripper Magdalen.

*L'osservatore romano* kept its head, declaring the film "a humanized Gospel but lacking messianic mystery . . . but it is already something that a Marxist-atheist even approaches such a subject and the divine personage of Jesus, and does so with respect . . . Pasolini's attempt to understand the poetic reality of the Gospel, even with its evident limitations, is among the most serious [ever]."

The press on the Right howled. *Il tempo* wrote: "They make a friar of the devil," for the devil presents himself that way to steal a soul. The Roman daily wrote that OCIC's prize was "to the immense profit of Communism" and asked what Don Rossi would think of a "Capital according to Karl Marx" in five acts. *Vita* claimed Pasolini's Christ dies "with a feeling much more of rebellion and desperation than of abandonment." While *Il telegrafo* of Livorno was content to exclaim "What an unpredictable man is Pier Paolo Pasolini!" *Napoli notte* sniped that the next step would be to give Pasolini a cardinal's hat and erect a temple in Rome dedicated to "San Carlo Marx."[47] One editorial said OCIC's reference to "sufficiency" was "a masterpiece of ambiguity and at the same time pious and ridiculous," and that the institute at Assisi ought to be renamed Pro Civitate Comunista.

On November 12 *Il borghese* ran a long mock-short story—a *racconto fantacattolica*, a "Catholic-fiction tale"—a takeoff of *fantascienza*, science fiction. It recounted how "Pietro Paolo" [sic] drove to the *borgata*, "hoping to find company for an hour or for the night." He gestures to a boy ("after all, it was a way to make money, like any other"), who gets into his car and they drive out to the fields. They park, and only then does the boy notice that Pasolini's head is encircled by "a halo." "Only the day before, the Marxist writer had written in a weekly of his party that he did not believe in God; and here he was, with this thing on his head, forced to take account of something which Marx had always denied but never explained."

In April the next year the *Nastro d'argento* (Silver ribbon)—Italy's near-equivalent to the Oscars, awarded by the film critics' association—went to Pasolini for best film, to Delli Colli for best director of photography, to Danilo Donati for best costumes.

*The Gospel*'s success infuriated Pasolini's enemies: It was simply unacceptable that Pasolini had made a film officially labeled by Catholic critics as "a fine film, a Christian film that produces a profound impression." Reviewers became apoplectic trying to decide whether to label the work Marxist or Catholic.

The magazine *Folla* wrote: "The fact is that this film is an authentic preaching of Communism, using the words of Matthew maliciously interpreted . . . to have given this work a prize, and even in the presence of Fathers [of the Church] was a humiliating concession to error . . . to confusion."

Pasolini's old adversary Guareschi took up his pen. His widely circulated cartoon showed two middle-aged men—solid citizens, both wearing hats, one in the sure-fire conservative identification of double-breasted suit—*due buoni padri di famiglia* ("two good family men")—each with a young son in tow. On the wall behind the *piazza* where they stand, a poster reads: "Parish Cinema—*Vangelo secondo Matteo* by P. P. Pasolini, 'enthusiastically recommended by the Civitas Cristiana, prizewinner of the International Catholic Center [for Cinema].' "

One turns to the other: "Aren't you going to take the boys to Mass?" The answer: "No, I'm afraid we'll bump into Pasolini."

On October 18 the MSI's *Il secolo d'Italia* ran a full page, complete with photo of Pasolini in dark glasses. It was headed, in large block letters: "WHO IS PASOLINI?" and answered:

> The Roman Association (of the M.S.I.) has distributed this flyer in order to illustrate the cultural and moral personality of Pier Paolo Pasolini.
>
> This is the man:
> —Tried on April 18, 1952, on the charge of SEXUAL
> ASSAULT (acquitted for insufficient evidence);
> —Accused on July 12, 1960, by the Commissariat of Anzio, of ATTEMPTED CORRUPTION OF MINORS (charges dropped due to insufficient evidence);
> —TRIED FOR DISORDERLY CONDUCT AND FOR GIVING AID AND COMFORT TO A CRIMINAL along with 13 other co-defendants (he alone was acquitted, on November 16, 1961)
> —SENTENCED by the Tribunal of Latina to 15 DAYS OF IMPRISONMENT AND HARD LABOR, 5 DAYS OF DETENTION AND 10,000 lire FINE FOR ARMED THREATS (freed from the criminal charge by amnesty of the Court of Appeals)
> —SENTENCED APRIL 28, 1964, TO FOUR MONTHS OF IMPRISONMENT WITH HARD LABOR FOR PUBLIC DEFAMATION OF RELIGION (acquitted in Appeals Court on grounds that the act did not constitute a criminal offense)
> —DRIVERS LICENSE SUSPENDED FOR TWO MONTHS according to Ordinance 23940/C of the Prefect of Rome for VIOLATION OF ARTICLE 105 of the Traffic Code.
>
> THIS IS THE WRITER:
> (a sampler from the book *Una vita violenta*, published by Garzanti)
> ". . . who were there every night, waiting for the faggots . . ." p. 160
> ". . . Goddam fruits . . . p. 167, in full.
> ". . . listen, tur' . . . he yelled, don't say my coc'ing mother"
> p. 193, in full.
>
> THIS IS THE MAN AND THE WRITER WHO IS PASSED OFF AS THE AUTHENTIC INTERPRETER OF THE DIVINE EVANGELICAL MESSAGE.[48]

The page was reprinted, and updated, in *Il camino* in Lodi during January 1964, in *Il meridiano* in Cagliari on May 11, 1965, and thereafter on fliers in several Italian cities.

*Il secolo* ran a still from the film, of Judas' kiss with copy: "Pasolini and his followers can kiss among themselves all they like but cannot burden the protagonists of the history of the world with their stuff."

Some serious observers charged that Pasolini had not been accurate enough, that all his talk of using only the words of the Gospel masked his own version-making pretending to be somehow scientific. He answered:

> I did not want to reconstruct the life of Christ as it really was. I wanted to do the story of Christ plus two thousand years of Christian translation, because it is the two thousand years of Christian history which have mythicized this biography, which would otherwise be almost an insignificant biography as such. My film is the life of Christ plus two thousand years of storytelling about the life of Christ. That was my intention.[49]

On November 26, 1964, in *Vie nuove*, Pasolini answered a letter from a most useful reader—Umberto Rossi, of Genoa—who argued that "There can be nothing in common between Marxists and non-Marxists." Pasolini dismissed the notion.

> I want you to consider that the great majority of the Marxist leaders are of bourgeois origin: many of them, as young or very young people were Fascists, even activists in the GUF [Gioventù Universitaria Fascista] and so on. Thus they were non-Marxists: and they became Marxists. You would not allow any non-Marxist to become a Marxist? If you do not make such an allowance you will find yourself a thousand times in a thousand contradictory situations, mortified by the reality of the facts.[50]

That same month an article appeared in the official church magazine *Civilità cattolica,* entitled "The Impossibility of Dialogue with the Communists." Pasolini attacked it on psychological grounds: "He who has fears of being destroyed has a bad conscience: and he feels that he deserves destruction." But he had fire too for Communists unwilling to engage in dialogue with the "advanced and progressive" wing of the Church: "[Only] fragile Marxists fear 'being destroyed' by a dialogue with the Church and cling to their old positions to be reassured."

Once again he who called himself "most ancient of the ancients" and "most modern of the moderns"—foiling both orthodoxies—intended to demonstrate the contradictions at the heart of things. He insisted one could be at the same time more pious than the clerics of the Church and more mature, and thus more revolutionary a Marxist, than the cautious clerks who ran the PCI.

Because the bourgeoisie was, he felt, bent on destroying "the elements which are anthropologically human, classic, and religious in man," he rose to defend those values even at the risk of confounding and annoying those on the lay Left who were his natural possible allies. The newly open-minded Church John had left behind, and the State censors and the party-line critics in the press, would have to come to terms with the success of a man who said, "I don't believe in the divinity of Christ, because my vision of the world is religious . . . a mutilated religion because it hasn't got any of the external characteristics of religion, but it is a religious vision of the world. . . ."[51]

Nothing less could be expected from a man who looked at slum boys from Donna Olimpia and saw "fourteen-year-old Christs" who make a "clamor . . . which the pale sun absorbs in a sickly halo of grass and air," whose "eyes burn" so that they "reveal their souls in their pupils . . ."[52]

Such matters were anything but hypothetical: Which of the armed camps was he loyal to, after all? Having awarded *Gospel* its Grand Prize, the Catholic Film Office arranged for the film to be screened in Paris, within the walls of Notre-Dame, in December, and Pasolini went along. Following a Mass in the cathedral, and projection, there came the inevitable round-table discussion: The church was filled with spectators, the Sorbonne's Professor of the History of Christianity, bishops, priests, choir. Some who spoke were for the film, others against.

Maria Antonietta Macciocchi, *L'unità*'s then correspondent in Paris, later wrote, with understatement, that Pasolini's encounter with the French intellectual Left was "tempestuous. For them, the film was a slap right in the face. They are laical, rationalist, like Voltaire."

Michel Cournet (who refused to shake Pasolini's hand), critic of *Le nouvel obervateur*, wrote: "It is a religious film and religious propaganda beneath the façade of a faithful transcription of the Gospel made by a Marxist . . . I do not know if M. Pasolini is a prodigy of unawareness or a little champion of publicity." Claude Mauriac wrote, "No, it is not sacred art, nor art. It is only a fantasy. It is nothing."[53]

Pasolini answered, "The French intellectuals are deaf, out of touch with the historic reality of the whole world . . . Sartre is the only one who has understood. . . ."

Sartre agreed to meet Pasolini the day following the Notre-Dame debacle, at his usual hangout, the Pont-Royal Café. Pier Paolo and Macciocchi set out but became lost; they arrived only after phoning Simone de Beauvoir, who explained that the place was not near a bridge, as Pasolini had assumed, but inside the Hôtel du Pont-Royal in Saint Germain-des-Près. "We arrived two hours late," Macciocchi later wrote. "Sartre was ensconced on a red velvet sofa, smoking his hundredth Gitane. 'Did you really think I wouldn't wait for you? Now, about Saint Matthew.' "[54]

He assured Pasolini that Marxism, at least in France, still had not confronted Christianity as it must: "Stalin rehabilitated Ivan the Terrible; Christ is not yet rehabilitated by Marxists." And he offered canny cultural-political advice: The only way to satisfy French critics was to show *Il Vangelo* in Italian, not the version dubbed badly by a French priest, and back-to-back with *La ricotta*, to establish Pasolini's credentials as anything but a Catholic apologist. Showing Stracci dying on the cross before Enrico Irazoqui would, Sartre thought, calm the fears of his fellow-countrymen's anticlerical thought-police. Pasolini told Sartre, "Had I been French, I would have set the *Gospel* in Algeria, and that would have shaken them, just as the Italians are shaken because I set my *Gospel* in Lucania. Maybe that way they would have understood." Sartre urged him to return to Paris the following January—after *Il Vangelo* had been shown in both Budapest and Prague—and open a debate on his film between the lay Left and those Catholics, many of them priests who had made a personal contribution to the fight to liberate Algeria.

Pasolini's enemies exulted in his problems. Already a year before, he had visited Naples to join a cultural association–sponsored debate on the theme "From *Accattone* to *Gospel According to Matthew*"; the meetings ended in slaps, fisticuffs and the local police condemning the actions of an MSI candidate to the Naples City Council for his trouble-making. When *L'unità*'s local correspondent defended Pasolini, *Il secolo d'Italia* replied:

> *L'unità*'s defense of Pasolini was to be expected. Pasolini's ideas have been known for some time, and that Marxism is now trying to sidle up to certain positions of liberal Catholics and circulated under their protection . . . but the next time, it will not be a case of young people accompanying Pasolini to his train but rather the whole populace, fed up by now with such a disgusting personality.[55]

His isolation was also literary. He wrote editor Geno Pampaloni in Florence: "I do no longer have 'requests' for poetry"; would his magazine, *Questo e altro*,[56] consider printing something from his coming book of poems? He tried to stay involved, proposing work by "another girl" (poet Sandra Mangini) for Leonetti to print in *Il menabò*; acting as intermediary between Garzanti (who "won") and Giulio Einaudi in the publishers' tug-of-war over the next work by poet Amelia Rosselli. And he was in the midst of efforts by Moravia (Leonetti and Roversi were also involved) to have *his* magazine, *Nuovi argomenti*, taken under the administrative wing of Garzanti, and when that stalled, backed by Left-wing publisher Giangiacomo Feltrinelli.

Pasolini sensed something important had changed: Culture, it seemed, had become an industry, not the product of individuals or ardent groups of friends motivated by the love of their work. Depressed at the publishers' callous treatment of Roversi, he wrote his friend in Bologna: "This cannot but be the symptom of something worse than the fouled-up publication of your book. It means we are not strong and united enough to confront the new Italian situation, that we are disappointed and discouraged, that what matters is death and not life."[57]


Political reconciliation and change were in the air during the months he made *Il Vangelo*. Prime Minister Aldo Moro, after a seven-hour speech to Parliament, effected an "opening to the Left," inviting socialist politicians into his Christian Democrat cabinet. In a single stroke, he cut the PCI off from its natural allies on the Left.

The "impossible" happened. Nenni, head of the Socialist Party, became Vice-Premier; after thirteen days of balloting (and expressions of concern by Paul VI), on the twentieth polling Giuseppe Saragat—president of the Constituent Assembly that had drafted the 1948 constitution, and founder of the Social Democratic Party—became the country's fifth postwar president. Seemingly intolerable tensions eased, pressures on the Christian Democrats were alleviated. Wages of all public employees leaped upward and some palpable reforms were made in housing, education, and medical care. Italy's commitment to NATO was reaffirmed.

Pasolini put the changes in his own context. The so-called historic compromise triggered in him an overview of Italy in "History," bonded to excruciating autobiography and the complaint of a poet condemned to write in a minor language.

In the long poem "Plan of Future Works," dated "November–December 1963," he returned to the poet-seer's voice of *Le ceneri di Gramsci:*

> Even today, in this melancholy physicality
> when the nation's occupied forming a government
> and 'Center-Left' causes the fragile linguists'
>
> normative organs to shudder—winter steeps
> distant objects in obscure light while barely
> kindling mauve-green closer ones,
>
> in an exterior lost deep in the Italian
> ages . . .
> with Piero's azure earths arising out of
> Languedoc's
> unsayable azurines . . . or perhaps the Sicilian
>
> azurities of the Beginnings . . . which here in
> the rough
> appendixes of the exquisite Centers, are
> green, mauve,
> for mud, sky, lemons, roses . . . eyes of
> Fredericks,
>
> half their heart in rings of rocky almond
> groves,
> lit by Arabian sun; other half
> in some fog-beaded valley, the distant Alps
> insanely new . . .
>
> I'm going mad! All my life I've been trying
> to express this dismay, like Proust
> —which I felt even as a child on the
> Tagliamento,
>
> or Po, closer to the matrixes—to the circle
> of
> those who speak my language—who, from
> habit,
> are deaf to every private, infantile, unsure
>
> pre-expressivity, where the heart is naked.
> But trusting that, before I die, my thousand
> efforts might bring something to the judges,
>
> in this epoch when Italian's about to end,
> defeated by either Anglo-American or Russian,

I return naked, and, as I said, mad, to
green April

to the green April of that illustrious language
(which, never was, never was!) High
Italian . . .

## And his role?

I transform myself back into a Catholic,
Nationalist, Romanesque, in my research for
"Blasphemy" or "The Divine Mimesis"—and, ah
mystic

philology!, in the vintage days,
I rejoice as one rejoices sowing seed
with a fervor that mixes irreconcilable

substances, magmas without amalgam, when
life is April's lemon and rose.
Shit! To try to describe the condition

of language without assuming
political accompaniments! linguistic
unity without base economic

motives, without the insensibility
of a class that doesn't give a shit about
slang—
literary choice! Fucking professors,

neo or paleo patriots, assholes up to their
ears
in all that knowledge, who see twelfth-to-
fourteenth-century texts only as functions

of other texts . . . Stop, my blind love!
I'll employ you in translinguistic
research, and to one text I'll oppose a
veto,

to three texts three saints, to a literary
circle, traditions of cooking, border
disputes; and in the year of the discovery

of a rarified text, by copyists
of the Paduan language, I'll search, driven
by

stupidity or vanity, for what the painters
were doing,

from farm to farm in the green-sublime light
of the lands of the Po . . . but above all for
what
the ruling class wanted, whatever, I don't
know.

I'll turn it into a monstrous work, contemporary
with the *lettera 22*'s Anti-Works, the very
latest fashion,
old figurative mode stuck in the side of the
young.

But one has to disappoint. Only a noble
mishmash
of mixed inspirations can demystify
when chaos miraculously come up on

a plastic clarity, for instance, Romanesque
griffins—huge thighs, necks, and thoraxes
swollen like breadloaves, grey stone to
codify

full Reality. . . .[58]

"What," he asked his *Vie nuove* readers, "will be the effect of
technocratic capitalism?" regardless of which parties oversee the
State? What will be the future of relations between the "great capitalist nations and the underdeveloped world"? He was convinced that
"only Marxists love the past . . . the bourgeoisie loves nothing." It
mattered that, in its mad dash for "modernity," Italy was throwing
away what he called "the great European and Italian tradition."

The political man was also a private man in anguish:

Oh intricate dark
twists that push one to a "destiny of opposition!"
But there's no other alternative to my future
works . . .

Opposition of one who can't
*be loved by anyone, and who can't love anyone*

. . .

In the end, oh I know,

never, in my haggard passion,
have I ever been such a cadaver as now

as I take again in hand my tables of the
present— . . .[59]

On October 15, at the height of the work on *Il Vangelo,* he wrote
in *Vie nuove,* "My pessimism pushes me to see a black future, intolerable to the humanistic perspective, dominated by a neo-imperialism
of forms which are, in reality, unpredictable."[60]

In May, during the shooting, Garzanti published Pasolini's fourth
volume of poetry, *Poesie in forma di rosa* (Poetry in the form of a
rose), collecting work from 1962 through diary-poems occasioned by
the search for locations for the film-in-progress. Pasolini dismisses
ideology as "a drug," and cries (in all capitals) "I REPUDIATE THE
RIDICULOUS DECADE," just closed.[61] From "The Beautiful Banners," a poem dated 1962:

Like a wife cast onto the pyre with the king
or buried alive with him
in a tomb that moves off like a skiff
toward the millennia—the faith of the 1950s,
is here with me, already slightly past time's limits,
and it too will be crumbled
by the furious patience of the sea's blue grains.[62]

*Poesie in forma di rosa* includes the poem "Plan of Future Works"
("Progetto di opere future"), which closes with a searing vision in
Dantean tercets. "The Jews," to whom he appeals, are all Italians.
Their refusal to heed his call (and his self-described "immobility")
guarantee his "opposition":

I verify the heartrending need for
allied minorities. Come back, Jews,
to the dawn of this Prehistory,

which for the majority smiles like Reality
and for the connoisseurs is
loss of humanity and cultural reconstitution

of the new man. And, in fact, here's the
point:
in the atmosphere of a small nation,
in this case, Italy—a false dilemma

is posed between Revolution and an Entity
called the Center-Left—making

the linguists blush . . . the new course of
reality

is thus admitted and accepted. Return,
Jews, to contradict it, with those
few who've finally clarified

their destiny: Power goes toward
the future, and the Opposition follows it,
in
the act of its triumph, power within power.

For one crucified to his tormenting
rationality,
butchered by puritanism, nothing makes sense
anymore
but an aristocratic and unpopular opposition.

The revolution is now just a sentiment.[63]

Later, he tried to soften *Poesie*'s bleak vision. He told the critic
Fernando Camon[64] that the book's diary form communicated his
thought only at any given moment, "making the contradictions extreme, never reconciled . . . ," that his "rejection" of the immediate
past—"a kind of destructive rage"—"ought to be read as one reads
poetry . . . 'the tone' of that rejection is poetic, not real." Backing
off even as he advanced, he suggested the feelings the poetry expressed were in "more rancorous terms" than he felt.

He also wrote (of himself, using the third person), that he accepted
"the exercise of his political / duty as the exercise of reason." He
had no choice but to remain the *poète engagé*, even though "Intelligence will never carry any weight, never, / in the judgment of this
public opinion . . ."[65] So, as though willed by a destiny he could
only obey and therefore chose to embrace—not to pull back from the
struggle—he reminded his readers that the important concerns of
1964 were "the Chinese question" and understanding better "the
phenomenon of Stalinism." As for Italy, he mourned John XXIII,
recently dead, "who was not only a good pope: because what he said
and did is *irreversible*." In *Vie nuove* he wrote: "With Papa Giovanni,
the Church bestirred itself. . . ."

Calvino wrote, praising one of the book's poems, "Vittoria" ("one
of your most beautiful . . ."), and asked "When are you going to stop
making movies?"[66] Even Laura Betti, who admitted she had read
only "half" his poetry ("because poetry tires me out, my intelligence
being of an absolutely uterine character and thus bizarre"), wrote,

saying she would rather see him "victorious as a poet or writer than as a filmmaker."

He was worried that fame was typecasting him as Rebellious Sage. To his column's readers, he wrote:

> Know then that I do not want to exert influence. If I should do so, it will be from time to time, through the possible strength of my arguments, at *that given moment,* in that *given* circumstance—and above all through sincerity. The monstrous thing about the influential man is his making use of the sincerity, commitment, and the total risk of his whole being through which he has been able to achieve influence, and which, it having been achieved, are mechanically reproduced in an *a priori* way.[67]

*Poesie in forma di rosa* includes the poem "A Desperate Vitality": The poet imagines himself "piloting his Alfa Romeo," returning from Rome's airport, presumably after a trip to Africa with Moravia. His friend remains there, "pure among his luggage." But Pasolini?

> —I'm like a cat burned alive,
> crushed by a truck's tires,
> hanged by boys to a fig tree,
>
> but still with at least eight
> of its nine lives, like
> a snake reduced to a bloody pulp,
> an eel half-eaten
>
> —sunken cheeks under dejected eyes,
> hair horribly thinned on skull,
> arms skinny as a child's,
> —a cat that doesn't die, Belmondo
> who "at the wheel of his Alfa Romeo"
> within the logic of the narcissistic montage
> detaches himself from time, and inserts in
> it
> himself
> in images that have nothing to do with
> the boredom of hours in a line,
> the slow splendid death of the afternoon.[68]

The poem "represents" the poet during the act of being interviewed on film. The reader is thus both eavesdropper and voyeur:

> Without a dissolve, in a sharp cut, I
> portray myself in an act—without historical
> precedents—of "cultural industry."

I, voluntarily martyred . . . and
she in front of me, on the couch:
shot and countershot in rapid flashes,
"You"—I know what she's thinking, looking
at me,
in a more domestic-Italian *Masculine-
Feminine*,
always *à la* Godard—"you, sort of a Tennessee!"

the cobra in the light wool sweater
      (and the subordinate cobra
        gliding in magnesium silence).
Then aloud: "Tell me what you're writing?"

"Poems, poems, I'm writing! Poems!"
(stupid idiot,
poems she wouldn't understand, lacking as
she is
in metric knowledge! Poems!)
poems NO LONGER IN TERCETS!

      Do you understand?
This is what's important: No longer in tercets!
I have gone back, plain and simple, to the
magma!
Neocapitalism won, I've
been kicked out on the street
  as a poet [boo-hoo]
  and citizen [another boo-hoo]
And the cobra with the ballpoint:
"The title of your work?" "I don't know . . ."
[He speaks softly now, as though intimidated,
assuming
the role the interview, once accepted, imposes
on him: how little it takes
for his sinister mug
to fade into
the face of a mama's boy condemned to death]
—perhaps . . . "The Persecution"
    or . . . "A New Prehistory (or Prehistory)
    or . . .
[And here he rears up, regaining
the dignity of civil hate]
    'Monologue on the Jews' . . ."
                [The discourse
flounders like the weak unaccented beat
of a jumbled octosyllable: magmatic!]

"And what's it about?"
"Well, my . . . your, death.
It is not in not communicating [death],
but in not being understood . . ."[69]

The "interview" closes with a heading: "(Funereal conclusion: with synoptic tables—for use of the writer of the 'piece'—of my career as a poet, and a prophetic look at the ocean of future millennia.)"

He laid it out on the page with an eye to words-as-design, exactly as the concrete poets proposed:

I came into the world at the time
of the Analogic.
I labored
in that field, as an apprentice.
Then there was the Resistance
and I
fought with the weapons of poetry.
I reinstated Logic, and I was
a civil poet.
Now is the time
of the Psychagogic.
I can only write, prophesying
in the rapture of Music
through an excess of seed or compassion.

If now the Analogic survives
and Logic has passed out of fashion
(and I with it,
I'm no longer asked for poetry),
there is
the Psychagogic
(to the disgrace of the Demagogy
ever more in control
of the situation).
And thus
I can write Themes and Trains
and even Prophecies;
as a civil poet, ah yes, always![70]

Almost a decade later, he told reporter Jean-Michel Gardair from *Le monde* that "after *Poesie in forma di rosa* I had the feeling of having exhausted a certain linguistic world, the pleasure of certain choices, certain words. . . ." In this his most desperate poem in a desperate book, he intoned the lines that came to be a kind of epitaph:

Death is not
in being unable to communicate
but in no longer being able to be understood.[71]

His next book of poems, his last, did not appear until 1971.

On December 27, 1964, he wrote to thank Don Giovanni Rossi at the Cittadella for Christmas greetings:

> As for my sins . . . the greatest of these is to think most deeply only about my work, something which makes me rather monstrous: but I can do nothing about it, it is an egoism which finds its excuse in an ironclad promise *("alibi")* which I have made with myself and with others and which I cannot undo. You could never absolve me from this sin, because I could never make a commitment not to do it again. The other two sins which you have intuited are my "public" ones: as for blasphemy, it isn't so. I said bitter words against a *certain* Church and a *certain* Pope: and how many believers, now, do not agree with me?
>
> The other sin I have so many times confessed in my poetry, and with so much clarity and so much terror, that I have ended up cohabitating with it inside me like a familiar specter, one I have become used to, and of which I no longer succeed in seeing the real, objective entity.
>
> I am "blocked," dear Don Giovanni, in a way which only Grace can resolve. My will and so on are helpless. And this I can only say objectifying myself, and looking from your point of view. Perhaps because I have always been fallen off the horse: I have never been defiantly in the saddle (like many powerful people in life, or many miserable sinners): I have always been fallen off, with one foot trapped in a stirrup, so that my course is not a cavalcade but a dragging along, with the head hitting on the dust and stones. I cannot either get back on the horse of the Hebrews and the Gentiles, nor fall definitively on the ground of God.[72]

Rossi answered: "Thank you for your letter! It was the best gift you could have given me. That which matters for your great soul [*la tua grande anima*] is not the past but the future. . . ."[73]

# 19

*Hope? I have none and furthermore I condemn it with everything
in my power. Hope is the flag, the special marker of hypocrisy . . . I don't believe in it. I believe only in my own vitality.*
—*Pier Paolo Pasolini*

# A TELLER OF FABLES

Italian literature's professionals pride themselves on a seismographic
function, attentive to sort out what is current, what avant-garde, what
retrograde or passé. A group of writers called Gruppo 63 (they took
their name from the year of their first conference, that October, in
Palermo) coalesced around the poet and critic Edoardo Sanguineti.
They wanted—and aggressively—to remake the face of Italian letters
by modernizing it and that meant displacing those who then set (or
appeared to set) its course. Pasolini was in this category; at only

forty-two, he seemed to them both a man of the old school and boss of a clique. He was dismissed as too elegaic, too discursive, neither sufficiently international nor sufficiently abstract. Gruppo 63 claimed it saw the future in the mass media and technology and dismissed his taste for making self-reference as so much solipsism, and ridiculed his lament over "the end of dialects" as crying over defeat in a battle long ago lost. Pasolini was not alone. The entire literary generation identified with neo-realism was to be buried: Alvaro, Vittorini, Pratolini, Moravia, Pavese, Piovene, Levi, Brancati.

As lines formed and "sides" hardened, magazines and people separated into the *avanguardisti* and their opposition. Social life replicated intellectual loyalty; the *Nuovi argomenti* people around Moravia wanted nothing to do with the Gruppo 63 gang, and vice versa. Fabio Mauri kept contact with both camps: "Pasolini was annoyed by the *neo-avanguardisti*'s bourgeois origins. I had to see him secretly, even when we were in public." [1]

Mauri recalls, "Pasolini's group (including Penna and Bertolucci) had more money than the painters: They went in the evening to the Bolognese in Piazza del Popolo and da Carlo." The visual artists of what Mauri calls "the School of Piazza del Popolo" (including friends Robert Rauschenberg and Cy Twombly, who had settled in Italy) gathered in the afternoon in the Rosati bar (next door to Bolognese) and cheap places in via della Penna, at Otello in via della Croce and in the via dell'Oca, where, coincidentally, Morante lived upstairs from Mauri at number 27. It was all a family affair: Pasolini's friend Adriana Asti was briefly Mauri's wife. [2]

The painters hovered around the Tartaruga gallery, talking of Jackson Pollock, of Gorky and De Kooning, who visited and announced "Painting is a word." A kid named Christo wrapped a statue in front of the Museum of Modern Art in the Villa Borghese. Mark Rothko and Franz Kline came to town. Mauri recalls, "America really seemed to loom with its skyscrapers directly behind Ostia"; his uncle Valentino published Harold Rosenberg's *The Anxious Object*. The literati of the Gruppo waged their polemics over much coffee and cheap wine out of a back room in the Feltrinelli bookstore, in via del Babuino."

Pasolini, who detested non-figurative art, as he did modern music, contended that the neo-avant-garde poets did not respect the cultural past not because they "refused" it, but because they were ignorant of it. Or that, when they did use it—sprinkling allusions—it was all surface, no more than the earlier and truer avant-garde of the twenties reheated and served up as though new. They answered that he was blind to the exciting present of the pregnant sixties.

He protested. Was it not he who first announced that the Italian language was in crisis? It availed him little. There was truth in their description. He had made his way in the world in the old-fashioned manner. It counted against him that he came from the bad, old provincial times when poets still paid to have their poems printed, as he had *Poesie a Casarsa*. The new *avanguardisti* had what seemed to them a more up-to-date perspective: They wanted literature to be free of Pasolini's beloved and anguishing History, which they saw only as a burden once again to be buried. Also, his cherished "culture of engagement" was, to them, old hat. They were tired of references to class struggle and the subproletariat, the urban periphery and Marxist ideology; instead, literature was to be about literature, and style was all.

They did not stop to notice that Pasolini's was not like anyone else's "poetry of commitment" of the fifties, nor that he had used the tradition to subvert it. He brought back the Dantean *terza*, the long medieval canon, ellipses—skipping over the nineteenth-century's long, closed lines. He used recognizable parts of speech to arrive at a sometimes indecipherable ambiguity; he used the building blocks of commonsense language to arrive at mirror-images, labyrinths of contradictory meaning, concepts at war with the face value of the words that expressed them. But it was crime enough that he wrote in the "bourgeois code," making poems that were "stories" rather than pure form as meaning, things unto themselves. Their taste ran to Expressionist painting and Pop Art; his to figuratives like Morandi, De Pisis, Guttuso, and Zigaina. They saw Futurism as a triumph; he agreed with Trotsky, who dismissed it as "the product of Italy and the Soviet Union—the two most backward countries in the world."

One cornerstone of their program for a new, more modern Italian poetry and prose for a new, more modern Italy was production of new anthologies for the schools. While their much-announced revolution did not come, a collection of verse—intended to rewrite "the cannon"—did: *I novissimi* (literally The very newest): *Poesie per gli anni '60* (Poetry for the sixties). The contents gave Pasolini short shrift; he wrote Einaudi, who had published it, that the book was "horrendous . . . Naturally, I speak as a man of culture (*uomo di cultura*), not as a publisher."[3]

For Pasolini himself to announce his own "retirement" from letters and commitment to cinema—that was one thing; but to be forced into early retirement, and by those whom he had reviewed when they were otherwise unknown—that was unacceptable. He reminded them that it had been he who wrote, ahead of others, "The centers for the

creation, development, and unification of language are no longer the
universities but the business firms." He had discovered for himself
the effect of television in flattening the regional dialects and the
power of technical language to make what he believed to be a completely new kind of consciousness. He wrote in *Vie nuove*, "I was the
first reviewer, for example, of Sanguineti, his first time out: a favorable reviewer."

> It was I who inaugurated in *Officina* the prehistoric and still inarticulate
> critical discourse on the avant-garde . . . as for the "leaders' of the avant-
> garde, they are plainly in a position of polemic with me although they do
> not go to the extremes they do when speaking of Cassola and Bassani. They
> accuse me of naturalism. But in bad faith, and the more intelligent of them
> know it. So I do not let it bother me, given the absolute arbitrary absurdity
> of the accusation.[4]

By 1966, his gloves were off:

> avant-garde men of letters . . . as they are and as they want to be . . . petit-
> bourgeois old men, reunited in groups according to a horrendous tradition
> (Freemasonry, Mafia, academies, bar-room brawls, congressional sessions,
> and the military spirit).[5]

Because everyone agreed that language was a mirror of politics
(and vice versa), a matter of power, the stakes were higher than
"mere" literature. Pasolini believed that the Italian his countrymen
spoke even through the fifties was something learned in school,
overlaid onto dialect. With the new decade came, late in the day as
compared with, say, France, "the language of advertising" and apro-
found infiltration of the industrial north's technical vocabularies. He
wrote that "the most important characteristics of this national Italian
[were] . . . (1) a certain bias in favor of the progressive sequence . . . (2) the end of osmosis with Latin . . . (3) the predomi-
nance of the communicative purpose over the expressive one."[6] To
him, the *neo-avanguardisti*'s highly publicized and so-called revolutionary literature was *informa* (unformed). He dismissed it as
"merely magma."
He instructed and warned his *Vie nuove* readers:

> I believe we confront a crisis which has no comparison in our past, neither
> immediate nor distant. We are at a "zero" moment of history (an ideal
> moment, we understand) (and thus the avant-garde have taken, it is true,
> the right position: but while they think it is one they have freely chosen, it

is in reality compulsory: the zero moment has arrived). That is to say a historical epoch has ended—and another is beginning. The pseudo-national Italy of monopolistic industry is ending, and a new Italy is beginning, which builds its own, real nationality of the real power of a neo-capitalistic and technocratic industry. Eash artist adapts himself through a complicated and dense latticework of projections which are born out of the historical moment which determined him and he knows how to express: when this historical moment is zero, the artist goes crazy: he is in a state of confusion and of pseudo-security of values by now overtaken.[7]

Not bothering with personalities, he went to the core of things as he saw them. He told French journalist Jean Duflot that the neo-avant-garde had "wasted too many young people's time," acted out of "pure snobbism" and "mental anarchy . . . in their end their literature was consumed, exactly that, consumed not read."[8]

The run-in with the Gruppo marked one more step in his path to impasse: His opposition to what was stridently new made him seem increasingly "nostalgic," even reactionary, an opponent of "progress." In the face of a claimed liberalism which he thought the ploy of cynical merchandising, he appeared moralistic; faced with politicized, public homosexuals gathering in ghettoed bars, he stuck (some thought defiantly) to rough trade he found on the streets and in the fields, where he began; faced with writers who wanted above all a market, not readers, he heaped scorn.

It was inevitable that he became fascinated by method and was soon speculating about the "languages" of cinema. The primitive pulled him, and Claude Lévi-Strauss entered his intellectual ambit. His discovery of the Third World continued—Christmas in Italy became impossible, so he went to non-Christian countries. It seemed he was taking Cézanne's advice, given at the turn of the century: "Everything is about to disappear. You've got to hurry up if you want to see things."[9]

After the *Vangelo* visit to Israel and Jordan, Pasolini joined Moravia in Africa. A picture of the two there emerges from Moravia's essay "The Culture That Presents an Understanding of Others," first published in the *Corriere della sera* and later collected as an African travel diary in book form.[10]

It is July 1963. The two are sitting in

the dining room of a big hotel in Mombasa: immaculate tablecloths, shining glass and cutlery, air-conditioning, a Viennese orchestra, waiters in white jackets with silk lapels, a buffet table with all the Western tidbits, a discreet bustle of conversation and of dishes. At a table not very far from ours there were about ten men without a single woman . . .

### Moravia's recollection:

The friend with whom I was sitting at table can actually listen to a conversation that is taking place at the other end of the room.

### Moravia (whose English was far better than Pasolini's) inquired what they were saying.

"Nasty brutes."

"What d'you mean?"

"Landowners, businessmen, company employees."

"And what are they talking about?"

"They're talking about the Africans, naturally."

"And what are they saying?"

"They're saying and they're not saying."

"But what *are* they saying?"

"They're saying nasty things."

"What d'you mean?"

He was silent for a short time, listening. Then he explained, continuing nevertheless to keep his ears open. "How is it possible," he said " to give a detailed account of an English conversation? It's a question of hints, of half-tones, of allusions, of accents. Apart from the words themselves, one would have to interpret the clearings of the throat, the stammerings, the hesitations, the hoarsenesses, the flatterings. So I can't give you a full account of what they're saying. I can give you a summary of it."

"Let's hear your summary."

He listened a little longer, then he resumed: "The summary of it is this: the Africans will prove themselves incapable of carrying on the administrative, economic, and social machine created by the Europeans in Africa. Once the whites have departed, everything will go to pieces. And this, not so much because the Africans are lacking in certain qualifications that can be acquired with time, as because they are essentially incapable of doing certain things, in other words because they are racially inferior."

"What arguments do they bring forward to prove that statement?"

"No arguments. They are convinced of it from the start. The whole conversation, in fact, is based on this presumption, which is tacitly shared by them all."

"And what else are they saying?"

I saw him prick up his ears again, with a look of malicious delight in his eyes. At last he said:

"They're now talking about someone named Harrison who has divorced his wife in order to marry someone named Maud." [11]

Pasolini now occasionally echoed Léopold Sédar Senghor, the poet-president of Senegal, whose work he had translated for the anthology *Letteratura negra:* "Negritude . . . will be the way." He cried, in the poetry: "Africa? My sole alternative!" Fleeing Italy seemed to make sense after the *La ricotta* trial. He told a reporter then, "The hard reality is that in Italy the ruling class defends itself against poets and intellectuals by *brutally sending them into exile or imprisoning them* [emphasis Pasolini's]. [12]

In November 1964 he explained to his *Vie nuove* readers that he was at work on "a long essay—now that I have a little free time and peace." It was called *Nuove questioni linguistiche* (New linguistic questions) and appeared first in the PCI magazine *Rinascita*, the day after Christmas. It "includes a paragraph dedicated to the neo-avant-garde:" "Beyond every ugly argument and every irritation and so on, I hope finally to have centered the argument."

His article opened a debate that lasted for months, drawing in Sereni, Eco, Moravia, Arbasino, Calvino, and others. Pasolini had a chance to reply, extending and refining his burial of the neo-avant-garde, in articles published in *L'espresso, Il giorno*, and *Rinascita*. He was accused of "stating the obvious"; he answered that there was indeed something new—a "technocratic bourgeoisie" replacing the old one of merchants, professionals, and academics, a new class which "at the same time radiates economic, cultural, and therefore linguistic power." He spent the last weeks of the year speaking on the subject in various cities, under the auspices of ACI, the Communist cultural association. He declined a friend's call to address a group at Arco Felice near Naples because "I have about ten [conferences and debates] over two weeks," including Messina.

As though with his left hand, Pasolini now wrote *Vivo e conscienza*, a "sung ballet" for the theater; it was to have music by Bruno Maderna, dance by Jerome Robbins, and premiere at the Twenty-fourth Festival of Contemporary Music in Venice. It was never staged, never published.

The Christmas of 1964 he went to ski in the mountains of the Abruzzi with Ninetto—a child of the Italian south descended from peasants from hot Catanzaro who had never seen snow. Pasolini wrote that "Nino" (as he now also called him), then sixteen, "was too small for the snowfall in Rome of '57, or perhaps he had not yet come from Calabria . . . "

> With nightfall, the sky suddenly turns white and, as we leave the hotel to take a stroll around the deserted village, suddenly the air comes alive; by a strange optical effect, even though the tiny flakes are falling to the ground, instead they seem to be climbing toward the sky . . . It looks as though the whole sky is falling on us, dissolving in this happy and naughty feast of Apennine snow. Just imagine Ninetto. No sooner does he perceive this unheard-of occurrence, the sky dissolving on his head, and knowing no obstacles of good upbringing to the manifestation of his feelings, than he abandons himself to a joy devoid of all modesty. Which has two phases, very rapid ones: first, a kind of dance, with well-defined rhythmic breaks (I am reminded of the Denka, who beat the ground with their heels, and who in turn made me think of Greek dances as one imagines them by reading the poets) . . . The second phase is oral: it consists of a childish and orgiastic cry of joy that accompanies the heights and breaks of that rhythm: "He-eh, he-eh, heeeeeh." In short, a cry that cannot be reproduced in writing . . . A vocalization stemming from a recollection *that joins in an uninterrupted continuum* the Ninetto of today in Pescasseroli with the Ninetto of Calabria, a marginal area and preserver of Greek civilization, with the pre-Greek, purely barbarian Ninetto who beats time with his heels the way the prehistoric naked Denka of the lower Sudan do today . . . [13]

With an apparent effortlessness that engendered fanatical envy in his contemporaries, he switched gears; he moved from poetry to linguistics in a Marxist vein, defining a linguist as "a scientist, not an esthete. Linguists who are occupied with beauty, correctness, the purity of language were always idiots. They were always, knowingly or not, the spokesmen for the dominant or managerial class which, among its other privileges, has also that of good taste, and is conservative also in the field of language, because its language is the mirror of its life."

He was careful to make distinctions, but—in the violence of his reaction—seemed to many to go too far:

> When kids talk about motors, they of necessity use a technical language: spare parts have no names in dialect, nor populist, nor Latinized, neither alive nor expressive. They have an ugly signal-like name and operate within a grammar that is strictly functional: and that name and that grammatical standard are diffused throughout the country.

In apocalyptic tone, he writes, "the solution to propose, one does not know."

> An abyss yawns before us. Even more horrible, to the extent that the language is only the external appearance of the real social and political situation.[14]

In March he visited Morocco and returned "not disappointed, no, but confused." He had expected "to verify" that the Third World was in a "scandalous dialectical relationship" with the industrial world, whether capitalism or Marxist. Instead, the Moroccans were "mired in an ugly reality: pragmatic, unaware. . . ." Still, the journey served; he was to return.

In early June a recently inaugurated film festival at Pesaro showcased the "New Cinema," complete with the usual round-table discussions. Pasolini offered a paper called "The Cinema of Poetry," the first of several studies meant to set right a deficiency: "It is my opinion that there exists no film criticism that possesses a precise diction with a stylistic critical set of rules as there is in literature."

He used a film of Ermanno Olmi's and Bertolucci's just-released *Prima della rivoluzione* (Before the revolution, 1964) to illustrate that the language of the cinema is "crude," "irrational," "barbaric"— and in this nothing less than reality itself, without the smoothing intermediate artifice of literature. The lexicon for philological analysis had simply not yet stabilized in film.

The "cinema of poetry" was forming in his mind:

> because it [the cinema] is dreamlike, because it is close to dreams, because a cinema sequence and a sequence of memory or of a dream—and not only that but things in themselves—are profoundly poetic; a tree photographed is poetic because physicality is poetic in itself, because it is an apparition, because it is full of mystery, because it is full of ambiguity, because it is full of polyvalent meaning, because even a tree is a sign of a linguistic system. Because who talks through a tree? God, or reality itself.[15]

All things are sacred: trees, the sea, boys. Communion with them is, in effect, therefore communication with the divine. Eros and art are the same: two overlapping routes to the sacred. Mere human objections grounded in hypocritical morality fade to insignificance.

The poet and the film *auteur* participate, Godlike, in the creation / rendition of reality. But poetry need not be—must not be—without ideology; both could be served, as Eisenstein had dreamed, by manipulating the lexicon of images rather than of words. It was a lexicon more vast and more universal than any spoken or written language.

At the time of *Accattone*, Pasolini told an interviewer that he was leaving literature for the cinema, but only partly because it offered a universal language. The camera provided the means for communicating in cinematic signs (regardless of the soundtrack) what his friend the poet Andrea Zanzotto has called "a hyper-space," free from the limitations of languages controlled by national power. As one student of his strategy has put it, "reality is already a totality of signs, and cinema is the writing of this totality.[16]

But he hedged, unwilling to claim that cinema was another, more attractive way of being a poet.

> Between my renunciation of novel-writing and my decision to make movies there was no breach of continuity. I took it as a change of technique.
>
> But was this the truth? Wasn't it actually a case of abandoning one language for another? Of abandoning an accursed Italy for one that could at least be trans-national? Of that old rabid desire to renounce my Italian citizenship (but which other one could I take on?)? Still, this was not really the case; no, it was not even a matter of adopting another language . . .
>
> By making movies I was finally living according to my philosophy. That's all.[17]

In the films from 1966 onward, Pasolini trained his camera on faces and bodies he believed "spoke" in the universal language of signs. Pasolini the filmmaker was coming to be, in action if not in declaration, in perfect accord with the words of Don Giovanni Rossi. In defending his collaboration with Pasolini, the priest had written: "Indeed in every human face we see reflected the wonderful face of the Lord."

Roland Barthes was present at Pesaro, as was the film theorist Christan Metz, both of whom were breaking new ground in *Cahiers du cinéma:* in Rome a group of young cineasts created a similar periodical, *Cinema e film*,[18] encouraged and aided by Pasolini. They all agreed on the importance of the business at hand: the search for a "grammar of cinematographic images." Pasolini argued: "*Reality is a language.* I would hardly want to speak of a "semiology of cinema; *what is needed is a semiology of reality* [italics Pasolini's]!" The "languages" of reality, "physical presence," "comportment," and "the written-spoken one" are, he argued, "summarized in that final and primary language, the language of action." [19]

He explained, for those who could follow, "In effect it has been my semiological research into the cinema which has explained to me why I make movies." [20]

The effect of Gruppo 63's attacks was in the background as he worked on a new book, returned to intermittently between 1963 and 1967. Only published after his death, it is complete only through two "cantos"—cantos because his project took nothing less than *The Divine Comedy* as its model. It became an obsession, something he said he "had" to write. Here was a contest worthy of him, one with no less than the greatest Italian poet of all. As so often, he mentioned it to his readers in *Vie nuove*, calling it "a project worth completing." In "Plan of Future Works" (dated November–December 1963), he called it "a work to finish / if ever one was . . ." He took the next twelve years to do so.

He called it *The Divine Mimesis:* [21] True to Dante (as in *La mortaccia*), it opens with a journey, and (apparently following a lead from Contini, in a letter about Dante) closed with an "iconography"— twenty-five photos Pasolini carefully assembled shortly before his death.

The poet's journey in the narrative is truncated because its author—the imaginary poet whom Pasolini pretends not to be—is murdered. Stepping back from himself, in an Editor's Note, someone understood to be "Pasolini" explains the circumstances that have led to the present incomplete book:

> This is not a critical edition. I am limiting myself to publishing everything which the author has left. My only critical effort, and a very modest one, is that of reconstructing the chronological sequence, as exactly as possible, of those notes at the foot of which the author has noted the date; in those cases it has, therefore, been easy to place them. But many of the notes, especially the shorter of them, some of them being only two or three lines and almost illegible, have no date. And not only that, they were found apart from the typed body of the work, either in drawers other than that where the main part was kept, or behind the pages of books which he had started to read but not finished. A note pad was even found in the inside pocket of the door of his car; and finally, a macabre but, one must admit, moving detail, a separated-off page (obviously torn from a notepad) covered with about ten very wavy lines, was found in the jacket of his corpse (he died, killed by blows on the ear, at Palermo, last year). . . . [22]

Palermo was the site of Gruppo 63's conference, where Pasolini-poet felt himself figuratively beaten to death. His publisher put *The Divine Mimesis* in the bookstores two weeks after its author's death. The difference: Pasolini's protagonist was "beaten to death with a stick."

The poet of *The Divine Mimesis*, the Pasolini whose figurative death was "in not being understood," visits the new Inferno of consumerist society. Pasolini's despair is that literature has no more authority, the "Demagogy [is] ever more in control of the situation." Since "the Revolution is nothing more than a feeling" and the *impegno* of a man born only to be young has passed from fashion, there is nothing left but a slow retreat. The poet—figuratively "dead". . . "in Palermo"—added these lines as preface to *La divina mimesis*, these not from the imaginary narrator but explicitly from Pasolini himself: "*The Divine Mimesis:* I give over for printing these pages as a 'document,' but also to show contempt for my 'enemies': in fact, offering them one more reason to despise me, I provide them one more reason to go to Hell." [23]

Pasolini caused certain parts of "A Desperate Vitality"—dated "1963/1964," the same time as the first canto of *The Divine Mimesis*—to be printed in alignment with a central axis, like a lapidary:

"As for the future, listen
your fascist sons
will sail
toward the worlds of the New Prehistory.
I'll be there, but by myself,
like someone dreaming of his own damnation
on the shores of the sea
in which life begins again.
Alone, or almost, on the old coastline
among ruins of ancient civilizations,
Ravenna,
Ostia, or Bombay—it's all the same—
with gods that peel off, old problems
—such as class struggle—
which
dissolve . . .
Like a Partisan
dead before May 1945,
I will begin little by little to decompose
in the tormenting light of that sea
as a poet and citizen, forgotten." [24]

Ravenna is the place of Carlo Alberto's birth, Bombay the city of Pasolini's dream of an intact peasant civilization, Ostia the place of his murder. [25]

In May 1964 (while working on *Il Vangelo*) he told an audience of students at the Centro Sperimentale di Cinematografia: "Talking a little relieves me of the desire to create. There was a book that, by talking about it first, I completely got rid of, and now I don't think I'll ever write it."

A year later he wrote in *Vie nuove* that there seemed to be "less interest" in his columns—the number of letters sent it was down from two years before. He was annoyed that so many readers seemed "stubbornly" unwilling to see his point of view on his film about Christ; a month later he wrote, "This column is often an exhausting interruption." He explained the reasons "outside of myself" included a change in the relationship "between intellectuals on the Left and the Communist base." The problem was not strictly political—not only and not merely—but larger: The common "system of allusions, of common references" had collapsed.

But he did not make of his departure from the pages of the PCI's magazine an occasion to blast the Party's leadership. He intended to influence them and their comrades from outside, to continue his polemics for a "cultural policy of the PCI [that is] a *real liberalization* [italics Pasolini's]." On the contrary, in his last *Vie nuove* columns he went out of his way to praise the PCI's bosses. For example, on June 24,1965, he explained that all Western Communist parties were "in crisis" but the "PCI is the one least touched and stricken." [26]

In mid-July: "The terms of the daily political struggle of the workers" and the "new mandate of the writer . . . coincide perfectly." They must work for the same goal together—and "through the mediation of the PCI."

Soon after, he offered his readers a melancholy farewell:

> It doesn't matter to me that I have lost a certain popularity within the workers' base and among the readers of *Vie nuove*. It is a risk I foresaw and accepted, from the very first letter. What is important is that I posed real questions, and that some readers of *Vie nuove* became conscious of them. That my writings are followed with less trust and sympathy . . . gives me great displeasure, that's another matter. [27]

As usual he moved without pause into a new project even more demanding than the old. His penultimate piece (September 23, 1965) announced his coeditorship, starting with the new year of 1966 of a "new series" of the magazine *Nuovi argomenti,* to be "published by [the PCI's book publishing arm] Editori Riuniti." He wrote, "It will be first and above all a contribution to clarification, to the exact framing of and search for a solution to the crisis of Marxism."[28]

He also described it as "an alternative to the avant-garde's regression" and a place to address the "new problems which have turned upside down and suddenly aged the Marxist thought of the fifties."[29]

He had agreed to join with Moravia in reviving the magazine his friend had founded in 1953, a periodical with a small but influential, highbrow circulation. Moravia had collaborated with Alberto Carocci in the founding. Pasolini wrote that he came "close, close" to "breaking the friendship" with Carocci over his refusal to accept an essay by Leonetti in May 1958.

Appearing about two to four times a year, *Nuovi argomenti* had been started to address the "new arguments" raised by the end of the war. It quickly earned respect with articles by Moravia on "An Inquiry into Art and Communism" and contributions by no less than Lukács on "The Aesthetic Writings of Marx and Engels." It was famous for its "inquiries," like the fairly courageously early "9 Questions About Stalinism" (No. 20, 1956) and "8 Questions About Sex and Literature" (Nos. 51–52, 1961), and for its "special issues"— on America (No. 4, 1953), colonialism in Algeria (No. 19, 1956), on the two Germanys (No. 34, 1958) and "the Right in Germany" (Nos. 47–48, 1960–61). Pasolini had participated in one called "9 Questions About the Novel" in the issue of May–August 1959. When *Nuovi argomenti* conducted a poll among intellectuals, the results were often reported by the mass media as news.

After a decade its fortunes were in evident decline and the "first series" ended, effectively ceasing publication in 1965. For Pasolini, brought in to reinvigorate its pages, coeditorship offered a chance to resume where *Officina* (and before it *Il setaccio, I eredi, Il stroligut*) had left off: Again he could rally those voices that demanded an "independent" (that is, non-PCI) Marxist line in culture, open to poetry and polemic. It was also, he explained to Leonetti, far less trouble than starting another magazine from scratch at a time when he was immersed in another film and putting the final touches on *Ali dagli occhi azzuri.*

The "new" magazine's inaugural issue ran Pasolini's essay on "A Poet's Notes Toward a Marxist Linguistics" and "The Script as a Structure Which Wants to Be Another Structure." Also, an essay from Moravia on his novel *L'attenzione,* Enzo Siciliano on Bassani, Leonetti's "Preamble for a Magazine of '64," poems by Amelia Rosselli (about whom Pasolini had written for Vittorini's *Il menabò*), and Sandra Mangini. Soon, the magazine printed young Giorgio Manacorda and Renzo Paris, both prominent in Italian letters well into the eighties.[30] Dario Bellezza—impoverished (Pasolini paid him to type some of his correspondence), brilliant, as outrageous as Laura Betti—also appeared; he joined the Garzanti list and won the Viareggio Prize for Poetry in 1976.

When Paris sent him galleys of his book *Frecce avvelenate* (Poison arrows),[31] Pasolini wrote him: "You . . . must simply forget the avant-garde, erase it from your minds as soon as possible. If not, you will end badly; enough of the avant-garde."[32] When his second cousin, Giulietta Chiarcossi (Graziella's sister), surprised him with a cycle of love poems (*Piccolo canzoniere d'amore*), he wrote that, save for some—he specified which and why—they were "sincere . . . delicate"; he printed them in the first issue of *Nuovi argomenti*'s "new series."[33]

*Nuovi argomenti* provided an outlet for his changing preoccupations. In *Laboratorio*, a section of the magazine set aside for experiments, he printed an essay on "Marxist linguistics," careful to label it a work *en poète*, that is, linguistics as practiced not by a scholar of the discipline but as a working poet.

His essay *Il cinema di poesia* (The cinema of poetry) appeared, from the Italian to French and then in the *Cahiers du cinéma in English* (No. 6); he gave space in *Nuovi argomenti* to papers delivered at the 1966 Pesaro Festival, which took issue with his paper presented there the year before.

The Tenth Congress of the PCI now drew Pasolini's fire for offering no cultural program to take the place of the school of "realistic commitment." He ridiculed its platform for giving "carte blanche to all possible literary experiments: 'Do what you like and then we'll see' is readable between the lines," he wrote. He scorned the Congress' official pronouncement that the artist was "free," remarking that "a liberty without confrontations is a mythical liberty, it is the liberty of bourgeois liberalism, in the end a pretext." He wanted something to buck up against, a boundary to defy, a prohibition to transgress, edges. He also wanted to keep what he thought Italy's last hope from repeating the obstinate provincialism of the Fascism of his youth.

In 1966 he wrote the last word on his enemies: "The End of the Avante-garde":

> The new "collective consciousness" in Italy does not include problems. Its ideology, as is well known, is in "the decline of ideology." Marxism, in a state of crisis, does not have the authority to validate those arguments that rightly oppose such a decline and oppose Marxism's continual use of pretext, the delinquent apathy of its appeals to the technical, etc. etc. And in that opposition not even rigidly Marxist groups like the "*piacentini*" have any real weight—as scattered groups operating in the provinces, in a Northern Italy whose mind is on something else somewhere else.[34]

If the "the decline of ideology" was at hand, it would be his satisfaction to film that decline his way and in all its complexity. His vehicle was a filmed fable he conceived in 1965. In one of his last columns in *Vie nuove* on May 6, 1965, he printed the film he imagined in three episodes. He called it *Uccellacci e uccellini* (Hawks and sparrows).

Now theory and praxis exactly overlapped; behind the camera, he could put to work his theory of "the cinema of poetry." Here was the same strategy as the critic-essayist alternating with the poet-novelist: for example, treating dialect as observer, and writing poetry and novels in dialect, all one seamless act of creation.

The first episode—called in French *L'aigle* (The eagle)—was written with what he called "a little anarchic-radical pamphletism and a little surrealism." He explained that it was also about

> the relationship between rationalism—one hopes advanced, one hopes even Marxist—and "savage thought"; or to put it another way between the West and the Third World. This rapport has presented itself as the most difficult and 'scandalous' of our time, and its lack of solution is the cause—at least in part—of Stalinism.[35]

The script recounted the antics of an odious horse-trainer at an equestrian club who tries to dominate the eagle of "the savage thought of the Third World" by reading extracts from Pascal and browbeating; instead, he himself ends turned into a beast. He stands for the arrogance of those who believed in "the civilizing mission of France" and also stood for a specific Frenchman: Pasolini called him "M. Cournot"—the very name of the critic from *Le nouvel observateur* who had attacked his *Gospel*. After screening the rushes, Pasolini decided the idea worked on paper but not as cinema, and the episode—and his revenge—was dropped from the film.

What ultimately emerged made an eighty-eight-minute black-and-white, produced by Bini and released as what Pasolini called his blast at "the obscene good health of neo-capitalism."

Pasolini said his intention was to make an "ideo-comic" film, "a formula I invented for fun." But as it ended, he admitted, it was melancholic more to make one smile ironically than to laugh. For the comic part, he relied on his protagonists: The elder of two was Totò, the great Neapolitan character actor, a speaking Keaton. Like Magnani, "Totò"—born Principe Antonio Vincenzo Stefano Clemente de Curtis Gagliardi—was in the closing days of a career that had seen him lead (a so-called *vedette*) in Italian variety shows as long ago as 1922, the year Pasolini was born. He was a living institution by the time they crossed paths: Totò, a household name, had already made more than a hundred films, a third of which bore titles like *Totò in Paris* and *Totò in the* [Bicycle] *Tour of Italy*, *Totò Against the Four*, and *Totò and the King of Rome*, *Totò Diabolicus*, and *Totò and Cleopatra*. His face was as famous as Chaplin's and as automatic a draw: his trademark jutting jaw, his rolled eyes and slightly raised brow—Jerry Lewis and Cantinflas rolled into one extraordinary talent.

"Totò was chosen for what he is as a man," Pasolini said, "and that is a poor Neapolitan with airs of nobility, but never of the lower middle class. Totò is sweet and lovable and not only as a buffoon appears."

> Poor Totò, he used to ask me very gently, almost like a child, if he could make a more serious film, and I used to have to say "No, no, I just want you to be yourself." The real Totò was, in fact, manipulated, he wasn't a straightforward ingenuous character like Franco Citti in *Accattone*. Totò was an actor who had been manipulated by himself and by other people into a type, but I used him precisely as that, someone who was a type.[36]

Ninetto Davoli made the perfect foil as his young son. "When I thought of doing *Uccellacci e uccellini* I thought of him and Totò at once, without the slightest hesitation."[37] In a turtleneck sweater, walking with a teenage bounce, Ninetto radiated the pure innocence of youth as counterweight to Totò's lovably foolish old age. "Ninetto is like Totò, there is this combination of humdrumness and something magical in both of them. There is no conflict of generations between them. The son is getting ready to be an ordinary man like his father was."[38]

When Pier Paolo took Ninetto to meet Totò, no sooner did the great comic open the door of his apartment than the boy broke out laughing. Ninetto recalled:

Pier Paolo elbowed me, and said "Oh, behave yourself, calm down" but Totò was not in the least put out, but told Pier Paolo that [Ninetto's reaction] was perfectly normal. We became friends immediately, although I heard later that since I had gone to his house without a tie, but in jeans—what I wear every day—after we left he sprayed the sofa where I had been sitting with DDT.

. . . during pauses in the filming, he told me stories. Since I am a big eater in the morning, especially when we were in Yugoslavia and it was cold, he told me to imagine a big steam oven out of which came hot pastries, and then he cut them, buttered them. . . . We got along very well.

With Pier Paolo he was less expansive. They were both timid men and called one another "*lei*." Pier Paolo was one who did not use actors because they were actors. Totò was useful because he had that face. Totò followed the script closely, but Pier Paolo, in time, left him free to do as he liked.[39]

Totò and Ninetteo, as father and son, were to illustrate important themes lightly, sugaring the pill of preaching with levity. Pasolini said, "I have never tried to treat of a theme explicitly this difficult." He also had never tried so hard to make "opera buffa, a writer's supreme ambition," but, he said, "I only succeeded in part, because I am a petit-bourgeois and I tend to dramatize everything."

Totò and Ninetto are symbols who illustrate through picaresque (mis)adventures the crisis in the postwar years—that Marxism of the Resistance and the fifties, the end of ideology in the time coinciding with the death of Palmiro Togliatti. "What we have now," he commented in 1968, "is the economic boom, the welfare state, and industrialization which is using the South as a reserve of cheap manpower and even beginning to industrialize it as well. There has been a real change which coincided more or less with Togliatti's death. It was a pure coincidence chronologically, but it worked symbolically."

He added:

In Italy, this transition [to industrial prosperity] has just taken place. What took a century in England has virtually happened in twenty years here. This explosion produced an ideological crisis which particularly threatened the position of Marxism, and coinciding with this there was a big cultural change here as well. That is what I was referring to.[40]

Pasolini told an interviewer that Totò and Ninetto are "all the unconscious Italians, mankind . . . two typical heroes of neo-realism . . . living out their life without thinking about it—humble, humdrum, and unaware." He added in 1969: " 'Everyone in Italy is a Marxist, just as everybody in Italy is a Catholic,' a phrase used by

Paul VI, which I put into *Uccellacci e uccellini* and everyone took to be from Marx."[41]

The film opens suddenly. On the road, the pair are walking from nowhere to nowhere, suddenly (as in a dream) they meet Togliatti. But he is a crow, who hops and talks; his argumentative torments of the two innocents are nothing less than the challenge of Communism to an Italian people who do not want to be bothered with dreams. The voice is Francesco Leonetti's, many of the ideas are from Franco Fortini; Pasolini thanked him in the book of the film[42] for providing—with an anthology and Fortini's book *Verifica dei poteri*—the texts needed to turn "a horrible muddle" into a "summarized poetic line."

The bird introduces himself, "My country is ideology and I live in the City of the Future." He hops along at the travelers' side, dispensing nonstop a pendantic and insistent monologue, something utterly over the heads of poor Totò and Ninetto who were, as Pasolini saw, "such a lovely couple, and so poetic per se." Ninetto excuses himself, "My parents are Mr. Doubt and Mrs. Go-Along, but I am just Ninetto."

The two at first listen patiently as the crow prates: "This is the crisis of the grand ideologies, of the great hopes." He suggests that Ninetto will "probably go and work at Fiat." Finally, Totò decides—and convinces his son (with riotously funny sign language)—that the bird will probably make a good meal. They strangle and cook him, leaving a mound of feathers. But just before the bird is slaughtered and consumed, he says, "Teachers are made to be eaten in *salsa piccante*." Teachers, like Pasolini, are to be killed, taken in and transcended, but with something of their presence integrated in those who ingest them, consumed in a "hot sauce."

Soon the two voyagers discover that they have killed the symbol and spokesman of the hopes of the working class. Before being silenced by those who need him most, the crow had warned: "Once upon a time, there was the beautiful color red . . . Oh, middle class, you have identified the whole world with yourselves; this identification means the end of the world. But the end of the world will also be your end."[43]

The result, for the first time not sequestered and Pasolini not hauled into court, was brilliant. Even he admitted, "I can, maybe with greater pride [than saying it is my "best"] say that it is . . . my most pure." He told English journalist Oswald Stack, "There is almost total identity between me and the crow."

Pasolini concentrated his obsessions in the footage: the degradation of language, the homogenization of humanity through the dominance of consumer culture, the end of class struggle, the innocence of the bourgeoisie, the subproletariat as History's victims. With virtually alchemic legerdemain he transformed the *materia* of the poetry and essays into effective screen dialogue that is at once intriguing and disturbing:

> Crow: Ha! ha! ha! They got together some statistics and found this rule, that "those who speak the same way consume the same way," thus everyone talking the same way will dress alike, will go around in cars all alike and so on. And, at last, everything can be done in series.
>
> Totò: Oh well, the will of the bosses be done.
>
> Crow: And you, Ninetto, would you like to speak the same, dress the same, eat the same, go around in the same car as everyone else?
>
> Ninetto: (with a laughing giggle of supreme certainty) Me? Sure I would. What do you think I am? Stupid or something?
> (the music sounds louder, the epic of music "*Scarpe rotte*") ["Broken Shoes," a Resistance ballad]
>
> Crow: Eh, I know a man who weeps for this, who says this means the end of mankind and who says that if the workers do not decide to take back in their fists the red banners, then nothing can be done . . . because they are the only ones who can give some soul to things . . . so that the products are humanized and the world therefore stays human . . . but the workers are sleeping, and produce in a dream-like state and the Ninettos consume . . . products without souls . . . which slowly sap the souls out of those who have them . . . [44]

In the book version of the film, Pasolini wrote that the crow "had to be eaten . . . because his mandate was over. He finished his task and he was, as one says, overtaken."

> They [Totò and Ninetto] perform an act of cannibalism, which Catholics call Communion: they swallow the body of Togliatti (or of the Marxists) and assimilate it; after they assimilate it, they carry it along the road, so that even though you don't know where the road is going, it is obvious that they have assimilated Marxism.

All this theory is beneath the surface, as with any skilled parable obvious only on reflection. At first viewing, the story functions as a comedy, even with moments of hilarity. Pasolini said, "It makes you think more than laugh . . . it is not a funny film" but when it was put on in Montreal and New York [where he traveled with it], the audiences laughed a lot, to my great astonishment, unlike in Italy, where they were a bit disappointed, mainly because they went to see Totò and have their usual laugh, which they gradually realized they weren't going to be able to do.[45]

Pasolini had another aim for this "film told in prose but with poetic moments, something typical of fables." He claimed the "real subject" was the encounter of Western culture, including the Marxist crow, with the Third World. Totò and Ninetto are normal people everywhere in the West, wanting what Ninetto wants, at the moment when they "clash with the new historical situations."[46]

In one sequence, his Quixote with flat feet and Sancho Panza in jeans ("national-popular in the Gramscian sense," Pasolini called this part) walk a road in the Italian urban periphery—the *borgata*'s shabby high-rises seen in the background. The locations were the Tuscania and Alberone rural districts at Rome's edge and parts of Fiumicino. They pass placards declaiming "Private Property" over garbage heaps. Ahead of them, a street sign announces "Cuba, 13,257 km": Its alternative reality is present, but very far away. Totò and Ninetto are "following a sign" toward a dream of something they have only heard about.

Pasolini explained:

> All the first part is an evocation of neo-realism, though naturally an idealized neo-realism. There are other bits . . . which are deliberately intended to invoke Fellini and Rossellini. Some critics accused me of being Fellinian in that episode, but they did not understand that it was a quotation from Fellini; in fact . . . immediately afterwards the crow talks to the two of them and says "The age of Brecht and Rossellini is finished." The whole episode was a long quotation.[47]

What he called "a poetic opera in the language of prose," first intended as three fables, had become instead a single story within a story—what he called "a single film with another short film within it." The brief film "within" sees the father (Totò) and son (Ninetto) become what they always were, but in the guise of Franciscan friars in the year 1200. They are under orders from Saint Francis to preach and convert the hawks and the sparrows. They are followers of that Francis who equated poverty with purity, who taught to go "naked to follow the naked Christ."

He said he meant the second episode to be "something light . . . as though from *The Magic Flute*": sweet Ninetto and Totò as friars trying to talk to the birds, waving their arms, finally engaging them in conversation and successful conversion to Christianity. When all their prayers and antics are rewarded, still the hawks—even converted—attack the smaller sparrows, themselves also Christians. Finally, innocence is overwhelmed despite religion; ideology is no use when the strong wish to exploit the weak. We arrive only at pathos, the state where (as Pasolini said in the last weeks of his life) "nothing is to be done."

Underestimating what collaboration with him had cost the Franciscan Cittadella, he approached them again, asking their advice on the Franciscan episode. On October 7, 1965, Caruso wrote:

> Following on your kind invitation that we suggest modifications in the screenplay . . . and with the fraternal desire to be truly useful, I applied myself to this work with Don Andrea.
>
> We studied the text carefully and have discussed it with our colleagues. But we find ourselves absolutely incapable of making modifications or corrections partial enough that would leave the film substantially as it is. It is a film which for us cannot be other than completely disapproved.[48]

They asked him, "for heaven's sake," to cut out Francis' "Beatitudes" and the "Canticle to the Animals." And they begged him "in the name of our real friendship" not to shoot "any scenes near Assisi or that might seem to be Assisi. You can understand the reasons." Caruso wrote the same day to Bini, asking that he not make the film at all and, if he must, come nowhere near the city of Saint Francis.

When the film was done—without the Cittadella's assistance— Pasolini claimed he was dissatisfied, a reaction by now as much part of a pattern as his excitement and satisfaction when a film (a poem, an essay, or an article) was in the making. "What happened is that when I finished . . . I realized that the ideology played a much greater part in it than I had expected: the ideology was not all absorbed by the story . . . when I first saw the film . . . I really felt quite sorry about it. . . ."

Bini had troubles of his own:

> Think of those poor theater owners to whom I had to propose Totò, whom no one wanted any more and was paid then only three or four million a film when, only a short time before, he had commanded fifty, and then a crow, and a certain Ninetto Davoli who was nothing more than Pasolini's friend, and about what? About the crisis of ideology! It was obvious that I'd get no more than a boot in the face. Luckily, I found intelligent people . . . [49]

Bini arranged what he rightly called "an experiment" for the film's release in France, where it was first shown on State television, not in commercial theaters. Pasolini published an "Open Letter" in the cultural journal *Occhio critico* timed to coincide with the film's Milan premiere:

> I have never sent forth a film as defenseless, as delicate and timid as *Uccellacci e uccellini* . . . I am not talking about its originality—which would be stupidly presumptuous—but its formula: that of a fable, its meaning hidden . . . fable which ends the way it ought not to . . . but one has to disappoint. "Leap always into the flames like martyrs, roasted and ridiculous" is what some poetry [his own "Project for Future Works"] says . . . I have never exposed myself as I do in this film . . . the crisis of Marxism . . . lived through and seen by a Marxist, from the inside, not at all willing to believe that Marxism is finished (the Crow says "Do not cry for the end of my ideas, because certainly there will come someone else to take up my banner and carry it forward. Cry only for me . . .."
>
> . . . It [Marxism] is not finished to the extent that it can accept many new realities (the scandal of the Third World, the Chinese and above all the immensity of human history and the end of the world, with its religious implications, which is the other theme of the film. . . .[50]

The Party, which represented Marxism in Italy, had to respond. Writing in the semiofficial *Rinascita*, Mino Argentieri listed what he called the film's "administrative classifications:"

> *Uccellacci e uccellini* is at the same time, fable, essay, confession, pamphlet, didatic representation, picaresque saga, an abandonment to the joy and magic of spectacle, refined figurative assemblage, mimesis of a stylistic primitivism which crosses cultures and—why not?—a freewheeling chat among friends meant to leave the references incomprehensible to outsiders . . . it needs a second reading from the viewer; one wishes even a third.[51]

In March, with *Uccellacci* in the works, Pasolini was felled by a long-building gastric ulcer. He was in a restaurant in Rome's Jewish ghetto, dining with Moravia and his companion, writer Dacia Maraini. Pasolini went to the toilet, failed to return. Maraini has recalled "the door flew open and he fell forward, into a pool of blood, hemorrhaging. He fainted three times in my arms, begging, 'Don't leave me. Don't let me die.' " He was rushed to a doctor, given an injection, and ordered to bed for a month.

He was put on a diet of milk and unspiced food; his weight fell to 110 pounds. He later explained that he "began rereading Plato with

an undescribable joy" and started to write—plays. "In bed I wrote
six tragedies," although he later said, "I don't know why I wrote them
in the first place . . . I just picked up a pen and the first thing I
wrote were these plays in verse." "The point is that I had not written
any poetry for several years, and then suddenly I started again, but
for the theater, and in fact I've never written with such ease . . .
nothing has ever been such fun." [52]

*Orgia* was first, then *Bestia da stile*—also called *Poesia* and *Il
poeta ceco* (The Czech poet) which he was rewriting at the time of his
death; by May and June he was working on "four or five plays," of
which one was *Pilade* (his particular reworking of a Greek myth) and
the others became *Calderón, Affabulazione* (the germ of *Teorema*,
ultimately both book and film) and *Porcile*, reworked as a film in
1969.

Despising the Italian theater, he went in search of a translator so
that the plays could be performed abroad. He told Alberto Arbasino
that he hoped to see them performed, with luck, in New York, to
avoid having them "tormented by the petit-bourgeois voices of our
horrible actors." [53] He had gone on record with remarks like, "The
[Italian] theater is dead because the people in it have no interest in
culture":[54] he dismissed Italy's as merely "the theater of conversation." During the height of the fling with happenings and the Living
Theater, he said "Italy seems to offer either 'the theater of gesture'
or 'the theater of shouting'—for the bourgeoisie, the first designed to
mirror, the second to shock." His position in this, as in much else,
parallels that of Godard who once told a reporter, "I hate the theater.
Perhaps because actors are shouting. Or because they are serfs. I
prefer sport, which is a more free kind of theater." [55]

So he set out to find another style, or (as Godard would say) to put
the questions differently. He wrote, "I want to get somewhere else,
closer to a religious rite, as in ancient times. I want to make a
'cultural rite.' "

As from his earliest youth, his critical and creative impulses ger-
minated and enhanced one another. In the January–March 1968
(ninth) number of *Nuovi argomenti*, he published *A Manifesto for a
New Theater*: "The fact that I had six tragedies sitting on my desk
forced me to adopt a position and formulate my theories . . ." [56]

In the *Manifesto*, he argued that only poetic language was the answer to the crisis of the stage; he proposed "the theater of the Word"
On December 1, 1968, he wrote in the Milanese daily *Il giorno*,
"This new type of theater, which I call 'the theater of the Word' is a
mixture of poetry declaimed loudly and the usual theatrical conven-

tions reduced to a minimum. . . ." Declamation of poetry (along lines of ancient Greece) and little action were the route to "the rebirth of the theater in a nation in which the bourgeoisie is incapable of making a theater which is not provincial and academic, and in which the working class is completely extraneous to the problem. . . ."[57]

On November 27, 1968, he directed *Orgia* (with Laura Betti) in Turin's Teatro Stabile. He seemed to change his attitude: He now said the theater offered a way to make an "active protest, dynamic, against mass culture" because (he said, as though the first to have thought it) "the theater cannot be reproduced in series . . . every evening this rite reproduces its physicality, in its virginity" and no matter how many spectators, they would always be fewer than "number X, which is the mass."

But when *Orgia* was not well received by the critics or public, he called it his effort "mistaken for my fault . . . an incomplete experience, half-realized." He decided one had to dedicate "a life" to the theater, "or it amounts to nothing."

At his death, his plays were in transition; critic Siciliano has written, "Only *Calderón*, published in book form in 1973 [by Garzanti] can be considered to have been completed by his own hand."[58] The posthumous edition of *Affabulazione* and *Pilade* of April 1977 includes the publisher's note: "The first draft of *Affabulazione* dates from the spring of 1966 and appeared in *Nuovi argomenti*, No. 15, July–Sept 1969. The text published here is the third—*not definitive* [publisher's italics]—draft."

The note reports a "first draft" of *Pilade* from May 1966. A second draft appeared in *Nuovi argomenti*, Nos 7–8, July–Dec. 1967. "The text that appears here is the third draft, of which the final ordering was in progress [at Pasolini's death]."

*Calderón* is a dream-piece, widely criticized as static, with actors who declaim but do not move, inspired by Calderón de la Barca, author of *La vida es sueño* (Life is a dream). Pasolini set the psychodrama in seventeenth-century Spain, complete with Velásquez at work on his *Las Meninas*.

*Affabulazione* (which Attilio Bertolucci called Pasolini's "most frightening and exquisite" work) is set on the outskirts of contemporary Milan and (like Eliot's *Cocktail Party*, performed in Italy in prose translation) makes its characters speak in verse, lending what Bertolucci senior called "a sinister ambiguity." The critic also wrote that probably "no one would have the courage to perform it."

Pasolini made no secret that he, bedridden, had "for the first time . . . felt old." At forty-four he thought again of Carlo Alberto and put their tragic misunderstanding into his plays. All six tragedies turn on the corrosive impact of "neo-capitalist power" on the family, especially on fathers and sons.

From the first Episode of *Orgia:*

> Man: And your family?
> Woman: It was like yours.
> Man: A father who opened his mouth to emit vile sounds of command, made surly like an old soldier by wine and half-poverty, AND DID NOT SPEAK? A mother, unconscious and far away like a little bird, who opened her mouth to defend herself or to cry and protest inopportunely—AND DID NOT SPEAK? [59]

*Affabulazione* exposes raw the generational conflict in an industrialist's family; its tormented crux explores the love-hate of a father and son, locked in conflict with no way out. The son flees the family home, challenging order, normalcy, and authority. He is found [in an odd twist on Tolstoy's flight] "at the train station at La Spezia" and is brought home by the police. The commissioner explains to his parents that their son was "dying of cold, like all the boys who run away from home. It's not a pretty place, that, for a boy from a family like yours. . . ."

The father takes back his errant son and even confesses that in his place he would have done the same. But the son is not really radical; on the contrary, he announces his goal is to be a "petit bourgeois"; it is the father who wants his son to challenge all limits. The roles are reversed. It had been Carlo Alberto who served as typist and secretary, errand-boy, and review-clipper to his son. And it was the son, Pier Paolo, who felt he held the family together through Carlo's drunken binges, his black depressions.

> Father: Don't holler, first of all. Pass all limits? Who knows, maybe instead we will pass them together. Look, I too lived the condition of being a son, youth. I had it and I lost it. Now, not to be young, what does that mean? Ah, simple: it means to be a child.
>
> Thus, before your youth full of semen and the desire to procreate, you are the father. And I am the baby. Now I have understood.
>
> It is I, not you, the poor beggar baby, who does not know what his youth is, and his loves, because he has yet to test them: and he is humbled in his sterility as though it were a guilt or an exclusion.
>
> Thus here I am, at the feet of your youth, and I ask of it, as one who is powerless, power. At the feet of your youth where youth still is, and your body, from the waist down.

[in Pasolini's italics]
*And this is what the father always wants to ignore in the son and for which he hates him: and I, instead, love you for it corrupt father! Have the patience you have with children.*

When the son rejects his plea ("Love is a sad victory / which never gives me any awareness of my rights"), the father draws a knife and stabs the son to death.

The father, so much like Carlo Alberto, addresses the audience:

> The fathers want to cause their sons' death (that's why they send them to war) while the sons want to murder the fathers (that's why, for example, they protest against war and hate, full of pridefulness, the society of the elders that seeks it).
>
> Now then I, instead of murdering my son . . . wanted him to kill me! Doesn't that seem strange to you? And he, instead of wishing to kill me—or let himself be killed willing and resigned like all those obedient ones of his generation—wanted neither to kill me nor let himself be killed! Neither one nor the other, understand *Cacarella* [roughly: "little shit"]. He didn't care at all about me, or about all the killings, old and new, which link a father and a son. . . . Thus he freed himself from everything, and went away, and lived on his own, he ignored me, he fled from me, he went elsewhere. [Pasolini's italics] *If this was the future, it was all unpredictable.*[60]

The plays, unperformed and published only in the small-circulation *Nuovi argomenti*, met with neither critical acclaim nor public attention. Pasolini, asked about the response to them, said, "Absolutely none. I might as well have published a hundred blank pages.[61]

*Affabulazione* was first performed in German translation in Austria; its Italian premiere came only after Pasolini's death, to inaugurate a new theater in Turin when Vittorio Gassman recited the three-hour near-monologue and then repeated the success in Rome before four thousand spectators. Ten years later he launched a new production in Pistoia, taking it to Florence, Lucca, Siena, Bologna, and Rome. This time Gassman played the father and the actor's own son, Alessandro, twenty, made his debut as the son. The production was filmed by the Italian State television (RAI)'s second channel (the "socialist" one), for television broadcast.

The play whose structure "wanted to become" *Teorema* was about that bourgeoisie that Pasolini told a BBC-TV interviewer he hated "with an almost physical repugnance." The "simple" plot is the not at all simple story of what happens to such a family when it "encounters a visitor, someone who comes into and out of [its] life like an ultra-terrestrial or metaphysical apparition."[62] As usual *Teorema*—both book and film—came hard on the heels of *Uccellacci;* while he worked at it, he was also writing scripts based on the ancient myths of Oedipus and Medea. Whatever happened on the level of chronicle in his life seemed never to interrupt the work. As though on a plane untouchable by daily life, the work surged forth, even faster than ever.

He had several projects under way. One called for working again with Totò. Perhaps to remake *Pinocchio* with Totò as Geppetto the cobbler, Ninetto as his beloved wooden boy. Pasolini apparently saw himself as the third point of a triangle: as the talking cricket, Pinocchio's conscience, who foretells disaster and laughs at himself. There was also talk of Totò in a film Pasolini would base on Moravia's *L'attenzione* or in a film-in-episodes to be called *Che cosa è il cinema?* (What is cinema?).

He returned to the Pesaro festival to deliver a paper, "La lingua scritta della realtà" (The written language of reality). He declaimed to Alberto Arbasino, "Between the cinema and reality there is the same difference as between the written word and the spoken word."[63]

Before turning to *Teorema*, he had to fulfill a commitment to Dino de Laurentiis to produce parts for two more episodic films. Both were to be fables starring Totò, made (Pasolini told a reporter) "under the sign of the Roman Phaedrus, or La Fontaine."

His episode for *Le streghe* (The witches)—one in the grouping was *La strega bruciata viva* (The witch burned alive), directed by Visconti from a script by Giuseppe Patroni Griffi and Cesare Zavattini—was called *La terra vista dalla luna* (The earth seen from the moon, 1967). Its cast: Totò, Ninetto, Laura Betti, and Silvana Mangano (since 1949, Mrs. Dino de Laurentiis)—an actress in whom he found what he called his "ideal of feminine beauty." In fact, each of the five parts of *Le streghe* featured Mangano. Besides Pasolini and Visconti, episodes were directed by Mauro Bolognini, Franco Rosi, and Vittorio de Sica to showcase her; one magazine called it "a Silvana festival . . . [her] recital." She was in her ascendancy, before competition from Lollobrigida and Loren, who were less demanding about the quality of their roles and far more accessible to the press.

Later, by way of unnecessary excuse for his segment's tone being so out of synch, Pasolini said De Laurentiis had approached him "after the others were finished." But Pasolini made a point of not seeing the others' episodes ("because I might have become demoralized") before he began work. The result was (again) to make him *contracorrente*—"against the current."

> All the other episodes of *Le streghe* are rather alike, they are all basically anachronistic products of neo-realism; even Visconti turned out something fairly poor. All the other episodes are set in a bourgeois milieu and have a brilliant or comic style, so my episode is unassimilable: when it has appeared audiences have just been disconcerted. The same goes for the critics—I don't think any of them have said anything sensible about it; they have treated it as though it were simply a kind of bizarre parenthesis in my work, whereas I consider it one of the most successful things I have ever made.[64]

Pasolini, the director of black-and white, now discovered color with a vengeance. Ninetto (called Basciu Miao, a nonsense name, sounding perhaps like a cat), son to Totò (called Ciancicato Miao), wears a carrot-orange punk wig and a turquoise sweatshirt with NEW YORK written across it. Totò wears a wig of two tufts of acid-yellow curls, like earmuffs bookending his bald head. Observers were struck by the vividness of the colors and asked if Pasolini had invented the then unseen combinations: "I was very lucky. I found two or three locations which had completely fabulous colors and I just used them. Everything is real . . . poor people's resorts, down at Fiumicino and Ostia, where people have built these huts and painted them fantastic colors."[65]

The film opens with father and son weeping at the grave of their wife and mother, who is depicted on her tombstone as a comic bookstyle play-dough statuette, complete with raised rolling pin. The two go off, down a road from nowhere in particular to nowhere designated, in search of a replacement. Every candidate proves unsuitable: a prostitute (who only says "That'll be a thousand"), a widow (who chases them off with an umbrella), and a blond mannequin (*É nordica!*," they exclaim, "She's Nordic!"), who is hauled away in the back of a truck.

A year passes and Totò advises his son, "Life is a dream." Finally, they come upon Assurdina Cai, praying by a roadside altar. Played by Mangano in an ash-blond wig, she has tears in her eyes, is deaf and dumb, pliable, and suits them both. Totò offers her a banana. The entire business infuriated one critic who said Pasolini's idea seemed to come from the *Corriere dei piccoli* (a comic strip), that ". . . so (under)using Mangano was enough to make one . . . lose one's mind."

She and Totò are wed in a funny episode with groom as a knockoff Harpo Marx, Mangano the takeoff of the petit-bourgeois bride in demureness and white and Mario Cipriani (Balilla in *Accattone*, Stracci in *La ricotta*), as officiating priest. Totò meows his assent (he is, after all, Signor Miao); Ninetto plays the harmonica.

Now they must set up housekeeping. But the shack to which they return is a mess, full of bats, a parody of the worst *borgata*. But as Totò points out, "It has running water." No matter: The ever-willing Assurdina sets to work. She tosses a hand grenade and a doll, a radio and a Manchu who sells neckties fly out. At one point, when Mangano is cleaning out a pile of incredible junk in the house (a shack Pasolini found in Ostia), she finds a photograph of Chaplin. Pasolini told a critic, "That's the key quotation, obviously."

Soon she has cheerfully made their abode spotless.

All seems to be well, when a voice-over injects that man is "never satisfied." Totò covets his neighbor's bigger house opposite and plots to get it. The solution is simple: Assurdina climbs to the top of the Colosseum and threatens to throw herself off. Her son and husband cry out for help—miming that she has four children with tuberculosis, has eaten only three or four times since marrying—and the foolish public gives money to convince her to descend, assured of having the home she wants. She indicates that checks are accepted and money rains down.

But something goes awry. Two tourists arrive: Laura Betti in male drag, done up as a British-style explorer with potbelly and pith helmet, accompanied by Luigi Leoni in female drag as a quivering English matron, constantly photographing the ever-so-charming and picturesque Italians. They try to climb to save her but somehow drop a banana peel; Assurdina gets on top of it, slips, and falls to her death.

We return to the almost Day-Glo cemetery, where Ninetto and Totò again weep at the demise of the woman of their house, this time buried beneath a stone depicting the Colosseum, a skeleton, and a banana peel.

Returned home, they are afraid to reenter their house because the dead Assurdina has reappeared, in her wedding gown. They ask, "Is she dead?" She nods yes. They ask if she can still do all she did for them before—cooking, cleaning, washing. She assents and lets them know that she is made of flesh and bone and willing to return to her former life, nothing changed.

She puts on the green dress and red shoes she wore when they met, and smiles, mute as always. They celebrate, and all ends well. The voice-over remarks, "Dead or alive, it is all the same," a line

Pasolini later described as "a kind of slogan of Indian philosophy."

For all its apparent levity and Fauve-inspired palette, *La terra vista dalla luna* communicates a sadness, the pathos of unconscious lives. The world Totò and Ninetto inhabit is like that of *Uccellacci and uccellini*—but without any substructure it is absurd, something "from the moon."

His deal with De Laurentiis called for contributing to another episodic product, this time a sextet: The other directors were Steno, Zac, Monicelli, and two were to be made by Pasolini's old ally Bolognini. This time Pasolini's "play within a play" lasted only twenty-two minutes. Returned from a second location-scout in Morocco, for *Oedipus Rex*, he shot *Che cosa sono le nuvole?* (What are the clouds?) ". . . in a week, because I was in a hurry."[66]

Instead of *La ricotta*'s filming of the Crucifixion, this time a troupe of traveling players—full-size human "puppets" but stringed—is enacting jazzed-up, truncated scenes from Shakespeare's *Othello* from a mobile stage in a poor district. Posters advertise the puppet play to be something called " 'What Are the Clouds?' by Pier Paolo Pasolini." Again, play within a play and again—as in Welles' dialogue with the reporter on the film set of *La ricotta*, as in the poetry of "A Desperate Vitality"—he is a player in the story he has made, *protagonista* in work that blurs narrative and narcissism.

Totò plays Iago (his last role—he died soon after), his jealous face grease-painted bright green, sporting a giant black top hat; Ninetto (now in his fourth film role, all for Pasolini) is a gallant Othello, wearing a wide sash and blackface; Laura Betti plays Desdemona in cherry earrings, a platinum blonde with heavy eyelashes.

Pasolini added two other famous comics, instantly recognizable to the Italian audience: as Cassio, Franco Franchi (a Sicilian who appeared in three or four films a year for many years, to have a major role in Fellini's *Amarcord* in 1974), and Ciccio Ingrassia as Rodrigo.The effect was Cheech and Chong as Hamlet and Horatio. "I don't think it's a problem because they are what they are whether they are known to be that or not. I chose them because of their plebeian quality, which is a bit vulgar . . . their comicness is a bit abject, maybe, but it's also immediate. In Italy people know about their being funny, abroad it will be unknown, but it's still the same thing."[67]

Other "puppets" were his regulars, Mario Cipriani and Piero Morgia, who played Pio in *Accattone* and Piero in *Mamma Roma*. In his third Pasolinian role, Francesco Leonetti played the unseen puppeteer. A Pasolini troupe had jelled.

The play-within-a-play turns Shakespeare around a bit: Cassio has been named lieutenant to Othello. Iago and Rodrigo plot behind Othello's back, and as they are doing so, Cassio arrives to announce the impending invasion of the feared Turkish fleet. The scene changes and the puppeteer explains that the Turkish armada has conveniently been destroyed by a storm. Iago finds a handkerchief of Desdemona's, thus the way to drive Othello mad and destroy him.

As though "behind the scenes" from the live audience—but in view of the film one—the characters (humans who are puppets in the hands of fate) live out a parallel story. Ninetto-Othello, at one point, finally asks the question that fascinated Pasolini, "Why must we be so very different from what we think we are?" The answer, from Totò-Iago, "Ah, my son, we are a dream inside of a dream." Pasolini returned to the "dream" theme many times later, culminating in *Thousand and One Nights*, made five years later, which declaims from the screen a frame of text: "Reality is not found in one dream but in many dreams."

In the "dream within a dream," Cassio is caught dallying with a Turkish woman and is stripped of his military rank. Desdemona, at Cassio's supplication, begs Othello to reinstate him. Iago plants suspicion in the disingenuous mind of Othello (Ninetto plays it in perfect, broad strokes) and passes the fatal handkerchief.

Suddenly, the line between representation and reality collapses, or seems to: The playgoing audience (who are "real"—or more real than people playing characters?) of "simple" factory workers and farmers hollers its disapproval at Iago's perfidy. Othello, stepping out of character (although he cannot, such being his fate), goes backstage to ask the always unseen puppeteer why it is that he is being forced to kill Desdemona, bringing down on himself the audience's wrath. It seems the common people, no more than judges or prosecutors, cannot tell the difference between a play and the truth, between actors and real people, between the content of art and the morality of artists who create it.

Leonetti, the puppeteer, answers, "Perhaps because, in reality, it is you who really wishes to kill Desdemona." To this, the stupefied Ninetto-Othello answers, "And how's that? I want to kill Desdemona. And why?" The puppeteer responds: "Maybe because it pleases Desdemona to be killed." Ninetto is stumped and asks (again transparently standing for Pasolini—who is also perhaps Desdemona: "pleased to be killed"), "But which is the truth? That which I think about myself or that which others think about me?"

Offstage, Totò—who as a man-puppet is as wise as his Iago char-

*Anna Magnani as Mamma Roma, 1962.* Photo: Divo Cavicchioli

*The Madeleine (Maria Bernardini) strips for the film-within-a-film's crew,* La ricotta, *1963.* Photo: Archivio Cinemazero

*Enrique Irazoqui as Christ in* Il vangelo secondo Matteo *(The Gospel According to Matthew), 1964. Photo: Angelo Novi*

*Silvana Mangano (Jocasta) and Franco Citti (Oedipus) in* Edipo re *(Oedipus Rex), 1967.* Photo: *Alfonso Avincola*

*On location at Cappadocia, Turkey, Pasolini directs Maria Callas (Medea) in* Medea, 1969. Photo: *Mario Tursi*

*Pasolini in East Africa, filming* Appunti per un'Orestiade Africana *(*Notes for an African Oresteia*), 1970. Photo: Gianni Pignat*

*Vincenzo Amato (Masetto) in the convent,* Decameron, *1971.* Photo: Mario Tursi

*Pasolini plays Chaucer in*
I racconti di Canterbury
(Canterbury Tales), *1972.*
*Photo: Deborah Beer*

*Salvatore Sapienza as Prince Yunan in the underground palace, fulfilling the prophecy, in* Il fiore delle mille e una notte (Thousand and One Nights), *1974. Photo: Deborah Beer*

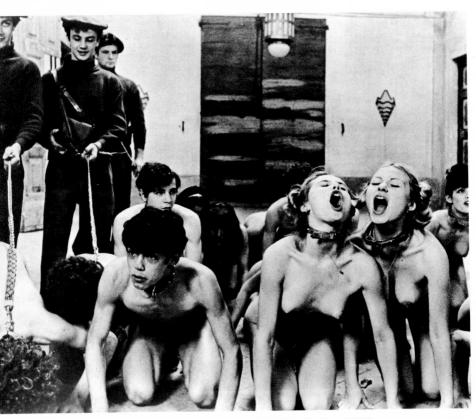

Salò, *1975. Photo: Deborah Beer. Courtesy of the Museum of Modern Art Film Archives*

acter is evil—counsels that what is true is what he, Ninetto, feels about himself. "But you must not name it, for as soon as you do that, it is gone." The beautiful, in order to be innocent (and to be good) must be unconscious of their nature and of their fate and of the plan of history (the bourgeoisie's History, to Pasolini), that will eliminate them.

Ninetto returns to the stage to enact his unavoidable mandate. But as he sets about strangling Betti-Desdemona, the public rushes the stage and kill both him and Iago. They hail the unjustly wronged Cassio in triumph. Innocent people presumably will not allow the good to suffer and evil to triumph, even in the name of art.

How to end the morality play? Desdemona says her farewell, and the dustman ("Pasolinian" symbol by now) arrives. In one of this exquisite film's sweetest moments, Domenico Modugno as the singing garbageman piles all the puppets onto the rear of his truck to drive them to the dump. Famous as the singer of "Volare," Modugno delivered in his cameo role a perfect parody of the jolly Italian manual laborer, complete with pencil mustache. As he pulls away (singing to himself, happy and indifferent in the face of tragedy), we see that the side of his so-mundane van is decorated with the most sophisticated commentary on beauty and art, on reality and depiction: the "Rokeby" Titian, the "Toilet of Venus." The nude goddess gazes at herself—as we gaze at her and at her representation of herself, which she also looks upon—in a mirror held for both the viewed and viewers by Cupid.

The moment of death alone brings insight: As the "puppets" are driven away, the camera moves to the back of the truck and we see Totò and Ninetto (somehow, as men, still alive) look up. They see overhead, as for the first time, the clouds. The film closes with their exclamation at what they call "the heartrending, marvellous beauty of creation."

The fables seem to have given Pier Paolo solace, if only as a pause. De Laurentiis paid well enough that in the summer of 1966 he bought a used red Maserati 3000GT. To many, it was a fatuous act, at least proof that he was no different from any other film director with some success. It seemed phony to his critics, like Lillian Hellman modeling fur coats for magazine ads. Others shrugged.

For Pasolini, though, success was more simple: He had been poor and now he was not. He could afford the car. Besides, it pleased Susanna, and Ninetto loved the electric windows. Pasolini took Susanna to the Carnian Alps, north of Casarsa, the region where Guido had been killed.

And the boys liked it. He was sure they noticed and were well disposed to its owner. It was "an erotic necessity," he said—like dyeing his hair, which came later.

In mid-September 1966 he visited the New World: The New York Film Festival had scheduled both *Accattone* and *Uccellacci*, with the latter's commercial release set for the Cinema Studio and the Seventy-second Street Playhouse.

Six years before, Elsa Morante had written him from Manhattan: "This is not *a* city, but *the* city, it is the universe, the firmament, the viscera of the earth. You would love it! Millions of Anglo-Saxons, Italians, Spaniards, Chinese, Negroes, Puerto Ricans running around on the streets. Everyone returns your greeting, as if they knew you. They ask your [first] name and right away start calling you by it. And all around, buildings like immense rocks, and cars like shooting stars."

As she predicted, he fell in love: "I'd like to be eighteen years old so as to be able to live a whole life over here," he told Oriana Fallaci, with whom he spent time. "I am sorry not to have come here before, twenty or thirty years ago, to stay. It has never happened to me like this, so to fall in love with a place. Except, maybe, for Africa." [68]

The reasons were several. One was "the most beautiful Left to be seen," one of white radicals and Black Panthers.

> In America, even in my very brief stay, I lived many hours in the clandestine climate of struggle, of revolutionary urgency, of hope that belonged to the Europe of '44 and '45. In Europe, everything is finished, in America, you get the feeling that it is about to begin . . . people are living there as on the eve of great things.

He ran the tourist gamut from the Automat, which he mentioned delightedly in an interview with the *New York Times*, to a boat trip around Manhattan. "One thing does surprise me about your city," he said. "Its deep humanism. The easy rapport we can have between people. Like Naples, in a sense. I even have the strange feeling that I have always been here." [69] He wrote later that in Harlem (which Oriana Fallaci warned him against visiting):

> One night . . . I shook hands (but they shook my hand suspiciously, because I was white) with a group of young blacks wearing on their sweaters the sign

of the panther—an extremist movement that is getting ready for a real armed
struggle . . . I accompanied a young black trade unionist who took me to
visit the cell of his movement.[70]

A "degraded and barbarized" Italian press wanted to hear what he
had to say about New York. *Paese sera* ran his rapportage ("Pasolini
in America") on November 18, 1966, and he wrote on the visit for
*Nuovi argomenti.* He began to talk about a film on Saint Paul.

A photograph shows him in Times Square, pausing in a light rain-
coat, jeans, and short boots at the foot of the statue of George M.
Cohan. Another caught him, alone, just having stepped off the curb,
the marquees of as-yet non-porno movie houses overhead. One advertised *The Group;* another, the Victoria, shouted a double bill: "LIZ
SIZZLES! in *Cat on a Hot Tin Roof* and *Butterfield 8.*"

He noted as "irony" many Americans' apparent revolt against consumer society. He quickly sensed "the life of conservatism, which
unfolds in a silence much more intense than the 'howls' reaching us
from the Left."[71] He saw the darker side of America's "pacifist and
nonviolent demonstrations, governed—by an intelligent spirituality."
He said, "Those who refuse to integrate themselves into the secure
workaday world, are committing something more than a series of old
and anarchistic acts—they are living a tragedy."[72]

He met Allen Ginsberg and wrote,

> I love Ginsberg
> it has been a long time since I've read poetry by
> a brother poet.

They met again the next year when Ginsberg visited Italy. Fascinated with the anarchic liberty Beat culture offered, Pasolini took
his new discovery—his poet friend from America—to meet Montale
and Quasimodo and "in my house, Umberto Eco and Enrico Filip-
pini." On October 18, 1967 (he was writing *Teorema* at the time)
Pasolini wrote to the fellow poet in New York:

> Dear angelic Ginsberg,
>     Last night I heard you say everything that came into your mind about
> New York and San Francisco, with their flowers. I have told you something
> about Italy, flowers only to be found in the forests. Your city is full of insane
> people, mine of idiots . . . All Americans are forced to be inventors of
> words! We here, instead (even those now sixteen years old) already have our
> revolutionary language, with its own ethics behind it. Even the Chinese
> speak like civil servants. Even myself—as you see. I have not succeeded

mixing prose and poetry (as you do) and I never succeed in forgetting, not even in this moment, that I have linguistic obligations. . . .

Nothing gives a sense, a feeling, of guilt more profound and incurable than retaining power. Is it incredible then if those who hold power want to die? And therefore everyone—from the divine Rimbaud to melting Cavafy, from the sublime Machado to the tender Apollinaire—all poets who have struggled against the pragmatism and reason, have done nothing else but prepare the ground, like prophets for the god War whom society invokes: a God exterminator . . . But, at the same time, to renounce, in that same stupendous mysticism of the Democracy of the New Left, to renounce, besides Holy Violence, also the idea of the conquest of power on the part of the just, signifies leaving power in the hands of the fascists who always and everywhere hold it. If these are the questions, I wouldn't know how to answer. And you? I kiss you affectionately on your thick beard.[73]

America joined Africa in the universe of at least poetic alternatives. The world of Italian culture, "in which I live because of a literary vocation" now seemed cut off, "extraneous" to a universe that mattered. "I cannot accept at all the world in which I live. Let me even say it, I remain isolated, left to yellow [as an old photograph] . . . and with a repugance at speaking both of commitment and its opposite [*sia di impegno che di disimpegno*]."[74]

## 20

*A protest without a program is little more than sentimentalism—this
is the epitaph of many of the great idealisms.*

*—Ernest Becker*

*Actors are only the annex of a film.*

*—Jean-Luc Godard*

# THE CINEMA OF POETRY:

## *OEDIPUS THE KING, TEOREMA,*

## AND A *SAINT PAUL* THAT WAS NEVER TO BE

In April 1960 in a poem entitled "Frammento alla morte," Pasolini
invoked Africa as symbol of the Third World. He called it "my sole
alternative."[1] When Leonetti reviewed *La religione del mio tempo* in
*Paragone* (October 1961) and ventured to guess what Pasolini meant
by "sole alternative," Pasolini quickly corrected him: "You have
misunderstood . . . Africa is not the Africa of Lumumba, but that of
Rimbaud." He was only being "decadent . . . in the nineteenth-
century sense," he explained. It was a romantic myth of Africa which

drew the poet, alienated in his own country, feeling there was nowhere one could really go to live.

In 1963 this seemed radical, if not yet radical-chic. Asked how he thought he could possibly survive in the Third World, he answered. "The details are difficult, not the substance." He talked about the "historical function" of Africa's masses. Perhaps there (but an imaginary "there,"all should understand), he could escape that "wave of formalism and empiricism of the great European neo-capitalist rebirth." That "rebirth," which others saw as postwar's ripened recovery, was to him like Yeats' "rude beast," something horrible, boding apocalypse. "Whether we let atomic bombs explode or arrive at complete industrialization of the world, the result will be the same: a war in which man will be defeated and perhaps lost forever."

The destiny of his escapist dreams was ironic, as he understood. What he was able to do was film a series of fables (myths, stories, tales) in exotic places, carrying exquisite pictures back to Italy and America—frames of fantasy to fill the screens of movie houses in Western cities. Their commercial sucess as "escapism," as "exotic" diversion, as scintillating entertainment masked what they also were: an artist's desperate attempt to find his way out of a cul-de-sac.

When the "national-popular" films, from *Accatone* through *Uccellacci*, were done, he turned to analogy. Having tried (and, in his view, failed) to instruct frontally by didactic preaching, he resorted to sweetening the medicine of ideology with what appeared to be nostalgia. The rest of the films are of a piece: It hardly mattered if the subject was from ancient Greece (Oedipus, Medea, the *Oresteia*), a modern "Greek tragedy" (*Teorema*) or tale-cycles (Boccaccio, Chaucer, *Arabian Nights*), or a nightmare fabulist—the Marquis de Sade.

Following an exquisite logic, in 1967 he took Oedipus—took himself—to Africa. The project's realization virtually overlapped *Teorema*.

*Edipo re* began as a hybrid of Sophocles' *Oedipus the King* with major input from *Oedipus at Colonnus*, but ended up filmed with Freud "inserted," as Pasolini himself said, "as a dilettante might insert him."

> I had two objectives: first to make a kind of complete metaphoric—and therefore mythicized—autobiography; and second to confront both the problem of psychoanalysis and the problem of the myth. But instead of projecting the myth onto psychoanalysis, I re-projected psychoanalysis on the myth. This was the fundamental operation in *Oedipus*.[2]

It was to be nothing like Universal Studios' production of *Oedipus the King*, shot in Greece and released in 1968 with polished Christopher Plummer in the title role and Orson Welles as Tiresias. In Pasolini's highly personal version, Franco Citti—not seen in a Pasolini work since *Mamma Roma*—played Oedipus. His Accattone and Oedipus have much in common: Both confront society's rules and suffer. Both are assigned to act out a destiny assigned before birth, within a social universe offering them no freedom. Both are Pasolini.

Early in the shooting, Citti—now an experienced actor, although many thought unimproved—was self-conscious. He told an interviewer he hoped people would stop calling him "Accattone" and instead "call me Oedipus." When he overacted, Pasolini joked, called him "Laurence Olivier" and instructed him to "be normal."

Silvana Mangano plays Oedipus' mother, later his wife, the queen Jocasta. Danilo Donati, following Pasolini's instructions, costumed her in copies of Susanna's clothes. "Mangano," Pasolini said, "has the perfume of primroses of my mother when young."

Besides Mangano (whom Citti found "spontaneous, genuine"[3]), Pasolini used more professional actors than ever before. He cast well-known Italian theater director Carmelo Bene as the king of Corinth. Alida Valli, whose fame was made in the Italian "white telephone" melodramas of the thirties, played Queen Merope. Often billed only as "Valli," she had launched an international career with *The Third Man* (1949). During a brief Hollywood phase, she played the female lead in Hitchcock's *The Paradine Case* (1947) with Gregory Peck, Charles Laughton, and a very young Louis Jourdan. In Italy her most famous role had been as the countess Livia Serpieri in Visconti's *Senso* (1954); Bertolucci cast her in *The Spider's Stratagem* in 1970.

For the blind Tiresias who—unlike Oedipus before his blinding can "see" reality—Pasolini chose Julian Beck of the Living Theater. The Becks had transferred their company to Europe, and after *Edipo* the Theater appeared in Bertoluccci's episode of a film first entitled *Vangelo 70* but renamed *Amore e rabbia* (Love and anger), released in 1969.

Ninetto's brother Giandomenico was cast as the shepherd to Polybus, who finds the abandoned infant Oedipus. Ninetto (whom Vincent Canby of the *New York Times* called "Pasolini's favorite aging-faun of an actor") played the messenger—in Greek *angelos*—the angel of annunciation. He was dressed by Donati in what seems macramé, a necklace of seashells; a brass bell (to announce his arrivals) hung from the brim of a straw hat.

Pasolini's first intention had been to shoot in Rumania, and he scouted locations but "the countryside is in the middle of an industrial revolution; all the old wooden villages are being destroyed, there's nothing old left." So the film's principal filming locations were the red deserts of Morocco, and its "intact" ancient cities.

Making his first full-length feature entirely in Technicolor, he now had a budget of 20 million lire; the production was by Bini's ARCO Film with participation by the Moroccan Somafis of Casablanca. When financing hit a snag, the troupe just waited in the south Moroccan desert without film stock. On April 13 he wrote Susanna from the Grand Hotel du Sud in Ouarzazate, in Morocco's interior, in the Anti-Atlas: "Here I am. Today I started shooting. It is atrociously cold, the wind blows off the Atlantic where it snowed. But they tell me the weather also turned bad in Rome. There were also a lot of organizational problems: but now it seems everything is straightened out. Try to be well, to eat and do all the things I always tell you."

Ninetto (signing "Nino") added *"Saluti affetuosi e felicità."*[4]

Before taking up Sophocles' story in his own translation (which he labeled "very straightforward and faithful to the original"), Pasolini offered a Prologue: The film opens on a just-born naked baby boy being tossed in the air, alive with a smack on the bottom and a scream. The script published by Garzanti says the viewer sees "the first experience of light (the provincial sunlight coming in through the blinds, through the unbleached canvas with its Idrian embroidery)." Embroidery from Idria because we are in fact not in Morocco, or in Greece, but in Italy.

Immediately, the camera cuts to the world as a child in the Italy of the twenties—say, one born March 5, 1922—would see it: feet and hands, then a lyrical passage of Silvana Mangano nursing the boy-child in one of the meadows Pasolini's poetry so often invoked, coddling him against a background of an elegaic cello solo from Mozart's Quartet in C Major. Alone together (in Friuli, it seems), mother and son are happy.

In an interview about his childhood, Pasolini told Dacia Maraini:

> I remember when I was one year old. I remember the room in which I slept. It was the dining room and my crib was in a corner by the wall. In front of that was a wooden alcove where my grandmother slept. I remember too a sofa which followed us around for years. The arm of this sofa lifted up and

showed the wooden structure beneath. I drew on this wood with a pencil. A car I called "Rupepe."[5]

Then, a long take on the face of an actor playing a handsome young officer of the Italian royal army, "wearing an infantryman's uniform of the nineteen-thirties."

> Maraini: What was your father like physically?
> Pasolini: A very handsome man. When I was born he was twenty-eight years old. He was not too tall, dark, very strong, dark and bright eyes, well-defined features.[6]

The young soldier-father, in the modern era, stares at his baby son in his pram. The script notes, "The father looks at him. . . . He is listening to his own inner voice. It is loud and solemn, as in a tragic drama."

> FATHER'S INNER VOICE: Here he is, the child who is gradually going to take your place in the world. Yes, he will hound you away and take your rightful place. He is here for no other reason. He knows it. The first thing he will rob you of is your wife, your sweet wife who you believe lives only for you. While instead there is love between this fellow here and her; and you are well aware that she returns it, that she is betraying you. Through love of his mother, this fellow will murder his father. And you can do nothing about it. Nothing at all.[7]

Reality and representation merge: Susanna and Jocasta, the soldier and Carlo Alberto, the baby of ancient Greece and Pier Paolo. He said as much: "The baby in the prologue is I, his father is my father, an infantry officer, and the mother, a schoolmistress, is my mother."[8]

Through a window the small boy watches his parents dancing. Here—as in *Accattone* and *Mamma Roma*, in the poems of *La nuova gioventù* rewritten from the *friulano* in 1974 and even in the closing shot of *Salò*—dance symbolizes human communion. From across a courtyard, a kind of military parade-ground, the child—now three or four—sees his parents embrace and kiss. Like Susanna, the wife-Mangano apparently acquiesces unenthusiastically to her husband's sexual insistence. The the camera records with brutal clear-sightedness the true relationship between husband and wife: He lies in bed beside her, dressed in his underwear, depressed and frustrated, staring at the ceiling; she lies apart and also stares at the ceiling. They do not touch.

The father-soldier hears a flute—the archaic flute of the Attic poets—and he grabs the baby boy by the ankles. As the flute continues to sound, the scene shifts to an ancient desert, where a slave of Laius, King of Thebes, executes his master's orders. The camera literally bounces with his step. He walks alone in a desert landscape, with the boy-child, bound hands and feet to a pole slung over his shoulder, being borne to a place to be killed. Only thus can the curse be foiled, that the child will grow to "murder his father and marry his mother."

Pasolini is faithful to Sophocles; the plot is that of the ancient play. Pasolini's Oedipus, in Citti's rendition, is no neo-classical beauty in muscles and wide brow but an impetuous, unthinking, and violent hunter-warrior, product of a preliterate society riddled with superstition, subject to forces beyond his understanding and control.

Pasolini cast himself as the High Priest, his head encircled by a corona of straw and seashells. He explains that only revenge for the murder of King Polybus, killed en route to the priests' temple, will quell the pestilence attacking Thebes.

Tiresius arrives, led by Ninetto. At first he resists telling what he knows, but—as Ninetto plays his flute—he explains that years before, servant-Leonetti had not killed the child, who grew up to enact a prophecy. At first, Oedipus tries to blame the messenger. Jocasta tells him about the child but says that the child is dead. At last, Oedipus knows she is wrong, and he understands. He calls her "mother," and again they make love. The consequence: Jocasta hangs herself; Oedipus puts out his eyes with the pin of her brooch. End of Sophocles as source. Pasolini comments, "I wanted all the central part of the film (which is almost the whole movie) to be a kind of dream, and this explains the choice of costumes and settings, the general rhythm of the work. I wanted it to be a kind of aestheticizing dream."[9]

The blind Oedipus is led by the angel-messenger, out of the archaic past onto the streets of Bologna of 1967. Citti remains in his ancient tunic, his eyes encrusted with dried blood. But now Ninetto, the spirit of innocence, wears a T-shirt with a wide necktie painted on it; he is in a "real" place the Italian audience instantly recognizes. Oedipus is now, and the place is here. Ninetto guides the blind man through the porticoed streets: They have come to "the richest city of the north, which development has made more opulent—opulent to the point of being like a French or German city," the Communist-run city where, Pasolini predicted, "the population would all be petit bourgeois, the workers having been anthropologically eliminated by the bourgeoisie."[10] Knowing what effect this jump would have, Pasolini ackowledged that "the audience is shocked by the transition."

The script:

> A wide square, bearing the marks of history and of civilization: an unfinished cathedral [Bologna's San Petronio], in red stone, a palace of the Commune opposite it, with its solemn arcade of pointed arches, and its marble mullioned windows . . . On the right side of the square is a long arcade, an elegant series of porticos laden with memories of rich families, of public events, of long-forgotten Sunday promenades. Here the bourgeoisie can celebrate its rites, and admire its own grandeur.[11]

At a corner of the Piazza Maggiore (in "a refuge away from the vortex of city life"), "Oedipus eases himself down and begins playing his flute." He starts to make music: "the only expressive action / perhaps as high and indefinable as the actions of reality."

Pasolini explained or, at least, provided one of the many keys into his metaphoric vision:

> Once Oedipus has blinded himself, he reenters society by sublimating all his faults. One of the forms of sublimation is poetry. He plays the pipe, which means, metaphorically, he is a poet. First he plays for the bourgeoisie, and he plays the old Japanese music connected with the Oracle—ancestral, private, confessional music . . . then, disgusted by the bourgeoisie, he goes off and plays his pipe (i.e., goes off and acts like a poet) to the workers, and there he plays a tune which was one of the songs of the Resistance.[12]

Finally, Oedipus "and the boy guiding him" walk along a village street, "in silence through the midday hush." It is a place that has "stagnated into a backwater" and near it runs a river, a "modest little river"—the "Livenza . . . shimmering green." The film ends here, with Oedipus playing music on the banks of the river, a spot that is "a jewel of nature . . . It was here that Oedipus first distinguished and recognized his mother." It is the Livenza that "let loose its green roses," the Livenza where Susanna had taken her boy-child, Pier Paolo.

Here, Pasolini dissolves back to the house where it all began, where Susanna-Mangano-Jocasta and Carlo Alberto-soldier-Laius conceived their son, Pier Paolo-Citti-Oedipus.

The film ends as did *Che cosa sono le nuvole?*: Pasolini points his camera skyward—is it protecting or indifferent?—as Pasolini on the sound track reads lines of his poetry: "Life ends where it began." The closing frame shows a field of grass, "the meadow on the banks of Livenza," the river near Casarsa where a mother first caressed her "cursed" baby boy.

Oedipus punishes himself for what has happened because of the curse. But he was innocent; he is punished even though he did not know, condemned even before birth. He was born what Pasolini called himself: "an adult foetus." His complete innocence is required if his punishment is to teach; his blinding is not useful pedagogy for others unless he is guiltless victim.

Using the language of Freud, Pasolini addressed the fact of Oedipus' incest—the very motor of the myth:

> Even if I understand it rationally, it is difficult to accept in all its fullness. Perhaps I was inhibited in representing it artistically while I let myself go in representing the parricide. This must be due quite simply to Freudian reasons, presumably. I hadn't realized it before. . . .[13]

The conflict between Oedipus and Laius is developed more than that between the son and Jocasta because

> The relationship between a son and his mother is not a historical relationship, it is a purely interior, private relationship which is outside history, indeed it is meta-historical, and therefore ideologically unproductive, whereas what produces history is the relationship of hatred and love between father and son. . . . Everything ideological, voluntary, active and practical in my actions as a writer depends on my struggle with my father.[14]

Soon after *Edipo*'s release Pasolini said,

> Quite recently, I've realized that my relationship with my father was very important too. I always thought I hated my father, but in fact I didn't hate him; I was in conflict with him, in a state of permanent, even violent tension with him. There are many reasons for this . . . he had a very difficult relationship with my mother. I only understand this now, but he probably loved her too much and then perhaps this was not reciprocated fully . . . like all children, I sided with my mother.[15]

But, according to family legend, Carlo Alberto was so much the model officer loved by his men that: "When he died, a soldier came specially from Sicily, bearing a crate of oranges." Pier Paolo's explanation for the dichotomy: "It is typical of paranoids, and of men who drink."[16]

In a conclusion, which must perhaps be seen as a staggering piece of necessary self-deception, he told *Cahiers du cinéma:*

> Being the most autobiographical of all my films, *Edipo* is the one I think of as most objective and disinterested . . . even though I recount personal experience it is also true that it is a phase of experience which is concluded, and hardly interests anymore.[17]

Determined to keep the pot at a hard boil, he wrote that in this story he was only telling "things . . . by now remote." He wrote in the screenplay's preface, "I am no longer terribly interested in the subject of the researches of Freud and Marx. I'm no longer at all seriously involved in that academic bog that turns Oedipus into a whipping post for Freudian or Marxist theories . . . I want to stress the fact that now, at forty-five years of age, I have emerged from the wilderness of Freudian and Marxist dogma. *But where have I got to?*"

> I have certainly never dreamed that I was making love to my mother. Perhaps I should refer the two or three readers who have stayed with me as far as this to a couple of lines from the *Usignolo della chiesa cattolica*
>
>     . . . *il sogno in cui mia madre*
> *s' infila i miei calzoni.*
>
> ( . . . the dream in which my mother
> slips into my trousers.)
>
> If anything, I have dreamed rather of making love to my father against the chest of drawers (in the wretched little bedroom my brother and I shared) and perhaps to my brother as well. And I have dreamed of making love to women of stone. Of course I'm not counting the dreams that have recurred several times throughout my life, where I climb endless, dreary flights of stairs in dreary homes. I am looking for my mother, who has disappeared.
>
> But after all it is some time since I have had such dreams. Silvana Mangano might have the same scent of primroses about her that my mother had when young, but Franco Citti has nothing in common with me—save his slightly raised cheekbones.[18]

As Pasolini's Queen of Thebes, Mangano is virtually encrusted with stones: Almost buried under topaz and seashells, she is wheeled about in a kind of wooden wheelbarrow carved with totemic figures. Pasolini allowed her very few lines and relied on her sharp-edged beauty, etched nose, exquisite mouth—the "sign" of her face would "speak." In his view, it hardly mattered what Queen Jocasta thought or said. Like everyone else, she was ordered by destiny beyond the bidding of human personalities.

And yet at a crucial junction in the film, when Oedipus might evidence a new self-awareness but does not, Pasolini takes a phrase from Sophocles which he found "absolutely mysterious . . . I cannot understand the phrase, but I find it wonderful, precisely because it is enigmatic and incomprehensible." The phrase is, "There, now all is clear, willed, not imposed by destiny."

Pasolini wrote that he was "inspired" by "the contrast between total innocence and the obligation to know." He wrote, "This is what I liked the most in Sophocles, that fact that the person who has to encounter all of these problems should be the person most unprepared for all this, someone who is completely innocent.[20]

"By the time Oedipus understands," Pasolini explained, "it's no use to him." One cannot help but be reminded of his frequent references to himself, in the poems, as "innocent" and "ignorant," unprepared for his "destiny." And is Pier Paolo, despite his protestations, then Oedipus? He said "I am basically irrational and innocent like Oedipus and, at bottom, ignorant. As a reaction, I concoct these endorsements of consciousness." A message, deeply hidden, was read by some sensitive Marxist critics, to the effect that the greatest programs and the merest maneuvers of human party politics (even of the PCI, which Pasolini still cited as a "hope") had near and impenetrable limits. The issues which mattered were existential, "bound up with blood and the destiny of blood . . . there where the great tragic myths have placed it."[21]

Garzanti had committed to publishing Pasolini's screenplays, understanding that they were distinct works of literature from that which was finally filmed and released. The series ultimately included more or less modified versions of the screenplays of *Il Vangelo, Uccellacci, Edipo,* and *Medea.* He also agreed to print other screenplays that Pasolini, as director of a collection called *Films and Discussion,* might choose. The first appeared in October 1966: Ermanno Olmi's script of *E vienne un uomo* (And there came a man), about Papa Roncalli; Pasolini's poetry preface was called "Versi e note d'occasione su Giovanni XXIII" and includes the line: "Pope John was a delicious peasant but also a grand Parisian." Also published under Pasolini's editorship was Marco Bellocchio's first feature *I Pugni in tasca* (literally, Fists in the pockets) (1967)—with an exchange of letters between Pasolini and Bellocchio as preface. Pasolini also brought to the bookstores the script of Sergio Citti's *Ostia* (1970), on which Pasolini collaborated.

In 1966 Garzanti added a line called *Laboratorio*, dedicated to film theory, again directed by Pasolini. For more than four years, he oversaw publication of *The Cinema and the Cinema* by Jean-Luc Godard (1968)—for which he wrote a preface, *The Russian Formalists in Cinema* by Giorgio Kraiski (1971), *The Semiology of Cinema* by Christian Metz (1972), and, that same year, *What Is the Cinema?* by André Bazin. The making of his films (which were also books), and the making of books about film and films by others, proceeded hand-in-hand. Before leaving for the Berlin Festival in June 1966 he wrote Garzanti: "I am in direct contact [about the series] with Godard, Barthes, and Metz." [19]

On September 3, 1967, *Edipo re* premiered at the Twenty-eighth Venice Film Festival, where it shared the Special Jury Prize with Buñuel's *Belle de jour* and Godard's *La chinoise*. But only after a fight. Bini accused Festival director Luigi Chiarini of having decided to honor Buñuel's film alone, even before the jury met. The charges were enthusiastically broadcast by the press, infuriated at what it saw as the Festival's high-handedness toward the media. Bini's accusations against the Festival and noisy polemics against it were only the tip of an iceberg of discontent; even conservative magazines accused Chiarini of exercising "a personal dictatorship"—he alone had decided no films would be accepted from America, the Soviet Union, or Japan. The Italian film critic's union awarded its Silver Ribbon to Bini for best producer, to Luigi Scaccianoce for "best decoration." According to Nico Naldini, *Edipo*'s greatest success over time was in France and Japan. [22]

It was the last of Pasolini's films Bini was to produce. In his eighth year in the business, he had made eighteen films, working not only with Pasolini but also with Lattuada, Rossellini, Bolognini, Gregoretti, Godard, and others.

Three weeks after Pasolini's murder, he recalled how he and Pasolini had lain on their backs gazing at the night sky, "looking for the Southern cross." They met a Father Calvini in Africa, who wanted most of all a Pellizzari brand pump (which Bini sent him) to water the desert and make lemon trees grow. And the priest arranged a mass—a *Messa luba* —the liturgy sung by Masai who worked under a broiling sun, breaking up rocks for a public works project. Pasolini used it in the sound track of *The Gospel According to Matthew*; years later, Bini recalled that Pasolini wept when he heard it, the "only time" in their years together.

After Pasolini's murder Bini wrote that in seven years' collaboration, his key director's private life never became an issue between them, "never a mention of homosexuality . . . never a gesture."As for the compulsive nature of Pasolini's sexual activity, Bini dismissed it ("addressing" Pasolini in a written reminiscence)—"It was just something stronger than you. I think it was a question of your damned suprarenal glands which dumped liters of stimulant into your blood!"

Bini knew and accepted Pasolini's unconventional work methods. "Most directors will shoot fifteen, at the most twenty takes a day. Pier Paolo literally ran from one to another, driven." Again, writing to him as though alive:

> Do you remember Matera? During the shooting of *Vangelo?* Seventy shots in a day, from four in the morning until eight, nine at night, you remember? With your feet all bandaged because they were hurting you. I said, "Will you come and eat something?" "No, no, I'm tired. I'm going to bed." O.K. You went up to bed. You threw yourself onto the bed with those sound blockers in your ears. "Alright," I said to myself, "at least until tomorrow morning he will be quiet."
>
> But what's this? When it was midnight, half past midnight, you got up . . . and went out like a thief. Where in the devil were you going at two in the morning in Matera? Where did you get inside, who did you get to let you in, huh?
>
> And the same thing, always, everywhere. You remember in Port Sudan, where you were dragged out of that Bedouin tent at one in the morning in a rocky desert where not even a crazy camel would have ventured?"[23]

But after *Edipo re*, Bini soured. His somewhat self-serving explanation of their break:

> I was just bored, and I thought he was already dead by then, as an artist. I wanted him to direct *The Inferno* but he was not interested. I thought *Teorema* was turning back on himself, reworking old stuff. . . . It was like Pygmalion. I made this creature, and after it was made there was nothing more to do. The job was done, my interest faded.[24]

But the explanation might be less high minded. Both men had found other partners for other projects, chances for doing (and earning) more apart than together. In 1967, the same year as *Edipo*'s release, Bini produced *The Rover* (*L'Avventuriero* in Italy), starring Anthony Quinn and Rita Hayworth, a combination that ought to have spelled box-office success but did not. And that year, Pasolini threw in his lot with Franco Rossellini (nephew of Roberto) and Manolo Bolognini, partners in Aetos Films, for his next project. They offered him budget enough to pay a real film star like Massimo Girotti, famous to Italian moviegoers since playing the young lead in Visconti's *Ossessione* in 1943. Pasolini was now offered a director's fee of 50 million lire per picture. *Teorema* was produced to full feature length, ninety-eight minutes, and in color.

"A work that would be more problematic, ambiguous, more for elites" than the brightly colored fables of the two episodic films. That is what he told Roman film school students he wanted to do after *Edipo re.* The result was *Teorema:* It proved to be what he proposed and became a cult film, one of the symbols of the European '68.

Shooting started in March 1968, two months before the Sorbonne exploded and the Italian universities caught fire. It was shot in five weeks (in English), edited in nine. Pasolini's first idea had been to film in New York, but instead he found a villa outside Milan. His new producer arranged for international distribution, including America. Garzanti released his book of the same title that spring, slightly ahead of the film. Pasolini intended it to stand alone, a work of literature and not just a script-in-print.

On set at San Angelo Lodignano, he offered an interviewer some striking comments. One senses Pasolini "living up to one's myth" in his overstatement, even stretching so as to shock: "This is the first film I have shot in a bourgeois milieu with bourgeois characters. Until now, I have never done this because I could not bear to have to live with people I could not stand for months on end, fixing the script and then shooting the film."[25]

He told an English television reporter about the characters: "I chose people who were not particularly odious, people who elicited a certain sympathy—they are typical of the bourgeoisie, but not the very worst bourgeoisie.[26]

"He added, "Besides all this, it is only right that I should feel something for all individuals, including bourgeois individuals."

Massimo Girotti and Silvana Mangano play the upper-middle-class couple. Ninetto was, again, cast as a messenger; Godard's wife, Anne Wiazemsky, as Odette, the daughter in the household; Andrés José Crux as her brother, Pietro. The literary critic Cesare Garboli had a small part; almost alone among the clique of literary critics, he defended the book of *Teorema.*

An important role went to Laura Betti, who plays the peasant servant Emilia, come from the countryside to be maid in the wealthy household. He explained to a reporter from *L'espresso* that Betti, cast against type, would play the deeply religious servant because "At her depths, there is something of the Apocalypse . . . something biblical, capable of powerful curses as of overwhelming blessings." And Susanna Colussi Pasolini was cast as an old peasant in a key cameo.

He first planned to cast as the mysterious, pansexual Guest the American actor Lee Van Cleef, then at the height of his Italian fame after a series of "spaghetti Westerns," including *For a Few Dollars More* and *The Good, the Bad and the Ugly*, both released in 1966. Van Cleef was probably too expensive. Without losing stride, Pasolini settled on the much less costly Englishman Terence Stamp, who had just completed *Toby Dammit* and a segment of Fellini's *Spirits of the Dead*, and was "hanging around a bit in Rome" with his brother, Chris.

> We were walking down the street and bumped into Piero Tosi, Fellini's [and Pasolini's] costume designer—he always called me by my name translated into Italian, *"Terencino Francobollo."* He was window-shopping with Silvana Mangano, whom I had worshiped since I saw her in *Bitter Rice*. He mentioned something about a director named Pasolini who was making a film soon, and then he said to Silvana that I would be just right for a certain part. I didn't think much about it, but later my brother, who knows all about such things, took me aside and said that Pasolini was a gay, Communist poet, very brilliant, that I had to get the role no matter what.[27]

Stamp believes "Mangano's recommendation of me was enough," and soon producer Rossellini contacted the actor's agent and a meeting was arranged in London.

"I remember Pasolini staring at me, from behind tinted glasses, studying my face. I remember thinking his head looked like a skull, the skin drawn so tightly over it. It was unnerving."

Stamp flew to Milan for the shooting of the interior scenes; he was lodged at the Principe Savoia Hotel and ferried by car-and-driver to the set every morning.

Not that Pasolini had much to say to him. "There was no script . . . it was nonacting. I spoke what lines I had in English and as for the rest, no direction was forthcoming at all. It seemed to me that it was being made like a B-movie, strictly cinema verité." But Stamp—an actor with credits but still only twenty-eight—was worried, and turned to Mangano for advice. "He is just a boy," she explained about Stamp's role, "but perhaps a boy with a divine nature."

Pasolini, who showed no sexual interest in Stamp, asked that the actor really undress completely and get into bed with Andrés José

Crux. "He [Crux] came and told me, 'Look, I think we're going to have to be naked in bed together in this scene. What about that?' and I told him not to worry and that was that."

Another scene sees Stamp reclined in a lounge chair on the lawn of the family house. "I remember Laura Betti came running over to me and started caressing my crotch and carrying on. Pasolini just kept filming, and used it. She was amazing, telling me how when we had to do our sex scene she would really make me fuck her, she would drive me mad with desire and all that . . . very vulgar." [28]

When the film was done, Pasolini wrote Betti, "I will never forget the shock your behavior during the shooting caused me." [29]

When Stamp attended the opening of the film at the Curzon theater in London, "People just laughed; the English are like that." In Paris the film opened to enormous clamor, generating long lines at five cinemas around the city. Stamp says, "I had to sneak into one near the drugstore on Boulevard Saint-Germain. The story was out that anyone who touched me was transformed [so runs the film plot]. It made my life wonderful in Italian restaurants but complicated in Turkish baths."

People expected Pasolini to deliver a straightforward if scathing attack on the bourgeoisie and its lack of religion. His apparently simple premise, the "theorem" of the film's title, was that when one family was faced with a power that constituted real liberation (by necessity sexual) and their values were revealed as bankrupt, its members would spin into "madness."

By 1968 he had decided that the "classical bourgeoisie" of Italy had changed. Since "the whole of mankind was becoming petite bourgeoisie," his "indignation and anger [at the Italian middle class] . . . no longer has any rationale behind it." Their sacred fortress of the family had collapsed before their eyes, in a process that left them almost sympathetic characters, perhaps more to be pitied that reviled.

Wife Lucia (Mangano) and husband Paolo (Girotti) live a quiet, privileged life in a luxurious villa in industrialized Lombardy: She tends to her duties as *grande dame*, he to managing his factory. All is static and has the air of permanence in a hierarchical society subject to "rationality," as defined by the powerful. Control over others and oneself is all.

A documentary-style Prologue, labeled as such and shot in black-and-white, shows interviews at a (real) factory gate with workers who have been given the plant by its owner. A *padrone* has acceded to the demands of labor, thrown it all over, let the workers try and see if they can do better. As the workers explain to an offscreen interviewer (critic Garboli) their varying attitudes toward the decision, a neat cut brings on screen a chauffeur-driven car. It exits from the gates: Inside sits the boss (Massimo Girotti), elegantly attired, his face composed but slightly sad, as though he is distracted, thinking of something nameless, something missing thus far in his life.

Such a short sequence of factory life is the closest Pasolini ever came to setting a film in an industrial workplace. When asked why by a correspondent in *Vie nuove*,[30] he answered that Chaplin had "exhausted the poetic potentials" of the setting in *Modern Times*.

We return with Girotti to his sumptuous house (from this point, the film switches into color) where we meet Lucia and their "advanced" ever-so-1968 son and daughter, products of the most enlightened upbringing a northern industrialist of the day could offer. They have everything and nothing. Pasolini told an interviewer that fall (significantly the fall of 1968), "There are no uncultured bourgeois who are not vulgar; only culture can purify."[31]

And we meet Emilia: silent, accommodating, crucial to the family's comfort and also crucial in Pasolini's frame of reference because she is a symbolic presence from another human universe.

While the family is at dinner—its atmosphere silent, repressed—the doorbell rings. Emilia answers to find Ninetto, delivering a telegram (literally, the herald, as Pasolini called him in the poetry), stating that soon a visitor will be arriving. We know no more. The family barely reacts: In fact, their passivity is like that of protagonists in a Greek myth, caught in the hands of Fate. Cause and effect are suspended; it is as though they were expecting this unknown, uninvited, and yet somehow desired visitation.

The Guest (Stamp) enters into a world both prepared and unready for him. A handsome young man, dressed casually, he is given to sweet smiles, a gentle manner, but an unsettlingly steady gaze. Like everyone in the film, he speaks very little but gently acts as though being within the family is perfectly natural. They take him in without question.

> Originally, I intended this visitor to be a fertility god, the typical god of preindustrial religion, the sun-god, the Biblical god, God the Father. Naturally, when confronted with things as they were, I had to abandon my original idea and so I made Terence Stamp into a generically ultraterrestrial

and metaphysical apparition: he could be the Devil, or a mixture of God and the Devil. The important thing is that he is something authentic and unstoppable.[32]

Pasolini said the Stamp character is not Christ: "It is an Old Testament, not a New Testament, visitor."[33]

The Guest's first extraordinary act is to save Emilia from suicide. She wants to escape from the deadly world of the family in which she will always be exploited. Or perhaps she wants to avoid bearing witness to the terrible events she "knows" will come and can predict with the intuition that is the monopoly of the "simple." Stamp prevents her self-destruction and she offers herself to him: Their intercourse (far from explicit on film) is the first sexual "revelation," and is conducted in almost complete silence.

Stamp proceeds to make love—to bring love—to every member of the family; at the least they offer hesitating acquiescence, at the most unspoken encouragement.

He has been given a bed in Pietro's room, the son who is in well-mannered rebellion and does not want to grow up to run his father's company nor live his father's life. Without words he and Stamp undress, lie in their separate beds. But Pietro wants to share his with Stamp, who accedes, silently and sweetly acting out his preordained role.

The "theorem"—Paolini's "What if?"—proceeds. The mother caresses the Guest's clothing. He is not only Divine Love but also Profane. He appears; she disrobes and draws him toward her for lovemaking. Neither visual nor verbal text explains whether this is to compensate for what seems a frigid marriage or altogether something else.

The father takes suddenly and mysteriously ill. Again, we are left to fill in the blanks, the obvious explanation (and Pasolini was not above the obvious) that an inner malaise is—like an ulcer, perhaps—taking its somatic toll. Immobilized with an unexplained but symbolic paralysis, he is comforted above all by Stamp, who touches his legs, takes them around his neck as though to transfer healing into them. Twenty years later Stamp says, "I did not then realize that the position in which I held him, with his [clothed] legs up on my shoulders, around my neck, was one used by homosexuals in intercourse." If the audience understood more than did Stamp, then with this behavior the Guest had now also made love to yet another member of the family.

Finally, the daughter, Odette, makes love with Stamp. The first phase of the "visit" is complete.

The family has—to use the Pasolinian word—"encountered" a

radically different reality. They must change. Throughout the erotic encounters, Pasolini allows the viewer to feel for the family's needs, to sense the fragility of their hold on a reality that appears false, deeply unsatisfying, one that holds them in tenuous rapport with one another and their own selves. The sound track, coming and going in snatches, is Mozart's Requiem and other music by Ennio Morricone.

Thus, Part One ends, announced on-screen, as though a morality play had concluded its first act—the Revolution before the Enlightenment.

Part Two opens with Angelo, "the angel"—messenger Ninetto, who even flaps his arms when he walks—delivering another telegram. It announces that the Guest will soon be leaving. The family members, in sequence, lose control, shedding their precious rationality, which has failed.

Each reacts differently to this disaster, to the loss of their salvation: Pietro says he does not "recognize himself," that he is "different now" and that what he "had in common with others is destroyed." He isolates himself in a room and paints—wild splashes, incoherent scribblings; Pasolini had his friend Zigaina produce these.

Odette explains that she has recovered from her obsession with her father but is now alone, unable to have any interaction with men. She falls into a comatose trance; as she stares, open-eyed at the ceiling, she is ministered to not by her mother but by another symbol of the poor (the innocent, with insight and human kindness), a servant played by journalist Adele Cambria. To no avail, a doctor comes to call, played by poet Alfonso Gatto.

The mother explains (rather too didactically for some) that the Guest had given meaning to her empty life. Once he is gone, she takes to picking up young men on the street. We see her stop her car at a curb and invite in two young men. First, she takes a pair to a hotel. She lies, her arms stiff and fists closed as handsome Carlo de Mejo, Alida Valli's son, mounts her. The other boy she picks up is played by Davide Grieco, a young PCI intellectual and budding cinema journalist at *L'unità*, whom Pasolini had known in the course of his debates at round tables.

Lucia-Mangano goes with another behind an abandoned church. Here the symbolism is double: They remain outside a church—which no longer serves its function of helping those in need—but the site is also autobiographical, a kind of quotation of Pier Paolo's preference for sex in the open air.

There remain the father and servant Emilia, the one whose values had not been corrupted by capitalist consumer society. Her reaction to the disappearance of the Guest is the most elaborate and poetic, and for her performance Betti received the Venice Festival's Volpi Cup as best actress of the year.

Emilia alone has been allowed to bid the Guest farewell, kissing his hand before she carries his simple suitcase to a waiting car. She immediately returns to her village to dedicate herself to a stoical life of meditation and what seems to be penance.

Her "sainthood," achieved through her exposure to the divine (or at least meta-human), is obvious to the peasants in her village; her status is reenforced when she begins to eat raw nettles. She sits for days and nights without end, unspeaking and subjecting herself to this scourge, as though a Father of the early Church, a female version of that Saint Jerome in the desert who, transformed by the vision of the cross, pressed a stone against his breast in self-abnegation. Soon her hair turns green, and she levitates, rising above the farmhouse where she had begun her vigil. The townspeople gather below in mute wonderment and veneration: Pasolini does not make the worshipers ridiculous. She then returns to Earth to be buried—not to die but to weep within the earth.

In a scene without dialogue, with only music and gesture—a poet's rejection of one kind of language for others—Emilia summons an old peasant woman (Susanna) to follow her. They walk away from the village, from humankind, and come to a spot where bulldozers have carved a hole in the earth. Betti lies down on her back and Susanna—without spoken instructions—starts to dig with a simple shovel. Soon Emilia-Betti is covered with soil, save for her eyes (the focus of religiosity, like Saint Clare's) which run with tears that become a pool, a stream of life-giving water.

After this, Pasolini cuts to the film's closing scene: the travail (perhaps en route to transformation) of the father. He is now "reborn" without prejudices, but aparently does not yet know what to believe in. At film's end he goes to the Milan Central Station, which Mussolini built and—in a trancelike state within his double-breasted suit—spots a hustler parked outside the public toilets. Slowly, Girotti undoes his tie, removes his shirt and suit. The camera follows his bare feet—not toward the hustler but out of the station; we see him nude, from the rear, crossing sand dunes. This vision of absoluteness has been intercut throughout the film: the sky, the sand, and a wind moving over it. *Teorema* ends with Girotti's ambiguous but anguished cry, a deep animal howl.

Pasolini offered some explanation: "The very irrationality of this cry conveys the absence of an answer" to the trauma Pasolini thought Europe was living in that spring of 1968.

> The bourgeoisie is at present undergoing a revolutionary change: it is assimilating everybody to the petit bourgeoisie: the whole of mankind is becoming petit bourgeois. So there are new problems, and these will have to be solved by the members of the bourgeoisie themselves, not the workers or the opposition. We dissident bourgeois cannot solve these problems, and neither can the "natural" bourgeois. That is why the film remains "suspended" . . . [34]

The Twenty-ninth Venice Film Festival, convened September 4, was caught in the maelstrom of international youth revolt: Its halls were occupied by students, and that brought the police. Franco Rossellini had submitted the film and then withdrawn it, claiming that the Festival's director had gone back on his assurance of a new kind of event, one without prizes and without police. Pasolini was expected to take first prize but instead announced, "Since the film was presented at the Festival against my will, I could not accept any prize."

Posturing notwithstanding, as part of its Venice premiere, the producers arranged a private screening for the critics. Before it could run, Pasolini rose and asked them to leave the room: The film, he said, was there because of the producer's choice, not his. Pasolini also refused to participate in the ritual press conference; rather, he convened his own at his hotel.

Producer Rossellini took a leaf from Bini's book. Working with the OCIC (the Catholic Film Office) he managed the situation so that the film received the Center's award, which Pasolini did accept. The Right-wing magazine *Vita* blasted what it called "this absurd behavior of the Catholic critics." The Vatican's official *L'osservatore romano* editorialized that the Guest smacked of Freud and Marx and "is almost a demon," and labeled the film "negative and dangerous." On September 13 it published the judgment of a national bishops' commission: They found that Pasolini's work should be "excluded for all [viewers]."

The OCIC jury was headed by a Canadian Jesuit, Marc Gervais, who later published a monograph on Pasolini's films. In defense of his jury's decision, he wrote, "Obviously the erotic atmosphere of the film and above all a certain homosexual sensibility make this film suspect. But its mystical character is incontestable. It is an inquiry into the human condition. It is a work about the demands of the absolute and about the refusal to be made bourgeois that alienates men." Put on the defensive by an outpouring of letters against the award to Pasolini, Gervais hedged, "The fact that OCIC has given a prize to the film does not mean that five hundred million Catholics are obliged to see it."

Pasolini was furious at the backsliding. He threatened to give back not only OCIC's *Teorema* prize but the one they had given him for *Gospel* as well. The *Corriere della sera* reported him as saying, "I will continue on my path, and nothing will impede me from pursuing my mystical dialogue. My only hope is to be able to resume a dialogue with priests who are cultured, young, and free." He added, "The representatives of this clerical Church have only one thought, that of leaving behind them an unchangeable world. So much the worse for them because the world has changed and will change even more. Industrial power has no need any more of that old Church. The only ones who still have use for it are Franco and the Greek colonels."[35]

As though scripted, a Roman public prosecutor now played out his role. Nine days later, or the same day as the *Osservatore romano*'s condemnation appeared, an order officially blocked the film from exhibition. A laundry list of outrage at the sexual scenes was offered by a citizen-denouncer, one Enrico Biamonti, who declared, "I often go to the cinema, especially to scabrous films, to inform myself of their content. . . ." Even the choice of music outraged him, "and the work of Mozart accompanying sexual scenes!"

The official charges read like a last gasp of an Italy challenged and soon to pass away. Pasolini was accused of making a film

> in which are contained various scenes and sequences offensive to decency, according to the common sense of it, among which for example are those relative to the contact and embraces between the guest and the maid, the mistress of the house and young people accosted on the street, as well as all those indicating sexual relations between the guest and the male members of the family and, following on these, homosexual tendencies in the father (specifically, the sequence at the station) and all this considered in the light of the theme and significance of the film, contrary to every moral, social, or family value.[36]

Another complaint was lodged in Rome, objecting to "the unimaginable sense of homosexuality which permeates the work."

The trial, convened in Venice on November 9, gave Pasolini a forum to distinguish what he considered gratuitous, and therefore "obscene" from what he deemed "authentic," and therefore not. When his judges asked whether the scenes showing Stamp naked might not have been cut, he answered:

In today's world, the individual, prey to alienation, lives with a false idea of the self, in an inauthentic way. The relationship between authenticity and inauthenticity is impossible on the level of language: in fact, the Guest never speaks at all to the other characters, he does not seek to convince them with words even though he has a love relation with each of them.

And it is in this that the film is completely symbolic. When the guest leaves, these characters are changed utterly; they are not able, each in a different way, to understand the authenticity that has come to them. Thus the eruption of authenticity in an inauthentic world only puts it in crisis, a crisis which is, however, a form of salvation. [37]

The answer seems not to address the question. Pasolini suggested that the court, which observed the objectionable scenes one by one, had to agree that "they are far from the least hint of obscenity, exactly because it is all an allegory and the erotic rapport is always symbolic, never naturalistic or realistic."

By convincing the court that the film was symbolic, Pasolini avoided the label "pornography." On October 10, 1969, after three hours in chambers, the appellate court in Venice absolved the film because "the fact as charged does not constitute a crime."

The debate over the Strega Literary Prize provided another battlefield. *Teorema*, born as a play written during his 1966 convalescence, had also become a book; he said that a piece for the theater, *Pilade*, had been "transformed into a film, and simultaneously into the story from which the film is taken and which has been corrected by the film." [38]

Irked at reports of his literary demise and looking for a way to vent long-pent-up frustrations with the literary scene, Pasolini acceded to Garzanti's submission of the book of *Teorema* for the much criticized but still-prestigious award. It was understood, as it had always been, that the Prize (only a million lire) was largely a matter of deal making among publishers, each avid for the virtually guaranteed fifty-thousand-copy sale that went to the winner. Pasolini and others decided to change the rules. When it appeared that he would take second place, he withdrew from the competition, taking several other leading contenders with him. In London the *Sunday Times* remarked, "Pier Paolo Pasolini seems determined not to let the new generation of protesters oust him from his position as the No. 1 bête noir of the Italian bourgeoisie." [39]

On June 24 he published an article in *Il giorno:* "In the name of culture, I withdraw from the Strega Prize [competition]." But the rules did not allow for withdrawing, and his book stayed among the candidates. Two weeks later he launched a polemical attack, entitled "Cast a blank ballot and culture will be the winner."[40]

He attacked the Strega as "completely and irreparably in the hands of an arbitrary neo-capitalism," in effect, a closed deal among the publishers. Just as he had solicited his friends to vote for him, now he asked them to back his embargo. His campaign was effective: Twenty-seven Strega jurors, including Moravia, quit "in light of the evident crisis surrounding the Prize."

President of the Prize-jury Luigi Barzini urged the electors to "forget the polemics and vote. You can make a friend happy." By only five votes, first place went to Rizzoli's author Alberto Bevilacqua, the sole official candidate remaining. His novel *L'occhio del gatto* (The cat's eye) was the sort of commercial fiction Pasolini dismissed as "summer reading for middle-class women to take to the seaside." *Faute de mieux*, Bevilacqua drew 122 votes, but Pasolini made his point—of 447 electors, 126 abstained altogether, 117 blank ballots were cast. The Strega changed its rules: Secret balloting was eliminated and the list of candidate books would not be by publishers' nomination but by a jury named by the Prize's organizing committee.

About the same time, Pasolini accepted the Saint Vincent award for the direction of *Edipo re*. Why attack one sort of prize and refuse another? His explanation seemed strained at best: Books, he contended, were a field "I still consider, even yet, in an old-fashioned way (*arcaicamente*) not industrial." Films, on the other hand, were commercial products whose surrounding exploitation one who makes them had to accept.


Despite (or perhaps because of) his attacks on the Italian stage, the directors of Turin's Teatro Stabile had approached him about "financing me a theater . . . it will be independent and all mine." Having tried for years to convince him to write for them, now they would literally give him a stage. Pasolini asked Sciascia: Would he be interested in writing a tragedy along Pasolini's theoretical lines, "or at least translate me a Greek one?"[41]

Sensing a giant adversary and vast work to be done, he threw himself into the project: "I want to do many things [in the theater]," he wrote Leonetti, asking him also for a translation of a classical play. He did the same with Attilio Bertolucci (who took on *Alceste*), Enzo Siciliano (for *Hippolytus*), and asked Leonetti to direct or act in a *Prometheus*.[42] He approached Andrea Zanzotto to translate Se-

neca. The theater was to be "beyond a theater also a cultural movement and in some way political (a component of a true New Left)."


Pasolini saw in the troubles of 1968 his chance "to throw my body
into the struggle." That spring Roman architecture students occupied
their faculty in the Valle Giulia on the grounds of the Villa Borghese.
On March 1, when the rector called in police to prevent a student
occupation, a pitched battle erupted on and around the ramparts of
the via Antonio Gramsci. The "forces of order" reported 160 injured,
the students only 53, although it was widely believed they numbered
far more, but they avoided state-employed doctors and municipal
hospitals so as not to enter into official records. The unexpected
revolution seemed to be starting on its own; it had not been ordered
by the PCI, still reeling by the disaster of the "Prague spring."

Nor had the students' revolt been sanctioned by the trade unions,
nor summoned by the intellectuals who scrambled onto its band-
wagon. By the end of May, 10 million French workers had gone on
strike. Among Italian intellectuals, very quickly those who were not
for the students were deemed to be against them—a position worse
than merely ideologically unfashionable but a kind of living death to
conformist academics and writers.

Pasolini's generation quickly took sides: Fortini and Leonetti, for
example, veered far to the Left, the former as advisor to Pasolini's
*bête noire*—the Quaderni Piacentini group—the latter as president of
a splinter party called the PC(ML)I (Partito Communista Marxista–Leninista Italiano), whose newspaper *Voce operaia* (The workers'
voice, later *Servire il popolo*—Serve the people) they were proud to
say was distributed even in Peking.

Pier Paolo had altogether another perspective on the phenomenon
of '68. It was unpredictable, infuriating, and rooted deep in the core
of his being. As an appendix to the book of *Teorema*, he published
a long poem about the students who made the "revolution." It reads,
in part:


> Sure, what else do young, intelligent
> kids from well-off families do except
> talk about literature and painting?
> Maybe even with lower-class friends
> —a little rougher, but also more tormented
> by ambition? Talk about literature and painting,
> sly and seditious, ready to upset everything,

already starting to warm up with their little
asses
barstools already warmed by the asses of the
Hermetics? . . .
What do the kids of 1968 talk about—with their
barbaric hair and Edwardian suits,
in a vaguely military style, that cover unhappy
cocks like mine,
except about literature and painting? And what
does this do except evoke from the darkest
depths of the petit bourgeoisie the
exterminating God, who strikes them once again
for sins even greater than those committed in '38?
Only we bourgeois know how to be thugs,
and the young extremists, skipping Marx and
outfitting themselves
at the flea market, do nothing but shriek
like generals and engineers against generals and
engineers.
It's an internecine struggle.
Someone who would really die of consumption
dressed like a *muzhik*, not yet sixteen
he might perhaps be the only one in the right.
*The rest cut each other's throats.*

On June 16 the weekly *L'espresso*, with a far wider readership than either *Nuovi argomenti* (where the poem also appeared) or the book of *Teorema*, published this, what Pasolini called his "ugly" verse on the "student May." [43] Entitled "Il PCI ai giovani!" (The Communist Party to youth!), it ran next to the transcript on a debate about the student movement, one in which Pasolini participated. It headlined *Vi odio cari studenti* (Dear students, I hate you).

It's sad. The polemics against
that party were all over in the first half
of the last decade. You're late, kids. . . .

When yesterday in the Valle Giulia you came to
blows
I sympathized with the cops!
Because the cops are the sons of the poor
They come from the outskirts, whether peasant or
urban

He called the students "spoiled kids." Their clamor had more to do with style and their fathers than with Mao or Ché. The police were dressed "like clowns, / and with that rough fabric that stinks of food rations . . . ; but the protesters, he was sure, would grow up to take the places of those they challenged ("your stupid fathers"). The police ("They're twenty years old, your age, dear boys and girls") would stay poor. As the students burned their books and set up "anti-courses" on Vietnam, Pasolini dismissed it as almost all empty gesture. It was nothing but a fight among the "haves," with the "have-nots" once again stuck with doing the dirty work.

This was a time for pedagogy, even then. And he did not change his mind.

> *Il PCI ai giovani!*
>
> Quit thinking about your rights,
> quit asking for power.
> A redeemed bourgeois must renounce his rights,
> and banish from his soul forever,
> the idea of power. All this is liberalism; leave
> it /
> to Bob Kennedy.

The truth about where he stood in the world of now, and of what he was capable, was almost hidden in an otherwise routine exchange of opinions about *Il Vangelo*, published on October 22, 1964, in *Vie nuove:* "*Mi sento libero, e non ho paura di scandalizzare nessuno*" ("I feel myself free, and I am not afraid of scandalizing anyone").

He addressed the student protesters:

> *Popolo* and *Corriere della sera, Newsweek* and
> *Le monde*
> kiss your asses. You are their sons,
> their hope, their future . . . Blandly,
> the times of Hitler return . . . the bourgeoisie likes
> to punish itself with its own hands . . .
> the student movement knows only one thing:
> the moralism of a father who is a magistrate or a
> professional,
> the violent conformism of an older brother
> (naturally started on the road of the father)
> hatred for the culture of their mothers, from the
> peasantry, even far off.
> This, dear children, you know.

He taunted: "Occupy the universities / but tell me the same idea occurs to young workers."
And if it did?

> *Corriere della sera* and *Popolo*, *Newsweek* and *Le monde*
> will have that much solicitude
> to try and understand their problems?
> Will the police limit themselves taking a few licks
> inside an occupied factory?
> This is a banal observation. But above all in vain:
> because you are bourgeois
> and thus anticommunists. The workers, they
> are stuck back in 1950 and before.
> An old idea like that of the Resistance
> (something fought over twenty years ago, and the
> worse for you if you were not then yet born)
> still thrives in the breast of the people, the one
> in the periphery.

The generation of '68's "moralism" gave them freedom but—as he later claimed—only within the confines of the heterosexual couple. It was all a fight in the family, and the family was the Other. He believed the radical transformation of society had to begin with the mutation of the self. Many thought this made him "reactionary."

> It is strange, abandoning the revolutionary language of the poor, old, Togliattian, official Communist Party. . . .
>
> I hope you have understood that making puritanism is a way of keeping yourselves from any real revolutionary action.
>
> Go, instead, kids, and seize the Federations!
> Go and invade the Cells!
> Go and occupy the offices
> of the Central Committee! Go, go and
> get yourselves to the via delle Botteghe Oscure!
> If you want power, go and make it yours,
> at least the power of a Party that is nevertheless
> in opposition

> (Even if badly served by the authority of gentle
> men
> in double-breasted suits, bowling enthusiasts,
> lovers of litotes,
> bourgeois gentlemen contemporary with your stupid
> fathers)
> and has as its theoretical objective the
> destruction of the State.

*Affabulazione*, his play that sides with the father against the son, was written in 1966; it marks the start of what can be seen as Pasolini's "rehabilitation" of Carlo Alberto. With the student uprising, he came to understand that he—never to be a father, always a son— was on the side of the fathers (and thus also Carlo's), even despite himself. And yet, after 1968, he felt himself to be one of the fathers whom the young rejected; and he rejected them. He found himself a "father" who saw the fathers as enemy and a "son" of the past who hated the new generation of sons.

In 1973 he dubbed the Italian '68 "an unexpected, violent revolution . . . of a technological type," an "intestinal struggle" between the bourgeoisie's fathers and sons, a "false revolution—which presented itself as Marxist while it was in reality only a form of self-criticism of the bourgeoisie (with the bourgeoisie using the young to destroy the myths that bothered it). . . ." That false revolution led, he came to decide, to a "flowering [of] all those conformist and moralistic attitudes which we had hoped ended once and for all." He believed the generation of '68 was ignorant of the past and less genuinely tolerant than their parents, who had survived Fascism and lived the Resistance. To him, they were fodder for "Moloch," a ghastly new type of man who came to adulthood by the mid-70's, not more than a horrible wave of "new consumers."

Because Herbert Marcuse was the students' idol, Pasolini took him to task in *Nuovi argomenti*. It was fine, he wrote, to call the students "the true heroes of our time" (a phrase attributed to the German philosopher) in America or in Germany but not in Italy or France. In those countries, such a view is simply absurd "because France and Italy have a Marxist cultural tradition." The students must see the Resistance not as they did—as only the end of the *Risorgimento*— but as a movement "in which workers and peasants participated. It was something, even partially and confusedly, revolutionary." Let the new ideologues see themselves within that tradition, not overturn it.

At a debate organized by *L'espresso*—on his poem and the violent response to it—Vittorio Foa, secretary of the trade union CGIL and Claudio Petruccio, then head of the FGCI (Federazione Giovanile Comunista Italiana), accused Pasolini of being a true and authentic reactionary. Others in the student leadership announced they had decided not to take him on "given that his poetry has been denied by history." But one wrote, "Before he writes another [poem about them], Pasolini ought to get to know the young people a bit better, for example by mounting the barricades." He seemed to many heretical for its own sake, an exhibitionist out for attention first with the Strega incident, now this.

The PCI hardly thanked him for his begrudging endorsement. The Communist monthly *Il calendario del popolo* wrote, "That there were actions in the student movement enough to provoke a reaction like Pasolini's is difficult to deny. But whatever they were, they can never justify taking the side of the police: Revolution and progress have always been on the other side." Groups to the left of the PCI were even more blunt and attacked him for "offering major assistance to the enemies of the Movement."

The students' *Mondo nuovo* attacked:

> Guts and heart, above all heart, never brains . . . it is logical that he [Pasolini] has never understood anything about history, the class struggle, the revolution . . . there remains only to say to Pasolini: we are not fellow travelers because, *caro*, we have no road in common; stay then on the sidelines in your compartment, puffing yourself up with the illusion that you understand and can represent, and give witness. . . .[44]

In early June, at the height of furor over the poem, *L'espresso* organized a round table, one that would serve to make copy. Two students rose and told Pasolini he knew nothing about Marxism, and began reading a page from Lenin. Then they looked at their watches and said, "We are expected at the Apollon factory, and if Pasolini wants to talk to us, he can come along." Fortini, also present, read a statement: "[For you, it is] not enough to be D'Annunzio, you want also to be Malaparte . . . with this poem Pasolini made an excellent flypaper and now is the time to toss out the paper and the flies." It marked the end of a friendship and a decade of battles. When Pasolini was dead, Fortini had a last word for the first and last time:

> I did not understand, or else did not want to, that he had to obey his interior demons and that any discipline, even of the smallest group, was foreign to him. It is also clear to me that Pasolini tended, with the violence of fatal

error, to assimilate any criticism of his ideological behavior with a moral stricture against his diversity [*diversità*, that is, homosexuality].[45]

*Rinascita* had to address Pasolini's poem's central agrument: that the police were the sons (and tools) of a repressive Establishment and the students were making a phony revolution. The PCI's spokesmen saw matters differently, not in terms of the consciousness of the cops but of their actions:

> The students do not find themselves facing some poor Tommassino come out from the *borgata* . . . but rather facing a repressive armed force, on the offensive, taking orders from the bourgeois State. One which today beats up students, yesterday killed peasants, the poor of the south and the workers of Modena and Reggio, and today will do what it is ordered to do. Thus "guardians of the people," yes; but the people allied with the guardians of capitalism, no.[46]

Almost twenty years before '68, when expelled, Pasolini had written Fernando Mantino: "I am a Communist despite you." And seven years after '68, in the address he did not live to deliver to the Radical Party, he wrote, "First of all, I must justify my presence here: I am not here as a Radical; I am not here as a Socialist; I am not here as a progressive; I am here as a Marxist who votes for the PCI and who believes in the new generation of Communists."

In April 1972 Pasolini reprinted his polemical poem in a last collection of essays, entitled *Empirismo eretico* (Heretical empiricism). And he appended an "Apology" that did not apologize. He asked, "Why was I so very provocative with the students (as much as I would have been with some greasy privately owned newspaper, you might speculate)?"

> The reason is this: up to and through my generation, young people had before them the bourgeoisie as an "object". . . we could look at the bourgeoisie . . . objectively, from outside (even if we were horribly implicated with it, history, school, church, anguish): the way in which to look at the bourgeoisie objectively was offered us, according to the typical scheme, by the "view" offered of them by those WHO WERE NOT BOURGEOIS: workers and peasants (that which later came to be called the Third World).
> . . . For a young person today, the situation presents itself altogether differently: for him it is much more difficult to look at the bourgeoisie objectively, through the viewpoint of another social class. Because the bourgeoisie is triumphant, is making bourgeois out of the workers on the one hand, out of the peasants and ex-colonialists on the other. In effect, through neo-

capitalism, the bourgeoisie is becoming the human condition. Whoever is born in this entropy cannot, by any means, metaphysically exit from it. It is all over. For this I provoke the youth: they are presumably the last generation who will see workers and peasants: the next generation will not see anything but bourgeois entropy.[47]

His critics charged him with *Manzonismo degli stenterelli*, a condescending romanticism like that of the nineteenth-century novelist Alessandro Manzoni, whose rural characters are always cheerful, obedient, and content, despite grinding poverty, subhuman conditions and no prospects.

As usual, he beat them to the punch. In the "Apology," he gently reprimanded "the intellectuals following Fanon and Marcuse, myself included," who "mythicize . . . the poor peasants." Pasolini, by his own admission not "humorous," was not grim. He was able and willing to debunk himself: It was, he felt, necessary so as better to teach. But that did not stop his arguing with increasing frequency and force that Italian society had sold its patronage for a pot of propaganda.

He invented a character called Gracchus, a "pirate," one who is willing to hold forth on almost any topic, who claims always to know better. Pasolini put himself inside him, this "new type of buffoon"; but nothing was to be done. This "Gracchus," he explained, had had authority thrust upon him—the press asked for articles and interviews, offered a platform. The only solution was to play the part, admit the ambiguity that he had sought it, but somehow try to undercut himself in the act of preaching. The way out was to make his role the subject of his role. Consciousness was all, self-consciousness included:

> This buffoon talks big. True,
> he writes in the same style I do.
> He needs applause from youthful hands,
> and is therefore forced to talk bigger than they
> but the content of demagoguery is demagoguery.
> In opposition, *I know*, and now *want*, every word to
> be useless.
> I'll throw this manuscript (in words only)
> into Lake Victoria, let's say in a Coca-Cola
> bottle . . . [48]

As early as December 1964, long before the events of Valle Giulia were clear on the horizon, he explicitly addressed his own "demagoguery." The words must be read alongside those about the "buffoon" who "talks big" to understand his all-consuming need to "be present," despite the risk of making enemies of one's friends, even a laughingstock of oneself.

> In reality, the right is given the artist to err, at least insofar as contradiction goes or hypotheses made too early or too late. He must hold back nothing, because in an artist the greatest sin is omission—expression being his function . . . [49]

Admitting the vulnerability of his identity and all the illogic of his stance toward the students of '68, he closed his "Apology" with another, most intimate kind of truth about his relation to them: "And so? Have I not the right to provoke them? How else can I hope to have a relationship with them if not in this way?"

This could be the father's voice from *Affabulazione*, the father who sees himself also as the son, who craves a connection, even if a flawed one.

During the hot days of May 1968 Pasolini finished work on the script for his next film. His publisher (by then Einaudi) added a note to the *Project for a Film on Saint Paul*, published in October 1977—specifying that *San Paolo* was written '22–28 May 1968," with "corrections"—in ink on Pasolini's customary typewritten pages—made "31 May–9 June." "Pasolini intended to publish this 'film not realized,' but it was also his intention to re-systematize it in a definitive version." [50]

Already on the shooting set of *Teorema* that year, he spoke of it:

> I've decided to scrap . . . all the . . . saint ideas I have had and do a life of Paul, which I'm going to start in the spring of 1969. It will be completely transported into modern times: New York will be Rome, Paris will be Jerusalem and Rome will be Athens. I've tried to find a series of analogies between the capitals of the world today and the capitals of the ancient world, and I've done the same thing for the actual events—e.g., the opening episode where Paul is a Pharisee, a collaborator, and a reactionary, is standing by at the murder of Saint Stephen, along with the executioners, is going to be done in the film with an analogous episode during the Nazi occupation of Paris, where Paul will be a reactionary Parisian collaborator who kills a Resistance fighter. The whole film's going to be transpositions like that.

But why Paul?

> With the simple strength of his religious message, Saint Paul in revolutionary fashion demolished a type of society founded on class violence, imperialism,

and above all slavery. And so it is clear that, by analogy, for the Roman aristocracy and various collaborationist ruling classes, one can substitute the present bourgeois class that has the capital in its hands, while for the humble and downtrodden should be substituted, by analogy, the advanced bourgeois elements, the workers, and the subproletarians of today.[51]

If the scheme is overly simple—dangerously close to a long polemic against "bourgeois entropy"—Pasolini would argue that the force of fable requires simplification. Had he made the film, his New York and Washington ("the seat of modern power over the rest of the world," but transposed "into the heart of the sixties") might have disappeared in a confusion of ideological heavy-handedness. No less a disaster struck Antonioni, whose *Zabriskie Point* (also of 1969) is an object lesson in how a Left-wing European's simpleminded comicbook vision of America can go grossly awry. MGM went so far as to take that film's rushes out of its director's hands, forcing an edit to try to save both director and producers from even greater embarrassment than they eventually suffered.[52]

Pasolini declared his intention was to show "current bourgeois civilization, both in its hypocritical and conventionally religious aspect analagous to that of the [ancient] Jews and its lay aspect, liberal and materialistic (analogous to that of the [ancient] Gentiles)."[53]

In 1968 the help of Church authorities would (again) be useful in lining up backers for *Saint Paul*. In his preface to the text (as posthumously printed), he announced that "the entire arc of the Apostolate will be gathered together (I will be helped in this by specialists, who [will] guarantee absolute fidelity to the sum of Paul's thought)." But his contacts in Sampaolofilm, a Church-affiliated cinema entity, hesitated, and fatally.

Yet more problems arose: Directors Valerio Zurlini and Vittorio De Seta announced that they, too, were using the subject. He complained, "I was displeased because this was not very loyal toward me, given that I have been speaking about making a film about Saint Paul for five years. They might have called and asked: 'Are you still making that film about Saint Paul?' After all, they are friends."

So the script he had virtually completed in the summer of 1968 remained in a drawer. He wanted to "leave the spectator free to choose and resolve the contradictions: and to establish whether this [film] . . . is a hymn to Sanctity or to the Church."[54] But he never made the film that he claimed would show that "Saint Paul is *here, today, among us* [italics Pasolini's]."

The project was revived seven years later, at the level of talk, when the world had much changed and *Salò* was done. Had he lived,

Pasolini's film following *Salò* would not, as so many predicted, have been part of a continuing black vision of horror but rather a return to his lifelong obsession with the spiritual in man in a world profoundly indifferent to matters spiritual. *Saint Paul's* "profound theme [would be] . . . the contraposition of actuality and sanctity." Pasolini's Paul was scripted to walk the edges of German autobahns in place of the byways of Ephesus and Antioch and is "asked questions by modern men, specific, based in circumstances, problematical, political, formulated in the language of our day." But in the film, as in the New Testament, Paul would respond in a manner "exclusively religious . . . in the language typical of Saint Paul, universal and eternal."

# 21

*The Italian intellectual is essentially an unpleasant figure, some-
thing already abstract, limited, so "local," so engulfed either in little polemics, little articles, little retributions . . . or else the
greatest Principles.*

*—A. Arbasino*, Fantasmi Italiani

# *MEDEA* AND CALLAS

Italian-Swiss television came to EUR in 1969, to interview Pasolini
for a series called "Works in Progress": the six-minute "visit" was
called "Pasolini Speaks." He explained to reporter Marco Blaser that
he had started writing poetry "at age seven" but now only did so "out
of a habit of self-expression," producing only two poems out of his
last trip to Africa. "I'd rather write in Swahili, the twelfth [most
spoken] language of the world," he said. He added that he was not
writing a novel and that the debates of literary circles bored him.

"To talk about the neo-avant-garde is like talking of something [that happened] twenty years ago," he said. His energies were going to critical prose and to film.

His distance from literary circles, and his disillusionment, now emerged in an acrimonious exchange with Eugenio Montale. Pasolini had been reviewing books in *Nuovi argomenti* throughout 1971; it was inevitable that he review Montale's long-awaited *Satura*. He might not have intended confrontation: by now he meant only to say what he thought, consequences be damned. In February 1965 he had declined an invitation to contribute to a special issue of the review *Letteratura* dedicated to Montale:[1] "It would displease me both to be hypocritical and to be sincere: it has been two or three years now that Montale has not inspired much liking in me (even though my admiration for his poetry remains unchanged)."[2]

His review of *Satura* appeared in the *Nuovi argomenti*'s January–March issue,[3] along with three other articles by him on literary topics. He did not hedge but rather (as he often did) took up a theme already broached in the preface to the book of *Edipo re*, elaborating it:

> All of *Satura* is basically an anti-Marxist tract. But if it were only that, I would limit myself to taking note of it (called into question by its satirical tone). If I disapprove of it, it is rather because Montale has tried to ignore the fact that bourgeois pragmatics, as well as Marxist praxis, is also founded on the illusion of *time*, and that the bourgeoisie, like the Communists, do nothing but talk about "tomorrow" . . . unlike Marxism, Montale does not, as a satirical poet, "free" himself from power. Indeed, he achieves a kind of identification of power with nature.
>
> His book is wholly based on the naturalness of power.[4]

Montale struck back in *Diario del '71*, calling Pasolini Malvolio (Ill-intender). And he did more—in a poem called "Letter to Malvolio." It reads like a wound long festered, at last sliced open to drain the resentment that had collected in the literary Establishment against Pasolini for years:

> It has never been a question of my fleeing, Malvolio,
> nor even of a flair for sniffing out the worst
> a thousand miles away. This is a virtue
> that you possess and I don't envy you, also
> because it would do me no good.
> > No,
> it wasn't ever a question of fleeing
> but only of taking up a respectable distance.

It wasn't very difficult at first,
when there was a clear separation,
horror on one side and decency,
oh just a very little decency,
on the other, No, it wasn't difficult,
it sufficed to slip away, fade out,
make oneself invisible,
perhaps be so. But later.

But later when the stables were emptied,
honor and indecency locked in a tight embrace
established the permanent oxymoron
and it was no longer a question
of fleeing and taking shelter. It was the hour
of conceptual phocomelia
and the crooked was straight, on everything else
derision or silence.

It was your hour and it's not over.
with what agility you've mixed
historical materialism and evangelical
pauperism,
pornography and redemption, nausea for the odor
of truffles, the money that came to you.
No, you're not wrong, Malvolio, the science of
the heart
is still unborn, each invents it as he likes.
But let's not talk about fleeing . . .[5]

The collision was probably unavoidable. Montale was a family man married to a wealthy woman, living in Milan's fancy via Bigli, making a journalistic career at the *Corriere della sera* because it pleased him, a cosmopolitan man in the old-fashioned style, even appointed by the President of the Republic a Senator-for-Life. Pasolini was as he was.

With 1972 Pasolini answered Montale in epigram, again in *Nuovi argomenti:* "I don't reproach you for having been / afraid, I reproach you for having made excuses / for it. / I may want evil [*mal voglio*]; but my own. / She has darkened your mind, your somewhat too / Italian / Dark Muse."[6]

With August 6, 1968, Pasolini began a new column, this time in the weekly *Il tempo.* It was called "Chaos" (Il caos); at first, his contributions appeared irregularly. Sometimes several weeks passed without a piece. At other times he delivered copy (this time without the near-fiction of responding to reader letters) every week. "The

Why of This Column" was his first. There followed his version of what happened at the 1968 Venice Film Festival (September 15); a piece on Panagoulis, the enemy (and later victim) of the Greek colonels; then "The Maturity of Dutschke (November 10); "Dialogues" with Moravia—whom he had first written about at age twenty-five, living in Casarsa—in *Libertà* of Udine[7]; then a piece on "my provocative independence[8]; on Prague; on "a day in Bologna"; on Franco Zeffirelli.

As though echoing Wilde, also very much in earnest at his most apparently flippant, Pasolini wrote in one of his first articles:[9] "Consistency is inhumanity; it is a language for fanatical monks, not for men," and "Seriousness is a quality for those who have no other qualities."[10]

The column ended abruptly with January 24, 1970. In the nervous days of the so-called *strategia della tensione*, after the bomb attack in Piazza Fontana, the magazine cut him off. Its new editor wrote him, "The column does not run because you take on specifically political subjects, even more than that I'd say the technically political, which do not enter into the subject matter of 'Caos'."[11]

And two months later, "I wanted to tell you face-to-face my decision to suspend 'Caos' permanently. The reasons are to allow us to look into the negative reaction (certainly not only) of *Il tempo*'s public to your column."[12]

New York's Museum of Modern Art invited him to visit. On March 27, following his remarks to the viewing public, *Teorema* was screened. This time he was disappointed in what he found in New York, or rather did not: no more pacifist marches as three years before, no flower-children: "Everything is over: there remains only a folklore like the stupendous peeled skin of a snake slipped away, gone underground [in English], leaving only used-up longhairs, small-time gangsters, crowds of the desperate to populate Nixon's America."[13]

First touted in 1967, another episodic film (again a French-Italian coproduction) called for assembling shorts from him, Lizzani (who produced), Bertolucci (who used The Living Theater), Godard, and Zurlini. At first it was called *Amore e rabbia*, then (echoing his *Matthew*) *Vangelo '70*. Pasolini's part was first called *Il fico innocente* (The innocent fig), a play on slang for the female genitals. Renamed *La fiore di campo* (The flower of the field) and finally *La sequenza del*

*fiore di carta* (The sequence of the paper flower), his twelve-minute
film, shot fast, during the spring of 1968, was built on a simple
premise, developed from an idea of Puccio Pucci and Piero Badalassi:

> Initally it was just one long tracking shot all the way up the via Nazionale
> in Rome . . . but I've cut it into two or three different shots. *Vangelo '70* is
> supposed to be inspired by parables or bits in the Gospels, so for my episode
> I chose the innocent fig tree—you remember Christ wants to pick some figs
> but because it's March the tree hasn't produced any figs yet so he curses it.
> That is an episode which has always been very mysterious to me and there
> are several contradictory interpretations of it. The way I've interpreted it
> goes like this: There are moments in history when one cannot be innocent,
> one must be aware; not to be aware is to be guilty. So I got Ninetto [called
> "Riccetto"] to walk up via Nazionale [carrying a giant, red crepe-paper
> flower] and while he's walking along and completely innocent [in jeans,
> unbuttoned shirt and classic Roman *borgataro*'s gold chain, complete with
> the "horn" against the evil eye] a number of images of some of the important
> and dangerous things happening in the world pass superimposed across the
> via Nazionale—things he is not aware of like the Vietnam War, the relations
> between the West and the East and so on: these are just shadows which pass
> above him which he does not know about. Then at a certain point you hear
> the voice of God [provided by Aldo Puglisi and Pasolini's cousin Graziella]
> in the middle of the traffic urging him to know, to be aware, but like the fig
> tree he does not understand because he is immature and innocent so at the
> end God condemns him and makes him die.[14]

Ninetto's sequences are in color, the documentary footage in black-
and-white; the sound track was "Pasolinian"—Bach's *Saint Matthew
Passion*. He also shot an under-titles sequence that was later cut: a
round-table discussion among the five directors about their assignments—Lizzani's was the Good Samaritan, Godard's the Prodigal
Son, Zurlini (later substituted for by Bellocchio) the Passion and
Crucifixion, and Pasolini's "innocent fig tree."

The film, released in May, garnered little attention from the critics
and soon vanished.

In May 1969 Gianfranco d'Aronco wrote from Udine, asking that
he collaborate on a new magazine, *Quaderni di letteratura popolare
friulana* (literally, Notebooks of popular Friulian literature), to be
published by Pier Paolo's old nemisis, the Friulian Philological Society. He answered:

> I would gladly collaborate if only I had some idea, but it has now been years
> since I have occupied myself seriously with popular literature (not even an
> article) and so, even presuming I found a few free hours, I would not know

what to write. I tell you this with a profound sense of shame: as though I had blamefully lost something entrusted to me.[15]

By that November, he had started a new film, *Porcile* (Pigsty). It became his most "difficult" to date, ancestor of *Salò*, a vision of corrupt power and human cruelty without punishment, and parricide, all within the framework of cannibalism and a protagonist who makes love to swine. His original plan was to make what he called "a normal film, in two parts." The first half was to be *Orgia*, the second *Porcile*—films grown out of the plays of the same names. But in the making, he put the two episodes under the single title of the second.

In the first half, a man lives on the slopes of a volcano (Mount Etna) sustaining himself on grass, snakes, and butterflies. He is played by French actor Pierre Clementi, not coincidentally cast by Bertolucci the previous year as the lead, Jacob, in *Partner* (1968) and the following year in *The Conformist* (1970). Suddenly, he comes upon the remains of a mysterious battle: weapons and skeletons. He takes a rifle for himself and a helmet.

Over the horizon comes a line of marching soldiers, and he encounters one at close range. Speechlessly, the two stare at each other—stare so long that the viewer is made to wonder if they will end in combat or embrace. They begin fighting and the mysterious Clementi figure disarms the other and—when he has the chance to show pity—slays his adversary. Thus far the film, without dialogue, proceeds with long tracking shots, long stills on faces and an air of foreboding.

Clementi decaptiates his enemy and eats his flesh. Another figure—Franco Citti—appears from nowhere and joins him in the horrible feast.

The two, now allies in survival, spot a group of men who are transporting a woman prisoner in a wagon. Somehow the duo manages to kill the men and enslave the woman. The group now becomes a savage tribe of cannibals, threatening all who come within their reach. In due course a man and a woman approach: The group kills the woman and throws her head into the volcano on whose flank they have made their base. The man escapes, fleeing in terror to a nearby city, where he alerts the populace to the danger lurking just beyond the walls.

The town sends a nude boy and girl onto the volcano's rocky landscape as decoys to lure the tribe. Clementi's band takes the bait and are captured, then are marched in chains as prisoners into the city.

There, a near-naked Clementi and Citti are brought to trial. The death sentence is read: Citti, the second cannibal, weeps before the cross on which he will be nailed, kisses it, and begs forgiveness. Clementi stands straight and announces three times, "I killed my father, I have eaten human flesh, and I tremble with joy." Clementi and Citti are staked to the ground under the broiling sun, left to be devoured by wild beasts. End of Part One.

The second episode, also centered on cannibalism and madness, takes place in a setting as specific as the first part is generalized. Before shooting began in November, Pasolini told English journalist Oswald Stack, "This takes place in the industrialized part of Germany, at Godesberg, near Cologne, which is where Adenauer used to live, in the villa of a big German industrialist like Krupp, say— one of the old industrial families." [16]

We meet Julian, played by Jean-Pierre Leaud, a veteran New Wave actor used by Truffaut and Godard. The time is the present, when protesters stood outside Milan's La Scala on opening night bearing placards: *"Ricci, godete! Sera l'ultima volta."*—"Rich, enjoy yourselves! This will be the last time."

Julian is the son of Signor Klotz, played by actor Alberto Lionello. Pasolini's first choice for the role was Jacques Tati, whose "Mr. Hulot" alter ego he adored in *Playtime*—written, acted, and directed by the French comedian. He wrote Tati in November 1968, assuring him that his signature character would remain intact, including the particular long gait. But it did not work out.

Filming in Padua, Pasolini told film historian Gian Piero Brunetta that Klotz's arch-rival ("more vital, more energetic") calls himself Herdhitze, played (rigorously against type) by the famous comic Ugo Tognazzi.

Pasolini set out to "crystallize horror": Klotz and Herdhitze, all smiles, jockey toward blackmailing one another, using Julian's obsession with swine as a playing card. They speak lines that sound like poetry, even epigraphs. The sound track includes a song of the Nazi stormtroopers, "Horst Wessel Lied."

The action is simple enough, simple as hallucination: Julian has a secret he will not tell even his girl friend, Ida (played by Anne Wiazemsky, the daughter Odette in *Teorema*). Trying to draw him out of himself, she suggests they attend a student demonstration in Berlin together [Pasolini wrote poems about Rudi Dutschke about this time], but Julian is indifferent to her politics, as he is to the prospect of taking over his father's business. Finally, he confesses to Ida, swearing her to secrecy. Then, in a fashion reminiscent of Odette, he lapses into a catatonic state. At his bedside, Ida and Julian's mother (played by Margherita Lozano) offer radically different views of his character. They neither really knew him, or each knew only half of his split personality.

Pasolini cuts to Signor Klotz, playing his harp (music often accompanies evil in Pasolini's films: the pianist in *Salò* accompanies the horrors because—like the sun—music is "indifferent") as his servant-adviser named Hans Günther (played by Marco Ferreri, with steadily smiling evil) delivers the "good news." At last, he has learned his enemy Herdhitze's true identity: He is the notorious Nazi called Hirt, passed easily into postwar Germany's respectable society after a mere facelift.

Hirt-Herdhitze (Tognazzi) arrives just then and the two men reminisce about the wonderful spring of 1938, the season when Hitler visited Italy. Prefiguring some lines in *Salò*, Hirt-Herdhitze remarks, "Contradictions are absolutely necessary."

Klotz, who now manufactures domestic appliances (a take-off of the ultimate in respectability), attempts to blackmail his old friend with the information about his identity. The ex-Nazi counters that he knows Julian's terrible secret, that the comatose boy has an erotic attachment to swine.

Ida comes to bid farewell to Julian, for she is about to marry: She tells him of the love that has suffused her life.

Meanwhile, Klotz and Hirt-Herdhitze decide their blackmails are equal enough to cancel, and they merge their industrial empires—"like Montedison," Pasolini said, referring to the merger of Montecatini chemical works and the Edison electric company, to create the first giant Italian conglomerate. While they celebrate at the villa (Pasolini used the Villa Pisani at Stra), toasting one another with beer, Julian rises and leaves the house. His path is followed by the eyes of a peasant-servant, Ninetto, symbol of the consciousness (and conscience: in Pasolini they become one) of an uncorrupted preindustrial world.

Julian enters his father's pigsty, his *porcile*. Pasolini's intention was to have him then converse with the ghost of Spinoza, "the first rationalist philosopher and thus guilty, in a certain sense, of bourgeois rationalism, which he, Julian, in that moment, rejects, saying that reason always serves a god but once God was discovered man ought to have stopped there, not going further to carry reason to the level of myth, where the bourgeoisie took it." But the Spinoza idea was dropped; in the film, Julian simply enters the sty.

Next, a delegation of peasants appears at the Klotz villa and reports that a witness has seen Julian devoured by swine. Herdhitze asks if any trace remains. Told that there is "not a tuft of hair, not a button," he offers to keep his "gentleman's agreement" and say nothing. The peasants are told to say nothing: "Shhh" is the word, and a finger is held to the lips. As in *Affabulazione*, the sins of the fathers are visited on the innocent-victim sons, who must vanish in silence.

The links to *Teorema* are strong: *Porcile* is, in effect, the previous film's nightmare flipside. Pietro becomes Julian; his sister, Odette, is Ida. Just beneath the polished surface, accomplices to the comfortable world of Girotti and Mangano, are the Signori Klotz and Hirt-Herdhitze.

But *Porcile*'s roots run deeper. In 1957, *Le ceneri di Gramsci* mourned "Our history is finished." *Porcile* portrays the "New Prehistory," what Pasolini called a "horrible universe" (*l'universo orrendo*) that comes after the world he loved had passed away but before a new era had yet dawned.

His cinematic reality could not longer reproduce a social reality which Italian prosperity had destroyed. The peasants in *Porcile* are an afterthought, a late walk-on to the action; reduced to helpless witnesses to History, they come to reproach, but respectfully so, at the gates of Klotz's villa. Clementi, from the first half, dies at the hands of "rational society," unable to accept the horror inside itself; Julian, too, dies, consumed by beasts kept by his father. We are at the threshold of *Salò*, where history disappears into the black hole of language's end.

After a disastrous screening in Venice, Pasolini organized a private viewing of *Porcile* for his writer friends in mid-October. It left them puzzled. "What is there to understand?" he asked.

> To understand the film you have to have more heart than head (better yet, if there is head used so much the better): because there is to understand the desperate story of a sinner who makes of his sin his sanctity . . . there is to understand the ambiguous and dramatic relationship between the old capitalism and the new which concludes, even if in the tones of an almost contemplative poem, with a condemnation of them both.

*Porcile* was the first of what he declared to be his new style, one of "difficulty," "enigma," and "stylistic complexity."

At a debate on *Teorema* convened by film students, he defiantly proclaimed that he accepted his cinema's "unconsumability." His films would—*like Teorema and Porcile*—be "difficult"; he would not try any more to "simplify my problems . . . to make them accessible to others." Pasolini-watchers should have been on notice right then that when he announced that he would not try to do "popular epics" for *Il popolo*, then *Decameron, Canterbury Tales,* and *Thousand and One Nights*—entertainment for what he called "mass culture"—were not far off. It is the zigzag of contradiction, of others and always and above all of himself, that charts the Pasolini trajectory.

Coinciding with *Porcile*'s release, he published an essay in the magazine *Cinema nuovo*, written in the form of an answer to a question posed by its editor, Guido Aristarco: "In the past few years, you seem committed more and more to the cinema (as opposed to literature). If this is so, would you explain to what extent you think the cinema offers today a means of expression pertinent to these times?" The studied blandness of the question invited the full blast of Pasolini's polemic:

> How to refuse to make cinema as a medium of mass culture?
>
> By making the cinema aristocratic: unconsumable . . . *Uccellacci, Teorema* and *Porcile* wanted to be unconsumable. The ferocious reductionists say to me: "It's not true. *Teorema* was widely viewed, it was a success. And it looks the same way for *Porcile.*" They were, or are being consumed, I answer, for a series of contradictory reasons. But they remain undigested or—even more the case—undigestible: their consumers put them in their mouths and then spit them out, or they pass the night with a bellyache.[17]

*Porcile* was screened at the Thirtieth Venice Film Festival on August 31, 1969; the critics were split. Pasolini, still furious with the Festival's administration over the previous year's troubles, stayed away. In his absence, Moravia (who called *Porcile* Pasolini's "best work since *Accattone* and *La ricotta*) read these lines the director left for the press:

> To crystallize horror. To make a Petrarchan sonnet on a theme from Lautréamont. A film atrocious and mild. The explicit political content of the film has as its subject, as its historical situation, Germany. But the film is not about Germany, but about the ambiguous relationship of old and new capitalism. Germany was chosen as a way to illustrate a case. The implicit political content of the film, instead, is a desperate mistrust of all historical societies: Thus it is a film of apocalyptic anarchism. The theme of the film being so horrible and upsetting, I could not help but treat it (a) with a distance that is almost contemplative, and (b) with some humor. I am certain that someone will ask me: "Is this an autobiographical film?" All right, I'll say "yes" to whoever asks me this question. The film is autobiographical to the extent that my autobiography has carried me to understand this horror

and to expound it with distance and also with humor. I don't hold too closely to this distance and this humor, but to the extent it is there, it is there. Further, the film is autobiographical for the following reasons: First: I identify in part with the character of Pierre Clementi (apocalyptic anarchy, and— let us say—total contestation in the existential plane); Second: I identify also with Jean-Pierre Leaud (eaten by the pigs, cannibalized rather than a cannibal)—ambiguity, fleeting identity, and everything which the boy says in that long monologue to his girl friend who then leaves. The simplified message of the film is this: society, every society, devours both its disobedient sons and the sons who are neither obedient nor disobedient. The sons must be obedient, and that's that. . . .

Up the Adriatic coast toward Trieste, Pasolini and his friend Zigaina had started their own anti-Festival in protest. Under Zigaina's direction, it ran three years in a seaside resort: The Grado International Weeks of the Cinema introduced *Porcile*, the next year *Decameron*, and after that offered the worldwide premiere of *Canterbury Tales*, forcing Europe's film press into the village's Cinema Cristallo. By 1972 Pasolini was powerful and angry enough to pull his version of Chaucer out of Venice over the strenuous objections of his producer. He told the international press that producers do not have the right to keep directors from sending films to the festivals of their choice. Bertolucci followed his old teacher; *Last Tango in Paris*, an even hotter ticket in 1972 than *Canterbury Tales*, also made its Italian premiere in Grado.

On October 11, 1969, more than a year after the events at issue, Pasolini and six other leaders of the Italian cinema were brought to trial in Venice. They were charged with "interfering with public order" for refusing to clear a Festival hall in 1968 when ordered to do so.

The events had been tragicomic, as often was the case in those years. Tensions over the management of the Festival had come to a point that a committee of protesters—made up mostly of directors— demanded that they be ceded the power to select films for the Festival and reorganize the prize system. After negotiations broke down, the Christian Democratic president of the Festival and the city's mayor both found themselves facing a likely occupation of the event's premises.

Pasolini was among the protesters who refused to leave the Volpi Hall of the Palazzo del Cinema. After shouts and shoving, a negotiated settlement was reached, one in which Pasolini was an active participant. The Festival management would run its buildings, but the directors' committee would have "cultural direction" over the events.

But as this was about to be implemented, the "cultural consultant" to the Christian Democrats arrived, bearing a scathing article in the Vatican's *L'osservatore romano*, which soundly chastised the officials for giving in to pressure. The deal unraveled.

Fistfights broke out. A crowd of recognized Right-wingers was waiting outside: The director Filippo de Luigi claimed he was literally thrown by the police beyond their cordon and into a mob armed with clubs and chains, where he was beaten. Even the boatmen, who could have ferried them to safety or the hospital, were intimidated. Cesare Zavattini, *éminence grise* of neo-realism, presiding over the now-chaotic meeting, refused to move, and was carried out by four policemen, chair and all.

A year later the charges included interfering with "the otherwise peaceful enjoyment of things immobile," that is, obstruction of property. Pasolini took advantage of the staggering slow pace of Italian justice to enjoy Venice at summer's height. After a one-day hearing, the charges were dropped because "the facts do not constitute a crime."

Between March and October 1969, during the pre-production of *Medea*, he traveled to Uganda, Tanzania, and Tanganyika. His friend Angelo Romanò from *Officina* days, now a producer at RAI-TV, commissioned a film about how Pasolini would go about setting the *Oresteia* trilogy of Aeschylus there. It was, as with the Indian project, "Notes" toward a film, toward an *African Oresteia* (*Orestiade Africana*). The "solution" to mass culture's destruction of the world he loved was to find the successor, poetic equivalent to the *borgate* and the Roman *sottoproletariato* in the Third World.

He had translated the work for Vittorio Gassman's theater in 1960. Now he returned, imparting to his fifty-five-minute "Notes for an *African Oresteia*" a "message": "Archaic civilization—superficially called folklore—must not be forgotten, despised, and betrayed. But it must be integrated within the new civilization."

The frightening Erinyes—the Furies of Aeschylus and of "archaic" Africa—must be won over to the man-made hearthside, brought into the era of reason, transformed into beneficent Eumenides. In his Author's Preface to the translation of a decade before, he had expounded the same idea: "The irrational, represented by the Erinyes, must not be dismissed (which would be impossible) but simply checked and dominated by reason, [by] productive and fertile passion. Curses transform themselves into Blessings."[18]

The film opens on African villagers listening to the tale of the tragedy of Agamemnon, returned from the Trojan War to be slain by his wife, Clytemnestra, and how their children, Orestes and Electra, swear revenge. The film-within-a-film chronicles the director's difficulty at finding the right girl to play Electra; Pasolini's voice-over explains that the Africans seem "deprived of the purity and pride and the hate which animate" the character.

He cuts to the lecture hall of the University of Rome, where the director—Pasolini himself—explains to a group of African students why he seeks to transpose the ancient plays to Kigoma, Kasalu, and Lake Victoria in Tanganyika, Kampala in Uganda, Dar es Salaam in Tanzania. He tells them, "It seems to me that African tribal society resembles the archaic Greek civilization."

Orestes discovers democracy, and the director asks the students and himself whether 1960—the focal year of colonial African independence—might not be a better year in which to place his story than 1969. It seemed late in the day for so much done to be undone.

How to depict the Furies, which he called "unrepresentable in human form"? His thought was to render tham as giant trees. He inserted footage of the war in Biafra, and, instead of screening scenes of war against sound-track silence, had the lines from Aeschylus sung by a black American jazz group. We go to a studio where this experiment is tried. Then the film cuts back to Africa as Pasolini asks people to repeat for the camera some gestures they had "enacted" in normal life, in what—to extend his analogies—might be called "the other film."

Cut to the University of Dar es Salaam—standing in for the Temple of Apollo, both dedicated to reason. To him, speaking for himself on the sound track, it "represents all the contradictions of the young African nations":

> Look at this plaque, over the door of the library. It says that this institution [exists] thanks to the aid of the people and of the People's Republic of China. But in the display cases is displayed the other alternative: the alternative that is, in fact, neo-capitalist and Anglo-Saxon. *Introduction to the Teaching of English.* Books for teaching the history of Africa . . . *The Sexual Education of the Adolescent . . . Julius Caesar . . . The Birth of Nationalism in Central Africa*, poems, indeed, in the dialects of Swahili and of Kenya, new grammars. And then a book about Russia, about Christ, on American education . . .[19]

At the university, he engages a group in discussion of how to depict the Furies' taming by Athena into Eumenides. Someone suggests a dance. The film ends with a scene of tribal dancing by the Wa-gogo in Tanzania, against choral music. The author says, "The work of a people knows neither rhetoric nor delay. Its future is an anxiety about the future, and its anxiety is a great patience."[20]

Although it had commissioned the work, the State network suddenly—and for vague "technical reasons"—refused to broadcast it. *Paese sera* speculated (April 17, 1970) that it was out of fear of censorship. The film was first shown in Venice only the month of Pasolini's death in a small Roman *cinema d'essai*.

Sailing with his friend Zigaina in the Laguna of Grado, he came upon the island of Safon: no more than a tuft of grass topped with a reed-walled, thatch-roofed hut. Pasolini rented the island from the commune and visited for a few weeks for a summer or two. It was to become home to the Centaur, in a story celebrating a society that was not "historical" but mythic, "archaic"—a world Pasolini could trust. He had begun work on *Medea*, his twelfth film in nine years, as soon as *Porcile* was done.

While he had been thinking of filming the Greek myth of Medea for some time, it was only when producer Franco Rossellini convinced his friend Maria Callas to star in it that the script became a reality. From its inception, the film was conceived as a showcase for her, a part written to order—as Bellini and Donizetta write operas to measure for the sopranos assigned them. It was intended for the most compelling actress among opera divas in living memory.

Not only was Pasolini the director least likely to put Callas finally on film, but he was far from the first candidate for the challenge and the honor. Between 1960 and her death in September 1977 (at fifty-three, Pasolini's age at his murder), she sang only three operas—*Norma*, *Medea*, and *Tosca*—any one of which would have served for a film version. Onassis had urged her for years to try her hand at acting. In 1961 a producer, a guest on Onassis' yacht, tried unsuccessfully to convince her to play opposite Gregory Peck in *The Guns of Navarone*. Five years later she turned down a part in the gigantic Italian-American coproduction of *The Bible*. She declined other offers or near-offers as well: to appear in an adaptation of a Poe story or in Tennessee Williams' *Boom*, both projects of Joseph Losey, whom she respected. (The part in the disastrous *Boom* and a staggering million-dollar fee went to Elizabeth Taylor.) Callas might also have made a *Medea* with Pasolini's hero Carl Dreyer, whom she called "an exceptional man," but he could not line up a producer to back him.

But by 1968 she was in crisis: On October 20, Onassis married Jacqueline Kennedy in the chapel of Panayitsa (Little Virgin) on his private island of Skorpios. Rather than appear in a projected life of Puccini, which Visconti wanted to film, or sing in Menotti's *The Consul*, Callas finally agreed to play a song-less Medea in a Italian-French-German coproduction, written and directed by Pasolini. She told an interviewer the exact date of the proposal: October 19, 1968. Putting the best face on a difficult decision, she said at the time, "When Franco Rossellini, *Medea*'s producer, proposed this one, I had no doubt. I knew immediately this was the occasion I'd been waiting for and I determined not to let it slip by."[21]

Her public stance about the coming collaboration was in marked contrast to her reaction to *Teorema*. Rossellini told a friend that Callas had walked out "in the middle of the screening."[22] According to her confidante-assistant Nadia Stancioff, Callas phoned her friend Jacques Bourgeois "at three A.M., and without prologue or apology launched into her version of *Teorema*": "Jacques . . . I have just seen something absolutely disgusting! Pasolini's latest film, *Teorema*. The man is mad! . . . A young man goes to spend the weekend with a family in the country. He makes love to the mother, then he makes love to the daughter, and then he makes love to the *son!*"

When her friend explained, "That's God," she answered "What do you mean, God?" "Maria, the young man in the story represents God. It is to be taken symbolically." A long silence followed. *"God? But that is blasphemous!"* Maria gasped.[23]

Before agreeing to take the part, Callas spoke with many friends and, according to Stancioff, "consulted . . . Joelle de Gravelaine, a respected Parisian astrologer."[24]

That would have suited Pasolini's conception of Medea perfectly. What he saw in her (and he explained so to the press and addressed it in poetry) was not the voice and not the star but the woman. He wanted her "for herself," in precisely the same way he had wanted Franco Citti and Magnani, Ninetto and Silvana Mangano.

Pasolini's plan was to present Medea through images, a film not directed to the obvious audience of Callas' opera fans.[25] Besides, he did not like opera anyway. At eighteen he went to the Teatro Duse in Bologna and saw his first performance, an "ugly" rendition of *Il trovatore*: "I suffered such a shock that I never went to the opera again"; but after going with Ninetto to hear Giuseppe di Stefano in *Rigoletto*, in the open air at the Baths of Caracalla during the mid-sixties, "From then on, I began to have a feeling and a love for opera." Nevertheless, he thought swooning over Callas singing "Vissi d'arte" was so much *ceccheria* (approximately: queenery); Callas as the darling of homosexuals all over the world interested him not at all. He said, "Here is a woman, in one sense the most modern of women, but there lives in her an ancient woman—strange, mysterious, magical, with terrible inner conflicts."[26]

Pasolini merged the "real" Callas, the Medea inside her but palpable to him, with the Medea of ancient myth, a personality quite as "real" as the living opera legend before him:

> This barbarian deep inside [Callas], who emerged through her eyes, her shape, does not manifest itself directly, on the contrary, the surface is almost smooth. Overall, the ten years [Medea] passes at Corinth are a bit the life of Callas. [Callas] comes out of a peasant world, Greek, antique, and then had a bourgeois formation. Thus in a certain sense, I tried to concentrate in her character that which she is, in her total complexity.[27]

If such a perspective helped Pasolini to work, so be it. Rossellini knew an international box-office draw when he saw one.

Pasolini also stated the mechanism of his strategy more baldly: "I'm aware of her professional abilities," he said, "but they are really of very little interest to me." He demanded that she start over and, for the first time in the public eye, be herself. She wrote that her involvement with Onassis left her with "nine years of meaningless sacrifice." Maybe acting the drama of a woman mad with love, and then betrayed by it, offered a way to ease her pain.

She decided Pier Paolo was not like other intellectuals "with their nose always in a book who do not see life."[28] He soon said, "I feel I've always known her. It's as if we'd been to school together." He told one reporter, "For me, Callas is like Franco Citti. The two extremes meet: The so-called 'sacred monsters' have something so authentic and personal about them, just as if they had been taken off the street."[29]

Pasolini treated her with kid gloves from their first meeting in March 1969, one that followed on exchanges of letters and telephone calls. He spoke softly and they struck it off immediately. She had been known to snap unpleasantly about "homosexuals and Marxists" (her friendships with both notwithstanding): Nothing unpleasant occurred. The production proceeded from the first day that summer with the calm of two professionals animated by mutual esteem, locked in their common task.

They worked through an unusually hot June and July 1969. Pasolini's reworking of Euripides was filmed first in Turkey, where the barren and primitive landscape (and conditions) of Cappadoccia stood for the ancient Colchis. Grado—where the wise Centaur tutors young Jason—and the Piazza dei Miracoli at Pisa were his analogues to "rationalist" Corinth. He used Pisa as he had Bologna in *Edipo re*, unperturbed at the impossibility of ancient Greeks amid Renaissance buildings. What mattered was that Pisa—Galileo's home—was the symbolic city of practical reason, and thus the enemy of all Medea stood for.

Consistent with his style from the time of *Accattone*, Pasolini wanted to shoot Callas' face in long, slow close-up. She was used to the opera audience at a distance and begged him not to. He won. She might have been convinced to sing at some length. He asked only that she sing a short lullaby, in Greek, to Medea's baby son. She agreed but asked that it be omitted when she saw the rushes with sound track.

The press followed them everywhere: to isolated Goreme in Turkey, where Pasolini liked the weirdly shaped rocks, suggestive of a world "outside of time," imbued with Medea-the-sorceress' magic and communion with the supernatural. To Grado, to Aleppo in Syria, to Tor Caldara and Tor Calbona outside Rome. Her assistant, Nadia Stancioff, has recalled the four weeks they spent at Goreme and the village of Uchisar:

> By comparison with those of the cast and crew, our accommodations were grand. Maria, Bruna [Callas' ladies-maid] and I were privileged. We were put up at the brand-new Club Mediteranee . . .We were its first guests and work was still in progress. The hallways smelt of fresh whitewash. The bathrooms were being completed and the kidney-shaped pool was bone dry. The aroma from the kitchen heralded fried brains for our inaugural midnight dinner, not everyone's favorite.[30]

Callas outworked everyone. She was always early, attentive, and willing. She never complained. Stancioff reports:

> In one scene, she was being taken in long shot, and had to run frantically on a dry riverbed. She was wearing a heavy gown with huge ropes of pagan jewels, the sun was beating down and she was running, running until she fainted and collapsed on the mud. Pasolini and the entire crew ran toward her, and as she came back to consciousness, her first words were "Please forgive me! I'm so stupid. I shouldn't have done that. It's cost everyone so much time and money."[31]

Moments not filming were spent studying the day's work just completed. To keep her shielded from the heat, Callas was transported by a special sedan-chair the production carpenters built for her.

> As we moved from place to place, Maria listened to taped music. She sang
> along with the Beatles, Frank Sinatra, or harmonized to Mexican ballads.
> Her favorite songs were "Stormy Weather" and "Hernando's Hideaway."
> The latter became the *Medea* theme song. We became so accustomed to her
> impromptu concerts that we soon forgot it was Callas singing.[32]

Director and star understood each other perfectly as to what Medea
was supposed to be. On the Turkish set, she told the press her role
was that of " . . . a semi-goddess who puts all her beliefs in a man.
At the same time, she is a woman with all the experiences of a woman,
only bigger—bigger sacrifices, bigger hurts. . . . You can't put these
things into words. . . ."

The film opens on the education of young Jason by the Centaur, who
is half-man, half-horse. The young hero is played (in his first and
only film role) by Giuseppe Gentile. The athlete, then a national hero
in his mid-twenties, had starred at the 1968 Olympic Games in Mex-
ico City, where his jump of 17-plus meters gained him (and Italy) a
gold medal. He was handsome (his costumes left him practically
naked from the waist down), but he hardly spoke a line in the film.
One obtuse critic complained, "One wonders why he was chosen,
since he is never given a chance to show off his athletic abilities."

His mythological tutor (Laurent Terzieff) teaches his charge about
the mystical origins of the earth, the gods, and a Golden Fleece,
which is the symbol giving authority to those in power. But as he
ages, the Centaur changes course and gives the boy a "rational"
education, one that sees the world bereft of the power of the gods.

As the Centaur predicts, the young adult Jason goes to his uncle
Pelias to reclaim the kingdom taken from him, the power that ought
to be his as the son of a king. Jason accepts his uncle's self-defending
challenge: He will hand over the throne if Jason returns with the
Golden Fleece. The stalwart heads for Colchis, a mysterious place
where primitive practices of great violence occur and the fields are
fertilized with the blood of human sacrifice.

Medea, the daughter of Colchis' king, has retired to the temple to
pray, to the sacred precinct where the fleece is stored. Part of the
audience would recognize in Medea's sacred role the Druid priestess
of Bellini's *Norma*, perhaps Callas' greatest role.

Jason, his arrival announced by a chorus of women, appears:
Medea is attracted to him and yet troubled by his presence. Callas
must show all this more with movement and facial expression than

speech. With the help of her brother, she agrees to steal the Fleece and gives it to Jason; but in doing so, she betrays her family and her people.

The city rises in revolt and the Argonauts barely escape, the enemy army in hot pursuit. Critic Gian Maria Guglielmino described their flight "not so much something heroic as the quick getaway of a bunch of petty thieves." Medea, who has given up all for love and fled with Jason, now murders her brother Absyrtus—who had stolen the Fleece for Jason—and quarters him. This slows down the advance of her father's army, who stop to gather up the pieces.

Medea is now separated from her sacred site and, among strangers and strange ways, becomes disoriented. She seeks refuge in her obsessive love for Jason. He brings the Fleece to his uncle, who breaks his promise. Jason and Medea flee again, taking refuge in Corinth.

Ten years pass. Medea is troubled and Jason (who had never wed her but fathered two sons by her) is about to marry Glauce (Margareth Clementi), the daughter of Creon, King of Corinth (played by Massimo Girotti).

In Corinth—where all is law, order . . . and consciousness— Medea is considered a barbarian, one capable of terrible acts and black magic. She is so feared and reviled that to protect Glauce from Medea's wrath, King Creon orders Medea, the foreign woman, from his city.

She is desperate: To lose Jason is not only to lose the man she loves to another woman but to lose her sole link to reality, he for whom she had abandoned her home and universe, for whom she had cut herself from her roots.

In Corinth, Jason again encounters his tutor the Centaur, this time rendered double—partly linked to the world of myth, partly to the world of reason. Jason explains how Medea is a woman from a world before rationality, now stranded in the "modern" world.

After a prescient dream, Medea summons Jason for a last encounter. She has had a vision in which she presents the new bride with a garment, which, as soon as Glauce dons it, bursts into flame. Awakened, she summons her sons and sends them with this very gift for Jason's betrothed, who wants to don it immediately, is seized by fright, leaves the palace courtyard, and falls to her death—in flames—from the parapet. She is followed by her father.

At sunset, Medea calls her sons to her. She bathes them, dresses them in white tunics, and then (all in silence) stabs each of them. Mad with grief, she sets her house afire. Jason appears, begging, "Let us caress once more their poor, innocent bodies." The film closes with fateful Medea's refusal: "No. Do not insist, for it is useless. By now, nothing more is possible."

In April 1970 Garzanti published *Medea* as a book: ninety-seven "scenes," always very short, some even a single line of dialogue. Pasolini had written it as though to be one sequence, then shuffled the pieces into another order for shooting. During that process he sat for long sessions of one-on-one talk with Rossellini, explaining his ideas. Their conversation offers an intimate view of the director's mind at work. The dialogues were the only guidance given Callas. Used to working with score and libretto, she found film difficult. Sometimes she complained that the dialogue was not Shakespearean enough; another time she claimed she could not memorize lines without music.

The producer, within limits, gave Pasolini free rein. A deepening fascination with cultural anthropology, rite and ritual, reading of Lévi-Strauss and Jung permeate Pasolini's vision of the film. He had discovered the great scholars of comparative mythology, including Mircea Eliade and Sir James Frazer. He later dismissed Eliade's *Myth and Reality*, writing that it was "not a great book . . . there is in it something gray, elementary, and fanatical which limits its fascination."[33]

He talked with Rossellini about the film he imagined:

Passolini: The film begins with a silent section and we'll shoot it in bits, sometimes in a soundstage, sometimes [outside] in Italy, wherever it happens to make sense. Let's leave the exact description of this part for later. What matters is to understand the beginning, starting with a human sacrifice where people cross a field, stop in the middle of it, like that red earth area we saw on this side of that church of St. Simon.

There, in the middle, they will be digging a grave, among them a naked girl, a naked boy, both of them drunk as though insane because they have known for many years that it would end this way. There is a brief ritual, and they throw them in a hole and bury them.

Franco Rossellini: And who is it that buries them?

PPP: This group of people, and we'll include a priest, two or three minor priests and a bunch of peasants—I'd say twenty to thirty people altogether. After the two have been buried, we'll take a long, still shot of this red earth, and this recurrent image of this red earth will perhaps work [as did clouds and shifting sands in other films] for dissolving from one episode to another. Maybe we'll use for the transitions not only this but frames of the sun and moon joined together, something like that. . . .

FR: Won't it be difficult to manage all this?

PPP: I know, but maybe we can do the whole thing when we start, or maybe there's no need . . . it's enough to shade it in. But it isn't even sure we'll do it . . . some of the orgy scenes we have to do later because I see them as an essential element of the peasant rites, of the earth, it is this orgy which makes vitality circulate within nature.

This is the start of the film, the silent and mythical part of it. We come back every time, returning to this fixed image of the earth which holds these victims, or maybe other sacrifices too, very briefly, to get us to the place of the gods, where the gods are . . . I see the camera rising up the sky like this, or if we have a helicopter some sort of ascent, and thus after the sacrifices we move upwards—after this the film opens, alternating these myths [linked to ] the gods, and then to the drama of Jason and the Golden Fleece.

## On the education of the child Jason by the Centaur:

PPP:  . . . We see Jason at five or six listening as he would to tales of a grandfather, and then again at about twelve . . . to give you a more concrete idea of the scene, the Centaur takes the boy into a cave and teaches him by the light of the fire. The Centaur likes to drink—downs nectar like wine— this is another detail, and we see him, Jason, on the beach, [then] jump then to Jason at twelve.

At his second and later appearance, when Jason is grown and the Centaur has taken the form of a man, instead of teaching the mythical aspects of religion and the occult, the teacher explains "a relationship with religion that is rational and practical." Pasolini explained to Rossellini his idea of a series of crosscuts, showing Jason as evermore practical (bourgeois), worldly, and "modern"; Medea in sharp contrast is part of another world.

Medea's universe is as important as her personality, or more so, for she is largely a symbol. To depict her prerational world, Pasolini planned to depict three rituals: one to do with the cult of the sun, which is also of death, but in cyclical fashion, of fecundity and rebirth. Medea is to officiate. "This one will probably finish with coitus with a bull—with a violence that is almost awful, showing the bull as it is." It was not filmed.

He then cast about for a way to illustrate the idea of rebirth, with the moon as a symbol of passing and returning. "Maybe in a moonlit sea nude girls strew white clay about and then become lunar themselves, but with luck we'll think of something better." They did not.

PPP: And the third ritual is connected to the earth, close to that seen at the start of the film, the burial or something similar. He outlines an orgy in which Medea does not participate but one in which the figures in authority do, including the priests, and they lose their authority during that time— as though everything returns to nothing, to the original chaos. This ritual could be like those that really happened, say instead of the live burial we saw at the beginning, instead they kill someone tied to a tree or onto the ground and cut them up and spread the parts on the earth—and when Medea cuts her brother into pieces, it becomes then a ritual act out of her religion and this removes the horror (for her) of the murder. So Medea will participate in these rituals and she will say something, they will be singing some sort of songs and so on.

This last ritual was filmed and later cut: The extras painted the victims' "blood" on the leaves of crops, their ashes thrown to the wind under Medea's supervision.

He tells Rossellini, "As soon as we are back in Rome, the first thing to do is research on hymns, preferably Indian ones." Pasolini did just that, but ended with folk music and music from the Greek Orthodox liturgy, again in collaboration with Elsa Morante, as he had done with *The Gospel According to Matthew*.

The producer must have worried that Pasolini was reviving the silent cinema.

FR: So, there will be words, music?

PPP: Not music, no (the accompaniment to these rituals will be spoken) . . . and one of these will be a ritual of initiation—I want to make the agriculture rite overlap with that of the initiation typical of the world of peasants, and in this one Medea can sing and recite these hymns as though liturgy, to underline here for the clarity of the storyline—everything involving Medea and the humans will be accompanied by sacred music, deeply sacred—even that of a mass. There, that's it.[34]

Rossellini balked at two rituals that end in human sacrifice: Would not one be enough? Pasolini agreed: "Maybe the first ritual, instead of being a burial, can be a decapitation or some other sort of martyrdom."

He turned to the questions of sets. Designer Dante Ferretti was to place statues around a sacred tree where Medea appears, "and those in the grotto where the Golden Fleece is stored, these must be phallic, erotic, recalling the orgies and the coitus of the bull and so on. And other bas reliefs ought to represent the rituals, accurate pictures of what happens, the same symbols and so on. When we get back to Rome, an urgent thing to look into is all this: the sun, vegetation, the moon, and so on."

This way, through improvisation, discussion, compromise, *Medea* was made. Some of what was planned was never shot. Other parts were shot but cut in editing, including a scene with Fabio Mauri as a king with seven daughters, all nude and in competition to show their affection for their father. "Pier Paolo made them shoot it over and over," Mauri recalls," because, he said, "'I see you are enjoying yourself.' " As usual, the scene was as much made in the editing as the filming: Pasolini shot several times what he needed and, back in Rome, boiled it all down to 118 minutes.

He believed that he had "a sacred relationship with objects";[53] they were the signs and symbols he could make speak through the language of the eye. He was, through things—places and bodies—communicating the unseen; his work, he believed, was to bridge from the material to the equally real that was invisible.

The month before Medea's shooting started, he told a reporter from Turin's *La stampa*, "I am an atheist. But my relationship with things is full of the mysterious and sacred. For me, nothing is natural, not even nature."[36] Talking with a student group about *Teorema*, he repeated the idea, "To me, everything seems invested with an important light, special, which is best defined as sacred. And this determines my style, my technique."

So the shots of sky, shifting sands, the red earth—and the characters his actors and nonactors played—were so much stuff to be shaped into a syntax, a grammar of sacred meaning. The first incarnation of the Centaur makes him train the young Jason to see the world as Pasolini still saw it: "All is holy, all is holy, all is holy. There is nothing natural in nature my boy, keep that in mind. When nature seems natural to you, all is over—and something else will begin. No more sky! No more sea!"[37]

Callas came to Rome to see the rushes in December 1969.[38] She was dismayed at how many shots of her she thought lovely had ended up on the cutting room floor. Too often, she thought, a camera angle emphasized her nose. The close-ups were not always kind to her forty-six years. But she said nothing, so in awe was she of Pasolini's art, so much did she trust him. More than a decade before, she had also been mesmerized by Visconti; when they disagreed, she sometimes held her tongue, and the result was perhaps her very best work.

The film was not—at least at first—a commercial success. From the start, it was labeled as something for film clubs and art cinemas. Many critics found the backdrops that quoted early Renaissance paintings, the costumes full of self-conscious pastiche somehow too decorative, "too esthetic." The mass magazine *Gente* called Pasolini "ambiguous and cerebral"; *Panorama* wrote that Callas' violence recalled "that of Malcolm X"; *Rinascita*'s reviewer was reminded of "the bloody feudal epics of Kurosawa." Callas, Moravia, Maraini, and Pasolini spent New Year's 1970 together in West Africa.

Rossellini scheduled a screening for March at the Argentine Film Festival in the resort of Mar del Plata. Pasolini was now forty-eight; he remarked, "There are happy little, old people; I will be one of those."[39] He and Callas were photographed in close-up at Rome's airport, kissing on the mouth. Headlines announced their imminent engagement to be married.

After all, the entire *Medea* production had sometimes been a media circus. One reporter had tried to enter Callas' hotel room in Turkey by climbing along an outside railing, only to be discovered hanging in midair. In Rome, journalist Adele Cambria besieged Callas for an interview to the point that the diva tried to substitute Stancioff as a trick. NBC, the RAI, *Life*, and *Look* sent reporters to cover the great Callas' film debut. The BBC shot an interview on the set, three minutes aired June 28, 1969, on *Omnibus*. No one wanted to miss making copy of the unusual Callas-Pasolini relationship.

Pasolini's enemies howled. Rome's satirical cabarets (revived in the wake of 1968) had a field day. Those artists and intellectuals, Pasolini among them, who had stepped into the spotlight in the time of troubles, to seize a microphone, were now to be jostled a bit. In the months when *Medea* was in the news, this scene was part of one theater's fare:

> The stage darkened and from the wings a woman's voice called out, small and plaintive, "Pier Paolo. Pier Paolo."
> From the opposite wings, a man's voice answered, also tentative, "Maria, Maria."

Laughter from the audience, alerted that this was the odd love couple of the year, the diva jilted by Onassis and the notoriously homosexual director.

> They call more loudly, and then again, and again as their excitement mounts, always in the dark. "Pier Paolo." "Maria." "Pier Paolo." "Maria." And then the deep breathing of sex, the sigh of satisfaction. And a voice booms over the audience: "*Che bella chiamata*" [What lovely calling to one another].

*Chiamata* is a close enough rhyme to *chiavata*—slang for fucking—to be the perfect takeoff of "What a lovely screw."

> And the voice offers an epilogue [to bring down the house and ice the cake of derision]: "Well, that's all we can manage."

*Medea* opened in Milan in December 1969; a month later, on January 28, 1970, a gala premiere was held at the Paris Opera. A selection of the international *beau monde* was in attendance: The Aga Khan, Maurice Chevalier, Mrs. Sargent Shriver (wife of the U. S. ambassador), various Rothschilds and ambassadors from eleven countries. Photographers recorded Pasolini in black tie, sitting with Susanna, Callas, and their hostess, Madame Georges Pompidou, wife of the president of France.

But between Callas and Pasolini was no more or less than a playful and tender mutuality of feeling. It began platonically and stayed that way during the filming and for several years afterward when they saw one another. She visited with Susanna and Graziella on via Eufrate. For a time, long phone calls passed between Paris and Rome.

In April 1970 Garzanti published the shooting script of *Medea* along with Pasolini's treatment for the film, an interview with Callas, and "poems written during the shooting. . . ."

Some were to, or about, Callas. On the set, Pasolini had given her a ring: an antique bronze coin set in silver. "On one side, there were the worn profiles of a man and a woman, and on the other a victorious warrior.[40] His poetry to her almost teasingly suggests heterosexual love. He wrote that she came into his life:

> bringing with you that odor from beyond the
> tomb,
> you sing arias composed by Verdi that have
> turned blood-red
> and the experience of it (without a word being
> uttered)
> teaches sweetness, pure sweetness.[41]

His was an attention she needed then. Not long before Onassis dismissed her talent as "a bird that had died" in her throat, Pasolini wrote that she was a "Little bird with the powerful voice of an eagle. A trembling eagle."

He wrote to her about her father, George Kalogeropolous, to explain that he could not love her as perhaps she might have wished:

> What counts is him, the Father, yes, him:
> so says one who does not know him,

knows nothing about him, has never seen him,
never spoke to him, never saw him, . . .

You, smiling at me, are smiling at him.

But I can never be him, because I do not know him,
I swear to you, Maria, I haven't the least experience of this;
and for you, it is so natural![42]

Their friendship survived and overcame ideology. She stopped lecturing him about his Communism. When the film was done, she stayed on in Rome; they went for long lunches together, sometimes at the Escargot on the via Appia Antica, one of her favorite restaurants. He told a reporter from *Le monde* that she had read some of his poems about her in *Nuovi argomenti:* "She was a bit upset by them, she doesn't know if she should be happy or unhappy about what I wrote about her. This has provoked a conflict in her we don't talk about much."[43]

In the summer of 1970 he joined Callas on Tragonisi, an Aegean island in the Petalii group owned by Perry Embiricos—a great music lover, heir to one of the great Greek shipping fortunes. The party on vacation included Callas, Nadia Stancioff, one of Onassis' partners from his early whaling business and his wife: an odd ensemble. As he and Callas talked on the beach, Pasolini sketched her, continuing the series of portraits he had started during the filming of *Medea* the year before. He folded a paper into squares and drew her profile on each, using transparent glue and flowers for color. Stancioff says that he exclaimed, "This is art in the making. Now it must dry in the sun for twenty-four hours. I shall make only three, and one will be for you."[44]

One undated sheet, believed to be from the drawings series of 1969–1970, repeats the abstracted image of a profile or a mountain—just lines running from lower-left to upper-right in sixteen squares of a folded page. It is an image repetitive, automatic. At the bottom of this sheet, he penned, "The world does not want me anymore and does not know it" (*Il mondo non mi vuole più e non lo sa*).

Between 1969 and 1971 Pasolini made fourteen drawings of Callas in all: a first group in Cervignano del Friuli and five more in Greece. In Italy he worked at the dinner table, combining the red and white wine at hand, a bit of candle-wax, crushed flower petals. On the beach he took the materials he found there and worked his alchemy with them.

He gave one to a Signor Citossi, who did some work on the Centaur's house on Safon. Two went to Callas, on the occasion of *Medea*'s Paris Opera premiere. Other versions were found among his papers at his death. In the first group Callas is seen full-face and lively; by 1970 she is only a profile, something distant.[45]

It seemed time for an inexpensive "selected poems," drawn from the three Garzanti-published volumes in print. The publisher had come to think that a substantial market existed for such a book (it would sell for only 1,000 lire), and it seemed as though Pasolini as poet had written the bulk of what he had to say.

In a sense, Pasolini agreed. He had written Garzanti in June 1966, "The selection of the poetry would be a concluding act to my literary 'period,' and the opening of another.[46] He suggested such an edition (noticing one had come out of Saba's work) because he believed it "well closed that period of my style," so a selection from his three volumes of verse could be presented as something historic. He cited as another reason: "I do not even have a single copy of *Poesia in forma di rosa*, a volume become unfindable, along with the other volumes of [my] poetry in Roman bookstores. (You remember that I once mentioned this?)"[47]

By 1970 when the selection was published, his feelings were more complex: "By now I no longer know how to separate the idea of a book from [that of] the smile of a lady who has a glass in her hand . . . I think of the case in point of the Strega Prize with that atrocious partnership between the well-mannered man of letters [*il letterato per bene*] and the well-mannered lady in the good *salone. . . .*[48]

And yet he wanted to wait. He wrote Garzanti that "ninety-five chances out of a hundred" he would have finished another new collection of verse for January 1971: *Trasumanar e organizzar*. Only after that, in 1972, did he want to proceed with an edition of "the complete corpus of my poetry, written over thirty years (my first little book came out in '42)," and with the title *Bestemmia* (Curse, or Blasphemy), its name after a previously unpublished "fragment" he wanted to include.

Instead, the retrospective paperback appeared in October 1970, as per the publisher's preference. In 1972 Garzanti brought out *Trasumanar*, poems of 1968–1971; and in September 1975, a second edition of the paperback selection, expanded to include fifteen previously unpublished poems and a selection from *Trasumanar e organizzar*.

For the 225-page economical pocket edition, Pasolini selected poems from *Le ceneri di Gramsci, The Religion of My Time,* and *Poetry in the Form of a Rose.* And he wrote an autobiographical essay ("To the New Reader") as well as a new poem, called *CHARTA (SPORCA)*—literally, Dirty Paper:

> [which] will certainly not contribute to the ordering of this anthology of old poems, nor to draw sympathy to me; it will tend, on the contrary, to put everything again into debate, which I absolutely refuse, whether consciously, or unconsciously, in any form of pacification . . .[49]

"To the New Reader" hides as much as it reveals. With the skill of an experienced anthologist of other poets, he moves quickly through his Friulian period, the discovery of Marx and Gramsci, the flight to Rome with Susanna "as in a novel," his first days in Rome. He closes:

> As I write this introduction for a nonspecialized reader, I'm working on a document about the [current] strike of Roman streetcleaners ("*Appunto per un romanzo sull'immondezza*" / "Notes on a novel about garbage") and it doesn't really seem that thirty years have gone by. It could be that the sentiments of class struggle of the young in 1968–70 have revived the great days (of *Sogno di una cosa*); and it's not important if this is an illusion. In fact, the class struggle is not a phenomenon that can be resolved in thirty years, and its characteristics are always the same.
>
> Finally, the poems selected here from the volumes representing the thirteen years between 1951 and 1964 form a coherent and compact block. What strikes me in them—I'm talking as if I'd been estranged from them, which is not true—is a widespread sense of discouraging unhappiness; an unhappiness that's part of the language itself, like a datum of its own, reducible in quantity and almost in[to] physicality. This sense (almost a right) of being unhappy is so predominant that the sensual joy (of which the book is full, although accompanied by guilt) is obscured by it; and so is its civic idealism. What strikes me further, on reading these poems, is the realization of how ingenuous was the expansiveness with which I wrote them: it is as if I were writing for someone who could only love me a great deal. I understand now why I have been the object of so much suspicion and hatred.[50]

*CHARTA (SPORCA)* is full of lines that end in ellipses, as though the poem were on a paper found after an accident or disaster, something retrieved. In italics, Pasolini ended some lines by writing "words illegible due to dirty spots": It is as though the poet cannot, or will not, round out a thought.

\*     \*     \*

In the spring of 1970 he moved to repay a substantial, long-standing debt to Sergio Citti. His early muse and constant helper wanted to direct his own film, so Pasolini helped him write the script of *Ostia* and was listed in the credits as coauthor with "supervision of the direction."

The film is about two brothers, professional thieves in the *borgate;* in addition to Franco (as Rabbino), it stars the Swedish actress Anita Sanders (whom Franco married) and Laurent Terzieff as Bandiera. Pasolini also helped Citti to make *Storie scellerate* (in English, Bawdy tales), which Sergio directed in 1973 and Alberto Grimaldi produced for PEA (Produzioni Europee Associate). On August 8 Pasolini accompanied Citti to Locarno and participated in a press conference and discussion held the next day at the Hotel America. Promoting those in whom he believed gave him great satisfaction.

Now his public remarks, in a constant stream of interviews, changed tone:

> Finally, living like the birds in the sky and the lilies in the field, that is not occupying myself with tomorrow, I am enjoying a little life and liberty (I enjoyed the latter very much especially erotically but dissociating myself . . . Enjoying life (in the body) signifies precisely enjoying a life which historically no longer exists: so living it is thus reactionary. I have been uttering reactionary propositions for some time. And I am thinking about writing an essay entitled *Come recuperare alla rivoluzione alcune affermazioni reazionarie?* (How to retrieve for the revolution certain reactionary claims?)[51]

He had taken no fee for either *Uccellacci e uccellini* or *Porcile; Medea* made money. In November 1970 he bought a medieval tower outside the hamlet of Chia in the province of Viterbo north of Rome, one he had probably first seen when filming the Baptism of Christ for *Gospel* six years before. He had rooms built at the base of the tower, in what were ruins that rose from the rubble of a supposedly Saracen fortress keep. They were modern and spare, all concrete block and wood and expanses of glass—looking over a ravine where the Chia torrent ran. It was sheltered from the main road, large enough for two people at most. He talked of making a trio of films and then retiring there. To study literature, he said, "and to paint."

# 22

*The unsatisfied yearnings of the artist reach back to the primordial image in the unconscious which is best fitted to compensate the inadequacy and one-sidedness of the present.*

—*C. G. Jung*

*The wise contradict themselves.*
—*Oscar Wilde*, **Phrases and Philosophies for the Use of the Young**

# THE *TRILOGY OF LIFE*

Pasolini told a reporter that the idea for *Decameron*—his tenth film in as many years—came to him "brusquely, with a kind of force, an evident presence, on the plane that was carrying me to Turkey for the shooting of *Medea*."[1] He explained, "It was a great desire to laugh which inspired *Decameron* . . . it was not I who chose the *Decameron*, it was the *Decameron* which chose me.[2] "It was the first of three films evoking a disappeared past based in "my nostalgia for an ideal people with its misery, its lack of political awareness and—

I know it is terrible to say this but it is true—for a people I used to know when I was a child."[3]

The *Trilogy* also represented his flight from the present, from the bitter conclusion to which he thought History had come. It was also a reminder because (as Theodor W. Adorno wrote) "All reification is forgetting." The not-at-all-brave new world of consumer culture was fast losing the memory of how it once had been.[4]

The years of the *Trilogy*, 1970–1974, are also those of *Scritti corsari*, a series of contestatory articles—journalism on current events, deeply topical and fiercely engaged in the violently unfolding present.

Lest anyone think he had abandoned his "career as a committed author" (*carriera di autore impegnato*), he pointed out that in the stressful year 1970 to make a film "happy, comic, without implicit problems"—one celebrating "the profound and ontological sense of reality" through "its naked symbol, which is sex"—was a statement sure so to "disappoint expectations" and keep his reputation as troublemaker intact.[5]

In December 1970—the same month the Chamber of Deputies followed the Senate's legalization of divorce—the "black" (that is, papal) Prince Valerio Junio Borghese organized a militia to stage a coup from the Right. It aborted, but the political climate was unstable: three different coalition cabinets came and went within twelve months. Exhausted by the political strife of '68 and after—but not yet in the clear—Italians craved escape. They welcomed Visconti's "German trilogy" (*Death in Venice, The Damned, Ludwig*) and Pasolini's "escapism" as well.

It seemed to the small film world that Pasolini's filming the great classic of Italian erotic literature was a natural. In retrospect, producer Alberto Grimaldi, who from the first sensed a box-office smash, called it "inevitable." And yet Franco Rossellini had encountered trouble arranging financing. When Grimaldi, proprietor of PEA—Produzioni Europee Associate—read about the project in the *Araldo dello spettacolo* (the Italian movie industry trade journal), he acted. "I called Rossellini, we met, and I proposed that I would produce the film. He would be 'line producer' and receive credit as executive producer in Italy."[6]

Rossellini agreed and a budget of $750,000 was set, a moderate amount for features of the time. According to Grimaldi, Pasolini received a director's fee of "about $50,000" and a small percentage ("not more than one or two percent, closer to two") of the Italian box-office gross. This share might prove substantial: The box-office

gross—raw ticket sales totals—is double or triple the so-called distributor's gross and much more than the bottom-line producer's profit.

Pasolini left negotiation to his lawyer-agent Theresa Niquesa
(called Esa) de Simone, and never himself discussed business with
the producer. "He understood that he was not yet a commercial director, that without me there would be no film," Grimaldi says; the
entrepreneur had a track record with Sergio Leone and access to the
worldwide distribution of the Americans of United Artists. *Decameron*
became part of Grimaldi's deal with UA for for coproduction and
distribution of nine films over several years.

A lawyer known for leaving his directors in peace, Grimaldi intended to build a long-term relationship with Pasolini. Throughout a
career that saw him produce Bertolucci, Fellini, Pasolini, Pontecorvo
and others, Grimaldi says Pasolini was "the best to work with of all—
genuinely sweet, enormously intelligent—a real man of culture, always reasonable."

Some discipline had to be imposed. Before shooting began, Pasolini wrote Rossellini that the film would run "at least three hours,"
and not with a few Boccaccian tales recounted but "as of this first
draft, fifteen." He wanted the Neapolitan stories to be only a core,
with others added in order to make "a kind of fresco of the entire
world [in transition] between the medieval and the bourgeois eras."
Pasolini announced he wanted to shoot throughout the Mediterranean,
"from Egypt to Spain." While the budget was enormous by Pasolini's
standards and certainly enough for the nonstar cast assembled, his
scope was scaled down, the script confined. As French casts and
crews did for Buñuel, Pasolini's troupe agreed to work for lower-than-
standard pay: It was, by now, deemed an honor in Rome to work on
one of his films.

Starting with *Decameron* (1971) and then with *Canterbury Tales*
(1972) and *Thousand and One Nights* (in Italian, *Il fiore delle mille
e una notte*) (1974), Pasolini definitively crossed a major boundary
and moved from a semi-obscure European film *auteur* to mainstream
moviemaker, complete with ballyhoo and distribution to match. What
could sell better than the risqué, famously ribald stories of Boccaccio
in the hands of homosexual "pornographer" Pasolini? Grimaldi says
even he had not imagined *Decameron* would become the highest-
grossing foreign film in the U.S. for 1971, but it did.

Pier Paolo set about making a decidedly upbeat film about uninhibited love, claiming that it was in defiance of the "hate and suspicion" he felt surrounding him. As with *Gospel*, he started a trend.
On the lucrative heels of his *Decameron* appeared every sort of

squalid knockoff, twenty-two in all: a *Black Decameron*, a *Decameron Sinners*, a *Racconti proibiti di niente vestiti*—which rhymes in Italian and in English as "Forbidden Tales of Bare Tails."[7] *Canterbury Tales* spawned at least fifteen knockoffs, *Thousand and One Nights* eight. "As an author I am not protected [against this]," Pasolini told *Panorama*.[8] "But I'd like to see what would happen if a car factory decided suddenly to call its products Fiat, Fiat Number Two, Fiat *all'italiana*."

The first of his several major alterations to Boccaccio was to eliminate any reference to the Florentine plague of 1348 or to the original text's ten storytellers. He wanted the tales recounted not through the voice of the then-emerging urban merchant class but rather from the altogether different perspective of a Neapolitan street bard. With an obscene gesture and wave of the hand, his alter-ego narrator dismisses the uppity Florentine language, demanding that the tales be passed along "in the Neapolitan way." Italy's poor southerners, dispossessed like their counterparts in Harlem and black Africa, were at last to take center stage. He used Naples and walled Caserta Vecchia as locales because he thought their people, kept so long in superstition and subservience by the Bourbons and the Church were still "cut off" from the history of Italy and of the world. Living as though in "an air pocket . . . the Neapolitans decided to stay the way they were . . . and thus allow themselves to die."

He wrote:

> I love their differentness. I love their desire
> to live alone in their world, among fields and
> buildings
> where the word of our world does not reach;
> between us and them;
> I love their dialect invented each morning
> to make oneself not understood
> if only not to share their happiness with any
> one.[9]

His love was for those who, like him, sensed a mark of destiny on themselves and who would rather "die" than change themselves. That their isolation came hand in hand with poverty was not evidence of their failing but simply proof of their victimization. As for that *miseria*, he was fast coming to think that in a horrible world of relative truths, poverty was not the worse thing that could befall a man or a people. As a matter of esthetic politics, he had argued for twenty years that describing the beauty of suffering, without moralizing, was not slumming but part of the artist's job and his particular moral calling.

In one stroke his three movies (their scale requires the term) made homage to the dialects of the underclass, saluted the Italian regional particularism he believed was in mortal danger, and offered a kind of hymn to the naked human body. It is as though Pasolini's personal trajectory, and the passing obsessions of the capitalist West, were in symmetry; two planets on a movie producer's idea of the perfect collision course. People went to see the naked bodies and hear "dirty" talk; they usually cared little and knew less that the film recorded the final section of a consistent thirty-year arc of Pasolini's mind.

> In a moment of profound cultural crisis (the last years of the sixties), which made one think (and still think) of the end of all culture—the situation reduced itself, in concrete terms, to the conflict between two subcultures: that of the bourgeoisie and the one in conflict with it . . . it seemed to me that the sole reality which remained was that of the body . . . thus the protagonist of my films is the corporeality of ordinary people . . . the symbol of this corporeal reality is the naked body and . . . sex.

Only after his death did someone wonder in print—using Pasolini's Frankfurt School vocabulary—if the bodies in the *Trilogy* were "objectified." Only when the full film of his life had run, and sense could be imposed on it, did someone ask whether these were not already the "bodies without souls" of *Salò*. Only in retrospect did one acute critic connect the *Trilogy* and *Salò* and call them all "the quartet of death."

At their release, liberals hailed the triad as "liberation" and as a "celebration" of sexuality; both their champions and adversaries called them soft-core pornography, couched in the guise of literary classics. It made "sense" that an outspoken homosexual would make such movies in the wake of '68, a counterpoint to *Hair* and *Oh, Calcutta!*

But in an interview given *Il tempo*, Pasolini threw cold water on the instant explainers:

> An author's "time" is never the time of the newspapers. To satisfy himself, he must always be exorbitant. Nor are an author's cultural problems those which the critics find it easy to recognize. Even the representation of Eros in my trilogy does not have the function they would like to attribute to it, i.e., it is not a plea for the liberalization of sexual relations. No. If my films should happen to contribute to the present form of "permissiveness" I would reject them. In fact, I find such permissiveness planned and programmed

by those in power: from above, then adopted by the people and above all by the young, who are rendered neurotic with the anxiety of being "up to" all the liberties which have been conceded to them.[10]

Those who only saw his movie and did not read his words found in *Decameron*'s ten episodes "a magnificently rendered tapestry of joyous medieval Italian life," an "exquisite" childlike paradise of unself-consciousness, uninhibited everyman characters without guilt or remorse who leave calculation's unhappiness to the bourgeoisie of an urban, industrial world not yet born. Almost all failed to see the films as also a homage to what was dead, a dirge for a world lost.

He told the press he wanted to avoid "escapism," and yet viewers saw first *Decameron*—and then his Chaucerian England and pastiche of Arabic and Nepalese *Thousand and One Nights*—as brilliantly just that. And they intended the description as praise. He claimed he sought to keep himself "outside ideologies"—and yet he pinpointed to interviewers just that agenda:

> But more than one "ideological" element is hidden in these three films I have made. The main one is the nostalgia for the past era which I have sought to recreate on the screen . . . to me [making the *Trilogy*] represents an entry into the most mysterious inner workings of the artistic process, an experiment with the ontology of narration, an attempt to engage with the process of rendering a film filmic, the kind of film one saw as a child.[11]

The experiment in narration attracted him as well, what he called "rendering a film filmic" in a way that has nothing to do with plot. Without success, he offered the part of Giotto to Sandro Penna and to Paolo Volponi, but both friends refused. Pasolini declared that *Decameron* would be "the least autobiographical of my films," but he eventually took up Sergio Citti's suggestion and played Giotto himself. He called it "part of the game" and enjoyed himself. In a funny sequence filmed in Chaplinesque fast-forward, he moves the scaffolding of the walls of the church he is frescoing, races through a meal with his friar-employers, and playfully daubs blue paint on the nose of a bare-torsoed male assistant of striking good looks. We are inside a work of art as it is being made by the artist, himself within the work about the work.

During *Decameron*, he repeatedly cut to Giotto (that is, to himself) seen painting a holy narrative, a counterpoint to the the human stories recounted in the film. It mattered not at all that Giotto, in fact, never appears in Boccaccio, nor that the fresco Pasolini reproduced was not contemporary to Boccaccio but was completed decades before the

*Decameron*'s composition. Pasolini closes his movie as Giotto completes his fresco; both artists are fresco-makers, both engaged in the transformation of imagination into reality.

Pasolini almost managed to bury in the juiciness of the narrative the political lesson he wanted to teach. *Uccellacci*, a mere four years before, is light-years behind. He claimed the *Trilogy* was to satisfy an unmet need for "the sheer joy of telling and recounting . . . away from ideology"; he achieved it, but only to a point. [12]

One film historian has found a political strategy in his reworking of two of Boccaccio's most famous tales: that of the young lovers Riccardo (played by Francesco Gavazzi) and Catarina (Elizabetta Davoli) who "listen to the nightingale" (the bird, *uccello*, slang for penis) and sleep together without marriage; and the tale of another pair of lovers, Lorenzo and Elizabetta, and a pot of basil:

> Two pairs of lovers brave the objections of their families to enjoy each other's favors, but the outcome of each tale is radically different. Because Riccardo comes from a wealthy family, when he and Caterina are discovered naked on the balcony with the famous "nightingale" in Catarina's hand, her father resolves the moral problem with a merchant's cleverness, forcing the well-born Riccardo to take his daughter as his wife. To establish a contrast to this triumph of "business logic," Pasolini then relates the tragic end of Lorenzo, who has been transformed from a Pisan into a Sicilian servant and part of a despised, exploited lower class: Lorenzo is murdered by Elizabetta's brothers because his origins provide no economic advantage to her family.
>
> With only a few subtle changes to the original, Pasolini is thus able to attack both a specific class (the bourgeoisie) and an institution (the family) that is its typical expression, thus completely reversing Boccaccio's habitual admiration for his practical merchants who guiltlessly reconciled economic interests and sexual drives. [13]

The fabric is seamless: The young Pasolini, who loved Catalan and *friulano*, who collected the poetry of Italian dialects in *Il canto popolare* (1954) and the *Canzoniere italiano* (1955) has merged into the mature student of Marx and Freud and perhaps, as he claimed, leaving them behind has gone in search of a lost world. His contemporary from *liceo* days, Renzo Renzi, contends that Pasolini chose the very tales their teacher Alberto Mocchino had taught in their class thirty years before.

Giotto's fresco cycle in Padua's Arena Chapel culminates in the Last Judgment. But instead of Christ weighing souls, Pasolini-as-Giotto dreams a dream of *Pietà*, a vision of the Madonna and Child: Silvana Mangano as the silently smiling Virgin appears to him with her son, dark-haired and dark-eyed, an Arab ancestry showing in a face of the contemporary Mezzogiorno. The holy pair are not surrounded by angels in a space beyond human access but appear on the roof of one of the countless Roman apartment blocks thrown up by speculators. Behind them, the camera frames more housing in the *borgate* in 1970; yet their heads are circled with golden halos.

Having introduced the Mother of God in human-made squalor, Pasolini takes the institutional Church to task. Fat, bejeweled ecclesiastical officials are willing to turn a pederast and thief like Ciappelletto into a saint in order to keep the population quiet. True to Boccaccio, the nuns of a country convent secretly and then openly line up to ‚be serviced by innocent, gentle, gap-toothed Masetto, a stud who pretends to be deaf and mute to secure work in their orchard. All ends happily and hilariously when the aged mother superior—the last to bed the boy—declares that the return of his speech (he finally begs for a rest) is a miracle sent by God.

A still of actress Angela Luce—clad only in medieval bedcap—performing fellatio on the mostly clothed and smiling Vincenzo Ferrigno (in the episode of *Peronella*) made for an effective cinema poster. The movie's bawdiness filled theaters around the world: *Variety* reported *Decameron's* first-year box office was about $5 million in Italy alone, seven times the producing French-Italian-German consortium's investment. It had cost not much more to make than Bini spent for *Gospel*. As of July 30, 1988, *Decameron's* worldwide gross from "film-rentals"—what theater owners pay distributors—reached $9,890,838.73.[14]

The fables recounted and his fresco complete, Giotto-Pasolini turns to the theater audience to close his story. He asks:

> *Perché realizzare un'opera*
> *quando è così bello sognarla*
> *soltanto?*
>
> ("Why realize a work of art / when it is so beautiful simply to dream it?")

During the shooting of *Porcile*, when *Decameron* was scripted and its shooting about to start, Pasolini told film historian Gian Piero Brunetta:

> At first, I used technique to affirm reality, devour it, represent it in a way that was more corporeal, heavier; I tried with my camera, to be true to the reality that belongs to other people, but no more. Now I use the camera to

create a kind of rational mosaic that will render acceptable—clear and absolute—aberrant stories.

The world will not be seen on screen through eyes of Accattone nor of Stracci, but through the unashamedly composing vision of a narrator (Giotto, Chaucer) who assembles the "rational mosaic."[15]

Once Pasolini accepted this notion of point of view, it was inevitable that he step from behind the camera and onto the set as himself—the artist inside his work in the cinema as he had always been in the poetry. He—the absolute narrator—reveals that he exists and shows just what he is doing. The nonactors and professionals are there, as before, but now we see their puppeteer. "Finally, with this film [Decameron], I not only played the game but understood that the cinema is a game, something very simple but which took me ten years to understand . . . in Decameron, I played with reality having fun with itself."[16]

Many people did not see Decameron as he did, as "reality having fun with itself." Some thirty legal complaints were lodged against it between August and November 1971. By the following February, eighty official "denunciations" had been registered with judicial authorities all over Italy. One newspaper reported: "Some use pre-stamped paper, others white paper or letterheaded to suggest importance. There's a surgeon in Venice, a Roman youth committee of the monarchical front, the national committee for the pubic morals in Naples . . . even two missionary sisters from the Sacred Heart in Milan."[17] Grimaldi, who has called Italian censorhip "barbaric," was not surprised. He expected to win on appeal, and the tumult made for free publicity.

On August 28, 1971, a citizen Di Bezzecca exercised his right under Italian law and filed a *denuncia* against the film, shown for the first time the day before. His request was that the district attorney "examine [it] and determine if it is opportune to move against it on grounds of obscenity, indecency, or any other crime." The next day the prosecutor in Trento held that "there cannot be penal action brought" and dismissed the matter.

Pasolini might have left it at that but did not. Instead, he took to the pages of the *Corriere della sera* to make an argument he had made before. The defiant tone of his argument galled many who agreed with his logic:

This so-called "pornography" and "obscenity" is not what we label a "work of art" in our penal code. Thus, Article 529 sanctifies and institutionalizes a privilege. The privilege of the artist. This is a spiritualistic-bourgeois idea of art which presupposes a structured society in which there are limited circles capable of having feelings and ideas not available to the masses.[18]

The dismissal of charges in Trento was only the start. Ignoring the decision there, the public prosecutor in Bari banned the film within his jurisdiction. In response, Trento's magistrates ordered it released, and Bari's magistrates ordered it re-seized and demanded a hearing in Italy's highest court. Others followed Bari's lead—the film was confiscated by order of the district attorney's offices of Sulmona and at Ancona after action by "female police and private citizens." At Campobasso, a week before screening was scheduled, the local police inquired of the court whether perhaps some penal code violation was imminent.

In Cremona, the film was seized following "phone calls from a variety of persons who preferred to remain anonymous." Bari's police chief told a reporter that *Decameron* was a film "of a hair-raising and disgusting obscenity"; at Ferrara the magistracy denounced the movie *sue sponte*; in Ancona, a group of "citizens and police officers" filed a complaint. Others were lodged in Milan, Pavia, Rome, Lucera, Padua, Venice, Naples, Chieti, and Verona. Matters reached such a point that *L'unità* editorialized against "magistrates who consider their district a little fiefdom where the law of Italy does not apply."

One complaint described the film: "Indecent, obscene, pornographic and thus absolutely not artistic, offensive to honest persons and serious people, extremely dangerous for the young who are already too corrupted and for mature adults as well."[19]

Another explained that seeing the movie was "simply nauseating, obscene, contrary to good manners, stimulating only to the basest and most ignoble animal instincts . . . please excuse me, gentlemen prosecutors, but I really think it is a sacred duty of every serious and civilized person to participate in the creation of movies for people, not for animals."[20]

Renata Danielle, identifying herself as *una mamma*, said she "came out of the movie theater wobbly on my feet. . . ."

A complaint was lodged against *Corriere della sera* for printing ads for the film's screening in a Milanese movie house. In that city, with the precision of a well-coordinated action, five separate complaints were lodged against the film, against Pasolini and his producer in the five days between October 20 and 25, 1971. In that most cosmopolitan of Italian cities, Signora Bice Allegretti implored the authorities: "Please intervene, in the name of God!"[21]

A National Committee for the Public Morality, widely understood to have the backing of certain ecclesiastics, went after *Decameron* as part of a campaign against Ken Russell's *The Devils*, released about the same time. The group was especially outraged at the depiction of the behavior of priests and nuns. Umberto Monti of Rome denounced the film without having seen it: "I agree with Mr. Ferrari [who had moved against the film to defend housewives], a great veteran of the last war who goes to the cinema every day without paying [as the law allowed]. *Decameron*, the most revolting and stomach-turning of all. Worse than *The Devils*! Naked men in close-up who copulate among themselves!"

In Naples, Giuseppe Barca and ten others stated their objections to "various close-ups in which is shown, from the front, the lower part of the male abdomen, the male organs all bandaged up to make them have more than respectable proportions."[22]

Also in Naples, Mirra Salvatore wrote (with an apparently straight face):

> because of its obscene sequences, [*Decameron*] must be closely looked at by the juridical authorities of Naples as it has been by others in cities throughout the south with an eye to its immediate banning, lest viewers of it, in the twenty-four hours after seeing it participate in coitus and so risk that their genital organs atrophy, after which they will have improper blood circulation, symptoms of mental imbalance and certain of them will be struck by mental thromboses difficult to cure.[23]

At first, *Decameron* was refused inclusion in the Twenty-first Berlin Film Festival in June. *Variety* wrote: "Pasolini has made the most sexplicit [sic] picture of the year and probably in the history of Italian cinema . . . the turndown from Berlin (where screenfare is pretty sexy) heightened speculation as to what Pasolini had wrought." The Germans reversed themselves, screened *Decameron* and awarded it the Festival's second prize, the Silver Bear. The citation read: "For artistic rigor, cinematographic maturity and full-bodied humor with which Pasolini has recreated the irreverent irony of Boccaccio, not only rendering a picturesque image of the medieval world, but translated, with a healthy vitality, into an image of the world of today."

New York critic Vincent Canby approved, writing in the *New York Times*, "The film might be offensive to ordinary senses of delicacy and decency but it would be difficult to find it 'morally offensive.' " He saluted Pasolini for one of "the most beautiful, turbulent, and animated views of the Renaissance ever brought to the screen."

> Dante Ferretti's scenery and Danilo Donati's costumes . . . click. The eye can dwell on the colors and the forms.

> As for the forms of male and female nudity, Pasolini provides plenty of
> both, sometimes with the penis erect, sometimes large enough to provide
> the audience an uncomfortable titter. It is difficult to know where show
> business smarts leave off and the poetry that eases the viewer out of his
> inhibitions takes up. Naked, and with mouths full of the bad teeth of the
> poor, his characters smile.[24]

In Paris a critic for *Le nouvel observateur* loved the peasants, out
of "Altdorfer and Brueghel." What did it all mean to Pasolini? He
remarked: "I said in *La ricotta*, 'I am a force of the past.' . . . I am
becoming this more and more."[25]

In the spring of 1971 Pasolini was at the end of his fifth decade;
the boys he wanted had stayed the same age for thirty years. He
began to color his hair, now noticeably thinning. A bald spot had
grown too large to cover easily; lines around his eyes and his skin,
tight over his skull, gave the lie to the youthful appearance of his
lean body.

He signed himself into the Budapest clinic of Dr. Ana Aslan;
founded in 1954 and named for its endocrinologist founder, the Par-
hon Institute of Geriatrics offered a "Gerovital revitalizing cure."

The outfit's procedures were never approved by either the American or British medical establishments, but that did not stop a steady
stream of clients among the wealthy and famous. Detractors asserted
Aslan offered "simply a solution of procaine, which under the brand
name Novocaine is widely used by dentists to block pain and also
administered as an antidepressant." Her patients, whose extravagant
claims Ana Aslan never denied, were "said to include Charles de
Gaulle, Nikita Khrushchev, Indira Gandhi, Josef Broz Tito, Konrad
Adenauer, Lillian Gish, and Marlene Dietrich."[26]

Another run-in with the law. For two months he had lent his name
as a *pro forma* matter to a group charged with violating Article 272
of the penal code, banning "propaganda and anti-national and subversive apologetics." The Turin court of Assizes threw out the case
against him, but some damage was done. His participation, scheduled
for July 27, 1971, on the popular round-table talk show "III-B Make
the Call" proceeded as planned (and was widely publicized); but after
it was filmed, nervous network executives of the RAI put the program
in the archives. A replay of the (then) Cassius Clay–Jimmy Ellis fight
was broadcast instead. The reason: Italian law forbade the appearance on the state's network of anyone who, at the time of the broadcast, was the subject of a judicial proceeding. *Paese sera* commented:

"Evidently the principle is utterly unknown at the RAI that an accused can only be considered guilty after having been condemned." The program was broadcast only after Pasolini's death and rebroadcast in 1989 as though something antique, a lesson in how things were in the bad old days.

For the broadcast, Pasolini had come to RAI's studio to find, according to the program's format, friends from his youth at the Liceo Galvani in Bologna: Agostino Bignardi, Sergio Telmon—classmates who had not seen one another for thirty years. They had sat in Mario Borgatti's classroom together, studying Latin and Italian, history and geography all from the same teacher. Pasolini might have absorbed a love for dialects even then, for his *professore* was an expert on that of Emilia and later a distinguished anthologist of the region's *canti popolari*.

All the broadcast's participants, including a Liberal member of the chamber of Deputies, wore dark suits, white shirts, and conservative ties. Pasolini, in an open shirt and casual jacket, looked sportive, much younger than his contemporaries. But he did not dress expensively: nothing from Rome's luxury haberdashers like Brioni or Carlo Palazzi where he could now afford to shop.

He gestured animatedly when he spoke, but his mouth drew tight when he listened. The vein on his left temple, always pronounced in adulthood, seemed to throb; he looked wound up, ready to explode. He was there because, as he wrote, he "had to enter this game—though not without a taste for adventure—precisely to be able to become truly public, placed in the piazza, in the mortal arena."[27] How else than through appearing on the ruling means of the present was he to explain the "revolutionary force which is in the past"? The entire television sequence lasted eleven minutes. In part:

Biagi: "What has been your greatest sorrow?"

Pasolini: "I can't answer—well, objectively, the death of my brother—the sorrow of my mother at news of his death."

Biagi: "You have said 'to grow old is to become happy.' Why?"

Pasolini: " . . . less future, fewer hopes . . ."

Biagi: "You have no hope?"

Pasolini: "No."

Biagi: "You live day to day?"

Pasolini: "Yes, I no longer have those hopes which are alibis, success is nothing."

Biagi: "For you, what is success?"

Pasolini: "Success is nothing. Success is the other face of persecution. It can exalt in its first moment, provide small satisfactions, but as soon as one has achieved it, one understands that success for a man is something horrible.

"For example, the fact of meeting my friends here, on television, is not beautiful. Happily, we could forget the microphones and the cameras, and we could reconstruct something sincere; but there remains the fact that the situation is false, horrible."

Biagi: "What do you find so abnormal about it?"

Pasolini: "Television is a mass medium which cannot but alienate."

Biagi: "But aside from advertising for cheese and so on, as you once wrote, the medium at this moment carries, into people's houses, also your words. We are all now discussing with the greatest liberty, without any constraint."

Pasolini: "No, that's not true."

Biagi: "Yes, it is true. You can say what you like."

Pasolini: "No, I cannot say what I wish."

Biagi: "Say it."

Pasolini: "No, I could not, because under the Italian Fascist [legal] code, I would be charged with outrage. In reality, I cannot say everything. And furthermore, objectively, faced with the ingenuousness and lack of preparation of certain listeners, I would not really want to say everything. As a result, I censure myself. But aside from that, it is the mass medium in and of itself: From the moment when someone hears us on television, there is a relationship set up around us of inferior and superior, which is something appallingly undemocratic."

## Changing topics, Pasolini continued:

Society tries to assimilate, to integrate, that is certain: it is an operation which it must effect to defend itself . . . but we cannot speak of poetry as of other merchandise: I produce, you say, and that is true, but I produce a merchandise which is, in reality, unconsumable . . . I will die, my publisher will die, we will all die, our society will die, capitalism will die, but poetry will remain unconsumed.[28]

During the making of *Decameron*, Grimaldi offered Pasolini a contract for two more pictures: *Canterbury Tales* and *Thousand and One Nights*. The budget for each was to be about $1.2 million and Pasolini's fee (plus a percentage of Italian box office) rose to "about $100,000, more or less." Grimaldi recalls this was "as much as any Italian director was receiving then, save perhaps for Bertolucci and Zeffirelli, who had bigger international names."[29]

*Decameron*'s staggering commercial success was not the point.

Lawyer De Simone accepted Grimaldi's offer, she says, "as an insurance policy." It was more money than Pasolini had ever seen, budget enough to travel over much of the world in search of the images he wanted. He used the money to buy an expensive sports car, reconstruct the Saracen tower at Chia, take friends to dinner. Grimaldi says, "There are directors who make their first big money and are never the same. Bertolucci, after *Last Tango*, became a completely different man. Pasolini not at all."

That winter of 1971 *Canterbury Tales* seemed a certain success. Even before it appeared, a squalid takeoff called *The Other Canterbury Tales* was released. But *Decameron* had Boccaccio's fame as the author of ribald tales and the novelty of Pasolini's first "epic"; *Canterbury*'s box office was respectable, about 2 billion lire but only half that of *Decameron*. By July 30, 1988, its worldwide film rental income was $6,335,171.88. Still, with Pasolini, Grimaldi had plainly struck gold.

But the reaction to *Decameron*, from those Pasolini would call "moralists," gave United Artists' parent company, Transamerica Corporation, cold feet: In all, 152 legal complaints had been filed against it and the print had been subject to four separate judicial seizures. Transamerica did not want its name on *Canterbury Tales*, *Thousand and One Nights*, and certainly not on *Salò*. The last two parts of the *Trilogy* were only distributed in the United States in 1980, under what one executive called the company's *nom-de-porn*, Aidart Distribution Corp.[30]

Pasolini started work in England the very day *Decameron* premiered in Italy. *Canterbury* was shot and ready for editing in nine weeks: He filmed exteriors in Cambridge, Bath, St. Osyth, Laver Marney, Lavenham, Warwick, Chipping Campden, interiors in the cathedrals of Wells and Canterbury. Even as he filmed that winter, he told *L'unità*'s Mirella Acconciamessa that he was already sure where he would make *Thousand and One Nights* "in Iraq, Yemen, and India . . . and I also know it will be almost completely silent."[31]

The far-from-silent *Canterbury* was filmed in English, dubbed into Italian for the home market, then back into English. For the Italian version, Pasolini hired twenty boys from Bergamo to dub what he thought the "equivalents" of the cockney of the "Cook's Tale" and Peterkin's story. Filming in the medieval center of Wells, he encountered the dialect of Somerset, so he used that too. For the "Pardoner's Tale," he told a reporter, "I found three boys on the road. Completely by chance, all three happened to be Scottish."[32] So he cast them, speaking their own heavy brogue, again to be dubbed for the Italian market into its counterpart.

In place of Giotto, now Pasolini played Chaucer, smiling at his desk, content in the reverie he had made in his *Tales*. He seems almost to lean back and dream them onto the screen.

The important continuities held: as assistant director, Sergio Citti; director of photography, Tonino delli Colli; Ferretti for sets: Donati for costumes; and composer Ennio Morricone to "collaborate" on Pasolini's selection of music. The familiar names made the cast: Laura Betti as the Wife of Bath, Ninetto as Peterkin, Franco Citti as a mysterious stranger. Hugh Griffith was hired to play old king January opposite Josephine Chaplin (Charlie Chaplin's daughter) as his young (and cuckolding) wife May. A Rome-based English journalist, John Francis Lane, played a monk. The rest of the large cast was about evenly split between Italian and English players.

A reporter from the French magazine *Jeune cinéma* asked why the poet of *engagement* seemed intent on making films set in the past, costume epics that the interviewer dismissed as "as archaic form." Pasolini quickly dismissed the question and answered one not asked, speaking as the poet of *Le ceneri di Gramsci*, telescoping history and autobiography:

> If you open a newspaper, you can see that it is nothing more than a series of stories, just like Chaucer or Boccaccio. I connect these stories with the regret I feel for the loss of the world of the past. I am a disenchanted man. I have always been at odds with society. I have fought with it, and it has persecuted me, but it has given me some success as well. Now I don't like it anymore. I don't like its way of life, its quality of life. And so I regret the past. At my age, my point in life, I suppose it's almost conventional.

He continued:

> The world of Chaucer and Boccaccio hasn't yet experienced industrialization. There wasn't any consumer society, there weren't any assembly lines. There was nothing in common with the society of today. Except there was a kind of demand for sexual freedom owing to the beginning of a bourgeois revolution in the context of medieval society. But periods of freedom like that are doomed to finish quickly. In his old age, Boccaccio became a bigot. The explosion of freedom lasted only a few years. The same is true of today; it will last only a few years.[33]

Before "sexual politics" came into currency, Pasolini was practicing his own version. He offered what he called "a confession": "I see [in sexual relations] an incomparable fascination, and their importance in life seems to me so great, so absolute as to be worth dedicating to this more than a film." But there was more to depicting the sexual worlds of Boccaccio and Chaucer than celebrating what the modern world had lost.

He wrote, in self-explanation:

> There is in my last film work also a provocation. A provocation on several fronts. Provocation against the bourgeois and public "right-thinkers" . . . provocation also of the critics who, removing the sex out of my movies, take out everything and find them empty, not understanding that there is plenty of ideology, and how, right there in that enormous cock on the screen, right there over their heads which they do not want to understand.[34]

Making *Canterbury Tales*, he cooperated with the British press who were hungry to know how this controversial Italian intellectual understood Chaucer, and how he was like and unlike Boccaccio. He told British interviewers:

> Chaucer foresees all the victories and triumphs of the bourgeoisie, but he also foresees its rotten-ness. He is a moralist but he is ironic too. Boccaccio doesn't foresee the future in this way. He catches the bourgeoisie in its moment of triumph, when it is being born. In Italy, the bourgeoisie was [later] blocked. There were the princely courts and there was the Counter-Reformation. There was no bourgeois revolution, as there was in England. This is what Gramsci described. The Italian bourgeoisie suddenly found itself in the modern world, after the end of Fascism, dragged there by others.[35]

About this time, he told a conference organized by ACI, the Communist Party's cultural arm:

> I began to work in an epoch when what was expected of products was that they last a long time, without which they would not even be seriously considered. Now today I continue to work (without having adapted myself to the times) in an epoch in which, on the contrary, what is expected of products is that they be rapidly consumed.[36]

Pasolini chose seven tales from Chaucer: those of the Merchant, the Friar, the Cook, the Miller, the Wife of Bath's Prologue, the Reeve's Tale, and the Summoner. They provided ample occasion for nudity and hilarity, for showing how people survive however they can in difficult situations—all to a rebuke to Pasolini's contemporary middle-class audience.

For example, a miller who tries to cheat two poor students come to buy flour finds out, too late, that with the help of his wife and daughter, they have the best of him and of the women as well.

In another episode, Dick, Jack, and Johnny find a treasure under a tree and motivated by greed, Jack and Johnny send Dick on an invented errand while they plot his murder, so better to divide the treasure between them. They poison his wine; he does the same to them and—as payment for their sin—all drink and all three die.

The movie's closing episode is dedicated to the story of a priest who works with visions of Hell to terrorize a dying man into bequeathing his money to a monastery. His payment for betraying his vow becomes Pasolini's surrealistic nightmare, filmed on Etna: a mountain landscape where giant devils with horns and batlike wings defecate priests. On this vision of an inferno centered on excretion, one worthy of Hieronymous Bosch, the *Canterbury Tales* ends—save for a still close-up on the face of Chaucer-Pasolini, silent and smiling.

In April, Garzanti issued *Empirismo eretico* (Heretical empiricism), 300 dense pages of essays about his three obsessions: language, literature, and cinema, each treated in a blend of research, polemics, and rationality, of outward-directedness and confession. He included no bibliography, no list of other authors, and what few footnotes there were referred only to his other writings. In a hurry to communicate his idea, his sentences are often fragmentary, mazes of parentheses, sometimes ending in "etc." or even "etc., etc." Even more than in *Passione e ideologia*, the reigning inspiration throughout *Empirismo eretico* is Gramsci; its missing god, Freud.[37]

In the second section, "Literature," he printed "Comments on Free Indirect Discourse," on the problem of narrative point of view:

> The most odious and intolerable thing, even in the most innocent of bourgeois, is that of not knowing how to recognize life experiences other than his own: and of bringing all other life experiences back to a substantial analogy with his own. It is a real offense that he gives to other men in different social and historical conditions. Part of the equation of the whole world with the bourgeois world is just such insensitivity, manifested in linguistic as well as other forms of oppression.[38]

Reviewing *Mito e realtà* (*Myth and Reality*) by Mircea Eliade,[39] Pasolini had written that he had found "inebriating . . . a direct confrontation with other ways of thinking and of being"; he said he "sought contact with 'archaic people' [who] . . . are contemporaneous to us, because it is clear that nothing in us is destroyed but everything coexists."[40]

He also reprinted "The PCI to the Young!! (Notes in Verse for a Prose Poem Followed by an 'Apology')" and an essay on socialist realism entitled "What is Neo-Zhdanovism and What Isn't."[41] In the "cinema" section, he recast in definitive form his ideas on the semiotics of film language: three essays on the "cinema of poetry" as "the written language of reality" and his theory of editing, matters on which he had been thinking and writing since the first Pesaro conference of 1965.

He simplified the ideas considerably for the Parisian magazine *Avantscène* in November 1969:

> They say I have three idols: Christ, Marx, Freud. These are only formulas. In reality, my idol is REALITY. If I chose to be a director [*cineasta*] at the same time as a writer, that is because rather than express this *reality* through those symbols which are words, I preferred the cinema as a means of expression: to express *reality* through *reality*.

As for film editing, it "establishes contexts in which the relationships of contiguity and similarity are analogous to those of every other language of Art. In such a context the material object as the sign itself comes to have multiple meaning. . . ."

*Empirismo eretico* was received in near-silence. Umberto Eco accused Pasolini, the self-described "dilettante" linguist, of "singular semiotic ingenuousness." He completely rejected Pasolini's conclusion that all life is language, the manifestation of a General Semiology of Reality, in which everything is an iconic sign of itself.[42]

It was, perhaps, too frightening to take Pasolini literally, which was the way he demanded the words of his Dantean idea read: "Until that time when I am dead, no one can guarantee really knowing me, that is, give sense to my action which, therefore, as a kind of linguistic moment, is poorly decipherable."[43]

After the book's critical and commercial failure, Garzanti began to wonder if Pasolini's day had passed, and Pasolini began to wonder whether his long-time publisher did not take him for granted, putting too little effort into promotion. Although the reaction was one he might have expected, Pasolini was struck hard nonetheless. In May he made a lecture tour of Turin, Milan, and Rome (sponsored by the Italian Cultural Association), and declared, "I must say that I do not find myself in a happy moment of my intellectual life. I have a vague feeling, for example, that my words here lack both originality and authority."

On July 14, 1972, he told a reporter from *Il mondo*: "I now live outside of literary society. I no longer vote in the Strega. I am voluntarily on the sidelines. Literature, in its social aspect, does not interest me very much. As for the silence which surrounds me, it seems to me only a symptom of incompetence, of cowardice, or simply of hatred. . . ."[44]

After the release of *Canterbury Tales* and its undeniable success, he told a reporter from the newsweekly *Panorama*, "I was very unhappy when I made the film. To make a film full of vitality and sex, when one's spirit is anguished, is difficult." That summer, while he was filming in Bath, Ninetto explained that on his return to Rome he intended to marry.

In August, Pasolini wrote Paolo Volponi:

> I would have jumped with joy reading what you say about my poetry if I were not in a period when I am insane with grief. Ninetto is finished. After almost nine years, there is no more Ninetto. I have lost the meaning of life. I think only of dying and similar things. Everything has collapsed around me: Ninetto with his girl friend, ready for anything, even to go back to being a carpenter (without batting an eye); and I, unable to accept this horrendous reality, which not only destroys the present, but casts in a painful light all those years when I believed in joy, at least thanks to his joyful, unchanging presence. I beg you, tell no one. I do not want it talked about. You and Elsa [Morante] (and Nico) are the only ones who know.[45]

On August 20 Pasolini began composing *L'hobby del sonetto:* 118 sonnets in various states of draft and revision, which one critic says "can be interpreted as a long ballad on the agony of love caused by a 'vile' betrayal."[46] Written during the filming of *Canterbury Tales*, they bear the completion date "February 1973"; they have never been published in full.

In those that were printed, he called himself "a rag of a man" and talked of hanging himself in his garden by "a faithful and reassuring cord." He mourned "years lost," and begged for pity, "it being by now my inveterate / custom, I masturbate, within the burned-out / windings of the sweat-covered bed."[47]

At first he wished Ninetto's wife-to-be dead and ridiculed the young man's need for a "nest," something "petit-bourgeois": "It escapes me / the reason for so much fury in your mind / against this so chaste love of ours."[48]

He wanted Ninetto for himself, on any terms: "Is it the thorn of sex that heightens such / revulsion? / It's not a matter of sex, as you know, / but of a love which, like death, has clutching / hands."

Ninetto promised that with his marriage nothing fundamental, as he saw it, would change. Pasolini could not even lose respect for the one he called "the Inexpressible." "You never lacked dignity," he wrote, but the wound was no less deep for being self-inflicted.

Pasolini insisted that his friends understand, that they take his side, that they try to talk Ninetto out of marrying. Elsa Morante disagreed and, finally, accused him of selfishness. Pasolini wrote, "Elsa has certainly not understood that / I might die; or that I was so weak as to wish / to be consoled, or treated like a madman."[49]

He did not forgive her and a chill set in between them.

At first he wrote in pain:

> It's true that love should be holy,
> Elsa was right, and one should want nothing
> but the happiness of the one who is loved. But
> it's also true
> that there is no right not matched by a duty.

With time he wrote in resignation:

> I on the other hand live the reality
> reserved for the different [*diversi*, with double
> meaning] who have no alternative
> but to wish well to those who love.[50]

After the wedding in January 1973 (Pasolini stayed away, searching for locations for *Thousand and One Nights*), the crisis passed, at least temporarily; their relationship transformed into another. Desire gave way to affection and loyalty. Pasolini cast Ninetto as Aziz in the last part of the *Trilogy*, as a character he described as "joy, happiness, a living ballet." The couple named their first son Pier Paolo; their second, they named Guido.

Ninetto—whom he called "Lord" in the sonnets, in Shakespearean style—had served in effect to keep him from incessant cruising and all the dangers it brought. Pier Paolo had focused his emotional love on Ninetto, leaving to the streets a simpler search for physical ecstasy. That focus gone—replaced by another sort of love, to be sure— he returned to frequent anonymous encounters; perhaps he was now searching for more, for another Ninetto.

He began to frequent the most notorious hustlers' hangouts in Rome, where he was sure to find someone for sale, the sort of people from whom he might need to defend himself with the crowbar that Ninetto urged him to keep under the driver's seat. "But Pier Paolo said that would only incite the fascists . . . only show them that when they said that I was violent they were right. It would only justify their escalating violence, only invite it."[51]

For money, boys could always be found. Enzo Siciliano has written: "It seems that at the same time [as Ninetto's pending marriage] he was indulging in severely masochistic erotic practices." That conjecture is only that: Countless shady characters came forward after his death, proudly claiming that they had been his partner. His cousin Nico kept the pot boiling with remarks like "Pasolini's biography ought to be written in the key of sadomasochism, something no one has done . . . they miss the point."[52] But all this is rumor, self-promotion, and exhibitionism. Pasolini's name was a magnet for every sort of fantasist and madman, people more than willing to bury this part of the truth with him. All one can know for certain is what he wrote and said himself.

> It was almost two in the morning—the wind
> screamed through the *Piazza dei Cinquecento*
> as in a church—there wasn't even any refuse
> the only life at that hour—on the grass
>
> prowled the last two or three boys,
> neither Romans nor rustics, in search of the usual
> thousand *lire*, but as though without cocks—I talked to one of them in the car—
>
> a fascist, poor kid, and I struggled to touch
> his desperate heart.[53]

The 111-minute version of *Canterbury Tales* put into circulation differs radically from the one Pasolini submitted in competition as one of three official Italian entries to the Berlin festival of July 1972.

Enzo Ottone, editing supervisor in charge of making the prints, has recalled what happened behind the scenes:

> It was one of those movies that ends up being long. In fact, it was two hours and twenty minutes. Both [Nino] Baragli (the film's official editor) and I put the same pressure on him [Pasolini] . . . but as usual, with a dreamy smile, he told us we were crazy.
>
> We left for Berlin and arrived the day before the showing. In the hotel, Pasolini was immediately seized upon by a swarm of reporters and television people. The showing was to be an hour after our arrival, and I went to keep

an eye on the projectionist and sound man, to be sure they were efficient.

During the showing, as time passed it became clear that it was a beautiful film, but boredom began to show on the faces of some of the viewers, confirming my fear. Some of them even got up and walked out halfway through.

I went back to the hotel and waited for the interviews with Pasolini to end. He noticed in my expression that something was wrong. He freed himself for a moment from the reporters and asked me what was up. With a bit of sadism, I told him what had happened and repeated my fears for the showing of the next night and the gala to follow.

I will never forget his total lack of amazement; with his usual benevolent smile he said to me, "O.K., let them wait. Let's get to work."

We labored all-night on a wooden movieola, something from about 1939. Out of all the all-night stints I have put in, this was the one I will never forget. We cut twenty minutes. The film won first prize.[54]

Reporters at the post-viewing Berlin press conference asked if Chaucer's last-frame smile was "ironical, or one of pity for the human race?" Pasolini's answer might serve to describe his feelings about Ninetto's marriage:

My psychological stance toward the characters and the action in the film is a mixture of irony and compassion. Irony corrects the compassion and the compassion does the same for the irony. This is how the ending has to be viewed: the irony of the *Inferno* with all the devils and so on, followed by a final "Amen," which corrects the ironical violence of the scene in Hell.[55]

*The Canterbury Tales* opened in Benevento, deep in Campania, on September 2, 1972. A month later a magistrate ordered the first of three seizures that withdrew it from circulation. United Artists had too big an investment at stake not to fight back. An Establishment Neapolitan lawyer of impeccable political credentials, Alfredo de Marsico, was retained for the defense. According to Nico Naldini (press officer to the production), every southern Italian intellectual of any weight at all was called as a defense witness.

De Marsico told the court that although he, personally, did not like the film, it must be defended any way as a work of art. That helped. The coup de grâce came with an appearance by Eduardo de Filippo, the playwright whose rank in and around Naples equalled that of Pirandello in Sicily. By now an old man, he was considered an Italian national treasure, a man who could do no wrong, who was nothing less than the symbol (like Totò, but intellectual) of the genius of southern culture. With great fanfare, he hailed his old friend De Marsico in full view of the bench. Naldini, who had phoned De Filippo to ask his help, has said, "At that moment the case was won."

Within a week after the complaint was filed, on September 8, 1972, the court dismissed the charges. *Canterbury Tales* reentered circulation and rang up another 4.5 billion lire in Italian ticket sales.

But no sooner had the Benevento incident cooled than other complaints were filed, each of which had to be addressed: in Mantua, Viterbo, Frosinone, Venice, Latina, Bari, and Ancona. A "group of magistrates" saw the film in Florence and made official inquiry to Benevento, asking that the inquest be reopened.

On October 18, 1972, a month after it had exonerated the film, the Benevento court reversed itself. Pasolini was brought to trial along with producer Grimaldi and (as the law provides) Salvatore Iannelli, manager of the cinema that first showed the film. The judicial bill of particulars read as follows:

> There are, for example, shameless scenes depicting oral copulation between homosexuals, and those [scenes] of the Pasolinian depiction of Hell in which friars are expelled from the anus of devils as though excrement . . . the repeated depiction of the male organ with a hand on it, the loud farts of two naked lovers in the face of [the character] Assalonne, the long masturbation of the wife of Giannozzo, the urination by a young man from the balcony of a tavern on the heads of the roughnecks below, the monsters and animals who copulate sodomically with men. The film continually depicts sexual encounters and gestures which, were they enacted in a public place, would lead to the arrest of those involved *in flagrante delicto;* there is a steady insistence on organs and gestures of intense libidinous nature and of a deviant character with vulgar wording and many double meanings.[56]

It serves perhaps to remember that *Canterbury Tales* was not the only film locked up in 1972 in the name of public order. Also removed from Italy's screens were Warhol's *Trash* and Bertolucci's *Last Tango in Paris* (also produced by Grimaldi), the latter described in court as "obscene, indecent and catering to the lowest instincts of the libido."[57]

But a field day seems to have been declared on Pasolini in particular. The pent-up resentment of the currents in Italian society who detested all he stood for was unleashed. His encounter with the priesthood over his scene on the slopes of Etna was especially nasty. A Father Antonio Gambale had filed a separate action, claiming that the episode offended the Franciscans. Grimaldi took the stand, contesting every point of the accusation. Pasolini sent a statement, reprinted in *Paese sera*:

> I have never had any reason to offend friars or argue with them. On the contrary, they are a group of people for whom I have had feelings of *simpatia*

and tenderness. I say this now especially that one of their order has accused me in the name of the "honor," "decorum" and "reputation" of the order: these are not religious concepts, but petit-bourgeois ones.

He called the controversial scene "substantially innocuous and purely comical"; "The expulsion of the friars from the anus of the Devil is found in Chaucer, and I reproduced it on the screen exactly to the letter." He also explained that Chaucer "is for the Anglo-Saxon world what Dante is for us." Theology students at the Monastery of the Little Brothers in Benevento organized to offer an *amicus* brief to the prosecution, but their offer was declined.

After two days of hearings, at part of which Pasolini spoke for himself, he was absolved on October 20 because, yet again, "the act charged does not constitute a crime."

But *Canterbury Tales* stayed out of circulation, on the theory that it was not truly cleared so long as any legal action anywhere was pending. Grimaldi appealed to Italy's highest tribunal, the Court of Cassazione: A definitive interpretation was called for to decide whether section 622 of the Code of Criminal Procedure (against obscenity) was incompatible with three articles of the Italian constitution: number 21 protecting "liberty of expression," number 27 the presumption of innocence until proven guilty, and number 33, guaranteeing "the free circulation of works of art."

The proceedings dragged from October 1972 to April 1973. In the interim, the movie was not shown in markets wherever a complaint had been filed. In March—even after the film had been cleared in Benevento and appeal was pending in Naples—the prosecutor in the town of Teramo, in the Abruzzi, piled on his own, a fresh act of sequestration.

When the high court spoke, it said only seven words: *"Annulla senza rinvio, per violazione di legge."*[58] The Benevento's court reversal, freeing the film, was effectively undone; the film would remain blocked until all judicial proceedings against it, at every level, had worked their way through the courts, a matter of years. A parallel strategy was being pursued at the same time against *Last Tango*: Although cleared in Bologna, it faced new blockage because of lack of an absolute and final sentence.

By now completely fed up with what seemed judicial efforts to whitewash Italian film, the Association of Film Actors met at the PCI's Casa Della Cultura in Rome, issuing a statement joined by almost every segment of the film world. Communist parliamentarians introduced legislation to limit the magistracy's power and reform the procedures surrounding film censorship.

Further legal maneuvering dragged through the summer. On June 20 Pasolini took the stand in his own defense, arguing that his intention was "to contribute to the liberation of man and of society from sexual taboos." A week later the appeals court in Naples convened behind the closed police-guarded doors of the Alcione Cinema to view *Canterbury Tales*—twice.

On July 2 the court confirmed the acquittal granted at Benevento, holding that the film was "art" not "pornography." Pasolini said, "I am, naturally, happy for myself personally and for the work of my immediate future. But I am even more pleased at the general import of this judgment, which reinforces liberty of expression and artistic thought. I am also happy this sentence issued in Naples, confirming that city's high juridical, cultural, and human rank, a city so dear to me."

But the treatment of *Canterbury Tales* had undermined even Pasolini's stoicism. He announced, "I will write a book about my courtroom trials." On July 6 he told the newspapers:

> My film *Canterbury Tales* was judged four times and absolved four times: a first ban on September 8, 1972, then on October 20, 1972, absolution of the charge of obscenity by the Benevento appeals court, absolution of the charge of vilification of religion by the same court on February 3, 1973, and absolution of the charge of "obscene spectacle" by the appeals court of Naples last July 2 . . . this last ought to be definitive, and yet the film remains sequestered . . . [this is] a hypocritical and brutal injustice which threatens and offends not only an artist's freedom of expression but the same liberty of all citizens.[59]

During the Benevento trial, Dacia Maraini interviewed him for *L'espresso*. He had said the world had changed for the worse, so she asked him, "What would you propose to a young person who is born now and knows no other world save that in which he was born and lives?" He answered:

> I know it is absurd to look to the past. I am not a reactionary. But unfortunately I know there is nothing one can suggest to change this world. Capital does what it wishes. The peasant-craftsman's preindustrial world is destroyed and thus also its vision of the world and its sexual morality. But this was the world in which I was born and grew up and which I love. One cannot love abstractions.

Maraini asked, "Well, then do you think repressing is to be preferred to liberty so far as sex is concerned?"

And he answered:

I would never say anything like that in a theoretical sense. I only know that for now the false permissiveness at the heart of a false democracy is even worse than a repression that is brutal and without euphemisms.

Pasolini told the American critic Gideon Bachmann,

While not believing other things, I do believe in the concreteness of a relationship between him who does and him who exploits or receives, betweeen writer and reader. And this is a relationship between an individual and a second individual. This kind of relationship I still believe in . . . Perhaps I am believing in something that is about to end.[60]

But before turning to *Thousand and One Nights*, he addressed one last time the politics of Italy torn by attempted Right-wing coups, growing rage from extra-Parliamentary parties, and a new terrorism. Early in 1971, between *Decameron* and *Canterbury Tales*, he detoured to make a political film.

*December 12 (12 dicembre)* was billed as "from an idea by Pier Paolo Pasolini," with "subject and screenplay" by Giovanni Bonfanti and Maurizio Ponti. The production was underwritten by a Comitato Cineasti Italiani Contro la Repression, "The Committee of Italian Filmmakers against Repression"; in September 1970, Pasolini had shot part of a collective documentary called *Lo sciopero degli spazzini* (The garbagemen's strike) under the auspices of the group.

On December 12, 1969, a powerful explosion shook central Milan just after four in the afternoon: Sixteen people were killed, ninety-one injured. At first, police assumed a boiler beneath a sidewalk had exploded. The focus went immediately to a bomb, planted in the Banca Nazionale dell'Agricoltura in the downtown Piazza Fontana. The search for those responsible for the "massacre" generated enormous tensions: Attacks from far Left and far Right seemed equally plausible; neo-Fascist gangs armed with knives and chains circulated on Milan's Piazza San Babila; the city's public university had been taken over by what the middle class called "the Reds." Right-wing youths gathered in front of the Duomo to sing Mussolini's anthem, "Giovinezza," in celebration of what they took to be the start of a State-sanctioned Red Scare. The Interior Minister felt the need to assure Parliament that the police were in control, although they frequently harassed people without reason or warrant.

On December 15 ballet dancer and self-described anarchist Pietro Valpreda was arrested, as was railroad worker Giuseppe (Pino) Pinelli. The latter somehow "jumped" to his death in the courtyard of the police station, where he was being interrogated. That was the police version of how he died. In *Accidental Death of an Anarchist,* playwright Dario Fo codified what many believed a case of murder. Eight people connected to the case died shortly after their police interrogations. The Left was convinced Pinelli was eliminated better to cover up and draw attention away from an officially blessed drive to liquidate the opposition. It was, they were convinced, part of a "strategy of tension" meant to set the stage for a reactionary coup, one that included train-bombings over the previous several months and widespread arrests of known militant Communists.

Pasolini's film, *12 dicembre,* named for the day of the bomb attack, is a documentary pastiche which argues that a repressive Christian Democratic regime was conducting a systematic persecution of the Left. It opens with an interview with an old Communist militant Augusto Lodovichetti, accused and then absolved of plotting to assassinate Mussolini at the Milan Trade Fair in 1928. The film cuts to an interview with Pinelli's wife, Lucia: The parallel is heavy-handed, as Pasolini meant it to be.

Then to Trento where Fascists assault workers outside factory gates, including a stabbing at a factory; then to Sarzana, where a group of ex-Partisans, now old, wonder whether they ought not to "do justice themselves," since the republic they fought to create orders its police to fire on workers.

In the second part of the film's 104 minutes, Pasolini (who, along with others, did the filming) visits the marble quarries of Carrara. The workers speak directly into his shoulder-held Arriflex camera, asking why no one seems to care about their terrible working conditions. They explain the extreme danger of their job, the indifference of both the bosses and the State. Similar encounters follow with workers at a Montedison and a Fiat plant, who spell out the abysmal health and safety conditions in the auto paint shops. Then some small children appear, singing "The Red Flag."

The scene shifts to the Mezzogiorno: Barricades are going up in Reggio Calabria, police arrive, the barricades ignite, tear gas is shot against demostrators—the terrible days of 1960, of police chief Scelba returned. Cut to peasants arriving at Turin's Porta Nuova station, the arrival of the uprooted and unwelcome in the inhospitable North, where the factories wait to turn them into what the sound track calls "robots."

Cut to the attorney for the anarchist charged with the Piazza Fontana attack, who reminds the audience that the probably innocent Valpreda has been imprisoned two years without trial. Cut to meeting of the Fascist group Ordine Nuovo and close with a rally of Lotta

Continua in their Emilian stronghold of Bologna, the crowd singing and the speaker calling for "elimination of the Fascists."

Joining forces now with the very youth he had vilified satisfied a need for Pasolini. He separated the protesting generation into subgroups, clearly distinguishing the *borgata* boys—become thugs, what he would soon call "anthropologically mutated" monstrous transformations of those he had loved—from the committed, "conscious" young people within and at the Left edges of the PCI.

He sought out the company of other "militants," of those he called "exceptions" to the degradation of Italian youth. They were "among the students, among those who read . . . they are few but one can still find them." The main place to find them was among the membership of the Roman Youth Federation of the PCI, the capital's branch of an organization then near its peak, with more than a hundred thousand members nationwide. He began to accept invitations to speak at their round tables, and he invited them to his house for discussions. And why? He wrote in the "Apology" to *"Il PCI ai giovani!"*: "How else can I hope to have a relationship with them if not in this way?"

He was not going to get away with helping the far-Left fringe so easily. On February 23, 1973, he and fourteen others of the crew that made *12 dicembre* were formally charged with "inciting delinquency" and "stirring up hatred between the social classes," sections of the Rocco Code that passed through fifty years of Italian history unchanged. A judicial action had been lodged against him in Siena by a local lawyer named Arturo Viviani, named in a pamphlet called *Some Names to Remember* (*Alcuni nomi da ricordare*), produced by the Comitato Rivoluzionario Antifascista (Revolutionary Anti-Fascist Committee) and distributed as a supplement to the radical publication *Lotta continua*. But at the time the pamphlet appeared, Pasolini was no longer listed on the masthead and had not collaborated with the group for some time.

Lotta Continua's members were charged, and he with them, with inciting members of the armed forces to desertion. The Siena court threw out charges against Pasolini and the other defendants, "for not having committed [a chargeable] act."

In fact, Pasolini's relations with Lotta Continua were rocky, and his assistance given grudgingly. Two weeks after the *12 dicembre* trial's end, he wrote in *Panorama*, condemning his apparent fellow travelers with faint praise:

> The young people of Lotta Continua are extremists, agreed, perhaps even fanatics and insolently brutish from the cultural angle, but they are yanking

on the rope and it seems to me for this alone they deserve a hand. One has to want too much to obtain a little. It is always with some form of extremism that one manages to make progress.[61]

That May, Italian television broadcast *Uccellacci e uccellini* as the closing piece of a Totò retrospective. When *Paese sera* asked what Pasolini thought of it, he said, "Nothing at all. If you had not asked me, its TV showing would have passed by me unnoticed. I don't want anymore to think about the bad conscience of those who run the television; and I don't want any more anguish about the ambiguous destiny of those who work today in cinema (or literature), finding themselves halfway against society as it is and halfway inside it." Television flattened and leveled everything, and those who watched it "like a child reduced to idiocy, accept everything in the same way."

To those literary friends who accused him of making costly films without the right ideology, of having compromised, he answered, "I deny it . . . all my friends are ready to say 'Look, you integrate yourself,' as if I had found myself in a house on fire and they said: 'Look, you are burning. Don't worry, friends, don't bother yourselves so.' "[62]

In 1969 he told interviewer Jean Duflot, "I have been discovering, slowly as I study the mystics, that the other face of mysticism is precisely 'to do,' 'to act'. . . ."[63] *Trasumanar e organizzar* (To transhumanize and to organize): The book's very title was a facing of opposites. "Transhumanize" is Dante's term to designate the impossibility of describing the mystic discipline undertaken in the *Paradiso*. And "organize" is its opposite: community rather than solitude, action rather than contemplation.

The poems in his last book address the effort to bridge this gap:

> In fact, I don't believe any more in dialectics and contradictions, but in pure opposition. I don't pretend at all to transcribe in verse the ineffability which only life permits us to live and apprehend. And since I myself am neither a mystic nor a saint, I don't have any experience of what a seventh-heaven rapture might be. But I am more and more fascinated with the exemplary union accomplished by the major saints, St. Paul, for instance, between active and contemplative life. And it is that double face of the human, that double aspiration of the imaginary to both embody and reflect itself, that I try to capture through these notes torn from my daily life.

The poems of the first part he called "civic," a second group "more decidedly political . . . about the ambiguity of my ties with the revolutionary youth of today," and the third "a diary of my most intimate life," including poems "inspired by my friendship with Maria Callas." With heavy irony, he characterized the collection with a play on his initials: *Piccoli poemi politici e personali* (Little political and personal poems).

Worried by his experience with *Empirismo eretico*, he solicited a review from his old friend Anna Banti (Mrs. Roberto Longhi), editor at *Paragone*. But he remained so dissatisifed with the book's overall critical reception that he reviewed it himself. On June 3, 1971, in *Il giorno*, he wrote "This work by Pier Paolo Pasolini . . . risks passing with less notice than it deserves because it is not (as is said, horribly) 'utilizable'—*strumentalizzabile*—by anyone."

He continued, even though he said he wrote "seriously" while knowing that the act bore "a substantial amount of absurdity." He wrote of his poetry and of himself in the third person:

> His nostalgia for a mode of being that belongs to the past (and which sometimes imparts to Pasolini almost a shy and awkward reactionary vehemence) and will never be restored, and for a final victory of evil, is transformed into a cosmic pity for those younger brothers destined to live from now on existentially, by values that to Pasolini seem intolerable.

*Trasumanar e organizzar* was about that

> stratum of reality where reality is about to lose and dissolve itself, but is not yet lost and dissolved: all of its exigencies and its excuses, its passions, are there, physically present: one more step, and, like a cadaver in decomposition, they will become unrecognizable. . . .
>
> May we, therefore, conclude affirming that this refusal to know, to search, to want the truth, any truth (not relative ones, for Pasolini continues, Don Quixote-like, to fight for these), this Oedipal terror at coming to know, to admit, is what determines the strange and unhappy fate of this book, and probably all of Pasolini's work?[64]

With November 26, 1972, he started a weekly book review in *Tempo illustrato;* it ran three years, until January 24, 1975. Six months into the column,[65] he printed an appreciation of the work of Marianne Moore, in it discussing Charles Olson, Andrea Zanzotto, Ezra Pound. He wrote that John Ashbery is "the best of the 'New York School.' " During the fourteen months the column appeared, he offered not only information and opinon but analysis and argument on Strindberg and Gottfried Benn, on the important Turinese critic Giacomo Debenedetti (who not only had aided him but had been a friend to Gramsci and Gobetti), on Céline and Bassani, Dostoevsky and Gabriel García Márquez. He reviewed with equal ease the dead

Greek homosexual poet Cavafy, civil servant in Alexandria's municipal "Third Circle of Irrigation," and the living Italian heterosexual one, Andrea Zanzotto.

On January 28 he reviewed Calvino's *Le città invisibili* (Invisible cities):

> The first observation which comes to me to make is that this book is the book of a boy. Only a boy could have on the one hand a humor so radiant, so crystalline, so willing to do beautiful things . . . on the other, have so much patience—that of an artisan who at all costs wants to finish and refine his work. Not the old, but boys, are patient.[66]

Two weeks later Calvino wrote, thanking him for the appraisal, writing that if they had grown apart over the previous ten years it was because Pasolini had chosen to immerse himself in the cinema and in addressing daily events, whereas Calvino had gone to live in Paris, "in a great city where I know no one and no one knows I exist . . . I pass twelve hours a day reading, most days of the year."[67]

Pasolini's ninety articles, reviewing a range from Forster's *Maurice* (November 26, 1972) through Leonardo Sciascia's *Todo modo* (January 24, 1975), were later collected by his cousin, Graziella Chiarcossi, and published in 1979 under the title *Descrizioni di descrizioni* (Descriptions of descriptions). After all, books were descriptions of the world, and his reviews were therefore "descriptons of descriptions."

His mind played freely over whatever drew it, the book to be reviewed sometimes reduced to mere occasion. Reviewing *Maurice*, he discussed Osip Mandelstam, whose poetry he was reading at the same time for a review to follow a week after the one on Forster. He stretched to make a point about timing common to the two: The Edwardian Englishman afraid to print and the Russian poet muzzled by Stalin each—for completely different reasons—"missed [their] time. In each case, their work appeared past its right moment." In another piece, he noted that Huysmans' *A rebours* (in English, *Against Nature*; in Italian *Contracorrente*) and Nietzsche's *Thus Spake Zarathustra* appeared the same year, 1884. Both, he argued, made the case for a Superman.

He was often generous, especially to old friends. Reviewing Bassani's volume of verse *Epitaffio* (June 21, 1974), he offered layman's psychologizing about the author's feelings toward his father, rounded with fulsome praise: "It is perhaps Bassani's most perfect book," one "linguistically perfect."

The *Tempo illustrato* reviews give the lie (or at least render ironical) Pasolini's comment to an interviewer in January 1971: "You know, my intellectual horizon has narrowed. I don't read as avidly as ten years ago. The movies have made me less civilized, less cultivated, like all directors."

A year into the column, his review was based on " . . . [my] rereading, in the past few days, selections, in a handsome inexpensive edition from Gogol's *Dead Souls*, Pushkin's *Novels and Stories*, Balzac's *Eugénie Grandet*, and Flaubert's *Madame Bovary*." A week later he took up the madness of Dino Campana and of Pound, but in the key of politics asking why it was that "the literary Right" had appropriated the Italian, but Fascism could not "swallow this enormous Easter lamb" of Pound's "extremely great culture, even if, in an American way, a bit elementary . . ." [68]

Only one book, a novel, held his attention for two consecutive reviews: *La storia* (*History*, 1974) by his longtime close friend, his intellectual intimate Elsa Morante. [69] She had been a famous writer, not just in Italy, since the 1957 publication of her novel *L'isola di Arturo* (*Arthur's Island*, published in the United States two years later), which had gone into its fourteenth Italian printing by 1972. But *History* was her last, biggest, and most ambitious undertaking, the project to which she gave years of her life.

Morante's magnum opus aimed to do nothing less than deliver a sprawling narrative of many characters against the background of Italy's most dramatic recent history. She aimed to bring the Second World War to life, recount what it did to a group of people between 1941 and 1967. But this time and this ground were also Pasolini's turf.

He opened his review with a gasp of admiration at the novel's scale, "a heavy volume of 661 pages, and its 'subject' is no less than its title, History. It is difficult to imagine a subject more ambitious than this. . . ." Then he divided her work into "three books," the first "extraordinary beautiful . . . I read it during a rereading of *Brothers Karamazov* and it stood up to the comparison." But "the second 'book' leaves much to be desired, for it is nothing more than a mass of information thrown together almost, one would say, without having thought about it; the third book is lovely, even if very discontinuous."

Pasolini praised how Morante set character and history against one another and her rendering of "the incompatibility of life and of death"; he said she produced —in her alternation between biography and annals—"hallucinatory effects." But he rejected some three hundred pages as "lacking the necessary madness to make it self-sufficient." For her long excursus to work, he argued [like critic Erich Auerbach, without naming him] it must be so complete and so engaging that the reader forgets the "main" story line. "I give two examples," he wrote, "but might have listed dozens."

He saved his harshest words for Morante's use of dialects: "One boy presents himself as Bolognese but is in fact from Mantua, but he speaks a kind of Veneto . . . the Roman spoken by Nino and his friends resembles even (Morante will excuse me, but here one must be hard) nothing so much as that of certain scribblers for *Il messaggero.*"

To many, likening her so carefully conjured dialogue to journalistic hackwork seemed to be going too far in the name of truth. He pressed on, almost with the cruelty of a lover betrayed, or one betrayed by a friend when betrayed by a lover:

> There is nowhere, not a corner of *Alta Italia* in which *"cadere"* [to fall] is said *"cader."* There, in upper Italy, it is *"cascare"* which has triumphed, eliminating every other competing form. That David says *"cader"* offends the reader: but it offends him even more. Where is Morante's great love for him [her character] if she is too lazy to make the slightest effort to listen to how he speaks? It means that there is something pre-constituted in this love, preventing the arrival of the detailed and the concrete, in the face of some sort of Law of Love.

He concluded that she ought to have worked on the novel "another year or two."

The second half of his two-part review effected the final demolition. Morante was simply not up to the ambition of her book. Her "personal ideology"

> shows itself to have extreme weakness and fragility at that moment when it becomes translated into a popular novel, applied, vulgarized. Even though masked behind a certain humorism, she screams in a childish way in the narrative part of the text; and when she "puts words into the mouths" of her characters, they become totally aphasic.

He closed this half of his critique—and their friendship, for they never spoke again—with the claim that she had lost "all credibility."

*Thousand and One Nights (Il fiore delle mille e una notte)* offered an antidote, both personal and intellectual, to Italian reality. The stories were long ago and far away; Pasolini had read the fables (some of which he had encountered as a boy) while shooting *Decameron*.

To film them, he spent from February through May 1973 in India, Iran, Eritrea, Ethiopia, Nepal, in places called Salif, Hodeida, and Zabid in "Arabia Felix"—the land of the Queen of Sheba, North Yemen. Box office for *Decameron* and *Canterbury Tales* made the producers dare to spend; Grimaldi and United Artists knew they had a sure thing. Imitations, sometimes pornographic, were already under way. The budget of $1.2 million was nothing excessive, as epics went. No stars, few expensive costumes, and as for the travel: "It is cheaper to film in such places than to reconstruct them," Grimaldi says. By mid-1988, the movie's worldwide film rentals had broken $6 million and the videocassette was released.

But there were far too many tales in the original *Alf Laylah wa-Laylah,* and Pasolini had to make what he called "a strange, critical reading" of the stories to generate a narrative axis around which to organize them. Specialization and scholarship were not the point: He used the story of Aladdin and of "Ali Baba and the Forty Thieves," which are not part of the official canon of the *Thousand and One Nights*. Method was all: He believed structuralism "allows one to analyze a text in its own right, how it relates to its context, how it works, how its universe is formed." It allowed him to make his pastiche.

If his *Oedipus* started in Africa and ended in Bologna, why could not his "Arab film" also include sequences shot in the Nepalese Himalayas? At a press conference at the Cannes Festival, following the film's premiere on May 20, 1974, he explained that locale hardly mattered:

> I had no intention of telling the stories from within the Arab world . . . one popular culture is, for these purposes, like another. My polemic was with the dominant Eurocentric classes. It is pointless to make distinctions between Syrian culture and Ethiopian when those societies are equally distant with respect to the Europe-centered one.

His working methods were closely studied and meticulously reported by film critic and historian Gideon Bachmann:

> Behind the camera, which he operates alone and himself, he seems hurried, tormented by the limits of space and time. He works fast, and with great precision, and he seems to want to do everything himself. Where other directors would do ten scenes in a day, he shoots forty: because the frames are already present in his head, and transferring them to film is only a slightly

boring operation, an obstacle to be overcome, standing between himself and the viewer. It is as though he wanted to rid himself of an obsession in the fastest possible way.

    Two cameras are always prepared and at the ready: a simple Arriflex 35s, without sound. While one is being loaded, he moves about with the other . . . the director of photography only measures the light. The camera operator's job is only to hand him various lenses. He organizes everything himself. The others help arrange matters, with minimal instructions, at the last moment. His technique is deeply simple. Nothing is fantastic or invented at all, save for the costumes and the countryside.[70]

But the fantastic—and perhaps something more, an alternative set of values—was there in the Third World, waiting for him in the unadorned everyday. While the seventies brought the committed film of social ideas and personal consciousness locked in conflict, now he seemed to be going the opposite direction with the *Trilogy*. When asked whether he had abandoned the social commitment of his earlier work, he became impatient: "I'd say that was shit. Just lazy. That person [making such an accusation] would plainly be unable to see that the most ideological films of my life are these three. Everything I am and am not, everything I love and do not, everything I wish existed and wish did not is in them."

He said he loved the Arabian tales' "telling for telling's sake, each time ending on an unexpected detail." That detail was often a quirk of destiny, not a result brought into being by rational human will. The many plots, and plots within plots, work as a series of Chinese boxes or Russian dolls, one tale passing, ever deeper, into another, whose meaning echoes those before and hints at what will come after.

Film historian Peter Bondanella: "In the original text, the narrative evolved from a series of stories, each told by a woman to her husband to escape execution . . . Pasolini frames his stories within a single episode in the original: the Tale of Nur-ed-Din and Zumurrud."[71]

The slave-girl Zumurrud (played by Ines Pellegrini) is sold at auction in an Arab square but refuses to accompany the ugly old man who has bought her, preferring instead to become the property of the boy Nur-ed-Din, played by Franco Merli. Pasolini described him to a reporter from *L'unità*[72] as "a boy from Corleone [in Sicily] who has the innocence of his sixteen years in the physique of an eighteen-year-old." Zumurrud consigns to Nur-ed-Din a cloth she has woven that under no circumstances is to fall into the hand of "a man with blue eyes."

Fate being what it is, it does just that: The mysterious blue-eyed stranger drugs the boy, kidnaps Zumurrud, and parks her with a merchant-collaborator. She is then stolen away by someone she does not know but, disguising herself as a man, escapes. In the fabulous way of fables, she arrives in a city, takes a wife, and is declared king.

Providence—always at work, never explaining nor explained—brings the blue-eyed man to her wedding feast, set in the opulence of a tiled, Moorish palace. He is taken and crucified.

The scene shifts, or rather tunnels, inward, to a tale anterior to the tale we have seen. A mysterious lady, engaged to help Nur-ed-Din out of his troubles, tells him the story of the princess Dunya (played by Abadit Ghidei) and her confusing dream of a dove captured, caught and struggling in a net. We meet a young prince named Tagi (Francesco Paolo Governale), who appears only to encounter the young Aziz (played by Ninetto); he tells a tale as well, that Aziz was going to marry his cousin Aziza, when he fell in love with a mysterious woman, seen at a window. The self-sacrificing Aziza assists him to interpret the strange hand signals of the woman so that he finally conquers her, makes love with her. He returns home—to exotic rooms with hunks of stained glass, the classic apartment of Sana'a, capital of Yemen—to find Aziza dead.

Aziz is taken prisoner by a woman who forces him to marry her. A year passes and Aziz-Ninetto returns to his beloved, and she gives him a parchment that Aziza had left behind. On it is a drawing by the princess Dunya, with whom Aziz is infatuated but in vain. The two tales, which seemed distant, intersect.

The prince Tagi hears about the parchment and the princess who drew it and announces he must know Dunya. He goes to the marketplace and recruits two workmen: Shahzman (a prince in disguise, played by Alberto Argentino) and Yunan (also a prince, played by Salvatore Sapienza). He orders them to construct a mosaic in the tower of Princess Dunya's garden.

As they work, a tale unfolds within this tale. Shahzman tells his story: One day, having escaped the assault of bandits, he falls through a trapdoor leading to an underground palace where a princess is being held against her will by a demon. He makes love with her and, in his haste to escape before the demon's return, leaves his shoes behind. The demon (played by Franco Citti in a bright red wig) returns to the scene of the princess' betrayal, and, before the young man's eyes, he slays her.

The demon-Citti then embraces (prince) Shahzman, which causes them to fly through the air (Pasolini purposely let the process shot show itself for what it was), landing in a desert, where the evil character turns the handsome prince into a monkey.

He is returned to human form by a king's daughter who captures him and lifts the curse. Shahzman tells his tale while laying the pieces of the mosaic. As the picture comes into completion, we see that it is the depiction of the dove caught in the net. Is the dream in reality or reality inside a dream?

Now Yunan, the other workman, recounts his story. In fact a prince, he is on an expedition to visit an island ruled by his father, a king. The expedition sails near a giant rock dominated by a gigantic warrior of bronze who draws all ships who pass him onto the rocks and their destruction. Yunan kills the monster, who topples into the sea, followed by his island which sinks without trace. Yunan comes to a safe landing and comes upon a trapdoor. Underground, he finds a splendid chamber, all gold and turquoise, and within a terrified boy whose father has hidden him there to avoid a terrible prophecy.

It seems the boy is cursed to die a the hand of "a man with no eyes." In fact, Yunan sleeps with the boy (protectively, without hint of sexual relations) and with his eyes closed—in a trance—stabs him to death. Despondent at what he has done, he—like Shahzman who has fled the riches of his father's court—rejects his past and his rank.

The mosaic is finished: Dunya comes to see it, recognizes her dream, and (as destiny wills) returns Tagi's love.

Meanwhile, the first pair of lovers—Zumurrud and Nur-ed-Din—are still apart and seeking one another. A lion and Nur meet in the desert and the beast (special effects again shown for what they are, not Hollywood-polished) leads the boy into the city where Zumurrud now reigns (in male drag) as king. She recognizes him, but he does not know her. After teasing him and threatening him with what seems to him male rape (they are both men, he thinks), she reveals herself and the two are joyfully reunited.

The twists and turns of the complex plot bring the viewer by film's end back to its start. Its very complexity and apparent irrationality appealed to Pasolini; the splendor of Arabian architecture, bareness of its landscapes, and sheer exoticism of scenes filmed at Kathmandu captured his eye, as they do the viewer's:

> I wanted to approach the irrational as the revelation of life which becomes significant only if it examined as a "dream" or a "vision." I have made a realistic film . . . but also a film where the characters are in a trance, beset by an involuntary anxiety regarding the events which happen to them. This anxiety makes their passivity somehow strangely erotic. [73]

The eroticism appears in scenes of lovemaking, which never come even close to contemporary notions of pornography. On the contrary, lovers couple with joy—naturally, even wholesomely. The nude body, both male and female, appears frontally and in full length, but never seems out of place or forced.

A polemicist by now ready to strike the first, preemptive blow, Pasolini raised the issue of nudity and sex in the very publicity brochure distributed at the time of the film's release.[73]

> How truly inferior are "religious interests" and "political interests" to sexual interests! The latter at least have the quality of being innocent, of preceding social conditioning, which often cheapens and lessens them. But even the feelings of guilt produced in the spectator who chooses to go and see a film which freely depicts sexual relations, even that is infinitely more free than any others, if for no other reason than that it concerns the thing which, in life, a man in some way always puts above all else.[74]

In September 1973 he showed *Thousand and One Nights* incomplete (the Nepalese sequence was added later) to a gathering in Venice called "Days of Italian Cinema," a group of filmmakers organized in protest against the institutions dominating film production. In the debate that followed, he was more or less accused (this time by intellectuals, not the pulp press) of being a pornographer. It was another way of saying he had "sold out" to mass culture, had become a success.

He answered:

> I am proud to be at the head of a school (or so they say) of pornographic films. Any pornographic film is better than any ordinary television program; there is much more reality in the ugliest porno film than in all the programming of a year of television. Another thing . . . they say that this genre of Boccaccioesque porno films is already exhausted. The reality is that I have, if anything, opened the door to the films of Bertolucci. . . .[75]

So much for *Last Tango in Paris*, which his former "student" made sure Pasolini saw before its general release in 1972. But Pier Paolo dismissed it and right to Bertolucci's face, calling it "merely mass entertainment," "a subcultural product."

That which Pasolini called "the quality of being innocent" contributed to *Thousand and One Nights'* winning the Cannes Film Festival's Special Jury Prize. On June 20, 1974, the film premiered at the Capitol cinema in central Milan, followed by a discussion in which Pasolini participated.

During shooting, he told a reporter that he expected this film, at long last, to pass unchallenged. "Those who make love [in the movie] are those whom the bourgeoisie consider racially inferior. If there are

two English people, as in *Canterbury Tales,* or two self-declared bourgeois as in *Last Tango in Paris,* the judges are severe. When those
making love are two blacks or two Arabs, the judges shut an eye."[76]
But it was not to be so simple.

Five days after the Milan premiere, Angelina Briosci of Milan
denounced the film to the local district attorney as "nothing more
than . . . vulgarity and exhibitionism of sexual organs, all very
clearly photographed."[77] She had somehow seen a sneak preview;
*Thousand and One Nights* was blocked even before its national release, a kind of record. But matters went better than in the past—
on August 7 the prosecutor threw out the complaint and the film was
officially free to circulate throughout the country.

But the press had copy about Pasolini as pornographer. Accusation, for many, equaled condemnation.

To praise it, a Milanese assistant State's attorney remarked that
*Thousand and One Nights* offered: "the representation of a sexuality
and affection [that in the film is] not sick . . . because liberated from
the notion of sin, out of the Christian tradition." *L'osservatore romano*
answered: "The idea of sin as product of some false morality, from
which to liberate oneself? Then immorality would not exist anymore . . . how many fewer crimes would pass through the hands of
district attorneys if the concept of sin had more consideration in
society! Could it be that these people cooperate in undervaluing it?"[78]


Filming the episode of Alibech for *Decameron* (it was later cut) on
his last Sunday morning in North Yemen,[79] Pasolini turned to use up
what he called "leftover film." His sixteen-minute documentary on
the threat to Yemen's "intact" cities was, he said, "an appeal to
UNESCO and to the authorities of the young Democratic Republic of
Yemen." Sana'a, the capital, was encircled by gigantic walls fast
disappearing under development; within them was a city whose fabric
had hardly changed in five hundred years—"a savage Venice in the
dust, with Saint Mark's without the Giudecca."

Writing to his mythical fifteen-year-old Gennariello two years later:
"Maybe it's a professional deformation, but I felt the problems of
Sana'a as my own."

But those who are conscious of the beauties of primitivism are not
the primitives.

> My estheticism is indivisible from my culture. Why deprive my culture of
> one of its elements even if it is spurious and perhaps even superfluous? It

completes a whole. I have no scruples about saying so, because in the last few years I have become convinced that poverty and backwardness are not by any means the worst ill. We are all mistaken on this score. Modern things which capitalism has introduced into the Yemen have not only made the Yemenites physically clowns; they have also made them more unhappy. The Iman, the banished king, was horrendous; but the disgusting consumerism which has taken his place is no less so.

This give me the right not to be ashamed of my "sense of the beautiful."[80]

He wrote that he could find "no Yemeni [who] knows that Sana'a is worthy, let's say, of Venice. One city, Taiz, has already been completely destroyed and rebuilt. It ought to be stupendous. Now it is instead one of the ugliest cities in the world. . . ."[81] He lent his support to an "Italo-Arab commission for the defense of Yemeni architectural heritage" and declared "Yemen is the most beautiful country in the world."[82]

In his commentary, sounding behind slow pans over the city, Pasolini says the "desire for modernity . . . had *entered* the country, was not *born* there." He continues:

in the midst of all this [indigenous beauty] the expressive, horrible presence of modernity—a leprosy of chaotically planted lamp-posts—huts of cement or corrugated iron put up without logic where once there were city walls— public edifices of a terrible twentieth-centruy Arab style, etc . . . plastic objects, tins, shoes, textiles of miserable cotton, tinned pears (from China), transistors.

Having declared in the voice-over that the city is of ". . . an unreal perfection, almost excessive and exalted . . . beautiful like Venice, or Urbino, or Prague," he cut to an interview with citizens of Orte, a medieval Italian town once intact but undergoing its first new construction, its so-called progress. One man says he is happy at the new buildings going up; another believes "they" are destroying the place.

Pasolini closed by appealing to UNESCO to "save the walls of Sana'a . . . in the name of the true, even if as yet inexpressed, will of the Yemeni people. In the name of simple men whom poverty has kept pure. In the name of the grace of obscure centuries. In the name of the scandalous revolutionary force of the past."[83]

The Orte footage came from a second documentary, made after his return from filming *Thousand and One Nights*. It was commissioned by the RAI for a series called *The Form of the City*; his was entitled *La forme di Orte*. This time an unseen camera recorded Pasolini as he looked through his camera pointed at the town skyline. He and we see a center of fewer than ten thousand inhabitants, its still preserved pre-Renaissance buildings rising over an Etruscan base, all perched on a rocky outcrop over a tributary of the Tiber. Ninetto is with him and listens as Pasolini explains, "Orte must be defended as the entire city of Orte, and not its single monuments. At this point a great palace, a great church are worth a little wall, a capital, a tabernacle, a logge . . . they are worth the farmhouses of the peasants . . . this had to be defended as [would be] a church."[84]

The film cuts to Sabaudia, on the sea south of Rome; there, in the summer of 1973, Pasolini had gone with Dacia Maraini to write *Thousand and One Nights*. The town was a centerpiece of Mussolini's public works program, raised in 1933–1934 from scratch, on land reclaimed from swamp. It had stayed almost intact since the war; one could still read the Fascist rhetorical texts carved on the faces of its buildings.

Pasolini now explains "to Ninetto" (who served as audience) that while that regime thought it was enforcing its values, they were "only a small bunch of stupid criminals" whose city reflects something deeper than they could conjure or control, something that predated and survived them. Sabaudia—too blithely rejected after the war, because a Fascist creation—is the product of a society "provincial" but intact, one that lived normal life and values, mostly ignoring the surface structure raised by Fascism. Much worse, he says, are the democratic regimes, which in the name of freedom and liberty in fact succeed—as Italian Fascism never did—in homogenizing human character and all of life. The process is happening fast, he says, and will be over "in the course of ten, twenty years . . . And one morning, we will wake up and it will be too late." With that, he turns and walks toward the sea, as though to disappear into it as in the poems. The film ends.

Before *Thousand and One Nights* was finished, he started making detailed notes on a film to be called *Ta kai ta*—from an ancient Greek, meaning "This and That"—later provisionally changed to the equally problematic *Porno-teo-kolossal*. It would star Ninetto and Eduardo de Filippo. He even summoned reporters to the set of *Salò* in May 1975, announcing that Eduardo and Ninetto would follow an "abstract comet, which represents ideology," through Naples, Milan, Rome, and Paris, that it would be a fable 'in the tone of *Uccellacci e uccellini*.' "

He also began to talk about *Saint Paul*. Its treatment was already written, left in publishable form at his death. And after that? As early as 1968 he told an interviewer, "A life of Socrates would be ideally my ultimate film—I would like it to be the culmination of my cinema experience."[85] He had told Dacia Maraini, "My mother was like Socrates for me. She had, and has, a vision of the world that is certainly idealistic and idealized. She really believes in heroism, in charity, in pity, in generosity. And I absorbed all this in a manner almost pathological."[86] What better farewell to "the language of reality" than one pedagogic pederast's story of the most famous of pedagogic pederasts? And after? Disappear? Like Rimbaud? He saw a giant boat for sale in a Persian Gulf port one day during the shooting of *Thousand and One Nights* and talked of buying it, of settling in the region.


He hardly noticed *Thousand and One Nights*' commercial fate. The *Trilogy* done, he seemed to accelerate even more: a human version of the phenomenon known to physics as "time dilation." According to this aspect of the theory of relativity, time appears to slow down almost to a stop for bodies that approach the speed of light.

Starting with the summer of 1972 he frequently traveled alone to Chia, shutting himself in his glass-walled study overlooking the trees. At a plain trestle-table, he worked at his peeling Lettera 22, writing his novel. And why *Vas*? Zigaina believes Pasolini took the word for the ancient alchemist's crucible, the container where "amplification" is conducted—the "vase"—spherical to imitate the cosmos, the egg, the uterus—where reality is forged. And Paul had called himself Vas—the container of the Spirit.

Pasolini wrote, "My hallucinatory, infantile, and pragmatic love for reality is religious to the extent that its base, somehow as though by analogy, is like some kind of immense sexual fetish."

That "fetish" would be given its performance in the novel. He spoke little about the book but intimate friends like Moravia knew he had 600 pages and intended to write a great many more. Its precedents would include Giacomo Leopardi's enormous daybook, the *Zibaldone*, run to 2,882 pages in the Mondadori edition; Leopardi, his fellow countryman and fellow Romantic, fellow lyric poet, and probably fellow homosexual. The Arab-Israeli war of 1973 figured in it, and the ensuing oil shortage in Italy. A working title was also *Petrolio* (Oil). He said that he intended to state in plainest terms how it all was: the repetition of oral sex, realistic scenes of the protagonist as both the "passive" partner "servicing" boys and the active partner as well.

The inevitable scandal would be merely incidental: The Crow had to be consumed to nourish, and the sinning Christian saint had to be butchered—just as in Medea's time when human limbs were spread of the fields to nourish the land and its people.

And political power—what he soon called "*Il Potere*"—would be exposed, names named, secrets revealed. He sketched a party at the Quirinal Palace, residence of Italy's presidents—a *mondano* gathering of literary and political figures. The scene was already predicted in *Plan of Future Works* at the end of 1963, a scene symbolizing (in Dantean Fashion) "the Vulgar." He asked Paolo Volponi, who had made a career at Olivetti, to explain the special language of senior executives and how big companies were structured. He told him the novel's main character was to be a manager "in crisis," another a banker. The background was to be the dependence of Italy's industrial society on (imported) oil and—these are the days of the first OPEC embargo—its collapse. "And there will be ordinary people, almost inarticulate . . . not speaking dialect because by now the dialects are finished [thanks to] the horrendous language of the television news, advertising, official statements. . . ."[87]

Just as *La divina mimesis* had required a "yellowed iconography" to be complete, so *Vas* needed photographs. He proceeded with the writing, waiting for Reality to make him that important "gift," sure in the knowledge that it would.

# 23

*There are two modes of knowing, those of argument and experience.*

—*Francis Bacon*

*Take them all in all, I detest the Italians beyond measure . . . they are Yorick's skull with the worms in it, nothing of humanity left but the smell.*

—*John Ruskin*, in a letter to his father, 1845

# *LUTHERAN LETTERS*
# TO THE ITALIANS

In Milan for a screening of *Thousand and One Nights*, Pasolini met Giulia Maria Crespi, heiress of the old-line family that owned the *Corriere della sera*. He had used her villa as the setting for *Teorema*, although she later said, "Had I any idea what it was about, I never would have given my permission." Gaspare Barbiellini Amidei, one of the daily's three vice-directors and its chief cultural and literary editor, was also present.

Crespi, like many members of the Italian *alta borghesia* (especially in publishing, the industry of ideas) was swept up in the radical-chic of the time. One seasoned reporter has said, "In those years, every elegant party had to have someone there who talked revolution. Pasolini fascinated—alone on the opinion-making Left, he was *contra-corrente* [against the current]."[1]

It was agreed that he would, on occasion, contribute a piece of a certain length to the newspaper, the topic to be of his choice; the space would be called "Tribuna Aperta." When his first article arrived, Barbiellini Amidei suggested to his boss, editor-in-chief Piero Ottone, that it run on the first page. The next day Crespi called and praised it, but she asked, "Why the first page?" Still, she accepted the explanation that it had been the editors' judgment that it belonged there.[2]

Piero Ottone (a bit more than two years in the editor-in-chief's job) wanted to make a "new" *Corriere:* less stuffy, more cosmopolitan. He faced pressure from *Il giorno* and, from 1976, a real challenge from a new daily, *La repubblica,* on the political center-Left. Journalistic innovation was in the air: In these months, the *Corriere* decided for the first time not only to print reader letters but to let editors answer them. Another innovation would be these regular articles from Pasolini: less frequent than those of staff columnist but more than just the occasional contributor. The Ottone model was a perhaps idealized disinterested press of Gladstonian Liberalism: He understood that the traditional working class was disappearing, that communism was entering the Italian mainstream at the ballot box—and that Pasolini (whom Ottone never met) was unique. His presence would sell newspapers. To calm and to explain to readers who were shocked to see the front page of the daily of Italy's *ben pensante* given over to such a figure, he wrote an Editor's Note:

> We came to do so precisely in our search for less conformist and less traditional voices. I have said that we believe in the circulation of ideas: who can promote the circulation of ideas if not the intellectuals, who are the first artificers of ideas in society?

The *Corriere* articles became, even as they appeared, the most discussed phenomenon in Italian journalism since Gabriele d'Annunzio's 1915 *Corriere* pieces, calling for Italian intervention in World War I. The symmetries, at least superficially, were noteworthy: Both "civil poets" (D'Annunzio on the Right, Pasolini the Left), both deeply narcissistic, both exceptional because they were poets become public figures, household names. But Pasolini hated everything

D'Annunzio stood for: bombast, rhetoric, posing. And yet he was now on the reverse side of the same coin.

On the tenth anniversary of Pasolini's death, the newspaper brought out a special supplement "Pasolini and the *Corriere*." As though they were already something of major historical note, it reprinted his most controversial pieces. The paper was proud to have published them—it was part of its claim to greatness. By then, these articles were understood to have set the agenda for Italy for several decades to come. His metaphors had finally bridged the gap between journalism and literature, between thought and action.

In 1973 Pasolini published only four "Tribuna Aperta" pieces in the *Corriere*. The first, "Contro i capelli lunghi" (Against long hair), claimed that the symbolism of long hair had changed. No longer did it mean Left; now it was "something equivocal, Left-Right": "Long hair says in its inarticulate and obsessed language of nonverbal signs, in its hooligan iconicity, the "things" [*cose*] of television or of commercials for products."

"Hooligan iconicity," on the front page of the nation's leading daily. A second article, on May 17, was called "Il folle slogan di Jesus jeans" (The crazy slogan of Jesus jeans): A clothing manufacturer took the Scriptural admonition "He who loves Me follows Me" and ran it with a close-up from the rear of female buttocks in tight jeans. If the ad campaign had not existed for Pasolini's excoriation, he would have had to invent it.

The third article, on December 12, was "Sfida ai dirigenti della televisione" (Challenge to the television executives), including what he told a French interviewer was "a Swiftian proposal—that the bosses of the RAI . . . and the professors . . . be eaten." Enlightenment antecedents to this, his program to give conformism a black eye, were Diderot and Voltaire. But the Enlightenment had made little headway in Italy. He did not cite the great rationalists or the German who hovers over the articles, Theodor W. Adorno, who had already emphasized the critical role of exaggeration, desirable because it "brought into bold relief the tensions in a force-field or constellation rather than smoothed them over."[3] Pasolini's disruption of the "force-field" of Italian life would bring other Swiftian proposals in the *Corriere* and in *Il mondo*, in poetry, debates, interviews, and on the screen; it was the working out of his destiny of opposition.

Starting in June 1974, Pasolini sped up his *Corriere* appearances. And in March he began the "letters" to the imaginary Gennariello in the *Corriere*'s sister magazine "of politics, culture, and economics," *Il mondo*. These were, like those in the daily, tied to the events of that day, to *attualità*. And this time the readership was not the converted, as with *Vie nuove*, but Italy's elites.

The procedure was that Pasolini would tell Barbiellini Amidei, on the telephone, what he proposed to address next, a few days before the column was due. They discussed his idea, always "serenely," according to Barbiellini Amidei, and the work always appeared on time.

Only two *Corriere* pieces he submitted did not run; one was on the "presumed" (and, for the editor, "absurd") homosexuality of Saint Paul and the other a profile ("of a hardness and irony really destructive," according to Barbiellini Amidei) "of another contributor to the *Corriere* whom he did not name but everyone could have identified." It was probably journalist and TV commentator Enzo Biagi. Ottone believed that piece libelous. According to Ottone, "When I told Pasolini what I thought, he dropped the idea immediately." Had it appeared, its target would have joined Pagliuca, Pedoti, Di Gennaro, and Cournot, those who attacked Pasolini at their own peril.

In one article satirizing the language of Italian politicians, Pasolini ended with a swear word. Barbiellini Amidei told him that he liked the piece very much but believed that single world "somehow contradicted what he had written about it."

> The author of novels where slang and liberty of expression had offered critics in the past so many occasions for saying that his was a vulgar literature, this author spoke to me for half an hour about that word without wanting to say it. At a certain point, I said to him, "Listen Pasolini, if you think I am going into all this because I think the word '*stronzo*' [shit] must never appear in the *Corriere*, then I take offense and let's leave it there." He said he never thought that and added, "Listen, take out the word."[4]

His articles had a theme, or rather several aspects of one grand disillusionment. One was the disaster modernism had brought to Italian cultural and regional diversity. A second was religious: exhortation to the Church to cut its ties to the economic state.

He wrote (September 22, 1974): "Never has Marx's statement that capitalism transforms human dignity into exchange goods made more sense than today." The Church, he argued, ought to become the leader, "the guide, grandiose but not authoritarian," of all who reject "the power of the new consumer society, which is completely irreligious." "It is this refusal that the Church could best symbolize by returning to its origins, i.e., to opposition and revolt. Either do this or accept a power that no longer wants it—that is, commit suicide.[5]

Two weeks later (October 6, 1974) he argued that because the Church was "no longer useful to Power," it might do well to consider separating itself from the state and bureaucracy of the Vatican:

> If—making a gift to the Italian State of the great (folkloristic) stage set of the present Vatican, and giving the junk (folkloristic) of stoles and capes, of *flabelli* and gestatorial seats to the workers of Cinecittà—the Pope outfitted himself like a *clergyman* [in English] with his collaborators in some cellar in Tormarancio or the Tuscolana [borgatas], not far from the catacombs of Saint Damian or Saint Priscella—would the Church then cease to be the Church?[6]

A third theme, wrapping over all, related to the other two as they were to each other: personal mores and sexuality. Taken together, the article articulated a kind of thinking vision groping toward what he called "a new way of being progressives."

Pasolini did not live to see the scandal of Lockheed's payoffs to Italian Cabinet ministers nor the exposé of "P2"—the "lodge" of politicians, senior police officers, and industrialists apparently intent on a coup d'état; nor the willingness of Christian Democracy to sacrifice Aldo Moro to keep him quiet and his accusing letters secret. Nor did he live to see the PCI's record high vote of April 1976 (38.7 percent for the Christian Democrats; 34.4 percent for the PCI) and the party's subsequent near-collapse in the following decade; he did not live past "the years of lead," to see suppression of the Red Brigades and a Socialist Prime Minister come to office.

But he was there when on May 12, 1974, Italians went to the polls to vote on legalizing divorce: A "yes" vote was to indicate opposition, while those in favor of the law's allowing this possibility were to vote "no." After an acrimonious public debate, Italy voted "no" and established divorce as law for the first time. Pasolini wrote in the *Corriere*'s "Open Tribunal" that it was a "victory of consumption and of consequent modernistic tolerance of the American kind."

Four months after the divorce referendum, he told an interviewer:

> The "no" vote was not put forward so much by the Left as by television. It is television which has made the Italian citizen into a consumer, and thus a layman, utterly irreligious; and it is the television which is totally, completely unreligious . . . a consumer *must* be for divorce. When I say these

things, I am looked at as a malcontent, but I say them because I once loved that Italian.[7]

He expanded the argument on June 10, in an article entitled _Gli italiani non sono più quelli_ (literally, The Italians are no longer those). He wrote:

My opinion is that a fifty-nine percent "no" vote does not miraculously demonstrate a victory of secularization, of progress and of democracy: not at all. It demonstrates two other things instead. The first: that the Italian middle class now lives only the values of a hedonistic ideology of consumerism and consequently of the American type of modernist tolerance, and second that the rural and paleoindustrial Italy has crumbled, has melted away, no longer exists, and in its place there is a vacuum waiting to be filled by a thorough bourgeoisization of the type that I mentioned a moment ago (modernizing, falsely tolerant, Americanizing, etc.)[8]

He was provocative, even outrageous and (people sensed) often correct. He wrote the preface to a book by Francesco Perego entitled _Divorziare in nome di Dio_ (literally, To divorce in the name of God). He accepted Garzanti's proposal that he ready a selection of the Bible for paperback edition. A Buenos Aires publisher issued the screenplays of _Accattone_ and _Mamma Roma_. The first Canto of _Divina Mimesis_, so closely following Dantean structure and reference as to be a kind of anti-_Divine Comedy_, appeared in _Il mondo_. Its sister publication, newsweekly _L'espresso_, immediately asked five intellectuals (among them Moravia and Fortini) to "reply." Leonardo Sciascia, called on for an opinion, disagreed with Pasolini. But he added, "He may be wrong, might contradict himself," but at least he knew "how to think with that liberty which very few today succeed in having or affirming."[9] An extended debate began: Calvino answered Pasolini who answered in an open letter in _Paese sera_. Moravia was drawn in, as were Umberto Eco, Fortini, the famous journalist Giorgio Bocca, and Natalia Ginzburg.[10]

Pasolini traveled to Morocco that June and returned to address a fundamental issue of modern Italian history: He wrote, "Italy has not had a great Right-wing movement because Italy has not had a culture capable of evolving it. Italy was able to call forth only that rough, ridiculous and ferocious right wing which is Fascism."[11]

That past, a new "mass culture" had performed an "anthropological mutation" such that the old definitions had blurred and "the heart of the left and the right" had become "indistinguishable." Angry readers reacted in large numbers when he wrote: "The social context has changed in that it has become extremely unified. The matrix that generates all Italians is now the same. There is, therefore, no longer, any appreciable difference—outside of a political choice—between a Fascist Italian and an anti-Fascist Italian citizen."

Within the year, he added that he hoped the "Fascists will continue to vote Fascist." *Il popolo* had had enough. "It is not possible to continue to give any credence to a personality like this." His opinions, the paper said, were more the stuff of "pathology" than of politics. "The question then is: Has Pasolini anything to say in the cultural sphere?" He was, they charged, not original at all but only a "warming-over [*rifrittura*], seven years after the fact, of Marcuseism . . . Pasolini would not scandalize a baby—in the sense he would like to scandalize—because he demonstrates that he has nothing to say. . . ." [12]

Next he declared that television was the tool through which "repressive tolerance" was being sold to the young, complete with images of a certain kind of couple who behave in a certain way. If he sounded "reactionary" and infuriated liberals of every sector, he welcomed it. The polemic was meant to provoke:

> You see young people suddenly seized by who knows what romantic impulse walking the streets hand in hand, perhaps embracing: "What is all this sudden romanticism?" you ask. It is nothing, only the new couple reintroduced by consumerism because this couple are consumers. They buy. They hold each other's hands and where are they going? To the Rinascita department store, to the Upim supermarket. [13]

The rich and the poor, the criminal and nascently so "are culturally, psychologically, and even more strikingly, physically interchangeable." He told a reporter from *L'Europeo*, "These boys have lost their individuality; they are all alike, Fascists, anti-Fascists, subproletarians, delinquents. If you go on foot into a Roman *borgata*, or the periphery of Milan and you walk and see the groups of young people, nothing, really nothing at all will tell you, looking at them, whether they are delinquents or not and whether within five minutes they will commit murder. I find this simply overwhelming." [14]

He called his *Trilogy* his "most ideological" films because they showed social reality before the bourgeoisie and its definition of reason had "conquered." He repeatedly denied that he wanted to return to a lost world, even that any such thing was possible. His was not, as it was taken to be, an argument rooted in nostalgia for a vanished golden age. But the future would be unavoidably worse—what Adorno called "the administered world" (the prototype for what Marcuse was later to make famous as "one-dimensional society"). It would be a world in which the permeation of official ideology had gone so far that all resistance is virtually eliminated.

The world that comes after the *Trilogy* (and it is that of *Salò*) is one where people live a false consciousness, such that they think and inevitably come to look the same—and eventually to act the same, conforming to what the Frankfurt School called "the authoritarian personality." In a phrase from Adorno, the argument from Pasolini was this: "Mass culture is 'psychoanalysis in reverse' because instead of curing authoritarian personalities, it helps spawn them."[15] He wrote: "I have arrived at saying that maybe at this moment Italy resembles Germany when Hitler came on the scene."[16] The "conformist" and "passive" young victims of *Salò* could not be far behind.

But how to impute backward from Italians of 1974 to 1944, the time of the film he was then making? That was simple enough: "What they are now, they were potentially even then," Pasolini wrote. The present, like some terrible black hole in space, was consuming the past and leaving only a horrible future.

He argued on: "Those responsible for the blurring, the degradation—what Gramsci called hegemony—were those in power. Power—*Il Potere* (he capitalized it)—meant the Christian Democratic regime that had governed Italy ever since the war. The institutions of the State were collectively *Il Palazzo* (The Palace). He wrote of the Italian political Establishment living "in the labyrinth of their Palace of Madmen."[17]

And "Outside the Palace"? "If one leaves 'the palace' one finds oneself 'inside' something else: the penitentiary of consumerism. And the chief characters in this penitentiary are the young."[18]

He published that on August 1, 1975, after a visit to "a bathing beach at Ostia between the morning shift and the afternoon one." He was, he wrote, "recovering from the insane darkness of the dubbing-theatre": *Salò*'s shooting was finished at the start of that summer.

> Ten years ago, I loved this crowd; today it disgusts me. And I dislike the young people in particular (with a pain and a sympathy which in the end cancels out in disgust); these imbecile and presumptuous youths who are convinced that they have had their fill of what the new society has to offer them; indeed to be almost venerable examples of it.[19]

But he cannot escape:

And I am here, alone, defenseless, thrown in the midst of this crowd, ir-
retrievably mixed up with it, its life displaying its 'characteristics' as in a
laboratory. Nothing shields me, nothing defends me. Many years ago, in the
epoch preceding this one, I myself chose this existential situation and now
I find myself there through inertia—because the passions admit of no solutions or alternatives. Besides, where is one to live physically?[20]

In the *Corriere* of November 14 he issued his challenge to the
entire political class linked to Christian Democracy:

I know.
I know the names of those responsible for what is called the *golpe* ["coups"]
(and which is in reality a series of *golpes* instituted by a system for the
protection of power).
I know the names of those responsible for the massacre in Milan [Piazza
Fontana] on December 12, 1969.
I know the names of those responsible for the massacres in Brescia and
Bologna in the first months of 1974. . . . [In May 1974, several people were
killed and injured in Brescia during a bomb attack on an anti-Fascist rally
held to protest against neo-Fascist violence.][22]
I know all these names and I know all the incidents (attacks on institutions,
massacres) of which they are guilty.
I know. But I have no proof. I don't even have clues.
I know because I am an intellectual, a writer . . .[21]

*Il popolo* sounded the reaction: "His whole approach is now characterized by an incurable and limitless presumption; the presumption
that he has the exclusive possession of truth, which he imposes on
others. A truth, let's be clear, not based on facts . . . but rather on
a total disdain for them."[22] One magazine took to calling him "our
little Homer of the *ragazzi di vita*."

Milder critics said all his talk of craving community was an abstraction, that he was an old-style elitist intellectual, a moralistic
(and also hedonistic) cultural mandarin-in-crisis for whom individual
people served only as foils, stimuli, challengers to be met. As for
"the masses," these critics pointed out that he had never spent a day
working on a factory floor, had never worked as an agricultural laborer, had never submitted even to office discipline and frustration.
He noted the criticism. At the end of October 1975, on the telephone
with Volponi, he remarked:

I have had no industrial experience. I do not know the world of industry, I
do not know the economy. I am a Marxist who has read little Marx. I read
Gramsci more. I do not know what a factory is, what are the tensions in a

factory, I do not know what it means to work today. I have glimpses of it. I see only this enormous, old, heavy bureaucratic confusion here in Rome. Maybe Rome is not the best vantage point from which to understand our country.[23]

Undeterred, over the course of a month from late August to late September, he dedicated four *Corriere* pieces and one in *Il mondo* to a call for putting the bosses of the DC—those who had passed ministerial portfolios among themselves for a generation—on trial. He wrote that they should be "handcuffed," brought to "a courtroom." He wanted to charge them with "a moral list of crimes" "—crimes which should drag at least a dozen political bosses into the docket in a proper criminal trial like, to be precise, the trial of Papadopoulos and the other colonels."[24]

The DC's weekly *La discussione* responded: "A trial of the DC equals a trial of Europe. To call for it might be amusing and also intellectually stimulating. But to do it would exact a price which certainly would not spare Pasolini's friends, nor Pasolini himself."[25]

He paid no attention. In the postwar decades of their party's hegemony, he wrote: "The Christian Democratic Party . . . has not realized that it has become, almost overnight, nothing but a surviving instrument of formal power, through which a new and real power has destroyed the country."[26]

After former Prime Minister Aldo Moro was kidnapped, taken out of his official car and five bodyguards murdered in broad daylight on March 16, 1978, some claimed the Red Brigades had taken the notion of his "trial" from Pasolini's worlds. But he did not want a kangaroo court of thugs but, rather, something institutionally regular, legitimate, public; he repeatedly called for "a proper trial."

The propagandist was still a poet. He wrote on February 1, 1975: "In the early sixties, due to the pollution of air, and, above all, in the countryside, due to the pollution of the waters (the blue rivers and transparent millstreams), the fireflies began to disappear . . . after a few years, there were no more fireflies."[27] The blue rivers included the Tagliamento, flowing through his heart and that of Friuli. Old, bad Fascism, which he did not defend, at least had left the rivers and the fireflies intact. He offered no solutions: His pedagogic task was to pose the questions for others to address after he was gone.

He exaggerated to get attention and to frame the debate: He wrote that young men used to break into song on the streets of Rome, even if only bits of melodies, but "No one sings on the street anymore."

Readers would have done well to remember his warning: "One must disappoint . . . one must hop onto / the coals . . . like roasted ridiculous martyrs: the Way / of Truth passes through even the most / appalling places of estheticism . . ."

In the course of his attacks on the DC, he called the PCI "a clean country in a dirty country, an honest country in a dishonest one, an intelligent country in an idiotic one, a cultured country in an ignorant one, a humanistic country in a consumerist one . . ."[28] During the first week of September 1975 he participated in the Party's "Festival of Unity" rallies in Milan and sat on a panel with PCI economics boss Giorgio Napolitano, Roberto Guiducci, and Renato Guttuso. ("Pasolini tried to understand the PCI and its position," Napolitano said later.) Their topic was "Development and Progress in a Changing Italy."

Pasolini again cited Marx's prophecy of "genocide," mentioned that he was at work on a book, which became _La divina mimesis,_ and talked about _Il Potere_—"a form of Fascism that is completely new and much more dangerous" making for "a substitution of values and models . . . Mine is certainly an apocalyptical vision." Guttuso dismissed Pasolini's "metaphor" as "a myth . . . an abstraction."

The _Corriere_ pieces of his last summer addressed what he called "Drugs—a real Italian tragedy":

> As far as my own and very limited experience goes, what I feel I know about the phenomenon of drugs is that they are always a surrogate. And, to be precise, a surrogate for culture . . . Even at a higher level . . . there are writers and artists who take drugs. Why do they do it? They too, I believe, do it to fill a gap; but this time it is not simply a case of a cultural void but rather a lack of compulsion and imagination. In this case the drugs serve to replace "grace" with despair, style with manner. I am not passing judgment: I am making a statement. There are some periods when the greatest artists are the most desperate mannerists.[29]

Drugs, politics, sexuality, religion, and culture—all are connected:

> The great phenomenon of the uncompensated loss of values, which includes the extreme mass phenomenon of the use of drugs . . . affects all the young people in our country (with the exception, as I have often said, of those who have made the only elementary cultural choice possible, the young people who have become members of the PCI). Taken as a whole, young Italians

constitute a social calamity which is perhaps no longer curable; they are either unhappy or criminal (or have criminal tendencies), extremists or conformists; and all that in a measure unknown until today.[30]

He was photographed on June 8 at a FGCI (PCI Roman Youth Federation) rally, Giorni Della Gioventù (Days of Youth) on the Roman hill of the Pincio, his hands held up in a forceful gesture, his dark glasses on the table before him, hair combed back, body lean within a zippered jacket. He told his audience that he would vote PCI in the regional elections that week, ones in which the party was to score what the *Economist* called "a major breakthrough by winning votes from members of the Christian Democrats' natural constituency—lower-middle and middle-class voters."

Pasolini told his young listeners:

> I know that suddenly there has come to pass around us and upon us the genocide that Marx prophesied in the *Manifesto:* not any longer a colonialist and partial one, but rather a genocide in the form of the suicide of an entire country . . . to alleviate this human slaughter there are neither hospitals nor schools, neither green spaces nor retreats for the young and the old, neither culture nor any possible human dignity. . . .[31]

On September 24 the FGCI asked him to address a conference on "permissiveness and drugs." He labeled these the joint breeders of criminality and again condemned "false tolerance." He was seen and heard in public speaking the arguments he was making at the same time in print. He had thrown his body into the struggle. About the same time, he invited the ten-member editorial board of the new magazine of the Roman FGCI to EUR. When they asked precisely what he did he mean by "genocide," he answered, "a subsitution of models . . . the acculturation by the power of Italian consumerism."As to how he knew this was happening, he offered his "evidence": "For example, in Rome, I found myself in a *borgata* where there was one of those cultures I spoke to you about, typical enough and exceptional enough as well; you see, when I go there, I do not find living beings but I find cadavers: they were killed."[32]

The following month he visited Barcelona very briefly. His reaction to the city living the last days of Franco: "a city of breathtaking *Angst.*"[33]

The *borgata* might be "dead" but not the great Italian tradition of open, extended, and trenchant debate. The most important names in

Italian culture now stepped forward to correct him, to suggest that he was painting with too broad a brush, perhaps overlooking important arguments. Impatient with the niceties of debate, he brushed them aside. He ran the risk of Adorno's complaint about Heidegger: "He lays around himself the taboo that any understanding of him would simultaneously be falsification."[34]

Some young Communist editors tried to reason in vain. One suggested that the result of 1968 was that Italian young people "desired spontaneity, liberty, a life without constrictions. . . ." He denied it: "What young people are you talking about? In the end, it is you ten and another four hundred or maybe four thousand . . . I am not talking about you, young Communists, who have your backs covered with consciousness and an ideology, but of the mass of the young, millions, not thousands." A writer in *L'unità* accused him of "irrationalism" and "estheticism"; *Paese sera* printed similar reservations, and he was widely dismissed as guilty of "nostalgia."

Calvino too emphasized this "nostalgic" aspect of Pasolini's analysis in an interview in mid-June. He was rather put off by what seemed to him Pasolini's mourning for a "little Italy" of the Mussolinian past (something not better, but that seemed in hindsight to be so) rendered roseate by Pasolini's present bitterness.

On July 8 Pasolini answered him in the pages of *Paese sera* in the now characteristic form of an "open letter":

> I mourn the *Italietta?* But then you haven't read a single line from *Le Ceneri di Gramsci* or *Calderón*, you haven't read a single line from my novels, you haven't seen a single frame from my films, you know nothing about me! Because everything I am and everything I have done *excludes* by its nature any mourning on my part for the *Italietta*. Unless you consider me radically changed—something that forms part of the miracle-minded psychology of the Italians, but for just that reason seems to me unworthy of you.[35]

He wrote "An Open Letter to the President of the Republic" (Giovanni Leone); it appeared first in the Milanese *Corriere d'informazion,* then in *Il mondo* on September 11:

> Italy—not only the Italy of the Palace and of Power—is a ridiculous and sinister country; its men of power are comic masks crudely smeared with blood, a contaminated cross between Molière and Grand Guignol. But the citizens of Italy are no better. I have seen them in crowds at *Ferragosto* [the national holiday in August]. It was a picture of frenzy at its most insolent. They invested so much energy in amusing themselves at all costs that they seemed to be in a state of rapture; it was difficult not to think of them as

contemptible or at least guiltily foolish. Especially the young people. All those stupid couples walking along hand in hand with an air alternately of romantic protection and inspired certainty of tomorrow.

They have been tricked, fooled. . . . lo and behold, well-being, the cause of their monstrous character, fails them while the dance of the marionettes continues.[36]

The force of his ideas, as well as their vulnerability, lay in their simplicity. For example, how could one account for the Far Left and its long string of then apparently successful attacks on fundamental entities of the States, like the police and judges? What about the evidence that seemed counterlogical to his argument? Wasn't "dance of the marionettes" the language of poetry and not to be taken seriously as politics or policy?

He continued his indictment of Leone and his Christian Democratic colleagues later that month (on September 28) in the *Corriere della sera*:

in the maze of corridors of their Madman's Palace, they continue to believe that they are serving the power structure set up by the clerico-Fascists. That led them to the tragic failures which have brought our country to that state which I have frequently compared to the ruins of 1945.[37]

And just in case one should think that only the Right came within his sights, just in case it was not understood that he wished a pox on all their houses, he claimed that the Red Brigades had a culture "the same as that of the enormous majority of their peers."

It all mattered and yet mattered not at all. The transformation of reality implied the transformation of language, and vice versa. The world had left him behind, and the proof was aphasia: "Death is not / in the not being able to communicate / but in no longer being able to be understood."[38]

Debating partners came forward to point out that consumerism was a new name for an old phenomenon, that only the surplus of goods made trade possible and trade, in turn, culture. Even Prime Minister Giulio Andreotti addressed him in the pages of the *Corriere*, arguing blandly enough that consumerism had done much to improve the lives of many. Pasolini's response was to put a finer point on his own argument, making a great leap, a leap subject to poetic verification only, not "scientific." He personalized. Humanity before its "anthropological mutation" consisted of:

consumers of extremely necessary goods. And it was perhaps this that made their poor and precarious lives extremely necessary. While it is clear that superfluous goods make life superfluous . . . Anyway, whether I mourn this peasant world remains my own business. This in no way keeps me from exercising my criticism on the present *as it is*—indeed, all the more lucidly the more I am detached from it, the more I agree only stoically to live in it.[39]

What, besides putting the entire DC on trial, was to be done? In the *Corriere* on October 18 he wrote perhaps his most controversial piece, calling for the "abolition" of television and the compulsory high school. It was reprinted in the posthumous edition of *Lutheran Letters* (1976) as "Two modest proposals for eliminating crime in Italy." On August 1 ("Outside the Palace"), he asked: "Do the journalists of *Paese sera* [who had reported a shooting incident as "absurd"] not know that it is the exception to find a seventeen-year-old in the working-class districts of Rome who does not have a revolver?" Now he wrote of "mass criminality" and offered "two Swiftian proposals . . . as their humorous definition makes no attempt to hide." Let them laugh, he seemed to argue, but at least think as well. He proposed that the mandatory system of secondary education be abolished—and away with television.

In the schools, young people were "in the best of cases . . . taught useless, stupid, false, moralistic things . . . I am literally anguished by the thought that 'sex education' might be added. The schools are all right until the point where they start teaching reading and addition . . . after that, they teach useless cretinism, imposed by a false modernity."

As for television, he stated: "What I have said about compulsory schooling is here multiplied to infinity, since it is not a case of teaching but of an 'example': that is to say, the models in television are not spoken but shown."[40]

The "proposals" engendered such an outcry (Moravia took the lead) in his by now enormous readership that he returned to the topic ten days later. Under attack, he called his "modest proposals" on schools and television "clearly intended to refer to temporary abolition." Having purposefully used hyperbole to get the public's attention, he now shifted to a liberal, reformist ground. He announced: "Abolition—once again—is merely a metaphor for a radical reform."

On October 21, 1975, he accepted an invitation to address a conference of teachers and students in Lecce. The site was the Palmieri *liceo* (high school), and the topic, "Dialetto e scuola" (Dialect and the schools). His hosts prepared for the encounter (which was tape-recorded) by careful classroom reading of his *Corriere* pieces; he opened by asking that he be allowed not to make a statement but rather to proceed directly to the questions-and-answers.[41] ("I do not know how to speak; I would never know how to make an address or a lesson.")

But first: "To give a preface to the conversation," he read from the closing monologue of *Bestia da stile*, the verse play he once called "a Poundian monologue," still in-progress after a decade. Since April 1966 he had returned to the manuscript, updating—stratum on interacting stratum—what he sometimes called his autobiography. "In the summer of 1974 I decided to stop—with the updatings, but not with the polishing." In fact, in the midst of the debates generated by his *Corriere* articles, he wrote a long appendix to the play.

Its working title had first been *Poesia*, or *The Czech Poet*; in *Bestia da stile*, as he finally left it, Pasolini's "double" is Jan Palach, the Czech who set himself on fire to protest the Soviet invasion of Prague in the summer of 1968. Pasolini put these words into his mouth:

> I want to be a poet and I do not distinguish
> this decision
> from the smells of the kitchen
> from the hour in winter that comes before dinner
> (and it hurts so much—a pain that is always
> unexplainable—
> in the heart of children) . . .
> I do not distinguish it from the silence of the granary
> from the rooms suspended in the night where the sons
> stay alone with all the sky before them.[42]

In Lecce he read that part of his play-in-progress which repeats ten "commandments" from Pound's *Cantos*, with his own after-comments to turn them on their heads: For example, "Never take the name of the Lord in vain (except often)."

Then, addressing an imaginary Fascist youth, dead long ago, he wrote: "In your Fascism without violence, ignorance, vulgarity, bigotry, / Sublime Right, / which is in each of us, / 'a relationship of intimacy with Power.' "

He told his listeners that this "sublime Right"—which he hastened to add bore no resemblance to historical Fascism—called on "values, themes, problems, loves, regrets which are, in the end, valid for all, if not appropriated by Fascists for rhetorical reasons." He hinted that there was in this "sublime Right" something utopian, which preceded and might have survived the disaster of the political Right, just as there was (or could be) a Marxism despite (or at least without) the PCI.

When a teacher named Buratti asked, "What must we [classroom teachers] do?" about the schools "aside from the 'radical solution' of their abolition?" Pasolini answered that it was "too late . . . by ten years" to do anything. Too late to make more than a "museum" of dialects, too late to offer sex education, since "the young people have sexual experience and an awareness of sex incommensurable with that of only a decade ago."

He said, "Horrendous television Italian" had made everyone talk like variety show–host Mike Bongiorno. The teachers and others who cared for language were only "a tiny elite." And as for fighting this "homologination," the alternatives were either to accept the protection of dialects as "conservation" or become "profoundly revolutionary." As for what that meant, he cited the Irish and the Basques. His listeners must have looked shocked or, at least, perplexed. In mid-response, he said, "Sometimes I speak using paradox and a bit extremistically, but you must try to understand me with moderation."

When the next questioner returned to his call for "abolition" of compulsory secondary education and of television, Pasolini said, "The exaggeration was Swiftian: They were two modest, humorous proposals." The dialects "in a museum" were "better than nothing." But "in reality, there is little to be done" (*in realtà c'è poco da fare*)."

Another professor was not convinced that the "culture of the *borgata*" was "happy" ten years before, nor that it even existed. Pasolini answered, "Although I am devoured by doubts, on this I have none." Instead of people smiling at one another—"There was no one who did not sing, no one who when looked at did not return the greeting with a smile"—now he found everyone "pale, neurotic, serious, introverted." And what did he expect this line to bring him? "I am not afraid . . . of being labeled conservative and reactionary because that is something that could terrorize someone ten years ago, but now things are completely changed and one cannot fear that; the truth must be said at all costs, and at any cost I say that the smile of a youngster ten years ago was one of happiness, whereas now he is an unhappy neurotic."

As for poverty and its conquest: "We have understood that misery is horrible, and we have understood that poverty is not the worst evil, we have clearly understood; the worst evil is the misery of a false well-being, they are much poorer than they were ten years ago. . . ."

A voice called from the back of the hall: "You are proposing the Arcadia of the proletariat . . ." Pasolini said he did not fear *illazioni* (inferences, deductions); people were free to make those as they wished. But he insisted he had never said going backward was the solution; in Frankfurt School terms, he did not believe the answer to modern societies (*Gesellschaften*) was in a return to lost communities, a mythically organic *Gemeinschaften*.

When a student asked about making a revolution from the Left "to empower the powerless," Pasolini responded that even for the PCI it was "also late, I believe" because "the Roman subproletariat, a large part of the proletariat of the North, enormous strata of the population of the South, have already undergone genocide; they are already dead [*cadaveri*]," in respect to what they were. "It seems to me that their historic destiny is to live this death-state . . . a Marxist revolution at this point, when genocide is already accomplished, seems to me fairly utopian."

As for "progressivism," he dismissed that as "antiquarian" and even the word "emancipation" as old-fashioned, something "yellowed" (*ingiallita*), like an old photograph. "One cannot use that word anymore." And Gramsci too was irrelevant because "he worked forty years ago, in an archaic moment which we do not even dare to imagine. . . ."

He returned to the question of abolishing the schools. Rather than return to the old "humanistic model," the schools ought to teach "how one pays taxes or not, hygiene, foods which are good and which bad, and also sex education to a certain level." To be done away with were the three years of obligatory Italian history: "Just think a bit of the history that is taught in those three years: it is something ridiculous, enough to make a person stupid for a lifetime."

When a teacher asked him not for "diagnosis" but for practical advice, he responded: "If I were in a school today, and I really do not envy your situation, because I would really not know what to say, what to teach. One has to start teaching from scratch." And he repeated, *"C'è poco da fare* ["there is little one can do"] . . . it is a battle between a culture which we do not accept and a culture which is finished."[43]

After Pasolini was dead, Calvino wrote that to debate him about the substance of the *Corriere* articles was "like hailing down a Formula One racedriver in the middle of his circles on the track, to ask for a ride." By now Pasolini did not bother scandalizing the bourgeoisie, who he believed would consume scandal like everything else. The ones to shock were the intellectuals, those who still believed "reason" would resolve all. He told the newsweekly *Panorama:* "The people I respect the most are those who haven't gone beyond the fourth grade."

His last articles are rooted in the most personal passions. He wrote, also of himself: "We are in the snake-pit." He embraced enigma and rejected pragmatism, the uses of experience, the cold comforts of progressive rationality. He understood that Italy's national income had quadrupled during his lifetime and took that fact as disaster, not success. His viscera (a most Pasolinian word) were engaged, not only his cognitive powers: "Taken as a whole, young Italians constitute a social calamity which is no longer curable; they are either unhappy or criminal (or have criminal tendencies), extremists or conformists; and all that in a measure unknown until today." [44]

The "progressivist" Radical Party had put forward eight referenda on civil rights issues, divorce the first, followed by legalization of abortion in certain circumstances. Inevitable objections were raised (and not only from feminists) when Pasolini wrote (June 19, 1975) for what he called "a stirring, tumultuous and chaotic series of reasons":

> I am for the eight referenda of the Radical Party, and I also would be willing to support an immediate campaign in their favor . . . However, I am traumatized by the legalization of abortion because like many I consider it a legalization of homicide. In dreams and everyday behavior—something common to all men—I live my prenatal life, my happy immersion in the maternal fluids, and I know that there I existed . . . [45]

He explained that he also opposed abortion because "it would make coitus—heterosexual coupling—easier, and there would practically no longer be any obstacles to it." But "this wonderful permissiveness" was not what it seemed—only something conceded by "the powers of consumption, by the new Fascism." He said: "My extremely reasonable opinion . . . is that instead of struggling on the level of abortion against the society that repressively condemns abortion, one should struggle against this society on the level of the cause of abortion, i.e., on the level of coitus."

The demystification of sex had passed directly to its predictable and obligatory merchandising. At Lecce, asked to explain the difference between pornography and art, he answered:

Now I have done a film called *Salò*, in which one sees terrible things, [things] which in reality, taken one at a time, would be pornography, [if] taken out of context; but in context I believe that they are not, because the context is that of the mercification [*mercificazione*] which power has made of bodies, that is the reduction of bodies to things, which Hitler did in the physical sense of the word and which today's new power has done in the sense of genocide, as I said before.[46]

Having won front-page, national attention, he retreated, writing in *Il mondo* on March 20, 1975: "I am for prudent and painful legislation [governing abortion]." But reasonableness coexisted with fury. He recommended homosexuality as the solution to unwanted children, to overpopulation. It would eliminate the need for abortion because "it is the heterosexual relationship that would appear to be a danger to the species, while the homosexual one represents its security."[47]

He had spent a lifetime as "Pasolini *il diverso*," feeling "like a black from Harlem when he walks on Fifth Avenue." He had had more than enough of it. To one critic, who argued that Pasolini's homosexuality disqualified him from being taken seriously on the subject, he answered: "Only a repressed homosexual could espouse such a vulgar and narrow-minded opinion."

And what did he imagine his arguments would bring him?

Finally: many—deprived of their virile and rational capacity for compre-hending—will accuse this—my intervention—of being personal, particular and of a minority. So what?

Those who appealed to him to be "reasonable" were trying to hail down a Formula One driver and ask for a ride. By now he believed that what was needed was "the full force of cold rejection, of des-perate useless denunciation."

On January 30, 1975, he addressed his friend Moravia, the quin-tessential rationalist, in the *Corriere:*

For you, consumerism exists and that's that, it doesn't touch you except, as one says, morally, while from a practical aspect it affects you as it does everyone else. Your deepest personal life is undamaged. But not, on the contrary, for me. As a citizen, it is true that I am touched, like you, and I undergo a violence which offends me; but it is as a person (and you know this well) I am infinitely more caught up in it than you. Consumerism is a real and true anthropological catastrophe: and I live, existentially, that cat-aclysm which is, at least for now, a pure degradation: I live it in my days, in the forms of my existence, in my body.

Since my bourgeois social life is completely exhausted in my work, my social life depends entirely on what people *are*. "I say "people" advisedly, meaning society, the people, the masses at the moment they come existentially (and let's hope only visually) in contact with me. It is from this existential, direct, concrete, dramatic, *physical* experience that all my ideological statements emerge in conclusion. . . ."[48]

The rhetoric of the articles and the message of the film he was shooting even as he wrote them now intersected. *Salò*'s production began in February 1975. On March 9 he published the first of the two months of letters to a fictional Gennariello. He wrote in the *Corriere* about what he was filming and also what he was teaching his Neapolitan *ragazzo:*

Its [the new consumer society's] permissiveness is false. It is the mask of the worst repression ever exercised by Power on the masses of citizens. In fact (it is a remark of one of my protagonists of my next film, which is taken from de Sade and set in the Republic of Salò): "In a society where all is forbidden, one can do everything; in a society where only some things are permitted, one can do only those things."

One can say that repressive societies . . . were in need of soldiers and, in addition, of saints and artists, while the permissive society needs only consumers . . .

The brood hens, the Italians have accepted the new unnamed sacredness of merchandise and its consumption . . . The new Italians do not know what to do with sacredness; they are all, pragmatically, if not consciously, very modern. And as far as sentiment is concerned, they tend to free themselves of it rapidly.[49]

As for his role, he said: "Many intellectuals like Calvino and myself risk being passed over by a real history that suddenly renders us obsolete, transforming us into wax statues."

On August 7 he published (in *Il mondo*): "Subject for a Film About a Policeman" based on the true story of Vincenzo Rizzi, reported in the *Corriere della sera* on July 19. He called policeman Rizzi "an obedient boy . . . from a decent Southern family" tricked by one Merletti, a prisoner who escaped. The criminal was reapprehended, but horrified at his breach of duty—of the values Pasolini argued had been turned into a mockery by cynical Italian society—Rizzi killed himself.

Pasolini began with the newspaper photo of Merletti's face. He wrote, admitting it was "on the basis of a single photograph":

His hair is sophisticated, full of sinister and vaguely indecent codes; in his eyes there is the mocking gleam of the well-heeled, together with a look that indicates an obsessive resolution (which in his archetypes was both madder and more noble). His dress follows fashion menacingly—or perhaps by now it is natural to him—the fashion of those younger than himself, who are as aphasic and as wicked as vipers.

As part of his scheme, Merletti had supper with Rizzi, as though they were friends,

in some *trattoria* or other in Centocelle, the very thought of which makes one's heart bleed. That spaghetti, that drop of bad wine, must have appeared in the last moments of Vincenzo Rizzi's life as an intolerable surrender to the base instincts, a criminal orgy.

Merletti had mentioned to Rizzi his need "to pass a couple of hours" with his woman. Rizzi agreed, giving Merletti the time he needed to escape. Pasolini argued that the use of a woman for sex in such a way—something to be expected, what he mockingly called "the most natural thing in the world"—was new, part of the mercenary, consumerist world. To old-fashioned Rizzi, the dupe, "Chastity was a part of a man's destiny. Woman was a dream and dreams wait or are waited for. Coitus would come in due time." Pasolini's thesis was that the inability to appreciate how the world had changed for the worse made Rizzi into Merletti's fool: "The myth of the woman shut away and alone (whose obligation of chastity implied the chastity of the man) has been replaced by the myth of the woman accessible and at hand, always accessible. The triumph of friendship between men and the erection has been replaced by the triumph of the couple and impotence."

He wrote that his film on the incident, if he ever made it, would demand a gold medal for Rizzi, "blackmailed . . . with a myth of the age of consumerism":

Young males are traumatized by the duty permissiveness imposes on them— that is to say the duty always and freely to make love. At the same time they are traumatized by the disappointment which their "sceptre" has produced in women who formerly either were unfamiliar with it or made it the subject of myths while accepting it supinely. Besides, the education for, and initiation into, society which formerly took place in a platonically homosexual ambiance is now because of precocious couplings heterosexual from the onset of puberty. But the woman is still not in a position—given the legacy of thousands of years—to make a free pedagogic contribution; she still tends to favor codification. And this today can only be a codification more conformist than ever, as is desired by bourgeois power, whereas the old self-education, between men and men or between women and women, obeyed popular rules (whose archetype remains Athenian democracy). Consumerism has therefore finally humiliated the woman by creating for her an intimidating myth. The young males who walk along the street laying a hand on the woman's shoulder with a protective air, or romantically clasping her hand, either make one laugh or cause a pang. Nothing is more insincere than the relationship to which that consumerist couple gives concrete expression. [50]

In late September RAI-TV broadcast *Accattone*. Pasolini watched his now "classic" first film on television and wrote of the experience in the *Corriere* on October 8. Again, he took the occasion to explain how the subproletarian world of Rome had been a "culture," a "race . . . left to itself for centuries . . . to its own immobility."

> In *Accattone* all this is faithfully reproduced (and one sees it above all if one reads *Accattone* in a certain way that excludes the presence of my gloomy estheticism). Between 1961 and 1975 something essential changed: A genocide took place. A whole population was culturally destroyed. And it is a question precisely of one of those cultural genocides which preceded the physical genocides of Hitler. If I had taken a long journey and had returned after several years, walking through the "grandiose plebeian metropolis" I would have had the impression that all its inhabitants had been deported and exterminated, replaced in the streets and blocks of houses by washed-out, ferocious, and unhappy ghosts. Hitler's SS, in fact. The young boys, deprived of their values and their models as if of their blood, have become ghostly copies of a different way and concept of life—that of the middle class.
>
> If I wanted to reshoot *Accattone* today I would be unable to do so. I could not find a single young man who in his "body" was even faintly like the young men who played themselves in *Accattone*. I could not find a single youth able to say those lines with that voice. Not only would he not have the spirit and the mentality to say them, he would quite simply not understand them. . . .[51]

On October 30—the day he stopped in Paris en route from Stockholm to Rome—*Il mondo* published the last article. He called it "A Lutheran Letter to Italo Calvino" (answering Calvino's piece of October 8, which responded to Pasolini). He called it "[a] brief article, which I have penned as a telegram."

> Only intellectual Platonists (I add: Marxists)—also lacking information but certainly lacking self-interest and complicity—have any probability of in-

tuiting the sense of what is really happening; naturally, however, provided that this intuition of theirs is translated—literally translated—by scientists, Platonists themselves, into the terms of the only science whose reality is as objectively certain as that of Nature, i.e., Political Economy.[52]

Calvino had told Sciascia, "He is trying to provoke me, but I will not answer."[53] But he did. His reply, entitled "A Last Letter to Pier Paolo Pasolini," appeared on the front page of the *Corriere* on Tuesday, the fourth of November. By then it was too late.

*Salò* intervened, "wanting to be made," as Pasolini would say, after the *Trilogy*. He told his hosts at the Lecce school, "I wanted to start from the beginning; I wanted to make a film in which there is always the problem of sexuality, but not understood as pure freedom, because this has been seized and falsified by consumerism, in the most problematic and dramatic way."

*Salò* took the place of *Porno-teo-kolossal*, which he had wanted to film next. As early as 1973 he had spoken of *Porno-teo-kolossal* as a kind of return to *Uccellacci*, the film Bini discouraged him from making. He wanted to cast Ninetto with Eduardo de Filippo as two Neapolitans who follow a comet, symbolizing ideology. The pair would visit three cities—Sodom (Rome), Gomorrah (Milan), Numantia (Paris)—which depict "permissiveness, intolerance, and neo-capitalist Fascism in power." In a later version, he added New York. They would end up in Ur, standing for India and the East; the comet would lead them there, after their Dantean tour and fablelike trials, to a new "good news." De Filippo would play a poet, a utopian.

They had to be Neapolitans because theirs had remained "the true large dialect city, [where] adjustment to models from the center, to rules imposed from above on language and behavior, is only superficial. For centuries the Neapolitans have been adapting themselves mimetically to whoever is over them."[54]

On September 24, 1975, he sent Eduardo a seventy-five-page, detailed treatment; he wrote the legendary actor-playwright that "for the first time in my life" he had also used a tape-recorder to outline the work. He added: "I have read it through—for the first time—earlier today. And I was traumatized: shaken by its 'ideological' commitment, in fact, as a 'poem,' and shocked by its organizational bulk."[55] Included were four or five pages recounting a story of a man martyred in a public square. At the beginning of October he told critic Gian Carlo Ferretti that as soon as *Salò* was finished, "within a week . . . I will immediately start *Porno-teo-kolossal*, the new one.[56]

Or just maybe—at long last—he would film the long-dreamt-of story of Saint Paul. In June 1966 he had written to the Church-affiliated production company, Sampaolofilm, "Must I always resign myself to not making this film? Or is there at least a chance to make it two or three years from now? Or must I consider that my person and my project are considered a risk, and so there exists no real possibility even in the most distant future?"[57] After passing through the title *Film teologico* (Theological film), he now called his confrontation between the saint and the cleric at war within himself *Bestemmia* (literally, "Curse") taking the name of his earlier screenplay in verse. How could Pasolini not confront the Church father who had written:

> Men did shameful things with men, and thus received in their own persons the penalty of their perversity. They did not see fit to acknowledge God, so God delivered them up to their own depraved sense to do what is unseemly. They are filled with every kind of wickedness: maliciousness, greed, ill will, envy, murder, bickering, deceit, craftiness. They are gossips and slanderers, they hate God, are insolent, haughty, boastful, ingenious in their wrongdoing and rebellious toward their parents. One sees in them men without conscience, without loyalty, without affection, without pity. They know God's just decree that all who do such things deserve death: yet they not only do them but approve them in others.[58]

But rather than the long-postponed film on Paul or the film of the comet of ideology, in the same months he was writing to "Gennariello" he turned to that film that can be read as the visit to the city of "neo-capitalist Fascism in power." He set it not in Paris but in Mussolini's last-stand Republic of Salò, a real Italian town on the real Lake of Garda in 1944. It had to be told through a fable: the one that served was Marquis de Sade's *120 Days of Sodom*.

He had been receiving more-or-less anonymous threatening letters for some time. During the first weeks of October, he got into an argument with a gang of youths in the Piazza di Spagna and right in the tourist heart of Rome, they dragged him from his silver Alfa and beat him, according to Laura Betti, "with chains." He was hurt; the boys vanished; he did not bring charges. No one knows whether he was singled out or, as was suggested by those who do resist conspiracy-making, had simply had the bad luck to have crossed the path of the wrong people at the wrong time.

# 24

All'ombra de' cipressi è dentro l'urne
confortate di pianto è forse il sonno della morte men duro?
            —*Ugo Foscolo*, **Dei Sepolcri**

*A people of artists, of heroes, of saints, of thinkers, of scientists, of*
*navigators . . .*
    —*Inscribed at Mussolini's order on the façade of the central build-*
        *ing at EUR, the exposition ground he built outside Rome*


# THE COLLAPSE OF THE PRESENT, A QUESTION OF GRIEF

In October 1975 Bolognese publisher Cappelli published the *Trilogy* filmscripts, the versions drawn from the final sound tracks. Pasolini furnished the editor, his Liceo Galvani schoolmate Renzo Renzi, with a preface in three sections. It was an introduction meant to bury all that followed it: Its title was "Disavowal of the *Trilogy of Life*." While few read it when it appeared, a month later, on Sunday, November 9, it was devoured when the *Corriere* ran it in full, starting on the front page in the lead column.

I reject my *Trilogy of Life*, although I do not regret having made it. I cannot, in fact, deny the sincerity and the necessity which drove me to the representation of the bodies in it and of the culminating symbol, their sex.

First of all, they are part of the struggle for that democratization of the "right to self-expression" and for sexual liberation which were two of the fundamental factors in the progressive tension of the Fifties and Sixties.

In the second place, during the first phase of the cultural and anthropological crisis which towards the end of the Sixties—in which the unreality of the subculture of the mass media and therefore of mass communication began to reign supreme—the last bulwark of reality seemed to be "innocent" bodies with the archaic, dark, vital violence of their sexual organs.

In the end, the representation of Eros as seen in a human environment which had not been quite yet overtaken by history (in Naples, in the Middle East) was something that fascinated me personally as an individual author and as a man.

Now all that has been turned upside down.

First: the progressive struggle for the democratization of expression and for sexual liberation has been brutally superseded and cancelled out by the decision of consumerist power to grant a tolerance as vast as it is false.

Second: even the "reality" of innocent bodies has been violated, manipulated, enslaved by consumerist power—indeed, such violence to human bodies has become the most macroscopic fact of the new human epoch.

Third: private sexual lives (like my own) have suffered the trauma both of false tolerance and of physical degradation, and what in sexual fantasies was pain and joy has become suicidal disappointment, shapeless torpor. . . .

Even if I wished to continue to make films like the *Trilogy of Life*, I would not be able to do so because I now hate the [Italian youths'] bodies and sex organs. That is to say the bodies of the new Italian youth and boys, the sex organs of the new generation of Italian youth and boys. People will object: "But you did not in fact show in *Trilogy* contemporary bodies and sex organs but those of the past." That is true—but for some years I have not been able to delude myself.

The present with its degeneration was compensated for not only by the objective survival of the past but consequently by the possibility of reinvoking it. But today the degeneration of bodies and sex organs has assumed a retroactive character. If those things which *then* were thus and thus have *today* become this and this, it means that they were already so potentially— so that their mode of existence even *then* is devalued by the present.

The boys and youths of the Roman subproletariat—which are incidentally those whom I projected into the old Naples that still survives and into the countries of the Third World—if *today* they are human garbage it means that they were potentially the same *then;* so they were imbeciles forced to be adorable; solid criminals forced to be pathetic; useless, vile creatures forced to be innocent and saintly, etc. The collapse of the present implies the collapse of the past. Life is a heap of insignificant and ironical ruins. . . .

Everyone has adapted to this situation either by not wishing to notice anything or by an inert process which takes the drama out of the situation.

But I have to admit that even if one had noticed or dramatized the situation that by no means saves one from adaptation or acceptance. So I am adapting to degradation and accepting the unacceptable. I maneuver to rearrange my life. I am beginning to forget how things were *before*. The loved faces of yesterday are beginning to turn yellow. Little by little and without any more alternatives I am confronted by the present. I readjust my commitment to a greater legibility (*Salò?*)[1]

He was publishing in the pages of *Il mondo*, his "pedagogic tract" in installments, addressed to the "imaginary" boy named Gennariello:

I shall have to explain briefly why I wished you to be Neapolitan . . . I prefer the poverty of the Neapolitans to the prosperity of the Italian Republic; I prefer the ignorance of the Neapolitans to the schools of the Italian Republic; I prefer the little dramas which one can see in the Neapolitan slums—even if they are somewhat naturalistic—to the little dramas of the Italian Republic's television.[2]

The series was an adolescent's "little instructional treatise," the new *Emile*, and appeared as fourteen installments from March 6 through June 5, 1975. And yet it was not *Emile* because the bourgeoisie was not emergent but cruelly triumphant:

I do not think there is anyone—at least in my world, the so-called world of culture—capable of minimally appreciating the idea of compiling a pedagogic treatise for a boy. An enormous vulgarity makes them think of such a treatise as a chat that is completely and perfectly "legible." All right: it means that instead of dedicating it to the monstrous shade of Rousseau we shall dedicate it to the scornful shade of de Sade.[3]

The *Trilogy* done and rejected, he took on new projects. One was to collaborate on an adaptation of *Trash* by Paul Morissey (whom he called "an unconfessed neo-realist"); it was produced by Andy Warhol and starred Italo-American Joe d'Allessandro, now a Roman regular.

His deep-seated disagreements with feminist Dacia Maraini hardly mattered to their friendship; on the contrary, they gave it spice. The two collaborated on the script of *Trash* and the next year on *Sweet Movie* by the Yugoslav director Duăn Makavejev. In January 1975 he welcomed journalists to his home to meet its director, and when

*Sweet Movie* ran afoul of the censors and was sequestered (after a first showing in La Spezia), he issued a statement. He dismissed as "arbitrary and utterly without scientific base" the magistrate's deciding for himself that the film offended "the common sense of decency." "Everything is in the head" of the official, "once again a magistrate takes it upon himself to be an esthete or a critic. They have evidently not understood that this film is an art film, not insofar as it is a story or a poem but insofar as it is a pamphlet or allegory, two particularly refined forms of expressive technique."[4] In the age of "total publicity,"[5] he could be counted on for a quotable line, a printable reaction. His dance with the media was in full swing.

Starting in February, he began shooting *Salò*, an allegory of his own. Pasolini did not invent the madness of *Salò*, a truth within a series of nightmares rather as *Thousand and One Nights* was "a truth . . . not in one dream but in many dreams." He found the film—one which retrospect decided "had" to be his last—waiting, ready-made by the Marquis de Sade. When it was done, released and banned, and Pasolini dead, *Le monde* opined: "It is difficult for the cinema to go further than this."[6] Donatien Alphonse François de Sade set his long (quarter of a millon words), numbingly repetitive litany of cruelties in the Château of Silling in the Black Forest, and populated it with forty-eight innocents who are confined for four months during the rule of Louis XV. The château is cut off from mankind by obstacles at once fairy-tale and nightmarish: a village of woodcutter-smugglers who allow no one to pass, a steep mountain, a dizzying precipice that is. destroyed once the Sadeans are inside, a thirty-foot wall, deep moat, and daunting quantities of snow.

The film, loosely based on the story, was originally Sergio Citti's project, to be directed by him. But Citti—even with two films to his credit made with Pasolini's assistance—could not carry off a story involving sexuality and violence on this order. To producers, the idea of Citti filming Sade was one commercial proposition, but the white-hot Pasolini was altogether something else. Only a very big name, with guaranteed international box office, could manage the press pressure around a closed set and deliver a product passable as art and not mere pornography. Pasolini learned of Citti's troubles and asked if he might take the project over. He agreed and received title credit for "story and screenplay" on *Salò*. For Citti just then, *Salò* was one of two possible next projects, the other a film of *L'histoire du soldat*. For Pasolini, it represented nothing less than what he called "a sort of horrible, sacred representation, to the very limits of legality."[7]

Pasolini explained that he had wanted for some time to do a work built on the principle of Dante's "theological verticalism": levels of blessing, layers of Hell. "Then I read the book by the contemporary French philosopher Maurice Blanchot, *Lautréamont et Sade*, and decided to launch myself into this venture. I have given up the idea of making a film about Saint Paul. Perhaps this is a more meaningful story for today."[8]

Pasolini could hardly fail to be fascinated by Sade's *Les 120 Journées de Sodome*, not as a sexual tract and not even because it asks where social corruption intersects individual cruelty. Sade's story was the "structure that wanted to be" film, inevitably following on the prose structures of *Scritti corsari* and *Lettere Luterane*. The bridge that connects the seemingly unconnectable *Decameron*, *Canterbury Tales*, and *Thousand and One Nights* to *Salò* is that of corrupted language, what Pasolini believed to be the shadow cast by power in society—in its relation to sexuality. The *Trilogy* films are, among other things, about storytelling and eroticism. So, too, *Salò* is (among other things) about narration and arousal, words and sex. Lost in the tumult over its images, *Salò* remains also a film about books, writing, the power of words. In the universal rush to explain *Salò* as the inevitable delight of a pervert, observers forgot Sade's story is also grist for a linguist, and in Pasolini's hands, a poet's work.

Financing was arranged: It was inexpensive to make—no travel, a few interiors, no stars. Press curiosity (managed by Nico, the production's press chief) was enormous. Pasolini now had as free a hand, as much power, as Visconti or Fellini: Producer Alberto Grimaldi never set foot on the set during the thirty-seven days of shooting, from March 3 to April 14. According to Pasolini's lawyer, Teresa de Simone, "From the late sixties, it was possible for Pasolini to have his own production company, but rather than business he was interested in artistic freedom." To protect and promote her client's interests, she drafted a contract provision specifying that he need furnish his producers with only the sketchiest treatment of a script, a so-called "idea base," which he could alter as he saw fit. In practice, Grimaldi saw a script as detailed as they come in Italy—with dialogue but without shooting directions.

The lawyer also drafted a thirteen-point "Disciplinary between the Producer and the Director": Pasolini had the right to choose the players and technical crew, director of photography, cameraman, and editor; he alone chose the music; his was the exclusive and personal right to make the final edit to which no alternations could be made without his express approval. Once such approval was given, such edits were to be effected by him or solely under his control and direction. Were cuts ordered by official censors, these too would be effected only by the director and within ten days of the producers' written request. In exchange, he agreed to hold the film to a maximum of two and a half hours projection time.

Grimaldi was consulted on casting of the major players. After every day's shooting, the rushes were sped to Rome for developing and printing at Technicolor and then brought to the producer's PEA offices (in EUR, not far from Pasolini's house) for his private screening. "If I did not like something, I told Pier Paolo on the phone, right away—never on the set in front of other people." But Grimaldi had no serious problems. "My differences with him about the making of the film were quite minor. It was the best working relationship of my career."[9]

Writing about the original *120 journées de Sodome* after Pasolini's murder, Italo Calvino explained that Sade's book "is a first draft written uninterruptedly for thirty-six days (according to the author himself)" in the autumn of 1785, while Sade was imprisoned in the Bastille. The manuscript was lost during the Revolution, but traces surfaced during the next hundred fifty years: something out of Jorge Luis Borges. It first appeared in print in 1935. Calvino reported seeing the manuscript at the palace of Fontainebleau, "a roll of hundreds of sheets pasted together . . . an extremely dense, straight, regular torrent of handwriting, in lines all equal, well aligned, without one erasure, one addition, one regret." Sade literally rolled out his mania, in the tone of a medical treatise, on paper four inches wide.[10]

In the original, Sade provides four narrators, each of whom recounts five brief episodes to amuse themselves and their prisoners every day for a hundred and twenty days. He calls for six hundred graphic stories of perversion in all, a hundred and fifty lewd anecdotes, many centering on excrement, recounted by Madame Duclos, "in very thin and elegant *déshabillé*, much rouge and many diamonds." Sade wrote thirty cases in detail, leaving detailed outlines of the rest. He also specified that thirty victims were to be massacred, divided among several categories. All this Pasolini changed.

As part of *Salò*'s opening titles in black letters on white background, he included "An Essential Bibliography." So that his public might better understand what is to come, Pasolini-pedagogue put his viewers on notice to read French theorists Pierre Klossowski, Maurice Blanchot, Philippe Sollers, as well as Simone de Beauvoir and Roland Barthes.

These interpreters emphasize that the rambling speeches and relentless repetition of the Marquis' work reduce it to ritual. Taken together, the action is not a "story" that moves as a conventional narrative; it is something still, frozen, sterile.

Pasolini preserves the isolation of the setting, for it is crucial to the horror. Inside the villa-château, the libertines can only take pleasure in knowing they are "solitary." Further, once isolated, the Sadean protagonists, their helpers, and their victims form a total society, one with "an economy, a morality, a language, and a time articulated into schedules, labors, and celebrations." It replicates Fascism.

Pasolini changed Sade's four characters—Curval, Blangis, Ducet, and the Bishop—into his own more generic types: a Magistrate (called the President, as of a French regional court), a Banker, a Duke, and a Monsignore. And he changed the time to 1944–45, the closing days of the war in Italy as Fascism collapsed, bringing down what it could with it. In the midst of that chaos, the four organize their rituals of torture on innocent young victims at an isolated villa understood to be somewhere not far from Mussolini's headquarters.

Pasolini sets the action in that puppet regime Hitler provided for Mussolini from September 17, 1943, after his liberation by SS commandos from the hilltop prison in the Abruzzi where he had been sent following the vote of the Grand Council and his final interview with the King. It was from here that Mussolini had established his "Italian Social Republic" on the shores of Lake Garda. His macabre regime held on until April 1945, when the representative of General Heinrich von Vietinghoff, German commander-in-chief in the southwest, surrendered all German troops in Italy and western Austria to General Mark Clark, commander of the U.S. Fifth Army Group. The so-called cleanup required almost two years of house-to-house fighting; as Clark bitterly observed in his memoirs: "Particularly after the Allied invasion of France, we were a forgotten front, which until the spring of 1945 never had enough men or enough equipment to mount a quick, decisive and fatal blow to the enemy."

Mussolini fled for the Swiss border on the seventeenth, only to be captured and machine-gunned against a villa's gate by a band of Partisans. This "Republic of Salò" was the bottle into which Pasolini poured Sade's wine.

The film's location-shots were at two villas in the hills north of Bologna toward Mantua, rebuilt by designer Dante Ferretti and exquisitely furnished in the height of Art Deco and Bauhaus taste, down to the yellow-black-and-white teacups and touches of Lalique. Ferretti, in consultation with Pasolini, hung the walls with Bauhaus

designs and Cubist paintings. The icy elegance of the settings reproduced perfectly in Technicolor; director of photography was, for the
last time, trusted Tonino delli Colli. To stand in for the real village
Marzabotto, southwest of Bologna—where the film opens and the
young victims are taken—Pasolini used Gardelletta.

He called his decision to transpose the eighteenth-century German
castle to the Salò of 1944 "an illumination." To this, Calvino voiced
one of his milder objections:

> It greatly displeases me to see appear on a street sign the name of the town
> where a terrible massacre actually took place, Marzabotto. [The Nazis exe-
> cuted the entire town.] The evocation of the Nazi occupation can only rea-
> waken a depth of emotions that is the complete opposite of the paradoxical
> ruthlessness that Sade poses as the first rule of the game, not only to the
> characters but to the readers as well.[11]

By taking Sade into Italy in 1945, by making the libertines look
like us (in Sade they are grotesque and therefore easily dismissed),
Pasolini tears away the book's abstraction. He explained: "Sade said,
in a phrase not so famous as others, that nothing is as profoundly
anarchic as power . . . so far as I know, there has never been in
Europe a power as anarchic as that of the Republic of Salò." As
always, he did not shrink from autobiography, telling one interviewer
during shooting how he, too, had lived the Republic of Salò in Friuli,
renamed the "Adriatic Littoral" after the fall of Mussolini, ruthlessly
administered by a German governor. "Our own Fascists in that region
were real cutthroats. And there were constant bombings; the Flying
Fortresses were overhead night and day, going up to Germany. It was
an epoch of sheer cruelty, searches, executions, deserted villages,
all totally useless, and I suffered a great deal."[12]

By transposing Sade's *Les journées* into a place and time real to
his viewers, he offers not the Marquis' *tableaux vivants* to be gazed
upon—but a mirror. Apparently without intending to, Calvino
praised Pasolini for accomplishing exactly what he set out to do.
During filming, Pasolini said, "It is the first time I am making a film
about the modern world."[13]

And yet, Pasolini was only depicting a ghastly game. He insisted
it was just that, a game, "a representation," a "story"; after all, he
used chocolate as excrement and phony blood. Or was he? The sexual
violence and perversion on screen were almost universally taken as
nothing less than his veiled sexual confessions in the *Corriere* and
the poetry made into pictures. When Calvino objected to the film in

the *Corriere* on November 30 (Pasolini had been dead a month), his words read like the *ad hominem* accusation they were:

> The only way to render believable and up-to-date the rapport established between the perverted gentlemen and their court was to make it clear that their principal instrument was money. Only in this way could Pasolini speak of the drama's fundamental theme: the role that money had taken in his life after he had become a successful filmmaker.[14]

Later, Calvino added lines to his critique, ones which he claimed the *Corriere* had omitted in its published version of the article, " . . .money that conditioned his artistic expression according to movie budgets; money that conditioned his relationship to the sub-proletarian youth: The boys he once met at a brotherly level, when he was almost as poor as they, now looked so changed—calculating, greedy, inclined to violence and robbery." He pulled back, not calling Pasolini "corruptor." He did not say he bought sex. "Conditioned his relationship" was enough. The identity is unambiguous: Calvino's reader is to understand that Pasolini *is* one of the "perverted gentlemen."

Moravia, so famous as to be almost above the fray, answered Calvino on December 6, again in the *Corriere:* "I read with some stupor the article in which Italo Calvino speaks of Pier Paolo Pasolini as a "successful *cineasta*."

> I believe I knew him well, having traveled and lived with him; and I feel the need to say most emphatically that the place taken by money in his life really did not exist. Pier Paolo Pasolini was not corrupted by money; that is he neither changed his vision of the world nor his way of life because he could earn more and more easily . . . Pasolini remained, in spirit, *un povero* . . . Pasolini was too complicated and intellectual to be corrupted by money . . . the tragedy of Pasolini was not that of a man corrupted by money but rather that of a patriot betrayed by his country.

Under fire, four days later Calvino beat a public retreat. "Answering" Moravia's answer, he explained, "What I wanted to say, above all: not that he was "corrupt,' something which makes no sense, but that he suffered from not being able to exit a mechanism of corruption." In death as in life, Pasolini was exactly where he wanted to be: at the center of the storm.

Pasolini cast professional actor Paolo Bonacelli as the Duke. The President was Aldo Valletti, a Latin teacher who, for decades, had barely a line as an extra at the Rome Opera and Cinecittà. Giorgio Cataldi, a product of the *borgata* and a friend of Pasolini's from the days of *Accattone*—owner in 1975 of a men's clothing store—plays the Monsignore. The writer Uberto Paolo Quintavalle was cast as Excellency. "*Personaggi* of my films are exactly the opposite of the ones you find in television or the so-called escapist cinema," Pasolini remarked. The majority's lack of professional experience was exactly what was wanted and the shooting style he adopted was simple: Hardly anyone had a script and if they did, it was only very sketchy. Pasolini told the players their lines just before they were to say them and how to move just before they moved. The players were never shown rushes, lest it make them self-conscious and make them play someone other than themselves.

He reduced Sade's narrators from four to three, substituting for one a silent pianist. According to Sadean strict rules of order, the whole day's activity at the château converges nightly on the storytelling séance. In Sade the narrator sits on a throne. In Pasolini the elegant lady *racconteuses* dominate the room (but without the elevated throne) but, true to the text, the four libertines and their victims are carefully disposed in groups about the Hall of Orgies, to listen. The stories are meant to excite the bosses to try out what they have heard, then and there, on their victims. As Roland Barthes explains: "Without formative speech, debauchery, crime would be unable to invent themselves, to develop: the book must precede the book, the story-teller is the only "actor" in the book, since speech is its sole drama." [15]

Pasolini found in Sade the symbolic system to illustrate his argument: The language of Power in Italy corrupted, degraded, and brought with it the objectification of the body. In a world where only things matter, people are made objects, to be used, abused, discarded. What Pasolini called the muteness of Italians in the face of consumer hegemony is analogous to the silence of Sade's victims, who are literally prohibited from speaking. Communication makes sex intimate; so, only by gagging the victims and enforcing their silence is violence on them possible. Naturally, only the four in power can speak. As Barthes explains, "Libertinage is a fact of language." [16]

Pasolini had already said that "one of the cornerstones of my way of seeing reality" was the idea that the "real structure of all work is its linguistic structure." [17] The philologist of Italy's dialects, the literary critic of *Passione e ideologia* who constantly honed in on language, had never abandoned that fixed pole just because he stepped behind a camera. *Salò* resists any effort to separate it as an aberration, as something inconsistent, unconnected to the many Pasolinis, all of them poet.

*Salò* becomes the iconography to accompany the articles in the *Corriere* on "genocide," the "instructional treatise" to Gennariello. It is horrible, polemical pedagogy. Pasolini wrote, "Power is a system of education that divides us into the subjugated and the subjugated"; in his logic, based on a "heretical empiricism," political power, consumerism of things and others and of self, sexuality in all its aspects (the couple, coitus, abortion, divorce), language, education, and television were connected, facets of a unitary "anthropological mutation" that constituted "genocide."

The world was now irremediably transformed into one in which he had come to feel he had no place. Like an aphasic, he did not understand the common code. Bred in the humanist idea that communication is meaningful and not simply mechanical, he felt himself condemned to irrelevance, redundancy, the opposite of "being present."

Here is Pasolini as the *poète maudit*—the Romantic vision of poet-seer of Shelley's "Defense of Poetry" passed through Rimbaud's poet as the great blasphemer, grand criminal, and supreme sage. The poet's duty is to realize his vocation through example; in other words, in a world where poetry counts for nothing, the poet is heard only when he dies. To confess and to scandalize were the same in a society where everything is said and nothing is heard. In Pasolini's pedagogy—its roots deep in the past (for he knew himself to be also the healthiest of all, the Goethean artist)—instruction follows scandal and does go inexorably, as in Greek tragedy, to its logical (necessary) limit—death.

The son of teacher/leaders—a schoolmistress and an army officer—Pasolini wanted to use what he called "the weapons of poetry" to educate the poor to consciousness and to reeducate the bourgeoisie. His "program," a lifetime in the execution, was to impart values, remaking those of the middle class to greater tolerance and liberality, bringing the poor to pride and self-empowerment, the intellectuals out of what he deemed their "new clericism." The "practical end" of his poetry seemed possible in the fifties, when corruption in high places found its mirror in desperation in the *borgata*. The poetry of commitment, fueled by private eros, was perfectly timed for the decade of Italy's chaotic scramble back after the war. But that moment passed, and sometime around 1968 the loving maestro came to think the game was over and that he had lost. He saw the underclass overwhelmed by false tolerance, panic for goods, and the bourgeoisie determined to sacrifice everything Pasolini valued in exchange for power. If right-thinkers and people of good sense thought him a charlatan, the only solution was to be "hysterical."

Of course, his was a "ridiculous" mannerism to make Silvana Mangano wear clothes copied from Susanna's, as it was to make Susanna the aged Madonna in *Gospel*. It was "too much:" an excessive emotionalism, a narcissistic romanticism to make a corpus of confessional poems and claim that his private experience was a social warning. Symbolic lives smack of programmed self-promotion in the age of manufactured fame; it was "too much" that he talked about the subproletariat and drove an Alfa, returned home after his adventures (Siciliano wrote of them as "crude") to the comfort of the EUR house or the Chia retreat. His argument that the Alfa was what the boys would have bought made no difference: his clique—those of his tribe—expected him to find social and sexual life inside his métier and among people of his rank and age, as everyone else did.[18]

Making claims about the "necessity for contradiction" did not hold, even when they stuck to only a part of what he did. The boys' willing participation made no difference. *Il borghese* on the far Right and *Il manifesto* on the far Left agreed: They resented him with different rhetoric but, in the end, felt the same. After the posturing and hedging were done, he was in their eyes still just a corruptor of minors. He would have answered them all the same way. The success he had sought had made him rich and famous; the boys knew that. He had changed, so had they, but his need had not. He loved them (and also now hated them) and that gave him a right: "Have I not the right to provoke them? How else can I hope to have a relationship with them except in this way?"

The boys were "sons become fond father," or not so fond, who

> little by little
> have become stone monuments
> thronging my solitude by the thousands.

At the end, the patient—even loving—teacher turned bitter and perhaps, perhaps violent. In crude terms, Riccetto ends up either as armed helper to the libertines of *Salò* or as one of their victims. In the course of Pasolini's descending trajectory of hope, he decided that the choices open to Gennariello and the other Neapolitan *scugnizzi* were retreat, Fascism, or helpless liberalism. History was "finished."

*Salò*'s "innocent"—but he made sure not too pitiable—victims (in the film and out) are "products" of Italy's schools. *Salò*'s is the good schoolmaster of Valvasone's declamation on the ethics of evil, for that too is a part of pedagogy. It is a lesson in which he counts himself both sadist and masochist, victim and (perforce) victimizer. His word is Sade's to the extent that in both the link between sex and love has been severed. And how has the world (and his) come to this? "The first tragedy: a common education, obligatory and mistaken, that pushes us all into the arena of having everything at any cost . . . In a certain sense, we are all weak because all victims. And are guilty because all are ready for the massacre game."

This from his very last interview, given to journalist Furio Colombo for the literary magazine *Tutto libri*, the afternoon of Saturday the first of November.


Who to "play" *Salò*'s shameless female narrators? Pasolini hired his friend Elsa dé Giorgi (for Signora Maggi), Catarina Boratto (for Signora Castelli) and the French actress Hélène Surgère (for Signora Vaccari), dubbed by Laura Betti. The fourth female figure of importance is the pianist, played by Sonia Saviange, whose music accompanies the narrators' performances. The French actresses, Saviange and Surgère, had appeared in Paul Vecchiali's *Femmes, femmes*, which Pasolini had admired at the 1974 Venice Festival.

The cast also numbers Ines Pellegrini (Zumurrud in *Thousand and One Nights*), who plays a servant, and sixteen victims: eight boys (including Franco Merli, *Thousand and One Nights'* Nur-ed-Din) and eight girls. Save for Pellegrini and Merli, the victims were hired by open casting (told they would appear nude), recruited from high schools in the area. Four soldiers guard the victims, carrying out the orders of the bosses; five servants make sure the horrors proceed in comfort. In addition, the bosses have the complicity of four "collaborators," a special set of guards.

One of these guards was played by Claudio Troccoli, the teenage son of peasants living near Chia. Pasolini had come to know him there and took him to Rome several times. His curly hair and pimpled skin reminded those who saw him of a less animated version of Ninetto. Pasolini called him Troccoletto. Sometime in 1974 Pasolini drew him looking out a window. The work—called *Una sera a Chia*—might have been the next sheet on the very pad where thirty years before he had sketched Tonuti, gazing from a window in Versuta.

When Naldini called Quintavalle to offer the role of *Eccellenza*, he objected that he had no experience. Pasolini, meeting with him, explained that it did not matter at all: He wanted him "for your physical aspect, which is perfect for the role of a decadent intellectual, which I need." Quintavalle emerges from the book[20] he wrote about the making of *Salò* as a master of self-delusion and self-revelation; he seems not to have been insulted by Pasolini's reasons for choosing him.

Quintavalle went to pains to explain how much he disapproved of Pasolini's decisions and working methods, and how he—unperturbed at having no cinema experience of any kind—would have made *Salò* differently. He recounts that Pasolini's authority on the set was absolute; people everywhere received him with respect and even obsequiousness; for example, the principal of a local high school approached Pasolini one night in a trattoria, asking if he would come to address the students. In Quintavalle's view, the principal asked as one does a famous man; and as a famous man who sensed himself obliged, Pasolini consented.

To the actor, that Pasolini had both worldly success and genital satisfaction was mildly stupefying. That he seemed, amid all that, "unhappy" was nothing less than infuriating. To Quintavalle, Pasolini was living in Henry Miller's mythical "Land of Fuck," a perverted one but no less paradise for that. Quintavalle was staggered: "At the height of his [Pasolini's] power, he felt himself someone persecuted, someone excluded . . . he nourished his anguish with the thought of enemies who mistreated him."

The nonactor actor argued "that the ideology of the film was confused seemed evident to me on more than one occasion"; Pasolini's approach, he wrote (in the midst of sycophantic praise) was "like wanting to play polo in tennis shoes." Quintavalle had no difficulty concluding that Pasolini's work was an exercise in Freudian projection: The director was simply one of the four libertines. Quintavalle's book was taken seriously in some quarters, or at least found useful. Writing in the English journal *Encounter*, François Bondy said that his impression, "reinforced for me by a book of memoirs recently published by one of the Italian actors in the film," was that *Salò* was no more than Pasolini "transferring his own erotic fantasies to the screen with vast self-indulgence and no artistic self-criticism at all."[21]

*Encounter*'s essayist had Italian company. *Gente*, the mass-circulation gossip tabloid, printed an extended excerpt from Quintavalle in February 1976, hailing his book as one written "without preconceptions" by an "author of successful novels." Pino Pelosi's lawyer unsuccessfully offered the memoir in evidence at Pelosi's trial, to prove the simple proposition that anyone who could direct actors in a film as Pasolini had was certainly capable of attacking his client first. Thus, "evidence" supporting Pelosi's claim of justifiable homicide on grounds of self-defense. Later, the defense attorney spelled it out: "The book shows it, that he [Pasolini] was violent and, equally, that he was obscene." [22]

Pelosi's lawyer, named Rocco Mangia, tried to fight fire with fire, stage-managing public opinion in the press, where rules of relevance are lax. In May 1976, within two weeks after Pelosi's first sentence and while his appeal was being prepared, he arranged access to Pino in prison for Francamaria Trapani, a journalist from *Gente*.

Mangia seemed sure she would take the right line. During the previous November her magazine had called Pino "a minor, born into a family of honest laboring people," and had written mildly that "the black sheep of the family" had begun to frequent friends "not wholly recommendable." *Gente*'s reporter speculated (but presented as fact) that Pelosi knew, "from newspapers and the television," who Pasolini was when they met. As for what happened "between ten-forty and the moment of death," *Gente* says no witnesses exist. So the relationship between "the strange couple" was passed along from Pelosi intact, with snickering. "Pasolini began to embrace me," Pino is reported as saying. The writer added: "One is not dealing here with generic embraces, and to define them without offending decency is difficult: It would do enough to say that Pasolini did not use only his hands." [23]

In December the magazine ran a full-page photo of Pasolini with Susanna over a caption describing *Salò* as "a sampler of horrors and perversions," part of an article on how the Soviet Union and Eastern European bloc countries deal with their homosexuals.

Trapani worked hard to cultivate Pelosi's parents from the start, comforting his mother during the trial, enthusiastically backing Mangia's line that Pino was not an experienced hustler but a *bravo ragazzo*, who simply had the misfortune to accept an invitation for dinner and a drive from a madman. Three weeks after the crime she published a long piece entitled "The Secret Life of a Boy Assassin," complete with shots of Pino at age five, furnished by his parents. Her "exclusive" interview with his parents included father Antonio recalling Pino saying, "When we spoke about homosexuals, he always said: 'Papa, don't worry. Those men disgust me.' " [24]

She even managed to get Pino to reenact, with the help of a fellow inmate, the gestures of the crime, playacting punches and blows with a stick. Trapani kept at it. Six months' work paid off: On May 10, two weeks after the sentence, she printed "Pino Pelosi: I Ask Forgiveness of Pasolini's Mother," complete with file photo of the boy in tears. It was a perfect follow-up to "They Hated Pier Paolo Pasolini," Trapani's visit with a *ragazzo di vita*, who recounted how the year before, Pasolini had tried to pick him up, offering a part in a film in exchange for sex. He also offered reminiscences about Pasolini as sadomasochist, of what was said on that score *in giro*.

In February *Gente* ran a lengthy excerpt from Quintavalle's book, headlined "the incredible behind the scenes of Salò" (*gli incredibili retroscena*) with a still of the author captioned, "Here Is the Witness" and another from the film headed "A Squalid Scene."

In March, during Pelosi's trial, Trapani called on the man from the *Ricotta* trial, Dr. Semerari. He bemoaned the fact that years before, "No one listened to me, starting with his [Pasolini's] friends." Trapani passed along to her readers the doctor's decade-old opinion that the dead man "must be considered someone mentally ill [*un malato mentale*]." The court trying Pino might not have admitted Semerari's report in evidence, but Trapani was free to quote from it, and did.[25]

Trapani's skill with kitsch ought not to mask the politics. *Gente*'s texts echo the line of the MSI's official *Il secolo d'Italia*, which quickly declared Pelosi the sole guilty party and the matter closed. Trapani and her colleagues delivered a character assassination on Pasolini to reinforce Pelosi's version of the crime: that Pasolini was a violent man who attacked first, that the boy acted alone and in self-defense. *Il secolo* charged that "certain press" (understood to include *L'Europeo*) were making "groundless charges" and complicating into a political crime a strictly personal one. For Trapani (as for the extreme Left, the opposite wing of Italian politics from *Gente*'s) the Communists were now crying "crocodile tears." "You know," she said, "the crocodile that eats its young and then weeps big tears."[26] But she shrugged, adding: "*Tutto fa brodo* [everything serves for soup]."

*Gente*'s predisposed public responded. One reader of the magazine wrote to Pino's parents, through Mangia: "God has struck a [human] being so that he will not ruin other youths . . . we are many who wish that Pino will return home soon and your Christmas will be serene. A hug to Pino." Perhaps the letter was sparked by the article: "The Memory of the Friends in Casarsa: He was a Corruptor of Boys"?[27]

But letters to Maria and Antonio Pelosi were not what Mangia wanted from Trapani's coverage. He claimed to be shocked and angered that she failed to give the Pelosis a gift, "not even a blouse, a pair of shoes." But worse, she did not once mention his name in her two longest articles. Thanking her in kind and reminding her who held the reins, he had her excluded from the courtroom the day of sentencing and declined her request for a post-verdict exclusive interview with Pino's parents.

She ought to have understood the demands Mangia's old-style *virtuosismo* made on his self-image. Mangia thought Marazzita and Calvi—lawyers representing Susanna Colussi and Pasolini's interests—"opportunists, only interested in making politics"; they retorted that he was a nobody whose only clients came from jail warden referrals.

Under attack, Mangia defended himself: "The television has come [to see me] from Germany, France, England, Belgium, Switzerland, some of my friends, clients, wrote and told me they had read all about this [case] with great interest in Australia, Argentina, Colombia, Brazil, they read about it and saw my picture, read my words, wrote to me and sent affectionate congratulations." He dismisses claiming the case served to build his practice: "I already had a great name . . . people already knew me, they come to me continually."[28]

The pulp press found fertile ground in the story of Pelosi in prison, material equal to the usual fare of royal weddings, starlets' divorces, and tales of natural disaster. On January 15, 1976, while the lawyers were building their cases for and against Pelosi (and Pasolini), the *Domenica del corriere* (which Pasolini had once called malodorous) sponsored and reported a roundtable on *Salò*. To make sure the intellectualizations of its guests did not limit readership, it also ran two sidebars: the first was an interview with one of the girl-victims in *Salò*, who said, "While I said my lines, I wept with shame." The other was an interview with the film's makeup artist, explaining how he made plastic breasts to be severed in the Circle of Blood, a phony eye to be gouged out, enormous penises of latex for the naked execution squad. He recalled Pasolini saying, "I want to make an evil film, one without hope. A film colored with violence but in which, however, one sees blood only rarely." No commentary was needed: Readers understood—a man who could make such a film was capable of anything. He was guilty of attacking Pelosi by artistic association.

The next month, not to be outdone by *Gente*'s Trapani, the *Domenica* also visited the Pelosis at home. Mentioning that the appellate hearing was approaching, the piece quoted Antonio Pelosi, who knew just what to say: "My son was simply one who said 'no' to Pasolini and to those like him. . . . Sometimes people stop me on the street to say Pino did well to do what he did. If you could see how many letters I've received, even many from America, many from emigrants; many priests have written me."[29] He may have had in mind a form letter sent on Monday, November 3, to his son from the World-Wide Christian Fellowship, Inc., from a post office box in Toledo, Ohio. It began, "Dear Troubled One. . . ."

Maria Paoletti Pelosi, Pino's mother, was interviewed on the sidewalk in front of her apartment in Setteville, a *borgata* "fraction" of Guidonia. By now she was not flattered by press attention and had taken to putting her hands over her face when a photographer appeared. Upstairs were two rooms and a kitchen, her son's bed a foldaway inside a piece of furniture that by day doubled as a bookcase. He had no space that was his own, no belongings save for the guitar he refused to learn to play, his clothes, the car. She told the reporter: "We want to be forgotten. We forget the dead, so why not forget the living? I do not want to speak because I am afraid anything I say will hurt my son. I don't want to know what people think; I don't want even to read the letters that come to the house."

Photos taken with a zoom lens ran with the text, shots of Pino laughing as he played soccer in the jailyard with fellow detainees. A caption explained that a girl named Luana was Pino's betrothed. He wears a sweatshirt on which he has written, "Luana, I love you." Luana's parents made sure the relationship terminated. Readers were not told whether he wore the "miraculous medallion" sent him the day of his capture by "a Christian woman," who wrote, "You will see, with the help of the Madonna, Giuseppe will become *good*."

Another photo caption explained that Pino passed his time awaiting trial working in the detention center's kitchen and laundry, washing windows, playing cards and soccer, and reading Mickey Mouse comics and a Western series called "Tex." He was described as "a boy of the *borgata*, one of so many young men of the Roman periphery who find work hard to obtain and sometimes make the wrong friends." Pelosi told *L'espresso*: "If I had been born in America, I would have been a Marine."

Inside the Casal del Marmo, he told the reporter, "They say that Pasolini was a poet, a writer, an important man. For me, he was just a person who had money, a car, and wanted to go into the fields like a lot of others." A social worker in contact with him explained that his mother, father, and sister were "always out working . . . virtually a case of abandonment."

*Amica* magazine offered the claims of a Bombay astrologer. He opined Pasolini was killed by two people.


*Salò*'s first images are of uniformed, armed Nazi-Fascists rounding up young people. It is a section Pasolini labels "the Anti-Inferno," a prelude to horror, filmed in pastels like those Pasolini used to paint Friulian fields *"de ca'l de l'aga"* (on this side of the water).

A town somewhere in the north of Italy has become a battlefield: Nazi soldiers kill a Resistance fighter and leave him lying in the *piazza*. The camera shows the four soldiers marching a prisoner away form the corpse. It is no different from the body Pier Paolo found in Casarsa in 1944.

The soldiers take eight adolescent prisoners, boys and girls, at random off the street and seal them in a villa. From here to its end, the film takes place in the claustrophobia of a sealed environment, a place from which there is no escape. Unlike Sade, Pasolini keeps punishers and victims clearly demarcated. The Marquis makes all the participants play all the parts; by turns, everyone at Sade's Château de Silling is both actor and spectator. In Pasolini's film there is no doubt that the eight are innocent victims. Pasolini told a press conference:

> They are taken by chance, they are more than innocent. They think at first that it is all a game and only realize what is happening when it is too late . . . but I don't want them to be politically superior or inferior [to their captors]. In fact, I believe them to be superior, but insofar as they are the victims in this film, I could not make them too tender, so good as to tear at the heart.[30]

And later, expanding on the idea,

> If I made them likeable victims who cried and tore at the heart then everyone would leave the movie house after five minutes. Besides, I don't do that because I don't believe it.[31]

After the roundup, all the film's action stays within a restricted group inside an enclosed, almost airless space. The four bosses and the beautiful (though not young) lady narrators are always dressed, some of the latter in sumptuous evening gowns and jewels, better to delight the eye as their ghastly stories assault the ear. The victims are immediately stripped naked and stay that way throughout the film.

Inside the chic villa, three Circles are acted out, ghastly renditions of Dantean madness—all in near silence, eerie inevitability, and studied cruelty.

Three Circles—that of the "manias," of "excrement," and of "blood"—consume most of the hundred seventeen minutes of *Salò*. Each starts with one of the ladies recounting, with much relish and studied coquettishness, the "greatest perversion she has witnessed." Pasolini found the idea in Sade. On screen, it makes for blood-chilling shock.

In the Circle of the Manias, labeled as such by a title-frame on screen, the lust for power is portrayed: Blond, toothsome Signora Vaccari—dressed in an extravagant white evening gown, many-stranded pearl bracelets at her wrists, and more pearl ropes at her neck—delivers her story. It stimulates the four to fondle their victims (without regard to sex) and toss off lines from Baudelaire and Nietzsche, or epigrams such as "The Fascists are the true anarchists." This "dialogue" was generally taken to be Pasolini's takeoff on European decadence, a commentary to the effect that Romanticism ends in totalitarianism. It might well be that: But such lines are also good history, nearly exact quotes from Fascist pamphlets and speeches of his youth. The claim that Fascism was the progeny of the anarcho-syndicalist movement he exterminated was one of Mussolini's gambits.

Now the victims are reduced to wearing dog collars, placed on leashes by the soldiers. They are forced to run up and down the villas' staircases on all fours, and—always naked—to bark and howl. A still from this sequence served as one of the film's publicity posters.

In this Circle, one of the soldiers named Ezio falls in love with the black servant-girl, played by Pellegrini. It is the only instance of heterosexual love in the film and, inevitably, must be eradicated, its participants punished with immediate execution. First the girl is shot before her lover's eyes. She slumps on the floor and the shock of the pistol shot gives way to a frame of a lovely, bloodless form, a body without mark, its arm extended over the seat of a chair. Violence has occurred, but what we see is beautiful, as graceful as an Ingres *odalisque*.

Before he, too, is murdered, Ezio stands naked and defiant, his fist clenched and held high. He has loved someone "of color" and defied the Power. His resistance is brief; he is shot dead and the corruption throughout the villa (the Palace?) is totally triumphant. Pasolini described Ezio's love and dying gesture as "a moment of political consciousness, which throws an unexpected light over the whole film."[32] This very brief moment is the only glimpse of hope Pasolini allows.

Now the four bosses force a heterosexual pair to copulate on the marble floor before them. Pasolini wrote in the *Corriere* on March 25 during shooting: "Sex today is the satisfaction of a social obligation, not a pleasure taken against social duty." During the making of *Salò*, is he remarked to a reporter: "Sex in *Salò* is a representation, or a metaphor of this situation: that which we are living in these years: sex as an obligation and ugliness."[33]

Now the four libertines compulsively caress their male and female victims alike, all of whom remain passive as though in a trance; like a Roman hustler, they neither resist nor join in. Had he not already written in *Calderón*: "We want to be the first helpers to our assassins"? During the shooting did he not tell a journalist: "Power . . . is that which manipulates bodies to reduce them to *things* and transforms victims and the innocent into accomplices and spies"?[34] The victims on *Salò*'s screen are objects—"reified," in Marxist terminology—their bodies gray and beautiful, robbed of their souls. When one girl cries for help, her fellow captives are as indifferent as her guards; her captors are amused. As punishment, she is made to kneel naked before the Duke and eat feces with a fork, from the floor. The screen goes to black.

Next, the Circle of Excrement, as in Sade. Signora Maggi has donned an elegant ballgown to tell her story. Following on the excitation her narrative of perversions engenders, the victims are corraled to a banquet table, where they must eat their own excrement. It is not farfetched to liken the scene's form and the filming's technique—the layout of the table, the location of the camera—to that of the happy opening wedding sequence in *Mamma Roma*, reversed.

The film is almost silent, its symbolism purposefully riddled with ambiguities, open to myriad interpretation. One critic explains the victims' consumption of their own feces (which they have been forced to save) as Pasolini's way of saying that consumer society must, finally, consume its own excretions, thus itself.

The four now line up their victims and make them bend over. The bosses will inspect their captives' anuses: One says, "They are culturally, psychologically, and even more strikingly, physically interchangeable." The victim with the best formed will be executed.

Not the anus but the vagina is always a loathsome absence in de Sade:

> Sadean misogyny is based on the libertine's view of the female genitalia as
> a scandalous offense to reason. Nature orders us to live only for the pleasure
> of our senses at the same time she continues to produce millions of creatures
> sexually equipped to repel us . . . The most intense Sadean—and sadis-
> tic—sexuality depends on symmetry, and with women Sade's men enjoy the
> diminished pleasures of asymmetrical sex . . . The appeal of pleasure is
> inseparable from the appeal of evil, and a crime against another version of
> ourselves—against someone "absolutely" like us—doubles our pleasure.[35]

They choose one boy but decide they must let the "winner" live
in order to be able to sodomize him repeatedly. Death is thus denying
the victim pain, better inflicted by letting him live; Pasolini asked,
"Where is one to live physically?"

The worst is yet to come: Eros ends in Thanatos. The Circle of
Blood is the ritual destruction of all the victims, to the pleasure of
their captors. "The larger point in Sade . . . has to do with the use
of violence, quite literally, to make the victim give birth to sexuality
in the torturer."[36] The boys and girls are herded into the courtyard
of the villa by their guards, graphically tortured, and killed. Three
of the bosses make a chorus line and kick their heels in the air with
joy. Pasolini explained: "In the executions . . . I have used the four
modes of killing still practiced by our legal institutions: hanging,
shooting, the garrote, and the electric chair."[37]

The camera moves fast but not too fast to prevent sufficient
glimpses to upset the viewer. The horror proceeds in silence.

Sade declared that there was philosophical pleasure in contemplation, in the "abject pleasure of complicity and the supreme pleasure
of action." One of the four is thus a killer, two are accomplices, and
one, the President, watches from a window. Pasolini placed the camera not on the ground where the murders occur but in the villa, up
one floor. We see what the President does, and as he does—framed
through binoculars. As the Sadean captor looks down into Hell, into
a narrative enacted for him as observer in a place of safety, so do
we. The binoculars' frame-in-a-frame is part of what has been called
the "distancing tactics" in the film; the torture is "real," on screen,
but isolated as though controlled. One can lower the glasses, turn
away. It is, by rough analogy, the sight of bombs exploding at night,
recorded from the air, or watching war in "just a movie." We are
forced to confront the pleasure of being a spectator. "Moral consciousness is the replica of esthetic consciousness";[38] Pasolini makes
of art the motor for moral outrage. The artist was the natural moralist.

He told a reporter who saw some bits of the final Circle's sequence:

"I must confess that even here I do not arrive at the heart of violence . . . the real violence is that of television. . . . For me, the
maximum of violence is a television announcer. In my films, violence
is a mechanism, never a real fact."

Scholars of Sade have written of "the perfect identity between the
masochistic and sadistic impulses: The slaves are killed so that the
masters may, as it were, appropriate their suffering as their own
sexuality . . . as Freud writes, 'be enjoyed masochistically by the
[sadistic] subject through his identification of himself with the suffering object.' "[39] Pasolini even has the Duke say, "Ideally, one
should be both the executioner and the victim."

Pelosi claimed Pasolini said, "I will kill you." Circumstantial evidence and massive gossip (only that) suggest the Pasolini pursued
masochistic practices. Had he not written to describe himself
"hanged by boys to a fig tree"? In the Sadean universe, masochism
equals sadism, and vice versa. Pursuing that line on a symbolic
plane—not to be minimized for that—Pasolini "killed" Pelosi. And
Pasolini (like Desdemona) "wanted" Pelosi to kill him. The crow is
only useful dead; only then does his poetry serve its "practical end."

Matters are not simple when art and life collide. The first of several
appeals courts in Pelosi's case held in its sentence of December 4,
1976, subsequently overturned, that Pino had not acted alone. He
was held at law to have lied when he claimed he had killed Pasolini
to defend himself from sexual assault.

Further, he acted without what the law accepts as provocation:

> The court notes that if one examines [Pelosi's] story in depth, even with no
> attempt to keep in mind its mass of incongruities, in whatever way the attack
> itself was manifested, one finds nothing to make one believe that the de-
> fendant's sexual freedom or his physical integrity had been truly endangered
> or could have seemed to him seriously threatened. Even if Pasolini had been
> demanding something that Pelosi, perhaps out of a change of heart or last-
> minute disgust, did not wish to agree to, no attempt at the violent subjugation
> of the boy to his wishes emerges from the story.[40]

Before their elimination, some of _Salò_'s victims rebel, if only
slightly. And others became collaborators with their captors; one boy
saves himself by becoming the Duke's favorite. Some of the victims
call on God by name—to no avail. The appeals court noted the "impossibility of identifying the motive for the crime."

The court might have found some "explanation" for everything in

Pasolini's 1965 short story about Brahin, an Arab boy in Paris. He has had sex with a prostitute and then considers murdering her:

> Gazing at the blonde, he begins saying once more that he's *like* a madman, a lone gypsy who goes about the world, and already there'd been times when he was about to jump out of the window, and now too he'd like to jump—or would she like to jump? And meanwhile he approaches the window, and touches it, as out of an old passion, which subsides a bit at the touch—or prepares to explode with more violence. The window, cracked and pitiful, with its shutters closed on the Rue du Loup Blanc, lets itself be touched.
> Brahin is in the middle of the room, at the foot of the bed. Something has curdled in his eyes that does not dissolve. If it's a question of grief, it's nevertheless replaced by that special feeling by which we blame our grief on someone else, and we provoke this someone else into insisting on being to blame, so that the grief will have good reason to be transformed into rage.[41]

When the last of *Salò*'s storytellers is done and the executions are to start, the pianist whose accompaniment has sweetened the narratives rises quietly from her bench (she has not spoken throughout), climbs a staircase, and steps—as always, wordlessly—from a window ledge to her death. As one witty critic has noted, she "plays along." Perhaps more than just "extra entertainment," she is the sound of the news reports that so infuriated Pasolini, the background noise we take to be normal.

Earlier in the film the libertines stage a mock wedding ceremony. The bosses dress in drag, and each "marries" one of the male victims. The pianist plays the accordion at the ceremony but abruptly drops it and screams. She quickly recomposes herself, picks up her accordion and goes on playing. The mysterious, silent figure—the sole character never touched in the film by anyone else—returns to her piano, and stays there until her suicide.

Pasolini does not close *Salò* on the executions. According to Quintavalle, he considered having the four executioners drive away from the villa, chatting, once their work was done. Another thought was to close with a shot of Red flags, suggesting, presumably, that the PCI was the antidote to Fascism and its sexual corruption, just as Ezio's fisted salute was the answer to his executioners. Both ideas were rejected. Pasolini does not leave a crack in the door open to hope. Adorno did (in an essay written in 1951 on "Freudian theory and the pattern of Fascist propaganda"), suggesting the increase in ideologically and psychologically controlled domination "may well terminate in sudden awareness of the untruth of the spell, and eventually in its collapse." [42] But the "spell" in *Salò* is not broken; Pasolini never allows the viewer to wake, in relief, from its nightmare.

Instead, Pasolini's camera returns to the room from which the bosses have been observing the executions. While Quintavalle watches the tortures and murders in the courtyard, one of the guard-collaborators puts a record on the phonograph and a dance tune, heard under the film's opening titles, is heard.

The production's still photographer caught Pasolini demonstrating to the actors what to do next—a foxtrot. He has his hand on the back of a woman member of the crew, demonstrating. He is smiling, but his mouth is closed, his narrow lips stretched so that his sunken cheeks fell into deep creases. He is wearing the striped shirt they found at the Idroscalo.

Like a boy on Saint Sabina's day in Ramuscello or on the Ciriola dance-boat tied up beneath Castel Sant'Angelo, Troccoletto takes a fellow guard as partner and they begin to dance. One says to the other, "Have you a girl friend?" and he answers, "Yes, her name is Margherita." So *Salò*, autobiography that is not autobiography, ends.

Short of opening the set, Pier Paolo cooperated with PEA's program for publicizing the film. On the day before the last day of shooting, he gave a press conference on the film's site. One questioner asked whether Pasolini thought the peasant world was all good, that nothing bad happened in that era? Pasolini responded impatiently:

> O.K., but everyone understands that, it's almost too obvious to say. I did not say that was a world only good: I said that it was a world that was neither good nor bad, but that it was also good . . . I don't believe in this business of a "good world": I am talking about a world that had certain values, which also gave great things. I don't know, they gave the Duomo of Orvieto and that sweetness of the Friulian peasants who, at the risk of their lives, took bread to the soldiers.

He was fascinated by the stylistic contrast between the *Trilogy* and *Salò*, in which the entire film was, he said, "a metaphor." "There is not in this film any room for any gratuitous image, anything not working." And what is the effect he aimed for? Is it only horror, only the obvious explanation that power corrupts? And that political power and sexual power are metaphors for one another?

He took boys from the *borgata* and Troccoli from Chia and cast them as accomplices to the four Sadean protagonists whose power unleashes anarchy. Does this means that they—not the characters, but the real boys—were accomplices now in the closed system of corrupting power? Where did they begin and end, and where did the characters they played take up and leave off?

Returning home from Stockholm on Friday, October 31, he stopped in Paris to meet with the organizers of the new Paris Film Festival where *Salò* was to premiere. Before leaving Paris, he granted an interview with Channel 2 of the French State-run television, for a program called *Dix de Der*. The well-known reporter, Philippe Bouvard, had followed *Salò*'s enormous pre-release publicity: rumors of explicit sexuality, naked youths on a closed set.

To the question "Why had he given up" being a militant, Pasolini looked both stupefied and annoyed. He answered "I have not at all given up. I am one more than ever." Bouvard asked whether Pasolini ever "felt nostalgia for the era when people insulted you on the street." He answered, "They still do today."

QUESTION: And does this give you a certain pleasure?

PASOLINI: I do not reject it, because I am not a moralist.

QUESTION: What description do you prefer: poet, novelist, writer of dialogue, scriptwriter, actor, critic, director?

PASOLINI: Simply writer.

QUESTION: Will *Salò* scandalize?

PASOLINI: I believe to give scandal is a duty, to be scandalized is a pleasure, and to refuse to be scandalized is moralism.

QUESTION: Why did you enshroud the making of the *120 Days* in so much mystery?

PASOLINI: It was filmed with so much mystery because every work [of art] comes out of mystery. I tried to defend it more than usual because there were immediate dangers, impediments, but nothing special.

QUESTION: What do you mean by "immediate dangers"?

PASOLINI: The appearance of some moralists who reject the pleasure of being scandalized.

There was another "immediate danger" Pasolini did not mention. On August 26, while the film was being processed at Cinecittà, pieces of it were stolen from the Technicolor lab in via Tiburtina—kidnapped for ransom—along with reels of Fellini's *Casanova* and parts of *Genius* directed by Damiano Damiani.

Pasolini refused to pay anything of the hundred million lire demanded; and, in any case, PEA had other copies. Then, on May 3
the next year, twenty-four of the seventy-six reels stolen were found
in a little-used soundstage on the movie lot.

To Pasolini's undisguised impatience, Bouvard then asked whether
the political system in _Salò_ is not like that of Vichy. The apparently
simple questions and Pasolini's brief answers contain worlds.

> QUESTION: Do you think it was a period of great decadence?
>
> PASOLINI: It was the decadence of the Hitlerian period, but not certainly
> that of great Western capitalism.
>
> QUESTION: One knows that in this film hundreds of boys and girls are kid-
> napped and subject to particularly cruel and violent treatment, torture, and
> also those outrages which seem to be the very worst: how did you recruit
> these hundred boys and girls?
>
> PASOLINI: The magic number in Sade . . . the total number of victims is
> about twenty, not a hundred; to select them I simply did as for all the other
> films: I met these young people and chose those I thought the best.
>
> QUESTION: Are they masochistic actors?
>
> PASOLINI: If I chose them, that means that they are.

Pasolini seemed hurried and Bouvard wrote later: "He answered
with short sentences and looked nervously at his watch." The last
word said, Pasolini raced off to Orly, and someone who accompanied
him said he mentioned having "a very important appointment in Italy
the next day." The interview at seven minutes, fifteen seconds' length
aired in France on Saturday, November 8, the day they buried him
in Casarsa.

Bouvard's final question and Pasolini's answer were widely interpreted to mean that Pasolini had, in fact, conducted a Sadean orgy
on his film set, that he had "crossed the line" between art and life.
Rocco Mangia worked hard to estabish this theory: The man who
made _Salò_ must have acted like one of the film's four libertines when
he met Pino.

But any understanding of his attitudes toward filmmaking—even
based on his interviews and to say nothing of the theoretical essays—
suggests altogether otherwise. The adolescents hired to play the victims in _Salò_ were, in his eyes, masochistic. Just as Franco Citti was
a _borgataro_ Accattone, Silvana Mangano was Lucia the bourgeois
matron, Maria Callas was the primitive Attic sorceress. He did be-

lieve the young people of Italy in 1975 to be passive, to be victims of a manipulative power that objectified them and destroyed the values he cherished, to be sexually neurotic. The *Corriere* and *Mondo* articles spelled it out; *Salò* filmed it. The rest is biographical fallacy. The truth of Nietzsche's insight is too soon forgotten: "Terrible experiences give one cause to speculate whether the one who experiences them may not be something terrible."

Sometime during August 1975 Pasolini called on photographer-painter Man Ray at Fregene, a seaside resort twenty miles west of Rome. The American expatriate, labeled "the Dada of us all" and "the shipwrecker of the predictable,"[43] was guest of his Italian art dealer, Luciano Anselmo, whose gallery Il fauno (The Faun) was in Turin. Anselmo's lover, twenty-five-year-old Dino Pedriali, came along. The *bello-brutto ragazzo di borgata*, raised in Donna Olimpia, was starting his photographic career that year with a series of portraits of Ray.

Pasolini had come to see a Ray 1938 painting "Imaginary Portrait of D.A.F. de Sade," in which the head of Sade (who was imprisoned by the Revolution, as he had been by the *ancien régime*) appears, gazing at the Bastille in flames. Pasolini thought the vivid image might be right for *Salò*'s publicity poster.

Pedriali recalls: "Pasolini talked in French, pretty badly, with Ray. I told him I was a photographer and we chatted a bit." Ray seemed to have no idea what *Salò* meant as a symbolic place in Italy's recent history. Pasolini mentioned that he was then writing a catalogue essay for a show of Warhol's serigraphs—he entitled it "Ladies and Gentlemen" (in English). Pedriali and Pasolini had something in common: Pedriali was photographing Warhol, whose path he had crossed in New York three years before, and Pasolini was writing about him.

Pedriali, who recalls taking a copy of *Ragazzi di vita* along for Pasolini to sign, asked if he might photograph its author. "He said he wasn't interested, but if I wanted to take some shots while he was editing *Salò*, that was all right. I told him right away that I was not at all interested in that, but only in recording him as a writer."

With that remark, according to Pedriali, "Everything changed." Pasolini, to that point "detached," warmed to the conversation, and soon it emerged that Dino knew one of the boys Pasolini had befriended years before in the *borgata*. Pasolini seemed only now to notice Pedriali's raspy cigarette voice and intense sexuality—as though seeing him for the first time. He asked Dino to call on him the following week in EUR.

When Pasolini returned from a short visit to the Frankfurt Book Fair, Pedriali arrived at via Eufrate. He found Ninetto there, hanging a picture, and recalls that Pasolini brought Davoli cartons of duty-free cigarettes from the airport. But, "He said good-bye soon after and left." Then Susanna appeared, and Pasolini brought out his typewriter. Mother and son talked a while in dialect. Then Susanna turned to Pedriali. "I am pleased you are here with Pier Paolo because that place [Chia] is too lonely." Then, says Dino, she said to Pier Paolo in Italian: "I am happy to see you going with a boy I like."

That day the two drove to the beachfront house Pasolini shared with Moravia. "I had my own room, and early the next morning went to get newspapers, coffee. Not knowing which paper he read, I bought them all: the *Corriere*, *L'unità*, *Messaggero*. He laughed very timidly and apologized, said he was supposed to do all that, since I was the guest." They went into Sabaudia's streets, laid out by Mussolini's architects, where the public buildings carry hortatory inscriptions. "He parked the Alfa and walked. I made sure other people were not around, since I wanted to capture his aloneness." Pedriali shot about forty frames of Pasolini standing and walking.

Then they returned to Pasolini's house. "He offered me a shower, but I declined. He offered me some wine and said I ought to have some, even though I do not drink. He was very interested in my life in Donna Olimpia, all about me. I recall that he asked me if I followed politics, and when I said I didn't, he remarked, 'That's wrong. A young person ought to be interested in politics.' " "He told me the soccer match was on and he had to watch it undisturbed. It didn't interest me at all, so I just sat next to him watching it until it was over." They went to eat in town: "When we entered the restaurant, everyone fell silent . . . it was incredible, how they looked at him." Pedriali says he, Dino, "stared them down, hard."

Pasolini mentioned he had an "appointment" in nearby Nettuno with "some boys," but they needed to go there in two cars, since Pasolini expected the battery of his to give out at any time. When it did, in fact, fail en route, they left it to recover later and proceeded in Pedriali's blue four-door Alfa Berlinetta. "That made us late, and by the time we arrived, the boys had left. He seemed perturbed at this, upset, so I suggested we go over to the train station and see if they were hanging around there. He was offended and said, 'What makes you think these are the kind of boys who frequent the station?' I mumbled something about how it was cold and maybe they had gone there to keep warm." But they found none, and Pedriali drove Pasolini back to his house in EUR.

They agreed to meet the following week at Pasolini's retreat outside Viterbo at Chia. "I have many *rifugi* [refuges], places I love, where I concentrate. You'll photograph me there." Pedriali says Pasolini was in charge: "He knew what he wanted. He was directing, as on a film set. My job was to execute it."

When they reached Chia, Pedriali dropped his luggage and Pasolini said they had to go and find a local boy. "If he finds out I had arrived and did not go to say hello, there will be a mess." This was Claudio Troccoli. The three went to a restaurant where the boy "talked only about a cross-country motorcycle." "I was wrong to give it to you," Pasolini said, "you'll hurt yourself; I told you over and over to go slowly and you never listen. You make me worry all the time." They took Claudio home and returned to Pasolini's place.

"We sat near the fireplace and he asked, 'Would you feel like working with me? It will be risky and once done, runs the risk of jail: Does this upset you? No one must know about this work, not even Laura can know about it; at the right moment, I will introduce you to my friends. But not even Moravia must know about it; the first thing to do is go to Livio Garzanti because I want to introduce you to him, and it is right that he, my first publisher, after so many years have my last work . . . I want to go and talk about this new project and sign a new contract for this manuscript on which so far I have roughed out six hundred pages and which you will illustrate, together with me. Don't worry, you will do this better than would anyone else.' "

He told Pedriali, "Tomorrow, you will photograph me nude . . . I only ask that you take the pictures as though I were surprised, or unaware of a photographer's presence. Only at a certain moment will I come to understand that someone unobserved is watching me."

Pedriali says he slept little, woke early, and went for a long walk in the country. Returned, he began to photograph Pasolini at his worktable. A folder bearing the heading *Lettere luterane, 1975*, is plainly visible; Pasolini, in a denim workshirt, inclines his head over the keys.

They paused to talk. Pasolini said, "You know, one of the things I love is to paint. Who knows whether if I had been a painter instead of a writer, I would have been happier?" He sat on the floor and began drawing portraits from memory of Longhi. He used wax pastels, dark green and violet or only black. As Dino snapped, Pasolini explained how Longhi had been his teacher, taught him the history of art. Now Pedriali took a close-up, head portrait: Pasolini stared straight into the 50mm lens, the fingers of his right hand closed (but not in a fist), covering his mouth. He gazed into the camera, direct and uncompromising.

Then Pasolini asked, "Are you ready to do those photos?" Pedriali said he would stand outside the window of his stonewalled bedroom in the *dépendance* built at the base of the old tower. Pasolini undressed. Using a Nikon FL, Pedriali shot eighteen pictures through the glass: Pasolini standing naked next to his single bed, sitting on the bed with a book in hand ("he just picked up something off the shelf"), lying down and reading. As planned, Pasolini did not look at the camera, which caught him as though unawares. Pedriali: "Then I told him I wanted to wait until it was dark and I could take the shots with him lit by a single lamp inside. It was to invade his intimacy more, capture the feeling of a spy outside." Pasolini thought it a good idea. Dino shot eighteen more frames: Pasolini standing and looking at the photographer with his hand over his brow, as though peering through the window to better distinguish a form he has only sensed there, someone unseen, outside. The trees reflected in the window glass overlay the image, but neither camera nor cameraman appears.

The photos done, Pasolini told him to put the rolls aside and show them to no one. "As soon as I have seen the pictures, I will explain the work in greater detail; meanwhile, you see if you can come back to Rome because the work will be very intense . . . remember that we will have many enemies, you will even make enemies because people will not understand."[44] According to Pedriali, at some point Pasolini (without showing him the pages) told him that the opening scene of *Vas* was a realistically described homosexual coupling.

Inside the house, Pedriali says he "confessed": "I told him that I was homosexual, that I loved the same boys he did but that they were only for having sex with, but I needed someone mature, only then could one really make love." Pedriali says Pasolini "stared, amazed."

He suggested Pedriali take a shower, "which made sense to me. I'd been working hard, sweating. As I did so, he came into the bathroom and shaved. I could see he was looking in the mirror at me. But nothing happened. When I went to bed in a guest room, he came in and sat at the end of the bed and very gently asked if I needed a blanket. I said that no, I didn't, and he wished me a good night and left the room."

Pedriali claims that as they were leaving the next morning, Pasolini offered him the keys to the tower at Chia. "I refused, not wanting to seem to take advantage." They parted. Pedriali had about forty shots at Sabaudia and seventy at Chia, of which thirty-six were nudes and the rest were of Pasolini at work, writing and drawing.

Pedriali developed the film and prepared to leave Turin to come to Rome. "On Sunday, November 2, I started to leave for the airport. My former lover [Anselmo] called and said, 'You don't need to go now' but refused to explain. Downstairs, I stopped for coffee in a bar, where everyone was discussing the news on the television. I would have saved him. I would have told him those boys were vicious, that he had to stop going after them—that he had to stay with me, work together, live."

A few weeks later Pedriali called on Silvana Mauri Ottieri in Milan. "He wanted to show me these pictures he had taken. I gathered he wanted me to put him in touch with Pasolini's circle in Rome. He seemed very disturbed."[45]

On the evening of November 11, 1975, the five-member censorship commission of the Ministry of Tourism and Spectacle, empowered by a law of 1962, gathered in a ministry projection room to view *Salò*. The board numbered a magistrate from the Supreme Court of Cassazione, a professor of ecclesiastical law, a "representative of the film industry" and—named by the Ministry itself without the collaboration of the appropriate unions or associations—a journalist and the brother of actor Rossano Brazzi.

Grimaldi told the commission he was willing to make cuts. But exercising the vast powers granted it by the Ministries of Spectacle and of Public Instruction, by unanimous vote the panel ordered *Salò* blocked from Italian theaters because "in all its tragedy, it brings to the screen images that are so aberrant and repugnant of sexual perversion as certainly to offend community standards."

The Minister of Spectacle, Adolfo Sarti, who had privately urged the Moro government to undertake major reform of the censorship system, was reported to have privately expressed his agreement with the commission's action. No sooner was this reported than an official announcement came from the Ministry press office; "The Minister denies in the most categorical and indignant manner having influenced the operation of the commission."[46] Grimaldi had twenty days in which to appeal to a combined panel of other censors; meanwhile, *Salò*'s Italian premiere, set for November 21 in Milan, was off.

Three days after announcement of the censorship commission's ban, Senator Delio Bonazzi, identified by the *Corriere della sera*[47] as a member of "the independent Left" rose on the floor of Parliament.

And did the Minister of Tourism and Spectacle not think, he asked, that those seeing the film premiered in Paris rather than in Milan would not find "yet another proof of our cultural and civic inferiority"? Not to be outdone, another member of Parliament, the Christian Democrat Giuseppe Costamagna, formally requested that the Ministry of Finance investigate Pasolini's taxes. "By now, there has been created the mythology of a poor man and a benefactor, trenchant enemy of the society of consumerism and opulence, whereas in other places it is written that he was the owner of houses and villas in Rome, in Soriano nel Cimino and in Casarsa in Friuli, that he owned luxury cars and for every film was paid, as director, not less than a hundred million lire."

*Salò* had been a French-Italian coproduction, and Grimaldi proceeded with its world premiere at the Paris Film Festival in an auditorium of the Palais de Chaillot on the evening of November 22. *Salò* shared the new Paris Festival's sold-out program with Rainer Werner Fassbinder's *Mamma Küster Goes to Heaven*, with Werner Herzog, with the Spanish director Carlos Saura, and with the world premiere of Miloš Forman's *One Flew Over the Cuckoo's Nest*. The program closed with a documentary on the last hours of Salvador Allende. The rock group Soft Machine provided entertainment. The room, which seats two thousand, was filled to overflowing an hour before the film's nine-thirty start. To accommodate those unable to enter, an extra showing was scheduled for eleven the next morning. At the Le Paris cinema the same morning, Parisian critics had a special viewing of their own.

On December 15, 1975, an editorialist for *Oggi* magazine wrote that he hoped *Salò* (slated to open in Milan the following January 11) would be shown to empty cinemas. He added:

> If I were the defense attorney for Giuseppe Pelosi . . . I would invite the judges, in the courtroom, to see the film before issuing their sentence. This film, which carries all the marks of an authentic testament, is in fact the most serious accusation against the director. Sweet and timid in appearance, of tender and gentle manners, Pasolini was in reality a violent man. With the violence of money (and the prestige of his name) he pushed young people to act out the shamefulness of his film and give into his unnatural proposals. The actors, for a few million [lire] and the mirage of a career, said yes. Pelosi, violated for a dinner and twenty thousand lire, said no. And rebelled.[48]

A few days after the article appeared, Pino's mother received this letter from a man from Messina:

In the magazine *Oggi* I read your story and your loving son's, and I confess it really moved me . . . I sympathize with Giuseppe . . . I believe in your son and in the heartfelt words of a mother; this is why I am writing to encourage you . . . If I can do anything for you, I would be happy to help you, even though I am poor . . . If you like, I would be happy to write to your son, become his friend, help him and encourage him . . . When you go to see him, please say hello for me and tell him that I would be happy to be his friend and older brother.[49]

Three days after *Oggi*'s publication, the ban was lifted by the censors' appeals division; they granted the "no objection" stamp, the *nulla osta*. The film's twelve-day run brought in 40 million lire at the box office; Salò had cost about 800 million lire to make.[49] The next month, Enzo Biagi wrote in the *Corriere della sera*: "Salò, for me, and again I declare myself no expert, is a sad and boring confession, the triumph of the backside as a message, the macabre joke of a deformed fantasy, an exercise which calls, more than for aesthetic judgment, that of a psychiatrist."[50]

Within forty-eight hours, on January 13, 1976, the Milan district attorney sequestered the film and commenced proceedings against producer Grimaldi for "commerce in obscene publications" and because Salò "is totally characterized by images and language which represent deviations and sexual perversions . . . homosexual and heterosexual couplings, coprophagia [the consumption of excrement], sadomasochistic relations." Grimaldi told the court that the scenes at issue could not offend the common sense of decency, since they were "not real, but symbolic," playacting and, in any case, a work of art.[51] The court viewed the film on January 26 and on the January 30 ordered a ban.

On February 19 state's attorneys in Rome charged Grimaldi with "corruption of minors" and "obscene acts in a public place" effected during the shooting of the film. Within a week the action was transferred to the competent authorities of Brescia and Mantua, where the alleged crimes occurred. On March 11 the National Association for Good Morals (Associazione Nazionale per il Buon Costume) brought an action in a Lazio regional court against the Ministry of Spectacle and Tourism, seeking annulment of the *nulla osta*. The next month this claim was dismissed; in September the prosecutor's office in Mantua dropped the charges against Grimaldi.

A new denunciation reopened the case: Grimaldi was again charged, the film again sequestered. The sentence this time called the film one of "breathtaking obscenity," "a horrid swamp, stinking slime." Again, Grimaldi was accused of having put a film "offensive to public morals" into circulation. On February 25, 1976, he was sentenced to two months in jail, a fine of 200,000 lire, and confiscation of the film. He won on appeal.

A petition was begun. Moravia was joined by Montale and others calling for absolving the banned film, which they called "the last important work of one of Italy's major intellectuals of this century."

In mid-July Milanese movie houses offered much to choose from in addition to Visconti's *Innocente*, then in its third month. The Diana cinema was showing *Troppo nude per vivere* (Too nude to live); at the Tonale was *Calde labbra* (Hot lips), at the Eden Rivoli *Le giornate intime di una giovane donna* (The intimate days of a young woman). The Puccini offered *Storia di Emmanuelle, o il trionfo dell'erotismo* (The story of Emmanuelle, or the triumph of eroticism), with *Una ragazza dal corpo caldo* (A girl with the hot body) announced as soon to open.[52]

In March *Salò* played briefly in Frankfurt and Stuttgart but was closed after protest by the Catholic Parents Association. Two major unions protested the ban, the German film community rallied and the matter went to court.

In Italy other judicial actions were brought against *Salò* during 1977. That January the film was again ordered blocked in Milan. On February 19 the Milan court of appeal lifted the ban; now the film—minus five minutes of court-ordered cuts, almost all of scenes depicting sodomy—ran three days in a Milanese cinema. New *denuncie* were filed.

During the same months as *Salò*'s fate worked its way through the courts, Pino Pelosi came to trial. Rome's Juvenile Court in via delle Zoccolette (the Street of the Whores)—next door to the Ministry of Justice, only yards from the Tiber's edge—convened on February 2, 1976. Fifty-year-old Alfonso Carlo Moro, member of the court of appeals with particular responsibility for the juvenile sector, presided. Under the terms of article 16 of law number 1404 of July 20, 1934, concerning the trials of minors, the press and all save lawyers and close relatives of the accused were excluded—not simply from the room but from the building. At one point, explaining his relationship with Pasolini, Pelosi turned to Moro and asked if his mother might be excused—he was "ashamed" to have her hear. Moro told Maria Paoletti Pelosi that she was free to do as she liked. She turned to her son, and said, "Well, if that's what you want," and left the room.

The first morning Rocco Mangia offered enough objections and procedural challenges to keep the judges in executive session for four hours. Acceding to objections of both the *parte civile* and the *pubblico ministero* (the state prosecuting attorney), the court declined Mangia's request that the courtroom be opened to the public, as well as his demand that every official document throughout Italy concerning Pasolini's private life be entered in the record, starting with Ramuscello. His request for seventy-five hostile witnesses testifying to Pasolini's character was also denied.

The four-judge panel (Moro, judge Giuseppe Salme, and two women—one a psychologist, the other a social worker) had first planned to hear testimony only twice a week, Mondays and Thursdays. But the first X ray of Pelosi's nose was thrown out because it had been effected in the absence of the defense attorney. It was Mangia's sole victory; another was ordered, despite expert medical testimony that the ensuing months would have repaired any damage done the previous November. The false hope was that some scientific evidence would decide once and for all whether the wound came from Pasolini's blow or Pelosi's striking his head against the Alfa's steering wheel.

More than thirty witnesses were heard during ten days; February 5, 7, 9, 12, 16, and 26, and March 4, 8, 9, and 11. The press managed to get detailed accounts of what went on behind closed doors; reporters ran tabs at bars on the via Arenula for witnesses who passed directly from the courtroom to the waiting reporters. Even the lawyers excused themselves "to take a breath of air"—in fact, to update the journalists outside. Everyone understood that public opinion would decide, if not Pelosi's fate then Pasolini's.

*Gente*'s Trapani (dismissed by a *Messaggero* reporter as "really stupid, unable to get work anywhere else") was summoned. Oriana Fallaci's turn came on March 8. Asked to name her sources, she declined, citing professional privilege against testifying to reveal confidential sources. She was, her argument went, protected by article 2 of the law of February 3, 1963, empowering the Order of Journalists: "Journalists and publishers are held to respect professional secrecy on the sources of information, when acting in a fiduciary relationship to such sources."

"Arrest me even, but I have given my word of honor," she said; Mangia asked that the court order that she be handcuffed immediately. His motion was contested both by Nino Marazzita (representing the Pasolini family) and Salvatore Guinta, the state's attorney at this first trial level. The Tribunal retired for an hour of deliberation and returned to announce that it agreed with Fallaci. An action for refusal to testify during the inquest had already been initiated by the new state's attorney, *sostituto procuratore della repubblica* Guido Guasco. In characteristically calm fashion, he remarked, "Fallaci is a person who likes to be seen, talked about. Her theory certainly found no confirmation. One does not understand why someone with information that could help to determine the truth refuses to give it."

Mangia's shouts could be heard by people in the street outside the Tribunal. "Do not be a whore," he shrieked at her, "but in the name of justice and of the dead man, tell the truth." Fallaci turned to Alfonso Moro: "I cannot endure this man," she said, and he dismissed her. Mangia later claimed that he had "promised her two black eyes, to her face" and that he "was disgusted" when a state's attorney named Sansarsiero "took her arm and led her to a bar for coffee."

Six months later, interviewed by Mike Wallace for "Sixty Minutes," Fallaci said:

> I hate objectivity; I have said so many times. I do not believe in objectivity. I believe in what I see, what I hear and what I feel which is some kind of blasphemy . . . especially for the American press when it predicates facts, not opinion. I don't put only my opinions but my feeling in it [her journalism] and they are dramas indeed. When I make an interview, I live it physically.

She closed the encounter with American TV journalism:

> And you know what scares me most in life, it is to get bored. Boredom . . . everything is better than nothingness. And boredom is nothingness. Above all in life, I do not want to get bored.

Hers was not the only drama. During a day of testimony, despite security guards, one Mario Appignani, twenty-five, a self-described ex-*ragazzo di vita*, managed to enter the courtroom; he approached Pelosi and said, "Decide to tell the truth. Everyone knows that night at the Idroscalo you were not alone." Pelosi rose in his place and made a gesture as though to strike him but was restrained by two guards.

Called to testify, Appignani told the bench a seventeen-year-old named Piero Centi had told him that Pelosi was present at the Idroscalo but that the killing was done by four boys who wanted to get even with Pasolini for driving off and leaving them stranded in Ostia after they had refused to allow him to *fare l'uomo*, "to play the man." The court also called Centi, but *Paese sera* suggested Appignani was "a mythomaniac . . . perhaps trying to publicize his book," which was soon to be published, entitled *La marchetta* (The hustler).

Under cross-examination on February 7 he retracted everything. But the MSI's *Il secolo* had already passed Appignani's fantasies along as fact: "The assassins must have decided to avenge themselves because Pasolini had tried to violate and sodomize them."[53] That same day one of those whom Appignani had named—Giuseppe Raffa—went to a police station and said Appignani had promised him money if he would swear to the existence of a *casa di appuntamento per soli uomini* (a house of appointment for men only) in via delle Vergini.[54]

It was widely believed that the only journalist who did not treat Appignani as a well-known *matto* (a crazy man) was Fallaci: Her many detractors in the Italian press speculated that he was her major source.

If the co-conspirators out to "teach Pasolini a lesson" had been at the station square the night of November 1, how difficult would it have been to tell Pelosi to suggest going to Ostia, following far enough behind not to be seen? Was there not time for just such a plan when Pelosi returned to settle the matter of the keys with Claudio Seminara? And even having Pelosi suggest Ostia would not have been needed: Would they not have acquired enough *furbizia* on the streets to have guessed that was where Pasolini would go?

Under cross-examination, Pelosi admitted that his friends had told him who the man in the Alfa was, and that he had agreed to have sex with him for a promised 20,000 lire. "I planned only to play the man [*fare il maschio*], and anyway I wanted to see whether having sexual relations with a man would disgust me."

On the sixteenth, *carabinieri* Colonel Giuseppe Vitali—*Il messaggero*'s Di Dio calls him *"un cretino"* (an idiot)—told the court that two boys believed to be accomplices had been detained: Franco Borsellino, fourteen, and his older brother Giuseppe, sixteen, also known as Pino. Mangia demanded that they be put on the stand immediately or Vitali quieted. The court, having decided they could not testify as witnesses if there was any chance they would become defendants themselves, adjourned for ten days until February 26 to allow police investigations to proceed.

The case against the boys was thin: The older Borsellino had lived two doors down the street from Pelosi, and he had written to him at the detention center. In one letter he had mentioned going to see "Johnny," a known killer and part of the hustlers' *giro*. Other than that, the case against the pair was mostly their claim to a reporter from *Il tempo* that they had been there and similar boasting to an undercover cop, posing as a hippie. A search of the Borsellino home at via dei Cristoldi 29 found nothing. Plainclothesmen handcuffed and carried off the brothers and confiscated Pelosi's letters to his friends, music tapes, a television, a stereo and record-player. The weekly magazines approached their mother, Luciana, for an exclusive serialization of their story.

On close examination, it became plain that they had made it all up—to seem *duro* (hard) in front of their friends. The police, now edgy, had jumped. Charges of incompetence in the national press were getting to them: In one of the Fallaci stories, *L'Europeo* ran a half-page headed "Six Mistakes Made by the Police." The brothers seemed to think it was all fun, like the *ragazzo di vita* who told a reporter he robbed because it gave him "the same sensation as going to the Luna [amusement] Park in EUR." On February 20 after five days at the Casal del Marmo, the younger Borsellino was set free. Hearings resumed; Marazzita's turn had come to insist on Pelosi's legal maturity. He did so, based on a psychological examination of the boy made by the *parte civile*'s retained expert, psychiatrist Luigi Cancrini.

During the trial, Marazzita received two anonymous letters from someone who identified himself as "a young friend of Pelosi's": They claimed that four well-known "protectors" of hustlers ("They beat us up and take our hard-earned cash") had decided Pasolini intended to write an exposé of male prostitution and the inroads made by pimps to organize the business around the Stazione Termini. He spelled out the first three digits of a Fiat 1500's license—from Catania in Sicily. Marazzita immediately filed a formal *denuncia* against the unknowns, the legal act needed to set an investigation in motion. It was almost immediately "archived," without explanation. *Paese sera* reporter Franco Rossi also received copies, and he printed both letters in his paper. Pelosi laughs them off as "*cazzate*" (bullshit).

Three days before the verdict, Mangia received an anonymous letter: "So he [Pelosi] is a murderer, thief, fag and an idiot . . . But not all idiots kill. There are those who end up being lawyers and defending killers." During the trial, Mangia went to dinner with one of the journalists who had assiduously cultivated his company for some time. After what the reporter calls "too much to eat and drink . . . an unguarded moment," Mangia acknowledged, "for all intents and purposes," that he believed at least one other assassin was present. The reporter felt he did not have enough of substance to print and said he—like Mangia—would deny the story if asked.

On April 24 Mangia delivered his closing speech, properly called *l'arringa* (literally, a harangue). He shouted for three hours against the witnesses, the press, Pasolini, the *parte civile* and the public prosecutor. Bystanders in the via delle Zoccolette outside heard him through closed and guarded doors: Part of the press "had written lies and unfounded information, contributing to the foment of hate and rancor"; others (understood to be Fallaci) had "neither the dignity nor the courage to carry their evidence before justice." He described Pasolini as a man "of a violent life, bitter, odd, dissipated," who took Pelosi to Ostia "with the premediated intention of violating him." He argued that Pelosi had killed "without wishing to" and passed over Pasolini's body "without realizing" that it lay beneath the wheels.

As for the forensic reconstruction of the crime by Susanna Paso-lini's retained consultant, Dr. Fausto Durante, Mangia called his version "the fruit of political ideas and absurd hypotheses." The lawyer had, as early as the first week after Pasolini's murder, appealed to the Juvenile Court to impose the same press gag on Durante as that which prevented the official coroners' going public. Mangia asked that Pelosi be acquitted of murder, and absolved of "obscene acts in public," since his sexual contact with Pasolini was within the car, and also be found innocent of the charge of auto theft because he had taken the car "only to flee from that place."[55]

Marazzita and Calvi, representing the *parte civile*, chose not to address to the court any closing statement. Instead, they submitted a four-part brief: first, why the *parte civile* came into being and chose not to participate in the appeal process; second, why Pelosi must be considered legally even though not chronologically mature; third, an analysis of the crimes charged and why Pelosi was guilty of them all; and finally, an homage to Pasolini as "man, poet, writer, director." In due course, this fifty-page memorandum to the court was printed in the magazine of the Communist Youth League, *Nuova generazione*.

Before retiring to chambers, court president Moro asked Pelosi if he had anything to say. "I am innocent," Pino responded, and that was all. "I could tell the judges' minds were closed," he said later.

On April 26, 1976, after six hours' deliberation, Moro began reading the sentence at 7:20 P.M. to a growing background of gasps from onlookers and Pelosi's cries. The court held "that Pasolini did not attack Pelosi" and that:

> On the basis of numerous elements taken together, one must hold as unac-ceptable Pelosi's version that Pasolini was the aggressor and instead hold that the act was performed by more than one person, and that having reduced

Pasolini to helplessness, they then caused him to be killed by passing over him with the car.

The accused was found "guilty of the crime of voluntary homicide in company with others not known," obscene acts, and theft and ordered to pay a fine of 30,000 lire and court costs. In addition, the Tribunal, "reducing for [his legal age of] minority" from the statutorily provided minimum (article 575 of the penal code) of twenty-one years [life for adults]," ordered Pelosi incarcerated for nine years, seven months, and ten days. The state had asked for ten years, eight months, and ten days. The sentence broke down thus: nine years and four months for voluntary homicide, a year and four months for auto theft, a month and ten days for obscene acts.

Marazzita and Calvi stood on the courthouse steps and told the press that they were satisfied; the *parte civile*, its point made, was now "retiring."

Journalist Di Dio, who had covered the case from Pelosi's first detention by the *carabinieri* on Ostia in the early hours of November 2, believes Judge Moro, like his brother, was "a liberal Catholic, open to the Left," but someone overwhelmed by the public campaign mounted against Pelosi, convinced by the mass media sympathetic enough to Pasolini as a rallying cry to campaign that he was not alone. Mario Coffaro of *Il messaggero* says Moro is "very slippery, a man impossible to classify, to pin down."

Perhaps most important, as *Il messaggero*'s Marcucci says, "It was a time of intellectual terrorism, before the real thing, an era of conspiracies. The public wanted plots and saw them everywhere. Those of us covering the story treated it as a crime like any other, but the readers were in a frame of mind that said if an *espresso* was not good, the CIA must be behind it."[56]

A certain "Rosa" wrote Pino's parents: "I heard about Pelosi's sentence, the poor boy . . . being Communist like Pasolini you can win all the battles . . . he was a filthy rotten pig in a pigsty, but even dead that monster had everyone's blessing, but only because that pig was a Communist."

Dino Sisti, from near La Spezia, wrote the next day: "No one of the ordinary people believes you are guilty" and offered a citation from the evangelist Luke (21:24), "Men are about to account to their grand judge for that which they have done."

Pino was sped away in a waiting police car, just as in the movie he claims he went to see at the Moderno. Even before he was gone, fistfights erupted at the courtroom door: Pino's baker uncle threw himself against some photographers, shouting, "It's all your fault." His aunt and mother did the same. Someone kicked Pelosi's cousin, who fell to the ground. Antonio Pelosi could be heard yelling: "They condemned him only because it was Pier Paolo Pasolini, that pig, that corruptor of minors. My son defended himself against that wretch and that's all." *Carabinieri* had to break up the battle; the photographers got their pictures. Mangia told reporters he would immediately appeal. An English journalist covering the trial called it "a Roman circus"; what started in tragedy ended in farce.

Under section 98 of the Italian Penal Code, a psychological profile must be made of juvenile offenders "more than fourteen years of age but less than eighteen" at the time of their crime. Those found to have "capacity to intend and to will" can be charged and tried as adults. Pino got off easy. The public prosecutor told the court: "We have certain proof that during the trial the boy behaved in a way both clever and smart. He understood what could damage him, and that which instead would help him; he is, indeed, rough and primitive, but he is not unable to understand and to will." Mangia had won a major victory: The court-appointed experts were unanimous in their prognosis that "taken together, both for psychological-emotional reasons and those environmental and familial, the boy finds himself in a stage of immature development." And yet the Tribunal exercised its authority to reject the finding. It could have gone better for him.

Or worse: Had the court chosen to make no allowance for Pelosi's age, he might have been sentenced—as an adult—for first degree murder with premeditation, receiving the life sentence (*ergastolo*) prescribed by law. Escaping that, neither was he deemed so immature as to be committed only to a reformatory (*riformatorio giudicario*), where after three years he might be released if found by a panel of experts to no longer be "a social menace."

The trial court had also held, as a matter of law, that the green sweater found on the back seat of the Alfa when police stopped Pelosi belonged neither to him nor to Pasolini, and that a foam-rubber insole had been inadvertently left behind when the unknown killer "removed his right shoe, to clean off the mud (or blood) and, in the confusion that necessarily accompanied the crime, forgot to recover it." No one was sure the prints left by rubber-soled shoes came from the soccer-players who swarmed over the site on Sunday morning. Both Pelosi and Pasolini wore leather-bottomed boots, with heels that would clearly have left their trace.

Pelosi and Pasolini arrived at the Idroscalo at 12:30 A.M., and

Pelosi was picked up by the police almost exactly an hour later. In the court's judgment, Pelosi's version accounted for a half hour at most, even erring in his favor. "Is it not more logical," the court asked rhetorically in the sentence, "that the blank time was used to decide on a common course of conduct by those who had participated in the crime?" On the night of November 1–2, 1975, Claudio Seminara (born July 4, 1956)—whom Pelosi's mother called her son's *amico di cuore* (bosom-buddy), Adolfo de Stefanis (born September 24, 1956), and Salvatore Deidda (born February 22, 1957) were all over eighteen, legal adults. Only Pino was not.

The full holding of one hundred typewritten, legal-length pages was formally entered into the record on May 21, 1976. Ten days later, to no one's surprise, *Paese sera* wrote praising Calvi, Marazzita, and especially Durante, who had been a journalist at the paper before turning to medicine. Leaping wildly to conclusions, the daily's Franco Rossi wrote: "The second, unknown assassin wore a green sweater, shoes with rubber soles, probably some sort of tennis shoe, and smoked Marlboros."

Three weeks later, on his eighteenth birthday (June 28), Pelosi was transferred, as the law required, to the adult prison at Rebibbia, built in 1971 to house 800 adult male inmates. Lawyer Calvi called it "a model prison, one without bars on the windows . . . a hotel."[57] *Pubblico ministero* Santarsiero disgreed: He believed that "people are better off at Regina Coeli with toilets than at Rebibbia without them." Pino was soon moved to the lower-security facility at Civitavecchia.

On June 21, 1976, Mangia filed a fifty-three-page appeal. Now a twenty-six-year veteran of criminal interrogations named Guido Guasco had been appointed by the head *procuratore generale* "Excellency" Raffaele del Guidice, replacing Giunta and Santarsiero. Guasco won the grudging admiration of reporters for his "seriousness" and resistance to press pressures. He seemed credible when he claimed, "I was not interested in the figure of Pasolini but in what happened." He was unmoved by the *parte civile*'s reconstruction of the crime. He believed Pasolini had provoked Pelosi, but not enough to rise to the level of legitimate self-defense. As for what Pasolini might have done to enrage Pelosi, Guasco says, "Pasolini was too well known as an active homosexual for it even to be discussed. It would be impossible to find out [what his practices were] and his friends would never tell the truth . . . he had transfused into himself the mentality of the *borgata*, also including the violence of the *borgata*. Even if he were not a violent man, he would have lived the violence of the *borgata* through his contact with its people."

Italian law accepts "temporary insanity" but not out of anger; it must be part of a "psychic infirmity," an ongoing pathology. Pelosi's sentence could be reduced on grounds of legal immaturity, and provocation could be taken into account. But Pasolini's action would not provide Pelosi with a legitimate defense enough to excuse the boy's actions in full; Guasco argued that the kick to the balls (a *violenza di reflesso*) incapacitated Pasolini and at that point Pelosi's legitimate defense ended. After that, Pino's acts constituted homicide.

Starting December 1, appellate arguments were heard, but it was (what Di Dio called) "a show" that passed with only about ten persons present. Marazzita and Calvi neither appeared nor filed documents. Guasco told the court the the first tribunal's sentence was "superficial, arbitrary, based on smoky hypotheses and . . . fantastic journalistic reconstructions."[58] Looking back, he says, "I wanted to establish a historic reality, the truth for itself."

When Mangia's turn came, he spoke for three hours nonstop. Court president Ferdinando Zucconi-Galli Fonseca asked Pelosi if he wished to speak. "I have always said the truth and I have nothing to add. I was alone with Pasolini and there was no one else."[59]

After seven hours' deliberation, on Saturday, December 4, the appellate tribunal of five—three judges, a sociologist, and a psychologist—confirmed Pelosi's guilt as regarded voluntary homicide and auto theft. In the course of a 124-page opinion, the court rejected Mangia's self-defense argument, but also overturned the first court's holding as to conspiracy. It dismissed the evidence which had convinced the court of first instance, calling it "a light residue of doubt" and merely "allegations."

In his brief, Guasco had written that if Pelosi was not alone, he could not be condemned as he had been at first instance. "I wrote that if the killing had been by more than one, we must go back and make further investigations and identify them. The conclusion: If Pelosi was not alone, the case could not be closed. Or he had to be condemned as sole assassin." "In this dilemma," he says, "the [appellate] court chose the latter." As for the mechanics of the crime, Guasco believes Pelosi's boots ("they were pointed and heavy") enough to incapacitate anyone from the kick Pasolini took. As for the lack of blood on Pino, the magistrate contends, "The plank left a distance between them and [Pasolini's] blood did not spurt. It would be different with a knife."

Following his theory, the appellate bench reversed the Moro court's finding. It held there was "lacking the proof that the crime of murder was committed together with other persons."

Mangia crowed that Guasco "quite rightly" decided that the mysterious green sweater was, in fact, only a rag, "all greasy." It was, Mangia had argued, actually found in the automobile's trunk and only by mistake of the police made its way later inside the passenger compartment. But the court rejected Mangia's call for hearing another thirty witnesses. It threw out the "obscene acts in a public place" change because Pelosi's sex with Pasolini was inside a car.

Mangia's difference with Guasco was that the lawyer insisted Pelosi had run over Pasolini's body in panic, by accident, and thus was guilty only of *omicidio colposo* (involuntary homicide), which carried a minimum sentence of five years. Guasco, who agreed that Pino was alone, contended that the boy drove over the body intentionally but only once, not backing up and repassing over Pasolini, as Durante had claimed.

Guasco won a confirmation of the conviction of voluntary manslaughter but not of intentional homicide (*preterintenzionale* but not *premeditato*), a major step for the worse from Mangia's claim of accidental killing.

The bottom line was that Pelosi's sentence was cut only by three months and ten days. Pelosi says he told Mangia "they might as well keep the three months." Officially, he was the assassin, who acted alone. Mangia had won small and lost big.

Following on this second verdict, the Italian press, save for the Left, was quick to announce the case definitively closed and declare Pelosi a proven sincere and accurate confessant. It was neat and clean: A confessed killer was being punished, with all difficult questions tabled indefinitely.

The *New York Times* characterized the hypothesis that Pelosi had accomplices as one now "destroyed at the second trial, in which it was established that the young assassin had acted alone."[60]

The State-owned television had done as much from the start, reassuring Italians that Pasolini had contended and broadcast his end essentially as Pelosi claimed. In his letter-lesson to Gennariello of April 10, 1975, Pasolini described the RAI-TV's personnel as "announcers, presenters and other dregs of humanity of that kind [who] talk—and talk horrendously."[61] The dead man's friends contended that the television he had attacked "could not resist the temptation of getting even" by dismissing the theory of accomplices. It blared the news of his murder and the verdicts with what Andrea Zanzotto called "a vile din . . . by a monstrous, slavering turbidity of 'information-by-redundance.'"[62]

Zanzotto also wrote of his fellow poet and friend: "He had been aware of the slaughter in the air for quite a while, like the ozone in a storm, and he had not noticed it on behalf of himself alone, but for his era."

Three years passed and on April 26, 1979, the First Section of the highest court in the land—the Corte di Cassazione—considered Mangia's call for Pelosi's acquittal. His claim, as always, was that Pasolini had not been beaten to death but rather was the victim of "an accident" that occurred when Pelosi mistakenly ran over Pasolini's body. His argument, as always: "voluntary manslaughter by a legally immature party, legitimate self-defense against provocation by beating."

A few days before the high court handed down its decision *L'espresso* ran the color photos of Pasolini's body in the morgue. They were presumably supplied to the magazine by Marazzita (who remained Susanna's lawyer of record); he must have had them from the photographer, Dr. Faustino Durante. The accompanying text listed the six points which the magazine's reporter claimed argued against the appellate alteration of the first verdict:

A The lack of "significant traces of blood" on Pelosi's hands and clothing.

B The presence in Pasolini's car of the pullover sweater and the in-sole, which belonged neither to him nor to Pelosi.

C The disappearance of the pack of cigarettes and a lighter which Pelosi asked the police to retrieve from the car.

D Bloody prints on the passenger side of the car roof, none on the driver side: suggesting either Pelosi's hands were bloody and he got in on the passenger side while someone else drove, or an accomplice got in on the passenger side and left the stains.

E The failure of police or *carabinieri* to question Pelosi's friends closely as to whether they had relations with Pasolini. Why did the judicial authorities hold it "not obligatory" (after the first sentence, from the Juvenile Court) to reopen the investigation in order to identify the so-called unknown accomplices?.

F And why did they not follow through with the lead on a car with a Catania license plate, of which an anonymous source provided the first two numbers, one said to have followed Pasolini's car that night?

After two hours' deliberation, the First Penal Section of the Corte di Cassazione rejected Mangia's claims: Not a trial court hearing evidence, the Cassazione's sole ambit is to pass on the "legitimacy" of lower-level rulings. They held the appellate verdict of December 4,

1976—modifying the first Tribunal's decision of the previous April 26—confirmed intact. Pelosi was alone, was mature, and killed voluntarily, not acting in justifiable self-defense.

Mangia commented that Pelosi would have fared better "if he had killed his own father and mother." Pelosi, more than a decade later, asks bitterly what would have happened "if the one who had killed Pasolini had been the son of [Prime Minister Giulio] Andreotti."

Pelosi served five years, and then asked that Mangia seek early release; Italian penal law allows such a request to be filed after half a sentence has been served: If the request is granted, the inmate's comings and goings are monitored by a *giudice di sorveglianza*, effectively a parole officer. Mangia thought it better to wait. A year passed. In the summer of 1982, six years and five months after the first sentence, he petitioned that his client be granted *libertà provvisoria* (parole) on grounds that Pelosi's behavior in prison had been exemplary, a claim now backed by Pino's prison supervisor, social worker Gaetano DeLeo.

"Pelosi has changed," Mangia argued, "he is penitent and has resumed studying, and he works." But the appeals section of the juvenile court denied the motion. Pelosi says it made into "symptoms of a not exhausted criminal tendency" the accidental breaking of a window playing Ping-Pong and a protest that lasted a few hours when an inmate committed suicide by gas inhalation.

As allowed by law, Mangia then appealed for clemency (*grazia*, literally, grace) in an open letter to the President of the Republic; the President chose not to intervene.

Pelosi asks: "If they did not find me insane—and they did not—then what was my motive for killing Pasolini, if not self-defense, tell me that." He asks why the psychologists appointed by the Tribunal (Busnelli and Giornale) were ignored, when they found him legally "immature." He asks why no one pays attention to the lie detector test he volunteered to take, administered by "an American professor," presumably a mark of quality. "He asked me whether I put the car into reverse, to pass over Pasolini's body a second time and I told him no, he asked whether I knew Pasolini before and I told him no, he asked whether I was alone that night and I told him yes. But they ignore all that."[63]

Its verdicts rendered, Italian justice considered the matter closed. The matter was "archived." Laura Betti began circulating petitions among ARCI clubs (PCI cultural associations) in sixty cities. In March 1979, writing with more hope than fact, *Panorama*[64] reported on "a movement . . . born out of anguish and suspicion," headed with "notable names" anxious to see the case reopened. From the floor of Parliament, PCI deputies Giovanni Berlinguer (brother of the party's General Secretary) and Gian Carlo Codrignani argued that the case had been "too quickly sent to the archives." Minister of Justice (DC) Francesco Bonifacio ignored them.

Similarly, the Minister of the Interior ignored demands from three senators of the "independent Left"—Giuseppe Branca, Judge Carlo Galante Garrone, and Pasolini's old *Officina* friend Angelo Romanò, as well as the former president of the Constitutional court—and two members of the Supreme Council of the Magistracy (Ettore Gallo and Michele Coiro, both Communists, at least by orientation), all demanding that the investigation be reopened, and the search for the "unknowns" resumed. They accused the Rome DA's office under Del Guidice (who retired in the summer of 1976, after Pelosi's first sentence) of incompetence, and the bench of not doing their duty.

The matter passed to Guasco, who checked the record and rejected the demand, specifying that everything they asked for had already been done by the police. Guasco stayed in that job until the end of 1979 and heard nothing more; from April 1978 until December 1979 he was occupied with the murder of Aldo Moro.

The legal matter of Pasolini's death was now deemed to be officially ended.

Gossip has it that one night at Moravia's, after too much wine, Berlinguer and others declared themselves a "Democratic Committee for Investigation into the Death of Pier Paolo Pasolini." Nothing happened; the matter stayed on the *livello di salotto* (small talk). Pasolini dead served again for the living to form ranks and show their flags. Like Feltrinelli, like Pinelli, his death "had" to be political; he "had" to be a "victim of the Fascists."

After Pelosi had served six years, about two-thirds of his sentence, Mangia (undeterred by his first rejection) approached the Juvenile Court again. This time, it heard recommendations from prison authorities at Civitavecchia who called Pino, now 24, "a model prisoner," who had worked peacefully in the institution's laundry and spent the 150 hours in class needed for his high school diploma. Satisfied that rehabilitation had been successful, the panel reduced his sentence by about a year and a half.[65]

On August 18, 1982, Mangia petitioned to grant his client "semi-liberty"; the judges agreed in December, stating of Pelosi: "He behaved well; he studied and collaborated in the work of maturation of his character." Under terms of the order, intended to "favor his reintegration into society," he was transferred from Civitavecchia to Rebibbia prison and allowed to work outside by day but required punctually to return by three every afternoon.[66] Pino had his old job waiting for him at his maternal uncle Italo's wood-burning bakery in Garbatella.

Altogether, Pelosi served seven and a half years in Civitavecchia for voluntary homicide, followed by six months of *semi-libertà* at Rebibbia, and after that ten months of *libertà condizionale*—free except he had to present himself at least twice a week to the *carabinieri*, reporting on his whereabouts. He was released (it was duly reported in the press)—apparently once and for all—in July 1983. In 1978 and 1981, he profited from an across-the-board reduction of sentences granted by the Italian State to relieve some of the over-crowding in its prisons.

In September 1985, Pino and accomplice Aldo Piacentini, 26, (with whom Pino would work again) were caught by *carabinieri* in the act of "carrying off various objects they had stolen from an apart-ment." Piacentini was "conditionally discharged." Pelosi, then 27, returned to Rebibbia.

On December 5, 1985, he was arrested with five others at the Stazione Termini, charged with attempting to rob a postal truck car-rying a billion lire, destined for an office in Milan. It was Pino's second such adventure: already in January 1984—only six months after completing his time for killing Pasolini—he was charged with trying to rob a postal truck. After five months in detention pending trial, he had been released for "insufficiency of evidence."

On the second occasion, police had stepped up surveillance around the Station and noticed "two suspicious men" walking back and forth between the Station post office in via Marsala (running parallel to the tracks) and the mail trucks stopped to await loading. After Pelosi's trial on these charges (Mangia was again his lawyer), Pino was set freed, but only for "insufficiency of evidence." Ten days later, the police arrived in via Fusinatti and revoked his driver's license. That year, Pino and his buddies hit a butcher shop (the owner was wounded), and a shop in Tivoli, apparently with plans to strike a furrier.

In June 1985, he held up a jewelry store in via Catania; under interrogation (he claims police struck him), Pelosi confessed to par-ticipating. His accomplice, Carlo Simone, held a pistol to the head of the owner's wife, Giovanna Lascari, who insisted she did not have the keys nor the combination to the safe. They took watches and small gold items—"not worth more then four or five million lire," Pelosi insists, not the eighty million lire the papers reported.

Mangia insisted Pelosi could not go to trial without first undergoing psychiatric examination. The youth claimed he suffered hallucinations, and "felt himself persecuted by Pasolini's ghost" (*Il progresso*, Oct 29, 1986). Sentenced to three and a half years, he served eighteen months in prison, followed by six in a halfway house—rehabilitation center; he was released in January 1988.

Next came an apartment break-in ("Someone I knew said there were two kilos of gold inside"); Pelosi explained it as an effort to acquire enough capital, fast, to set up a vendor's stand in the market, to traffic in old clothes, fur coats bought cheap and sold dear. But an alarm sounded, police arrived and Pelosi was found crouching in a nearby doorway. Condemned to six months, he served three.

During 1985, he was free for three weeks; he remembers it was November and December. On December 9, *La repubblica* opined, "At this point, charged with theft, armed robbery, fencing stolen goods, illegal possession of firearms both military and civilian, forgery of documents, and *associazione a delinquere* (association for delinquent ends) for "Pino the Frog" the doors of Regina Coeli may not open for a long time."

Six weeks later he was arrested for kiting false checks, a charge he contends grew out of the avidity of the police to catch a famous fish and the perfidy of one of the two true criminals. Pending trial, he was sentenced to six months' house arrest. *Carabinieri* passed daily in a squad car to confirm that he was in and not gone out, not even for a coffee.

To earn money the only way he could while under house arrest, Pelosi sold interviews: "The television came here once. They paid me a million [lire]," he says proudly. With the callousness that excuses itself as clear-eyed, Reporter Di Dio says, "Those people live for publicity. If the press stop interviewing and writing about them, they'd throw themselves from a window."

Of the thirteen years following that night at the Piazza dei Cinquecento, Pelosi lived only one not behind guarded walls. Released, his life was a constant shuttling between unemployment at home (maintained by his parents) and ever more serious crimes he imagined would make him free but served only to put him back inside.

Within days after serving his last term of house arrest, he volunteered to enter a halfway house founded by Don Mario Picchi to treat drug addicts ("I'm not one of those," Pelosi says, thrusting out his arms to show they are clean); but he liked the place after his first time there because it only allows ten cigarettes a day, two glasses of wine a week, demanded regulated work, provided group therapy, and "promised never to leave me alone." He needed, he said, someone to help him put what he called (perhaps mimicking his psychologists) "structure" into his character. Now no one would hire him; he said he felt he had nothing to lose if he committed another major crime. He had to put himself away to keep from doing something terrible. With time, he came to decide that "outside'" was worse than confinement; "inside," at least he was provided companionship, security, and identity.

What would *not* have served Pasolini was a "mistaken death"—that would be like a battle lost. He wanted—needed—to die in the market square, making an instructive lesson of the consumption of his body. The only way to end the film of his life and make sense of it (to edit chaos into cosmos) was a violent death, seen to be so by the public. "Because only the death of the hero is a spectacle," he wrote, "only that is useful." [67] The hero, out of an archaic civilization, one whose memory is in "pre-History," part of the discarded world, unremembered and unwanted by modern, consumerist History.

In a poem entitled "Communiqué to ANSA (Suggestions)" (ANSA is the State-run national news service), printed in the almost ignored *Trasumanar e organizzar,* Pasolini predicted:

> I drank a glass of water at three in the morning
> while Arezzo seemed to be absolutely independent.
> Once the omission of principal responsibilities has been decided
> (of poet, of citizen)
> my verses will be *completely practical*
> (even though I know that without God practice is surrealistic)
> As Euripides says: "Democracy consists of these simple words:
> who has some useful counsel to offer his country?"
> And so, my counsels will be of a moderately mad man.
> After my death, therefore, my absence will not be felt:
> ambiguity matters as long as the Ambiguous lives. [68]

Only by useful spectacle could his life become a story, an example, the stuff of pedagogy. He pinpointed the nexus where art, life, and death converge and the esthetic becomes the ethical: "If we were immortal we would be immoral, because our example would never come to an end, it would be indecipherable." "Legibility," as he would call it, was only possible through dying. Only by negating himself could the the antihero of his own film-life prove it all worthwhile, that he was right all along.

He was one of the "director-martyrs" of the cinema whom he described in *Empirismo eretico*, who "in their fury to *expose themselves* [*esporsi*, the same verb used in "run the risk of danger"] end up getting that which they so aggressively desired: to be wounded and killed with the very weapons they offer to their enemy."[69] Only that way can "liberty" be had, and liberty he defined as "the freedom to choose one's own death." He who so exposes himself does so with scandalous and contradictory technique, scandalous and contradictory life, and —with his own body—to a scandalous and contradictory death.

He described the editing process on the moviola as "similar to the choice of death," and wrote that "at the moviola there is the liberty of the author." The film director, making the film of his own life, has liberty to edit, that is to say, to choose the death that alone gives signifying shape to his life as art.

He wrote that "man expresses himself above all through his actions." He meant something far more profound than the proverb, "Italians don't just live their lives; they enact them." The creation myths require that the passage from chaos to cosmos include a sacrifice, preferably violent; the greatest act of scandal also allows the greatest expression.[70]

To say Pasolini "wished his death" is banal. But what is one to make of his declaration, "One's time is not that time in which one lives, but that of life after death: as such, it is real, it is not an illusion and might very well be that of the plot of a film"?[71]

Perhaps with "A Desperate Vitality" in mind, Zanzotto wrote:

> After two verdicts, and perhaps precisely because of the absurdity of the second, [Pasolini's murder] appears more and more the effect of an intrigue, of a conspiracy (in a political and social climate which by now is itself a conspiracy), [yet this] does not remove the feeling of a lack of defense on the part of one who knew very well how every trap was ready to spring at any moment, and who exposed himself, unarmed, obstinate, even "resigned," there where the danger was greatest.[72]

On April 27, 1977, the *Corriere della sera* reported "*Izvestia* Attacks *Salò*": "The Rome correspondent of *Izvestia* writes that Pier Paolo Pasolini's film *Salò or the 120 Days of Sodom* constitutes the worst accumulation of sadism and masochism as well as perverse and disgusting deviations that has ever been seen in the cinema.' "

Along with Bertolucci's *Novecento*, *Salò* was shown at the Fifteenth New York Film Festival in October 1977. The *New York Times*, which editorialized in favor of its screening, reported: "At the Saturday night screening, gagging noises from spectators were heard . . . about two dozen members of the largely male audience walked out. Still, at the end of the film, the cheers and applause drowned out the hisses and boos." Vincent Canby wrote on October 1, "As Mr. Pasolini's vision of the world became increasingly bleak, his films became more arid. *Salò* is the bitter, empty end."[73] Rex Reed wrote the same day, in the *New York Daily News*, the film "is . . . a despicable and nauseating piece of garbage that would disgust the denizens of a 42 St. grind house. After this insult hits the screen, the Festival director . . . will have a lot of explaining to do." There followed a short commercial run at the Festival Cinema, which advertised, "A disturbing motion picture for mature audiences who are prepared to view it."

On January 16, 1980, another "commission of experts," without a single film critic or scholar in its ranks, convened in Rome under the aegis of the authorities charged with administering the laws on censorship, and decreed that film exhibitors were not obliged to accept *Salò* for viewing—a rare exception to the system in place in Italy which guarantees some showing of even the most squalid product.


As usual, with *Salò* finished, in the fall of 1975 Pasolini turned to new projects already in the works. It seemed, at one moment, that *Salò* might have been the first part of another trilogy, the reverse image of a trilogy "of life," a triad with *Porno-teo-kolossal* (at one point, called simply *Il cinema*) and *Saint Paul*, or *Bestemmia* (Curse), which he said he had been "thinking of five or six years." In January 1967, when he left off, he had brought its screenplay to one hundred fifty typewritten pages with many handwritten corrections; partly screenplay, partly narrative poem.[74]

He wanted to finish the novel called sometimes *Petrolio*, sometimes *Vas*. And had accepted an invitation to a new international film festival in Chicago. There was an address to the Radical Party's annual conference to prepare for delivery on Tuesday, November fourth. He planned to tell them he was going to continue to vote PCI, and why. He would urge the Radicals "to demand, to want, to identify with him who is different, to scandalize, to curse." First, he had to go to Stockholm. There he bumped into Francesco Saverio Alonzo, for whose book of poems he had written a preface years before. "Wasn't he afraid of being 'punished' for his statements against the neo-Fascists?" "I am amazed that they haven't already tried it," he answered, "once and for all."

He was home from Stockholm and Paris by early evening on Friday, October 31, and rose late on Saturday. He lunched in EUR with Graziella, Nico, and Susanna, who prepared the meal. About noon, he phoned Norberto Valentini of the tabloid *Domenica del corriere*. The weekly magazine was planning a roundtable on "censorship in television," and Pasolini wanted to accept their invitation. "I also want to come to answer the insults of so many people."

"When is it?" he asked. "November 6? Couldn't you move it up to Monday the third? I've come back to Rome because I understand two copies of my film *Salò* are finished and I'm in a hurry to see it and discuss it with friends. Maybe I'll see it today, why don't you come along? I'll call you back later."

Two weeks before, he had given an interview to that magazine's Giovanna Grassi: "A day doesn't pass when I do not feel myself accused. My niece, Graziella, who lives with me and my mother, goes down to collect the mail, and there are letters with insults, threats, blackmail . . . After my article in the *Corriere della sera*, where I wrote that the middle school and television were absolutely harmful to young people, I received infamous phone calls. I have been attacked on the street. And no one seems to want really to discuss it with me!"[75]

Grimaldi stopped by the via Eufrate apartment at about one o'clock. The treatment of their next film together was already in his hands. Their "brief and amiable" chat done, he left. The next morning Sergio Leone passed by Grimaldi's house in EUR with the news.

Sometime after two, Ninetto and Laura Betti arrived. Laura tried to convince Pier Paolo to go to the cinema with her and another friend; Pasolini said only, "We'll see." She tried to phone her friend to explain no decision was made, but the phones were out; she went to the movies alone.

Sometime during the afternoon of Saturday, November 1, Graziella washed the Alfa 2000 and cleaned the inside as well. Later, she was certain that she had cleaned thoroughly, and had not seen what the police found: a rubber orthopedic sole under one of the seats and a green sweater Graziella was sure was not Pasolini's. Maybe someone had left them there in the course of that afternoon, when he went alone on an appointment no one could later reconstruct.

At four o'clock, Furio Colombo came to conduct an interview. A widely respected star writer at Turin's *La stampa*, Colombo later recalled that Pasolini's tone struck him as "correct." The transcript of the question-and-answer session appeared under a banner heading—"Pasolini: The Last Interview"—on Wednesday, November 5, the day of the salute in the Campo dei Fiori. Pasolini suggested the story's headline: "We Are All in Danger."

From the start, he directed his remarks "to the lovely troupes of intellectuals, sociologists, experts, and journalists of the most noble intentions":

> I want to spit it out: I want to descend to Hell and see things that do not disturb others. But pay attention. Hell is mounting up also toward you. It is true that it comes wearing masks and carrying various banners . . . Don't delude yourselves . . . you are—with the schools, television, the quietness of your newspapers—you are the conservators of this horrible order based on the idea of possession and the idea of destruction. Lucky you who are content to put a nice label on the crime. To me, this seems one more of the many gestures of a mass culture . . . maybe I am wrong, but I will continue to say that we are all in danger.

He asked Colombo to delay publication so he could think overnight, and add "some notes" the next day. "It is easier for me to write than to talk," he said; they agreed the journalist would pass by via Eufrate and collect Pasolini's additions the following morning, on Sunday the second. The interview ended by six; Pasolini looked foward to dinner with Ninetto and his family at the Pommidoro in San Lorenzo.

"A Desperate Vitality" is Pasolini's 1963 poem cast as imaginary interview, autobiography, and hallucination. To apologize to his conjured interviewer-judge, to explain "never having had any lucidity"—and much more—the poet reaches back to the flight from Friuli and far beyond:

> I was alone:
> with my bones, a shy frightened
> mother, and my will.

> The objective was to humiliate the already
> humiliated.
> I must tell you they've succeeded,
> and without even much effort. Perhaps
> if they'd known it was so simple,
> they, and fewer of them, would have taken less trouble!

> (aha, notice, I'm using the generic plural: They!
> with the winking love of the madman toward his illness.)

The results of this victory, then,
even they, count for very little: one authoritative
signature fewer on the petitions for peace.
Well, from the object's viewpoint, it's not much.
As for the subject . . . But let's leave it at that;
I've described too much even,
but never orally,
my sorrows of a crushed worm
who raises its little head and struggles,
with repugnant ingenuousness, etc.

A fascist victory!
Keep writing: let them (*them!*) know that I know:

with the consciousness of a wounded bird
that meekly dying doesn't forgive."
. . .
Doesn't forgive!

There was a soul, among those that
still had to descend into life
—so many, and all alike, poor souls—
a soul, in the light of whose brown eyes,
in the modest forelock combed up by a maternal idea
of male beauty, burned
the desire to die.

He saw it at once, he
who dos not forgive.

He said, "Come closer." He took it,
and like an artisan
up there in the world that precedes life,
laid hands on its head
and pronounced the malediction.

It was an innocent clean soul,
like a little boy at his first Communion,
wise in the wisdom of his ten years,
dressed in white, in a material
chosen by the maternal idea of male grace, with,
in his warm eyes, the desire to die.

Ah, he saw it at once, he
who does not forgive.

He saw the infinite capacity to obey
and the infinite capacity to rebel:
he called it to him—and as it looked

at him, trustful, like a lamb looking at
its rightful executioner, he performed on it
the consecration in reverse, while,
over the fading light of his gaze,
a shadow of compassion was rising.

"You shall go down into the world,
and you shall be innocent, gentle, well-balanced and faithful,
you shall have an infinite capacity to obey
and an infinite capacity to rebel.
You shall be pure.
Therefore I curse you."

I still see his gaze
full of pity—as well as the mild horror
that one shows for him who inspires it
—the gaze with which one follows
him who goes off, without knowing it, to die,
and, from a need that governs him who knows and him who doesn't,
no one says anything to him—
I still see his gaze,
as I was turning away
—from Eternity—toward my cradle.[76]

# NOTES

## 1. THE WHITE BOATS OF WAXHOLM

**1.** Author's interview with Ulla-Britt Edberg, Stockholm, October 1988.

**2.** Arne Lundgren, "A Last Meeting with Pasolini," *Goteborgsposten*, Nov. 7, 1975.

**3.** Betty Skawonius, *Dagens Nyheter*, Oct. 31, 1975.

**4.** Pier Paolo Pasolini, *Lettere, II* (1955–1975), *Cronologia* clxv; taped at Italian Cultural Institute, Oct. 30, 1975.

**5.** Ibid., 664–65.

**6.** Author's interview with Carl-Johan Malmberg, Stockholm, September 1988.

**7.** Nov. 3, 1975.

**8.** Pasolini having fun with Latin: *in ore* means "for hours," but also suggests "spoken"—as opposed to "written"—from the Latin for mouth—thus, "orally."

## 2. AL POMMIDORO

**1.** Pier Paolo Pasolini, *Lutheran Letters* (henceforth cited as *Lutheran Letters*) (trans. Stuart Hood), Manchester, Carcanet New Press, 1983, from "Gennariello: More About Your Teacher," 22; first in *Il mondo*, Mar. 20, 1975.

**2.** Giuseppe di Dio, *Playmen*, January 1976.

**3.** Pasolini, "Lines from the Testament" from *To Transfigure, To Organize* (*Trasumanar e Organizzar*), 1971, in *Selected Poems* (ed. and trans. N. MacAfee and L. Martinengo), New York, Random House, 1982 (henceforth cited as MacAfee), 211–13; also in Pasolini, *Le poesie*, Milano, Garzanti, 1976, 652–53.

**4.** Pasolini, "Reality," from *Poetry in the Form of a Rose* (*Poesia in forma di rosa*, 1964) in MacAfee, *Selected Poems*, 115–19; in *Le poesie*, 352–68.

## 3. IN SEARCH OF GENNARIELLO

**1.** Pier Paolo Pasolini, "Gennariello: How I Imagine You," in *Lutheran Letters*, 18.

**2.** Ibid., "More About Your Teacher," 21, Mar. 20, 1975.

**3.** Pasolini, "The Beautiful Banners," in MacAfee, 145.

**4.** Pasolini, "Unhappy Youths," in *Lutheran Letters*, 11.

**5.** Pasolini, "The Beautiful Banners," MacAfee, 145.

**6.** Alfredo Bini, "I primi passi del regista Pasolini," *L'Europeo*, Nov. 28, 1975, 52–55.

**7.** Author's interview with Antonio Nori, Rome, 1988.

**8.** From transcript of Giuseppe Pelosi's statement to inquiring magistrate, taken at Casal del Marmo detention center, November 1975.

**9.** Ibid.

**10.** Author's interview with Giuseppe Pelosi, Rome, 1988.

**11.** From transcript of Giuseppe Pelosi's statement to inquiring magistrate, taken at Casal del Marmo detention center, November 1975.

**12.** Pasolini, *Lettere, II* (1955–1975), ed. N. Naldini, Torino, Einaudi, 1988 (henceforth cited as *Lettere, II* [1955–1975]), undated letter of October–December 1975 to Antonello Trombadori, 745.

## 4. THE IDROSCALO, OSTIA

**1.** Pier Paolo Pasolini, *A Violent Life* (*Una vita violenta;* trans. William Weaver), Manchester, Carcanet Press Limited, 1985, 251.

**2.** From transcript of Giuseppe Pelosi's statement to inquiring magistrate, taken at Casal del Marmo detention center, November 1975.

**3.** Ibid.

**4.** Statements by Giuseppe Pelosi to the Juvenile Court (*Tribunale per i Minorenni*), in transcript (*Processo verbale di dibattimento*) during his trial. Court sessions February 2, 5, 7, 9, 12, 16, 26; March 4, 8, 11, April 5 and 12, 1976.

**5.** Ibid.

**6.** Ibid.

**7.** Ibid.

**8.** Ibid.

**9.** Ibid.

**10.** Carla Rodotà, "Massacro di un poet," *L'espresso*, Feb. 11, 1979, 18–21.

**11.** "Indagini di laboratorio sui reperti relativi alla morte di Pasolini Pier Paolo," autopsy report by Professors Silvio Merli, Giancarlo Umani Ronchi, Enrico Ronchetti.

**12.** Ibid.

**13.** Author's interview with Giuseppe di Dio of the Rome daily *Il messaggero*, September 1988.

**14.** Statements by Giuseppe Pelosi to the Juvenile Court, in transcript during his trial. Court sessions February 2, 5, 7, 9, 12, 16, 26; March 4, 8, 11, April 5 and 12, 1976.

**15.** Ibid.

**16.** Author's interview with Leonardo Sciascia, Racalmuto, September 1988.

**17.** Pasolini, "Prayer to My Mother," in L. Ferlinghetti and F. Valente, ed. and trans., *Roman Poems: Bilingual Edition*, San Francisco, City Lights Books, 1986, 97; also in *Le poesie*, Milano, Aldo Garzanti Editore, 1975, 1976, 347.

**18.** Giancarlo del Re, "Parlano Sergio e Franco Citti: Era allegro e contro la violenza/ Ci ha insegnato cos' è l'amicizia," Il messaggero, Nov. 3, 1975, 5.

**19.** Official testimony (*processo verbale*) by officers Luigi Vitale, Giuseppe Gugliemi, and Antonio Cuzzupè before Juvenile Court (Tribunale per i Minorenni) at hearing of Feb. 9, 1976.

**20.** Ibid.

**21.** Ibid.

**22.** Ibid.

**23.** Ibid.

**24.** Ibid.

**25.** First reported (but later much repeated and embroidered) in Ulderico Munzi, "Pasolini assassinato a Ostia/ L'omicida (17 anni) catturato confessa," *Corriere della sera*, Nov. 3, 1975, 2.

**26.** Official testimony (*processo verbale*) by officers Luigi Vitale, Giuseppe Gugliemi, and Antonio Cuzzupè before Juvenile Court (Tribunale per i Minorenni) at hearing of Feb. 9, 1976.

**27.** Davoli's comments to the press were widely reprinted. See, for example, Catarina Dubini, "Parla Ninetto Davoli che ha riconosciuto la salma: Quando ho visto gli occhiali ho capito che Pierpaolo era morto," in *Il tempo*, Nov. 3, 1975, 5. Davoli's remarks were also reported in Franco Tintori, "La madre: Perchè lui e non io?" in *Paese sera*, Nov. 3, 1975, 4.

**28.** Pelosi's principal testimony before the Juvenile Court, one full of contradictions and claimed lapses of memory, was on Feb. 7, 1976.

## 5. LUNEDI, 3.xi.75

**1.** Ulderico Munzi, "Pasolini Assassinato a Ostia," *Corriere della sera*, Nov. 3, 1975.

**2.** Pier Paolo Pasolini, "Prayer to My Mother," in *Roman Poems: Bilingual Edition*, 97; in *Le poesie*, 347.

**3.** Author's interview with Gino Colussi, Rome, September 1988.

**4.** See "Your Interview Confirms That There Must Be a Trial," in *Lutheran Letters*, 60–95, first appeared in *Il mondo*, Sept. 11, 1975; and "Why the

Trial?" in *Lutheran Letters*, 95–99, first appeared in *Il mondo*, Sept. 28, 1975.

**5.** Pasolini, "Intervention at the Radical Party Congress," in *Lutheran Letters*, 119–26.

**6.** Piero Citati, "Tutta la vita per una morte violente," *Corriere della sera*, Nov. 3, 1975, 3.

**7.** Carlo Bo, "Poesia nel fiume della miseria umana," *Corriere della sera*, Nov. 3, 1975, 3.

**8.** Giovanni Grazzini, *Corriere della sera*, Nov. 3, 1975, 3.

**9.** Lietta Tornabuoni, "La difficile scelta di essere 'contro,' " *Corriere della sera*, Nov. 3, 1975, 3.

## 6.   CAMPO DEI FIORI

**1.** Unsigned article, "La vita e la violenza," *L'unità*, Nov. 3, 1975, 1.

**2.** Ibid.

**3.** Ibid.

**4.** Paolo Volponi, "Con civile coscienza di fronte allo 'scandalo,' " *L'unità*, Nov. 3, 1975, 1.

**5.** Author's interview with Giuseppe Zigaina, Cervignano del Friuli, 1988.

**6.** Luigi Pintor, "Un po' di confusione," *Il manifesto*, Nov. 6, 1975, 6. Also see Laura Betti, ed., *Pasolini: cronaca giudiziaria, persecuzione, morte*, Milano, Garzanti, 1977 (henceforth cited as Betti), 210–13.

**7.** Costanzo Costantini, "Fine della pietà," *Paese sera*, Nov. 4, 1975, 3.

**8.** Betti, 210–13.

## 7.   COLUS DI BATISTON

**1.** Pamphlet of Circolo di Informazione Culturale del Centro Communitario di Casarsa.

**2.** Author's interview with Silvana Mauri Ottieri, Milan, September 1988.

**3.** The author is grateful to Enrichetta Colussi Naldini, Casarsa, for her recollections of her family.

**4.** Enzo Siciliano, *Pasolini* (trans. John Shepley), New York, Random House, 1982 (henceforth cited as Siciliano, *Pasolini*), 54; recounted in full in Pier Paolo Pasolini, *Empirismo eretico*, Garzanti, Milano, 1972, 72.

**5.** Pasolini always was willing to explain the biographical sources of his film in terms of childhood memories from this period. For example, he explained to *Cahiers du cinéma* that he wanted to shoot that film's prologue "in the exact places of my childhood, at Sacile" but was unable "for production reasons." See Jean-André Fieschi, *"Pier Paolo Pasolini, 'Edipo re,' " Cahiers du cinéma*, No. 195, November 1967, 16.

**6.** Sigmund Freud, *The Interpretation of Dreams* (trans. and ed. James Strachey; present volume ed. Angela Richards), The Penguin Freud Library: 4, London, Penguin Books, 1962, 364.


## 8. A MODEL BOY

**1.** Dacia Maraini, *E tu chi eri?* Milano, Bompiani, 1973, 267.

**2.** Pier Paolo Pasolini, *Lettere, I* (1940–1954), N. Naldini, ed., Torino, Giulio Einaudi Editore, from *Cronologia*, xx–xxi (henceforth cited as *Lettere, I* [1940–1954]). Along with other important recollections of Pasolini's youth, from an eyewitness, this story of the tiger and the adventure is also recounted in N. Naldini, *Nei campi del Friuli (La giovinezza di Pasolini)*, Milano, All' Insegna del pesce d'oro, 1984, 12.

**3.** *Lettere, I* (1940–1954), *Cronologia*, xx–xxi.

**4.** Pasolini, "Due fulgurazioni," *Rotosei*, Roma, May 16, 1958.

**5.** Author's interview with Gianni Scalia, Bologna, September 1988.

**6.** *Lettere, I* (1940–1954), *Cronologia*, xxxi.

**7.** Ibid., letter to Luciano Serra, Aug. 1, 1941, 62.

**8.** Ibid., *Cronologia*, xxxiv–xxxv.

**9.** Siciliano, 63.

**10.** Ibid.

**11.** Gianfranco Contini, "Testimonianza per Pier Paolo Pasolini," *Il ponte*, Apr. 30, 1980, 339–45; also see *Lettere, I* (1940–1954), *Cronologia*, xl–xli.

**12.** Pasolini, "Appendix: to the New Reader," in *Poesie*, Milano, Garzanti, 1970; and in MacAfee, 223.

**13.** *Lettere, I* (1940–1954), *Cronologia*, xxxv.

**14.** The author is grateful to Leonardo Sciascia, now deceased, for sharing his *Architrave* archive.

**15.** *Architrave*, Dec. 31, 1942, No. 1.

**16.** *Il setaccio*, March 1943; also see *Lettere, I* (1940–1954), *Cronologia*, xlviii.


## 9. FRIULIAN RAPTURE

**1.** *Lettere, I* (1940–1954), 154 (letter to Fabio Mauri, February 1943).

**2.** Ibid., 156–58 (letter to Fabio Luca Cavazza, February 1943).

**3.** Ibid., *Cronologia*, xlvii.

**4.** Pier Paolo Pasolini, "A Desperate Vitality," from *Poesia in forma di rosa* (1964) in MacAfee, 159.

**5.** Pasolini, "Ode a un fiore, a Casarsa," *Il belpaese*, No. 2, July 1941.

**6.** From the *Quaderni rossi* (Red Notebooks) of 1946; see *Lettere, I* (1940–1954), *Cronologia*, xiv.

**7.** *Lettere, I* (1940–1954), letter to Franco Farolfi, Spring 1943, 169–71.

**8.** Ibid., letter to Franco Farolfi, June 4, 1943, 172–73.

**9.** Ibid., letter to Luciano Serra, June 4, 1943, 174–75.

**10.** Ibid., letter to Luciano Serra, June 24, 1943, 176–77.

**11.** Ibid.

**12.** From the *Quaderni rossi* of 1947; see *Lettere, I* (1940–1954), *Cronologia*, xivii.

**13.** From the second and third volumes of the *Quaderni rossi*; also see *Lettere, I* (1940–1954), *Cronologia*, xlix–lii; also see Pasolini, *Atti impuri*, ed. C. D'Angeli, Milano, Garzanti, 1982 (also includes *Amado mio*).

**14.** Pasolini, "The Religion of My Time" from the volume of the same title, in MacAfee, 61–67.

**15.** Oswald Stack, *Pasolini on Pasolini*, Bloomington, Indiana University Press, 1970, 19 (henceforth cited as Stack).

**16.** Pasolini, *Poesie e pagine ritrovate*, ed. A. Zanzotto and N. Naldini, Roma, Lato Side, 1980, 45.

**17.** Friedrich Nietzsche, "Notes, 1874," ed. and trans. Walter Kaufmann, *The Portable Nietzsche*, New York, Penguin, 1982, 49.

**18.** Norman Lewis, *Naples '44*, New York, Pantheon Books, 1978, 135.

**19.** For Naldini's account of Guidalberto's first acts in the Resistance, see N. Naldini, *Nei campi del Friuli* (La giovinezza di Pasolini), Milano, All' insegna del pesce d'oro, 1984, 34.

**20.** Pasolini's detailed account of the events leading to Guido's death is in his letter of Aug. 21, 1945, to Luciano Serra, then still in Bologna, in *Lettere, I* (1940–1954), 197–201.

**21.** From the *Quaderni rossi* of 1944; see *Lettere, I* (1940–1954), *Cronologia*, lix.

**22.** *Lettere, I* (1940–1955), *Cronologia*, lxii.

**23.** Pasolini, *Poesie e pagine ritrovate*, 37.

**24.** Ibid.

**25.** From the *Quaderni rossi* of 1947; see *Lettere, I* (1940–1954), *Cronologia*, lxix–lxx.

**26.** *Lettere, I* (1940–1954), *Cronologia*, lxii–lxiii.

**27.** Ibid., letter of Nov. 27, 1944, from Guido Pasolini to his brother, lxiii–lxix.

**28.** Ibid., letter to Luciano Serra, Aug. 21, 1945, 197–201.

**29.** Ibid.

**30.** Ibid., 201.

**31.** Guido Pasolini (Ermes, pseud.), "Il martire ai vivi," *Il stroligut*, San Vito, Stamperia Primon, August 1945, No. 1, iv.

**32.** Pasolini et al., *Pasolini e Il Setaccio*, ed. Mario Ricci, Bologna, Cappelli, 1977; also see *Lettere, I* (1940–1954), *Cronologia*, xc.

**33.** On the death of Nico's mother, Enrichetta Colussi Naldini, in 1990, plans were set in motion by the province and municipality to convert the house into a Pier Paolo Pasolini library and study center.

**34.** *Lettere, I* (1940–1954), *Cronologia*, lxxxvii.

**35.** Ibid., lxxxviii.

**36.** Ibid.

**37.** Pasolini, "Lingua," in *L'usignolo della chiesa cattolica*, Milano, Longanesi, 1958, 93–95.

**38.** Siciliano, 98.

**39.** *Lettere, I* (1940–1954), letter to Franco de Gironcoli, Dec. 7, 1945, 216.

**40.** Ibid., letter to Sergio Maldini, Dec. 27, 1945, 223.

**41.** Ibid., letter to Luciano Serra, Jan. 22, 1946, 234.

**42.** Ibid., letter to Gianfranco Contini, Mar. 27, 1946, 241.

**43.** Ibid., letter to Tonuti Spagnol, Apr. 3, 1946, 244.

**44.** Gianfranco Contini, "Testimonianza per Pier Paolo Pasolini," *Il ponte*, Apr. 30, 1980, 339–45.

**45.** Siciliano, 98.

**46.** From the *Quaderni rossi* of 1947; see *Lettere, I* (1940–1954), *Cronologia*, xcii–xciii.

## 10.   THE PARTY'S FOOT SOLDIER IN THE GARDEN OF ALCINA

**1.** Pier Paolo Pasolini, *Lettere, I* (1940–1954), letter to Tonuti Spagnol, Oct. 25, 1946, 268.

**2.** Ibid., letter to Ehnio de Concini, Nov. 18, 1946, 272–73.

**3.** Ibid., letter to Gianfranco d'Aronco, Jan. 19, 1947, 279.

**4.** Ibid., letter to Giovanna Bemporad, 281.

**5.** Ibid., letter to Gianfranco Contini, Feb. 5, 1947, 285.

**6.** From the third Quaderno rosso (Red Notebook), 1947; see *Lettere, I* (1940–1954), *Cronologia*, xciii–xcv.

**7.** Recollections of Silvana Mauri Ottieri, in *Lettere, I* (1940–1954), *Cronologia*, xcv–xcvi.

**8.** *Lettere, I* (1940–1954), letter to Ennio de Concini, Feb. 22, 1947, 293.

**9.** Ibid., letter to Silvana Mauri, Mar. 11, 1947, 296.

**10.** Ibid., letter to Sergio Maldini, Mar. 27, 1949, 298.

**11.** Pasolini, "Adulto? Mai—mai, come l'esistenza," in *Roma 1950: diario*, Milano, All' insegna del pesce d'oro, 1960, 7.

**12.** *Lettere, I* (1940–1954), letter to Gianfranco Contini, 307–8.

**13.** Pasolini, *Poesie e pagine ritrovate*, ed. A. Zanzotto and N. Naldini, Roma, Lato/Side, 1980, 63–65.

14. *Lettere, I* (1940–1954), *Cronologia,* ciii, from *Libera Stampa* prize jury statement, written by Gianfranco Contini.
15. Ibid., letter to Silvana Mauri, Aug. 15, 1947, 313–16.
16. Recollections of Silvana Mauri Ottieri, in *Lettere, I* (1940–1954), *Cronologia,* xcvi–xcvii.
17. From the *Quaderni rossi,* 1947; see *Lettere, I* (1940–1954), *Cronologia,* xcviii.
18. Ibid.
19. Ibid., xcviii–xcvix.
20. Ibid., c, from the *Quaderni rossi* entry of Oct. 7, 1949.
21. Ibid.
22. Pasolini et al., *Pasolini in Friuli (1943–1949),* Udine, *Corriere del Friuli* in collaboration with the Comune di Casarsa della Delizia, Arti Grafiche Friulane, 1976.
23. A. Zanzotto, "Pedagoy," in B. Allen, ed., *Pier Paolo Pasolini: The Poetics of Heresy,* Saratoga, CA, ANMA Libri, 1982, 35.
24. *Pasolini in Friuli (1943–1949).*
25. Pasolini, "Appendix: To the New Reader," in *Le poesie,* Milano, Garzanti, 1970; see MacAfee, 225 and *Lettere, I* (1940–1954), *Cronologia,* ciii.
26. See L. Betti, ed., *Pasolini: cronaca giudiziaria, persecuzione, morte,* Milano, Garzanti, 1977, for photo reproductions of Pasolini's wall posters at San Giovanni di Casarsa, for the period Feb. 20–May 15, 1949.
27. Siciliano, 101–2.
28. Pasolini, "Appendix: To the New Reader," in MacAfee, 225.
29. *Lettere, I* (1940–1954), letter to Luciano Serra, January 1948, 328.
30. Ibid., Aug. 7, 1948, 338.
31. For Naldini's recollections of the young Pasolini, see N. Naldini, *Nei campi del Friuli (La giovinezza di Pasolini),* Milano, All' insegna del pesce d'oro, 1984.
32. See editor's note to *Lettere, II* (1955–1975), 499–500.
33. Pasolini, *Il sogno di una cosa,* Milano, Garzanti, 1962, 5. Sole English translation is *A Dream of Something* (trans. Stuart Hood), London, Quartet, 1988.
34. Pasolini, *A Dream of Something,* 12.
35. Ibid., 34.
36. Pasolini, *Amado mio/Atti impuri,* ed. C. D'Angeli, Milano, Garzanti, 1982, 191–92.

## 11.  SAINT SABINA'S DAY IN RAMUSCELLO

1.  See Betti, 73–95 for photo reproductions of Pasolini's wall posters at San Giovanni di Casarsa, for the period Feb. 20–May 15, 1949.

2. Norman Kogan, *A Political History of Italy: The Postwar Years*, New York, Praeger Special Studies, 1983, 28.

3. In *friulano:*

L'ANIMA NERA

*Se esia duta sta pulitica ch'a fan i predis cuntra di nualtris puares? A saressin lour cha varessin da ver il nustri stes penseir; a me par che nustris sintimins a sedin abastansa cristians! Sers democristians a si fan di maraveja se i comunise a van de messa quant che i comunisc a podaressinfassi a mondi di pi marajeva par jodi chei democristians ch'a van a messa cu l'anima nera coma il ciarbon.* (From Betti, 86; also Siciliano, 101).

4. Betti, 80.

5. Ibid., 81.

6. Ibid., 88.

7. Giovanni de Luna, *Hanno sparato a Togliatti*, Milano, Grupo Editoriale Fabbri, 1984, passim.

8. *Lettere, I* (1940–1954), letter to Luciano Serra, Aug. 7, 1948, 338.

9. Pasolini, article, "Per la pace e il lavoro," in *Bollettino sul Primo Congresso della Federazione Comunista di Pordenone*, March 1949, 3.

10. Ibid.

11. *Lettere, I* (1940–1954), letter to Silvana Mauri, March 1949, 352–54.

12. Ibid., letter to Gianfranco Contini, July 7, 1949, 361.

13. Transcript of interrogations made by the Legione Territoriale dei Carabinieri di Padova, Stazione di Cordovado, Oct. 14, 1949.

14. The author thanks Avv. Bruno Brusin, San Vito al Tagliamento, for transcripts of depositions and sentences in the Ramuscello case.

15. Author's interview with Enrichetta Colussi Naldini, Casarsa, 1988.

16. *Lettere, I* (1940–1954), *Cronologia*, cx–cxi.

17. Ibid., cix. A notice written by Ferdinando Mautino, of the Udine Communist Federation, appeared in *L'unità*, Oct. 29, 1949.

18. See Norman Kogan, *A Political History of Italy: The Postwar Years*, for the changing role of women in postwar Italian public life.

19. *Lettere, I* (1940–1954), letter to Ferdinando Mautino, Oct. 31, 1949, 368–69.

20. Statement by prosecuting State's attorney (Procuratore della Repubblica) Dr. Ramiro Udira, in appeals court brief, Jan. 9, 1951, 2.

21. *Lettere, I* (1940–1954), letter to Teresina Degan, Nov. 10, 1949, 371.

22. Ibid., letter to Franco Farolfi, Dec. 31, 1949, 374.

23. Ibid., letter to Silvana Mauri, Jan. 27, 1950, 384–85.

24. Ibid., *Cronologia*, cxii.

## 12.   "AT THE CITY'S FAR EDGE"

**1.**   Pier Paolo Pasolini, "Rital and Raton" in *Roman Nights and Other Stories* (trans. John Shepley), Marlboro, VT, Marlboro Press, 1986, 110; first appeared as "Rital e raton" (1965), in Pasolini, *Alì dagli occhi azzurri*, Milano, Garzanti, 1965, 494–515.

**2.**   Author's interview with Antonello Trombadori, Rome, September 1988.

**3.**   Pasolini, "Roman Nights" in *Roman Nights and Other Stories*, 4–5; first appeared as "Squarci di notti romane" (1950), in *Alì dagli occhi azzurri*, 5–33.

**4.**   Pasolini, "I Work All Day . . . in *Roman Poems* (ed. and trans. L. Ferlinghetti and F. Valente), San Francisco, City Lights Books, 1986, 95; from "Poesie mondane," first in *Poesia in forma di rosa* (1964), reprinted in *Le poesie*, Milano, Garzanti, 1975, 1976, 364.

**5.**   *Lettere, I* (1940–1954), letter to Silvana Mauri, Feb. 10, 1950, 388–93.

**6.**   Ibid., 390–91.

**7.**   Ibid., 391–92.

**8.**   Ibid., Feb. 11, 1950, 401.

**9.**   Ibid., 402.

**10.**   Ibid., 403.

**11.**   Ibid., letter to Nico Naldini, March 1950, 418.

**12.**   Ibid., spring 1950, 420.

**13.**   Ibid., June 1950, 429.

**14.**   Ibid., letter to Susanna Pasolini, Aug. 28, 1950, 431.

**15.**   Ibid.

**16.**   Postcard from Susanna Pasolini to Pier Paolo Pasolini, dated Sept. 7, 1950, in *Lettere, I* (1940–1954), editor's note to 433–34.

**17.**   Postcard from Susanna Pasolini to Pier Paolo Pasolini, dated Oct. 4, 1950, in *Lettere, I* (1940–1954), editor's note to 438.

**18.**   *Lettere, I* (1940–1954), letter to Susanna Pasolini, Oct. 7, 1950, 437.

**19.**   Ibid., letter to Nico Naldini, August 1951, 452.

**20.**   Giuseppe Zigaina, *Pasolini e la morte*, Venice, Marsilio Editore, 1987, 23, citing Pasolini, *Passione e ideologia*, Milano, Garzanti, 1973, 324.

**21.**   Gianfranco Contini, "Testimonianza per Pier Paolo Pasolini," *Il ponte*, Apr. 30, 1980, 339.

**22.**   Pasolini, *The Ragazzi* (trans. Emile Capouya), Manchester and New York, Carcanet Press, 1986, 8–9.

**23.**   Ibid., 17.

**24.**   Pasolini, "A Night on the Tram," in *Roman Nights and Other Stories*, 54–55; first appeared as "Notte sull'ES" (1951), in *Alì dagli occhi azzurri*, 64–79.

**25.** Ibid., 58–59.

**26.** Pasolini, "Studies on the Life of Testaccio" in *Roman Nights and Other Stories*, 68; first appeared as "Studi sulla vita del Testaccio" (1951), in *Alì dagli occhi azzurri*, 80–88.

**27.** Pasolini, *Roman Nights and Other Stories*, 69–70.

**28.** Ibid., 78.

**29.** Siciliano, 168; in *Le poesie*, 23–31.

**30.** Pasolini, "The Tears of the Excavator," MacAfee, 29–31; from *Le ceneri di Gramsci*, in *Le poesie* (1975, 1976), 91–114.

**31.** Pasolini, "Memories of Misery" in *Roman Poems*, 23–25.

**32.** *Lettere, I* (1940–1954), letter to Tonuti Spagnol, "end of 1951," 460.

## 13. IN REBIBBIA EXILE

**1.** *Lettere, I* (1940–1954), letter to Giacinto Spagnoletti, March 1952, 472.

**2.** Pasolini, "The Religion of My Time," in MacAfee, 71–73; in *Le poesie* (1975, 1976), 223–24.

**3.** *Lettere, I* (1940–1954), letter to Giacinto Spagnoletti, "summer 1952," 485.

**4.** Ibid., letter to Silvana Mauri, July 1952, 486–88.

**5.** Ibid., letter to Luciano Serra, "summer 1952," 492.

**6.** Ibid., letter to Carlo Betocchi, August 1952, 494–95.

**7.** Ibid., letter to Giacomo Noventa, Oct. 17, 1952, 500.

**8.** Ibid., letter to Nico Naldini, December 1952, 510.

**9.** Ibid., letter to Nico Naldini, autumn 1952, 498.

**10.** Ibid., letter to Nico Naldini, January 1953, 530.

**11.** Ibid., letter to Enrico Falqui, Mar. 27, 1953, 552–54.

**12.** Ibid., letter to Giacinto Spagnoletti, Jan. 1, 1953, 519.

**13.** Elio Bartolini, *Due ponti a Caracas*, Milano, Mondadori, 1953.

**14.** *Lettere, I* (1940–1954), letter to Nico Naldini, Apr. 23, 1953, 565.

**15.** Ibid., letter to Cesare Padovani, May 16, 1953, 573–74.

**16.** Uberto Paolo Quintavalle, *Giorante di Sodoma*, Milano, SugarCo Edizioni, 1976, 29.

**17.** *Folder*, 2: 1, 1954–1955.

**18.** *Lettere, I* (1940–1954), letter to Francesco Leonetti, Oct. 29, 1953, 612.

**19.** Ibid., 640.

**20.** *Lettere, I* (1940–1954), letter to Vittorio Sereni, Jan. 2, 1954, 627.

**21.** Ibid., *Cronologia*, cxxvii–cxxviii.

**22.** Ibid., letter to Leonardo Sciascia, May 30, 1954, 662.

**23.** Ibid., letter to Vittorio Sereni, Aug. 7, 1954, 673.

**24.** Ibid., letter to Livio Garzanti, November 1954, 703–7.
**25.** Ibid., letter to Gianfranco Contini, Dec. 17, 1954, 717.


## 14. *ANNI MIRABILI: RAGAZZI DI VITA, OFFICINA, LE CENERI DI GRAMSCI*

**1.** *Il popolo di Roma*, Sept. 9, 1951.
**2.** Ibid.
**3.** Unpublished letter, Pier Paolo Pasolini to Livio Garzanti, Nov. 27, 1954.
**4.** *Lettere, I* (1940–1954), letter to Livio Garzanti, Nov. 6, 1954, 700.
**5.** Ibid., letter to Livio Garzanti, Nov. 15, 1954, 703–7.
**6.** Ibid.
**7.** *Lettere, II* (1955–1975), letter to Livio Garzanti, Apr. 13, 1955, 54.
**8.** Ibid., letter to Silvana Mauri, May 23, 1955, 69.
**9.** Ibid., letter to Livio Garzanti, May 11, 1955, 65–66.
**10.** Ibid., letter to the editors of *Officina*, June 6, 1955, 71.
**11.** Ibid., letter of May 19, 1955, 62.
**12.** Ibid., letter to Livio Garzanti, July 2, 1955, 80–81.
**13.** Ibid., *Cronologia*, xii.
**14.** Ibid., letter to Livio Garzanti, Aug. 17, 1955, 113–14.
**15.** Ibid., letter to Nico Naldini, Dec. 2, 1955, 138.
**16.** Ibid., letter to Gianfranco Contini, Sept. 16, 1955, 121.
**17.** Pasolini, *The Ragazzi* (trans. Emile Capouya), Manchester and New York, Carcanet Press, 1986, 37.
**18.** Ibid., 154–55.
**19.** *Lettere, II* (1955–1975), letter to Gianfranco Contini, June 15, 1956, 208.
**20.** *Letteratura*, Nos. 17–18; editor's note No. 3, *Lettere, II* (1955–1975), 209.
**21.** Betti, 66.
**22.** Ibid., 65–66; Pasolini's statement to the bench, July 4, 1956.
**23.** *Lettere, II* (1955–1975), letter to Livio Garzanti, Aug. 1, 1956, 229.
**24.** Ibid., *Cronologia*, xiii, comments by critic Carlo Salinari on *Ragazzi di vita*.
**25.** The author thanks the Hon. Antonello Trombadori for sharing his archive of letters concerning his role in Pasolini's life in this period.
**26.** Charley Shively, ed. *Calamus Lovers: Walt Whitman's Working Class Camerados*, San Francisco, Gay Sunshine Press, 1987; also see Justin Kaplan, *Walt Whitman: A Life*, New York, Simon and Schuster, 1980.
**27.** For Carlo Salinari's extended and insightful analyses, with much change of perspective over time, see Salinari, *La questione del realismo*, Firenze, Parenti Editore, and *Preludio e fine del realismo in Italia*, Morano

Editore, 1967. In the second, Salinari acknowledges that Pasolini was correct to call the critic's charges against him "disproportionate" but insists "the provocation was serious." The author thanks Antonello Trombadori for his analysis of the complex relationship between Pasolini and his Communist critics during this period.

**28.** For exchange of letters, Leonetti to Pasolini (Oct. 18, 1954) and Pasolini to Leonetti (Oct. 20, 1954), see *Letttere, I* (1940–1954), 691–93.

**29.** Ibid.

**30.** *Lettere, II* (1955–1975), letter to Francesco Leonetti, Feb. 2, 1955, 14.

**31.** Ibid., letter to Vittorio Sereni, Mar. 2, 1955, 25.

**32.** Pasolini, "La posizione," *Officina*, No. 6, April 1956, Bologna, Libreria Palmaverde.

**33.** Paolo Volponi, "Officina prima dell'industria," Belfagor, No. 6, Nov. 30, 1975, 723.

**34.** Ibid.

**35.** *Lettere, II* (1955–1975), letter to the editors of *Officina*, Feb. 5, 1957, 279–81.

**36.** The definitive work on *Officina*, including a masterful introduction and commentary followed by an anthology of the magazine's most important articles, is Gian Carlo Ferretti, *Officina: cultura, letteratura e politica negli anni cinquanta*, Torino, Giulio Einaudi Editore, 1975.

**37.** *Lettere, II* (1955–1975), letter to Franco Fortini, Dec. 1, 1956, 254.

**38.** Siciliano, 215.

**39.** *Lettere, II* (1955–1975), letter to Antonello Trombadori, June 7, 1956, 204–5.

**40.** Siciliano, 216, from "Una polemica in versi" (1956), in *Le poesie* (1975, 1976), 117–25.

**41.** *Lettere, II* (1955–1975), letter to Leonardo Sciascia, Mar. 31, 1956, 183.

**42.** Ibid., letter to Livio Garzanti, Apr. 9, 1956, 186–87.

**43.** Ibid., letter to Livio Garzanti, 301.

**44.** Pasolini, "The Ashes of Gramsci," in MacAfee, 5; in *Le poesie* (1975, 1976), 68. The extracts following (with the author's commentary) end on text page 303; MacAfee, 53; *Le poesie*, 114.

**45.** Ibid., "The Tears of the Excavator," 27; in *Le poesie*, 94–95. The extracts following (with the author's commentary) end on text page 308; MacAfee, 53; *Le poesie*, 114.

**46.** *Lettere, II* (1955–1975), letter to Livio Garzanti, June 3, 1957, 323.

**47.** Ibid., letter to Livio Garzanti, June 12, 1957, 327.

**48.** Ibid., letter to Livio Garzanti, June 18, 1957, 331.

**49.** Ibid., letter to Livio Garzanti, July 17, 1957, 333.

**50.** Ibid., editorial note 1, 334.

**51.** Ibid., *Cronologia*, xxxv.

**52.** Ibid., letter to Antonello Trombadori, August 1957, 336.

**53.** Pasolini, "A un ragazzo (1956–1967)" in *La religione del mio tempo*, Milano, Garzanti, 1961, 201–10.

**54.** Attilio Bertolucci, "Piccola ode a Roma," in *Viaggio d'inverno* (1955–1970), Milano, Garzanti, 1971, 31.

**55.** *Lettere, II* (1955–1975), letter to Roberto Roversi, Nov. 7, 1958, 394.

**56.** Ibid., letter to the editors of *Officina*, Dec. 13, 1958, 402–3.

**57.** "Ad alcuni radicali," in *Le poesie*, 251.

**58.** "A me," in *Le poesie*, 253.

**59.** "A un Papa," in *Le poesie*, 260–61.

**60.** Siciliano, 189, from Ferretti, 472–73.

**61.** *Lettere, II* (1955–1975), letter to Franco Fortini, Dec. 20, 1958, 404–5.

**62.** *Officina*, new series, No. 2, May–June 1959, 69–73.

**63.** The contretemps is spelled out in *Lettere, II* (1955–1975), letters between Fortini and Pasolini of June 1959, 441–45.

**64.** *Lettere, II* (1955–1975), letter to Nico Naldini, Jan. 10, 1958, 364.

**65.** Ibid., letter to Roberto Roversi, July 1959, 446.

**66.** *Paese sera*, June 3, 1975.

## 15. *LACHRYMOSA:* A VIOLENT LIFE

**1.** *Lettere, II* (1955–1975), letter to Franco Fortini, Dec. 20, 1958, 404.

**2.** Stack, 13.

**3.** Dacia Maraini, *E tu chi eri?* Milano, Bompiani, 1973, 198.

**4.** *Lettere, II* (1955–1975), letter to Carlo Pasolini, July 18, 1955, 106.

**5.** Ibid., letter to Susanna Pasolini, July 30, 1955, 108.

**6.** Ibid., letter to Francesco Leonetti, Dec. 21, 1958, 406.

**7.** Siciliano, 198.

**8.** Author's interview with Laura Betti, Rome, May 28, 1976.

**9.** *Lettere, II* (1955–1975), letter to Massimo Ferretti, Dec. 20, 1956, 259.

**10.** Born Laurent Tchemezine.

**11.** *Lettere, II* (1955–1975), letter to Livio Garzanti, Jan. 12, 1957, 269.

**12.** Ibid.

**13.** Ibid., letter of Jan. 21, 1957, 273.

**14.** Ibid., 274.

**15.** Pier Paolo Pasolini, *A Violent Life* (trans. William Weaver), London, Panther, 1970 (henceforth cited as *A Violent Life*), 257–64.

**16.** *Lettere, II* (1955–1975), letter to Livio Garzanti, Jan. 10, 1958, 366.

**17.** Ibid., letter to Giacinto Spagnoletti, January 1959, 408.

**18.** Ibid., letter to Giulio Einaudi, Mar. 9, 1959, 415.

**19.** "Il portico della morte," *L'illustrazione italiana*, Milano, LXXXVIII, January 1961.

**20.** *Lettere, II* (1955–1975), letter from Livio Garzanti, May 15, 1959, in *Cronologia*, xliv.

**21.** *A Violent Life*, 257–64.

**22.** Ibid.

**23.** Ibid.

**24.** *Lettere, II* (1955–1975), letter to Livio Garzanti. Mar. 2, 1956, 171.

**25.** "Pier Paolo Pasolini: An Epical-Religious View of the World," transcript of conference at Centro Sperimentale di Cinema (CSC), Rome, November 1964, in *Bianco e nero* (trans. Letizia Ciotti Miller and Michael Goldman), 35–36.

**26.** *A Violent Life*, 319–20.

**27.** Ibid., 320.

**28.** *Lettere, II* (1955–1975), letter to Livio Garzanti, August 1959, 448.

**29.** Ibid., *Cronologia*, xlix.

**30.** Ibid., li.

**31.** Ibid.

**32.** Ibid., letter from Livio Garzanti, Sept. 1, 1959, 453.

**33.** Siciliano, 220–21; from *Le poesie*, (1975, 1976) 243–44.

**34.** *Lettere, II* (1955–1975), *Cronologia*, lv.

**35.** *Rinascita*, January 1960.

**36.** *Lettere, II* (1955–1975), *Cronologia*, lv.

**37.** "Pier Paolo Pasolini: An Epical-Religious View of the World," 37.

**38.** *Lettere, II* (1955–1975), *Cronologia*, xlviii.

**39.** Betti, 102–3.

**40.** Ibid., 103.

**41.** Ibid., 101–6.

**42.** Ibid., 108.

**43.** Ibid., 263–64; from *Il tempo*, July 14, 1960.

**44.** Betti, 264.

## 16.  *ACCATTONE*

**1.** Peter Bondanella, *Italian Cinema: From Neorealism to the Present*, New York, Frederick Ungar Publishing Co., 1983, 142.

**2.** *Lettere, II* (1955–1975), letter to Luciano Anceschi, January 1960, 467.

**3.** Siciliano, 223; from Massimo D'Arack, *Cinema e letteratura*, Roma, 1964, 111.

**4.** "Pier Palo Pasolini: An Epical-Religious View of the World," 37 (see n. 25, Chapter 15).

**5.** *Vita*, Dec. 7, 1961, 55.

6. Luciano de Giusti, ed. *Pier Paolo Pasolini: Il cinema in forma di poesia*, Pordenone, Edizioni Cinemazero, 1979, 47.

7. Ibid., 22.

8. "Pier Paolo Pasolini: An Epical-Religious View of the World," 42.

9. *Lettere, II* (1955–1975), *Cronologia*, lxiii–lxiv.

10. Milano, Garzanti, 1965.

11. Siciliano, 219; in *Le poesie* (1975, 1976), 238.

12. Luigi Barzini, *The Italians*, New York, Atheneum, 1964, 180.

13. Siciliano, 218: from *Le poesie*, 235.

14. Ibid., 201; from *Le poesie*, 267.

15. Ibid., 194; from *Le poesie*, 277.

16. Pasolini, *La religione del mio tempo*, Milano, Garzanti, 1982 (henceforth cited as *La religione del mio tempo*), 134.

17. *Le poesie*, 280.

18. Siciliano, 227; from Pasolini, *Il padre selvaggio*, Torino, Einaudi, 1975, 60. Pasolini's remarks on Mother Teresa are to be found in *Lettere, II* (1955–1975), *Cronologia*, lxvi. His published, idiosyncratic travel recollections of India ("It is extraordinary, the vigor which that unlikeable institution called the Rotary Club has in India") are to be found in Pasolini, *L'odore dell'India*, Parma, Ugo Guanda Editore, 1990.

19. Pasolini, *Le belle bandiere*, ed. G. Ferretti, Roma, Editori Riuniti, 1977, 132–33.

20. *Vita*, Sept. 14, 1961, 58–59.

21. Ibid., Dec. 7, 1961.

22. Siciliano, 229; from Pasolini, *Accattone*, F.M., Roma, 1961, 7.

23. *Lettere, II* (1955–1975), *Cronologia*, lxi.

24. Siciliano, 238; from Alberto Moravia, *"Immagini al posto d'onore,"* *L'espresso*, Oct. 1, 1961.

25. Stack, 64.

26. De Giusti, ed., *Pier Paolo Pasolini: Il cinema in forma di poesia*, 42.

27. Maria Antonietta Macciocchi, *Duemila anni di felicità*, Milano, Mondadori, 1983, 328–29.

28. Ibid., 329.

29. Ibid., 330.

30. Interview with Fabio Mauri, Rome, 1988.

31. *Vie nuove*, No. 28, July 9, 1960, 53–54.

32. Ibid.

33. *Le belle bandiere*, 57; *Vie nuove*, No. 29, July 16, 1960.

34. Ibid.

35. Ibid., 135; *Vie nuove*, No. 27, July 8, 1961.

36. Ibid., 60; *Vie nuove*, No. 30, July 23, 1960.

37. Carlo Salinari, *Preludio e fine del realismo in Italia*, Firenze, Morano Editore, 1967, 144.

38. Salinari, *La questione del realismo*, Firenze, Parenti Editore, 183.

**39.** Siciliano, 230; from *Le poesie* (1975, 1976), 283–89.

**40.** *Lettere, II* (1955–1975), *Cronologia*, lviii; from Maria Bellonci, *Come un racconto gli anni del Premio Strega*, Milano, Club degli Editori, 1969, 55–56.

**41.** Siciliano, 231; from *Le poesie*, 283–89.

**42.** *Le belle bandiere*, 64; *Vie nuove*, No. 31, July 30, 1960.

**43.** Ibid., 76; *Vie nuove*, No. 40, Oct. 8, 1960.

**44.** Ibid., *Vie nuove*, No. 39, Oct. 1, 1960, 71.

**45.** Ibid., 77; *Vie nuove*, No. 41, Oct. 15, 1960.

**46.** Ibid., 78; *Vie nuove*, No. 41, Oct. 15, 1960.

**47.** Ibid., 94; *Vie nuove*, No. 50, Dec. 17, 1960.

**48.** Ibid., 95; *Vie nuove*, No. 50, Dec. 17, 1960.

**49.** Pasolini, *Il portico della morte*, ed. C. Segre, Roma, Associazione "Fondo Pier Paolo Pasolini," 1988, 205–11; "Un passo a Gadda," in *L'Europa letteraria*, Rome, 4:20–21, April–June 1963.

**50.** Pasolini, *Il portico della morte*, "Prefazione," vii–xxvii.

## 17. *MAMMA ROMA*, THE GOLDEN BULLET OF BERNARDINO DE SANTIS, BLASPHEMY

**1.** *Lettere, II* (1955–1975), *Cronologia*, lx.

**2.** Nov. 19, 1962.

**3.** Siciliano, 244. Pasolini's verses of 1966.

**4.** B. Allen, *Pier Paolo Pasolini: The Poetics of Heresy*, Saratoga, CA, ANMA Libri, 1982, (henceforth cited as Allen), 29.

**5.** Siciliano, 246.

**6.** *Le belle bandiere*, 207–10; *Vie nuove*, No. 28, July 12, 1962; Betti, 132–33.

**7.** Betti, 138.

**8.** Siciliano, 248.

**9.** MacAfee, 111–37.

**10.** Betti, 138.

**11.** *La religione del mio tempo*, 101–3.

**12.** MacAfee, 104–5.

**13.** Ibid., 111–37.

**14.** Pier Paolo Pasolini, *Mamma Roma*, "Diario al registratore" [Tape-recorded diary], Milano, Rizzoli, 1962, 139–40.

**15.** Ibid., 142–43.

**16.** *Lettere, II* (1955–1975), *Cronologia*, lxxi.

**17.** Stack, 53.

**18.** *Le belle bandiere*, 230; *Vie nuove*, No. 40, Oct. 4, 1962.

**19.** Pasolini, *Mamma Roma* [script], Milano, Rizzoli, 1962, 130.

**20.** Pasolini, "Diario al registratore" [diary], 139–40.

**21.** Ibid., 142–43.

**22.** Luciano de Giusti, *I film di Pier Paolo Pasolini*, Roma, Gremese Editore, 1983, henceforth cited as De Giusti, *I film*, 54; from *Filmcritica*, XIII, 225, September 1962.

**23.** Pasolini, *Mamma Roma* [diary], 138–41.

**24.** Ibid., 146.

**25.** Ibid., 146–49.

**26.** Ibid., 149–50.

**27.** De Giusti, *I film*, 50; from *Bianco e nero*, 26, Rome, June 1964, 6.

**28.** Siciliano, 260; from *Le belle bandiere*, 232; *Vie nuove*, No. 40, Oct. 4, 1962.

**29.** Ibid., 252; also in Pasolini, *Empirismo eretico*, Milano, Garzanti, 1972, 1977, 30.

**30.** *Le belle bandiere*, 219; *Vie nuove*, No. 36, Sept. 6, 1962.

**31.** Stack, 55–56.

**32.** Betti, 154.

**33.** Stack, 59.

**34.** Siciliano, 252; from Alberto Moravia, "L'uomo medio sotto i bisturi," *L'espresso*, Mar. 3, 1963; also in De Giusti, *I film*, 58.

**35.** Stack, 62.

**36.** A version of the script of *La ricotta* is in Pasolini, *Alì dagli occhi azzurri*, Milano, Garzanti, 1965, 473–77.

**37.** Stack, 62.

**38.** Betti, 162.

**39.** Ibid., 160.

**40.** Siciliano, 255; from Betti, 162–63.

**41.** Pasolini, *Lettere luterane*, Torino, Giulio Einaudi Editore, 1977, 48; in "Gennariello," article in *Il mondo*, June 5, 1975.

**42.** Stack, 63.

**43.** *Lettere*, *II* (1955–1975), *Cronologia*, lxxxi–lxxxii.

**44.** Siciliano, 287; *Le poesie* (1975, 1976), 348.

**45.** Author's interview with Antonello Trombadori, Rome, Sept. 10, 1988.

**46.** Stack, 51.

**47.** Ibid., 52.

**48.** Ibid.

**49.** From the *Avvertenza* of *Alì degli occhi azzuri*, 515–16.

## 18. THE CINEMA OF IDEOLOGY: *RAGE, LOVE MEETINGS,* AND *THE GOSPEL*

**1.** Siciliano, 270–71.

**2.** *Lettere*, *II* (1955–1975), letter to Dr. Lucio Caruso, February 1963, 508–9.

**3.** Ibid., 509.

**4.** Ibid., letter to Alfredo Bini, May 12, 1963, 514–15.

**5.** Stack, 75–76.

**6.** Ibid., 90–91.

**7.** MacAfee, 179.

**8.** *Lettere, II* (1955–1975), *Cronologia*, lxxxii.

**9.** Alfredo Bini, "I primi pasti del resista Pasolini," *L'Europeo* 31: 48 (Nov. 28, 1975), 53–54.

**10.** Pier Paolo Pasolini, *Il padre selvaggio*, 59–61, unpublished translation by J. C. Dillon.

**11.** Letter from Dr. Lucio Caruso to Alfredo Bini, May 12, 1963; in *Lettere, II* (1955–1975), *Cronologia*, lxxxiv.

**12.** Siciliano, 272; from Pasolini, *Il vangelo seconde Matteo*, Milano, Garzanti, 1969, 265.

**13.** Carlo di Carlo (writing in December 1978) in A. Bertini, *Teoria e tecnica del film in Pasolini*, Roma, Bulzoni, 1979, 148–50; in Luciano de Giusti, *I filmi di Pier Paolo Pasolini*, 61.

**14.** Stack, 70–72.

**15.** Ibid., 70.

**16.** Narrative of *La rabbia* from typescript, with Pasolini's handwritten annotations, for which the author thanks the Associazione "Fondo Pier Paolo Pasolini," Rome.

**17.** Ibid.

**18.** Stack, 70.

**19.** Ibid., 72.

**20.** Ibid., 65.

**21.** Ibid., 65–66.

**22.** Ibid., 82.

**23.** Ibid., 75.

**24.** Ibid., 77.

**25.** Ibid., 79.

**26.** MacAfee, 70–71.

**27.** *Le belle bandiere*, 257–58; *Vie nuove*, No. 44, Oct. 29, 1964.

**28.** Ibid., 258–60.

**29.** *Lettere, II* (1955–1975), *Cronologia*, lxxxv.

**30.** Ibid., *Cronologia*, lxxxvi.

**31.** Ibid., undated letter of 1963 to Yevgeny Yevtushenko, 518–19.

**32.** Ibid., letter to Guido Davice Bonino, March 1964, 540.

**33.** Siciliano, 271.

**34.** Stack, 78.

**35.** *Le belle bandiere*, 259; *Vie nuove*, No. 44, Oct. 29, 1964.

**36.** Stack, 87.

**37.** Ibid., 84–86.

**38.** De Giusti, *Pier Paolo Pasolini: Il cinema in forma di poesia*, 72.

**39.** Stack, 95.

**40.** *Lettere, II* (1955–1975), *Cronologia*, xciii, from *"Settimana incom,"* No. 38, 1964.

**41.** Number of July–September 1964.

**42.** *Lettere, II* (1955–1975), letter to Piergiorgio Bellocchio, Oct. 16, 1964, 561.

**43.** Siciliano, 276.

**44.** *Le belle bandiere*, 284; *Vie nuove*, No. 1, Jan. 7, 1965.

**45.** The word "joyful" (*lieta*) was cut from the dedication and "Saint" added to the title, against Pasolini's clear intentions, by his English-language distributors. See Stack, 97, note 2.

**46.** *Lettere, II* (1955–1975), *Cronologia*, xciii.

**47.** Allen, 7.

**48.** Betti, 151.

**49.** Stack, 83.

**50.** *Le belle bandiere*, 264; *Vie nuove*, Nov. 26, 1964.

**51.** Stack, 77.

**52.** MacAfee, 73.

**53.** Macciocchi, *Duemila anni di felicità*, 331–32.

**54.** Ibid., 332–35 for Pasolini-Sartre encounter.

**55.** Betti, 148.

**56.** Its life was brief (1962–64); Fortini published a column in its pages.

**57.** *Lettere, II* (1955–1975), letter to Roberto Roversi, 538.

**58.** MacAfee, 183–87; also "Plan of Future Works" in Pasolini, *Poesia in forma di rosa*, 1964, 68.

**59.** MacAfee, 199–201.

**60.** *Le belle bandiere*, 249–53; *Vie nuove*, Oct. 15, 1964.

**61.** *Le poesie* (1975, 1976), 439.

**62.** *Le belle bandiere*, 145; *Poesie in forma di rosa; Le poesie*, 444.

**63.** *Le belle bandiere*, 201–3; from "Plan of Future Works" in *Poesia in forma di rosa; Le poesie*, 531.

**64.** Fernando Camon, *Il mestiere di scrittore*, Milano, Garzanti, 1973, 99–100; *Lettere, II* (1955–1975), *Cronologia*, lxxxviii.

**65.** Siciliano, 279; *Le poesie*, 333.

**66.** *Lettere, II* (1955–1975), *Cronologia*, xcii.

**67.** *Le belle bandiere*, 249–53; *Vie nuove*, Oct. 15, 1964.

**68.** MacAfee, 151, from "A Desperate Vitality;" in *Poesie in forma di rosa; Le poesie*, 449.

**69.** Ibid., 153–73; *Le poesie*, 451–53.

**70.** Ibid., 173–75; *Le poesie*, 467–68.

**71.** *Le poesie*, 449–50.

**72.** *Lettere, II* (1955–1975), letter to Don Giovanni Rossi, Dec. 27, 1964, 576–77.

**73.** Ibid., letter of Rossi to Pasolini, Dec. 27, 1964, 577.

## 19.  A TELLER OF FABLES

**1.**  Fabio Mauri, "Nel 1950 gli anni 50 avevano 10 anni," 36, *Flash Art*, 112.

**2.**  Author's interview with Fabio Mauri, Rome, 1988.

**3.**  Author's interview with Gianni Scalia, Bologna, 1988. Scalia: "In 1964, Feltrinelli approached me to assemble an anthology to be called *Poesie italiana del dopoguerra* and I included a poem of Pasolini's. But Feltrinelli, the Group's publisher, was unhappy with that. It seems postwar poetry started with Sanguineti. They refused to have Pasolini in it."

**4.**  *Le belle bandiere*, 261; *Vie nuove*, Nov. 5, 1964.

**5.**  Pier Paolo Pasolini, "The End of the Avant-garde" (trans. K. J. Jewell), 1966, in Allen, 17; also in Pasolini, *Heretical Empiricism*, ed. L. K. Barnett (trans. Barnett and B. Lawton), Bloomington and London, Indiana University Press, 1988 (henceforth cited as *Heretical Empiricism*), 121–41.

**6.**  Siciliano, 292; also in *Heretical Empiricism*, 22.

**7.**  *Le belle bandiere*, 271; *Vie nuove*, Dec. 3, 1964.

**8.**  *Lettere, II* (1955–1975), *Cronologia*, xcvii; also, J. Duflot, ed., *Il sogno del centauro*, Rome, Editori Riuniti, 1983, 102 ff.

**9.**  S. Lotringer, *Overexposed: Treating Sexual Perversion in America*, New York, Pantheon Books, 1988, 10.

**10.**  In Italy, 1972; in English as *Which Tribe Do You Belong To?*, London, Panther, 1976.

**11.**  Ibid., 55–57.

**12.**  "Roma Giovani," reprinted from interview in *L'unità*, October–November 1963.

**13.**  Siciliano, 294–95; from Pasolini, *Empirismo eretico*, Milano, Garzanti, 1972 (henceforth cited as *Empirismo eretico*), 73–74.

**14.**  *Le belle bandiere*, 303–5; *Vie nuove*, Feb. 25, 1965.

**15.**  Stack, 153.

**16.**  B. Allen, "The Shadow of His Style" in Allen, 3.

**17.**  Ibid., 19, from Pasolini, "The End of the Avant-garde."

**18.**  Siciliano, 298.

**19.**  Allen, 21.

**20.**  Stack, 149.

**21.**  Pasolini, *La divina mimesis*, Torino, Einaudi, 1975.

**22.**  Ibid., "Prologue."

**23.**  Ibid.

**24.**  "A Desperate Vitality," in *Le poesie* (1975, 1976), 468.

**25.**  Giuseppe Zigaina, *Pasolini e la morte*, Venezia, Marsilio Editore, 1987, 93.

**26.**  *Le belle bandiere*, 350; *Vie nuove*, June 24, 1965.

**27.**  Ibid., 352; *Vie nuove*, July 15, 1965.

**28.** Ibid., 364–67; *Vie nuove*, Sept. 23, 1965. Also see *Lettere, II* (1955–1975), *Cronologia*, ciii.

**29.** Ibid., 367; *Vie nuove*, Sept. 30, 1965.

**30.** Elisabetta Mondello, *Gli anni delle rivisti*, Lecce, Edizioni Milella, 1980, 147–48.

**31.** Published by Valentino Bompiani Editors, Milano, 1974.

**32.** *Lettere, II* (1955–1975), letter to Renzo Paris, Spring 1970, 673.

**33.** January–March 1966.

**34.** Pasolini, "The End of the Avant-garde," in Allen, 13.

**35.** Stack, 101.

**36.** Ibid.

**37.** Ibid., 103.

**38.** Ibid.

**39.** O. Caldiron, *Totò*, Rome, Gremese Editore, 1983, 52.

**40.** Stack, 110.

**41.** Ibid., 22.

**42.** Pasolini, *Uccellacci e uccellini*, Milano, Garzanti, 1966, 59.

**43.** Ibid., 207.

**44.** Ibid., 181.

**45.** Stack, 107.

**46.** Ibid., 103.

**47.** Ibid., 99–100.

**48.** *Lettere, II* (1955–1975), letter from Don Lucio Caruso to Pasolini, Oct. 7, 1965.

**49.** Alfredo Bini, "La città del cinema," *L'espresso*, 1979, 102.

**50.** Luciano de Giusti, *Pier Paolo Pasolini: Il cinema in forma di poesie*; from *Cahiers du cinéma*, No. 179, June 1966, 39; also in Marc Gervais, *Pier Paolo Pasolini*, Paris, Seghers, 1975, 142–43; and "Open Letter," in *Occhio critico*, No. 2, 1966.

**51.** *Rinascita*, 23: 21, May 21, 1966.

**52.** Stack, 143.

**53.** *Lettere, II* (1955–1975), *Cronologia*, cviii.

**54.** Stack, 144.

**55.** Penelope Gilliatt, "The Urgent Whisper" [profile of Jean-Luc Godard], *The New Yorker*, Oct. 25, 1965, 49.

**56.** Stack, 143.

**57.** *Pier Paolo Pasolini: Una vita futura*, Roma, Associazione "Fondo Pier Paolo Pasolini," 1985, 123.

**58.** Siciliano, 301.

**59.** Pasolini, *Orgia*, in *Porcile/Orgia/Bestia da stile*, Milano, Garzanti, 1979, 114.

**60.** Pasolini, *Affabulazione*, in *Affabulazione/Pilade*, Milano, Garzanti, 1977, 107–14.

**61.** Stack, 143.

**62.** Ibid., 155, from interview on BBC-TV ("Release").

**63.** *Lettere, II* (1955–1975), *Cronologia*, cvii.

**64.** Stack, 112.

**65.** Ibid., 114–16.

**66.** Ibid., 116.

**67.** Ibid., 118.

**68.** *L'Europeo*, Nov. 21, 1975, 28.

**69.** Howard Thompson, " 'Gospel' Director Plans St. Paul Film," *New York Times*, Aug. 9, 1966; also see *Empirismo eretico*, 149.

**70.** Oriana Fallaci, "Un marxista a New York," *L'Europeo*, Oct. 13, 1966.

**71.** Siciliano, 307; from *Empirismo eretico*, 150.

**72.** Ibid., 308; from *Empirismo eretico*, 150.

**73.** *Lettere, II* (1955–1975), letter to Allen Ginsberg, 631–33; letter reprinted, in English, in the magazine *Lumen/Avenue A* (trans. A. Ginsberg and A. Galvano), New York, Vol. 1, No. 1.

**74.** *Lettere, II* (1955–1975), *Cronologia*, cxi.

## 20. THE CINEMA OF POETRY: *OEDIPUS THE KING, TEOREMA,* AND A *SAINT PAUL* THAT WAS NEVER TO BE

**1.** *Le poesie* (1975, 1976), 304–5.

**2.** Pier Paolo Pasolini, *Edipo re*, from the Introduction, "Perchè quella di Edipo è una storia," Milan, Garzanti, 1967, 13.

**3.** *Lettere, II* (1955–1975), *Cronologia*, cxii; from preface by G. Gambetti, "Franco Citti, attore da sempre," in *Edipo re*, 23–36.

**4.** Ibid., letter to Susanna Pasolini, April 13, 1967, 628.

**5.** Dacia Maraini, *E tu chi eri?*, 259.

**6.** Ibid., 260.

**7.** *Edipo re*, 50.

**8.** Lettere, II (1955–1975), *Cronologia*, cxiv.

**9.** Stack, 122.

**10.** *Lutheran Letters*, 39; first appeared as "Bologna, a consumerist and Communist city" in *Corriere della sera*, May 8, 1975.

**11.** *Edipo re*, 139.

**12.** Stack, 129.

**13.** Ibid., 119–20.

**14.** Ibid., 120.

**15.** Ibid., 13.

**16.** Maraini, 268.

**17.** *Cahiers du cinéma*, July–August, 1967, 172.

**18.** *Edipo re*, Pasolini's introduction, "Perchè quella di Edipo è una storia," 14.

19. *Lettere, II* (1955–1975), letter to Livio Garzanti, 618.
20. Stack, 124.
21. Siciliano, 306; from Guido Piovene, "Fino in fondo nel sangue nel buio," *La fiera letteraria*, Sept. 14, 1967.
22. *Lettere, II* (1955–1975), *Cronologia*, cxiv.
23. Alfredo Bini, "I primi passi del regista Pasolini," *L'Europeo*, No. 48, Nov. 28, 1975, 54.
24. Ibid.
25. Stack, 155; extract from an interview on BBC-TV ("Release").
26. Ibid.
27. Author's interview with Terence Stamp, London, Aug. 25, 1988.
28. Ibid.
29. *Lettere, II* (1955–1975), *Cronologia*, cxv.
30. *Le belle bandiere*, 273; *Vie nuove*, Dec. 10, 1964.
31. Stack, 158, citing L. Peroni, *Inquadrature*, 15–16, autumn, 1968.
32. Ibid., 156–57; from interview on BBC-TV ("Release").
33. Ibid., 162.
34. Ibid., 157.
35. *Corriere della sera*, Mar. 23, 1969.
36. Betti, 164–65.
37. Ibid.
38. Siciliano, 313; from Pasolini, *Teorema*, Milano, Garzanti, 1968, jacket cover.
39. J. F. Lane, "Pasolini's Prizes," *Sunday Times*, July 21, 1968.
40. *Il giorno*, July 4, 1968.
41. *Lettere, II* (1955–1975), letter to Leonardo Sciascia, dated "1958," 644.
42. Ibid., letter to Francesco Leonetti, June 1968, 645.
43. *L'espresso*, June 16, 1968.
44. Leopoldo Meneghelli, *Mondo nuovo*, June 23, 1968.
45. *Lettere, II* (1955–1975), *Cronologia*, xxiii.
46. Betti, 168.
47. *Empirismo eretico*, 162–63.
48. Siciliano, 330; also *Le poesie*, 601. Theodor Adorno called Pasolini's "critical thinking" "bottles thrown into the sea for addressees whose future identity is still unknown." See M. Jay, *Adorno*, Cambridge, Harvard, 1984, 54 ff.
49. *Le belle bandiere*, 269; *Vie nuove*, Dec. 3, 1964.
50. Pasolini, *San Paolo*, Torino, Einaudi, 1977, 169.
51. Ibid., 6–7.
52. P. Bondanella, ed., *Italian Cinema from Neorealism to the Present*. New York, Frederick Ungar, 1983, 224–26.
53. *San Paolo*, 6.
54. *Lettere, II* (1955–1975), letter to Don Emilio Cordero, June 9, 1968, 639.

## 21. *MEDEA* AND CALLAS

**1.** No. 28–81, January–June 1966.
**2.** *Lettere, II* (1955–1975), 585.
**3.** Pier Paolo Pasolini, "Satura," *Nuovi argomenti*, January–March 1971, 17–20.
**4.** Siciliano, 353.
**5.** Ibid., 354–55; also see E. Montale, "Diario del '71," *L'espresso*, Dec. 19, 1971.
**6.** Ibid., 355; from Pasolini, "Outis," *Nuovi argomenti*, May–June 1972, 149–50.
**7.** June 15, 1947.
**8.** Jan. 11, 1969.
**9.** "Il Caos," *Tempo illustrato*, Dec. 19, 1969.
**10.** Siciliano, 360.
**11.** *Lettere, II* (1955–1975), *Cronologia*, cxxx.
**12.** Ibid.
**13.** Ibid., cxxv.
**14.** Stack, 130–31.
**15.** *Lettere, II* (1955–1975), letter to Gianfranco d'Aronco, May 2, 1969, 657.
**16.** Stack, 142.
**17.** *Cinema nuovo*, 18: 201, September–October 1969, 363–64.
**18.** Luciano de Giusti, *I film di Pier Paolo Pasolini*; from Esohilo [Aeschylus], *Orestiade*, Torino, Einaudi, 1960, 3.
**19.** *Pier Paolo Pasolini: Una vita futura*, Roma, Associazione "Fondo Pier Paolo Pasolini," 1987, 248.
**20.** De Giusti, *I film di Pier Paolo Pasolini*, 114.
**21.** Arianna Stassinopoulos, *Maria Callas: The Woman Behind the Legend*, New York, Ballantine Books, 1981, 281.
**22.** Nadia Stancioff, *Maria Callas Remembered*, New York, E. P. Dutton, 1987, 170.
**23.** Ibid.
**24.** Ibid., 172.
**25.** Siciliano, 332.
**26.** De Giusti, *I film di Pier Paolo Pasolini*, 111; from Marc Gervais, *Pier Paolo Pasolini*, Paris, Seghers, 1973, 114.
**27.** Pasolini, *Medea*, Milano, Garzanti, 1970; from Preface by G. Gambetti, "Maria Callas: Sono per una Medea non aggressiva," 13–24.
**28.** Stancioff, 172.
**29.** *Vita*, May 14, 1969.
**30.** Stancioff, 174.
**31.** Ibid., 285.
**32.** Ibid., 32.

**33.** Pasolini, *Descrizioni di descrizioni*, ed. Graziella Chiarcossi, Torino, Einaudi, 1979, 367; review in *Tempo*, Aug. 30, 1974.

**34.** Transcript of taped conversation between Pasolini and Franco Rossellini, courtesy of Rodolfo Sonigo.

**35.** Siciliano, 331; from Piero Sanavio, "Porcile o no, tiriamo le somme su Pasolini," *Il dramma*, Sept. 12, 1969.

**36.** De Giusti, *I film di Pier Paolo Pasolini*, 110; from *Cineforum*, 85, May 1969, 318.

**37.** *Medea*, 92.

**38.** Stancioff, 174.

**39.** *Lettere, II* (1955–1975), *Cronologia*, cxxx.

**40.** Stancioff, 173.

**41.** "Rifaciamento" from *Trasumanar e organizzar*, Milano, Garzanti, 1971; in *Le poesie* (1975, 1976), 719.

**42.** Ibid., "Timor di me?" 718.

**43.** Allen, 51; from J.-M. Gardair, "January 1971, via Eufrate 9, Rome, EUR" (trans. D. Kormos).

**44.** Stancioff, 204.

**45.** Zigaina, 49.

**46.** *Lettere, II* (1955–1975), letter to Livio Garzanti, June 1966, 617.

**47.** Ibid., 611.

**48.** Ibid., *Cronologia*, cxxix.

**49.** Garzanti paperback edition (1970), reprinting *Le ceneri di Gramsci, La religione del mio tempo*, and *Poesie in forma di rosa*, 12. In *Trasumanar e organizzar*, 649–51.

**50.** MacAfee, 221–26.

**51.** *Lettere, II* (1955–1975), *Cronologia*, cxxx–cxxxi.

## 22.  THE *TRILOGY OF LIFE*

**1.** De Giusti, *I film di Pier Paolo Pasolini*, 118; from *Cinema 72*, 164, March 1972.

**2.** *Lettere, II* (1955–1975), *Cronologia*, cxxxi.

**3.** P. Willemen, ed., *Pier Paolo Pasolini*, London, British Film Institute, 1977; from R. Lomax and O. Stack in *Seven Days*, London, Nov. 17, 1971.

**4.** Martin Jay, *Adorno*, Cambridge, Harvard, 1984 (henceforth cited as Jay), 38, footnote 32 to ch. 1.

**5.** *Cinema*, Nos. 88–89, 60, January 1972.

**6.** Author's interview with Alberto Grimaldi, Los Angeles, Nov. 28, 1988.

**7.** P. Bondanella, *Italian Cinema from Neorealism to the Present*, New York, Frederick Ungar, 1983, 291.

**8.** March 5, 1974.

**9.** P. Panicali and S. Sestini, eds., *Pier Paolo Pasolini: Testimonianze*, Florence, Nuovo Salani, 1982, "Saluto e Augurio," 102.

**10.** De Giusti, *I film di Pier Paolo Pasolini*, 128; from Pasolini, "Tetis," in *Erotismo, eversione, merce*, Bologna, Cappelli, 1974, 100–11.

**11.** Willemen, 77.

**12.** De Giusti, *I film di Pier Paolo Pasolini*, 119; from *Filmcritica*, 22: 214, March 1971.

**13.** Bondanella, 288–89.

**14.** Author's interview with Alberto Grimaldi, Los Angeles, Nov. 28, 1988. "Film rentals" account for 50 percent of ticket sales (called "box-office gross" in North America), about half the world market. Because of government tax on tickets, it accounts for only one-third in Italy, 10 percent in the world market overall. To arrive at "gross worldwide revenue" from ticket sales alone, a conservative procedure is to double the film-rental amount.

**15.** De Giusti, *I film di Pier Paolo Pasolini*, 119; from *Cahiers du cinéma*, 212, May 1969.

**16.** Ibid., 120; from Dario Bellezza, interview in *L'espresso*, No. 47, Nov. 22, 1970.

**17.** *La stampa*, Feb. 11, 1972.

**18.** Betti, 180; from *Corriere della sera*, Feb. 4, 1973.

**19.** Ibid., 183.

**20.** Ibid.

**21.** Ibid., 185.

**22.** Ibid.

**23.** Ibid.

**24.** Oct. 6, 1971.

**25.** De Giusti, *I film di Pier Paolo Pasolini*; from *L'espresso/colore*, 47, Nov. 22, 1970.

**26.** *New York Times*, May 20, 1988.

**27.** A. Zanzotto, "Pedagogy" (trans. B. Allen), in Allen, 39.

**28.** *Pier Paolo Pasolini: Una via futura*, ed. Laura Betti and Sergio Vecchio, Rome, Associazione *"Fondo Pier Paolo Pasolini"* and Ente Autonomo Gestione Cinema, 1987, 374–79.

**29.** Author's interview with Alberto Grimaldi, Los Angeles, Nov. 28, 1988.

**30.** *Variety*, Feb. 13, 1980.

**31.** Dec. 14, 1971.

**32.** Willemen, 70.

**33.** Ibid., from interview in *Jeune cinema*.

**34.** De Giusti, *I film di Pier Paolo Pasolini*, 128; from Pasolini, "Tetis," 101.

**35.** Willemen, 71–74; from R. Lomax and O. Stack, *Seven Days*, London, Nov. 17, 1971.

**36.** Enzo Siciliano, "L'odiato Pasolini," *Il mondo*, July 14, 1972.

**37.** L. K. Barnett, "Introduction" to Pasolini, *Heretical Empiricism*, trans. and ed. L. K. Barnett, Bloomington, Indiana University Press, 1988.

**38.** Ibid., xx.

**39.** Mircea Eliade, *Mito e realtà*, Rome, Borla, 1985.

**40.** G. Zigaina, *Pasolini e la morte*, Venezia, Marsilio Editore, 1987, 79; citing Pasolini, *Descrizioni di descrizioni*, ed. Graziella Chiarcossi, Torino, Einaudi, 1979, 370.

**41.** A. A. Zhdanov (1896–1948) was Stalin's enforcer of the tenets of Socialist Realism.

**42.** Barnett, xvii.

**43.** Zigaina, 19–20.

**44.** Siciliano, 356; from Pasolini's lectures on behalf of the Associazione Culturale Italiana in Turin, Milan, Rome, May 1972.

**45.** *Lettere, II* (1955–1975), letter to Paolo Volponi, August, 1971, 707.

**46.** Siciliano, 338.

**47.** Ibid., 339.

**48.** Ibid., 340.

**49.** Ibid.

**50.** Ibid., 341.

**51.** Author's interview with Ninetto Davoli, Rome, 1976.

**52.** Author's interview with Nico Naldini, Refrontolo, July 1986.

**53.** Siciliano, 341.

**54.** A. Bertini, "Memories of a Production Director," in *Teorie e tecnica del film di Pasolini*, Bulzoni Editore, 1979, 153–54.

**55.** De Giusti, ed., *Pier Paolo Pasolini: Il cinema in forma di poesie*, Pordenone, Edizioni Cinemazero, 1979, 143; Pasolini's remarks at press conference, Berlin Film Festival, 1972.

**56.** Betti, 192.

**57.** In 1988 it was broadcast on Italian television with its hard-core scenes—including the anal fornication with butter—cut altogether. Bertolucci was reported as saying he deemed the six minutes of cuts "nothing serious" (*La repubblica*, Sept. 21, 1988).

**58.** Betti, 193.

**59.** *Paese sera*, July 6, 1973.

**60.** G. Bachmann, *Take One*, May/June 1973, reprinted in *Invisible City*, No. 15, February 1975.

**61.** Betti, 194; from *Panorama*, Mar. 8, 1973.

**62.** *Lettere, II* (1955–1975), *Cronologia*, cxl.

**63.** Ibid., cxxxv.

**64.** Pasolini, "Pasolini Reviews Pasolini," *Il portico della morte*, ed. C. Segre, Roma, Associazione "Fondo Pier Paolo Pasolini," 1988, 283–85; first appeared in *Il giorno*, Milano, June 3, 1971.

**65.** Pasolini, *Descrizione di descrizione*, review of May 20, 1973.

**66.** Ibid., 35.

**67.**    *Lettere, II* (1955–1975), *Cronologia*, cxlviii.

**68.**    Pasolini, *Descrizioni di descrizioni,* "*Campana e Pound,*" 235–40, review of Dec. 16, 1973.

**69.**    Ibid., 353–62, reviews of July 26 and August 2, 1974.

**70.**    De Giusti, *I film di Pier Paolo Pasolini,* 137–38; from interview with Pasolini by Gideon Bachmann, *Il messaggero,* Rome, Aug. 24, 1973.

**71.**    Bondanella, 292–93.

**72.**    Dec. 6, 1972.

**73.**    Willemen, 77; adapted from publicity handout version of an interview in *Il tempo,* 1974.

**74.**    Ibid.

**75.**    De Giusti, *I film di Pier Paolo Pasolini,* 138; from *La fiera letteraria,* Nov. 10, 1974.

**76.**    M. Giovannini, "Pasolini mille e uno," *Panorama,* Mar. 3, 1974.

**77.**    Betti, 197.

**78.**    July 31, 1974.

**79.**    Oct. 18, 1970.

**80.**    *Lutheran Letters,* 32; from "Gennariello: Our Impotence in the Face of the Pedagogic Language of Things."

**81.**    De Giusti, *I film di Pier Paolo Pasolini,* 142; from Pasolini, "Pasolini racconta con rabbia l'assurda rovina di una città," *Corriere della sera,* June 20, 1974.

**82.**    *Lettere, II* (1955–1975), *Cronologia,* cxlix.

**83.**    *Lutheran Letters,* 31–32.

**84.**    De Giusti, *I film di Pier Paolo Pasolini,* 142; from TV program "Io e . . ."

**85.**    Stack, 144.

**86.**    Dacia Maraini, *E tu chi eri?* Milano, Bompiani, 1973, 262.

**87.**    *Lettere, II* (1955–1975), *Cronologia,* clvii.

## 23.   *LUTHERAN LETTERS* TO THE ITALIANS

**1.**    Author's interview with Moreno Marcucci, Rome, Sept. 9, 1988.

**2.**    Pier Paolo Pasolini, "Il discorso dei capelli" in Pasolini, *Scritti corsari,* Milano, Garzanti, 1975, 16; appeared as "Contro i capelli lunghi," *Corriere della sera,* Jan. 7, 1973.

**3.**    Jay, author's "Introduction," 15.

**4.**    G. Barbiellini Amidei, *Corriere della sera,* Oct. 5, 1984.

**5.**    Siciliano, 374; from Pasolini, *Scritti corsari,* 101; "Lo storico discorsetto di Castelgandolfo," first appeared as "I dilemmi di un Papa, oggi," *Corriere della sera,* Sept. 22, 1974.

**6.**    *Scritti corsari,* 110; "Nuove prospettive storiche: la Chiesa è inutile al potere," first as "Chiesa e potere," in *Corriere della sera,* Oct. 6, 1974.

**7.** Interview with Gideon Bachmann at Chia, Sept. 13, 1974.

**8.** *Scritti corsari*, 51–52, "Studio sulla rivoluzione antropologic a in Italia," first as "Gli italiani non sono più quelli," *Corriere della sera*, June 10, 1974.

**9.** *L'espresso*, June 23, 1974.

**10.** *Lettere, II* (1955–1975), *Cronologia*, cliv.

**11.** *Scritti corsari*, "La prima, vera rivoluzione di destra," 29–30, from *Tempo illustrato*, July 15, 1973.

**12.** *Il popolo*, Apr. 24, 1975.

**13.** *Scritti corsari*, "Acculturazione e acculturazione," 31–39, from *Corriere della sera*, Dec. 9, 1973.

**14.** Sept. 19, 1974.

**15.** Leo Lowenthal, in Jay, 122.

**16.** De Giusti, *Il cinema in forma di poesia*, 153; from interview by Gideon Bachmann at Chia, Sept. 13, 1974.

**17.** *Lutheran Letters*, 66; first in *Corriere della sera*, Aug. 1, 1975.

**18.** Ibid.

**19.** Ibid., 63.

**20.** Ibid.

**21.** Ibid., 128.

**22.** Article by Alfred Vinciguerra, Apr. 24, 1975.

**23.** *Lettere, II* (1955–1975), *Cronologia*, clx.

**24.** *Lutheran Letters*, 79; first in *Corriere della sera*, Aug. 24, 1975.

**25.** Betti, 207; from *La discussione*, Sept. 29, 1975.

**26.** Siciliano, 379; also in *Scritti corsari*, "I Nixon italiani," 73; first as "Gli insostituibili Nixon italiani," in *Corriere della sera*, Feb. 18, 1975.

**27.** Siciliano, 378; also in *Scritti corsari*, "L'articolo delle lucciole," 161; first as "Il vuoto del potere in Italia," *Corriere della sera*, Feb. 1, 1975.

**28.** Siciliano, 378; also in *Scritti corsari*, "Il romanzo delle stragi," 114; first as "Che cos' è questo golpe?" *Corriere della sera*, Nov. 14, 1974.

**29.** *Lutheran Letters*, 59; first in *Corriere della sera*, July 24, 1975.

**30.** Ibid., 62.

**31.** Gianni Borgna in *Rinascita*, Nov. 14, 1975, 32.

**32.** *Roma giovani*, No. 1, Nov. 15, 1974.

**33.** *Lutheran Letters*, 62.

**34.** Jay, "Introduction," 12, from *Adorno, The Jargon of Authenticity* (trans. K. Tarnovski and F. Will), London, 1973, 93.

**35.** Siciliano, 372; also in *Scritti corsari*, "Limitatezza della storia e immensità del mondo contadino," 64–69; first in *Paese sera*, "Lettera aperta a Italo Calvino: Pasolini: Quello che rimpiango," July 8, 1974.

**36.** *Lutheran Letters*, 91; first in *Il mondo*, Sept. 11, 1975.

**37.** Ibid., 99; first in *Corriere della sera*, Sept. 28, 1975.

**38.** MacAfee, 151; from "A Desperate Vitality," in *Poesie in forma di rosa; in Le poesie* (1975, 1976), 449–50.

**39.** Siciliano, 372; in *Scritti corsari,* "Limitatezza della storia e immensità del mondo contadino," 64–69; first in *Paese sera.*

**40.** *Lutheran Letters,* 109–14, "My Proposals for Schools and Television"; first in *Corriere della sera,* Oct. 29, 1975.

**41.** Transcript of the discussion in Pasolini, *Volgar'eloquio,* ed. A. Piromalli and D. Scafoglio, Naples, Athena, 1976.

**42.** *Volgar'eloquio;* also in *Rinascita,* Nov. 5, 1976; and *Pier Paolo Pasolini, Una via futura,* Rome, Associazione "Fondo Pier Paolo Pasolini," 1985, 125.

**43.** *Volgar'eloquio,* 60–61.

**44.** *Lutheran Letters,* 62.

**45.** Siciliano, 374; from *Scritti corsari,* 123–31, "Il coito, l'aborto, la falsa tolleranza del potere, il conformismo dei progressisti"; first as "Sono contro l'aborto" in *Corriere della sera,* Jan. 19, 1975.

**46.** *Volgar'eloquio,* 73.

**47.** Siciliano, 376; from Siciliano, "Non rimpiango l'età dell'oro, rimpiango l'età del pane," *Il mondo,* Aug. 14, 1975.

**48.** *Scritti corsari,* 132–37; in *Corriere della sera,* "Pasolini replica sull' aborto," Jan. 30, 1975.

**49.** Allen, 122–26, from Pasolini, "Heart" (trans. J. Schiesari); also *Scritti corsari,* "Non aver paura d'avere un cuore," 152–59; first in *Corriere della sera,* Mar. 1, 1975.

**50.** *Lutheran Letters,* "Subject for a Film About a Policeman," 72; first in *Il mondo,* Aug. 7, 1975.

**51.** Ibid., "My 'Accattone' on TV After the Genocide," 100–102; first in *Corriere della sera,* Oct. 8, 1975.

**52.** Ibid., "A Lutheran Letter to Italo Calvino," 119; first in *Il mondo,* Oct. 30, 1975.

**53.** Author's interview with Leonardo Sciascia, *Racalmuto,* Sept. 17, 1988.

**54.** Siciliano, 384; from Enzo Golino, *Letteratura e classi sociali,* Bari, 1976, 112. Interview first published in *Il giorno,* Dec. 29, 1973.

**55.** *Lettere, II* (1955–1975), letter to Eduardo de Filippo, Sept. 24, 1975, 742.

**56.** Ibid., letter to Gian Carlo Ferretti, early October 1975, 744.

**57.** Ibid., letter to Don Emilio Cordero, June 25, 1966, 619.

**58.** Rom. 2: 27–32.

## 24.    THE COLLAPSE OF THE PRESENT, A QUESTION OF GRIEF

**1.** *Lutheran Letters,* 49–52; first in *Corriere della sera,* Nov. 9, 1975.

**2.** "Gennariello: How I Imagine You," *Il mondo,* Mar. 6, 1975.

**3.** "Gennariello: Scheme of Work," ibid., Apr. 3, 1975.

**4.** *Paese sera*, Feb. 1, 1975.

**5.** A phrase coined by Gore Vidal.

**6.** *Le monde*, Nov. 23, 1975, 1; reported in "Giudizi contrastati su salò," *Corriere della sera*, Nov. 25, 1975.

**7.** *Lettere, II* (1955–1975), *Cronologia*, clv.

**8.** Gideon Bachmann, "Pasolini on De Sade," *Film Quarterly*, Winter 1975–76, 39–45.

**9.** Author's interview with Alberto Grimaldi, Los Angeles, Nov. 28, 1988.

**10.** Italo Calvino, "Sade Is Within Us," in Allen, 108 (trans. M. Pietralunga); first in *Corriere della sera*, Nov. 30, 1975.

**11.** Ibid., 109.

**12.** Bachmann, 41.

**13.** Ibid., 45.

**14.** Calvino, "Sade e dentro di noi," *Corriere della sera*, Nov. 30, 1975.

**15.** R. Barthes, *Sade/Fourier/Loyola*, New York, Hill and Wang, 1976, 35.

**16.** Ibid., 137.

**17.** *Heretical Empiricism*, Editors' "Introduction," xvii.

**18.** See Lietta Tornabuoni, article from *Corriere della sera*, Nov. 3, 1975, reprinted in Allen, 99.

**19.** *Le poesie* (1975, 1976), 444.

**20.** U. P. Quintavalle, *Giornate di Sodoma: Ritratto di Pasolini e del duo ultimo film*, Milano, SugarCo Edizioni, 1976.

**21.** François Bondy, "Pasolini's Murder," *Encounter*, June 1976, 55.

**22.** Author's interview with Avv. Rocco Mangia, Rome, Aug. 3, 1976.

**23.** Article by P. Palumbo, *Gente*, Jan. 17, 1975.

**24.** F. Trapani, *Gente*, Nov. 24, 1975.

**25.** Ibid., Feb. 9, 1975.

**26.** Author's interview with F. M. Trapani, Rome, Aug. 3, 1976.

**27.** Nov. 11, 1975.

**28.** Author's interview with Avv. Rocco Mangia, Rome, Aug. 3, 1976.

**29.** Giovanni Grassi, "Nostro figlio ha ucciso Pasolini ma non ci vergogniamo di lui," *Domenica del corriere*, Feb. 12, 1976, 13–14.

**30.** De Giusti, *Pier Paolo Pasolini: Il cinema in forma di poesie*, 172–73; from Pasolini's comments at a press conference on the *Salò* set, the day before the end of filming.

**31.** Ibid., 173.

**32.** *Pier Paolo Pasolini: Una vita futura*, Rome, Associazione "Fondo Pier Paolo Pasolini," 1985, 149.

**33.** Bachmann, Apr. 29, 1975.

**34.** Ibid.

**35.** L. Bersani and U. Dutoit, "Merde alors," in Allen, 82–95.

**36.** Ibid., 85.

**37.** Bachmann, 41–42.

**38.** B. Allen, "The Shadow of His Style," in Allen, 1–7.

**39.** Bersani and Dutoit, in Allen, 83.

**40.** Siciliano, 394.

**41.** Pier Paolo Pasolini, "Rital and Raton" in *Roman Nights and Other Stories* (trans. John Shepley), Marlboro, Vt., Marlboro Press, 1986, 130.

**42.** Jay, 44; from "Freudian Theory and the Pattern of Fascist Propaganda" in *The Essential Frankfurt School Reader*, ed. A. Arato and E. Gebhardt, New York and Oxford, 1978, 137.

**43.** Andre Bretón on Man Ray. See *Perpetual Motif: The Art of Man Ray*, New York, Abbeville Press, 1988. One wonders whether Pasolini knew that Ray rose from his sickbed in November 1922, to photograph Proust dead, the year Pasolini was born.

**44.** Author's interview with Dino Pedriali, Rome, September 1988. Also see D. Pedriali, "Seconda settimana di ottobre 1975" in *Omaggio a Pier Paolo Pasolini: Foto di Pier Paolo Pasolini*, exhibition catalogue, Agrigento: Centro Culturale Editoriale Pier Paolo Pasolini, ed. Giuliana Scime.

**45.** Author's interview with Silvana Mauri Ottieri, Milan, Sept. 10, 1988.

**46.** *Il giornale*, Nov. 13, 1975.

**47.** Nov. 14, 1975.

**48.** V. Buttafava, *Oggi illustrato*, Dec. 15, 1975, 5.

**49.** Author's interview with N. Naldini, Rome, July 1976.

**50.** Betti, 215; from *Corriere della sera*, Jan. 10, 1976.

**51.** *Avanti*, Jan. 22, 1976.

**52.** *Corriere della sera*, July 18, 1976, 18.

**53.** *Il secolo d'Italia*, Feb. 2, 1976.

**54.** Literally. "The Street of the Virgins," *Giornale di Brescia*, Feb. 8, 1976.

**55.** *Il messaggero*, Apr. 25, 1976.

**56.** Author's interview with M. Marcucci and G. Di Dio, Rome, Sept. 9, 1988.

**57.** Author's interview with Avv. Rocco Mangia, Rome, July 20, 1976.

**58.** P. Menghini, in *Corriere della sera*, Dec. 5, 1976, 9.

**59.** *Il messaggero*, Dec. 2, 1976.

**60.** Oct. 1, 1977.

**61.** *Lutheran Letters*, "Gennariello: The First Lesson, Given to Me by a Blind Man," 30, Apr. 10, 1975.

**62.** A. Zanzotto, "Pedagogy," in Allen, 39.

**63.** Author's interview with Giuseppe Pelosi, Rome, Sept. 6, 1988.

**64.** Mar. 6, 1979.

**65.** *La repubblica*, Nov. 27, 1982.

**66.** Ibid., July 18, 1983.

**67.** *Empirismo eretico*, 275; first in *Nuovi argomenti*, No. 20, 1970.

**68.** Pasolini, "Communiqué to ANSA (suggestions)" (trans. B. Allen), in Allen, 45.

**69.** Zigaina, 98.

**70.**    Ibid., 101.

**71.**    *Empirismo eretico*, 247.

**72.**    Zanzotto, "Pedagogy," in Allen, 34.

**73.**    Vincent Canby, *"Salò* is disturbing . . . ," *New York Times*, Oct. 1, 1977.

**74.**    *Lettere, II* (1955–1975), *Cronologia,* clxxiv, note 71.

**75.**    *Domenica del corriere,* Nov. 13, 1975.

**76.**    MacAfee, 169–73, translation of "A Desperate Vitality"; from *Poesie in forma di rosa,* 1964; in *Le poesie* (1975, 1976), 463–66.

# SELECT BIBLIOGRAPHY

Many newspapers and periodicals were consulted in the writing of this work. Some of them, and some books on Pasolini, are not listed below but are credited in the Notes.

## I. WORKS BY PIER PAOLO PASOLINI

*Dates are of first, followed by date of most recent, Italian editions. "G" indicates those published by Aldo Garzanti Editore, Milano.*

### Poetry

*Poesie a Casarsa*. Bologna, Libreria Antiquaria Mario Landi, 1942.

*Poesie*. San Vito al Tagliamento, Stamperia Primon, 1945.

*I pianti*. Casarsa, Pubblicazioni dell'Academiuta, 1946.

*Dov'è la mia patria*. With thirteen drawings by Giuseppe Zigaina. Casarsa, Pubblicazioni dell'Academiuta, 1949.

*I parlanti* (1948). *Botteghe Oscure*, 8, Roma, 1951.

*Sonetto primaverile* (1953). Milano, All'insegna del pesce d'oro, 1960.

*Tal cour di un frut*. Tricesimo, Edizioni "Friuli," 1953.

*Dal "diario" (1945–1947)*. Caltanissetta/Roma, Salvatore Sciascia Editore, 1954, 1979.

*La meglio gioventù*. Firenze, Sansoni, 1954.

*Le ceneri di Gramsci*. (G), 1957; Torino, Giulio Einaudi Editore, 1981.

*L'usignolo della chiesa cattolica*. Milano, Longanesi, 1958; Torino, Giulio Einaudi Editore, 1982.

*La religione del mio tempo*. (G), 1961.

*La violenza*. 24 drawings by Attardi, Calabria, Farulli, Gianquinto, Guccione, Guerreschi, Guttuso, Vespignani, with 12 ballads by Pier Paolo Pasolini, Rome, Editori Riuniti, 1962.

*Poesia in forma di rosa*. (G), 1964.

*Poesie* (selection chosen by the author). (G), 1970.

*Trasumanar e organizzar*. (G), 1971.

*La nuova gioventù: poesie friulane, 1941–1974*. Torino, Giulio Einaudi Editore, 1975, 1981.

*Le poesie [Le ceneri di Gramsci, La religione del mio tempo, Poesie in forma di rosa, Trasumanar e organizzar, Poesie inedite (1950–1951)]*. (G), 1975, 1976

*Poesie dimenticate*. Udine, Società Filologica Friulana, 1976.

*Poesie e pagine ritrovate*. Edited by A. Zanzotto and N. Naldini, Roma, Lato/Side Editori, 1980.

### Narratives, Plays, and Screenplays

*Ragazzi di vita*. (G), 1955; Torino, Giulio Einaudi Editore, 1981.

*Una vita violenta*. (G), 1959; Torino, Giulio Einaudi Editore, 1979.

*Donne di Roma*. Milano, Il Saggiatore, 1960.

*Giro a vuoto, le canzoni di Laura Betti* (with various authors). Milano, Scheiwiller, 1960.

*Roma 1950, diario*. Milano, All' insegna del pesce d'oro, 1960.

*Accattone*. (G), 1961.

*Mamma Roma*. Milano, Rizzoli, 1962.

*L'odore dell'India*. Milano, Longanesi, 1962, 1979.

*Il sogno di una cosa*. (G), 1962, 1978.

*Il Vangelo secondo Matteo*. Edited by G. Gambetti. (G), 1964.

*Alì dagli occhi azzurri*. (G), 1965, 1975.

*Potentissima signora, canzoni e dialoghi per Laura Betti*. Milano, Longanesi, 1965.

*Uccellacci e uccellini*. (G), 1966, 1975.

*Edipo re*. (G), 1967.

*Teorema*. (G), 1968, 1974.

*Medea*. (G), 1970.

*Ostia, un film di Sergio Citti*, subject and script by Sergio Citti and Pier Paolo Pasolini. (G), 1970.

*Calderón*. (G), 1973, 1974.

*La divina mimesis*. Torino, Giulio Einaudi Editore, 1975.

*Il padre selvaggio*. Torino, Giulio Einaudi Editore, 1975.

*Trilogia della vita (Decameron, I racconti di Canterbury, Il fiore delle mille e una notte)*. Edited by G. Gattei, Bologna, Cappelli, 1975, 1978.

*Pasolini in Friuli (1943–1949)* (with various authors). Udine, *Corriere del Friuli*, in collaboration with the Comune di Casarsa della Delizia, Arti Grafiche Friulane, 1976.

*I turcs tal Friùl*. Edited by L. Ciceri, Udine, Doretti, "Forum Julii," 1976.

*Affabulazione, Pilade*. (G), 1977.

*Pasolini e "Il setaccio"* (with various authors). Edited by Mario Ricci. Bologna, Cappelli, 1977.

*San Paolo*. Torino, Giulio Einaudi Editore, 1977.

*Porcile-Orgia-Bestia da Stile*. (G), 1979.

*Amado mio / Atti impuri*. Edited by C. D'Angeli. (G), 1982.

*Il portico della morte*. Edited by C. Segre. (Quaderni Pier Paolo Pasolini) Roma, Associazione Pier Paolo Pasolini, 1988.

*Teatro: Calderón, Affabulazione, Pilade, Porcile, Orgia, Bestia da stile.* (G), 1988.

### Social and Literary Criticism

*Passione e ideologia (1948–1958).* (G), 1960, 1977.
*La poesia popolare italiana.* (G), 1960.
*Empirismo eretico.* (G), 1972, 1977.
*Scritti corsari.* (G), 1975, 1981.
*Le belle bandiere: Dialoghi, 1960–1965.* Edited by Gian Carlo Ferretti. Roma, Editori Riuniti, 1977.
*Lettere luterane, il progresso come falso progresso.* Torino, Giulio Einaudi Editore, 1977, 1980.
*Il caos.* Edited by Gian Carlo Ferretti. Roma, Editori Riuniti, 1979.
*Descrizioni di descrizioni.* Edited by Graziella Chiarcossi. Torino, Giulio Einaudi Editore, 1979.
*Volgar' eloquio.* Edited by A. Piromalli and D. Scarfoglio. Napoli, Athena, 1976; Edited by Gian Carlo Ferretti. Roma, Editori Riuniti, 1987

### Correspondence

*Lettere agli amici (1941–1945).* Edited by Luciano Serra, Milano, Ugo Guanda Editore, 1976.
*Lettere, I (1940–1954).* Edited by N. Naldini, Torino, Giulio Einaudi Editore, 1986.
*Lettere, II (1955–1975).* Edited by N. Naldini, Torino, Giulio Einaudi Editore, 1988.

## II. TRANSLATIONS AND CRITICAL EDITIONS BY PIER PAOLO PASOLINI

*Poesia dialettale del Novecento* (with M. Dell'Arco). Parma, Guanda, 1952.
*Il canto popolare.* Milano, La Meridiana, 1954.
*Eschilo* (Aeschylus), *Orestiade.* Urbino, Edizioni Urbinate, 1960; Torino, Giulio Einaudi Editore, 1960.
*La poesia popolare italiana.* (G), 1960.
*Il vantone di Plauto* (from Plautus, *Miles gloriosus*). (G), 1963.
*Canzoniere italiano.* Bologna, Guanda, 1955; 2 vols., (G), 1972.

## III. ENGLISH TRANSLATIONS OF WORKS BY PIER PAOLO PASOLINI *(in alphabetical order)*

*The Divine Mimesis.* Translated by Thomas E. Peterson. Berkeley, Double Dance Press, 1980.

*A Dream of Something*. Translated by Stuart Hood, London, Quartet, 1988.
*Heretical Empiricism*. Edited by Louise K. Barnett, Translated by Louise K. Barnett and Ben Lawton. Bloomington and London, Indiana University Press, 1988.
*Lutheran Letters*. Translated by Stuart Hood, Manchester, Carcanet New Press; Dublin, Raven Arts Press, 1983.
"Observations on the Long Take/ What is Neo-Zhdanovism and What is Not." *October* No. 13, summer 1980.
*Oedipus Rex*. Translated by John Matthews. New York, Simon and Schuster, 1971.
*The Ragazzi*. Translated by Emile Capouya, Manchester and New York, Carcanet Press Ltd., 1986.
"Rital and Raton." *October* No. 31, winter 1984.
*Roman Nights and Other Stories*. Translated by John Shepley. Marlboro, Vt, Marlboro Press, 1986.
*Roman Poems: Bilingual Edition*. Translated by Lawrence Ferlinghetti and Francesca Valente. San Francisco, City Lights Books, 1986.
*Selected Poems*. Selected and translated by Norman MacAfee and Luciano Martinengo. New York, Random House, 1982; New York, Riverrun, 1988.
*A Violent Life*. Translated by William Weaver, London, Cape, 1968; Panther, 1970; Manchester and New York, Carcanet Press Limited, 1985.

## IV.  SELECTED ARTICLES AND BOOKS ABOUT PIER PAOLO PASOLINI CONSULTED BY THE AUTHOR

ALLEN, B., ed. *Pier Paolo Pasolini: The Poetics of Heresy*. Saratoga, Calif., ANMA Libri, 1982.
ANZOINO, Tommaso. *Pasolini*. Firenze, La Nuova Italia, 1975.
BELLEZZA, D. *Morte di Pasolini*. Milano, Arnoldo Mondadori Editore, 1981.
BETTI, Laura, ed. *Pasolini: Cronaca giudiziaria, persecuzione, morte*. (G), 1978.
BORGHELLO, G., ed. *Interpretazioni di Pasolini*. Roma, Savelli, 1977.
BREVINI, F., ed. *Per conoscere Pasolini*. Milano, Arnoldo Mondadori Editore, 1981.
CAMON, Ferdinando. *Il mestiere di scrittore*. (G), 1973.
———. *Letteratura e classi subalterne*, Venezia/Padova, Marsilio, 1974.
CAROTENUTO, Aldo. *L'autunno della conscienza: ricerche psicologiche su Pier Paolo Pasolini*. Torino, Borighieri, 1985.
CASI, Stefano, ed. *Desiderio di Pasolini: Omosessualità, arte e impegno intellectuale*. Torino/Milano, edizioni Sonda, 1990.

*Cinema & Cinema*. Issue dedicated to Pasolini, *anno* 12, maggio-agosto 1985, No. 43. Bologna, Marsilio Editore.

*Da Accattone a Salò, 120 scritti sul cinema di Pier Paolo Pasolini. (Quaderni della Cineteca.)* Bologna, Edizioni della tipografia Compositori, 1982.

DE GIUSTI, Luciano. *I film di Pier Paolo Pasolini*. (Effetto Cinema series.) Roma, Gremese Editore, 1983.

————, ed. *Pier Paolo Pasolini: Il cinema in forma di poesia*. Pordenone, Edizioni Cinemazero, 1979.

DE SANTI, G.; LENTI, M.; and ROSSINI, R., eds. *Perché Pasolini*. Firenze, Guaraldi Editore, 1978.

DUFLOT, Jean. *Entretiens avec Pier Paolo Pasolini*. Paris, Pierre Belfond, 1970.

————, ed. *Il sogno del centauro*. Roma, Editori Riuniti, 1983.

FERRERO, Adelio. *Il cinema di Pier Paolo Pasolini*. Venezia, Marsilio Editore, 1977.

FERRETTI, Gian Carlo. *Letteratura e ideologia: Bassani, Cassola, Pasolini*. Roma, Editori Riuniti, 1974.

————. *"Officina": cultura, letteratura e politica negli Anni Cinquanta*. Torino, Giulio Einaudi Editore, 1975.

————. *Pasolini: l'universo orrendo*. Roma, Editori Riuniti, 1976.

*Galleria*. Issue dedicated to Pasolini. Edited by Rosita Tordi. January–August 1985. Palermo, Salvatore Sciascia Editore.

GERVAIS, Marc. *Pier Paolo Pasolini*, Paris, Seghers, 1975.

GOLINO, Enzo. *Pasolini, Il sogno di una cosa: pedagogia, eros, letteratura dal mito del popolo alla società di massa*. Bologna, Il Mulino, 1985.

GROPPALI, Enrico. *L'ossessione e il fantasma: il teatro di Pasolini e Moravia*. Venezia, Marsilio, 1979.

MACCIOCCHI, Maria Antoinetta. *Duemila anni di felicità*. Milano, Arnoldo Mondadori Editore, 1983.

MANNINO, V. *Invito alla lettura di Pasolini*. Milano, U. Mursia Editore, 1974.

MARAINI, Dacia. *E tu chi eri?* Milano, Bompiani, 1973.

MARTINELLI, L. *Pier Paolo Pasolini*. Firenze, Le Monnier, 1984.

MARTINELLI, L., ed. *Il Dialogo, il potere, la morte: Pasolini e la critica*. Bologna, Cappelli, 1979.

MUZZIOLI, Francesco. *Come leggere "Ragazzi di vita."* Milano, U. Mursia, 1975.

NALDINI, Nico. *Nei campi del Friuli, la giovinezza di Pasolini*. Milano, Scheiwiller, 1984.

————. *Pasolini, una vita*. Torino, Giulio Einaudi Editore, 1989.

PANICALI, Anna, and SESTINI, S. eds. *Pier Paolo Pasolini: Testimonianze*. Firenze, Salani, 1982.

"Pasolini e il Corriere." Milano, *Corriere della sera*, 1986.

PEDRIALI, Dino. *Pier Paolo Pasolini, Photographs*. Roma, Editrice Magma, 1975.

PETRAGLIA, Sandro. *Pier Paolo Pasolini. Il Castoro Cinema*, July–August 1974, No. 7–8. Firenze, La Nuova Italia.

*Pier Paolo Pasolini: Una vita futura*. Roma, Associazione "Fondo Pier Paolo Pasolini," 1985.

QUARANTOTTO, Claudio. *Il cinema, la carne e il diavolo*. Milano, Le Edizioni del *Borghese*, 1963.

QUINTAVALLE, Uberto P. *Giorante di Sodoma*. Milano, SugarCo Edizioni, 1976.

SANTATO, Guido. *Pier Paolo Pasolini: L'opera*. Vicenza, Neri Pozza Editore, 1980.

———, ed., *Pier Paolo Pasolini: L'opera e il suo tempo*. Padova, CLEUP, 1983.

SCALIA, Gianni. *Mania della verità: dialogo con Pier Paolo Pasolini*. Bologna, Cappelli, 1978.

SICILIANO, Enzo. *Vita di Pasolini*. Milano, Rizzoli, 1978; in English, *Pasolini*. Translated by John Shepley. New York, Random House, 1982; London, Bloomsbury Publishing Ltd., 1988.

STACK, Oswald. *Pasolini on Pasolini: Interviews with Oswald Stack*. (Cinema One series.) Bloomington and London, Indiana University Press in association with *Sight and Sound* and the Education Department of the British Film Institute, 1970.

VANNUCCI, S. *Pier Paolo Pasolini: Il colore della poesia*. Roma, Associazione "Fondo Pier Paolo Pasolini," 1985.

VOLPONI, Paolo, et al. *Pasolini nel dibattito culturale contemporaneo*. Pavia, Amministrazione Provinciale di Pavia, Commune di Alessandria, 1977.

WATSON, William van. *Pier Paolo Pasolini and the Theatre of the Word*. Ann Arbor, UMI Research Press, 1989.

WILLEMEN, P., ed. *Pier Paolo Pasolini*. London, British Film Institute, 1977.

ZIGAINA, Giuseppe, ed. *Pasolini, I disegni (1941–1975)*. Milano, Scheiwiller, 1978.

———. *Pasolini e la morte: mito, alchimia e semantica del "nulla lucente."* Venezia, Marsilio, 1987.

———. *Pasolini ou la traversée des emblèmes*. Basel, Balance Rief, 1985.

———, ed. *Pier Paolo Pasolini: Mito e sacralità della tecnica*. Moscow, Istituto Italiano di Cultura a Mosca, 1989.

## V. FOR FURTHER READING ON PIER PAOLO PASOLINI

ALFIERI, Dino, and FREDDI, Luigi. *Mostra della rivoluzione fascista* (1932). Milano, Edizioni del Nuovo Candido, 1982.

BARBARO, U. *Neorealismo e realismo*. 2 vols. Edited by G. P. Brunetta. Roma, Editori Riuniti, 1976.

BARTHES, Roland. *Sade/Fourier/Loyola*. Translated by R. Miller. New York, Hill and Wang, 1976.

BARZINI, Luigi. *The Italians*. New York, Atheneum, 1964.

BERLINGER, G., and DELLA SETA, P. *Borgate di Roma*. Roma, Editore Riuniti, 1976.

BETTINI, F., and BEVILACQUA, E., ed. *Marxismo e critica letterari*. Roma, Editori Riuniti, 1978.

BONDANELLA, P., ed. *Federico Fellini*. Oxford, London, New York, Oxford University Press, 1978.

————. *Italian Cinema from Neorealism to the Present*. New York, Frederick Ungar, 1983.

BRUNETTA, G.P. *Forma e parola nel cinema*. Padova, Liviana Editrice, 1970.

————. *Cinema italiano tra le due guerre, Fascismo e politica cinematografica*. Milano, Mursia, 1975.

————. *Storia del cinema italiano, 1895–1945*. Roma, Editori Riuniti, 1979.

BUCI-GLUCKSMANN, C. *Gramsci and the State*. Translated by D. Fernbach. London, Lawrence and Wishart, 1980.

CALDIRON, O. *Totò*. Roma, Gremese Editore, 1983.

CALVI, Guido. *Giustizia e potere*. Rome, Editori Riuniti, 1973.

CAMMETT, J. M. *Antonio Gramsci and the Origins of Italian Communism*. Stanford, Calif., Stanford University Press, 1967.

CODIGNOLA, L.; CRISPOLTI, F. C.; RANGSTROM, T.; SODERSTROM, G.; STRINDBERG, A.; AND ZOLLA, E. *Images from the Strindberg Planet*. Venezia, Edizioni La Biennale di Venezia, 1981.

CONTINI, Gianfranco. *Schedario di scrittori italiani moderni e contemporanei*. Firenze, Sansoni Editore, 1978.

DANEO, Camillo. *La politica economia della riconstruzione, 1945–1949*. Torino, Giulio Einaudi Editore, 1975.

DE FELICE, R. *Mussolini il duce: Gli anni del consenso, 1929–1936*. Torino, Giulio Einaudi Editore, 1974.

————. *Intervista sul Fascismo*. Edited by Michael Ledeen. Roma-Bari, Laterza, 1975.

DE GIUSTI, L. *I film di Luchino Visconti*. Roma, Gremese Editore, 1985.

DE LUNA, Giovanni. *Hanno sparato a Togliatti*. (*I Grandi Eventi*.) Milano, Gruppo Editoriale Fabbri, 1984.

DE SANTI, G. *Sandro Penna*, Firenze, La nuova Italia, 1982.

FALDINI, F., and FOFI, G. *L'avventurosa storia del cinema italiano*, vol. 1, *1935–1959*, vol. 2, 1960–1969. Milano, Feltrinelli, 1979, 1981.

FALLACI, Oriana. *Interview with History*. Translated by John Shepley. New York, Liveright, 1976.

———. *Lettera a un bambino mai nato*. Milano, Rizzoli Editore, 1976.

FERRERO, A.; GRIGNAFFINI, G.; and QUARESIMA, L. *Il cinema italiano degli anni 60*. Firenze, La Guide Guaraldi, 1977.

FERRERO, E. *I gerghi della malavita*. Milano, Arnoldo Mondadori, 1972.

FERRETTI, G. C. *Introduzione al neorealismo: I narratori*. Roma, Editori Riuniti, 1974.

———. *Letteratura e ideologia*. Roma, Editori Riuniti, 1976.

FORTINI, F. *L'ospite ingrato*. Casale Monferrato, Marietti, 1985.

———. *Questioni di frontiera: scritti di politica e di letteratura, 1965–1977*. Torino, Giulio Einaudi Editore, 1977.

FRASER, R. *1968: A Student Generation in Revolt*. New York, Pantheon Books, 1988.

GALASSI, J., ed. and trans. *The Second Life of Art: Selected Essays of Eugenio Montale*. New York, The Ecco Press, 1982.

GARRETT, George, ed. *Botteghe Oscure Reader*. Middletown, Conn., Wesleyan University Press, 1974.

GOLDONI, Luca, and SERMASI, Enzo. *Fiero l'occhio, svelto il passo*. Milano, Arnaldo Mondadori Editore, 1979.

GRAMSCI, Antonio. *Lettere dal carcere*. Torino, Giulio Einaudi Editore, 1947, 1971.

———. *Gli intellettuali*. Rome, Istituto Gramsci, 1975.

———. *Letteratura e vita nazionale*. Roma, Istituto Gramsci, 1975.

———. *The Modern Prince and Other Writings*. New York, International Publishers, 1975.

HOCHKOFLER, M. *Anna Magnani*. Roma, Gremese Editore, 1984.

JAY, Martin. *Adorno*. Cambridge, Harvard University Press, 1984.

JOLL, James. *Gramsci*. London, Fontana/Collins, 1977.

KOGAN, Norman. *A Political History of Italy: The Postwar Years*. New York, Praeger Special Studies, 1983.

LEICHT, P.S. *Breve storia del Friuli*. Tolmezzo, Edizioni "Aquileia," 1977.

LEWIS, Norman. *Naples '44*. New York, Pantheon Books, 1978.

LOTRINGER, S. *Overexposed: Treating Sexual Perversion in America*. New York, Pantheon Books, 1988.

MONACO, J. *American Cinema Now*. New York, New American Library, 1979.

MONDELLO, Elisabetta. *Gli anni delle riviste: Le riviste letterarie dal 1945 agli anni ottanta*. Lecce, Edizioni Milella, 1985.

MONTALE, E., *Otherwise: First and Last Poems of Eugenio Montale*. Translated by J. Galassi. New York, Random House, 1984.

MORANTE, Elsa. *History: A Novel*. Translated by William Weaver. New York, Alfred A. Knopf, 1977.

MORAVIA, Alberto. *Which Tribe Do You Belong To?* Translated by A. Davidson. London, Panther, 1976.

NALDINI, Nico. *La curva di San Floriano*. Torino, Giulio Einaudi Editore, 1988.

REDI, R. *Cinema italiano sotto il Fascismo*. Venezia, Marsilio, 1979.

SILVA, U. *Ideologia e arte del Fascismo*. Milano, Gabriele Mazzotta Editore, 1973.

SMITH, L. R., ed. and trans. *The New Italian Poetry: 1945 to the Present*. Berkeley, University of California Press, 1981.

STANCIOFF, Nadia. *Maria Callas Remembered*. New York, E. P. Dutton, 1987.

STASSINOPOULOS, Arianna. *Maria Callas: The Woman Behind the Legend*. New York, Ballantine Books, 1981.

# FILMOGRAPHY OF
# PIER PAOLO PASOLINI

## COLLABORATION ON SCENARIOS AND SCRIPTS

**1954** *La donna del fiume*
Director: Mario Soldati
Script: Basilio Franchina, Giorgio Bassani, Pier Paolo Pasolini, Florestano Vancini, Antonio Altovitti, and Mario Soldati
Produced by Excelsa-Carlo Ponti
Distributed by Minerva Film
With Sophia Loren

**1955** *Il prigioniero della montagna*
Director: Luis Trenker
From the novel by C. G. Bienek
Script: Luis Trenker, Giorgio Bassani, and Pier Paolo Pasolini
Produced by Bardo Film
Distribution: regional in Italy
With Marianne Hold, Luis Trenker

**1956** *La notti di Cabiria*
Director: Federico Fellini
Subject and script: Federico Fellini, Ennio Flaiano, and Tullio Pinelli
Adviser/collaborator on the script: Pier Paolo Pasolini
Produced by Dino de Laurentiis Cinematografica
Distributed by Paramount
With Giulietta Masina

**1957** *Marisa la civetta*
Director-scenarist: Mauro Bolognini
Script: Mauro Bolognini, Pier Paolo Pasolini, and Titina Demby
Produced by Carlo Ponti (Rome/Balcazar) (Barcelona)
Distribution: Cei-Incom

**1958** *Giovani mariti*
Director: Mauro Bolognini
Subject: Massimo Franciosa and Pasquale Festa Campanile
Script: Enzo Curreli, Luciano Martino, Mauro Bolognini, and Pier Paolo Pasolini

Produced by Nepi Film
Distributed by Lux Film

**1959**    *La notte brava*

Director: Mauro Bolognini
Subject: from *Ragazzi di vita* by Pier Paolo Pasolini
Script: Pier Paolo Pasolini and Laurence Bost
Produced by Antonio Cervi and Oreste Jacovoni for Ajace Film
    (Rome)/Franco-London Film (Paris)
Distributed by Euro International Films
With Rosanna Schiaffino, Laurent Terzieff, Jean-Claude Brialy,
    Franco Interlenghi, Antonella Lualdi, Mylène Demongeot, and
    Elsa Martinelli

**1960**    *Morte di un amico*

Director: Franco Rossi
Subject: Giuseppe Berto, Oreste Biancoli, Pier Paolo Pasolini, and
    Franco Riganti
Script: Franco Riganti, Ugo Guerra, Franco Rossi
Produced by Alfredo Bini for Cino Del Duca-Arco Film-Lyre Ciné-
    matographique
Distributed by Cino Del Duca

*Il bel Antonio*
Director: Mauro Bolognini
Subject: from the novel by Vitaliano Brancati
Script: Pier Paolo Pasolini, Gino Visentini, and Mauro Bolognini
Produced by Alfredo Bini
Distributed by Cino Del Duca
With Marcello Mastroianni, Claudia Cardinale

*La canta delle marane*
Director: Cecilia Mangini
Story: from a chapter in *Ragazzi di vita* by Pier Paolo Pasolini
Commentary by Pier Paolo Pasolini
Produced by Giorgio Patara

*La giornata balorda*
Director: Mauro Bolognini
Subject: Pier Paolo Pasolini and Alberto Moravia from *Racconti ro-
mani* and *Nuovi racconti romani* by Alberto Moravia
Script: Pier Paolo Pasolini, Alberto Moravia, and Mario Visconti
Produced by Paul Graetz for Produzioni Intercontinentali
Distributed by Euro International Films

*La lunga notte del' 43*
Director: Florestano Vancini

Subject: from the story "Una notte del '43" (part of the cycle *Le Storie Ferraresi*) by Giorgio Bassani
Script: Ennio De Concini, Pier Paolo Pasolini, and Florestano Vancini
Produced by Antonio Cervi and Alessandro Jacovoni for Ajace Film-Euro International Films
Distributed by Euro International Films

*Il carro armato dell' 8 settembre*
Director: Gianni Puccini
Subject: Rodolfo Sonego, Tonino Guerra, Elio Petri
Script: Gianni Puccini Baratti, Elio Bartolini, Pier Paolo Pasolini, and Giulio Questi
Produced by Film Napoleon
Distributed by Euro International Films

**1961** *La ragazza in vetrina*
Director: Luciano Emmer
Subject: Emanuele Cassuto, Luciano Emmer, and Rodolfo Sonego
Script: Luciano Emmer, Pier Paolo Pasolini, Luciano Martino, and Vincio Marinucci
Produced by Nepi Film-Sofidetip-Zodiaque
Distributed by Lux Film

**1962** *Una vita violenta*
Directors: Paulo Heusch and Brunello Rondi
Subject: from the novel *Una vita violenta* by Pier Paolo Pasolini
Treatment: Ennio De Concini, and Franco Brusati
Script: Paulo Heusch, Brunello Rondi, and Franco Solinas
Produced by Zebra Film (Rome/Aera Films) (Paris)
Distribution: Variety

*La commare secca*
Director: Bernardo Bertolucci
Subject: from a story by Pier Paolo Pasolini
Script: Bernardo Bertolucci and Sergio Citti
Produced by Antonio Cervi for the Compagnia Cinematografica Cervi-Cineriz
Distribution: Cineriz

## ACTED IN

**1960** *Il gobba*
Director: Carlo Lizzani
**1964** *Comizi d' amore*

**1966** *Requiescant*
Director: Carlo Lizzani
**1967** *Edipo re*
**1971** *Il Decameron*
**1972** *I racconti di Canterbury*


## DIRECTED

**1961** *Accattone*
Production Company: Arco Film-Cino Del Duca
Producer: Alfredo Bini
Director: Pier Paolo Pasolini
Script: Pier Paolo Pasolini
Assistant Directors: Bernardo Bertolucci and Leopoldo Savona
Assistant for Script: Sergio Citti
Director of Photography: Tonino delli Colli
Editor: Nino Baragli
Music: Johann Sebastian Bach, coordinated by Carlo Rustichelli

Franco Citti (*Accattone*), Franca Pasut (*Stella*), Silvana Corsini (*Maddalena*), Paola Guidi (*Ascenza*), Adriana Asti (*Amore*)
Location: Rome
Running time: 120 min. (115 min. in Great Britain)
Distributors: Cino Del Duca (Italy), Connoisseur (G.B.)
Shown in Great Britain in 1962; not yet shown commercially in U.S.A.

**1962** *Mamma Roma*
Production Company: Arco Film-Cineriz
Producer: Alfredo Bini
Director: Pier Paolo Pasolini
Script: Pier Paolo Pasolini
Assistant for Script: Sergio Citti
Director of Photography: Tonino delli Colli
Editor: Nino Baragli
Music: Vivaldi, coordinated by Carlo Rustichelli

Anna Magnani (*Mamma Roma*), Ettore Garofolo (*Ettore*), Franco Citti (*Carmine*), Silvana Corsini (*Bruna*), Luisa Loiano (*Biancofiore*), Paolo Volponi (*Priest*), Luciano Gonini (*Zacaria*), Vittorio La Paglia (*Signor Pellissier*), Piero Morgia (*Piero*)
Location: Rome
Running time: 110 min. (106 min. in Great Britain)
Distributors: Cineriz (Italy), Gala (G.B.)

Shown in Great Britain in 1964; not yet shown commercially in U.S.A.

*La ricotta*

(episode in *Rogopag* or *Laviamoci il cervello*; other episodes directed by Rossellini, Godard, and Gregoretti).

Production Companies: Arco Film-Cineriz (Rome) and Lyre (Paris)

Director: Pier Paolo Pasolini

Subject and Script: Pier Paolo Pasolini

Director of Photography: Tonino delli Colli

Costumes: Danilo Donati

Musical coordinator: Carlo Rustichelli

Orson Welles (*The Director*), Mario Cipriani (*Stracci*), Laura Betti (*The Star*), Edmonda Aldini (*Another Star*), Vittorio La Paglia (*The Journalist*), Ettore Garofolo (*An Extra*), Maria Bernardini (*Extra Who Does Striptease*)

Running time: 40 min.

Distributor: Cineriz (Italy)

Shown in U.S.A. in 1963; not yet shown commercially in Great Britain

At first banned in Italy because of the Pasolini episode, *Rogopag* was re-released under the new title of *Laviamoci il cervello*, with some cuts in *La ricotta*.

**1963** *La rabbia* First part

(Second part by Giovanni Guareschi)

Producer: Gastone Ferrante

Production Company: Opus Film

Director: Pier Paolo Pasolini

Script: Pier Paolo Pasolini

Commentary spoken by: Giorgio Bassani, Renato Guttuso

Editor: Nino Baragli

Running time: 50 min.

Distributor: Warner Bros.

The film was withdrawn by Warners immediately because of Guareschi's episode and has never been commercially released anywhere since.

**1963**
**—64** *Sopraluoghi in Palestina per "Il Vangelo secondo Matteo"*

Production Company: Arco Film

Cameraman: Aldo Pennelli

Speakers: Pier Paolo Pasolini and Don Andrea Carraro

Commentary: Pier Paolo Pasolini

Running time: 50 min.

Never distributed commercially anywhere

Edited and with commentary by Pasolini for the VIII Spoleto Festival, July 1965.

**1964** *Comizi d'amore*

Production Company: Arco Film

Producer: Alfredo Bini

Production Manager: Eliseo Boschi

Director: Pier Paolo Pasolini

Commentary written by: Pier Paolo Pasolini

Commentary spoken by: Lello Bersani and Pier Paolo Pasolini

Participants: Pier Paolo Pasolini, Cesare Musatti, Giuseppe Ungaretti, Susanna Pasolini, Camilla Cederna, Adele Cambria, Oriana Fallaci, Antonella Lualdi, Graziella Granata (and, suppressed in the editing, Giuseppe Ravegnani and Eugenio Montale)

Directors of Photography: Mario Bernardo, Tonino delli Colli

Camera Operators: Vittorio Bernini, Franco delli Colli, and Cesare Fontana

Editor: Nino Baragli

Locations: Palermo, Calabria, Naples, the Po Valley, and various other sites throughout Italy

Running time: 90 min.

Distributor: Titanus (Italy)

Not yet shown commercially in Great Britain or U.S.A.

*Il Vangelo secondo Matteo*

Production Companies: Arco Film (Rome), Lux Cie Cinématographique de France (Paris)

Producer: Alfredo Bini

Production Manager: Eliseo Boschi

Director: Pier Paolo Pasolini

Director of Photography: Tonino delli Colli

Camera Operator: Giuseppe Ruzzolini

Editor: Nino Baragli

Music: Johann Sebastian Bach, Wolfgang Amadeus Mozart, Sergei Prokofiev, Anton Webern, and Luis E. Bacalov

Costumes: Danilo Donati

Sound: Mario Del Pezzo

Enrique Irazoqui (*Christ*), Margherita Caruso (*The Young Mary*), Susanna Pasolini (*The Old Mary*), Marcello Morante (*Joseph*), Mario Socrate (*John The Baptist*), Settimio Di Porto (*Peter*), Otello Sestili (*Judas*), Ferruccio Nuzzo (*Matthew*), Giacomo Morante (*John*), Alfonso Gatto (*Andrew*), Enzo Siciliano (*Simon*), Giorgio Agamben (*Philip*), Guido Cerretani (*Bartholomew*), Luigi Barbini (*James, the Son of Alphaeus*), Marcello Galdini (*James, the Son of Zebedee*),

Elio Spaziani (*Thaddeus*), Rosario Migale (*Thomas*), Rodolfo Wilcock (*Caiphas*), Alessandro Clerici (*Pontius Pilate*), Amerigo Bevilacqua (*Herod I*), Francesco Leonetti (*Herod II*), Paola Tedesco (*Salome*), Rosanna di Rocco (*Angel*), Eliseo Boschi (*Joseph of Arimathaea*), Natalia Ginzburg (*Mary of Bethany*)
Locations in southern Italy (Calabria, Lucania, Puglie)
Running time: 140 min. (135 min. in Great Britain)
Distributors: Titanus (Italy), Compton (G.B.), Continental (U.S.A.)
Shown in U.S.A. in 1964 and in Great Britain in 1967, title *The Gospel According to Saint Matthew*
The word "Saint" was introduced against Pasolini's express wishes into the English title. The dedication to John XXIII was likewise truncated in English.
Christ's voice: Enrico Maria Salerno

**1966**   *Uccellacci e uccellini (Hawks and Sparrows)*
Production Company: Arco Film
Producer: Alfredo Bini
Production Manager: Fernando Franchi
Director: Pier Paolo Pasolini
Assistant Director: Sergio Citti
Script: Pier Paolo Pasolini
Directors of Photography: Mario Bernardo and Tonino delli Colli
Camera Operators: Franco di Giacomo and Gaetano Valle
Editor: Nino Baragli
Music: Ennio Morricone
Costumes: Danilo Donati
Sound: Pietro Ortolani

Totò (*Innocenti Totò and Brother Ciccillo*), Ninetto Davoli (*Innocenti Ninetto and Brother Ninetto*), Femi Benussi (*Luna*), Rossana di Rocco (*Friend of Ninetto*), Lena Lin Solaro (*Urganda La Sconosciuta*), Rosina Moroni (*Peasant Woman*), Renato Capogna and Pietro Davoli (*Medieval Louts*), Gabriele Baldini (*Dante's Dentist*), Riccardo Redi (*Ingegnere*)
Filmed on location around Rome—at Ruscania, near Fiumicino, near the EUR, and various other places
Running time: 86 min.
Distributor: Marchio (Italy)
Not yet shown commercially in Great Britain. Released in the U.S.A. in 1966, title *The Hawks and the Sparrows*
The crow's voice is that of Francesco Leonetti.

*Le streghe*
(episode in *La terra vista dalla luna*)

Other episodes by Luchino Visconti, Mauro Bolognini, Franco Rossi, and Vittorio de Sica
Production Company: Dino de Laurentiis Cinematografica
Director: Pier Paolo Pasolini
Script: Pier Paolo Pasolini
Director of Photography: Giuseppe Rotunno
Color Process: Technicolor
Costumes: Piero Tosi
Sculpltures: Pino Zac
Editor: Piero Piccioni
Assistant Director: Sergio Citti

Totò (*Cianciato Miao*), Ninetto Davoli (*Basciù Miao*), Silvana Mangano (*Assurda Cai*), Laura Betti (*Tourist*), Luigi Leone (*Tourist's Wife*), Mario Cipriani (*Priest*)
Location: Rome and surroundings (Fiumicino)
Distribution: Dear Film/United Artists (Italy), Lopert (U.S.A.)
Shown in U.S.A. in 1969; not yet shown commerically in Great Britain.

*Capriccio all'italiana*
(episode in *Che cosa sono le nuvole?*)
Other episodes by Steno, Mauro Bolognini (2), Pino Zac, and Mario Monicelli
Production Company: Dino de Laurentiis Cinematografica
Producer: Dino de Laurentiis
Director: Pier Paolo Pasolini
Script: Pier Paolo Pasolini
Director of Photography: Tonino delli Colli
Editor: Nino Beragli
Song: "Cosi sono le nuvole": Domenico Modugno and Pier Paolo Pasolini
Color Process: Technicolor

Totò (*Iago*), Franco Franchi (*Cassio*), Ciccio Igrassia (*Roderigo*), Domenico Modugno (*Dustman*), Ninetto Davoli (*Othello*), Laura Betti (*Desdemona*), Adriana Asti (*Bianca*), Carlo Pisacane (*Brabantio*), Francesco Leonette (*Puppeteer*)
Distributors: Euro International Films (Italy)
Not yet shown commercially in Great Britain or U.S.A.

**1967** *Edipo re*
Production Company: Arco Film
Producer: Alfredo Bini
Production Manager: Eliseo Boschi
Director: Pier Paolo Pasolini

Script: Pier Paolo Pasolini, inspired by *Oedipus Rex* and *Oedipus at Colonus* by Sophocles
Director of Photography: Giuseppe Ruzzolini
Camera Operator: Otello Spila
Assistant Director: Jean-Claude Biette
Editor: Nino Baragli
Music: Rumanian and Japanese folk-music, plus original music co-ordinated by Pier Paolo Pasolini
Costumes: Danilo Donati

Franco Citti (*Oedipus*), Silvana Mangano (*Jocasta*), Alida Villa (*Merope*), Carmelo Bene (*Creon*), Julian Beck (*Tiresias*), Luciano Bartoli (*Laius*), Francesco Leonetti (*Servant*), Ahmed Bellashmi (*Polybus*), Giandomenico Davoli (*Shepherd of Polybus*), Ninetto Davoli (*Messenger*), Pier Paolo Pasolini (*High Priest*), Jean-Claude Biette (*Priest*)
Shot in northern Italy, Morocco, and Bologna
Running time: 110 min. (104 min. in Great Britain)
Distributors: Euro International Films (Italy), Eagle (G.B.)
Shown in Great Britain in 1969, entitled *Oedipus Rex*

*Amore e rabbia*
(episode in *La fiore di campo*)
Other episodes directed by Lizziani, Bertolucci, Godard, and Bellocchio
Production Company: Castoro Film (Rome), Anouchka Film (Paris)
Director: Pier Paolo Pasolini
Director of Photography: Giuseppe Ruzzolini
Color Process: Technicolor
Music: Giovanni Fusco; J. S. Bach: *St. Matthew Passion*
With Ninetto Davoli
Shot in Rome (Via Nazionale)
Running time: 12 min.

**1968**    *Teorema*
Production Company: Aetos Film
Producers: Manolo Bolognini and Franco Rossellini
Director: Pier Paolo Pasolini
Subject and Script: Pier Paolo Pasolini
Director of Photography: Giuseppe Ruzzolini
Color Process: Eastmancolor
Set Design: Luciano Puccini
Music: W. A. Mozart (Requiem Mass) and Ennio Morricone
Editor: Nino Baragli

Terence Stamp (*guest*), Silvana Mangano (*Lucia, the mother*), Massimo Girotti (*the father*), Anne Wiazemsky (*Odetta*), Andrés José Crux (*Piero*), Laura Betti (*Emilia*), Ninetto Davoli, Alfonso Gatto, Carlo de Mejo
Running time: 98 min.
Distributor: Euro International Films.

*Che cosa sono le nuvole?* (*What are the clouds?*)
(episode in *Capriccio all'italiana*)
Production Company: Dino de Laurentiis Cinematografica
Producer: Dino de Laurentiis
Director: Pier Paolo Pasolini
Subject and Script: Pier Paolo Pasolini
Director of Photography: Tonino delli Colli
Editor: Nino Baragli
Color Process: Technicolor
Set Design and Costumes: Jurgen Henze
Music: Dominico Modugno and Pier Paolo Pasolini

Totò (*Jago*), Ninetto Davoli (*Otello*), Laura Betti (*Desdemona*), Adriana Asti (*Bianca*), Franco Franchi (*Cassio*), Ciccio Ingrassia (*Roderigo*), Francesco Leonetti (*the puppeteer*), Domenico Modugno, Carlo Pisacane
Running time: 22 min.
Distributor: Dear-United Artists.

*Appunti per un film sull' India* (Notes for a film on India)
Short plan for a film project on India (made for transmission on TV
    7)
Producer: Gianni Barcelloni
Running time: 25 min.

1969    *La sequenza del fiore di carta* (*The sequence of the paper flower*)
(episode in *Vangelo '70*, then, *Amore e rabbia*)
Production Company: Castoro Film and Anouchka Film (Italy-
    France)
Director: Pier Paolo Pasolini
Subject and Script: Pier Paolo Pasolini
Director of Photography: Giuseppe Ruzzolini
Color Process: Technicolor
Music: J. S. Bach (*St. Matthew Passion*), and Giovanni Rusco
With Ninetto Davoli
Running time: 12 min.
Provisional title: *Il fico innocente* (*The innocent fig*)

*Porcile* (*Pigsty*)
Production Company: Idi Cinematografica, a film of Orso, Capac (Italy-France)
Producer: Gian Vittorio Baldi
Director: Pier Paolo Pasolini
Subject and Script: Pier Paolo Pasolini
Directors of Photography: Tonino delli Colli, Armando Nannuzzi, and Giuseppe Ruzzoli
Color Process: Technicolor
Set Design: Danilo Donati
Music: Benedetto Ghiglia
Editor: Nino Baragli

Pierre Clementi (*desert man*), Jean-Pierre Léaud (*Julian*), Alberto Lionello (*Klotz*), Ugo Tognazzi (*Herdhitze*), Anne Wiazemsky (*Ida*), Marco Ferrerri (*Hans Günther*), Franco Citti, Ninetto Davoli, Margherita Lozano
Running time: 100 min.
Distributor: Indief (Cineteca Nazionale).

**1970**   *Appunti per un' Orestiade Africana* (Notes for an African Orestaia)
Producer: Gian Vittorio Baldi
Subject: Pier Paolo Pasolini
Director and Commentator: Pier Paolo Pasolini
Director of Photography: Giorgi Pelloni
Music: Gato Barbieri
Running time: 55 min.

*Medea*
Production Company: San Marco film number one, Janus Film (Italy, France, Germany)
Producer: Franco Rossellini
Director: Pier Paolo Pasolini
Subject and Script: Pier Paolo Pasolini (from Euripides)
Director of Photography: Ennio Guarniere
Color Process: Eastmancolor
Set Design: Dante Ferretti
Costumes: Piero Tosi
Music: Coordinated by Pier Paolo Pasolini with the collaboration of Elsa Morante
Editor: Nino Baragli

Maria Callas (*Medea*), Giuseppe Gentile (*Jason*), Laurent Terzieff (*the centaur*), Massimo Girotti (*Creon*), Margarethe Clementi (*Glauce*), Paul Jabara, Gerard Weiss

Running time: 118 min.
Distributor: Euro International Films

Notes for (*Appunte per*) *un romanzo dell' immondezza* (Notes for a novel on garbage)
Documentary on the strike of Roman garbage collectors, a project of the Committee against Repression.
Production Company: Unitelefilm

**1971** *Il Decameron*
Production Company: PEA (Produzioni Europee Associate—Rome)
Les productions Artistes Associés, Artem film (Italy, France, Germany)
Producer: Franco Rossellini
Director: Pier Paolo Pasolini
Subject and Script: Pier Paolo Pasolini (from Boccaccio's *Decameron*)
Director of Photography: Tonino delli Colli
Color Process: Technicolor
Set Design: Dante Ferretti
Costumes: Danilo Donati
Music: Pier Paolo Pasolini, with the collaboration of Ennio Morriconi
Editor: Nino Baragli and Tatiana Morigi

Franco Citti (*Ser Ciappelletto*), Ninetto Davoli (*Andreuccio*), Angela Luce, Jovan Jovanovic, Giuseppe Zigaina, Pier Paolo Pasolini
Running time: 111 min.
Distributor: UA-Europa.

**1972** *12 Dicembre*
Directors: The direction was credited only to Giovanni Bonfanti, but it was a collective effort, controlled by Pier Paolo Pasolini who directed the sequences of Carrara, Sarzana, Reggio Calabria, and Viareggo (la Bussola); others are by M. Ponzi, G. Bonfanti, and A. Brand
Directors of Photography: Giuseppi Pinori, Sebastiano Celeste, Enzo Tosi, and Roberto Lombardi
Production Company: Circoli Ottobre-Lotta Continua
Music: Pino Masi
Running time: 104 min.
Distributor (commercial): Circoli Ottobre-Lotta Continua

*I racconti di Canterbury* (*Canterbury Tales*)
Production Company: PEA
Producer: Alberto Grimaldi
Director: Pier Paolo Pasolini
Subject and Script: Pier Paolo Pasolini (from Chaucer's *Canterbury Tales*)

Director of Photography: Tonino delli Colli
Color Process: Technicolor
Set Design: Dante Ferretti
Costumes: Danilo Donati
Music: Ennio Morricone and Pier Paolo Pasolini
Editor: Nino Baragli

Hugh Griffith (*Gennaio—January*), Laura Betti (*the Wife of Bath*), Ninetto Davoli (*Perkin*), Josephine Chaplin (*Maggio—May*), Franco Citti (*a mysterious youth*), Alan Webb (*an old man*), Pier Paolo Pasolini (*Chaucer*)
Running time: 111 min.
Distributor: UA-Europa.

**1974**  *Il fiore delle mille e una notte* (*The Thousand and One Nights*)
Production Company: Alberto Grimaldi for PEA (Rome)/Les Productions Artistes Associés (Paris)
Producer: Alberto Grimaldi
Director: Pier Paolo Pasolini
Subject and Script: Pier Paolo Pasolini (from *The Thousand and One Nights—Alf Laylah wa-Laylah*)
Collaborator on Script: Dacia Maraini
Director of Photography: Giuseppe Ruzzolini
Color Process: Technicolor
Set Design: Dante Ferretti
Costumes: Danilo Donati
Music: Ennio Morricone
Editors: Nino Baragli and Tatiana Casini Morigi

Ninetto Davoli (*Aziz*), Franco Citti (*the demon*), Franco Merli (*Nur-ed-Din*), Ines Pellegrini (*Zumurrud*), Tessa Bouché (*Aziza*), Fessazion Gherantiel (*Berhané*), Gianna Idris (*Gianna*), Abadit Ghidei (*Princess Dunya*), Alberto Argentino (*Prince Shahzmah*), Francesco Paolo Governale (*Prince Tagi*), Salvatore Sapienza (*Prince Yunan*)
Running time: 130 min.
Distributor: UA-Europa.

*Le mura di Sana'a (The walls of Sana'a)*
(documentary in the form of an appeal to UNESCO)
Production Company: Rosina ANSTALT srl
Producer: Franco Rossellini
Director: Pier Paolo Pasolini
Director of Photography: Tonino delli Colli
Commentary: Pier Paolo Pasolini
Running time: 16 min.

**1975**   *Salò, o le 120 giornate di Sodoma (Salò, or the 120 Days of Sodom)*
Production Company: PEA and Les Productions Artistes Associés
    (Italy, France)
Producer: Alberto Grimaldi
Director: Pier Paolo Pasolini
Subject and Script: Pier Paolo Pasolini and Sergio Citti (from the
    work by De Sade)
Director of Photography: Tonino delli Colli
Color Process: Technicolor
Set Design: Dante Ferretti
Costumes: Danilo Donati
Music: Coordinated by Ennio Morricone
Editor: Nino Baragli

Paolo Bonacelli (*the Duke*), Giorgio Cataldi (*the Monsignore*), Uberto
    Paolo Quintavalle (*His Excellency*), Aldo Valletti (*the President*),
    Caterina Boratto (*Signora Castelli*), Elso de Giorgi (*Signora
    Maggi*), Hélène Surgère (*Signora Vaccari*), Sonia Saviange (*the
    pianist*), Ines Pellegrini (*a maid*)
Running time: 117 min.
Distributor: UA-Europa.

# INDEX

## About the Author

BARTH DAVID SCHWARTZ was born in Dayton, Ohio, in 1947. He graduated *magna cum laude* from Harvard College (1969), held a Rhodes scholarship at Magdalen College, Oxford, and took his Juris Doctor degree at Yale Law School (1974). He lives in San Francisco.